Public School Law
Teachers' and Students' Rights

Second Edition

Martha M. McCarthy
Indiana University

Nelda H. Cambron-McCabe
Miami University

Allyn and Bacon, Inc.
Boston London Sydney Toronto

7 Wells Avenue, Newton, Massachusetts 02159

Library of Congress Cataloging-in-Publication Data

McCarthy, Martha M.
Public school law.

Includes bibliographies and index.
1. Teachers—Legal status, laws, etc.—United States. 2. Students—Legal status, laws, etc.—United States. I. Cambron-McCabe, Nelda H. II. Title.
KF4119.M38 1987 344.73'078 87-1110
ISBN 0-205-10489-4 347.30478

Printed in the United States of America

10 9 8 7 6 5 4 3 2 1 92 91 90 89 88 87

Contents

Preface

The second edition of *Public School Law: Teachers' and Students' Rights* provides a comprehensive treatment of the evolution and current status of the law governing public schools. Chapters on church-state relations and desegregation have been added to this edition, and all other chapters have been restructured to reflect emerging issues of legal concern.

Since World War II, lawmakers have significantly reshaped educational policy. Most school personnel are aware of the burgeoning litigation and legislation, and some are familiar with the names of a few landmark Supreme Court decisions. Nonetheless, many teachers and administrators harbor misunderstandings regarding the basic legal concepts that are being applied to educational questions. As a result, they are uncertain about the legality of daily decisions they must make in the operation of schools. Information provided in this book should help alleviate concerns voiced by educators who feel that the scales of justice have been tipped against them.

Public School Law differs from other legal materials currently available to educators because it addresses legal principles applicable to practitioners in a succinct but comprehensive manner. Legal aspects of topics that tend to be more relevant to educational policymakers than to practitioners, such as school property and finance, are not covered. Rather, topics with a direct impact on teachers and students are explored, and the tension between governmental controls and the exercise of individual rights is examined within the school context. The analysis of specific school situations relies on applicable constitutional and statutory law and judicial interpretations of these provisions. Implications of legal mandates are discussed, and guidelines are provided for school personnel. We have attempted to present the material in a nontechnical manner, avoiding the extensive use of legal terms. However, the topics are thoroughly documented should the reader choose to explore specific cases or points of law in greater detail. Numerous explanatory notes are included at the end of each chapter to provide additional information on selected cases and to assist the reader in understanding specific concepts. Also, a glossary of basic terms and a table of cases are provided at the end of the book.

A few comments about the nature of the law might assist the reader in using this book. Laws are not created in a vacuum; they reflect the social and philosophical attitudes of society. Moreover, laws are made by individuals who have personal opinions and biases. While we may prefer to think that the law is always objective, personal considerations and national political trends do have an impact on the development and interpretation of legal principles.

Also, the law is not static but rather is continually evolving as courts reinterpret constitutional and statutory provisions and legislatures enact new laws. In the 1960s and early 1970s courts and legislative bodies tended to focus on the expansion of personal rights through civil rights laws and constitutional interpretations favoring the individual's right to be free from unwarranted governmental intrusions. However, since 1975 legislative bodies have been less assertive in expanding protections for individuals, and judicial rulings have supported governmental authority to impose restraints on individual freedoms in the interest of the collective welfare. While the themes of educational equity and individual rights, which dominated litigation in the 1960s and early 1970s, remain important, efforts to attain educational excellence have generated a new genre of legal activity pertaining to teachers' qualifications and performance standards for students. Moreover, the educational agendas promoted by the religious and political right, such as prayer in public schools, curriculum censorship, and tuition tax credits, have provoked substantial legal activity.

Throughout this book, much of the discussion of the law focuses on court cases, because the judiciary plays a vital role in interpreting constitutional and legislative provisions. Decisions are highlighted that illustrate points of law or legal trends, with particular emphasis on recent litigation. A few cases are pursued in depth to provide the reader with an understanding of the rationale behind the decisions. Reviewing the factual situations that have generated these controversies should make it easier for educators to identify potential legal problems in their own school situations.

As this book goes to press, judicial decisions are being rendered and statutes are being proposed that may alter the complexion of the law vis-a-vis teachers and students. Additionally, some questions confronting school personnel have not yet been addressed by the Supreme Court and have generated conflicting decisions among lower courts. It may be frustrating to a reader searching for concrete answers to learn that in some areas the law is far from clear.

In spite of unresolved issues, certain legal principles have been established and can provide direction in many school situations. It is important for educators to become familiar with these principles and to use them to guide their decisions. While the issues generating legal concern will change over time, knowledge of the logic underlying the law can make school personnel more confident in dealing with legal questions that have not been clarified by courts or legislatures.

We have attempted to arrange the chapters in a logical sequence for those reading the book in its entirety or using it as a text for school law courses. An introductory chapter establishes the legal context for the subsequent examination of students' and teachers' rights, and a concluding chapter provides a summary of the major legal principles. Subheadings appear within chapters to facilitate the use of this book for reference if a specific topic is of immediate interest. The reader is encouraged, however, to read the entire text, because some topics are addressed in several chapters from different perspectives, and many of the principles of law transcend chapter divisions. For example, litigation involving various aspects of teachers' rights has relied on precedents established in students' rights cases; the converse also has been true. Throughout the text, various sections are cross-referenced to alert the reader that a particular concept is discussed more fully elsewhere in the book. Taken together, the chapters provide an overall picture of the relationship among issues and the applicable legal principles.

Although the content is oriented toward practicing educators, the material should be of equal interest to educational policymakers because many of the legal generalizations pertain to all educational personnel. In addition, this book should serve as a useful guide for parents who are interested in the law governing their children in public schools. Given its comprehensive coverage of students' and teachers' rights, this book also is appropriate for use as a basic text for university courses or in-service sessions.

The material should assist school personnel in understanding the current application of the law, but it is not intended to serve as a substitute for legal counsel. Educators confronting legal problems should always seek the advice of a competent attorney. Also, there is no attempt here to predict the future course of courts and legislatures. Given the dynamic nature of the law, no single text can serve to keep school personnel abreast of current legal developments. If we can provide an awareness of rights and responsibilities, motivate educators to translate the basic concepts into actual practice, and generate an interest in further study of the law, our purposes in writing this book will have been achieved.

ACKNOWLEDGMENTS

A number of individuals contributed to the completion of this book. Gail Sorenson, State University of New York at Albany, provided an excellent critique of the section pertaining to students' free speech rights, and Monique Clague, University of Maryland, provided insightful comments on the affirmative action section. We are also indebted to our students who reacted to various drafts of the chapters. Particular thanks go to Carol Bobek, Andrew Cameron, Gayle Hall, Nancy Hanson, Carla Iacona, Daniel Lindemann, James McGillivray, Thomas Newby, Karen Sanchez, Deanna Shirley, Charis Snyder-Gilbert, Scott Tarter, and Anne Waltermann, who spent many hours reviewing the manuscript and checking citations in the law library at Indiana University. In addition, we are very grateful to Martha McGillivray and Jan Clegg, whose excellent word processing skills facilitated production of the numerous drafts of this manuscript.

This book would not have been completed without the support of our families. Our parents offered constant encouragement as they do in all our professional endeavors. The contributions of our husbands, George Kuh and Harry McCabe, simply cannot be measured. Not only did they assume more than their share of family responsibilities during the preparation of the book, they also provided valuable editorial suggestions. Kari and Kristian Kuh never complained about their mother's involvement in this project, and special acknowledgment must be given to Patrick Harrison McCabe who was born during the preparation of the book. He seemed to sense immediately that he had to be an especially good baby, and for this we are truly thankful.

1

The Legal Foundation of Public Education

The authority for the establishment and control of American public education is grounded in law. State and federal constitutional and statutory provisions furnish the framework within which daily operational school decisions are made. Policies and practices at any level of the educational enterprise must be consistent with legal mandates from higher authorities. The overlapping jurisdictions of federal and state constitutions, Congress and state legislatures, federal and state courts, and various governmental agencies (including local school boards) present a complex environment for educators who are attempting to comply with legal requirements in their respective roles. In an effort to untangle the various legal relationships, this chapter describes the major sources of law and how they interact to form the legal basis for public education. This overview establishes a context for the subsequent chapters in which legal principles are discussed more fully as they apply to specific school situations.

STATE CONTROL OF EDUCATION

The tenth amendment to the United States Constitution stipulates that "the powers not delegated to the United States by the Constitution, nor prohibited by it to the states, are reserved to the states respectively, or to the people." The Supreme Court has recognized that this amendment was intended "to allay fears that the new national government might seek to exercise powers not granted, and that the states might not be able to exercise fully their reserved powers."[1] Since the Federal Constitution does not authorize Congress to provide for education, the legal control of public education resides with the state as one of its sovereign powers. The Supreme Court repeatedly has affirmed the comprehensive authority of the states and school officials "to prescribe and control conduct in the schools" as long as actions are consistent with fundamental federal constitutional safeguards.[2] The state's authority over education has been considered comparable to its powers to tax and to provide for the general welfare of its citizens. While each state's educational system is unique in some respects, there are striking similarities among states regarding the basic features of public education.

Legislative Power

All state constitutions specifically address the legislative responsibility for establishing public schools.[3] For example, the Arizona Constitution stipulates: "The legislature shall . . . provide for the establishment and maintenance of a general and uniform public school system. . . ."[4] The state legislature has plenary, or absolute, power to make laws governing education. In contrast to the federal government, which has only those powers stipulated in the United States Constitution, state legislatures retain all powers not expressly forbidden by state or federal constitutional provisions. In an early case, the Supreme Court of Virginia acknowledged the breadth of the state's plenary power regarding education:

> The legislature . . . has the power to enact any legislation in regard to the conduct, control, and regulation of the public free schools, which does not deny to the citizen the constitutional right to enjoy life and liberty, to pursue happiness and to acquire property.[5]

Courts have recognized the state legislature's authority to raise revenue and distribute educational funds, control teacher certification, prescribe curricular offerings, establish pupil performance standards, and regulate other specific aspects of public school operations. Legislatures are empowered to create, reorganize, consolidate, and abolish school districts, even over the objections of affected residents.[6] Moreover, states can mandate school attendance to ensure an educated citizenry. Presently, all fifty states require students between specified ages (usually six to sixteen) to attend a public or private school or to receive equivalent instruction that must be approved by the state education agency.

In some instances, state laws are subject to several interpretations, and courts are called upon to clarify the legislative intent. If the state judiciary misinterprets the law's purpose, the legislature can amend the law in question to clarify its intent. However, if a state law is invalidated as abridging state or federal constitutional provisions or federal civil rights laws, the legislature must abide by the judicial directives. Also, a state's attorney general may be asked to interpret a law and to advise school boards on the legality of their actions. The official opinion of an attorney general should be followed by school personnel, unless overruled by the judiciary.

Although the state legislature cannot delegate its law-making powers, it can delegate to subordinate agencies the authority to make rules and regulations that are necessary to implement the law. These administrative functions must be carried out within the guidelines established by the legislature. State laws are either mandatory (pertaining to essential state interests in providing education) or permissive (allowing local discretion in providing programs and services).[7] Some states are quite liberal in delegating administrative authority, whereas other states stipulate detailed standards that must be followed by subordinate agencies.[8] While it is a widely held misconception that local school boards control public education within this nation, local boards have only those powers conferred by the state. Courts consistently have reiterated that the authority for education is not a local one, but is a central power residing in the state legislature.[9] School buildings are considered state property, and local school board members are state officials. School funds, regardless of where collected, are state funds.

State Agencies

Since it has not been feasible nor desirable to include in statutes every minor detail governing public schools, all states have established some type of state board of education. This board often supplies the structural details necessary to carry out broad legislative mandates. In most states, members of the state board of education are elected by the citizenry or appointed by the governor, and the board usually functions immediately below the legislature in the hierarchy of educational governance.

Licensure is an important tool used by state boards of education to compel local school districts to abide by their directives. School districts often must satisfy state licensure or accreditation requirements as a condition of receiving state aid. Models for licensure and the standards that schools must satisfy vary among states. The most common approach involves the establishment of minimum standards in areas such as curricular offerings, teacher qualifications, instructional materials, and facilities. In some states, different grades of accreditation are established with financial incentives to encourage local school districts to qualify for the highest licensure level.

Within legislative parameters, the state board of education can issue directives governing school operations. In some states, rules pertaining to such matters as competency testing for students and the education of handicapped children are embodied in state board directives rather than state law. Courts generally have upheld decisions made by state boards of education, unless the decisions have violated legislative or constitutional mandates.[10] For example, the Kansas Supreme Court recognized that the state constitutional grant of general supervisory power to the state board of education was self-executing in that enabling legislation was unnecessary for the board to require local school districts to develop regulations pertaining to student and employee conduct.[11] Also, the Sixth Circuit Court of Appeals upheld the Ohio State Board of Education's authority to compel a school district to be annexed to a neighboring district because it failed to meet minimum standards under state law.[12] The appeals court reasoned that the annexed district had no federal constitutional right to remain in existence.

The Supreme Court of Pennsylvania has recognized the state board of education's authority to issue and enforce uniform student disciplinary regulations governing all schools within the state.[13] Even though local school districts asserted that uniform guidelines were impractical and that local boards were entitled under state law to apply their own disciplinary codes, the Pennsylvania high court held that "far reaching and unequivocal powers" were granted by the legislature to the state board. The court reasoned that the board's authority to establish standards governing all educational programs included the right to enact statewide disciplinary policies.

In addition to the state board, generally considered a policy-making body, all states have designated a chief state school officer (often known as the superintendent of public instruction or commissioner of education) to function in an executive capacity. Traditionally, the duties of the chief state officer have been regulatory in nature. However, other activities, such as research and long-range planning, have been added to this role. In some states, the chief school officer is charged with adjudicating educational controversies, and citizens cannot evoke judicial remedies for a grievance pertaining to the internal operations of schools until such administrative appeals have been exhausted. For example, in New York, the commissioner of education is authorized to adjudicate educational grievances. Courts have held that, when considering an appeal from a chief school officer's decision, they will not judge the wisdom of the decision or overrule such a decision unless it is clearly arbitrary or against the preponderance of evidence.[14]

Each state also has established a state department of education, consisting of educational specialists who provide consultation to the state board, chief state school officer, and local school boards. State department personnel often collect data from school districts to ensure that legislative enactments and state board policies are properly implemented. Most state departments also engage in research and development activities to improve educational practices within the state.

Local School Boards

Although education is state controlled in this nation, it is for the most part locally administered. All states except Hawaii have created local school boards in addition to state education agencies and have delegated certain administrative authority over schools to these local boards. There are approximately 15,800 school districts in this country, some with only a few students and others with several hundred thousand pupils. Many operational decisions governing the day-to-day activities of schools are made by local boards of education. Some states, particularly those with a large number of small local school districts, have established intermediate or regional administrative units which perform primarily regulatory or service functions for several local school districts.

As with the delegation of authority to state agencies, delegation of powers to local agencies is handled very differently among the states. In some states with a deeply rooted tradition of local control over education (e.g., Colorado), local school boards are given a great deal of latitude in making operational decisions about schools. In other states that tend toward centralized control of education (e.g., Florida), local boards must function within the framework of detailed legislative directives.

Local school board members usually are elected by the citizenry within the school district, and such elections must be conducted in conformance with state statutes. The Supreme Court has recognized that the equal protection clause requires each qualified voter to be given an opportunity to participate in the election of board members, with each vote given the same weight as far as practicable.[15] When board members are elected from geographical districts, such districts must be established to protect voting rights under the "one man, one vote" principle. If "at large" elections result in a dilution of the minority vote, an abridgment of the federal Voting Rights Act may be found.[16]

The state legislature can specify the qualifications, method of selection, and terms and conditions of local school board membership. Board members are considered to be public school officers and to possess a delegation of sovereign power, in contrast to school employees, who are hired to implement directives. Public officers cannot hold two offices if one is subordinate to the other, and in some states they cannot occupy two lucrative offices.[17] Public officers also are prohibited from having an interest in contracts made from their agencies.[18] Generally, statutes stipulate procedures that must be followed in removing public officers from their positions. Typical causes for removal include neglect of duty, illegal performance of duty, breach of good faith, negligence, and incapacity.

A local board must act as a body; individual board members are not empowered to make policies or perform official acts on behalf of the board. Local boards have some latitude in adopting operational procedures, but they are legally bound to adhere to such procedures once they are established. While courts are reluctant to interfere with decisions made by boards of education and will not rule on the wisdom of such decisions, they will invalidate any board action that is arbitrary, capricious, or outside the board's legal authority (*ultra vires*).

School board meetings and records must be open to the public. Most states have enacted "sunshine" or "open meeting" laws. The rationale for such statutes is that the public has a right to be fully informed regarding the actions of public agencies, including school boards. What constitutes a meeting is sometimes defined by statute, and certain exceptions to open meeting requirements are usually specified. For example, in many states, school boards can meet in executive session to discuss matters that threaten public safety or pertain to pending or current litigation, sensitive personnel matters, collective bargaining, or the disposition of real property. While discussions on these matters may take place in closed meetings, statutes usually stipulate that formal action must take place in open meetings.[19]

Local school boards hold powers specified in state law, powers implied by law, and other powers reasonably necessary to achieve the purposes of the granted powers.[20] These delegated powers generally encompass the authority to determine the specifics of the curriculum offered within the school district, to raise revenue to build and maintain schools, to select personnel, and to enact other policies necessary to implement the educational program pursuant to law. Courts have ruled that the rights to alter attendance zones and close schools are properly within a local school board's delegated discretionary authority.[21] Courts also have recognized the implied rights of local boards to establish and support secondary schools, kindergartens, nongraded schools, and various school-related programs, without specific legislation granting such authority.[22]

Decisions made by local boards of education often have been challenged on the grounds that the board has acted beyond its lawful scope of authority. In such cases, courts assess whether the act in question is within the implied powers of local boards under state law. The New York high court reasoned that, in the absence of any state regulations specifying a minimum length of instructional time for schools, the New York City Board of Education acted within its legal powers by shortening the school instructional period by two forty-five-minute periods each week.[23] The Wyoming Supreme Court, however, held that the statutory requirement of 175 school days was violated by a school district's practice of compressing the school week into four days, even if the amount of contact time was not substantially altered.[24]

Local school boards cannot exercise powers that are not at least implied in state law. For example, the Supreme Court of Washington ruled that a school board could not maintain a clinic offering medical, surgical, and dental treatment for needy pupils because there was no implied statutory authority for such activity.[25] State legislatures retain the legal responsibility for education and can restrict the administrative authority of local boards by enacting legislation to that effect.

Furthermore, local school boards cannot delegate their decision-making authority to other agencies or associations. In an illustrative case, a New Jersey court ruled that a school board could not relinquish responsibility for determining courses of study or settling classroom controversies to the teachers' association.[26] Also, the Iowa Supreme Court held that a school board could not delegate its rule-making authority to a state high school athletic association.[27]

Local boards are authorized to perform discretionary duties (i.e., involving judgment), while school employees, such as superintendents, principals, and teachers, can perform only ministerial duties that are necessary to carry out policies. Hence, a superintendent can recommend personnel to be hired and propose a budget to the board, but the board must actually make the personnel decisions and adopt the budget. Although it might appear that school administrators and teachers retain little decision-making authority, this is not actually the case. Administrators as well as classroom teachers can enact rules and regulations, consistent with board policy and law, to ensure the efficient operation of the school or class under their supervision.

FEDERAL ROLE IN EDUCATION

In contrast to state constitutions, the Federal Constitution is silent regarding education; hence, individuals do not have an inherent federal right to an education.[28] The Federal Constitution does, however, confer basic rights on individuals, and these rights must be respected by school personnel. Furthermore, Congress exerts control over the use of federal education aid and regulates other aspects of schools through legislation enacted pursuant to its constitutionally granted powers.

United States Constitution

A constitution, by definition, is a body of precepts providing the system of fundamental laws of a nation, state, or society. The United States Constitution establishes a separation of powers among the executive, judicial, and legislative branches of government. These three branches form a system of checks and balances to ensure that the intent of the Constitution is respected. The Federal Constitution also provides a systematic process for altering the document, if this is deemed necessary. Article V stipulates that amendments may be proposed by a two-thirds vote of each house of Congress, or by a special convention called by Congress upon request of two-thirds of the state legislatures. Proposed amendments must then be ratified by three-fourths of the states in order to become part of the Constitution.

Since the Federal Constitution is the supreme law in this nation, state authority over education must be exercised in a manner consistent with its provisions. In 1958, the Supreme Court declared:

> It is, of course, quite true that the responsibility for public education is primarily the concern of the States, but it is equally true that such responsibilities, like all other state activity, must be exercised consistently with federal constitutional requirements as they apply to state action.[29]

The Supreme Court has interpreted various constitutional guarantees as they apply to educational matters. While all federal constitutional mandates affect public education to some degree, the following provisions have had the greatest impact on public school policies and practices.

General Welfare Clause. Under Article I, Section 8 of the Constitution, Congress has the power "to lay and collect Taxes, Duties, Imposts and Excises, to pay the Debts and provide for the Common Defense and General Welfare of the United States. . . ." In 1937 the Supreme Court declared that the concept of general welfare is not static: "Needs that were narrow or parochial a century ago may be interwoven in our day with the well-being of the nation. What is critical or urgent changes with the times."[30] Although historically this clause has been the subject of much debate, the Supreme Court has interpreted the provision as allowing Congress to tax and spend public monies for a variety of purposes related to the general welfare.[31] The Court has stated that it will not interfere with the discretion of Congress in its domain, unless Congress exhibits a clear display of arbitrary power.[32]

Using the general welfare rationale, Congress has enacted legislation providing substantial federal support for research and instructional programs in areas such as science, mathematics, reading, special education, vocational education, career education, and bilingual education. In the interest of the general welfare of the nation, Congress also has provided financial assistance for the school lunch program and for services to meet the special needs of various groups of students, such as the culturally disadvantaged. In addition, Congress has responded to national health and safety concerns with legislation such as the 1980 Asbestos School Hazard Detection and Control Act, which requires local education agencies to inspect buildings and, if necessary, to take remedial action to assure the safety of school children and employees.[33]

Commerce Clause. Congress is empowered to "regulate Commerce with foreign Nations, among the several States, and with Indian tribes" under Article I, Section 8, Clause 3 of the Constitution. Safety, transportation, and labor regulations enacted pursuant to this clause have affected the operation of public schools. Traditionally, courts have favored a broad interpretation of "commerce" and an expanded federal role in regulating commerce activities to ensure the prosperity of the country. Interpreting congressional powers to regulate commerce, in 1985 the Supreme Court held that a municipal mass transit system was subject to the minimum wage and overtime requirements of the federal Fair Labor Standards Act (FLSA).[34] This decision, *Garcia v. San Antonio Metropolitan Transit Authority,* overturned a precedent established in 1976 when the Court limited congressional authority to enforce federal minimum wage requirements in areas of "traditional" state governmental functions.[35] Concluding that attempts to identify such traditional state functions that would be immune from federal requirements had been unworkable and inconsistent with established principles of federalism, the Court majority in *Garcia* found nothing in the FLSA that is destructive of state sovereignty.[36] This 1985 decision may revive federal efforts to regulate other aspects of public employment, such as a national collective bargaining law for public employees.[37]

Obligations of Contract Clause. Article I, Section 10 of the Constitution stipulates that states cannot pass any law impairing the obligation of contracts. Administrators, teachers, and noncertified personnel are protected from arbitrary dismissals by contractual agreements. School boards also enter into numerous contracts with individuals and companies in carrying out the daily business activities of schools. The judiciary often is called upon to evaluate the validity of a given contract or to assess whether one party has breached its contractual obligations.

First Amendment. The Bill of Rights, comprised of the first ten amendments to the Federal Constitution, protects individual liberties from governmental encroachment.[38] The most preciously guarded of these liberties are contained in the first amendment which states:

> Congress shall make no law respecting an establishment of religion, or prohibiting the free exercise thereof; or abridging the freedom of speech, or of the press; or the right of the people peaceably to assemble, and to petition the Government for a redress of grievances.

The religious freedoms contained in this amendment have evoked lawsuits challenging governmental aid to and regulation of nonpublic schools and contesting public school policies and practices as advancing religion or impairing free exercise rights. Cases involving students' rights to express themselves freely and to distribute student literature have been initiated under first amendment guarantees of freedom of speech and press. Also, teachers' rights to academic freedom and to speak out on matters of public concern have generated numerous legal challenges. The right of assembly has been the focus of litigation involving student clubs and employees' rights to organize and engage in collective bargaining.

Fourth Amendment. This amendment guarantees the right of citizens "to be secure in their persons, houses, papers, and effects against unreasonable searches and seizures." The Supreme Court has recognized that the basic purpose of this amendment is "to safeguard the privacy and security of individuals against arbitrary invasions by governmental officials."[39] Since the late 1960s, this amendment has frequently appeared in educational cases involving searches of students' lockers and cars as well as personal searches. A few cases also have involved alleged violations of teachers' fourth amendment rights by school officials.

Fifth Amendment. In part, this amendment provides that no person shall be "compelled in any criminal case to be a witness against himself, nor be deprived of life, liberty, or property without due process of law; nor shall private property be taken for public use, without just compensation." Several cases have addressed the application of the self-incrimination clause in instances where teachers have been questioned by superiors about their activities outside the classroom. The last clause of the fifth amendment has been used in educational litigation to protect citizens' rights to appropriate compensation for property acquired for school purposes. Due process litigation concerning schools usually has been initiated under the fourteenth amendment, which pertains directly to state action. However, many cases in the District of Columbia (involving topics such as desegregation and the rights of handicapped children) have relied on the due process guarantees of the fifth amendment, because the fourteenth amendment does not apply in this jurisdiction.[40]

Ninth Amendment. The ninth amendment stipulates that "the enumeration in the Constitution, of certain rights, shall not be construed to deny or disparage others retained by the people." This amendment has appeared in educational litigation in which teachers have asserted that their right to personal privacy outside the classroom is protected as an unenumerated right. Also, grooming regulations applied to teachers and students have been challenged as impairing personal rights retained by the people under this amendment.

Fourteenth Amendment. The fourteenth amendment is the most widely used constitutional provision in school litigation because it pertains specifically to actions of the states. In part, the fourteenth amendment provides that no state shall "deny to any person within its jurisdiction the equal protection of the laws." This clause has been particularly significant in school cases involving alleged discrimination based on race, sex, ethnic background, and handicaps. In addition, school finance litigation often has been grounded in the equal protection clause.

The due process clause of the fourteenth amendment, which prohibits states from depriving citizens of life, liberty, or property without due process of law, also has played an important role in school litigation. Property rights are legitimate expectations of entitlement created through state laws, regulations, or contracts. Compulsory school attendance laws confer upon students a legitimate property right to attend school, and the granting of tenure gives teachers a property entitlement to continued employment. Liberty rights include interests in one's reputation and fundamental rights related to marriage, family matters, and personal privacy. In addition, the Supreme Court has interpreted fourteenth amendment liberties as *incorporating* the personal freedoms contained in the Bill of Rights.[41] Thus, the first ten amendments, originally directed toward the federal government, have been applied to state action as well. The principle of "incorporation" has been criticized,[42] but Supreme Court precedent supports the notion that the fourteenth amendment restricts state interference with fundamental constitutional liberties. This principle is particularly significant in school litigation because education is a state function; claims that public school policies or practices impair personal freedoms (e.g., first amendment free speech guarantees) are usually initiated through the fourteenth amendment.

The federal judiciary has identified both procedural and substantive components of due process guarantees. Procedural due process ensures fundamental fairness if the government threatens an individual's life, liberty, or property interests; minimum procedures required by the Federal Constitution are notice of the charges, an opportunity to refute the charges, and a hearing that is conducted fairly. Substantive due process requires the state action to be based on a valid objective with means reasonably related to attaining the objective. In essence, substantive due process shields the individual against *arbitrary* governmental action that impairs life, liberty, or property interests.

Since the fourteenth amendment protects personal liberties against unwarranted *state* interference, private institutions, including private schools, may not be subject to these restrictions. For private school policies and practices to be successfully challenged under the fourteenth amendment, there must be sufficient governmental involvement in the private school to constitute "state action." The Supreme Court has not articulated a precise standard by which to assess how much state involvement is necessary to trigger fourteenth amendment guarantees; rather, specific controversies are assessed on a case-by-case basis.[43]

Federal Legislation

Congress is empowered to enact laws to translate the intent of the Federal Constitution into actual practices. Laws reflect the will of the legislative branch of government, which, in this nation, represents the citizenry. Since the states have sovereign power regarding education, the federal government's involvement in public schools has been one of indirect support, not direct control.

Federal legislation affecting public education actually was enacted prior to ratification of the Federal Constitution. The Ordinances of 1785 and 1787, providing land grants to states for the maintenance of public schools, encouraged the establishment of public education in many states. However, it was not until the mid-twentieth century that Congress began to play a significant role in stimulating *targeted* educational reform through its spending powers under the general welfare clause. The most comprehensive law offering financial assistance to schools, the Elementary and Secondary Education Act of 1965 (ESEA), in part supplied funds for compensatory education programs for economically disadvantaged students. With passage of ESEA, federal aid to education doubled, and the federal government's contribution increased steadily until reaching its high point of over 9 percent of total public education costs in 1981.

Congress and federal administrative agencies have exerted considerable influence in shaping public school policies and practices through categorical funding laws and their accompanying administrative regulations that must be followed for schools to be eligible to receive the federal aid. Individual states or school districts have the option of accepting or rejecting such federal assistance, but if categorical aid is accepted, the federal government has the authority to prescribe guidelines for its use and to monitor state and local education agencies to ensure fiscal accountability.

Much of the federal categorical legislation enacted during the 1960s and 1970s established funding sources to assist school districts in attaining equity goals and addressing other national priorities. For example, the Bilingual Education Act of 1968 and the Education for All Handicapped Children Act of 1975 have provided federal funds to assist education agencies in offering services for students with special needs. Although in the 1980s Congress has shifted away from its heavy reliance on categorical federal aid by consolidating some categorical programs into block grants with reduced funding and regulatory activity, aid for economically disadvantaged, handicapped, and English-deficient students has remained categorical in nature.

In addition to laws providing financial assistance to public schools, Congress has enacted legislation designed to clarify the scope of individuals' civil rights. Unlike the discretion enjoyed by state and local education agencies in deciding whether to participate in federal funding programs, educational institutions must comply with the provisions of these civil rights laws. Federal antidiscrimination laws are grounded in two distinct sources of federal authority. Some are enacted to enforce constitutional rights and have general application. Others are based on the federal government's authority to place restrictions on the expenditure of federal funds. The latter laws apply only to recipients of federal financial assistance. Various federal agencies are charged with monitoring compliance with these laws, and these agencies can bring suit against noncomplying institutions. Under most civil rights laws, individuals can also initiate private suits to compel compliance and to obtain personal remedies.

Several laws enacted in the latter part of the nineteenth century to protect the rights of black citizens were seldom the focus of litigation until the mid-twentieth century. These laws, particularly the Civil Rights Act of 1871, Section 1983, recently have been used by students and teachers to gain relief in instances where their federal rights have been violated by school policies and practices. Section 1983 provides a private right to bring suit for damages against any person who, acting under color of state law, impairs rights secured by the Federal Constitution and laws.[44] Although Section 1983 does not confer specific substantive rights, it has been significant in school cases because it allows individuals to obtain damages from school officials and school districts for abridgments of federally protected rights.

Subsequent civil rights laws enacted during the 1960s and early 1970s do confer substantive rights to protect citizens from discrimination. The vindication of individual rights in school settings has generated substantial litigation involving Title VI of the Civil Rights Act of 1964 (prohibiting discrimination on the basis of race, color, or national origin, in federally assisted programs), Title VII of the Civil Rights Act of 1964 (prohibiting employment discrimination on the basis of race, color, sex, religion, or national origin), the Age Discrimination in Employment Act of 1967 (barring age discrimination in federally assisted programs), Title IX of the Education Amendments of 1972 (prohibiting sex discrimination against participants in educational programs receiving federal funds), and the Rehabilitation Act of 1973 (prohibiting discrimination against handicapped persons in federally assisted programs). Courts often have been called upon to interpret these acts and their regulations as they apply to educational practices.

Other federal laws have been enacted to protect individual rights in educational settings. For example, the Family Educational Rights and Privacy Act and the Pupil Protection Act of 1974, respectively, guarantee personal rights in connection with school record keeping practices and federally assisted research projects. Courts have played an important role in interpreting the protections included in these laws and assuring compliance with the federal mandates.

Federal Administrative Agencies

Similar to state governments, much of the regulatory activity at the federal level is conducted by administrative agencies. The Office of Education was originally established in 1867, and it became part of the Department of Health, Education, and Welfare when this department was established in 1953. In 1980 the Department of Education was created with a Secretary who serves as a member of the President's cabinet. The Secretary is appointed by the President with the advice and approval of the Senate.

The primary functions of the Department of Education are to coordinate federal involvement in education activities, to identify educational needs of national significance, to propose strategies to address these needs, and to provide technical and financial assistance to state and local education agencies. Approximately half of the federal aid to education is administered by the Department of Education, and its regulations promulgated to implement funding laws have had a significant impact on schools. Public comments are solicited on proposed regulations, and Congress reviews them to ensure that they adhere to the legislative intent behind the law. The Department of Education administers over 200 sets of regulations for 128 different programs.[45] The remaining educational programs are administered by other departments such as the Department of Agriculture and the Department of Health and Human Services.

Through their regulatory activities, numerous federal agencies have a significant influence on state and local educational policies. For example, the Office of Civil Rights and the Equal Employment Opportunity Commission have reviewed claims of discrimination in public schools and initiated suits against school districts found in noncompliance with civil rights laws. Also, the Environmental Protection Agency has placed obligations on schools in connection with asbestos removal and ensuring safe school environments. School districts can face the termination of federal assistance if they do not comply with regulations promulgated by federal administrative agencies.

FUNCTION AND STRUCTURE OF THE JUDICIAL SYSTEM

Judicial decisions are usually cited in conjunction with statutory and constitutional provisions as a major source of educational law. Alexis de Toqueville noted in 1835 that "scarcely any political question arises in the United States that is not resolved, sooner or later, into a judicial question."[46] Courts, however, do not initiate laws as legislative bodies do; courts apply appropriate principles of law to settle disputes. The terms "common law" or "case law" are used to refer to judicially created legal principles that are relied upon as precedent when similar factual situations arise.

Although most constitutional provisions and statutory enactments never become the source of litigation, some provisions must be clarified by the judiciary. Since federal and state constitutions set forth broad policy statements rather than specific guides to action, courts serve an important function in interpreting such mandates and in determining the legality of various school policies and practices. It has been firmly established that the United States Supreme Court has the ultimate authority in interpreting federal constitutional guarantees.[47] Consequently, the Supreme Court occupies a powerful position as the "final arbiter of the nature and limits of state power under the Constitution."[48]

The United States Supreme Court has articulated specific guidelines for exercising the power of judicial review. The Court will not decide hypothetical cases and will not render an opinion on issues in a nonadversarial proceeding. There must be a genuine controversy initiated by a party with standing to sue. To achieve such standing, the party must have been adversely affected by the challenged practice to establish a real interest in the outcome of the case.

The Supreme Court also has declared that it will not anticipate a constitutional question in advance of the necessity of deciding the question. Further, the Court will not decide a case on constitutional grounds if there is some other ground upon which the case may be decided. When an act of Congress is questioned, the Court always attempts to "ascertain whether a construction of the statute is fairly possible by which the question may be avoided."[49] In applying appropriate principles of law to specific cases, the Court attempts to follow the doctrine of *stares decisis* (abide by decided cases), and thus relies on precedents established in previous decisions.

When a suit is initiated, the trial court holds a hearing to make findings of fact based on the evidence presented. The trial court then applies legal principles to the specific factual situation in rendering a judgment. If the ruling is appealed, the appellate court must accept the trial court's findings of fact unless they are clearly erroneous. The appeals court reviews the written record of the evidence but does not hold a hearing for witnesses to be questioned. The appeals court may accept the trial court's findings of fact but disagree with the conclusions of law. In such instances, the case is usually remanded to the trial court for reconsideration in light of the appropriate legal principles.

In addition to individual suits,[50] educational cases often involve class action suits brought on behalf of all similarly situated individuals. To be certified as a class action, the suit must satisfy rules of civil procedure that specify prerequisites to establish commonality of injury and circumstances among class members. If a suit is not properly certified as a class action, and the circumstances of the original plaintiff change (e.g., a student graduates from school before a judgment is rendered), the court may find that the issue has become moot as the plaintiff is no longer being injured by the contested practice. Such a finding would result in dismissal of the suit.

Various remedies are available through court action. In some suits, a court-ordered injunction is sought to compel school officials to cease a particular action or to remove restraints they have imposed on protected freedoms. For a court to issue an injunction, evidence must indicate that the complainant is likely to prevail when the trial court reviews the merits of the case. Judicial relief also can take the form of a declaration that specific rights must be respected. In addition, courts can order personal remedies such as reinstatement and removal of material from personnel records. Courts also can award damages to compensate individuals for the deprivation of their rights, and punitive damages can be assessed against state officials if such deprivations constitute a willful or reckless disregard of protected rights. Under certain circumstances, attorneys' fees can also be awarded.

In interpreting constitutional and statutory provisions, courts have developed various criteria to evaluate whether the law has been breached. These judicially created standards or "tests" are extremely important and in some instances appear to go beyond the original intent of the constitutional or statutory provision in question. The judiciary occupies a powerful position in shaping the law through its interpretive powers. Judicial standards for assessing claims under various constitutional and statutory provisions are continually evolving and being refined by courts.

Courts have assumed an increasingly significant role in determining educational policy since the landmark desegregation decision, *Brown v. Board of Education of Topeka,*[51] was rendered in 1954. Much of this judicial intervention has involved the protection of individual rights and the attainment of equity for minority groups. During the past two decades, courts have addressed nearly every facet of the educational enterprise, including students' rights to free expression, compulsory attendance and mandatory curriculum offerings, school finance reform, employment practices, student discipline, educational malpractice, sex discrimination, collective bargaining, employees' right to privacy, desegregation, and the rights of handicapped and non-English-speaking students.

Courts, however, will not intervene in a school-related controversy if the dispute can be settled in a legislative or administrative forum. In 1973, the Supreme Court emphasized that in situations involving "persistent and difficult questions of educational policies," the judiciary's "lack of specialized knowledge and experience counsels against premature interference with the informed judgments made at the state and local levels."[52] All state educational systems provide some type of administrative appeals procedure for aggrieved individuals to use in disputes involving the internal operations of schools. Many school-related controversies never reach the courts because they are settled in these administrative forums. Under most circumstances, courts require such administrative appeals to be pursued before court action is brought,[53] but a suit can be initiated after administrative appeals are exhausted without relief.

In evaluating the impact of case law, it is important to keep in mind that a judicial ruling applies as precedent within the geographical jurisdiction of the court delivering the opinion. It is possible for two state supreme courts or two federal courts to render conflicting decisions on an issue, and such decisions are binding in their respective jurisdictions until the United States Supreme Court rules on the issue. Only decisions of the Supreme Court have national application.

State Courts

State courts are established pursuant to state constitutional provisions, and the structure of judicial systems varies among states. In contrast to federal courts, which have only those powers granted in the United States Constitution, state courts have the authority to settle most types of controversies, unless restricted by state law. State judicial systems usually include trial courts of general jurisdiction, courts of special jurisdiction such as juvenile courts, and appellate courts. All states have a court of last resort in the state appeals process; decisions rendered by state high courts can be appealed to the United States Supreme Court.

In most states, the court of last resort is called the supreme court or supreme judicial court, but in New York and Maryland the highest court is the Court of Appeals, and in West Virginia it is the Supreme Court of Appeals. Courts occupying the next level in the state judiciary usually are referred to as appeals courts or superior courts. State trial courts of general jurisdiction often are called district or circuit courts, but in New York, trial courts are referred to as supreme courts of their respective counties. The most common special jurisdiction courts are juvenile, probate, domestic relations, and small claims courts. State judges are usually elected on partisan or nonpartisan ballots or appointed by the governor.

Federal Courts

Article III, Section I of the Federal Constitution establishes the United States Supreme Court and authorizes Congress to create other federal courts as necessary. Traditionally, the federal judiciary did not address educational concerns; less than 300 cases involving education had been initiated in federal courts prior to 1954.[54] Today, however, hundreds of school cases are initiated in federal courts each year. The federal judiciary no longer exhibits a hands-off posture toward schools and will intervene to protect individual rights and to clarify governmental authority in educational settings.

The federal court system contains courts of special jurisdiction such as the Claims Court, Tax Court, and Court of International Trade. There are three levels of federal courts of general jurisdiction—district courts, circuit courts of appeal, and the United States Supreme Court. Each state has at least one federal district court. Many states have two or three, and

California, New York, and Texas have four each. Judgments at the district court level are usually presided over by one judge.

On the federal appeals level, the nation is divided into twelve geographic circuits, and each circuit has a federal circuit court of appeals.[55] A thirteenth federal circuit court has national jurisdiction to hear appeals regarding specific claims (e.g., customs; copyrights, patents and trademarks; international trade). Federal circuit courts have from three to fifteen judges, depending on the workload of the circuit. Decisions rendered at the federal circuit level are extremely important, particularly if the Supreme Court has not addressed a specific issue. Although a federal circuit court decision is binding only in the states within that circuit, such decisions often influence other appellate courts when they deal with similar questions. The jurisdiction of the federal circuits is as follows:

- First Circuit: Maine, Massachusetts, New Hampshire, Rhode Island, and Puerto Rico
- Second Circuit: Connecticut, New York, and Vermont
- Third Circuit: Delaware, New Jersey, Pennsylvania, and the Virgin Islands
- Fourth Circuit: Maryland, North Carolina, South Carolina, Virginia, and West Virginia
- Fifth Circuit: Louisiana, Mississippi, Texas, and the Canal Zone
- Sixth Circuit: Kentucky, Michigan, Ohio, and Tennessee
- Seventh Circuit: Illinois, Indiana, and Wisconsin
- Eighth Circuit: Arkansas, Iowa, Minnesota, Missouri, Nebraska, North Dakota, and South Dakota
- Ninth Circuit: Alaska, Arizona, California, Idaho, Hawaii, Montana, Nevada, Oregon, Washington, and Guam
- Tenth Circuit: Colorado, Kansas, New Mexico, Oklahoma, Utah, and Wyoming
- Eleventh Circuit: Alabama, Florida, and Georgia
- D.C. Circuit: Washington, D.C.[56]
- Federal Circuit: National jurisdiction on specific claims.

The United States Supreme Court is the highest court in the nation, beyond which there is no appeal. If the Supreme Court concludes that a specific practice violates the Federal Constitution (e.g., intentional school segregation), the Court will prohibit continuation of the practice, and this judicial mandate will have national application. However, if the Court concludes that a given activity (e.g., corporal punishment) does not impair federal constitutional guarantees, states and local school boards retain discretion in placing restrictions on the activity. In the latter instances, legal requirements will vary across jurisdictions. Where the interpretation of a federal law is at issue, Congress can amend the law if the Supreme Court misinterprets congressional intent.[57] In contrast, Congress is not empowered to nullify the Court's interpretations of the Federal Constitution.

The Supreme Court has original jurisdiction in cases in which a state is a party or involving federal ambassadors and other public ministers. The Court has appellate jurisdiction in other cases arising under the United States Constitution or federal laws or entailing disputes between states or parties residing in different states.[58] The Supreme Court disposes of approximately 5,000 cases a year, but renders a written opinion on the merits in less than 5 percent of these cases. The Court often concludes that the topic of a case is not appropriate or of sufficient significance to warrant Supreme Court review. Denial of review does not infer agreement with the lower court's decision. Since the Supreme Court has authority to determine which cases it will hear, many issues are left for resolution by lower courts. Accordingly, precedents regarding some school controversies must be gleaned from federal circuit courts or state supreme courts and may differ from one jurisdiction to another.

An individual need not exhaust state administrative appeals before initiating a federal suit if the abridgment of a federally protected right is involved,[59] but some federal laws specify administrative procedures that must be pursued before commencing court action. Suits involving federal issues also may be heard by state courts, and the interpretation of federal rights by the state judiciary may be reviewed by the United States Supreme Court. While individuals have a choice as to whether to initiate a federal or state suit in these circumstances, they cannot relitigate an issue in federal court if they have been denied relief by the state judiciary. In essence, a federal suit cannot be initiated if an issue has already been adjudicated by the state judiciary or could have been raised in the prior state litigation.[60]

CONCLUSION

American public schools are governed by a complex body of regulations that are grounded in constitutional provisions, statutory enactments, agency regulations, and court decisions. During recent years, legislation and litigation pertaining to schools have increased dramatically in both volume and complexity. Although rules made at any level must be consistent with those of higher authorities, administrators and teachers retain considerable latitude in establishing rules and procedures within their specific jurisdictions. As long as educators act reasonably and do not impair protected rights of others, their actions will be upheld if challenged in court.

School personnel, however, cannot plead "ignorance of the law" as a valid defense for illegal actions.[61] Therefore, educators should be aware of the constraints placed on their rule-making prerogatives by school board policies and federal and state constitutional and statutory provisions. In the subsequent chapters of this book, an attempt is made to clarify the major legal principles that affect teachers and students in their daily school activities.

NOTES

1. United States v. Darby, 312 U.S. 100, 124 (1941).
2. Tinker v. Des Moines Independent School Dist., 393 U.S. 503, 507 (1969).
3. For a list of state constitutional provisions pertaining to the establishment of public schools, *see* Martha McCarthy and Paul Deignan, *What Legally Constitutes an Adequate Public Education?* (Bloomington, IN: Phi Delta Kappa, 1982), Appendix B, pp. 120–126.
4. Arizona Const., art. 11, § 1.
5. Flory v. Smith, 134 S.E. 360, 362 (Va. 1926). *See also* Board of Educ. of Aberdeen-Huntington Local School Dist. v. State Bd. of Educ., 189 N.E.2d 81 (Ohio App. 1962), *appeal dismissed,* 189 N.E.2d 86 (Ohio 1963); State Tax Comm'n v. Board of Educ. of Jefferson County, 179 So. 197 (Ala. 1938).
6. *See, e.g.,* Kaupas v. Regional Bd. of School Trustees of Mason County, 361 N.E.2d 1157 (Ill. App. 1977); In re Township No. 143 North Range, 183 N.W.2d 520 (N.D. 1971); DeJonge v. School Dist. of the Village of Bloomington, 139 N.W.2d 296 (Neb. 1966); Schwartzkopf v. State, 204 N.E.2d 342 (Ind. 1965); Alexander v. Randall, 133 N.W.2d 124 (Iowa 1965).
7. *See* William Hazard, *Education and the Law* (New York: The Free Press, 1978), p. 3.
8. *Compare* School Dist. No. 3, Town of Adams v. Callahan, 297 N.W. 407 (Wis. 1941); Sunnywood Common School Dist. v. County Bd. of Educ., 131 N.W.2d 105 (S.D. 1964) with State *ex rel.* Donaldson v. Hines, 182 P.2d 865 (Kan. 1947).
9. *See* Board of Educ. of Aberdeen-Huntington Local School Dist. v. State Bd. of Educ., 189 N.E.2d 81 (Ohio App. 1962); Child Welfare Society of Flint v. Kennedy School Dist., 189 N.W. 1002 (Mich. 1922); State *ex rel.* Clark v. Haworth School Trustee, 23 N.E. 946 (Ind. 1890). *See also* Kern Alexander and M. David Alexander, *American Public School Law,* 2nd ed. (St. Paul, MN: West, 1985), pp. 85–86; Newton Edwards, *The Courts and Public Schools* (Chicago: University of Chicago Press, 1955), pp. 27–28.
10. *See* Bell v. Board of Educ. of Shelby County, 215 S.W.2d 1007 (Ky. 1948); Board of Educ. of City of White Plains v. Rogers, 15 N.E.2d 401 (N.Y. 1938); Wiley v. Board of School Comm'rs of Allegheny County, 51 Md. 401 (1879).
11. State *ex rel.* Miller v. Board of Educ. of Unified School Dist. No. 398, Marion County, 511 P.2d 705 (Kan. 1973).
12. Wilt v. State Bd. of Educ., 608 F.2d 1126 (6th Cir. 1979), *cert. denied,* 445 U.S. 964 (1980). *See also* Board of Educ. of Bratenahl Local School Dist. v. State Bd. of Educ., 373 N.E.2d 1238 (Ohio 1978), *cert. denied,* 439 U.S. 865 (1978).
13. Girard School Dist. v. Pittenger, 392 A.2d 261, 264 (Pa. 1978).

14. *See* Craig v. Board of Educ. of City of New York, 19 N.Y.S.2d 293, 301 (Sup. Ct., New York County, 1940), *aff'd mem.*, 27 N.Y.S.2d 993 (App. Div. 1941).
15. *See* Hadley v. Junior College Dist. of Metropolitan Kansas City, 397 U.S. 50 (1970).
16. 42 U.S.C. § 1971, *et seq.* Section 1973 states that "no practice or procedure shall be imposed or applied . . . in a manner which results in a denial or abridgment of the right . . . to vote on account of race . . ." *See* United States v. Marengo County Comm'n, 731 F.2d 1546 (11th Cir. 1984), *cert. denied,* 105 S. Ct. 375 (1984), *on remand,* 623 F. Supp. 33 (S.D. Ala. 1985); United States v. Uvalde Consol. Independent School Dist., 625 F.2d 547 (5th Cir. 1980), *cert. denied,* 481 U.S. 1002 (1981).
17. *See, e.g.,* Ind. Const., art. 2, § 9.
18. *See* People v. Becker, 246 P.2d 103, 105 (Cal. App. 1952).
19. For a discussion of open meeting requirements, *see* James A. Rapp, ed., *Education Law,* vol. 1 (New York: Matthew Bender, 1984), chapter 3, pp. 95–96.
20. *See* Hazard, *Education and the Law,* p. 4.
21. *See* Beegle v. Greencastle-Antrim School Dist., 401 A.2d 374 (Pa. 1979).
22. *See* Schwan v. Board of Educ. of Lansing School Dist., 183 N.W.2d 594 (Mich. App. 1970); Sinnott v. Colombet, 40 P. 329 (Cal. 1895); Stuart v. School Dist. No. 1 of the Village of Kalamazoo, 30 Mich. 69 (1874).
23. New York City School Bds. Ass'n v. Board of Educ., School Dist. of City of New York, 347 N.E.2d 568 (N.Y. 1976). *See also* Morgan v. Polk County Bd. of Educ., 328 S.E.2d 320 (N.C. App. 1985) (county school board was authorized to implement an experimental program lengthening the school day and term).
24. Johnston v. Board of Trustees, 661 P.2d 1045 (Wyo. 1983).
25. McGilvra v. Seattle School Dist. No. 1, 194 P. 817 (Wash. 1921).
26. Board of Educ. v. Rockaway Township Educ. Ass'n, 295 A.2d 380 (N.J. Super. 1972).
27. Bunger v. Iowa High School Athletic Ass'n, 197 N.W.2d 555 (Iowa 1972). *See* note 155, chapter 4.
28. *See* San Antonio Independent School Dist. v. Rodriguez, 411 U.S. 1 (1973).
29. Cooper v. Aaron, 358 U.S. 1, 19 (1958).
30. Helvering v. Davis, 301 U.S. 619, 641 (1937).
31. *See* United States v. Gettysburg Electric Railway Co., 160 U.S. 668 (1896); United States v. Butler, 297 U.S. 1 (1936); Helvering, *id.*
32. Helvering, *id.* at 644–645.
33. For a discussion of litigation pertaining to asbestos removal in schools, *see* Kristin Olson, "Legal Issues in Asbestos Litigation," in *School Law Update—Preventative Law,* T. Jones and D. Semler, eds. (Topeka, KS: National Organization on Legal Problems of Education, 1984), pp. 124–133; text with note 59, chapter 12.
34. 105 S. Ct. 1005 (1985). *See also* Equal Employment Opportunity Comm'n v. Wyoming, 460 U.S. 226 (1983).
35. National League of Cities v. Usery, 426 U.S. 833 (1976). The *Usery* decision halted proposals that were pending before Congress to establish a national collective bargaining law for public school teachers. *See* text with note 16, chapter 11.

36. The four dissenting justices argued that the majority opinion weakens the concept of federalism and reduces the tenth amendment to "meaningless rhetoric." Garcia v. San Antonio Metropolitan Transit Auth., 105 S. Ct. 1005, 1022 (1985) (Powell, J., dissenting).
37. *See* Floyd Delon and Mark Van Zandt, "The Pendulum Continues to Swing: Garcia v. San Antonio Metropolitan Transit Authority," *Education Law Reporter,* vol. 26 (1985), pp. 1–11.
38. Several of the original states were reluctant to ratify the Federal Constitution without the promise of a statement of individual liberties. *See* Robert Rutland, *The Birth of the Bill of Rights, 1776–1791* (Chapel Hill, NC: University of North Carolina Press, 1955), chapters 7, 8. For a discussion of the application of the Bill of Rights to state governmental action, *see* text with note 41, *infra.*
39. Camara v. Municipal Court, 387 U.S. 523, 528 (1967).
40. *See* note 56, *infra.*
41. *See* Cantwell v. Connecticut, 310 U.S. 296, 303 (1940); Gitlow v. New York, 268 U.S. 652, 666 (1925).
42. *See* James McClellan, *Joseph Story and the American Constitution* (Norman, OK: University of Oklahoma Press, 1971), pp. 144–145.
43. *See* Burton v. Wilmington Parking Auth., 365 U.S. 720 (1961).
44. School boards as well as school officials are considered "persons" under 42 U.S.C. § 1983. *See* text with note 172, chapter 8.
45. *See* "The Making of Federal Education Regulations," *Education Daily Special Supplement,* October 1985, pp. 1–3.
46. Alexis de Tocqueville, *Democracy in America,* rev. ed. (New York: Alfred A. Knopf, 1960), vol. 1, p. 280.
47. *See* Marbury v. Madison, 5 U.S. (1 Cranch) 137 (1803).
48. John Coons, William Clune, and Stephen Sugarman, *Private Wealth and Public Education* (Cambridge, MA: Harvard University Press, 1970), p. 287.
49. Crowell v. Benson, 285 U.S. 22, 62 (1932). *See also* Ashwander v. Tennessee Valley Auth., 297 U.S. 288, 348 (1936) (Brandeis, J., concurring).
50. Most educational litigation involves *civil* suits, initiated by individuals alleging injury by another private party. Civil suits often involve claims for damages or requests for specific conduct to cease because it impairs the individual's protected rights. In contrast, *criminal* suits are brought on behalf of society to punish an individual for committing a crime, such as violating compulsory school attendance laws.
51. 347 U.S. 483 (1954).
52. San Antonio Independent School Dist. v. Rodriguez, 411 U.S. 1, 42 (1973).
53. *See* School Dist. No. 12, Phillips County v. Hughes, 552 P.2d 328, 332 (Mont. 1976). If a federally protected right is involved, state administrative appeals need not always be exhausted before initiating a federal lawsuit. *See* text with note 59, *infra.*
54. John Hogan, *The Schools, the Courts, and the Public Interest* (Lexington, MA: D.C. Heath, 1985), p. 11.
55. In 1981 the fifth federal circuit was divided into the fifth and eleventh circuits.
56. Washington, D.C., has its own federal district court and circuit court of appeals because only federal laws apply in this jurisdiction.

57. *See* text with note 94, chapter 9, for a discussion of congressional reaction to the Supreme Court's misinterpretation of congressional intent.
58. *See* text with note 183, chapter 8, for a discussion of eleventh amendment restrictions on federal lawsuits brought by citizens against the state.
59. *See* Loudermill v. Cleveland Bd. of Educ., 105 S. Ct. 1487 (1985); Patsy v. Florida Board of Regents, 457 U.S. 496 (1982); Holley v. Seminole County School Dist., 755 F.2d 1492 (11th Cir. 1985).
60. *See* Migra v. Warren City School Dist. Bd. of Educ., 465 U.S. 75 (1984).
61. *See* Wood v. Strickland, 420 U.S. 308 (1975); text with note 174, chapter 8.

2

Church-State Relations

Identifying the appropriate governmental relationship with religion has generated substantial controversy, and since the mid-twentieth century, schools have provided the battleground for some of the most volatile disputes. With the exception of school desegregation, church-state-school issues have elicited more active involvement of all three branches of government than any other educational topic. This chapter provides an overview of the constitutional framework and legal developments pertaining to church-state relations involving education.

CONSTITUTIONAL FRAMEWORK

The first amendment to the United States Constitution stipulates in part that "Congress shall make no law respecting an establishment of religion or prohibiting the free exercise thereof." Although this amendment was directed toward the federal government and was silent regarding state intrusions on individual religious freedoms, the fourteenth amendment, adopted in 1868, placed restrictions on state action impairing personal rights. In the twentieth century the Supreme Court has recognized that the fundamental concept of "liberty" embodied in the fourteenth amendment incorporates first amendment guarantees and safeguards them against state interference.[1] Since education is primarily a state function, most church-state controversies involving schools have been initiated through the fourteenth amendment.

Constitutional scholars have engaged in substantial debate over whether the framers of the establishment and free exercise clauses intended to sever civil and sectarian affairs or merely to prohibit religious discrimination and governmental promotion of a particular sect.[2] While this debate seems likely to continue, the ultimate responsibility for interpreting the restrictions imposed on governmental action by the first amendment resides with the United States Supreme Court. The vast majority of constitutional law governing church-state relations has evolved since World War II, and the Supreme Court has developed separate judicial tests for assessing claims under the establishment and free exercise clauses.

In the first major establishment clause decision, *Everson v. Board of Education,* the Supreme Court in 1947 reviewed the history of the first amendment and concluded that the establishment clause (and its fourteenth amendment application to states) means:

> Neither a state nor the Federal Government can set up a church. Neither can pass laws which aid one religion, aid all religions, or prefer one religion over another. . . . Neither a state nor the Federal Government can, openly or secretly, participate in the affairs of any religious organizations or groups and vice versa. In the words of Jefferson, the clause against establishment of religion by law was intended to erect 'a wall of separation between Church and State.'[3]

Since 1970 the Supreme Court has applied a tripartite test in assessing most establishment clause claims. To withstand scrutiny under this test, governmental action must: (1) have a secular purpose; (2) have a primary effect that neither advances nor impedes religion; and (3) avoid excessive governmental entanglement with religion.[4] If governmental action fails any of the prongs of this *tripartite test,* it will be struck down under the establishment clause. Some justices on the high court have faulted the tripartite test and urged flexibility in assessing challenged governmental action,[5] but this three-part test is still applied in most establishment clause cases.

While the establishment clause primarily is used to challenge governmental *advancement* of religion, free exercise suits usually focus on *secular* (nonreligious) governmental regulations that allegedly have a coercive effect on the practice of religious beliefs. In establishment clause cases, the legality of the governmental action itself is at issue, whereas in free exercise claims, individuals generally accept the legitimacy of the governmental regulation but assert a right to special treatment for religious reasons.

To evaluate free exercise claims, the judiciary applies a balancing test that includes an assessment of whether practices dictated by a sincere and legitimate religious belief have been impeded by the governmental action, and if so, to what extent. If such an impairment is substantiated, the court then evaluates whether the state action serves a *compelling* interest that justifies the burden imposed on the free exercise of religious beliefs. Even if such a compelling interest is shown, the judiciary will require the government to attain its objective through means that are the least burdensome on free exercise rights. Applying this balancing test, the judiciary must make sensitive judgments as to what constitutes a sincere religious belief and a burden on its practice, and what types of governmental interests are required to override free exercise rights.

In the most significant school case involving a free exercise claim, *Wisconsin v. Yoder*, the Supreme Court exempted Amish children from compulsory school attendance after successful completion of eighth grade. Noting that the assurance of an educated citizenry ranks at the "apex" of the functions of the state, the Court nonetheless concluded that parental rights to practice their legitimate religious beliefs outweighed the state's interest in mandating an additional two years of formal schooling for Amish youth. The Court declared that "a State's interest in universal education, however highly we rank it, is not totally free from a balancing process when it impinges on fundamental rights and interests."[6] The Court cautioned, however, that its ruling was limited to the Amish who offer a structured vocational program to prepare their youth for a cloistered agrarian community rather than mainstream American society.

Not only do courts apply different criteria to assess free exercise in contrast to establishment clause claims, they also impose different remedies for violations of the two clauses. If an establishment clause violation is found, continuation of the unconstitutional governmental activity is prohibited. If governmental action is found to impair free exercise rights, accommodations to enable individuals to practice their beliefs may be required. The remedy for a free exercise impairment often entails an exemption from the religiously offensive practice, but the practice itself would not have to be eliminated as it would if the state action were found to abridge the establishment clause.

The most troublesome church-state controversies involve competing free exercise and establishment clause claims because there is an inherent tension between the two clauses. Both "are cast in absolute terms, and either of which, if expanded to a logical extreme, would tend to clash with the other."[7] The principle that the first amendment demands wholesome governmental neutrality toward religion has been easier to state than to apply. Accommodations to respect free exercise rights can be viewed as an advancement of religion in violation of the establishment clause, but overzealous efforts to guard against state sponsorship of religion can impinge upon free exercise rights. The line is sometimes blurred between accommodation and advancement and between separation and hostility. The Supreme Court has not yet viewed a case as involving a clash between the two religious guarantees; thus, it has avoided specifying a hierarchy of first amendment freedoms. However, the tension between the clauses has complicated the judiciary's task in assessing claims regarding governmental relations with sectarian schools and the role of religion in public schools. In the remainder of this chapter, applicable legal principles are identified and unresolved issues are highlighted in connection with various facets of church-state relations involving education.

RELIGIOUS INFLUENCES IN PUBLIC SCHOOLS

From colonial days until the mid-twentieth century, religious (primarily Protestant) materials and observances were prevalent in many public school classrooms. In two precedent-setting decisions in the early 1960s, the Supreme Court prohibited public schools from sponsoring daily prayer and Bible reading, concluding that such activities advance religion in violation of the establishment clause.[8] The Court reasoned that the voluntary participation of students in the religious activities was irrelevant to the constitutional impairment. The fact that daily devotional activities were conducted under the auspices of the public school was sufficient to abridge the first amendment.

These decisions, however, left many issues unresolved, and the judiciary continues to grapple with sensitive, emotionally charged questions pertaining to religious influences in public education. Is the constitutional violation lessened if students rather than teachers initiate the devotional activities? If religious observances are occasional rather than daily, is the threat of an establishment clause impairment reduced? Do student religious groups have a free exercise or free speech right to hold devotional meetings in public schools if other student groups are allowed such access to school facilities? Can religious speech be distinguished from other types of speech in the imposition of restrictions? To date, only partial answers have been provided to these and related questions in the public school context, as illustrated by the following discussion of the legal status of silent and verbal prayer, student-initiated devotional meetings, religious holiday observances, the display of religious symbols, and religious instruction.

School-Sanctioned Prayer

Students have a free exercise right to engage in private devotional activities in public schools if they do not interfere with regular school activities. Indeed, it would be difficult to monitor whether students were engaging in silent prayer. It is generally accepted that individual students can even engage in audible prayer (e.g., before lunch) as long as the activity is private and nondisruptive. Controversies have focused on state laws or school board policies that condone student devotionals, thus placing the stamp of public school approval on such activities.

It was traditionally assumed that state laws calling for a period of silent meditation or prayer in public schools were constitutional.[9] Recent decisions, however, indicate that the judiciary is becoming more reluctant to accept the asserted nonreligious purpose for these laws. Since 1982 a West Virginia constitutional amendment and laws in four states calling for a period of silent meditation or prayer in public schools have been struck down under the establishment clause.[10] Although the New Jersey silent meditation law did not mention "prayer" per se, the federal district court, and subsequently the Third Circuit Court of Appeals, found that the law was intended to return religious observances to public schools. The appeals court reasoned that the law had a sectarian purpose in that it was designed to accommodate the sectarian beliefs of some students—those who worship through silent prayer.[11]

In 1985, the United States Supreme Court rendered its first decision on this issue, affirming the Eleventh Circuit Court of Appeals' conclusion that a 1981 Alabama law, calling for a daily period for silent meditation or voluntary prayer, violated the establishment clause.[12] In this case, *Wallace v. Jaffree,* the Supreme Court relied heavily on an assessment of the legislative history of the law in concluding that it was intended to convey a clear preference for students to engage in prayer during the moment of silence. The Court noted that under a 1978 Alabama law, authorizing a period of silent meditation in public schools, students already had the right to pray silently if they so desired. Thus, the Court majority concluded that the only logical reason for adding the phrase "or voluntary prayer" in the 1981 law was to encourage public school students to pray.

However, the Court in *Jaffree* indicated that laws calling for silent meditation or prayer in public schools without a legislative intent to impose prayer on students would probably withstand scrutiny under the establishment clause. Thus, a determination of the constitutional status of such laws (which almost half of the states have enacted) will have to be made on a case-by-case basis.

Even more controversial than silent prayer periods are disputes over various types of voluntary *audible* devotional activities in public schools because free speech rights as well as religious liberties are at issue. Several states currently have laws that allow voluntary spoken prayer in public education. However, such laws or school board policies have not withstood judicial scrutiny when challenged. Since 1980, the Supreme Court has affirmed without an opinion or declined to review decisions in which federal appellate courts have struck down two state laws calling for voluntary spoken prayer in public schools, a school board's attempt to permit student-led prayers in school assemblies, and state-condoned devotional activities initiated by teachers.[13] The appeals courts reasoned that there was little constitutional distinction between such practices and the state-imposed devotional activities barred under the establishment clause by the Supreme Court in the early 1960s. The assertion that students have a free exercise right to engage in devotional activities conducted under the auspices of the public school has not been persuasive.

School personnel might be vulnerable to liability if they encourage or even permit violations of the establishment clause in public schools.[14] In an Iowa case, a teacher was successful in obtaining $300 in damages for "emotional distress" resulting from exposure to prayers led by the principal during school assemblies.[15] The teacher also sought punitive damages, but the court reasoned that punitive damages were not warranted without evidence that the principal's unlawful actions were motivated by malicious and wanton intent. More recently, the Tenth Circuit Court of Appeals recognized that "plaintiffs are entitled to recover compensatory damages for the loss of the inherent value of their rights under the Establishment Clause, even if they are unable to demonstrate consequential injury."[16] The court further held that punitive damages might be warranted if the conduct of school authorities is shown to represent reckless or callous indifference toward substantive constitutional rights.

Traditionally, the judiciary appeared less inclined to find an establishment clause violation in connection with baccalaureate services and prayers during graduation ceremonies than in connection with routine devotional activities in public education. There has been no contention that baccalaureate programs and invocations are instructional rather than religious; instead, the activities have been defended primarily because of their transient, ceremonial nature. A Michigan federal district court recently upheld the inclusion of invocations and benedictions in the graduation ceremonies of two school districts, concluding that the longstanding practices, partly ceremonial and partly religious, do not pose a danger of religious indoctrination.[17] Other courts have reasoned that such fleeting events pose far less danger of influencing students' beliefs than do daily religious observances in public schools.[18]

However, since 1982 state appellate courts in California and Oregon[19] and an Iowa federal district court[20] have struck down such religious observances in graduation programs. Also, a Texas federal district court has enjoined the recitation or singing of a school prayer at extracurricular events and graduation ceremonies.[21] In all of these cases, the courts found evidence of governmental action to advance a particular religious creed; neither the extracurricular nature of the events nor the voluntary participation of students reduced the establishment clause impairments.

Despite the ambiguity regarding prayers in graduation ceremonies, the Supreme Court consistently has interpreted the establishment clause as prohibiting state endorsed devotional activities during instructional time in public schools. As a result, attempts have been made to restrict the authority of federal courts to review school prayer cases[22] and to amend the Federal Constitution to authorize prayer in public education.[23] If the Supreme Court continues to rely on the first amendment in barring devotional activities from public schools, efforts to secure a constitutional amendment to allow such activities seem destined to escalate. Should such an amendment receive congressional endorsement and be ratified by the necessary thirty-eight states to become part of the Federal Constitution, the ramifications for the vitality of the first amendment's religion clauses would undoubtedly reach far beyond the issue of public school prayer.

STUDENT-INITIATED DEVOTIONAL MEETINGS

Particularly sensitive first amendment questions are raised in connection with student groups holding devotional meetings in public school facilities before or after school, because this issue pits free speech, free exercise, and association rights against establishment clause restrictions. Since 1980 five federal appellate courts have ruled that the establishment clause bars such devotional meetings under the supervision of public school personnel.[24] Rejecting both free exercise and free speech claims of the students, the appellate courts have concluded that students' rights to assemble and express religious views during noninstructional time are limited by overriding establishment clause considerations in public school settings. The courts have not been persuaded that student religious groups must be treated like any other student organizations; indeed, they have reasoned that the establishment clause *demands* differential treatment.

In 1981, however, the Supreme Court upheld the right of college students to hold prayer meetings on state-supported campuses. In this case, *Widmar v. Vincent,* the Court ruled that state college campuses constitute an open forum for student expression and that any infringement on student access to this forum to express views—including religious views—must be justified by a compelling governmental interest.[25] Acknowledging that compliance with the establishment clause is a compelling state interest, the Court concluded that a policy allowing *all* student groups the same access to campus facilities would satisfy the tripartite test. An "equal access" policy would have the secular purpose of making campus facilities available to student organizations; it would not advance religion because the institution's endorsement of religious groups would not be implied any more than would its endorsement of student political groups, and it would avoid excessive governmental entanglement with religion because minimal supervision of student organizations is required on college campuses.

A comparison of the *Widmar* decision with the federal appellate court rulings involving public school students suggests that a distinction between religious expression and other types of speech may be *required* by the establishment clause in public elementary and secondary schools, but such a content distinction *cannot be made* in the open forum for student expression created by state-supported institutions of higher education.

Perhaps this double standard is partially explained by the differences in the respective students as to their maturity, vulnerability to indoctrination, and need for faculty supervision; the compulsory nature of at least part of high school; and the fact that college students often reside on campus and do not have the option of holding devotional meetings in their homes.

Yet, advocates of public school prayer have capitalized on the *Widmar* decision in asserting that high school students, and perhaps *all* public school pupils, have a free speech right to engage in devotional activities in public schools during noninstructional time. Because the Supreme Court has recognized that high school as well as college students have a constitutional right to express ideological views in a nondisruptive manner,[26] it has been argued that religious expression, like other forms of speech, deserves the same protection in public secondary schools as in higher education. This controversy has divided civil libertarians, with some asserting that free speech rights should prevail and others contending that the establishment clause is controlling.

In 1986 the Supreme Court sidestepped these sensitive first amendment issues in *Bender v. Williamsport Area School District*.[27] In *Bender* the federal district court ruled that a student club, formed for the purpose of promoting spiritual growth and positive attitudes among its members, had a free expression right to hold devotional meetings during the high school's activity period. According to the district court, the activity period constituted a forum created by school authorities for student expression, and religious speech could not be treated differently from other types of student expression. Reversing the decision, the federal appellate court held that the establishment clause precludes school authorities from allowing student-initiated devotional meetings under the auspices of the public school. Similar to the reasoning of four other federal appeals courts, the Third Circuit Court of Appeals concluded that a minimal restriction on free expression rights is justified by the overriding state interest in guarding against the advancement of religion.

Declining to address the merits of the case, the Supreme Court vacated the appellate court's decision on technical grounds, thus reinstating the federal district court's ruling. The majority held that the plaintiff, a member of the school board, lacked standing to appeal the federal district court's order; his status as a board member did not entitle him to bring suit on behalf of the board, and he could not appeal in his individual capacity since an act of the board was at issue. Furthermore, the majority reasoned that the plaintiff did not have standing to appeal as a parent because nothing in the record indicated that he or his children had been injured by the contested practice. Although the Court majority avoided the first amendment issues in *Bender*, four dissenting justices indicated that they would have addressed the merits of the case and relied on *Widmar* in upholding the student religious group's free speech right to meet in public school facilities during noninstructional time. Until the Supreme Court clarifies the governing legal principles, however, the constitutional status of such religious meetings remains unresolved.

Ambiguity also surrounds the constitutionality of the Equal Access Act (EAA), enacted by Congress in 1984. The act stipulates that if federally assisted public secondary schools provide a limited open forum for noncurriculum student groups to meet during noninstructional time, "equal access" to that forum cannot be denied based on the "religious, political, philosophical or other content of the speech at such meetings."[28] Under the EAA, school authorities have a choice; they can deny school access during noninstructional time to student groups that are not an extension of the curriculum, or they can create a limited forum for student expression and provide equal access to all student groups.[29] In essence, once a limited forum is created, the act extends the *Widmar* rationale to the high school level and thus is in conflict with the appellate court rulings discussed above.

Compliance with the EAA, which became effective in 1984, has been plagued by definitional questions such as what constitutes a noncurriculum student group, and to what extent can nonschool personnel participate in student-initiated meetings for such meetings to be protected under the act.[30] The EAA was championed by the religious right, but homosexual groups, religious cults, and antinuclear war protesters already have attempted to use the act to gain access to public school facilities. In the only federal appellate decision addressing the EAA to date, the Third Circuit Court of Appeals ruled that Congress intended to give students a private right to file lawsuits under the act to force school authorities to comply with the law.[31] In this case, involving a student group's request to hold a peace exposition on public school grounds, the appeals court also interpreted the EAA as applying to student-initiated groups involving nonstudents as long as the nonstudents neither control nor regularly attend the groups' activities.

Of course, the threshold question pertaining to the EAA is whether it violates the establishment clause. Although the act itself was not at issue in *Bender*, the students' claim focused on their asserted right to hold devotional meetings in a forum created for student expression during noninstructional time. If the Supreme Court had affirmed the appellate court's decision, it would have cast serious doubt on the constitutionality of the federal law. But since the Supreme Court declined to address the "equal access" concept in *Bender*, the legal status of the EAA under the establishment clause has not been clarified. In federal circuits where appellate courts have barred student-initiated devotional meetings in public schools, some attorneys are advising educators to disregard the EAA, at least in connection with student religious meetings.[32] In other jurisdictions, high schools are complying with the act by providing school access to all student-initiated groups or eliminating *any* forum for groups that are not curriculum-related.

Observance of Religious Holidays and Display of Religious Symbols

Most courts have not condoned the distribution of religious literature, such as Gideon Bibles in public schools,[33] but the display of religious documents and the observance of religious holidays remains controversial. For example, in 1980 the Supreme Court declined to hear an appeal of a decision allowing religious holiday observances and the temporary display of religious symbols in public education,[34] but a week later, the divided Court struck down a Kentucky law calling for the posting of the Ten Commandments in public school classrooms.[35] In the first case, the historical and cultural significance of Christmas convinced the Eighth Circuit Court of Appeals that the prudent and objective observance of this holiday in public schools does not serve to advance religion, even though songs such as Silent Night are sung and the nativity scene is displayed.[36] The appeals court reasoned that the school board's policy, allowing the observance of holidays with both a religious and secular basis, has the nonreligious purpose of improving the overall instructional program. The court noted that much of the art, literature, and music associated with Christmas has acquired a cultural importance that is no longer strictly religious.

In contrast, the five-member Supreme Court majority in the second case was not persuaded that the asserted cultural significance of the Ten Commandments justifies posting this religious document in public schools.[37] Distinguishing the posting of religious texts from the permissible use of religious literature in academic courses, the majority reasoned that the purpose behind the Kentucky legislation was to advance a particular religious faith in violation of the establishment clause. The majority rejected the state judiciary's conclusion that the constitutional impairment was neutralized because the copies were purchased with private donations and carried the disclaimer that "[t]he secular application of the Ten Commandments is clearly seen in its adoption as the fundamental legal code of Western Civilization and the Common Law of the United States."[38]

It should be noted, however, that in a subsequent decision the Supreme Court upheld the use of municipal funds to erect a Christmas display with the nativity scene in a private park. Reasoning that the nativity scene is a traditional holiday symbol, the majority concluded that such a display does not advance religion nor entangle the government in religious affairs.[39] The Court also divided evenly in a 1985 case, thus affirming the Second Circuit Appellate Court's decision in which two citizens' groups successfully challenged a municipality's denial of their request to display a crèche in a public park during the Christmas season.[40] The appeals court reasoned that the accommodation requested in a public park, a traditional public forum, did not implicate the establishment clause. Although the federal judiciary has appeared more sensitive to potential establishment clause violations in connection with vulnerable school children than it has outside the school domain, these decisions upholding the use of public funds or grounds to display the nativity scene will likely be relied on in future efforts to secure judicial endorsement of the observance of religious holidays and the posting of religious symbols in public schools.

Religious Instruction

Public school educators must adhere to establishment clause restrictions on governmental promotion of a religious creed. Because teachers have a captive audience in public schools, their actions have been carefully scrutinized to ensure that the classroom is not used as a forum to indoctrinate sectarian beliefs. Choper has noted that the academic study of religion cannot "take the form of teaching 'that religion is sacred' nor present religious dogma as factual material."[41] The establishment clause clearly prohibits teachers from using their position of authority to influence students' freedom of religious belief or choice.

As early as 1918 the Iowa Supreme Court concluded that Catholic nuns who were serving as public school teachers were unconstitutionally proselytizing students by teaching sectarian subjects.[42] More recently, the Supreme Court declined to review a decision in which the Eleventh Circuit Court of Appeals enjoined teacher-initiated devotional activities in an Alabama school district. The appeals court held that the absence of a state law or school board policy authorizing the activities did not negate the constitutional violation. The court reasoned that since public school teachers function as agents of the state, their actions—whether self-initiated or directed by the school board—are subject to establishment clause restrictions.[43] A Michigan federal district court similarly held that teachers violated the establishment clause by praying in their classrooms, reading from the Bible, and telling Bible stories. The court rejected the assertion that parents' and students' liberty interests were impaired by prohibiting teachers from promoting religious activities in public school classrooms.[44]

In several cases, teachers have been discharged for crossing the line from teaching *about* religion to proselytization. For example, a New York tenured teacher was dismissed based on evidence that she had tried to recruit students to join her religious organization, conducted prayer sessions in her office, offered to transport pupils to religious meetings, and used her classroom to promote tenets of her religious faith.[45] The New York appeals court concluded that such actions were in clear violation of the establishment clause and constituted valid grounds for termination. Similarly, a Pennsylvania commonwealth court upheld the dismissal of a public school teacher for refusing to comply with the superintendent's directives to cease opening classes with the Lord's Prayer and a Bible story.[46] Rejecting the teacher's assertion that the dismissal interfered with his free exercise of religious beliefs, the court held that public school teachers' free exercise rights do not entitle them to conduct religious activities in the classroom. The court recognized that while the teacher's freedom to *hold* religious beliefs is absolute, an individual's use of the "power, prestige, and influence" of the position as a public school teacher to lead devotional activities is barred by the establishment clause.[47]

The South Dakota Supreme Court also upheld the nonrenewal of a biology teacher for devoting too much instructional time to the biblical theory of creation.[48] The teacher received repeated warnings to follow the school board's adopted guidelines for teaching biology and to limit his discussion of the Genesis account. After the teacher persisted in violating the guidelines, the board refused to renew his contract. The teacher challenged the action as arbitrary, capricious, and in violation of his constitutional due process, free speech, and free exercise rights. Rejecting these assertions, the court concluded that the teacher willfully disregarded the board's guidelines and that all procedural requirements were met prior to the nonrenewal action.

Teachers also can be discharged for disregarding selected aspects of the curriculum that conflict with their religious values. For example, the Seventh Circuit Court of Appeals upheld a school board's dismissal of a kindergarten teacher who refused to teach patriotic topics, and the United States Supreme Court declined to review the case.[49] The teacher, who interpreted literally the Biblical prohibition against worshiping graven images, refused to teach about the American flag, the observance of patriotic holidays, and the importance of various historical leaders such as Abraham Lincoln. Upholding the dismissal, the appellate court noted that although the teacher enjoys the freedom to believe, she has "no constitutional right to require others to submit to her views and to forego a portion of their education they would otherwise be entitled to enjoy."[50] The court further recognized that if all teachers were allowed to design their own curriculum based on their personal beliefs, students would receive a "distorted and unbalanced view of our country's history."[51] Teachers possess constitutionally protected free exercise rights, but their conduct is subject to regulation in the interest of maintaining an appropriate educational environment.[52]

While it violates the establishment clause for public school teachers to proselytize students, it is permissible to teach the Bible and other religious documents from a literary, cultural, or historical perspective. If no mention of religion were allowed in public education, an accurate portrayal of historical events would not be possible. When daily Bible reading was barred from public schools in 1963, the Supreme Court emphasized that the academic study of religion is permissible, and indeed, desirable.[53]

However, the line is not always clear between teaching *about* religion and *instilling* religious tenets. While comparative religion courses have seldom been controversial, numerous Bible study courses have been challenged as a ploy to advance sectarian beliefs. Courts have carefully evaluated curricular materials and even reviewed video tapes of lessons in determining whether such instruction fosters a particular creed. Courts consistently have struck down programs where private groups have controlled the hiring and supervision of personnel and the selection of curricular materials.[54] With evidence that religious tenets are being advanced in a course, the judiciary has required the curriculum to be redesigned to ensure that the subject matter is approached from an objective academic perspective. Most courts have reasoned that Bible study courses which can pass first amendment scrutiny should be offered on an elective rather than required basis because even the academic study of religion may interfere with the tenets of some faiths.[55]

EXCUSAL FROM PUBLIC SCHOOL FOR RELIGIOUS INSTRUCTION AND OBSERVANCES

Although the Supreme Court has struck down the release of public school students from their regular instruction to receive religious training from clergy in public school classrooms,[56] the Court has recognized that the school can accommodate religion by releasing students during the school day to receive such religious training *off* public school grounds. Noting that the state must not be hostile toward religion, the Court declared in 1952 that "when the State encourages religious instruction or cooperates with religious authorities by adjusting the schedule of public events to sectarian needs, it follows the best of our traditions."[57] A release-time program has even been upheld in a school district where students receive an hour of religious instruction each week in a mobile unit parked on the edge of school property.[58] Courts have not been persuaded that academic instruction comes to a halt during the period when students are released for religious instruction, thus denying nonparticipating pupils their state-created right to an education.[59] Courts also have not found that release-time programs advance religion because students are confined to a single choice of attending religious classes or remaining in the public school.[60]

While upholding a release-time program in Utah, the Tenth Circuit Court of Appeals enjoined the school's practice of awarding course credit in the public high school for the secular aspects of instruction received at a Mormon seminary.[61] The seminary program entailed an hour of instruction each day oriented toward the tenets of the Church of the Latter Day Saints; most of the high school's students participated in the release-time program. The court reasoned that the award of credit for portions of the religious instruction would entangle school officials with the church because of the monitoring required. However, the court noted that under certain circumstances (where monitoring of course content is not necessary to ascertain secular components of the instruction), public schools might recognize release-time classes as satisfying elective hours. The court also reasoned that the time spent by students in the seminary program could be counted in calculating the school's eligibility for state aid.

Requests for students and teachers to be excused from public school to observe religious holidays raise particularly delicate issues because such requests usually are made by members of minority sects; schools are closed when the majority of teachers and students are observing their religious holidays. Courts have been called on to determine how far public school authorities *must go* in accommodating religious holidays and how far they *can go* before such accommodations abridge the establishment clause.

Most litigation in this arena has involved claims by teachers that personnel leave policies are discriminatory in their treatment of religious absences; these claims are addressed in chapter 9. A few cases, however, have focused on students. In 1982 the Fifth Circuit Court of Appeals affirmed a federal district court's decision striking down a school's policy that allowed students only two excused absences for religious holidays.[62] The policy was challenged by student members of the Worldwide Church of God, a sect that requires observance of several holy days and a week-long religious convocation. The court reasoned that the school's interests in ensuring regular school attendance and protecting teachers from extra work were not sufficiently compelling to justify requiring students to take unexcused absences to observe their religious holidays. The court also rejected the school's contention that by allowing excused absences the school would be advancing a particular faith in violation of the establishment clause. The court concluded that the school would be following a course of neutrality toward religion by granting excused absences for religious holiday observances.

The judiciary has not, however, condoned excessive student absences for religious reasons. For example, a Pennsylvania court rejected a parental request for their children to be absent every Friday, which is the sacred day of the Muslim religion.[63] Finding that the state could not assure an adequate education for a child who misses one-fifth of the instruction, the court held that the state's interest in providing continuity in instruction prevailed over the parents' free exercise rights in this case.

Also, courts have not been receptive to attempts to avoid school attendance altogether for religious reasons. The Virginia Supreme Court recognized that "no amount of religious fervor . . . in opposition to adequate instruction should be allowed to work a lifelong injury" to children.[64] Although parents can select private education for their children, courts have rejected parental claims that they have a first amendment right to *disregard* compulsory attendance laws in order to shield their children from the secular influences in public schools.[65] As discussed previously, the one judicially endorsed exception to compulsory attendance pertains to Amish children who have successfully completed eighth grade. In exempting the Amish from an additional two years of compulsory education, the Supreme Court recognized the uniqueness of the Amish lifestyle.[66]

RELIGIOUS EXEMPTIONS FROM PUBLIC SCHOOL ACTIVITIES

Teachers and other school employees have initiated a few requests for exemptions from religiously offensive public school activities, but most exemptions have been sought for students. Parents have asked for their children to be excused from particular requirements that allegedly impair the practice of their beliefs. In evaluating whether such requests must be honored by school authorities, courts have been called on to balance parents' interests in directing the religious upbringing of their children against the state's interest in assuring an educated citizenry.

Courts have found free exercise rights overriding in striking down required student participation in certain public school activities and observances. In a landmark 1943 case, *West Virginia State Board of Education v. Barnette,* the United States Supreme Court ruled that students could not be required to salute the American flag in contravention of their religious beliefs.[67] This decision overturned a precedent established by the Court only three years earlier.[68] In *Barnette,* the Court reasoned that refusal to participate in the flag salute ceremony does not interfere with the rights of others to do so or threaten any type of disruption. Thus, state action to compel this observance "transcends constitutional limitations on [school authorities'] power and invades the sphere of intellect and spirit which it is the purpose of the First Amendment to our Constitution to reserve from all official control."[69] Based on *Barnette,* several courts subsequently have protected students' rights not only to decline to participate for religious or philosophical reasons in the flag salute ceremony, but also to register a silent protest by remaining seated during the observance.[70] Of course, if a student should carry the silent protest to an extreme, such as lying down or standing on his hands during the observance, the threat of classroom disruption would justify curtailing such conduct.

Although the Supreme Court has not directly addressed teachers' free exercise rights in connection with patriotic observances in public schools, several lower courts have adopted the *Barnette* rationale in concluding that teachers, like students, have a first amendment right to refuse to pledge their allegiance as a matter of personal conscience. For example, in upholding a teacher's refusal to participate in this activity, the Second Circuit Court of Appeals declared that "the right to remain silent in the face of an illegitimate demand for speech is as much a part of First Amendment protections as the right to speak out in the face of an illegitimate demand for silence."[71] However, teachers cannot deny students the opportunity to engage in the flag salute and Pledge of Allegiance. Teachers have the right not to participate, but they do not have the right to eliminate this observance from their classrooms.

Patriotic observances have not been the only source of controversy; religious exemptions also have been sought from components of the curriculum. Whereas teachers cannot assert a free exercise right to disregard aspects of the state-prescribed curriculum,[72] the judiciary has been more receptive to students' requests for exemptions from instructional requirements. Students, unlike teachers, are compelled to attend school, and for many this means public school. Accordingly, the judiciary has been sensitive to the fact that certain public school policies may have a coercive effect on the practice of religious beliefs. In balancing the interests involved, courts consider the extent that the school requirement burdens the exercise of sincere religious beliefs, the governmental justification for the requirement, and the alternative means available to meet the state's objectives. School authorities must substantiate a compelling interest to deny students an exemption from a requirement that impairs their free exercise rights.

Students have been successful in securing religious exemptions from various instructional activities, such as sex education courses, officers' training programs, and specific class assignments where alternative assignments can be used to satisfy the objectives in a given course.[73] The relief ordered in these cases has entailed the excusal of specific children, but the secular activities themselves have not been disturbed. Also, schools have not been required to make special arrangements or to alter their programs to protect students from the embarrassment associated with nonparticipation.[74]

Requests for exemptions from physical education classes have generated several lawsuits. In 1962 the Alabama Supreme Court affirmed a trial court's conclusion that a high school student could be required to take a course in physical education even though some aspects of the course offended her religious beliefs. The court found that the school had a compelling interest in assuring the physical fitness of all pupils and that the school's concessions to the student's beliefs were adequate in that she was excused from participating in specific exercises and wearing attire considered religiously offensive.[75] Although generally assumed that the state can require all students to participate in physical education instruction, in 1978 an Illinois federal district court ruled that free exercise rights prevailed over the governmental interest in mandating coeducational physical education. The court reasoned that the plaintiff Pentecostal students were entitled to be excused from the coeducational instruction and noted that the state retained other options to ensure student participation in physical education; the school could offer sex-segregated classes or individualized instruction for the students who found coeducational classes religiously offensive.[76]

In a recent Tennessee case, fundamentalist parents secured an exemption for their children from being exposed to the broad range of ideas contained in a reading series that offended their religious beliefs.[77] The controversial series was used by all students in grades one through eight in the school district. The parents claimed that mandatory use of the books violated free exercise rights and their constitutional right to direct the upbringing of their children. They sought an alternative reading program and excusal of their children from any class where the controversial readers were being used. While the federal district court initially dismissed the parents' claim, the Sixth Circuit Court of Appeals reversed and remanded the case for a trial. The appeals court reasoned that there were genuine factual disputes regarding the sincerity of the religious beliefs, whether exposure to the books impaired those beliefs, whether an alternative reading program for the offended students would impede the teaching of reading, and whether the requested accommodation would advance religion in violation of the establishment clause. On remand, the trial court ruled that the fundamentalist children were constitutionally entitled to an exemption from exposure to the reading series that impaired their sincerely held religious beliefs. Recognizing the compelling state interest in assuring a literate citizenry, the court reasoned that this interest could be advanced through less restrictive means than the uniform, compulsory use of the reading series in question. The court, however, did not order the school district to establish a separate reading program for the offended students, concluding that such an accommodation would advance religion in violation of the establishment clause. Instead, the court held that the fundamentalist children must be excused from the controversial school program and allowed to study reading at home with their parents as long as they perform satisfactorily on state-prescribed standardized reading tests.

Religious exemptions have not been honored where courts have concluded that the exemption is unnecessary to the practice of religious tenets or where the exemption would substantially disrupt the school program or the student's academic progress. In an illustrative case, parents were unsuccessful in obtaining an exemption for their children from health and music courses and from classes whenever instructional media were used. The New Hampshire federal district court reasoned that the requested exemption would substantially disrupt the public school's instructional program.[78] Courts also have denied religious exemptions for student athletes if an excusal from specific regulations might pose a safety hazard or interfere with the management of athletic teams.[79]

While requests for specific exemptions have been traditionally handled at the local school level and have been relatively rare in the past, such requests have increased recently because of efforts of conservative parents' organizations to secure legislation granting such exemptions. As discussed in chapter 3, these groups have pressed for state pupil protection laws that require parental permission for children to participate in certain instructional activities that might offend the parents' religious, moral, or social values.[80] They also have urged parents to rely on the 1978 amendment to the General Education Provisions Act (Hatch Amendment) which entitles their children to be excused from federally funded instruction involving psychiatric or psychological testing or treatment designed to reveal information in specified sensitive areas.[81] Thus, parents may be able to secure an exemption for their children from a specific instructional activity, even if they cannot substantiate that the activity impairs free exercise rights.

RELIGIOUS CHALLENGES TO THE SECULAR CURRICULUM

Some parents have not been content with securing religious exemptions for their own children; they have pressed for specific courses, activities, and instructional materials to be eliminated from public schools. While courts often have been receptive to requests for individual exemptions from certain public school activities, the judiciary has not been inclined to allow the restriction of the secular curriculum to satisfy parents' religious preferences. In 1968, the Supreme Court recognized that "the state has no legitimate interest in protecting any or all religions from views distasteful to them."[82]

Recent challenges to the curriculum, however, raise complex questions involving the definition of "religion" under the first amendment. Increasingly, allegations are being made that aspects of the public school curriculum violate the establishment clause because they advance an antitheistic belief or "secular humanism," which disavows God and exalts humans as controllers of their own destiny.[83] Evolution, sex education, and values clarification have been central targets, but few aspects of the curriculum have remained untouched by such claims.[84] Those who have attacked humanistic aspects of the curriculum often have asked for the elimination of the offensive secular activities and their replacement with observances and instruction that promote the Christian faith. It has been asserted that because "secular humanism" is so pervasive in the public school curriculum, Christian doctrine should be taught to give students a choice.[85] Courts, however, have not yet concluded that if, in fact, a secular religion is being unconstitutionally advanced, the introduction of theistic instruction will reduce the constitutional infirmity.

Perhaps one of the most troublesome questions facing the judiciary is determining what constitutes religious beliefs and practices that are subject to first amendment protections and restrictions. As noted, the federal judiciary is being pressed to broaden the application of the establishment clause to nontraditional faiths. While the Supreme Court has adopted an expansive view toward religion in protecting the free exercise of beliefs,[86] it has not yet found an establishment clause violation in connection with a nontheistic creed.[87] Only one federal appellate court has ruled that a public school curricular offering (instruction in transcendental meditation) unconstitutionally advances a nontraditional religious belief,[88] but several other courts have suggested that secular religions should be subjected to the same standards that are applied to theistic religions in determining whether the establishment clause has been breached.[89]

Sex education classes have been particularly vulnerable to charges that an anti-theistic faith is being advanced, but courts have not yet been persuaded that such instruction promotes the religion of "secular humanism." In rejecting challenges to the school board's authority to include sex education in the curriculum, courts consistently have found that the courses in question present public health information that furthers legitimate educational objectives.[90] The judiciary also has concluded that the establishment clause precludes the state from barring such instruction simply to conform to the religious beliefs of some parents. In an illustrative case, the New Jersey Supreme Court unanimously endorsed the state's comprehensive sex education mandate, and the United States Supreme Court declined to review the decision. The state high court found nothing in the curriculum guidelines suggesting antagonism toward the Christian religion or support of nonreligion.[91] However, the judiciary has reasoned that students have a free exercise right to be excused from sex education classes if such instruction conflicts with their sectarian beliefs.[92]

Instruction pertaining to evolution also has been challenged as advancing a secular faith. Historically, some states by law barred evolution from the curriculum because it conflicted with the Biblical account of creation. In the famous *Scopes* "Monkey Trial" in 1927, the Tennessee Supreme Court upheld such a law, prohibiting the teaching of any theory that denies the Genesis version of creation or suggests "that man has descended from a lower order of animals."[93] In 1968, however, the United States Supreme Court struck down an Arkansas anti-evolution statute under the establishment clause, reasoning that evolution is science (not a secular religion), and a state cannot restrict student access to such information simply to satisfy religious preferences.[94]

Since creationists have not been successful in convincing the judiciary that evolution unconstitutionally advances a secular faith, recent efforts have focused on securing court orders, requiring evolution to be presented as a theory rather than scientific fact, and laws, requiring equal instructional emphasis on the Biblical account of creation whenever evolution is taught in public education. While a California court ruled that evolution cannot be presented as fact in public schools within the state and that textbooks must be screened accordingly,[95] laws requiring equal emphasis on the Genesis account and evolution have been consistently invalidated. Striking down such an "equal time" law in Arkansas, the federal judge reasoned that creation-science is a sectarian belief, not science, and that the only real effect of the law was to advance religion.[96] In 1985 the Fifth Circuit Court of Appeals reached a similar conclusion in striking down a Louisiana statute that required equal emphasis on the Genesis account whenever evolution was taught.[97] Despite the fate of the Arkansas and Louisiana statutes, similar "equal time" measures continue to be considered in other states, and whether the Biblical account can be taught at all in public school science classes remains unclear.

Although courts have not condoned parental attacks on various aspects of the public school curriculum that do not conform to their religious values, more difficult legal questions are raised when efforts to restrict the curriculum for religious reasons receive legislative or school board support. Conservative parent organizations have pressed for state and federal legislation and school board policies barring instruction that allegedly disavows Christianity. In 1984 Congress amended the federal law providing grants for magnet schools to prohibit the money from being used for instruction in "secular humanism."[98] The law did not specify what activities were proscribed, and the restriction subsequently was removed from the law; nonetheless, legislative bodies continue to consider similar provisions. There is some concern among educators that neutral, *nonreligious* instruction in public schools may be threatened by such efforts.

GOVERNMENTAL REGULATION OF PRIVATE SCHOOLS

It has long been established that parents have a legitimate interest in directing the upbringing of their children, including their educational experiences. In 1925, the United States Supreme Court upheld the right of parents to select private education as an alternative to public schooling. However, in this case, *Pierce v. Society of Sisters,* the Court also recognized that the state has a general welfare interest in mandating school attendance and regulating private education to assure an educated citizenry which is essential to safeguard our democratic form of government.[99] It is generally accepted that the state can require parents to ensure that their children are educated so as not to burden society with illiterate citizens. Volatile disputes have resulted from conflicts between the state's exercise of its *parens patriae* authority to protect the welfare of children and parental interests in having their children educated in settings that reinforce their religious and philosophical beliefs. If the government interferes with parents' childrearing decisions, it must show that the intervention is necessary to protect the child or the state.[100] State regulation of home education programs is addressed in chapter 3, so the discussion here is confined to regulatory activity in connection with private schools, the vast majority of which are church-related.

Recent controversies over state regulation of religious schools have focused primarily on fundamentalist Christian academies and their refusal to comply with state standards. Enrollments in evangelical academies have increased substantially over the past two decades,[101] and refusal of these schools to comply with state regulations often has resulted in the prosecution of parents for violating compulsory attendance mandates. The parents have asserted that the first amendment's prohibition against governmental action interfering with the free exercise of religion precludes the state from imposing regulations that threaten the sectarian mission of religious schools. The Supreme Court has not clarified the scope of the state's authority and duty to regulate the *means* by which all children receive an education, and state courts have rendered conflicting opinions in this domain.

For example, the Ohio Supreme Court invalidated comprehensive state regulations governing practically all aspects of the educational process in private schools as interfering with free exercise rights.[102] The Kentucky Supreme Court also struck down the application of certain state regulations to private schools, reasoning that the regulations interfered with the state constitutional guarantee that parents cannot be compelled to send their children to a school to which they may be conscientiously opposed.[103] The court suggested that the state should monitor the quality of secular education in private schools by requiring all students to take an examination; if students from a particular school consistently score poorly, grounds might be established for closing that school.[104]

However, other courts, such as the supreme courts of Hawaii, Nebraska, North Dakota, and Iowa, have upheld state minimum requirements (e.g., teacher certification standards, prescribed courses, maintenance of pupil records) for private schools, recognizing the state's obligation to assure an educated citizenry.[105] The Iowa Supreme Court rejected the assertion that the state's interest could be satisfied by the occasional testing of private school students, noting that deficiencies might not be discovered until the end of the school year.[106] While several of these decisions have been appealed to the United States Supreme Court, the high court has declined to render an opinion on this subject.

Efforts to secure the autonomy of religious schools have not been confined to judicial forums; substantial activity has taken place in state legislatures. States vary greatly in their regulatory activity in connection with private education. In 1982 it was reported that half of the states imposed no mandatory regulations on the operation of private schools, while twenty-six states required private schools to register with the state.

Eighteen states had some type of mandatory institutional regulations, but only thirteen states required private school faculty members to be certified.[107] Even where states have established regulations, the requirements often are not enforced systematically.

While most controversies over governmental regulation of private schools have involved state efforts to impose personnel and curriculum requirements, some disputes have focused on whether the first amendment entitles religious schools to special treatment under legislation governing other private employers. Church-operated schools have asserted a first amendment right to be exempt from a variety of state and federal laws pertaining to labor relations, unemployment tax programs, and employee protections against discrimination. The Supreme Court has interpreted the Federal Unemployment Tax Act as exempting from the cooperative federal-state tax program (to provide benefits for unemployed workers) those religious schools with no separate identity from the parent church.[108] The Court also has ruled that the National Labor Relations Board does not have jurisdiction over lay faculty in religious schools, in the absence of a clear statement that Congress intended such jurisdiction.[109] In both of these cases, the Court resolved the controversies based on its assessment of congressional intent, thus avoiding the issue of whether such exemptions would be *required* by the first amendment.

However, several lower courts have addressed church-operated schools' assertions that the religion clauses entitle them to special treatment under state or federal laws. The Second Circuit Court of Appeals concluded that neither the establishment clause nor free exercise clause precludes the New York Labor Relations Board from exerting jurisdiction over lay faculty in religious schools. But the appeals court did recognize that the Board could not inquire into asserted religious motives for personnel actions and that reinstatement of a lay teacher could be ordered only if the teacher "would not have been fired otherwise for asserted religious reasons."[110] Several state high courts also have ruled that religious schools are not excluded from state unemployment tax laws and thus are subject to tax assessments under such statutes.[111] In addition, courts have rejected the assertion that compliance with federal minimum wage and equal pay provisions of the Fair Labor Standards Act by religious schools would necessitate excessive governmental entanglement with religion or impair free exercise rights.[112]

In 1986 the Supreme Court addressed a controversy involving whether the Ohio Civil Rights Commission was authorized to investigate a claim of sex discrimination against a private religious school.[113] A pregnant teacher was told that her contract would not be renewed because of the school's religious doctrine that mothers should stay home with preschool children. After the teacher contacted an attorney and threatened litigation, she was terminated for violating the stipulation in her contract that all disputes would be resolved through the internal grievance procedure ("Biblical Chain of Command"). The teacher filed charges with the

Ohio Civil Rights Commission, and the school brought suit for an injunction, asserting that the Commission's investigation into the school's personnel practices violated the religion clauses of the first amendment. The Sixth Circuit Court of Appeals agreed with the school's contention, but the Supreme Court reversed, concluding that the school would have an adequate opportunity to raise its constitutional claims in the state proceedings. Noting that religious schools are not totally free from state regulation, the Court reasoned that the Commission would consider the school's religious justification for what would otherwise be considered illegal conduct and that the school could seek judicial review if not satisfied with the Commission's conclusion.

An issue that has generated substantial controversy pertains to whether the federal government can compel private schools to conform to national public policy as a condition of receiving federal tax-exempt status. In a widely publicized case, the Supreme Court held in 1983 that private schools operating in violation of national policy barring race discrimination cannot receive recognition as a tax-exempt entity which would in effect confer a governmental benefit on such institutions. Recognizing that "determinations of public benefit and public policy are sensitive matters with serious implications for the institutions affected," the eight-member Supreme Court majority concluded that the government's overriding, fundamental interest in eradicating racial discrimination outweighs any burden that the denial of tax-exempt status places on the schools' free exercise rights.[114] The Court declared that it would be "wholly incompatible with the concepts underlying tax exemption to grant the benefit of tax-exempt status to racially discriminatory private educational entities."[115]

This decision has raised some concerns that sectarian schools might be required to conform to other national policies, such as prohibitions against sex discrimination, even if such mandates interfere with the religious mission of the private schools. However, few schools have actually been denied tax-exempt status because of their discriminatory practices. In 1984 the Supreme Court ended an eight-year-old federal suit brought by minority parents seeking to force the Internal Revenue Service to be more assertive in withdrawing tax exemptions from racially discriminatory private schools. The Court majority reasoned that the parents did not have standing to sue the executive branch to induce more stringent regulatory activity.[116] Considerable ambiguity still surrounds the scope of public policy considerations that must be satisfied by private schools as a condition of tax-exempt status.

GOVERNMENTAL AID TO PRIVATE SCHOOLS

Particularly in states with large private school populations, such as New York, Ohio, and Pennsylvania, there have been regular legislative attempts to provide public support for private schools. According to a 1985 study, thirty-eight states provided public aid to private education.[117] The primary types of state aid to private school students were for transportation services (twenty-three states), the loan of textbooks (eighteen states), state-required testing programs (fourteen states), special education for handicapped children (thirteen states), and guidance counseling (ten states).

Although many private schools continue to seek various types of governmental financial support, some of the fundamentalist academies desire absolute autonomy from the government, fearing that government control is a condition of any type of financial assistance. Thus, there is a division among private school advocates in that some are seeking greater public support and adherence to government standards, while others eschew any type of aid and its accompanying regulations.[118]

Advocates of state aid to private education assert that parents should have a choice in selecting education for their children, a choice foreclosed to all but the wealthy without governmental assistance. It also is argued that private schools deserve governmental aid because they perform an important educational service in providing high quality instruction and offering some relief to overburdened public schools. Critics of governmental aid to nonpublic schools have voiced concerns that such aid undermines public education and nurtures class and racial segregation in schools. However, the central argument against government support of private education is that the aid advances religion in violation of the establishment clause, since approximately 85 percent of private schools are church-related.

The future prospects for governmental support of private education hinge to a large degree on the Supreme Court's assessment of whether specific types of aid violate the first amendment. Some of the most significant Supreme Court decisions interpreting the establishment clause have pertained to the use of public funds for private—primarily sectarian—education. Indeed, since 1970 there has generally been at least one case involving state aid to nonpublic schools on the Supreme Court's docket.

The following discussion focuses on two types of governmental assistance for nonpublic education. Initially, the legality of using public funds to support student services in parochial schools is explored. Then the legal status of governmental aid to encourage family educational choice is addressed.

Aid for Student Services

Although the Supreme Court in the mid-twentieth century adopted Thomas Jefferson's metaphor that the establishment clause was intended to create a wall of separation between church and state,[119] several types of public assistance that primarily benefit *students* rather than the religious *institutions* have received judicial endorsement. For example, the Supreme Court has relied on the child benefit doctrine in upholding the use of public funds to provide transportation services for nonpublic school students.[120] The Court has equated the provision of school transportation with other public services such as police and fire protection. Some courts even have upheld provisions that include special transportation accommodations for nonpublic school students, such as transporting these pupils when public schools are closed for vacation and providing private school transportation beyond public school district boundaries.[121]

However, the fact that courts have interpreted the establishment clause as allowing public aid to transport nonpublic school students does not mean that states *must* use public funds for this purpose. Courts in Alaska, Missouri, Oklahoma, and Washington have ruled that such transportation aid to private school students violates state constitutional provisions prohibiting the use of public funds for sectarian purposes.[122]

Similar to transportation aid, the Supreme Court has relied on the child benefit doctrine in upholding the use of public funds to loan textbooks for use by private school children. In 1968 the Court recognized that books are integral to the instructional program, but nonetheless the majority concluded that the loan of textbooks to private school students aids the child and not the religious enterprise.[123] Although this type of aid is permissible under the establishment clause, a number of state courts have invalidated the use of public funds to loan textbooks to parochial school students as violating state constitutional mandates.[124] In 1981 the California Supreme Court called the child benefit doctrine "logically indefensible" in striking down a state law that provided for the loan of textbooks to nonpublic school students.[125]

In addition to finding that the establishment clause does not prohibit governmental assistance in providing transportation and textbooks for private school students, the Supreme Court has concluded that several other types of aid are constitutionally permissible. For example, in 1977 the Court upheld a state law allowing the purchase of reusable workbooks or manuals used in public schools for loan to private schools and the provision of diagnostic services in nonpublic schools. The Court also endorsed the provision of therapeutic services for private school students, but concluded that such services must be performed in a public school or at a neutral site off private school premises. The Court reasoned that occasional diagnostic services performed in a sectarian school pose little threat of advancing religion, whereas regular therapeutic services might be used for religious purposes if performed in a "pervasively sectarian atmosphere."[126]

In 1980 the Court also upheld New York's distribution of up to $20 million to private schools for the cost of record keeping and testing services mandated by the state.[127] The Court distinguished this decision from its 1973 ruling striking down a New York law that provided state aid for teacher-developed tests as well as standardized tests.[128] The Court reasoned that teacher-developed tests would be extremely difficult to monitor and would necessitate excessive government entanglement to ensure that the tests were not used for sectarian purposes. In contrast, the subsequent law providing state aid *only* for standardized tests and record keeping practices was found to pose little danger of advancing the religious mission of sectarian schools.

While the Supreme Court has upheld several types of state aid to private school students, aid that directly subsidizes religious schools or excessively entangles the state with sectarian affairs has not been allowed. Applying the tripartite test during the 1970s, the Court struck down measures allowing direct reimbursement for the costs of teachers' salaries, textbooks, and instructional materials in specified secular subjects;[129] salary supplements for nonpublic school teachers of secular subjects;[130] grants for the maintenance and repair of school facilities;[131] tuition reimbursements to parents of nonpublic school pupils;[132] the direct loan of instructional materials and audiovisual equipment to nonpublic schools;[133] the provision of auxiliary programs, such as guidance counseling, speech and hearing services, and remedial instruction on private school premises;[134] and state aid for field trip transportation.[135] In most of these cases, the Court majority concluded that the proposed aid would provide a direct subsidy to religious schools or would necessitate extensive governmental monitoring of the parochial schools to ensure that the aid would support only secular activities.[136]

In 1985 the Supreme Court delivered two significant decisions in which a majority of the Court maintained a commitment to the tripartite test and to church-state separation in connection with the use of public funds to provide services for parochial school students. In the first case, *School District of City of Grand Rapids v. Ball,* the Court affirmed a decision in which the Sixth Circuit Court of Appeals invalidated an extensive shared-time program in the Grand Rapids, Michigan, School District.[137] Under the challenged program, the public school district rented space from forty parochial schools and one independent private school to offer a variety of enrichment and remedial courses to students who were enrolled in the private schools for the remainder of their instruction. Approximately 10 percent of a given nonpublic school student's instruction during the academic year was provided by the public school district. The shared-time teachers were full-time employees of the public schools, and a "significant portion" previously taught in the nonpublic schools where they were assigned under the shared-time arrangement. Also at issue was a community education program in which classes were taught at the close of the regular school day in classrooms leased from the private schools. Teachers in the community education program were part-time public school employees; virtually all of the teachers were otherwise employed by the nonpublic schools where the community education classes were taught.

Rejecting the argument that the challenged governmental aid flowed to the students rather than the religious institutions, the majority held that aid for the provision of instructional services by teachers in the parochial school building inescapably has the primary effect of providing a "direct and substantial advancement of the sectarian enterprise." [138] The majority reasoned that both the shared-time arrangement and the community education program impermissibly advanced religion in three ways. First, the teachers involved in the programs might intentionally or inadvertently promote religious tenets because no attempt had been made to monitor either program to ensure the avoidance of religious content. Second, the programs pose in effect "the symbolic union of government and religion," thereby conveying to impressionable students that the government is supporting the religious denomination operating the school. Third, the programs may have the effect of directly subsidizing the religious institution by having the public school assume responsibility for a significant portion of the secular instruction.[139] Although the Supreme Court in *Ball* invalidated shared-time programs under which public school districts are in effect subsidizing parochial schools, private school students can participate in publicly supported auxiliary services provided at the public school or at neutral sites.

In the second case, *Aguilar v. Felton,* the Supreme Court ended over a decade of litigation involving New York City's use of federal funds to provide services for private school students under Title I of the Elementary and Secondary Education Act of 1965.[140] Title I (which is now Chapter I of the Education Consolidation and Improvement Act of 1981) provides funds for compensatory education programs in school districts with concentrations of low-income families. To receive these funds for disadvantaged students, local education agencies must meet certain requirements, including the provision of comparable services for eligible students in private schools.

The controversy that eventually led to the 1985 Supreme Court decision focused on New York City's use of public school teachers to provide Title I services in parochial schools, a strategy employed by numerous school districts throughout the nation to satisfy the comparability mandate. Although a suit challenging the New York program was unsuccessful in 1980,[141] in 1984 the Second Circuit Court of Appeals struck down the arrangement, concluding that "the establishment clause . . . constitutes an insurmountable barrier to the use of federal funds to send public school teachers and other professionals into religious schools to carry on instruction, remedial or otherwise, or to provide clinical guidance services of the sort at issue here." [142]

Affirming this decision, the Supreme Court reasoned that the use of publicly funded instructors to teach classes composed exclusively of private school students in private school buildings advances religion and creates excessive governmental entanglement between church and state because of (1) the frequent contacts between public and private school personnel required to implement the program, and (2) the monitoring necessary to guarantee that only secular instruction is provided by public school teachers in religious schools. The Court declared that "the scope and duration of New York's Title I program would require a permanent and pervasive state presence in the sectarian schools receiving aid."[143]

The Supreme Court did not invalidate the provision of comparable services for private school children under Title I/Chapter 1, but it did eliminate one option for providing such services. In light of this decision, remedial programs provided for parochial school students must be offered at public schools or neutral sites, or some other arrangement will have to be devised to meet the comparability requirement. It is generally assumed that the *Aguilar* holding affects other federal aid programs that have a comparability mandate for private school students, such as the Education for All Handicapped Children Act and Chapter 2 of the Education Consolidation and Improvement Act which consolidates twenty-eight former categorical programs into block grants.[144]

While the 1985 rulings indicate that at least a majority of the Supreme Court adheres to a strict interpretation of the establishment clause in cases involving governmental aid for services in religious schools, a discernible trend in Supreme Court decisions in this area is difficult to identify. It appears that aid constituting a direct subsidy to religious schools violates the establishment clause, but criteria have not been provided to distinguish such impermissible aid from permissible aid that benefits the child. The Court's opinions in this domain have been criticized as "ad hoc," lacking theoretical consistency and firm constitutional grounding.[145] In 1985 Supreme Court Justice Rehnquist noted some of the anomalies:

> For example, a State may lend to parochial school children geography textbooks that contain maps of the United States, but the State may not lend maps of the United States for use in geography class. A State may lend textbooks on American colonial history, but it may not lend a film on George Washington, or a film projector to show it in history class. A State may lend classroom workbooks, but may not lend workbooks in which the parochial school children write, thus rendering them nonreusable. A State may pay for bus transportation to religious schools but may not pay for bus transportation from the parochial school to the public zoo or natural history museum for a field trip. A State may pay for diagnostic services conducted in the parochial school but therapeutic services must be given in a different building; speech and hearing 'services' conducted by the State inside the sectarian school are forbidden, but the State may conduct speech and hearing diagnostic testing inside the sectarian school. Exceptional parochial school students may receive counseling, but it must take place outside of the parochial school, such as in a trailer parked down the street. A State may give cash to a parochial school to pay for the administration of State-written tests and State-ordered reporting services, but it may not provide funds for teacher-prepared tests on secular subjects.[146] (citations omitted)

Recent decisions have been characterized by a severely divided Court, with the legality of given practices often hinging on one vote. There is some sentiment that the child benefit doctrine is not as viable as it once was, but without clear Supreme Court directives distinguishing permissible from prohibited types of governmental aid for private school services, continued legislative activity to provide assistance for nonpublic education seems assured.

Aid to Encourage Educational Choice

Since direct subsidies to private schools have been judicially struck down under the establishment clause, private school advocates have pressed for indirect aid to make private schooling a more viable choice for families. Tax relief measures for private school tuition and educational vouchers have received considerable attention in legislative forums.

Tax Relief Measures. Tax benefits in the form of deductions or credits for private school expenses have been proposed at both state and federal levels. While Congress has not yet endorsed any of the proposals for federal income tax credits for private school tuition,[147] several states have enacted tax relief measures for educational expenses. These state laws have generated two Supreme Court decisions and considerable activity in lower courts. The central constitutional question is whether such tax relief measures advance religion in violation of the establishment clause because the primary beneficiaries are parents of parochial school children and ultimately religious institutions.

In 1973 the Supreme Court struck down a New York statute that allowed parents to subtract from the adjusted gross income for state income tax purposes a designated amount for each dependent for whom they had paid at least $50 in nonpublic school tuition.[148] Recognizing that over 85 percent of New York's private schools were sectarian, the Court concluded that the measure aided religion. The Court declared that since the program rewarded parents for sending their children to parochial schools, it had the primary effect of advancing religion.

From 1973 until 1982, several other courts struck down various types of tax relief measures,[149] but in 1983 the United States Supreme Court upheld a Minnesota tax benefit program allowing parents of public or private school students to claim a state income tax deduction of up to $500 for educational expenses for each elementary school dependent and $700 for each secondary school dependent.[150] The five-member Supreme Court majority in *Mueller v. Allen* found the Minnesota law "vitally different" from the earlier New York provision which bestowed benefits *only* on parents of private school students. The majority declared that "a state's decision to defray the cost of educational expenses incurred by parents—regardless of the type of schools their children attend—evidences a purpose that is both secular and understandable."[151] The majority reasoned that such state assistance to a "broad spectrum of citizens" does not have the primary effect of advancing religion, noting that most recent decisions in which state aid to parochial schools has been struck down have involved the direct transmission of public funds to such schools.

Given the Supreme Court's decision in *Mueller,* it seems likely that future tax relief proposals introduced at both state and federal levels will broaden the tax benefit to expenses associated with public as well as private schooling and will take the form of deductions rather than tax credits. Seventeen states considered such tax benefit packages within a year after the *Mueller* decision, but none was enacted. Despite recent polls indicating considerable public support for tuition tax credits,[152] where such measures have been subjected to a referendum, voters consistently have not endorsed the concept.[153] Nonetheless, continued debate over this issue at all levels of government seems assured.

Educational Vouchers. Proposals to fund education through vouchers have been introduced in Congress and several state legislatures, but no extensive experiment with a voucher system has been implemented to date. Under a basic voucher plan, each elementary and secondary school student would be entitled to a voucher for a designated amount that could be redeemed at qualifying public or private schools.[154] Parents could supplement the voucher to provide a more expensive education for their children. Variations of this basic proposal have been suggested that would strengthen state regulatory activities and/or foster equity through variable vouchers based on family income level.[155] Also, proposals have been introduced in Congress to provide federal funds for compensatory education through vouchers that could be used at public or private schools.[156]

Whether such voucher proposals violate the establishment clause by advancing religious schools has not been litigated. However, the likelihood that voucher systems could survive an establishment clause challenge has been strengthened by the Supreme Court's recent decision in which all justices concurred that a visually handicapped individual could receive vocational rehabilitation aid to use for training at a Christian college to prepare for the ministry.[157] The Court in *Witters v. Washington Department of Services for the Blind* reasoned that since the aid went directly to the student who then transmitted the funds to the educational institution of his choice, there was no advancement of sectarian education. The aid was not considered a governmental subsidy to religious schools, and the student's *personal* choice to use rehabilitation aid to pursue religious education was not found to confer state endorsement on sectarian institutions.

This decision may simply be another illustration that the Supreme Court is not as likely to find an establishment clause violation in connection with governmental aid that flows to institutions of higher education than it is with aid to elementary and secondary schools.[158] However, possibly the Court will follow this precedent in upholding proposals for governmental aid to foster family choice in selecting private education below the college level. Since the Court already has ruled that state tax deductions for educational expenses do not implicate the establishment clause[159] (even though the primary beneficiaries are religious school patrons), the Court might apply similar reasoning in reviewing voucher proposals. The Court may be more receptive to aid that flows to the individual family to encourage educational choice than it is toward aid that directly supports student services in private schools.

CONCLUSION

For the past forty years, church-state controversies have generated a steady stream of educational litigation, and there are no signs of diminishing legal activity in this domain. While some suits have involved claims under the free exercise clause, most school cases have focused on an interpretation of establishment clause prohibitions. Recent judicial action cannot easily be classified into "separation" or "accommodation" categories, but it appears that the federal judiciary is more committed to enforcing establishment clause restrictions in elementary and secondary school settings than elsewhere.[160] The balance on the current Supreme Court is extremely tenuous, but certain principles can be identified that govern church-state-school relations at the current time.

1. State-imposed devotional activities in public schools, regardless of voluntary participation, violate the establishment clause.
2. Students have a free exercise right to engage in silent prayer in public schools; however, school officials cannot promote such silent devotionals.
3. Holidays, with both secular and religious significance, can be observed in an objective and prudent manner in public schools.
4. The Ten Commandments and other religious symbols cannot be permanently posted in public schools, and religious literature cannot be distributed.
5. Student devotional meetings held on state-supported college campuses do not abridge the establishment clause; content restrictions cannot be imposed on student-initiated meetings in such a designated open forum for expression.
6. The constitutional status of student-initiated devotional meetings in public schools during noninstructional time remains unresolved; five federal appeals courts have struck down such a practice as violating the establishment clause, but a federal law authorizes student religious groups to meet in federally assisted public high schools if other types of student groups are allowed such access.

7. The academic study of religion is permissible in public schools, but such instruction cannot be used as a ploy to instill religious beliefs.
8. Students can be released from public school to receive religious instruction *off* public school grounds.
9. Students are entitled to excused absences to observe religious holidays as long as the absences do not place an undue hardship on the instructional program.
10. Requests to evade compulsory school attendance mandates for religious reasons have been unsuccessful, but Amish children have been excused from mandatory schooling after successful completion of eighth grade.
11. Students can be excused for religious reasons from specific public school observances and activities if the management of the school or the students' academic progress is not jeopardized.
12. "Secular humanism" may constitute a religion for first amendment purposes, but no court to date has ruled that public school instruction (e.g., sex education, evolution) advances this faith.
13. Laws requiring equal emphasis on the Genesis account of creation when evolution is taught violate the establishment clause.
14. States have a general welfare interest in mandating school attendance to ensure an educated citizenry; however, parents have the right to select private schooling for their children.
15. States can regulate private education, but restrictive regulations may impair free exercise rights.
16. Direct public subsidies to religious schools or aid that necessitates extensive governmental monitoring (e.g., auxiliary services provided in private schools, loan of audiovisual equipment, field trip transportation) violate the establishment clause.
17. Public aid for certain services that benefit the child and not the religious institution (e.g., transportation, loan of textbooks, standardized testing programs) does not violate the establishment clause.
18. Shared-time programs, under which parochial school students receive some instruction from public school teachers in facilities leased from a private school, unconstitutionally advance religious institutions.
19. Income tax deductions that cover educational expenses associated with both private and public elementary and secondary schooling are permissible, but income tax credits for *only* private school tuition violate the establishment clause.
20. Governmental aid that encourages individual choice in education (e.g., vouchers that can be redeemed at public or private schools) seems less vulnerable to first amendment attack than aid that directly flows to sectarian institutions.

NOTES

1. *See* Cantwell v. Connecticut, 310 U.S. 296, 303 (1940); Gitlow v. New York, 268 U.S. 652, 666 (1925). The first three sections of this chapter are adapted in part from Martha McCarthy, "Religion and Public Schools: Emerging Legal Standards and Unresolved Issues," *Harvard Educational Review,* vol. 55 (1985), pp. 278–317.
2. As noted in chapter 1, the notion that the fourteenth amendment incorporates first amendment guarantees and applies them to state action has been criticized. *See* James McClellan, *Joseph Story and the American Constitution* (Norman, OK: University of Oklahoma Press, 1971), pp. 144–145; Felix Morley, *Freedom and Federalism* (Chicago, IL: Regnery, 1959), pp. 59–71; Edward Dumbauld, *The Bill of Rights and What It Means Today* (Norman, OK: University of Oklahoma Press, 1957), pp. 132–139.
3. 330 U.S. 1, 15–16 (1947). *See* note 119, *infra.*
4. Walz v. Tax Comm'n of the City of New York, 397 U.S. 664 (1970). The tripartite test was first used in an education case the following year in Lemon v. Kurtzman, 403 U.S. 602 (1971), and is often called the *Lemon* test.
5. Justices O'Connor, Rehnquist, White, and Chief Justice Burger have called for modifications in establishment clause analysis. *See* Wallace v. Jaffree, 105 S. Ct. 2479 (1985) (concurring and dissenting opinions).
6. 406 U.S. 205, 214 (1972).
7. Walz v. Tax Comm'n of the City of New York, 397 U.S. 664, 668–669 (1970).
8. School Dist. of Abington Township v. Schempp, 374 U.S. 203 (1963); Engel v. Vitale, 370 U.S. 421 (1962).
9. *See* Gaines v. Anderson, 421 F. Supp. 337 (D. Mass 1976); Opinion of the Justices, 307 A.2d 558 (N.H. 1973).
10. Jaffree v. Board of School Comm'rs of Mobile County, 554 F. Supp. 1104 (S.D. Ala. 1983), *rev'd sub nom.* Jaffree v. Wallace, 705 F.2d 1526, 1535–1536 (11th Cir. 1983), *aff'd,* 105 S. Ct. 2479 (1985); Walter v. West Virginia Bd. of Educ., 610 F. Supp. 1169 (S.D. W.V. 1985); Duffy v. Las Cruces Public Schools, 557 F. Supp. 1013 (D.N.M. 1983); May v. Cooperman, 572 F. Supp. 1561 (D.N.J. 1983), *aff'd,* 780 F.2d 240 (3rd Cir. 1985); Beck v. McElrath, 548 F. Supp. 1161 (M.D. Tenn. 1982), *appeal dismissed, vacated and remanded,* 718 F.2d 1098 (6th Cir. 1983).
11. May, *id.,* 780 F.2d at 252.
12. 705 F.2d 1526 (11th Cir. 1983), *aff'd,* 105 S. Ct. 2479 (1985). Although several state practices were contested in this case, the Supreme Court agreed to address only the silent prayer statute. *See* note 13 for the disposition of the other issues.
13. Jaffree v. Board of School Comm'rs of Mobile County, 705 F.2d 1526 (11th Cir. 1983), *cert. denied in part,* 466 U.S. 926 (1984) (teacher-initiated devotional activities); Jaffree v. Wallace, 705 F.2d 1526 (11th Cir. 1983), *aff'd mem. in part,* 466 U.S. 924 (1984) (Alabama voluntary prayer law); Karen B. v. Treen, 653 F.2d 897 (5th Cir. 1981), *aff'd mem.,* 455 U.S. 913 (1982) (Louisiana voluntary prayer law); Collins v. Chandler Unified School Dist., 644 F.2d 759 (9th Cir. 1981), *cert. denied,* 454 U.S. 863 (1981) (student-led prayers in school assemblies).

14. In Wood v. Strickland, 420 U.S. 308, 322 (1975), the Supreme Court announced that ignorance of the law cannot be used by public school officials as a defense under Section 1983 of the Civil Rights Act of 1871 for violating an individual's clearly established federal rights. For a discussion of liability under Section 1983, *see* text with note 174, chapter 8.
15. Abramson v. Anderson, No. 81–26W (D. Iowa 1982).
16. Bell v. Little Axe Independent School Dist. No. 70, 766 F.2d 1391, 1408–1413 (10th Cir. 1985).
17. Stein v. Plainwell Community Schools, 610 F. Supp. 43 (W.D. Mich. 1985).
18. Upholding invocations and benedictions during the graduation ceremony, *see* Wiest v. Mt. Lebanon School Dist., 320 A.2d 362 (Pa. 1974), *cert. denied,* 419 U.S. 967 (1974); Grossberg v. Deusebio, 380 F. Supp. 285 (E.D. Va. 1974). Upholding baccalaureate programs, *see* Goodwin v. Cross County School Dist. No. 7, 394 F. Supp. 417 (E.D. Ark. 1973); Chamberlin v. Dade County Bd. of Public Instruction, 160 So. 2d 97 (Fla. 1964), *rev'd,* 377 U.S. 402 (1964).
19. Kay v. David Douglas School Dist. No. 40, 719 P.2d 875 (Ore. App. 1986); Bennett v. Livermore, No. H–91312–6 (Cal. App. 1983).
20. Graham v. Central Community School Dist. of Decatur County, 608 F. Supp. 531 (S.D. Iowa 1985). *See* Clifford Hooker, "Prayer at Graduation Ceremonies," *Education Law Reporter,* vol. 27 (1985), pp. 649–661.
21. Doe v. Aldine Independent School Dist., 563 F. Supp. 883 (S.D. Tex. 1982).
22. *See* Lawrence Sager, "The Supreme Court 1980 Term, Forward: Constitutional Limitations on Congress' Authority to Regulate the Jurisdiction of the Federal Courts," *Harvard Law Review,* vol. 95 (1981), pp. 17–89. Senator Jesse Helms of North Carolina has been a central proponent of such "court stripping" measures. *See* S. 481, 97th Congress, First Session (1981). In August 1985, the Senate rejected another measure that would have removed school prayer cases from the jurisdiction of federal courts.
23. The amendment proposed by President Reagan in 1982 provided: "Nothing in this Constitution shall be construed to prohibit individual or group prayer in public schools or other public institutions. No person shall be required by the United States or by any State to participate in prayer." Several petitions asking for a school prayer constitutional amendment have been presented to President Reagan, and national polls have indicated that a majority of Americans favor prayer in public schools and a constitutional amendment to that effect. *See* "The 16th Annual Gallup Poll of the Public's Attitudes Toward the Public Schools," *Phi Delta Kappan,* vol. 66 (1984), p. 35; "Prayer in Public Schools," *Journal of Law & Education,* vol. 12 (1983), pp. 452–456.
24. Bender v. Williamsport Area School Dist., 741 F.2d 538 (3d Cir. 1984), *vacated,* 106 S. Ct. 1326 (1986); Bell v. Little Axe Independent School Dist. No. 70, 766 F.2d 1391 (10th Cir. 1985); Nartowicz v. Clayton County School Dist., 736 F.2d 646 (11th Cir. 1984); Lubbock Civil Liberties Union v. Lubbock Independent School Dist., 669 F.2d 1038 (5th Cir. 1982), *cert. denied,* 459 U.S. 1155 (1983); Brandon v. Board of Educ. of Guilderland Cent. School Dist., 635 F.2d 971 (2d Cir. 1980), *cert. denied,* 454 U.S. 1123 (1981). *See also* Ford v. Manuel, 629 F. Supp. 771 (N.D. Ohio 1985) (school district's practice of renting elementary school buildings to religious council immediately before and after school violated the establishment clause by creating the appearance of official school support of religion).

25. 454 U.S. 263 (1981). *See* Martha McCarthy, "Student-Initiated Prayer Meetings in Public Secondary Schools and Higher Education: An Apparent Double Standard," *Education Law Reporter,* vol. 1 (1982), pp. 481–488.
26. Tinker v. Des Moines Independent Community School Dist., 393 U.S. 503 (1969). In Clergy and Laity Concerned v. Chicago Bd. of Educ., 586 F. Supp. 1408, 1412 (N.D. Ill. 1984), the court noted in dicta that a policy allowing religious groups the same access as secular groups to the forum for communication created in public high schools would not violate the establishment clause. For a discussion of this case, *see* text with note 31, chapter 4.
27. 741 F.2d 538 (3d Cir. 1984), *vacated,* 106 S. Ct. 1326 (1986). The school board subsequently voted to allow the student religious group to meet during the high school's activity period. *See Education Week,* June 11, 1986, p. 1.
28. 20 U.S.C. § 4071. The proposal to tie compliance to the receipt of federal funds was withdrawn from the final version of the Equal Access Act. Thus, the law contemplates a judicial remedy for noncompliance, with aggrieved individuals bringing suit in federal court to force school authorities to observe the law.
29. In addition to the EAA, numerous measures calling for voluntary devotional activities in public schools have been introduced in Congress. Some members of Congress, who have regularly opposed such efforts to legislate public school prayer, were willing to support the EAA as a compromise to defuse the congressional momentum to enact a law sanctioning some type of daily prayer during the school day. *See Education Daily,* July 27, 1984, p. 3.
30. The American Association of School Administrators (AASA) has provided its interpretation of the EAA and guidelines to assist school personnel in complying with the law. *See* "Equal Access: Interpretation and Implementation Guidelines," AASA, 1984.
31. Student Coalition for Peace v. Lower Merion School Dist., 776 F.2d 431 (3d Cir. 1985). For a discussion of this case, *see* text with note 68, chapter 4.
32. *See Education Week,* August 22, 1984, pp. 1, 11.
33. *See* Hernandez v. Hanson, 430 F. Supp. 1154 (D. Neb. 1977); Goodwin v. Cross County School Dist., 394 F. Supp. 417 (E.D. Ark. 1973); Tudor v. Board of Educ. of Borough of Rutherford, 100 A.2d 857 (N.J. 1953), *cert. denied,* 348 U.S. 816 (1954). *See also* Meltzer v. Board of Public Instruction of Orange County, Florida, 577 F.2d 311 (5th Cir. 1978), *cert. denied,* 439 U.S. 1089 (1979); Martha McCarthy, *A Delicate Balance: Church, State, and the Schools* (Bloomington, IN: Phi Delta Kappa, 1983), pp. 41–42.
34. Florey v. Sioux Falls School Dist. 49–5, 619 F.2d 1311 (8th Cir. 1980), *cert. denied,* 449 U.S. 987 (1980). In an unusual case involving religious holiday observances, a chorus student missed two required Christmas performances, one of which was held at a local church. The student, who received an F for the grading period because he missed the performances, argued that his required attendance at "religious ceremonies" violated the first amendment. Upholding the failing grade, the court noted that the student could have been excused from the performances if he had raised his religious objection prior to the events. He had not sought an excused absence; instead he was vacationing with his family in Hawaii when the programs took place. R.J.J. by Johnson v. Shineman, 658 S.W.2d 910 (Mo. App. 1983).
35. Stone v. Graham, 599 S.W.2d 157 (Ky. 1980), *rev'd,* 449 U.S. 39 (1980).

36. Florey v. Sioux Falls School Dist. 49–5, 619 F.2d 1311 (8th Cir. 1980), *cert. denied,* 449 U.S. 987 (1980).
37. Stone v. Graham, 449 U.S. 39 (1980).
38. *Id.* at 41. *See* K.R.S. 158.178. *See also* Nartowicz v. Clayton County School Dist., 736 F.2d 646 (11th Cir. 1984) (barring the use of public school bulletin boards and public address systems to announce church-sponsored secular activities).
39. Lynch v. Donnelly, 465 U.S. 668 (1984).
40. McCreary v. Stone, 739 F.2d 716 (2d Cir. 1984), *aff'd by equally divided court sub nom.* Board of Trustees of Village of Scarsdale v. McCreary, 105 S. Ct. 1859 (1985).
41. Jesse Choper, "Religion in the Schools: A Proposed Constitutional Standard," *Minnesota Law Review,* vol. 47 (1963), p. 382.
42. Knowlton v. Baumhover, 166 N.W. 202, 206 (Iowa, 1918). *See also* Zellers v. Huff, 236 P.2d 949 (N.M. 1951).
43. Jaffree v. Board of School Comm'rs of Mobile County, 705 F.2d 1526 (11th Cir. 1983), *cert. denied in part,* 466 U.S. 926 (1984).
44. Breen v. Runkel, 614 F. Supp. 355 (W.D. Mich. 1985). *See also* May v. Evansville-Vanderburgh School Corp., 615 F. Supp. 761 (S.D. Ind. 1985), *aff'd,* 787 F.2d 1105 (7th Cir. 1986) (school authorities were upheld in barring teachers from the use of the public school building to hold prayer meetings for staff members before school), text with note 55, chapter 8.
45. LaRocca v. Board of Educ. of Rye City School Dist., 406 N.Y.S.2d 348 (App. Div. 1978), *appeal dismissed,* 386 N.E.2d 266 (N.Y. 1978).
46. Fink v. Board of Educ. of the Warren County School Dist., 442 A.2d 837 (Pa. Commw. 1982), *appeal dismissed,* 460 U.S. 1048 (1983).
47. *Id.*, 442 A.2d at 842. *See also* Lynch v. Indiana State Univ. Bd. of Trustees, 378 N.E.2d 900 (Ind. App. 1978), *cert. denied,* 441 U.S. 946 (1979).
48. Dale v. Board of Educ., Lemon Independent School Dist. 32–2, 316 N.W.2d 108 (S.D. 1982).
49. Palmer v. Board of Educ. of the City of Chicago, 603 F.2d 1271 (7th Cir. 1979), *cert. denied,* 444 U.S. 1026 (1980).
50. *Id.* at 1274.
51. *Id.*
52. Teachers have used the free exercise clause to challenge restrictions on the wearing of religious attire in public schools, and courts have rendered conflicting opinions on this issue. Some courts have concluded that the wearing of religious garb by public school teachers does not present a threat of state advancement of religion as long as the teachers are not attempting to proselytize students. *See* Rawlings v. Butler, 290 S.W.2d 801 (Ky. 1956); Gerhardt v. Heid, 267 N.W. 127, 135 (N.D. 1936); Hysong v. School Dist. of Gallitzin Borough, 30 A. 482 (Pa. 1894). Other courts have recognized the state's authority to enact legislation prohibiting public school teachers from wearing religious garb as a proper exercise of legislative power to guard against promoting a religious atmosphere in public schools. *See* Cooper v. Eugene School Dist. No. 4J, 723 P.2d 298 (Ore. 1986) (revocation of a teacher's certificate for violating the law did not represent hostility toward religion); Zellers v. Huff, 236 P.2d 949, 963 (N.M. 1951); Commonwealth v. Herr, 78 A. 68, 72 (Pa. 1910).

53. School Dist. of Abington Township v. Schempp, 374 U.S. 203, 225 (1963).
54. *See* Hall v. Board of School Comm'rs, 656 F.2d 999 (5th Cir. 1981), *appeal after remand,* 707 F.2d 464 (11th Cir. 1983); Crockett v. Sorenson, 568 F. Supp. 1422 (W.D. Va. 1983); Wiley v. Franklin, 497 F. Supp. 390 (E.D. Tenn. 1980); Vaughn v. Reed, 313 F. Supp. 431 (W.D. Va. 1970).
55. However, in Vaughn, *id.*, the court reasoned that the excusal provision for students desiring not to participate in the contested Bible study course supported the conclusion that the course entailed indoctrination rather than the academic study of religion.
56. McCollum v. Board of Educ., 333 U.S. 203 (1948).
57. Zorach v. Clauson, 343 U.S. 306, 313–314 (1952).
58. Smith v. Smith, 523 F.2d 121 (4th Cir. 1975), *cert. denied,* 423 U.S. 1073 (1976).
59. Holt v. Thompson, 225 N.W.2d 678 (Wis. 1975).
60. There is some sentiment that programs in which all students are released early from school one day a week would be easier to defend constitutionally because under such programs students would not be confined to a choice between remaining at the public school or attending sectarian classes. *See* McCarthy, *A Delicate Balance,* p. 112.
61. Lanner v. Wimmer, 662 F.2d 1349 (10th Cir. 1981).
62. Church of God v. Amarillo Independent School Dist., 511 F. Supp. 613 (N.D. Tex. 1981), *aff'd,* 670 F.2d 46 (5th Cir. 1982) (per curiam).
63. Commonwealth v. Bey, 70 A.2d 693 (Pa. Super. 1950).
64. Rice v. Commonwealth, 49 S.E.2d 342, 348 (Va. 1948).
65. Jernigan v. State, 412 So. 2d 1242 (Ala. Crim. App. 1982). *See also* Johnson v. Charles City Community Schools Bd. of Educ., 368 N.W.2d 74 (Iowa 1985), *cert. denied sub nom.* Pruessner v. Benton, 106 S. Ct. 594 (1985); text with note 18, chapter 3.
66. Wisconsin v. Yoder, 406 U.S. 205 (1972).
67. 319 U.S. 624 (1943).
68. Minersville School Dist. v. Gobitis, 310 U.S. 586 (1940).
69. Barnette, 319 U.S. at 642.
70. *See* Lipp v. Morris, 579 F.2d 834 (3d Cir. 1978); Goetz v. Ansell, 477 F.2d 636 (2d Cir. 1973); Frain v. Baron, 307 F. Supp. 27 (E.D. N.Y. 1969).
71. Russo v. Central School Dist. No. 1, 469 F.2d 623, 634 (2d Cir. 1972), *cert. denied,* 411 U.S. 932 (1973). *See also* Opinion of the Justices to the Governor, 363 N.E.2d 251 (Mass. 1977).
72. *See* text with note 49, *supra.*
73. *See* Valent v. New Jersey State Bd. of Educ., 274 A.2d 832 (N.J. Super. 1971); Spence v. Bailey, 465 F.2d 797 (6th Cir. 1972).
74. *See* Mitchell v. McCall, 143 So. 2d 629 (Ala. 1962).
75. Mitchell, *id. See also* Hardwick v. Board of School Trustees, 205 P. 49 (Cal. App. 1921) (students could not be required to participate in dancing instruction over parents' objections).
76. Moody v. Cronin, 484 F. Supp. 270 (C.D. Ill. 1979).
77. Mozert v. Hawkins County Public Schools, 765 F.2d 75 (6th Cir. 1985), *on remand,* CIV-2-83-401 (E.D. Tenn. 1986).
78. Davis v. Page, 385 F. Supp. 395 (D.N.H. 1974). While governmental interests prevailed over free exercise rights in denying the exemption from aca-

demic classes, the court recognized that the students could be excused when audiovisual equipment was used solely for entertainment purposes. *See also* Ouimette v. Babbie, 405 F. Supp. 525 (D. Vt. 1975); McCarthy, *A Delicate Balance,* pp. 59–64.

79. *See* Menora v. Illinois High School Ass'n, 683 F.2d 1030 (7th Cir. 1982), *cert. denied,* 459 U.S. 1156 (1983); Keller v. Gardner Community Consol. Grade School Dist. 72C, 552 F. Supp. 512 (N.D. Ill. 1982).
80. *See Education Week,* May 29, 1985, pp. 1, 19.
81. 20 U.S.C. § 1232h; 34 C.F.R., Parts 75, 76, and 98. For a discussion of the controversy surrounding the Hatch Amendment, *see Education Daily,* March 4, 1985, p. 3; February 20, 1985, p. 3; note 156, chapter 3.
82. Epperson v. Arkansas, 393 U.S. 97, 107 (1968), quoting Joseph Burstyn, Inc. v. Wilson, 343 U.S. 495, 505 (1952).
83. For a discussion of allegations that public schools are promoting a secular creed, *see* McCarthy, *A Delicate Balance,* pp. 89–92.
84. In a widely publicized Alabama case, Governor Wallace and the Mobile County School District signed a consent decree recognizing that "secular humanism" is a religion and calling for new textbook selection procedures to eliminate censorship of the contributions of Christianity to American culture. The state board of education, however, has not endorsed the decree and thus is being sued by a group of fundamentalist parents in Mobile County. The trial is attracting national attention because the court is being asked to rule that the public schools are unconstitutionally advancing "secular humanism." *See* Smith v. Board of School Comm'rs of Mobile County, cited in *Education Week,* March 12, 1986, p. 4; *Education Week,* October 15, 1986, pp. 1, 18. *See also* text with note 80, chapter 3, for a discussion of Grove v. Mead School Dist. No. 354, 753 F.2d 1528 (9th Cir. 1985), *cert. denied,* 106 S. Ct. 85 (1985) (parents unsuccessfully argued that Gordon Park's *The Learning Tree* advances "secular humanism" in violation of the establishment clause).
85. *See* Jaffree v. Board of School Comm'rs of Mobile County, 554 F. Supp. 1104, 1129–1130, n. 41 (S.D. Ala. 1983).
86. *See* Thomas v. Review Bd. of the Indiana Employment and Security Division, 450 U.S. 707, 714 (1981); United States v. Seeger, 380 U.S. 163, 175 (1965); United States v. Ballard, 322 U.S. 78, 87 (1944).
87. Several lower courts have explicitly rejected claims that instruction in evolution or sex education advances an antitheistic belief. *See* text with notes 90, 94, and 96, *infra.*
88. Malnak v. Yogi, 592 F.2d 197 (3d Cir. 1979). The court reasoned that instruction in transcendental meditation unconstitutionally advances the Science of Creative Intelligence which was found to possess many attributes of a religion.
89. *See* Jaffree v. James, 544 F. Supp. 727, 732 (S.D. Ala. 1982); Fink v. Board of Educ. of the Warren County School Dist., 442 A.2d 837, 843 (Pa. Commw. 1982), *appeal dismissed,* 460 U.S. 1048 (1983); Reed v. VanHoven, 237 F. Supp. 48, 53 (W.D. Mich. 1965). The Supreme Court also has noted that "the State may not establish a 'religion of secularism' in the sense of affirmatively opposing or showing hostility to religion, thus 'preferring those who believe in no religion . . .' " School Dist. of Abington Township v.

Schempp, 374 U.S. 203, 225 (1963). *See also* Torcaso v. Watkins, 367 U.S. 488, 495, n. 11 (1961).

90. *See* Citizens for Parental Rights v. San Mateo County Bd. of Educ., 124 Cal. Rptr. 68 (Cal. App. 1975), *appeal dismissed,* 425 U.S. 908 (1976); Hobolth v. Greenway, 218 N.W.2d 98 (Mich. 1974); Valent v. New Jersey State Bd. of Educ., 274 A.2d 832 (N.J. Super. 1971); Hopkins v. Hamden Bd. of Educ., 289 A.2d 914 (Conn. C.P. 1971); Medeiros v. Kiyosaki, 478 P.2d 314 (Hawaii 1970); Cornwell v. State Bd. of Educ., 314 F. Supp. 340 (D. Md. 1969), *cert. denied,* 400 U.S. 942 (1970).
91. Smith v. Ricci, 446 A.2d 501, 507 (N.J. 1982), *appeal dismissed sub nom.* Smith v. Brandt, 459 U.S. 962 (1982).
92. For a discussion of this issue, *see* Valent v. New Jersey State Bd. of Educ., 274 A.2d 832, 840–841 (N.J. Super. 1971).
93. Scopes v. State, 289 S.W. 363, 364 (Tenn. 1927).
94. Epperson v. Arkansas, 393 U.S. 97 (1968). *See also* Wright v. Houston Independent School Dist., 486 F.2d 137 (5th Cir. 1973), *cert. denied sub nom.* Brown v. Houston Independent School Dist., 417 U.S. 969 (1974); Moore v. Gaston County Bd. of Educ., 357 F. Supp. 1037 (W.D.N.C. 1973).
95. Segraves v. California, No. 278978 (Cal. Super. 1981).
96. McLean v. Arkansas Bd. of Educ., 529 F. Supp. 1255 (E.D. Ark. 1982). *See also* Daniel v. Waters, 515 F.2d 485 (6th Cir. 1975).
97. Aguillard v. Treen, 634 F. Supp. 426 (E.D. La. 1985), *aff'd sub nom.* Aguillard v. Edwards, 765 F.2d 1251 (5th Cir. 1985), *rehearing en banc denied,* 778 F.2d 225 (5th Cir. 1985), *cert. granted,* 106 S. Ct. 1946 (1986). The judiciary also has invalidated the adoption of a biology textbook with an avowedly creationist orientation, Hendren v. Campbell, No. 5577–0139 (Ind. Super. 1977). *See also* text with note 48, *supra.*
98. Education for Economic Security Act, Title VII—Magnet Schools Assistance, 20 U.S.C. § 4059. *See also* 34 C.F.R. Part 280. Neither the law nor its regulations defined "secular humanism." Before the restriction was removed, a group of prominent authors initiated a lawsuit, alleging that the prohibition against "secular humanism" was unconstitutional. *See Education Week,* August 21, 1985, p. 6.
99. 268 U.S. 510 (1925).
100. *See* Wisconsin v. Yoder, 406 U.S. 205, 214 (1972); text with note 6, *supra.*
101. *See* K. Forbis Jordan, "Issues in State Aid to Private Religious Schools," paper presented at the Annual Meeting of the American Educational Research Association, Chicago, 1985, p. 9. *See also Private Elementary and Secondary Education,* vol. 2, Congressionally Mandated Study of School Finance, School Finance Project, United States Department of Education, 1983, pp. 3–8. It should be noted that sources differ regarding whether private school enrollments declined more rapidly than did public school enrollments during the 1970s. The United States Bureau of the Census reported a greater loss for private schools, while the National Center for Educational Statistics reported an opposite trend. However, most sources are in agreement that the proportion of students attending private schools has steadily increased since 1979.
102. State v. Whisner, 351 N.E.2d 750 (Ohio 1976). *See also* State *ex rel.* Nagle v. Olin, 415 N.E.2d 279 (Ohio 1980).

103. Kentucky State Bd. for Elementary and Secondary Educ. v. Rudasill, 589 S.W.2d 877, 879 (Ky. 1979), *cert. denied,* 446 U.S. 938 (1980).
104. *See also* Bangor Baptist Church v. Maine Dep't of Educ., 576 F. Supp. 1299 (D. Maine 1983) (state compulsory school attendance law does not bar the operation of "unapproved" private schools; mere operation of an unapproved private school does not violate state law prohibiting action that induces truancy, and state defendants were enjoined from bringing suit against the plaintiff pastors, administrators, and religious schools for inducing truancy by "preaching" that the Bible commands fundamentalist Christians to attend fundamentalist academies).
105. Johnson v. Charles City Community School Bd. of Educ., 368 N.W.2d 74 (Iowa 1985), *cert. denied sub nom.* Pruessner v. Benton, 106 S. Ct. 594 (1985); State v. Rivinius, 328 N.W.2d 220 (N.D. 1982), *cert. denied,* 460 U.S. 1070 (1983); State by Minami v. Andrews, 651 P.2d 473 (Hawaii 1982); State *ex rel.* Douglas v. Faith Baptist Church of Louisville, 301 N.W.2d 571 (Neb. 1981), *appeal dismissed,* 454 U.S. 803 (1981); North Dakota v. Shaver, 294 N.W.2d 883 (N.D. 1980).
106. Johnson, *id.*, 368 N.W.2d at 81. *See also* Attorney General v. Bailey, 436 N.E.2d 139 (Mass. 1982), *cert. denied,* 459 U.S. 970 (1982) (supervisory officers of private schools could be required to report the names, ages, and residences of all private school students). Most courts have ruled that religious schools can be required to satisfy health, safety, and zoning regulations. *See* State v. Corpus Christi People's Baptist Church, 683 S.W.2d 692 (Tex. 1985), *cert. denied,* 106 S. Ct. 32 (1985); Faith Baptist Church of Boca Raton v. City of Boca Raton, 402 So. 2d 1381 (Fla. App. 1981), *cert. denied,* 454 U.S. 1147 (1982). *But see* City of Sumner v. First Baptist Church of Sumner, 639 P.2d 1358 (Wash. 1982) (exemption for church school from city's building and zoning codes would be required if state has other means to achieve its objectives that are less burdensome on free exercise rights).
107. R.M. Kyle and E.J. Allen, *Public Funding of Private Education, Contexts and Review 1970–1982,* Final Report to School Finance Project, United States Department of Education, 1983.
108. St. Martin Evangelical Lutheran Church v. South Dakota, 451 U.S. 772 (1981).
109. National Labor Relations Bd. v. Catholic Bishop of Chicago, 440 U.S. 490 (1979).
110. Catholic High School Ass'n of the Archdiocese of New York v. Culvert, 753 F.2d 1161 (2d Cir. 1985).
111. *See* Baltimore Lutheran High School Ass'n v. Employment Security Administration, 490 A.2d 701 (Md. 1985); Salem College and Academy v. Employment Div., 695 P.2d 25 (Ore. 1985).
112. *See* Donovan v. Shenandoah Baptist Church, 573 F. Supp. 320 (W.D. Va. 1983); Donovan v. Central Baptist Church, 96 F.R.D. 4 (S.D. Tex. 1982).
113. Ohio Civil Rights Comm'n v. Dayton Christian Schools, 106 S. Ct. 2718 (1986). *See also* Equal Employment Opportunity Comm'n v. Mississippi College, 626 F.2d 477, 487–488 (5th Cir. 1980), *cert. denied,* 453 U.S. 912 (1981) (federal agency's investigation into college's hiring practices under Title VII of the Civil Rights Act of 1964 would not constitute "ongoing interference" with the institution's religious practices).
114. Bob Jones Univ. v. United States, Goldsboro Christian Schools v. United

States, 461 U.S. 574, 592 (1983). In 1970 the Court held that tax exempt status for church property does not violate the establishment clause, Walz v. Tax Comm'n of the City of New York, 397 U.S. 664 (1970). For a discussion of the application of other federal laws and regulations to sectarian schools, *see* McCarthy, *A Delicate Balance,* chapter 7.

115. *Id.*, 461 U.S. at 595. *See also* Norwood v. Harrison, 413 U.S. 455 (1973) (state funds could not be used to provide textbooks for private school students attending racially discriminatory private schools); Virginia Educ. Fund v. Commissioner of Internal Revenue, 799 F.2d 903 (4th Cir. 1986) (fund created to solicit monies for segregated private schools was not entitled to a tax exemption as a charitable organization without evidence that the schools operated under nondiscriminatory admissions policies).
116. Allen v. Wright, 468 U.S. 737 (1984).
117. Center for State Legislation and School Law, "Aid to Private Schools," Alexandria, Virginia, National School Boards Association, 1985.
118. *See* Chester Finn, "The Politics of Public Aid to Private Education," in *The Changing Politics of School Finance,* Nelda Cambron-McCabe and Allan Odden, eds. (Cambridge, MA: Ballinger, 1982), pp. 183–210.
119. This statement was made in 1802 in a letter refusing a Baptist association's request for a day to be established for fasting and prayer in thanksgiving for the nation's welfare. *See* Saul Padover, *The Complete Jefferson* (New York: Duell, Sloan, and Pearce, 1943), pp. 518–519; Robert Healey, *Jefferson on Religion in Public Education* (New Haven, CT: Yale University Press, 1962), pp. 128–140.
120. Everson v. Board of Educ., 330 U.S. 1 (1947).
121. *See* Members of Jamestown School Comm. v. Schmidt, 699 F.2d 1 (1st Cir. 1983), *cert. denied,* 464 U.S. 851 (1983). McKeesport Area School Dist. v. Pennsylvania Dep't of Educ., 392 A.2d 912 (Pa. 1978), *appeal dismissed,* 446 U.S. 970 (1980); Cromwell Property Owners Ass'n v. Toffolon, 495 F. Supp. 915 (D. Conn. 1979); Hahner v. Board of Educ., 278 N.W.2d 474 (Wis. App. 1979).
122. *See* Matthews v. Quinton, 362 P.2d 932 (Alas. 1961), *cert. denied,* 368 U.S. 517 (1962); McVey v. Hawkins, 258 S.W.2d 927 (Mo. 1953); Visser v. Nooksack Valley School Dist. No. 506, 207 P.2d 198 (Wash. 1949); Gurney v. Ferguson, 122 P.2d 1002 (Okla. 1941), *cert. denied,* 317 U.S. 588 (1942).
123. Board of Educ. v. Allen, 392 U.S. 236 (1968).
124. *See* Elbe v. Yankton Independent School Dist. No. 63-3, 372 N.W.2d 113 (S.D. 1985); Fannin v. Williams, 655 S.W.2d 480 (Ky. 1983); Bloom v. School Comm. of Springfield, 379 N.E.2d 578 (Mass. 1978); In re Advisory Opinion, 228 N.W.2d 772 (Mich. 1975); Paster v. Tussey, 512 S.W.2d 97 (Mo. 1974), *cert. denied,* 419 U.S. 1111 (1975); Gaffney v. State Dep't, 220 N.W.2d 550 (Neb. 1974); Dickman v. School Dist. No. 62 C, 366 P.2d 533 (Ore. 1961), *cert. denied sub nom.* Carlson v. Dickman, 371 U.S. 823 (1962). In two states, measures providing aid for textbooks used by private school students have been struck down because of technical details regarding the manner in which the aid was provided. *See* Public Funds for Public Schools of New Jersey v. Marburger, 358 F. Supp. 29 (D.N.J. 1973), *aff'd mem.,* 417 U.S. 961 (1974); People *ex rel.* Klinger v. Howlett, 305 N.E.2d 129 (Ill. 1973).
125. California Teachers' Ass'n v. Riles, 632 P.2d 953, 962 (Cal. 1981).

126. Wolman v. Walter, 433 U.S. 229, 247 (1977). *See also* Meek v. Pittenger, 421 U.S. 349 (1975).
127. Committee for Public Educ. and Religious Liberty v. Regan, 444 U.S. 646 (1980).
128. Levitt v. Committee for Public Educ. and Religious Liberty, 413 U.S. 472 (1973).
129. Lemon v. Kurtzman, 403 U.S. 602 (1971) (Pennsylvania statute).
130. *Id.* (Rhode Island Statute)
131. Committee for Public Educ. and Religious Liberty v. Nyquist, 413 U.S. 756 (1973).
132. *Id.*
133. Wolman v. Walter, 433 U.S. 229 (1977).
134. Wolman, *id.*; Meek v. Pittenger, 421 U.S. 349 (1975).
135. Wolman, *id. See also* McCarthy, *A Delicate Balance,* chapter 6.
136. It should be noted that the Supreme Court has been more receptive to governmental aid to institutions of higher education than to private elementary and secondary schools. *See* Roemer v. Board of Public Works of Maryland, 426 U.S. 736 (1976) (upholding noncategorical grants to private colleges and universities); Hunt v. McNair, 413 U.S. 734 (1973) (approving the use of state revenue bonds to finance private college and university construction); Tilton v. Richardson, 403 U.S. 672 (1971) (allowing federal grants for private college and university construction.) *See also* text with note 157, *infra.*
137. 718 F.2d 1389 (6th Cir. 1983), *aff'd,* 105 S. Ct. 3216 (1985). Six months prior to the Supreme Court's decision in *Ball,* the Michigan high court upheld a shared-time program in which parochial school students received nonessential elective instruction in a public school. This situation differed from the Grand Rapids shared-time program in that the class in question, band, was offered in the public school and served primarily public school students. Snyder v. Charlotte Public School Dist., 365 N.W.2d 151 (Mich. 1984). For a discussion of other litigation involving shared-time programs, *see* McCarthy, *A Delicate Balance,* pp. 103–108.
138. *Id.*, 105 S. Ct. at 3228, citing Wolman v. Walter, 433 U.S. at 250.
139. *Id.* at 3227, 3230.
140. Felton v. Secretary, United States Dep't of Educ., 739 F.2d 48 (2d Cir. 1984), *aff'd sub nom.* Aguilar v. Felton, 105 S. Ct. 3232 (1985).
141. National Coalition for Public Educ. and Religious Liberty v. Harris, 489 F. Supp. 1248 (S.D.N.Y. 1980), *appeal dismissed sub nom.* National Coalition for Public Educ. and Religious Liberty v. Huffstedler, 449 U.S. 808 (1980). *See also* Wheeler v. Barrera, 417 U.S. 402 (1974), *judgment modified,* 422 U.S. 1004 (1975).
142. Felton v. Secretary, United States Dep't of Educ., 739 F.2d 48, 49–50 (2d Cir. 1984). The school district subsequently was granted a one year stay of the judgment, given the logistical problems involved in formulating and implementing an alternative plan, Felton v. Secretary, 787 F.2d 35 (2d Cir. 1986).
143. Aguilar v. Felton, 105 S. Ct. at 3233.
144. For a discussion of post-*Felton* legal developments, *see* Martha McCarthy, "The Use of Public Funds for Private Education," *Journal of Education*

Finance, vol. 11 (1985), pp. 278–293; *Education Week*, December 11, 1985, p. 9; *Education Week*, April 30, 1986, p. 6.

145. *See* Committee for Public Educ. and Religious Liberty v. Regan, 444 U.S. 646, 671 (1980) (Stevens, J., dissenting); Steve Gey, "Rebuilding the Wall: The Case for a Return to the Strict Interpretation of the Establishment Clause," *Columbia Law Review*, vol. 81 (1981), pp. 1463–1490.
146. Wallace v. Jaffree, 105 S. Ct. 2479, 2518–2519 (1985) (Rehnquist, J., dissenting). For a discussion of criticism of the Supreme Court's recent establishment clause decisions, *see* McCarthy, "Religion and Public Schools: Emerging Legal Standards and Unresolved Issues," pp. 310–315.
147. In 1982 President Reagan revealed his proposal for federal income tax credits up to 50 percent of each child's tuition costs to a maximum of $500 and with a limitation that only families earning $50,000 or less would be entitled to the full credit. Similar measures have regularly been introduced in Congress since 1977, but none has yet been enacted.
148. Committee for Public Educ. and Religious Liberty v. Nyquist, 413 U.S. 756 (1973).
149. *See* Rhode Island Fed'n of Teachers AFL/CIO v. Norberg, 630 F.2d 855 (1st Cir. 1980); Public Funds for Public Schools of New Jersey v. Byrne, 590 F.2d 514 (3d Cir. 1979), *aff'd*, 442 U.S. 907 (1979).
150. 676 F.2d 1195 (8th Cir. 1982), *aff'd*, 463 U.S. 388 (1983).
151. *Id.*, 463 U.S. at 395.
152. For a discussion of the School Finance Project's survey of parental choice of schooling and tuition tax credits, *see Private Elementary and Secondary Schooling*, pp. 49–59.
153. For a discussion of unsuccessful referenda in nine states and the District of Columbia, *see* James Catterall, "Politics and Aid to Private Schools," *Educational Evaluation and Policy Analysis*, vol. 6 (1984), pp. 433–440. The soundest defeat was in Washington, D.C., where almost 90 percent of the voters rejected a 1981 tuition tax credit proposal.
154. Milton Friedman proposed vouchers to fund education in the latter 1950s. *See* Milton Friedman, *Capitalism and Freedom* (Chicago, IL: University of Chicago Press, 1962), chapter 6.
155. For a discussion of various voucher models, *see Private Elementary and Secondary Education*, pp. 35–37.
156. *See Education Daily*, November 22, 1985, p. 3; March 6, 1985, pp. 1–2; *Education Week*, March 6, 1985, p. 1.
157. 106 S. Ct. 748 (1986).
158. *See* note 136, *supra*.
159. Mueller v. Allen, 676 F.2d 1195 (8th Cir. 1982), *aff'd*, 463 U.S. 388 (1983).
160. *See* Lynch v. Donnelly, 465 U.S. 668 (1984) (upholding use of public funds for nativity scene display); Marsh v. Chambers, 463 U.S. 783 (1983) (upholding public support of a chaplain to open state legislative sessions with a prayer); Widmar v. Vincent, 454 U.S. 263 (1981) (upholding student-initiated devotional meetings at state-supported universities). However, in 1985 the Supreme Court struck down a state law that gave employees a right not to work on their chosen day of worship, reasoning that the law violated the establishment clause because it gave an absolute preference to employees on religious grounds. Thornton v. Caldor, 105 S. Ct. 2914 (1985).

3

School Attendance and Instructional Issues

Although there is no inherent right to a public education under the United States Constitution, once a state establishes an educational system, such opportunities must be made available to all children on equal terms. Not only can children within the state assert an entitlement to attend school, but also the state can mandate school attendance and specify curricular offerings to ensure an educated citizenry. Substantial litigation has resulted from the collision of state interests in guaranteeing the general welfare and individual interests in exercising rights protected by constitutional and statutory law. In these instances, the judiciary must weigh the public and private interests involved. This chapter focuses on legal mandates pertaining to various requirements and rights associated with school attendance and the instructional program. Other aspects of students' rights and responsibilities are explored in more detail in subsequent chapters.

COMPULSORY ATTENDANCE

Presently, all fifty states have some type of compulsory school attendance statute that includes penalties for noncompliance. The legal basis for compulsory education is grounded in the common law doctrine of *parens patriae* which means that the state, in its guardian role, has the authority to enact reasonable laws for the well-being of its citizens. An enlightened citizenry is considered necessary to ensure the well-being of the state, and the individual has a legal obligation to give up a measure of personal freedom in the interest of the state's welfare. Kentucky's compulsory attendance law is typical in requiring "each parent, guardian or other person residing in the state and having in custody or charge any child between the ages of seven and sixteen" to send the child to school for the full school term.[1]

Parents can be prosecuted in criminal or civil suits for failing to fulfill their legal obligations under compulsory school attendance laws; their children can be expelled for excessive truancy or judicially ordered to return to school and held in contempt of court if they defy the court's order.[2] In some instances, truant children have been made wards of juvenile courts, with school attendance supervised by probation officers. In 1985 a California appeals court ruled that courts possess inherent power to enforce their lawful orders by imposing sanctions for willful violations. Noting that the state, in its *parens patriae* role, may enact special laws for the care, protection, safety and guidance of minors within its jurisdiction, the court held that a student, who persisted in truancy after a court ordered him to attend school, could be held in a secure facility during nonschool hours.[3]

While states can require schooling, it was settled in 1925 that private school attendance can satisfy such compulsory attendance mandates. In *Pierce v. Society of Sisters,* the United States Supreme Court invalidated an Oregon statute requiring children between eight and sixteen years of age to attend public schools. The Court concluded that by restricting attendance to public institutions, the state interfered with private schools' rights to exist and with parents' rights to govern the upbringing of their children. The Court recognized that "the fundamental theory of liberty upon which all governments in this union repose excludes any general power of the state to standardize its children by forcing them to accept instruction from public teachers only."[4] In essence, parents do not have the right to determine *whether* their children are educated, but they do have some control over *where* such education takes place. Legal developments pertaining to state regulation of private schools, 85 percent of which are church-related, are covered in chapter 2.

In many states, compulsory attendance laws permit pupil instruction outside of formal school settings as well as in public and private schools. In a 1984 study, the Education Commission of the States reported that over half of the states and the District of Columbia expressly allowed home education. Only four states required home tutors to be certified, but five states required the students to be tested for mastery of basic skills.[5]

Where state laws require attendance at a public or private school, but do not specifically authorize home education, controversies have arisen over the definition of a "school." Some courts have interpreted such statutes as precluding home education as a means to satisfy compulsory attendance mandates.[6] For example, in 1983 a New Mexico appeals court ruled that the exclusion of home instruction from satisfying compulsory school attendance mandates did not violate parents' equal protection rights.[7] However, in 1985 the North Carolina Supreme Court interpreted the state law requiring attendance at a public or nonpublic school, with teachers and curricula approved by the state board of education, as authorizing home education programs that meet state standards.[8] The supreme courts of Wisconsin and Georgia found compulsory attendance statutes to be unconstitutionally vague because they required parents to enroll their children in a public or private school but did not define what constitutes a private school.[9] Neither court questioned the state's authority to regulate alternatives to public education, but they reasoned that statutory mandates must provide adequate guidance as to what options are available to satisfy compulsory attendance mandates.[10]

In states where home education is authorized, courts have differed regarding whether the state or parents have the burden of proving the equivalency of home education programs to public school offerings. In two recent cases, Missouri appellate courts placed the burden on state officials to prove that home education (authorized by state law) was not comparable to the public school program.[11] Similarly, in 1985 a New York family court held that the state could not prosecute parents for violating the compulsory attendance law without evidence that the instruction they were providing their children at home was not equivalent to the public school curriculum.[12] In contrast, other courts have placed the burden of persuasion on those asserting a right to instruct children at home. For example, the Iowa Supreme Court held that parents had to substantiate that their children were entitled to be exempt from school attendance because they were receiving home instruction equivalent to the public school program.[13] Also, the Fourth Circuit Court of Appeals held that parents choosing to educate their children at home must prove that the instruction would prepare the children "to be self-sufficient participants in our modern society or enable them to participate intelligently in our political system," which is a "compelling interest of the state."[14]

States have considerable latitude in establishing standards for alternatives to public education, but there is wide variance among states in the requirements imposed. Some states preclude home instruction entirely or require home education programs to satisfy specific standards (e.g., certified tutors) to ensure equivalency, even if such requirements are more stringent than those applied to private schools.[15] Other states, however, permissively regulate home tutoring. It seems likely that parents will continue to assert a right to instruct their children at home, and the legal status of specific instructional programs will depend on judicial interpretations of applicable state statutes and administrative regulations.

Exceptions to Compulsory Attendance

State laws generally recognize certain exceptions to compulsory attendance mandates. The most common exemption pertains to married students. It is reasoned that students assume adult responsibilities when they marry, and thus should be emancipated from compulsory school attendance. Statutes often include other exceptions. In Indiana, for example, students who are serving as pages for the state legislature for a limited period of time and children who have reached age fourteen and have obtained lawful employment certificates are exempted from compulsory attendance requirements.[16]

In addition to statutory exceptions, an exemption from compulsory attendance mandates has been granted on first amendment religious grounds to Amish children who have successfully completed the eighth grade.[17] However, most other attempts to keep children out of school based on religious convictions have not been successful. In 1985 the Supreme Court declined to review a decision in which the Iowa high court refused to extend a statutory religious exemption from compulsory school attendance to children of the Baptist faith.[18] Under the state law in question, members of a recognized religious denomination, whose tenets conflict substantially with Iowa's stated educational goals and philosophy, can request from the state superintendent an exemption from the compulsory education law that requires children to be instructed by certified teachers. The Iowa Supreme Court reasoned that the exemption was intended to be limited to the Amish, who lead isolated lives, and thus was not available to students whose religious tenets are not threatened by exposure to American culture. The court rejected the assertion that the state's position in limiting the exemption to the Amish violates the establishment clause by favoring a particular religious sect.

Reasons other than religious convictions also have been unsuccessfully proffered as justification for noncompliance with compulsory attendance laws. For example, a North Carolina appeals court ruled that a "deep-rooted conviction for Indian heritage was an insufficient basis for keeping children out of school."[19] The father, who was an American Indian, testified that he would not send his children to school because they were not taught about Indian history and culture. The court concluded that the children were "neglected" within the meaning of state law, because they were not permitted to attend public school or provided with any alternative education.[20] Also, the Tenth Circuit Court of Appeals rejected the assertion that the conflict between a school's grooming restrictions and Indian customs, traditions, and religious beliefs justified noncompliance with compulsory education mandates.[21]

Some parents have defended noncompliance with compulsory school attendance laws because of the asserted unsafe conditions of the schools to which their children have been assigned. Courts in general have rejected such claims that fear of unsafe school conditions justifies an exemption from mandatory school attendance.[22] In a few situations, however, courts have rules that students' absences based on a history of physical harassment by classmates have warranted alternative placements for the victimized children.[23]

Health Requirements

State agencies have the power not only to mandate school attendance, but also to require students to be in good health so as not to endanger the well-being of others. In an early case the United State Supreme Court rejected a federal constitutional challenge to a Texas law authorizing local school officials to condition public and private school attendance on vaccination against communicable diseases.[24]

Numerous courts subsequently have upheld mandatory vaccination requirements, even when challenged on religious grounds, and have reasoned that there need not be a pending epidemic to justify such requirements. Parents have been convicted for indirectly violating compulsory attendance laws because they have refused to have their children vaccinated as a prerequisite to school admission. In a typical case, a New Jersey school board policy, requiring immunization against diphtheria as a condition of school attendance, was challenged by a group of Christian Scientists.[25] A state superior court upheld the policy, noting that the school board had the authority to mandate immunization without waiting for an epidemic to occur. Similarly, the New Hampshire Supreme Court held that parents' views, "whether 'conscientious,' 'religious,' or 'scientific,' " could not justify refusal to have their child vaccinated.[26] The Supreme Court of Arkansas also declared that religious freedom does not mean that parents can "engage in religious practices inconsistent with the peace, safety, and health of inhabitants of [the] state."[27]

In some states, statutes provide for an exemption from required immunization for members of religious sects whose teachings oppose the practice as long as the welfare of others is not endangered by the exemption. These statutory religious exemptions have evoked a range of judicial interpretations. For example, some courts have interpreted such statutes broadly, reasoning that parents can qualify for a religious exemption for their children in situations where vaccination is not specifically prohibited by official church doctrine,[28] or where the individuals objecting to immunization on religious grounds are not members of an organized church.[29] Other courts have narrowly interpreted such statutory exemptions and found them unconstitutional because they discriminate against individuals who have religious objections to vaccination but are not church members.[30] The Massachusetts high court noted that the legislature could remedy such a defect in the state law by expanding the exemption to cover individuals who objected to immunization based on sincere religious beliefs irrespective of their church membership.[31] A Kentucky federal district court, however, ruled that a parent could not rely on the statutory religious exemption merely because he was "philosophically opposed" to having his children immunized.[32] The court was not persuaded by the argument that the law was discriminatory because it granted an exemption to members of religious groups while denying the same privilege to those opposed to immunization on nonreligious grounds. An Ohio federal district court applied similar reasoning in holding that parents' belief in "chiropractic ethics" did not entitle their children to a religious exemption from vaccination.[33]

At least one court has questioned the rationale for such religious exemptions from mandatory vaccination. The Supreme Court of Mississippi concluded that a statutory exemption discriminated against parents who opposed immunization for nonreligious reasons, and further held that such an exemption defeated the purpose of an immunization requirement, which is to protect all students from exposure to communicable diseases. Accordingly, the court ruled that the state law requiring immunization as a prerequisite to school attendance must be applied to all students, regardless of the religious beliefs of parents.[34] Most other courts have reasoned that states are empowered to enact such statutory exemptions, but they clearly are not obligated to do so.

While it is well established that school attendance can be conditioned on vaccination against communicable diseases, states cannot abdicate their responsibility to educate children with such diseases. Children can be denied attendance in the regular school program if their presence would pose a danger to the health of others, but it is generally assumed that an alternative educational program (e.g., home instruction by computer) must be provided.

Substantial controversy has focused on school attendance by students with acquired immune deficiency syndrome (AIDS), a life-threatening disease that is not generally believed to be transmitted through casual contacts. Several states have adopted policies, modeled after guidelines issued by the National Centers for Disease Control (CDC), stipulating that students with AIDS should be allowed to attend public school unless they have open lesions, cannot control their bodily secretions, or display behavior such as biting. The CDC has suggested that determinations of whether individual students pose a health risk to others should be made on a case-by-case basis by a team of appropriate health and educational personnel.

Despite considerable evidence that AIDS is not communicated except through blood transfusions or sexual contact, some school boards have attempted to bar AIDS victims from attending public school classes. In such situations, infected students have sought judicial relief, asserting a right to attend school with their classmates. Several courts have reasoned that children suffering from AIDS are protected by federal statutes barring discrimination against the handicapped. Accordingly, these courts have ordered public schools to enroll children with AIDS upon certification by health officials that they pose minimal risk of infecting others.[35]

RESIDENCY REQUIREMENTS

In general courts have ruled that public schools have an obligation to educate school-age children who reside within the school district with the intention of remaining. In a significant 1982 decision, *Plyler v. Doe,* the United States Supreme Court held that school districts could not deny a free public education to resident children whose parents had entered the United States illegally.[36] Recognizing the individual's significant interest in receiving an education, the Court ruled that classifications affecting access to education would have to be substantially related to an important governmental interest to satisfy the equal protection clause.[37] The Court reasoned that the state's interest in deterring aliens from entering the country illegally was not important enough to deny students an opportunity to be educated.

In contrast to the judiciary's position in requiring school boards to provide free public schooling for students who reside in their districts with the intent of remaining, courts in general have not required public schools to admit nonresident students tuition-free. In 1983 the Supreme Court upheld a Texas residency requirement allowing local school boards to deny tuition-free schooling to any minor who lives apart from a parent or legal guardian for the primary purpose of attending public school.[38] The court ruled that the requirement advances the substantial state interest of assuring the high quality of public education enjoyed by residents (those living in a school district with the current intent of remaining).[39] Subsequently, a Texas appeals court upheld a school district's residency policy, even though it was more stringent than the state law in that it did not make an exception for minors living apart from their parents or guardians for noneducational purposes.[40]

Other courts similarly have upheld residency requirements, reasoning that tuition must be paid when students' legal residence is outside the school district, even though they may live in the district with someone other than a legal guardian.[41] Also, the judiciary has ruled that students have no property right to attend public school tuition-free in the school district in which they formerly resided prior to changing their legal residence.[42]

Departing from the prevailing judicial posture, however, in 1985 the Eighth Circuit Court of Appeals found that an Arkansas school district's residency requirement violated due process and equal protection guarantees.[43] The requirement denied tuition-free enrollment to minor students whose parents or guardians were not domiciled in the school district. Regarding the equal protection claim, the court held that the school district produced no evidence that a substantial state interest was advanced by the policy which discriminated against the class of students who live apart from their parents and have no control over this situation. The court further concluded that the policy violated due process guarantees by creating an irrebuttable presumption that a student who does not reside with a parent or guardian is not living in the school district with the intent to remain.

Some legal controversies have focused on students attending public school in neighboring school districts. In the absence of hardship conditions, students residing in one school district do not have a right to attend school in another district (even if tuition is paid) without the consent of both the sending and receiving school districts.[44] The Supreme Court of Washington addressed a claim that children from an allegedly inadequate school district were entitled to attend school in another district. The superior court held that all children should be able to attend school in the district that affords them the greatest potential for academic and social growth, but the high court reversed this decision. The Washington Supreme Court held that the parents did not prove that their children's enrollment in the allegedly inadequate school district would be detrimental to the children's welfare and thus their state constitutional entitlement to an "ample education" had not been abridged.[45] Where special hardship conditions have been proven, however, enrollment in a neighboring school district has received judicial endorsement.[46] Also, if school officials have erred in making a school district assignment, the affected student can assert a right to remain in the assigned school after the mistake is discovered.[47]

As discussed in chapter 4, several cases involving residency disputes have involved student athletes, and courts consistently have rejected efforts to establish limited guardianships to enable students to attend school tuition-free for athletic reasons. For example, an Indiana appeals court refused to recognize, for purposes of residency, a guardianship that was created to make a student eligible to participate in interscholastic sports in a school district where his parents did not reside.[48]

In some situations, however, courts have found that there are legitimate reasons for children to live apart from their parents. In an early case, the Colorado Supreme Court concluded that a child was placed in the home of another family to give him desirable influences and not primarily for educational reasons. Thus, the school district was ordered to consider the child a resident student.[49] More recently, the New Hampshire Supreme Court found that the major reason a child was living with his father during the school term, rather than with his mother who had legal custody, was based on health rather than educational considerations. Because the child's asthma problems were exacerbated by the humidity where his mother lived, the school district of his father's residence was ordered to admit the student tuition-free.[50]

As a result of reductions in federal "impact aid" to compensate public school districts for pupils associated with tax-exempt federal property (e.g., military installations), there has been some controversy over the authority of school districts to charge tuition to these students who are temporary residents. The Fourth Circuit Court of Appeals in 1984 invalidated such a tuition policy, noting that the school district had a contract with the federal government to provide educational opportunities for federal dependents as a condition of receiving impact aid.[51]

From litigation to date, it appears that school districts have considerable latitude in establishing residency requirements for students as long as protected rights are respected. Although tuition can be charged to students who temporarily reside away from their parents for the sole purpose of attending school, students who are bona fide residents of the district (even those whose parents are temporarily assigned to federal installations or whose parents entered the country illegally) cannot be denied a free public education.

REQUIRED FEES FOR TEXTBOOKS AND COURSES

The legality of charging students for the use of public school textbooks has been contested with some regularity. In 1972, the United States Supreme Court was asked to determine whether the Federal Constitution prohibits the imposition of such fees. This case involved a New York law that allowed local school districts to decide by election whether to charge elementary school students a book rental fee. The law was challenged in a school district that had elected to impose a rental system. The Second Circuit Court of Appeals concluded that the law did not violate fourteenth amendment rights to equal protection of the laws, even though it served to disadvantage children from poor families. The United States Supreme Court agreed to review the case, but before it had the opportunity to address the constitutional issue, voters in the district under litigation decided to assess a tax to purchase all textbooks in grades one through six. The Supreme Court, therefore, vacated the court of appeals' judgment since no controversy remained for judicial resolution.[52]

Because the Supreme Court has not ruled on the validity of textbook fees under federal equal protection guarantees, resolution of this issue has been handled on the basis of each individual state's consitutional and statutory mandates. In several states, such as Virginia, Colorado, Arizona, and Indiana, constitutional provisions have been interpreted as allowing fees to be charged for public school textbooks.[53] While authorizing public school textbook fees, an Indiana federal district court ruled that students could not be suspended from school for their parents' failure to pay the fees. Such action was found to impair the state student disciplinary code and federal equal protection guarantees.[54] The Ninth Circuit Court of Appeals also recognized that students have a constitutional right not to be subjected to embarrassment, humiliation, or other penalties for failure to pay textbook fees.[55]

In some states, courts have interpreted state constitutional provisions as precluding the imposition of fees for textbooks. For example, the Supreme Court of North Dakota held that the legislature is prohibited from authorizing public school districts to charge book fees, and the Illinois Supreme Court similarly interpreted state law as requiring school boards to furnish textbooks without charge.[56] Even in states where textbook fees have been judicially upheld, a waiver is usually provided for students who cannot afford to pay the assessed amount. The West Virginia high court interpreted the state constitution as requiring textbooks, workbooks, and other materials necessary for use in the state-prescribed curriculum to be provided free for students who cannot afford to purchase the materials.[57]

In addition to fees for textbooks, fees for courses and supplies also have been challenged. The Illinois Supreme Court sanctioned the imposition of supply fees for courses, but not tuition fees.[58] The Supreme Court of Missouri also ruled that the practice of charging course fees as a prerequisite to enrollment in academic classes impaired students' rights to free public schooling.[59] The court, however, did not address the issue of whether students could be required to furnish certain materials and equipment for use in classes. The New Mexico Supreme Court interpreted its state constitution as prohibiting fees for courses required of every student, but allowing reasonable fees for elective courses.[60] The Supreme Court of Montana similarly ruled that fees could not be assessed for courses or activities "reasonably related to a recognized academic and educational goal of the particular system," but that fees could be assessed for those courses or activities that were optional.[61]

In some cases, the concept of charging parents for materials and other supplies has received judicial endorsement, but the manner of fee collection has been invalidated. A New York appeals court struck down a school district's annual supply fee for classroom materials, reasoning that while parents could be asked to furnish supplies for the children, imposition of a charge on parents who were unwilling to purchase the supplies through the school district violated state law.[62] The North Carolina Supreme Court ruled that parents who were financially able could be required to furnish supplies and materials for pupils' personal use or to pay "modest, reasonable" supply fees, but the court invalidated the school district's waiver policy for students who could not afford the fees.[63] The court reasoned that the policy was unconstitutional because it failed to provide a mechanism for notifying students or their parents of the availability of the waiver and of the process for applying for such a waiver. The court noted that a revised policy could easily remedy these infirmities.

In a somewhat unusual school fee case, an Illinois appeals court upheld a lunchroom supervision fee for students who were not provided bus transportation, lived within close proximity (.7 of a mile) of the school, and ate at school.[64] The court reasoned that the fee did not violate the state constitutional mandate requiring the provision of a free education because lunchroom supervision was considered a noneducational service for which reasonable charges could be assessed.

Currently, school districts in many states solicit fees from students for various consumable materials. The legality of such practices varies across states and hinges primarily on the state judiciary's assessment of state constitutional provisions. An issue that is receiving increasing attention is the imposition of fees for participation in extracurricular activities; litigation pertaining to this topic is discussed in chapter 4.

THE SCHOOL CURRICULUM

State legislation pertaining to the public school curriculum has become increasingly explicit, and some of these enactments have been challenged as violating individuals' protected rights. Also, curriculum policies enacted by local school boards have been controversial. This section focuses on legal developments regarding curriculum requirements/restrictions and instructional censorship.

Curriculum Requirements and Restrictions

Courts repeatedly have recognized that the state retains the power to determine the public school curriculum as long as federal constitutional guarantees are respected. Although a few state constitutions include specific curriculum mandates,[65] more typically the legislature is given responsibility to make such curricular determinations. States vary as to the specificity of legislative directives, but all states require instruction pertaining to the Federal Constitution. Most legislatures also mandate the teaching of American history. Other subjects commonly required are English, mathematics, drug education, health, safety, and physical education. Some state statutes specify what subjects will be taught in which grades, and many states provide detailed legislation for the provision of vocational education, bilingual education, and special services for handicapped children. State laws usually stipulate that local school boards must offer the state-mandated minimum curriculum and may supplement this curriculum unless there is a statutory prohibition.[66] In about half of the states, local boards of education are empowered to adopt courses of study, but often they must secure approval from the state board of education.[67]

In addition to authority over the public school curriculum, the state also has the power to specify textbooks and to regulate the method by which such books are obtained and distributed. In most states, textbooks are prescribed by the state board of education or by a textbook commission. A list of acceptable books usually is developed at the state level, and local school boards then select from this list the specific books to adopt for various course offerings within the district. However, in some states, such as Colorado, the local board is given almost complete authority to make textbook selections.

Parents often have challenged specific curricular offerings or prohibitions and have asserted a right to control their children's course of study in public schools. As discussed in chapter 2, courts have upheld free exercise claims for specific children to be excused from course offerings (e.g., sex education) that offend their religious beliefs, as long as the exemption does not impede the student's academic progress or the management of the school.[68] Religious challenges to the courses themselves, however, have not found a receptive judicial forum. Courts consistently have held that the state and its agents (e.g., state and local boards of education) are empowered to determine the components of the public school curriculum within consitutional parameters.

While the state has considerable latitude in curricular matters and has received judicial backing in efforts to *expand* offerings for students, some legislative attempts to *ban* certain types of instruction have run afoul of federal constitutional rights. The first curriculum case to reach the United States Supreme Court involved a 1923 challenge to a Nebraska law that prohibited instruction in a foreign language in any private or public school to children who had not successfully completed the eighth grade.[69] The state high court had upheld the dismissal of a private school teacher for teaching reading in German to elementary school students. In striking down the statute, the Supreme Court reasoned that the teacher's right to teach, the parents' right to engage him to instruct their children, and the children's right to acquire useful knowledge were protected liberties under the due process clause of the fourteenth amendment. More recently, the Supreme Court held that states are precluded by the first amendment from barring instruction simply because it conflicts with certain religious views. Invalidating an Arkansas law prohibiting the teaching of Darwin's theory of evolution in public schools, the Court in 1968 declared that "the First Amendment does not permit the State to require that teaching and learning must be tailored to the principles or prohibitions of any religious sect or dogma."[70]

If constitutional rights are not implicated, however, courts will uphold decisions of state and local education agencies in curricular matters. Courts have deferred to state authorities not only in determining courses of study but also in establishing standards for pupil performance[71] and imposing other instructional requirements.[72] For example, school districts can establish prerequisites and admission criteria for particular courses as long as such criteria are not arbitrary and do not serve to disadvantage certain groups of students. The Fifth Circuit Court of Appeals ruled in 1980 that in the absence of an independent source, such as a state law entitling students to a particular course of study, students have no property right to be admitted to any class that is offered in the public school.[73] A New York court also rejected a student's assertion that he had a mandatory right to early graduation since he had accumulated sufficient credits. Noting that the program in question required completion of the twelfth grade, the court held that the judiciary does not have the power to review the competence of educational institutions in making academic judgments as to whether a student is entitled to a degree.[74]

Given the state's plenary power over education and the judiciary's lack of expertise in this arena, courts are generally reluctant to interfere with instructional decisions made by state and local education agencies. Only if such decisions are clearly arbitrary or impair constitutional rights will courts intervene.

Censorship of Instructional Materials

Attempts to remove books from classrooms and libraries and to tailor curricular offerings and methodologies to particular religious and philosophical values have led to a substantial amount of litigation. With the multiple actors and interests involved in censorship disputes, the issues do not lend themselves to simplistic resolution. There is general agreement that schools transmit values, but there is little consensus regarding *which* values should be transmitted or *who* should make this determination. In 1980 it was estimated that approximately 200 organizations were involved in efforts to purge public schools of "immoral, anti-Christian" materials and course offerings.[75] Between 1982 and 1986, the number of challenges to the public school curriculum increased by 117 percent according to a survey conducted by People for the American Way.[76] Few aspects of the public school program remain totally untouched by recent censorship activities. Since efforts to restrict *course offerings* for religious reasons have been addressed in chapter 2, the discussion here focuses on censorship of *instructional materials*.

One of the first widely publicized censorship cases involved Kanawha County, West Virginia. In 1974, parents protested the school board's adoption of a series of English materials that they considered to be godless, communistic, profane, and otherwise inappropriate for use in the schools. National attention was focused on Kanawha County as the parental protests evolved into school boycotts, a strike by coal miners, shootings, bombing of the courthouse, and even public prayer calling for the death of school board members. Although the federal district court upheld the board's authority to determine curricular materials and rejected the parents' contention that these books represented an infringement of constitutionally protected rights, book burnings and other public demonstrations continued.[77]

To date, courts have not allowed mere parental displeasure over instructional materials to dictate the public school curriculum, noting that parents' "sensibilities are not the full measure of what is proper education."[78] In rejecting a parental challenge to the use of Kurt Vonnegut's *Slaughterhouse Five* in the public school curriculum, a Michigan appeals court declared: "Our Constitution does not command ignorance; on the contrary, it assures the people that the state may not relegate them to such a status and guarantees to all the precious and unfettered freedom of pursuing one's own intellectual pleasures in one's own personal way."[79]

More recently, the Supreme Court declined to review a case in which the Ninth Circuit Court of Appeals rejected a parental challenge to the school board's use of Gordon Park's *The Learning Tree* in the high school curriculum.[80] The parents claimed that the book promoted "secular humanism," a religious creed that disavows God and exalts humans as controllers of their own destiny.[81] The court, however, ruled that the book was religiously neutral and related to legitimate educational objectives. Upholding the use of the book in the curriculum, the court noted that the school was willing to excuse offended students from reading the book and participating in classroom discussions.[82]

While courts have not been receptive to challenges to school boards' curricular decisions simply because some materials or course content offend the sensibilities of specific students or their parents, more difficult legal issues are raised when the policymakers themselves support the censorship activity. Bills calling for instructional censorship have been introduced in Congress and numerous state legislatures, with the central target being instruction that allegedly advances "secular humanism."[83] In addition, conservative parent groups have focused efforts on securing school board support in eliminating "objectionable" materials from public school classrooms and libraries.

The Supreme Court has recognized the broad discretionary authority of school boards to make decisions that reflect the "legitimate and substantial community interest in promoting respect for authority and traditional values, be they social, moral, or political."[84] Thus, the judiciary has been reluctant to interfere with school boards' prerogatives in selecting and eliminating instructional materials. For example, the Second Circuit Court of Appeals on two occasions upheld a school board's right to remove particular books from public school libraries. In 1972 the court noted that a book does not acquire tenure and therefore can be removed by the same authority that made the initial selection.[85] In 1980 the court reiterated that a school board's decision to remove "vulgar" and "obscene" books and to screen future library acquisitions did not create a risk of suppressing ideas.[86]

Similarly, in 1980 the Seventh Circuit Court of Appeals endorsed an Indiana federal district court's conclusion that "it is legitimate for school officials to develop an opinion about what type of citizens are good citizens, to determine what curriculum and materials will best develop good citizens, and to prohibit the use of texts, remove library books, and delete courses from the curriculum as a part of the effort to shape students into good citizens."[87] Recognizing that challenges by secondary school students to educational decisions made by local authorities can sometimes be valid, the court emphasized that such complaints must "cross a relatively high threshold" before implicating constitutional rights to justify federal court intervention. According to the Seventh Circuit Court of Appeals, the judiciary should not interfere with a school board's broad discretion in making curricular determinations unless there is a "flagrant abuse" of that discretion.[88]

In 1981 the Third Circuit Court of Appeals also held that performances by the high school drama club were a part of the school program and, therefore, the school board had a legitimate interest in assuring that the group did not perform a play at variance with the goals of the school's educational offerings.[89] Accordingly, the school board was upheld in prohibiting the performance of the musical *Pippin* because of its explicit sexual scenes.

Although the judiciary has attempted to uphold the right of school board members to apply social and moral values in determining curricular materials and offerings, some courts have found that specific censorship activity has impaired students' protected rights to have access to information. For example, in 1976, the Sixth Circuit Court of Appeals ruled that a school board acted beyond its scope of authority in removing books from the school library.[90] In this case, the board refused to accept the recommendation of the teaching staff to purchase several novels for the English curriculum and ordered the controversial books removed from the school library shelves. Students challenged the board's action, claiming that it created an unconstitutional censorship of classroom materials and impaired their protected freedom to learn. While upholding the board's right to override faculty judgments regarding the selection of books for academic courses and the school library, the court rejected the board's contention that it could remove books that had already been placed in the library. Since there was no claim that the books were obscene or that they lacked literary value, the court concluded that the board failed to demonstrate any compelling reason for removing the books. The court stated that the board was not forced to establish a library, but having done so, it could not place restrictions on the use of the library simply to conform to preferences of school board members.[91]

Other courts have intervened if specific censorship activity has clearly been motivated by a desire to suppress particular viewpoints or controversial ideas. In 1979 the New Hampshire federal district court held that the removal of *Ms.* magazine from the school library violated students' first amendment rights.[92] Echoing the Sixth Circuit Court of Appeals, the district court held that once a library is established, arbitrary conditions cannot be placed on its use. The court concluded that board members' disapproval of the political orientation of *Ms.* was not a sufficient justification for removing the magazine from the high school library.

Also, in 1982 the Eighth Circuit Court of Appeals afforded constitutional protection to students' rights to be exposed to controversial ideas when it struck down a Minnesota school board's attempt to ban certain films from the public school.[93] The court noted that the board's suppression of the films because of their ideological content had an obvious "chilling effect" on teachers and students.

A Mississippi federal district court found evidence of racial bias on the part of a Mississippi textbook-rating committee that barred from the approved book list a history textbook because of its controversial treatment of racial matters, particularly the reconstruction period and civil rights movement.[94] In addition to finding that the textbook committee's action violated civil rights statutes, the court held that the statutory scheme, which authorized the textbook approval committee to ensure that no unauthorized ideas were introduced in the classroom, deprived authors, educators, and students of the constitutionally protected rights to freedom of speech, freedom of press, and due process of law. The scheme precluded further review of the committee's decisions and foreclosed any involvement by those affected by the decisions.

While there has been substantial activity in lower courts, the Supreme Court has rendered only one decision involving the legality of censorship activity in public schools. This case, *Board of Education, Island Trees Union Free School District v. Pico,*[95] unfortunately, did not provide significant clarification regarding the scope of school boards' authority to restrict student access to particular materials. In fact, seven of the nine Supreme Court justices wrote opinions, conveying a range of viewpoints as to the governing legal principles.

At issue in this case was the school board's removal of certain books from junior high and high school libraries and the literature curriculum, despite the contrary recommendation of a committee appointed to review the books.[96] The federal district court ruled in favor of the school board without a trial, reasoning that the board had acted within its authority in removing the controversial books. Reversing the lower court's decision, the Second Circuit Court of Appeals remanded the case for a trial to determine whether the school board's action impaired students' first amendment rights. The United States Supreme Court, by a slim majority, affirmed the appellate court's remand of the case for a trial because of irregularities in the procedures followed in removing the books and factual questions regarding the school board's motivation. However, only three of the Supreme Court justices in *Pico* endorsed the notion that students have a protected right to receive information.[97] And even those justices recognized the broad authority of school boards to remove materials that are "pervasively vulgar" or educationally unsuitable and indicated that a trial might have been unnecessary if the school board had employed regular and unbiased procedures in reviewing the controversial materials.

After the Supreme Court's *Pico* decision, the Island Trees School Board voted to return the nine books to the school libraries, thus averting the need for a trial regarding the board's motivation for the original censorship. Although the *Pico* decision did not provide definitive guidelines for educators to follow in censorship controversies, a majority of the justices indicated that the first amendment might be breached by specific censorship activities where school boards act arbitrarily in censoring materials because of displeasure with the ideas contained in the books. In short, while school boards have broad discretion in such matters, this discretion is not unlimited.

Presumably, as long as public schools exist, there will be controversy surrounding the selection of materials for the curriculum. The debated issues will change to reflect shifts in public sentiments, but parental assaults on the public school curriculum undoubtedly will continue. Judge Rosenn of the Third Circuit Court of Appeals has noted the "inherent tension" between the school board's two essential functions of "exposing young minds to the clash of ideologies in the free marketplace of ideas" and instilling basic community values in our youth.[98] School boards would be wise to establish procedures for reviewing objections to course content and library materials,[99] and such procedures should be established *before* a controversy arises. Criteria applied in making decisions about the acquisition and elimination of instructional materials should be clearly articulated and educationally defensible. Once a process to evaluate complaints pertaining to the instructional program is in place, school boards should follow it carefully, as courts will show little sympathy when a school board ignores its own established procedures.

COMPETENCY TESTING

The state has the authority to establish academic standards for students, including mandatory examinations. The judiciary traditionally has been reluctant to interfere with academic assessments of pupil performance. In 1978 the United States Supreme Court distinguished an academic determination from a disciplinary action, noting that the former "judgment is by its nature more subjective and evaluative than the typical factual questions presented in the average disciplinary decision."[100] The Court emphasized that academic performance is properly assessed by professional educators who have expertise in this area. More recently, the Court rejected a claim that an academic dismissal from medical school violated a student's constitutional rights, reiterating that "when judges are asked to review the substance of a genuinely academic decision . . . , they should show great respect for the faculty's professional judgment."[101]

Courts have recognized that assurance of an educated citizenry is an appropriate state goal and that the establishment of criteria to give value to a high school diploma is considered a rational means to attain that goal. In 1981 the Fifth Circuit Court of Appeals had "nothing but praise" for the state's authority to determine educational policies and establish minimum performance standards for students to improve the quality of education.[102] Courts also have endorsed local school boards' authority to go beyond state minimum standards in establishing testing requirements for promotion[103] and/or high school graduation as long as the additional requirements are not prohibited by state law. In 1982 an Illinois federal district court noted that "local boards of education and their staffs have the right, if not a positive duty, to develop reasonable means to determine the effectiveness of their educational programs with respect to all individual students to whom they issue diplomas."[104]

The concept of proficiency examinations is not new, but the current use of minimum competency testing (MCT) as a condition of promotion or the award of a high school diploma has a relatively brief history. In 1976 only four states had enacted student competency testing legislation. By 1982, however, thirty-eight states had enacted laws or administrative regulations pertaining to MCT for diagnostic or promotion purposes, and by 1985, twenty of those states were conditioning the receipt of a high school diploma on passage of a competency test.[105] All remaining states currently have studies or proposals under consideration regarding student minimum competency requirements. Without question, MCT for students has become a pervasive and controversial national phenomenon.

While the state's authority to assess student proficiency has not been questioned, the implementation of specific MCT programs has been legally challenged as impairing students' protected rights to fair and nondiscriminatory treatment. Litigation involving MCT programs to date has focused primarily on tests used as a prerequisite to receipt of a high school diploma, but principles established in these cases have implications for testing programs used for grade promotion as well. There are five major areas of legal vulnerability: (1) sufficiency of notice; (2) racial impact; (3) adequacy of preparation; (4) participation of handicapped pupils; and (5) remedial opportunities.

Challenges to the *adequacy of notice* of competency test requirements have been grounded in the due process clause of the fourteenth amendment. To trigger constitutional due process guarantees, it must first be established that a liberty or property interest is at stake. Property rights are created through state laws or regulations, and the Supreme Court has ruled that students have a state-created property right to attend public school.[106] Some courts similarly have ruled that students have a property interest in receiving a high school diploma. Thus, when conditions are attached to high school graduation, students are entitled to notice of the standards and an opportunity to satisfy those standards before a diploma can be withheld. The Fifth Circuit Court of Appeals found that thirteen months from the time a statewide proficiency testing requirement was adopted until it was used as a graduation requirement was insufficient notice for students to prepare for the test.[107] Other courts have found that from two to four years' notice of a competency testing requirement for graduation is sufficient,[108] but the Seventh Circuit Court of Appeals indicated that lengthier notice may be required for handicapped pupils.[109]

Courts have not yet clarified how much notice must be given if a test is used for promotion purposes or to determine remediation needs. In 1984 the Eleventh Circuit Court of Appeals upheld a school board's policy requiring students to exhibit reading proficiency at grade level for promotion, reasoning that students do not have a property right to expect promotion based on substandard scholastic achievement.[110] However, if a test is used as the *sole* basis for denying grade promotion, possibly the judiciary would view such action as implicating a property right and would require at least two years' notice of the testing program before its implementation.

Where students have been successful in challenging competency testing programs as *racially discriminatory*, the test has been accompanied by evidence of purposeful racial discrimination, such as the lingering effects of a dual school system or a discriminatory tracking scheme. In some cases, school authorities have been enjoined from using proficiency tests as a prerequisite to high school graduation until the effects of prior racial discrimination have been eliminated. For example, courts have enjoined the use of competency tests as a prerequisite to receipt of a high school diploma until all students subjected to the requirements have entered first grade under desegregated conditions.[111] Even in these cases, however, courts have condoned the use of the tests to identify remediation needs. To successfully challenge the implementation of an MCT program on racial discrimination grounds, plaintiffs must prove that use of the test is accompanied by purposeful discrimination or that it perpetuates the effects of past school segregation; the mere fact that minority students are disproportionately identified for remediation programs is not sufficient to establish a violation of the equal protection clause.

Competency testing programs are possibly most vulnerable to a successful legal challenge in connection with the *adequacy of preparation* of students for the test. In 1981 the Fifth Circuit Court of Appeals received national publicity when it placed the burden on the state of Florida to substantiate that a proficiency test used as a graduation requirement covered material that actually had been presented to students.[112] While this standard has been referred to as instructional or curricular validity, in essence the appeals court required proof that pupils had been adequately prepared for the examination. The case was remanded to the federal district court to give the state an opportunity to present evidence that the test was fundamentally fair in that it covered material that had been taught to Florida students. Using data from a survey of all teachers and a sample of students, interviews with teachers and administrators, and an analysis of curriculum guides and other documents, the state ultimately was able to convince the court that students were adequately prepared for the test, and the injunction against using the proficiency test as a prerequisite to receipt of a diploma was lifted.[113] Nonetheless, the judicial willingness to require that competency examinations used as a graduation requirement cover material that has been taught may portend greater judicial intervention in reviewing the adequacy of preparation for tests used for promotion purposes or to determine remediation needs.

Another area of potential vulnerability pertains to the *application of competency tests to handicapped children.* Courts in general have ruled that the state does not have to alter its academic standards for handicapped children; thus, handicapped students can be denied grade promotion or a diploma if they do not meet the specified standards.[114] Handicapped children, however, cannot be denied the *opportunity* to satisfy requirements (including test requirements) for promotion or a diploma.[115] Whether handicapped children who are taken out of regular classroom instruction to receive special services could successfully assert that they are not being prepared to pass the competency examination remains to be clarified by the courts.

In some situations, handicapped children are given the option of not participating in an MCT program if the team charged with planning a given child's individualized education program (IEP) concludes that there is little likelihood that the child could master the material covered on the MCT. Under such circumstances, handicapped children are usually awarded a certificate of school attendance or some other alternative diploma. If handicapped children were awarded regular diplomas based on successful completion of their IEPs, while nonhandicapped students who failed the MCT were denied diplomas, equal protection rights of the nonhandicapped might be impaired.[116]

As mentioned previously, the Seventh Circuit Court of Appeals has ruled that handicapped children may need lengthier notice of a competency test requirement than necessary for the nonhandicapped to ensure an adequate opportunity for the material on the test to be incorporated into their IEPs.[117] Handicapped students also are entitled to special accommodations in the administration of examinations to ensure that their actual ability, rather than the handicapping condition, is being assessed. Since most competency tests have been validated with nonhandicapped children, the examinations may be vulnerable to legal challenge under the Education for All Handicapped Children Act which stipulates that tests must be validated for the specific purpose for which they are used and must be selected and administered to "accurately reflect the student's aptitude or achievement level or whatever other factor the test purports to measure, rather than reflecting the student's impaired sensory, manual, or speaking skills. . . ."[118] Although numerous accommodations for handicapped children are being implemented in MCT programs, whether alternative test formats (e.g., braille tests for the visually impaired) and alternative settings (e.g., private rooms or flexible time frames) provide a *comparable* opportunity for such children to display their knowledge remains to be substantiated.

The other major area of legal vulnerability pertains to the provision of appropriate *remediation opportunities* for those who fail the proficiency examination. It is generally agreed that students are entitled to remediation and the opportunity to retake the proficiency examination to demonstrate their competence. Indeed, if a student's deficiencies are identified and appropriate remediation is not provided, the grounds for a successful instructional negligence suit may be strengthened.[119]

School authorities cannot avert lawsuits, and specific competency testing programs seem likely to continue to generate litigation on the grounds discussed above. However, educators can take steps to avert *successful* legal challenges by ensuring that: (1) students are adequately prepared for the test; (2) sufficient notice of the test requirement is provided; (3) the test is not designed for discriminatory purposes; (4) appropriate accommodations for handicapped children are made; and (5) students who fail are provided remedial opportunities and the chance to retake the examination.

EDUCATIONAL MALPRACTICE

A topic that has generated litigation since the mid-1970s is instructional negligence, commonly referred to as educational malpractice.[120] Initial suits focused on whether students have a right to attain a predetermined level of achievement in return for state-mandated school attendance; parents asserted a right to expect their children to be functionally literate upon high school graduation. More recent cases have involved allegations that school authorities have breached their duty to diagnose students' deficiencies and place them in appropriate instructional programs. This section includes an overview of malpractice claims in which plaintiffs have sought damages from school districts for instructional negligence.

In the first educational malpractice suit to receive substantial attention, *Peter W. v. San Francisco Unified School Board*, a student asserted that the school district was negligent in teaching, promoting, and graduating him from high school with the ability to read only at the fifth-grade level.[121] He also claimed that his performance and progress had been misrepresented to his parents, who testified that they were unaware of his deficiencies until he was tested by a private agency after high school graduation. Both the trial court and California appeals court dismissed the charges against the school district. The appellate court reasoned that the complexities of the teaching/learning process made it impossible to place the entire burden on the school to assure student literacy. Noting "public policy considerations," the court concluded that the school district did not have a duty to guarantee that the student mastered basic academic skills. Finding no legitimate connection between the school district's conduct and the injury suffered, the court reasoned that to hold the school district liable would expose all educational agencies to countless "real or imagined" tort claims of "disaffected students and parents." [122]

Subsequently, the New York Court of Appeals dismissed a $5 million educational malpractice suit brought by a learning-disabled high school graduate who claimed that he was unable to complete job applications and cope with the problems of everyday life.[123] As in the California case, the New York high court concluded that the school could not be held accountable for ensuring that all students, with their varying abilities to learn, attain a specified reading level before high school graduation. The court reasoned that disputes over proper educational placements should not be resolved by the judiciary.

In 1979, the same court dismissed what had appeared to be the only successful educational malpractice suit. A state appellate court had awarded a former public school student $500,000 in damages after concluding that the New York City Board of Education had negligently diagnosed his needs and erroneously instructed him in a program for the mentally retarded.[124] At age five, the child's intelligence was assessed by the school psychologist using a test that required verbal responses, despite the fact that he had a severe speech defect. He scored one point below the score required for placement in a regular class, and his intelligence was never reevaluated through twelve years of public school, during which time he was instructed in classes for the retarded. The thrust of the negligence claim was that the school psychologist's report, recommending reassessment of the child within two years of the original evaluation, was ignored for the next eleven years—even though he scored in the ninetieth percentile on reading readiness tests at ages eight and nine. Upon high school graduation, he was required by Social Security to have his intelligence tested in order to continue receiving payments after his eighteenth birthday. At that time he scored one-hundred and thus became ineligible to remain in the occupational training program for the retarded. According to a psychologist and psychiatrist who testified at the trial, the plaintiff suffered a lengthy depression caused by his awareness that he was in essence uneducated and could not earn a living.

Distinguishing this case from previous educational malpractice suits, the lower court noted that school personnel committed affirmative acts of negligence (i.e., ignoring the psychologist's report) that placed crippling burdens on the student. Nonetheless, the New York Court of Appeals, in a four to three decision, reversed the lower court's ruling and held that it was not the role of the judiciary to make such educational determinations. The New York high court emphasized that instructional negligence claims, as a matter of public policy, should not be entertained by the judiciary. Instead, the court reasoned that such allegations should be handled within the administrative appeals network of the state educational system.

Other courts also have indicated a reluctance to intervene in educational policy decisions. For example, in 1984 a California appellate court dismissed a negligence suit in which parents sought damages for the school district's alleged breach of its duty under state and federal statutes to evaluate and develop an individualized education plan for their handicapped child.[125] Rejecting the contention that there was an implied duty which had been breached, the court observed that the societal interest in providing special education to handicapped students is not advanced by transforming special education laws "into springboards for private damages suits."[126] Similarly, the Supreme Court of Alaska refused to allow damages against a school district for the alleged misclassification of a student with dyslexia, reasoning that the courtroom is not the appropriate forum to address such educational concerns.[127] The Maryland high court also rejected a malpractice claim by a student who allegedly was misdiagnosed and instructed in classes for the mentally retarded;[128] and a New Jersey superior court ruled that a school district's failure to provide remedial instruction for a student was not actionable in a tort suit for damages.[129]

Although no educational malpractice claim has yet been successful, some courts have recognized circumstances under which plaintiffs possibly could recover damages in an instructional tort action. In a Maryland case, in which plaintiffs did not prevail in establishing instructional negligence, the state high court nonetheless noted conditions that might give rise to a successful damages claim. The court acknowledged that parents could maintain an action to prove that the defendants *intentionally* engaged in acts which injured a child placed in their educational care. While recognizing that the parents' burden of proof would be substantial, the court indicated that they had a right to attempt to prove such an allegation. Distinguishing intentional from unintentional acts, the court rejected the damages claim for the allegedly *unintentional* negligent action in evaluating a child's learning disabilities and inappropriately instructing the child, noting the availability of administrative remedies to settle such disputes.[130]

The Supreme Court of Montana went further, holding that unintentional acts might result in liability where school authorities have violated mandatory statutes pertaining to special education placements.[131] Reasoning that school districts have a duty to exercise reasonable care in testing and placing exceptional students in appropriate programs, the court concluded that damages could be assessed for injuries resulting from a breach of that duty. Accordingly, a trial was ordered to determine if a child's asserted misplacement in a segregated special education class warranted an award of damages. On remand, the trial court ruled that the plaintiff failed to present evidence substantiating the alleged injury caused by the school district, and the state high court subsequently affirmed this summary judgment.

In 1984 the New York high court unanimously allowed damages in a medical malpractice suit, even though the consequences were educational, but it barred damages in an instructional negligence suit by a one-vote margin. In the latter case, which the Supreme Court declined to review, the New York high court ruled that a student who was incorrectly diagnosed at age ten, after having been tested in English although he understood only Spanish, was not entitled to damages from the child care agency for its alleged failure to obtain suitable instruction to enable him to learn to read.[132] The plaintiff attempted to distinguish his claim from prior malpractice suits against schools, because his charges were against the child care agency responsible for his upbringing after his mother abandoned him at age seven. Rejecting this contention, the court reasoned that the issue involved educational policy matters regarding which instructional programs might have been preferable and was not actionable in a negligence suit.

In the other case, the same court awarded damages to an individual who was admitted to a state school at age two and diagnosed as retarded when he was actually deaf.[133] The failure to reassess the student upon learning that he was deaf was considered a "discernible act of medical malpractice on the part of the state" rather than a mere mistake in judgment pertaining to the student's educational program.[134] Concluding that the state school resembled a hospital and the students' records resembled medical records, the court held that damages for medical malpractice were appropriate.

The New York high court distinguished the two cases based on the age of the students when institutionalized, the nature of the institutions, and the kinds of care administered. These distinctions have been questioned by legal commentators, however, and there is some sentiment that prospects for a successful educational malpractice suit involving *placement negligence* may be more promising than they appeared a decade ago.[135] Even though it seems unlikely that public schools in the near future will be held accountable for a specified quantum of student achievement, it is plausible that schools will be held legally accountable for diagnosing pupils' needs, placing them in appropriate instructional programs, and reporting their progress to parents.[136]

INSTRUCTIONAL PRIVACY RIGHTS

The protection of students' privacy rights has become an increasingly volatile issue in political forums. State and federal laws have been enacted to ensure the confidentiality of students' records. In addition, laws have been enacted to protect students from mandatory participation in research projects or instructional activities designed to reveal personal information in sensitive areas. This section includes an overview of legal developments pertaining to students' privacy rights in instructional matters.

Student Records

The Supreme Court has recognized that constitutional protection is afforded to a zone of personal privacy;[137] thus, there must be a compelling justification for governmental action that impairs privacy rights, including the right to have personal information about oneself kept confidential. As a result of this recognized right, questions about who has access to a public school student's permanent file and what can go into a student's file have been the source of much controversy.

Legal challenges to school record keeping procedures have resulted in school officials being ordered to expunge irrelevant information from students' permanent folders. In an early case, the Supreme Court of Oklahoma ordered removal from the school register of a notation that a pupil had been "ruined by tobacco and whiskey."[138] Finding no evidence to support the veracity of the statement, the court concluded that the student was unjustly defamed. In some situations, students have brought libel suits for damages against school authorities who allegedly have recorded and communicated false defamatory information about them.[139]

Because of widespread dissatisfaction with educators' efforts to ameliorate abuses associated with student record keeping practices, the Family Educational Rights and Privacy Act (FERPA), commonly known as the Buckley Amendment, was passed in 1974, and final regulations became effective in 1976.[140] This law stipulates that federal funds may be withdrawn from any educational agency or institution that: (1) fails to provide parents access to their child's educational records; or (2) disseminates such information (with some exceptions) to third parties without parental permission. Upon reaching age eighteen, students may exercise the rights guaranteed to parents under this law.

Education officials may assume that a parent is entitled to exercise rights under FERPA unless state law or a court order bars a parent's access to his or her child's records under specific circumstances and the education agency has been instructed accordingly.[141] In 1981 a New York court ruled that the noncustodial father of a fifth-grade child was still a "psychological guardian" and was entitled to inspect the education records of his child despite the contrary wishes of the child's mother.[142] It should be noted, however, that in 1983 nearly three-fourths of the school counselors responding to a national study indicated that a noncustodial parent was not routinely allowed access to the child's records; thus, their schools were not in compliance with FERPA.[143]

After reviewing a student's permanent file, the parent or eligible student can request that the information be amended if it is believed to be inaccurate, misleading, or in violation of the student's protected rights. If school authorities decide that an amendment is not warranted, the parent or eligible student must be advised of the right to a hearing. The hearing officer may be an employee of the school district, but may not be an individual with a direct interest in the outcome of the hearing. Either party may be represented by counsel at the hearing, and the hearing officer must issue a written decision summarizing the evidence presented and the rationale for the ruling. If the hearing officer concludes that the records should not be amended, the parent or eligible student has the right to place in the file a personal statement specifying objections. Individuals can file a complaint with the Department of Education if they believe that a school district is not complying with the provisions of FERPA.[144]

Other federal laws include additional protections pertaining to the confidentiality and accessibility of student records. For example, the Education for All Handicapped Children Act of 1975 stipulates that records of handicapped children must be accessible to their parents or guardians.[145] Furthermore, interpreters must be hired, if necessary, to translate the contents of students' files for parents, and parental consent is required before such records can be disclosed to third parties.

Many states also have enacted legislation pertaining to the privacy of student records. Indiana law is typical in stipulating that school boards must maintain a list of all persons or agencies having access to personal files, furnish prior notice before such information is disclosed to a third party, and inform individuals of their right to access to their records and their right to contest the accuracy or appropriateness of the material in such files.[146]

Both state and federal laws recognize certain exceptions to disclosure provisions. For example, a teacher's daily records pertaining to pupil progress are exempt as long as the records are kept in the sole possession of the faculty member. However, private notes become education records and are subject to legal specifications if they are shared, even among educators who have a legitimate need for access to such information.

Certain public directory information, such as the student's name, address, date and place of birth, major field of study, and degrees and awards received, can be released without parental consent. A student's records also can be released to officials of a school to which the student is transferring if the parents or eligible student are notified, or the sending institution has given prior notice that it routinely transfers such records. A Maryland appeals court rejected a claim that a school's release of a student's records, including psychological reports, to the school where the student was transferring represented an invasion of privacy actionable in a suit for damages. There was no evidence that any unauthorized individuals had access to the information in the records or that any unwarranted publicity resulted from the release of the records.[147]

Similarly, students' privacy rights do not preclude federal and state authorities from having access to data needed to audit and evaluate federally supported education programs. These data, however, are to be collected in a way that prevents the disclosure of personally identifiable information. Also, composite information on pupil achievement can be released to the public as long as individual students are not personally identified. A Louisiana appeals court rejected a claim that the release of composite achievement data by school officials violated students' privacy rights, reasoning that the public had the right to examine the rankings of schools participating in a school effectiveness study conducted by the state department of education.[148] A New Jersey appeals court also concluded that a school district's curriculum reports prepared by a consultant were common law public records subject to disclosure to the newspaper. The court, however, remanded the case for a determination of whether the newspaper's interest in examining the report outweighed the school district's interest in maintaining confidentiality of the evaluation material contained in the reports.[149]

Students' records must be disclosed if subpoenaed by a court. In compelling a school district to reveal records of individual pupils, a New York federal district court reasoned that FERPA does not preclude the disclosure of student records where a genuine need for the information outweighs the students' privacy interests. In this case, data on the performance of individual students were needed to substantiate charges that inadequate instructional programs were being provided for children with English language deficiencies.[150] Also, a New York appeals court ruled that the records of students in a teacher's class would have to be disclosed (obliterating identifying data) for use by the teacher in defending charges pertaining to his competence. The court reasoned that "any degree of confidentiality accorded to the students' records must yield to the [teacher's] right to prepare his defense to the charges made against his reputation and his competence in his profession."[151]

Since Congress, state legislatures, and the judiciary have indicated a continuing interest in safeguarding the privacy rights of students in connection with school records, school boards would be wise to reassess their policies and ensure that they are adhering to the mandates included in federal and state laws. School personnel, however, should use some restraint before purging information from student files. Pertinent material that is necessary to provide continuity in the instructional program for a student *should* be included in a permanent record and should be available for use by authorized personnel. It is unfortunate that fear of federal sanctions under FERPA has resulted in deletion of useful information (along with irrelevant material) from student records.

The mere fact that information in a student's file is negative does not imply that the material is inappropriate. Courts have held that school authorities have an obligation to record relevant data pertaining to students' activities as long as such information is accurate. In an illustrative

Pennsylvania case, students sought to enjoin school officials from noting in their permanent records and communicating to institutions of higher education that they had participated in a demonstration at graduation ceremonies.[152] The federal district court denied the injunction, reasoning that the objective account of what occurred at the graduation exercises, with no reference as to the propriety of the demonstration, did not result in any "immediate, irreparable harm" to the students. Furthermore, the court held that school officials have a *duty* to record and communicate true factual information about students to institutions of higher learning in order to present an accurate picture of applicants for admission.

Pupil Protection Laws

Increasing attention has focused on the protection of public school students involved in research projects and experimental treatment programs. Parents have voiced concern over what they perceive to be nonacademic programs that invade family privacy. In 1973 a Pennsylvania federal district court enjoined implementation of a project in which potential student abusers of drugs were to be identified (through a questionnaire) and subjected to peer and faculty counseling. The court reasoned that such an invasion of privacy without informed consent violated protected rights of subjects and their parents.[153]

State legislatures as well as Congress have considered laws to protect students' privacy in connection with research activities in public schools. Under federal law, human subjects are protected in research supported in part under federal grants and contracts in any private or public institution or agency.[154] Informed consent must be obtained before placing subjects at any risk of being exposed to physical, psychological, or social injury as a result of participating in research, development, or related activities. All education agencies are required to establish review committees to ensure that the rights and welfare of all subjects are adequately protected.

In 1974 two amendments to the General Education Provisions Act required among other things that all instructional materials in federally assisted research or experimentation projects (designed to explore new or unproven teaching methods or techniques) be made available for inspection by parents of participating students. The amendments also stipulated that no child could be required to participate in such research or experimentation projects if the parents of the child objected in writing. In 1978 an additional amendment, referred to as the Hatch Amendment after its sponsor, was passed by Congress. The Hatch Amendment retained the provision giving parents the right to examine instructional materials in experimental programs and further required parental consent before students participate in federally supported programs involving psychiatric or psychological examination, testing or treatment designed to reveal information in specified sensitive areas pertaining to personal beliefs, behaviors, and family relationships.[155] The Department of Education issued final regulations pursuant to this amendment in 1984. The regulations broadly define psychiatric or psychological examination or treatment as including activities that are not directly related to academic instruction and are designed to obtain personal information or affect behaviors or attitudes. The Department of Education is charged with reviewing complaints under this law and ensuring compliance. If an educational institution is found in violation and does not comply within a reasonable period, federal funds can be withheld.

After the Hatch Amendment's regulation became effective in 1984, this previously obscure provision became extremely controversial, pitting conservative parents' groups against professional associations of educators. The dispute focused *not* on the protection of students' rights in research and experimental programs, but on ambiguities in the regulations regarding the scope and intent of the amendment and the federal government's role in resolving curriculum complaints. A coalition of more than thirty education and civil rights organizations has asserted that the regulations are so vague that they provide "inroads for conservatives aiming to gain control of local curriculum and instruction" by interpreting "psychological treatment" as covering any subject matter that is controversial or may require a value response from students.[156] The coalition has developed guidelines in an attempt to clarify the limited scope of the Hatch Amendment and avert its regulations' possible "chilling effect" on the instructional program.[157]

The coalition has voiced concerns that the Hatch Amendment and similar pupil protection provisions being enacted or considered by numerous state legislatures[158] will negate local school boards' prerogatives in curriculum matters. Although these pupil protection measures are couched in terms of protecting students' privacy rights by granting them *exemptions* from particular instructional activities, if a substantial number of exemptions are requested, a given instructional activity itself may be eliminated from the curriculum. The coalition, while supporting students' privacy rights in experimental programs, is opposed to the conservative groups' reliance on pupil protection provisions to force *alterations* in the public school program.[159]

CONCLUSION

The state and its agents are granted considerable latitude in regulating various aspects of public education, but any requirements that restrict students' activities must be reasonable and necessary to carry out legitimate educational objectives. Whenever students' or parents' protected rights are impaired, school authorites must be able to substantiate that there is an overriding public interest to be served. From an analysis of court cases and legislation pertaining to general requirements and rights associated with school attendance and the instructional program, the following generalizations are warranted.

1. The state can compel children between specified ages to attend school.[160]
2. Students can satisfy compulsory attendance mandates by attending private schools and, in most states, by receiving equivalent instruction (e.g., home tutoring) that is comparable to the public school program.
3. School officials can require immunization against diseases as a condition of school attendance.
4. Students cannot be excluded from public school because of particular health conditions, unless school attendance would endanger the health of others.
5. Public school districts must provide an education for bona fide resident children (even those who have entered the country illegally), but children who live apart from their parents for educational purposes are not entitled to tuition-free schooling.
6. Fees can be charged for the use of public school textbooks and for supplies associated with courses unless such fees are prohibited by state constitutional or statutory provisions.
7. The state and its agencies have the authority to determine public school course offerings and instructional materials, and such curricular determinations will be upheld by courts unless they are clearly arbitrary or in violation of constitutional or statutory rights.
8. School boards cannot arbitrarily censor instructional materials based on mere displeasure with the ideas contained in the materials; however, school boards can eliminate materials considered educationally unsuitable if objective procedures are followed in making such determinations.
9. Courts defer to school authorities in assessing student performance, in the absence of evidence of arbitrary or discriminatory academic decisions.
10. Proficiency examinations can be used to determine pupil remediation needs and as a prerequisite to high school graduation if students are given sufficient notice prior to implementation of the test requirements and if they are provided adequate preparation for the examinations.
11. Public schools do not owe students a duty to ensure that a specified level of achievement is attained.
12. Parents and eighteen-year-old students are entitled to access to the student's school records and an opportunity to contest the contents.
13. School personnel must ensure the accuracy of information con-

tained in student records and maintain the confidentiality of such records.

14. Parents have the right to inspect materials used in federally funded experimental projects, and students have a right to be excused from participation in such programs involving psychiatric or psychological testing or treatment designed to reveal information in specified sensitive areas pertaining to personal beliefs, behaviors, and family relationships.

NOTES

1. Ky. Rev. Stat. § 159.010. For an analysis of compulsory education laws across states, *see* Patricia Lines, *Compulsory Education Laws and Their Impact on Public and Private Education* (Denver, CO: Education Commission of the States, 1985).
2. *See* Trower v. Maple, 774 F.2d 673 (5th Cir. 1985); In the Interest of C.S., 382 N.W.2d 381 (N.D. 1986); New Mexico v. Edgington, 663 P.2d 374 (N.M. App. 1983), *cert. denied*, 464 U.S. 940 (1983); People v. Berger, 441 N.E.2d 915 (Ill. App. 1982); Williams v. Board of Educ., Marianna School Dist., 626 S.W.2d 361 (Ark. 1982). *See also* Pennsylvania v. Hall, 455 A.2d 674 (Pa. Super. 1983), in which parents were convicted for their children's truancy because they violated the school district's policy which allowed excused absences for one educational trip per year not to exceed five school days. Finding this policy reasonable, the court further noted that the educational value of additional trips made by the student was not relevant to the issue of whether the compulsory attendance law was violated.
3. In re Michael G., 214 Cal. Rptr. 755 (Cal. App. 1985). *See also* In the Interest of K.M.B., 452 N.E.2d 876 (Ill. App. 1983).
4. 268 U.S. 510, 535 (1925).
5. Patricia Lines, "Home Instruction," *Issuegram No. 49*, Education Commission of the States, August 1984.
6. *See* Burrow v. Arkansas, 669 S.W.2d 441 (Ark. 1984); State v. Garber, 419 P.2d 896 (Kan. 1966), *cert. denied and appeal dismissed*, 389 U.S. 51 (1967).
7. New Mexico v. Edgington, 663 P.2d 374 (N.M. App. 1983). Subsequently, the court recognized that the need for a child to be exposed to at least one other set of values was an important consideration in concluding that home instruction could not satisfy the state's compulsory school attendance law. *See* Strosnider v. Strosnider, 686 P.2d 981 (N.M. App. 1984) (instruction qualified as a private school, even though provided primarily to benefit the instructor's own child, where three other students were enrolled and classes were not offered at home).
8. Delconte v. State of North Carolina, 329 S.E.2d 636 (N.C. 1985).
9. Wisconsin v. Popanz, 332 N.W.2d 750 (Wis. 1983); Roemhild v. Georgia, 308 S.E.2d 154 (Ga. 1983).
10. The Minnesota Supreme Court also ruled that the term "essentially equivalent" as used in the compulsory attendance statute (requiring home instructors' qualifications to be essentially equivalent to the minimum standard for public school teachers) was unconstitutionally vague for purposes of imposing criminal liability on parents for noncompliance. Minnesota v. Newstrom,

371 N.W.2d 525 (Minn. 1985). But see Mazanec v. North Judson-San Pierre School Corp., 614 F. Supp. 1152 (N.D. Ind. 1985), *aff'd*, 798 F.2d 230 (7th Cir. 1986) (constitutional challenge to Indiana's compulsory attendance law was rejected where parents were prosecuted for thwarting efforts to verify compliance; the district court's finding that the home education program was essentially equivalent to public school instruction did not entitle the parents to injunctive or monetary relief).

11. In re Monnig, 638 S.W.2d 782 (Mo. App. 1982); State v. Davis, 598 S.W.2d 189 (Mo. App. 1980).
12. In Matter of Chapman, 490 N.Y.S.2d 433 (Fam. Ct., Delaware County, 1985). *But see* In the Matter of Kilroy, 467 N.Y.S.2d 318 (Fam. Ct., Cayuga County, 1983) (parents did not meet their burden of establishing the equivalency of their home education program because they refused to allow public school officials to conduct a necessary and reasonable on-site evaluation of the instructional program).
13. State v. Moorhead, 308 N.W.2d 60 (Iowa 1981). *See also* State v. Garber, 419 P.2d 896 (Kan. 1966); Knox v. O'Brien, 72 A.2d 389 (N.J. Super. 1950); Rice v. Commonwealth, 49 S.E.2d 342 (Va. 1948).
14. Duro v. District Attorney, 712 F.2d 96, 99 (4th Cir. 1983), *cert. denied,* 465 U.S. 1006 (1984). *See* Ralph Mawdsley and Steven Permuth, "Home Instruction for Religious Reasons: Parental Right or State Option?" *Education Law Reporter*, vol. 4 (1984), pp. 941–952.
15. *See* Trower v. Maple, 774 F.2d 673 (5th Cir. 1985); State v. Patzer, 382 N.W.2d 631 (N.D. 1986), *cert. denied*, 107 S. Ct. 99 (1986); Maine v. McDonough, 468 A.2d 977 (Me. 1983); Grigg v. Commonwealth, 297 S.E.2d 799 (Va. 1982); Oregon v. Bowman, 653 P.2d 254 (Ore. App. 1982); Jernegan v. State, 412 So. 2d 1242 (Ala. Crim. App. 1982); State v. M.M. and S.E., 407 So. 2d 987 (Fla. App. 1981); State v. Riddle, 285 S.E.2d 359 (W.Va. 1981); State *ex rel.* Shoreline School Dist. No. 412 v. Superior Court, 346 P.2d 999 (Wash. 1959), *cert. denied sub nom.* Wold v. Shoreline School Dist., 363 U.S. 814 (1960); People v. Turner, 263 P.2d 685 (Cal. App. 1953), *appeal dismissed*, 347 U.S. 972 (1953).
16. Ind. Code Ann. §§ 20–8.1–3–18; 20–8.1–4–3.
17. Wisconsin v. Yoder, 406 U.S. 205 (1972).
18. Johnson v. Charles City Community Schools Bd. of Educ., 368 N.W.2d 74 (Iowa 1985), *cert. denied sub nom.* Pruessner v. Benton, 106 S. Ct. 594 (1985). In this case, parents of children attending a fundamentalist school challenged the state's authority to require instruction by certified teachers to satisfy the compulsory school attendance law.
19. Matter of McMillan, 226 S.E.2d 693 (N.C. App. 1976).
20. *See also* Matter of Baum, 401 N.Y.S.2d 514 (App. Div. 1978).
21. Hatch v. Goerke, 502 F.2d 1189 (10th Cir. 1974). (however, expulsion of the student without a hearing for refusing to cut his hair impaired due process rights).
22. *See* In the Matter of Gregory B., 387 N.Y.S.2d 380 (Fam. Ct., Kings County, 1976); Commonwealth v. Ross, 330 A.2d 290 (Pa. Commw. 1975); School Dist. of City of Pittsburgh v. Zebra, 325 A.2d 330 (Pa. Commw. 1974).
23. *See* People v. Y.D.M., 593 P.2d 1356 (Colo. 1979); In the Matter of Foster, 330 N.Y.S.2d 8 (Fam. Ct., Kings County, 1972).

24. Zucht v. King, 260 U.S. 174 (1922). *See also* Jacobson v. Commonwealth of Massachusetts, 197 U.S. 11 (1905).
25. Board of Educ. of Mountain Lakes v. Maas, 152 A.2d 394 (N.J. Super. 1959), *aff'd*, 158 A.2d 330 (N.J. 1960) (per curiam), *cert. denied*, 363 U.S. 843 (1960).
26. State v. Drew, 192 A. 629, 631–632 (N.H. 1937). *See also* Calandra v. State College Area School Dist., 512 A.2d 809 (Pa. Commw. 1986) (mandatory tetanus immunization as a condition of participating in interscholastic baseball did not impermissibly burden a student who opposed immunization on religious grounds).
27. Cude v. State of Arkansas, 377 S.W.2d 816, 818–819 (Ark. 1964). *See also* Mannis v. State of Arkansas *ex rel.* Dewitt School Dist., 398 S.W.2d 206 (Ark. 1966) (parents could not evade mandatory vaccination requirement by withdrawing their child from public school and starting a parochial school which the parents asserted was not subject to the state health requirement).
28. *See* State v. Miday, 140 S.E.2d 325 (N.C. 1965).
29. *See* Maier v. Besser, 341 N.Y.S.2d 411 (Sup. Ct., Onondaga County, 1972).
30. *See* Davis v. State, 451 A.2d 107 (Md. 1982); Dalli v. Board of Educ., 267 N.E.2d 219 (Mass. 1971).
31. Dalli, *id. See also* Avard v. Dupuis, 376 F. Supp. 479 (D.N.H. 1974) (statutory religious exemption was unconstitutionally vague because it vested complete discretion in local school boards to determine whether an exemption would be granted).
32. Kleid v. Board of Educ. of Fulton, Kentucky Independent School Dist., 406 F. Supp. 902 (W.D. Ky. 1976).
33. Hanzel v. Arter, 625 F. Supp. 1259 (S.D. Ohio 1985) (claims that the immunization requirement impaired constitutional privacy and due process rights were also rejected). *See also* Heard v. Payne, 665 S.W.2d 865 (Ark. 1984) (statement from chiropractor could not satisfy medical exemption from immunization).
34. Brown v. Stone, 378 So. 2d 218 (Miss. 1979), *cert. denied*, 449 U.S. 887 (1980).
35. *See* In re Ryan White, No. 86–144 (Ind. Cir. Ct., Clinton County, 1986) (middle school AIDS victim was entitled to attend school); District 27 Community School Bd. v. Board of Educ. of the City of New York, 502 N.Y.S.2d 325 (Sup. Ct., Queens County, 1986) (automatic exclusion from school of all children with AIDS would violate their rights under the Rehabilitation Act of 1973 and the equal protection clause of the fourteenth amendment); Martha McCarthy, "The AIDS Crisis and Schools," *The Indiana Elementary Principal*, vol. 11, no. 1 (1986), pp. 5, 23–24. *See also* New York Ass'n for Retarded Children v. Carey, 612 F.2d 644 (2d Cir. 1979) (handicapped children with hepatitis B cannot be excluded from or segregated in public school). *But see* Board of Educ. v. Cooperman, 507 A.2d 253 (N.J. Super. 1986) (guidelines promulgated by the state board of education and orders of the Commissioner of Education directing local school boards to admit children with AIDS were null because provisions of the state Administrative Procedure Act were not followed and local boards of education were not afforded requisite procedural due process).
36. 457 U.S. 202 (1982). *See* text with note 9, chapter 5.

37. For a discussion of standards of judicial review under the equal protection clause, *see* text with note 2, chapter 9.
38. Martinez v. Bynum, 461 U.S. 321 (1983).
39. *Id.* at 328. Justice Marshall faulted the majority for not drawing a distinction between "residence" (having a well-settled connection in a locale) and "domicile" (one's true, fixed, permanent home), arguing that an individual may have more than one residence and that states should not be allowed to deny free schooling to all but domiciliary students. He asserted that the Court's use of a domicile requirement to establish residence for school purposes is not supported by prior Supreme Court decisions, *id.* at 338–342 (Marshall, J., dissenting).
40. Rodriguez v. Ysleta Independent School Dist., 663 S.W.2d 547 (Tex. App. 1983). *See also* Jackson v. Waco Independent School Dist., 629 S.W.2d 201 (Tex. App. 1982).
41. *See* Harris v. Hall, 572 F. Supp. 1054 (E.D. N.C. 1983); State *ex rel.* Henry v. Board of Educ., Madison Plains Local Schools, 485 N.E.2d 732 (Ohio App. 1984); Connelly v. Gibbs, 445 N.E.2d 477 (Ill. App. 1983); Matter of Proios, 443 N.Y.S.2d 828 (N.Y. Surrogate Ct. 1981).
42. *See* Daniels v. Morris, 746 F.2d 271 (5th Cir. 1984). It should be noted that children who live in orphanages or other state facilities are usually considered residents of the school district where the facility is located. State *ex rel.* Doe v. Kingery, 203 S.E.2d 358 (W.Va. 1974); University Center v. Ann Arbor Public Schools, 191 N.W.2d 302 (Mich. 1971). However, a state facility can charge tuition for children who are legal wards of another state. East Texas Guidance and Achievement Center v. Brockette, 431 F. Supp. 231 (E.D. Tex. 1977).
43. Horton v. Marshall Public Schools, 769 F.2d 1323 (8th Cir. 1985).
44. *See* Delta Special School Dist. v. McGehee Special School Dist., 659 S.W.2d 508 (Ark. 1983).
45. Ramsdiel v. North River School Dist. No. 200, 704 P.2d 606 (Wash. 1985).
46. *See* Pat v. Stanwood School Dist., 705 P.2d 1236 (Wash. App. 1985).
47. *See* Burdick v. Independent School Dist. No. 52 of Oklahoma County, 702 P.2d 48 (Okla. 1985) (there was an overriding public interest in promoting continuity of attendance once a residence status was honestly established and maintained in a given school system with no intervening change in legal boundaries).
48. Kris v. Brown, 390 N.E.2d 193 (Ind. App. 1979). *See also* In re United States *ex rel.* Missouri State High School Activities Ass'n, 682 F.2d 147 (8th Cir. 1982); text with note 156, chapter 4.
49. Fangman v. Moyers, 8 P.2d 762 (Colo. 1932). *See also* Matter of Curry, 318 N.W.2d 567 (Mich. App. 1982).
50. Luoma v. Union School Dist. of Keene, 214 A.2d 120 (N.H. 1965). *See also* Takeall by Rubinstein v. Ambach, 609 F. Supp. 81 (S.D. N.Y. 1985) (an eighteen-year-old student was entitled to notice of the basis for the school board's decision to deny him tuition-free admission as an emancipated student and to notice of the availability of administrative appeals).
51. United States v. Onslow County Bd. of Educ., 728 F.2d 628 (4th Cir. 1984).
52. Johnson v. New York State Educ. Dep't, 449 F.2d 871 (2d Cir. 1971), *vacated and remanded*, 409 U.S. 75 (1972) (per curiam).

53. *See* Foster v. County School Bd. of Prince William County, Cir. Ct., Prince William County, 1979, *appeal refused*, 219 Va. LXXVII (Va. 1979), *cert. denied*, 444 U.S. 804 (1979); Marshall v. School Dist. Re No. 3 Morgan County, 553 P.2d 784 (Colo. 1976); Carpio v. Tucson High School Dist. No. 1 of Pima County, 524 P.2d 948 (Ariz. 1974), *cert. denied*, 420 U.S. 982 (1975); Chandler v. South Bend Community School Corp., 312 N.E.2d 915 (Ind. 1974).
54. Carder v. Michigan City School Corp., 552 F. Supp. 869 (N.D. Ind. 1982).
55. Canton v. Spokane School Dist. No. 81, 498 F.2d 840 (9th Cir. 1974).
56. Cardiff v. Bismarck Public School Dist., 263 N.W.2d 105 (N.D. 1978); Beck v. Board of Educ. of Harlem Consol. School Dist., 344 N.E.2d 440 (Ill. 1976).
57. Vandevender v. Cassell, 208 S.E.2d 436 (W.Va. 1974).
58. Beck v. Board of Educ. of Harlem Consol. School Dist., 344 N.E.2d 440, 442 (Ill. 1976).
59. Concerned Parents v. Caruthersville School Dist., 548 S.W.2d 554 (Mo. 1977).
60. Norton v. Board of Educ. of School Dist. No. 16, Hobbs Mun. Schools, 553 P.2d 1277 (N.M. 1976).
61. Granger v. Cascade County School Dist., 499 P.2d 780, 786 (Mont. 1972).
62. Sodus Cent. School v. Rhine, 406 N.Y.S.2d 175 (App. Div. 1978).
63. Sneed v. Greensboro City Bd. of Educ., 264 S.E.2d 106, 114 (N.C. 1980) (reasonable user fees for musical instruments, gym uniforms, etc. were also upheld).
64. Ambroiggio v. Board of Educ., 427 N.E.2d 1027 (Ill. App. 1981).
65. For example, the Utah Constitution, art. X, § 11, requires teaching of the metric system, and the Oklahoma Constitution, art. XIII, § 7, stipulates that agriculture, horticulture, stock raising, and domestic science must be taught.
66. *See* Martha McCarthy and Paul Deignan, *What Legally Constitutes an Adequate Public Education*? (Bloomington, IN: Phi Delta Kappa, 1983), chapter 3.
67. *See* Dinah Shelton, "Legislative Control Over the Public School Curriculum," *Williamette Law Review*, vol. 15 (1979), p. 475.
68. *See* text with note 73, chapter 2.
69. Meyer v. Nebraska, 262 U.S. 390 (1923).
70. Epperson v. Arkansas, 393 U.S. 97, 106 (1968).
71. *See* text with note 100, *infra*, for a discussion of the judicial reluctance to interfere with academic assessments of student performance.
72. In two early cases, courts upheld disciplinary action against students who refused, on their parents' orders, to participate in instructional activities. State v. Webber, 108 Ind. 31 (Ind. 1886); Lander v. Seaver, 32 Vt. 114 (Vt. 1859).
73. Arundar v. Dekalb County School Dist., 620 F.2d 493 (5th Cir. 1980).
74. Fiacco v. Santee, 421 N.Y.S.2d 431 (App. Div. 1979). *See also* Bennett v. City School Dist. of New Rochelle, 497 N.Y.S.2d 72 (App. Div. 1985) (students have no protected right to be admitted to full-time program for the gifted); text with note 90, chapter 5.
75. *See* "Censorship: The Rules Have Changed," *Education U.S.A.*, March 24, 1980, p. 227; Stephen Arons, "The Crusade to Ban Books," *Counterpoint*

(November 1981), p. 19; "Newsnotes," *Phi Delta Kappan*, vol. 61 (1980), p. 722.

76. The survey indicated that censors were becoming more effective in that 39 percent of the challenges during the 1985–86 school year resulted in removal or restriction of the targeted materials, up from a 23 percent success rate in 1982–83. *Education Daily*, August 29, 1986, p. 3.
77. Williams v. Board of Educ. of County of Kanawha, 388 F. Supp. 93 (S.D. W.Va. 1975), *aff'd*, 530 F.2d 972 (4th Cir. 1975). For a discussion of the Kanawha situation, *see* Ralph N. Fuller, "Textbook Selection: Burning Issue?" *Compact*, vol. 9, no. 3 (1975), pp. 6–8; *Censoring Textbooks: Is West Virginia the Tip of the Iceberg?* (Washington, DC: Institute for Educational Leadership, 1974).
78. Right to Read Defense Comm. of Chelsea v. School Comm. of Chelsea, 454 F. Supp. 703, 713 (D. Mass. 1978), citing Keefe v. Geanakos, 418 F.2d 359, 361–362 (1st Cir. 1969).
79. Todd v. Rochester Community Schools, 200 N.W.2d 90, 93–94 (Mich. App. 1972).
80. Grove v. Mead School Dist., 753 F.2d 1528 (9th Cir. 1985), *cert. denied*, 106 S. Ct. 85 (1985).
81. For a discussion of allegations that public schools are advancing the faith of "secular humanism," *see* Martha McCarthy, *A Delicate Balance: Church, State, and the Schools* (Bloomington, IN: Phi Delta Kappa, 1983), pp. 89–92; text with note 83, chapter 2.
82. *See also* Mozert v. Hawkins County Public Schools, 765 F.2d 75 (6th Cir. 1985), *on remand*, No. CIV-2-83-401 (E.D. Tenn. 1986); text with note 77, chapter 2.
83. A controversial measure, enacted by Congress in 1984 and rescinded the following year, prohibited school districts from using federal grants for magnet schools to teach "secular humanism." Education for Economic Security Act, Title VII - Magnet Schools Assistance, 20 U.S.C. § 4052, 34 C.F.R., Part 280. *See Education Week*, August 21, 1985, p. 6; text with note 98, chapter 2. *See also* text with note 155, *infra*, for a discussion of the controversy surrounding the 1978 Hatch Amendment to the General Education Provisions Act.
84. Board of Educ., Island Trees Union Free School Dist. No. 26 v. Pico, 457 U.S. 853, 864 (1982). *See also* Bethel School Dist. No. 403 v. Fraser, 106 S. Ct. 3159, 3164–3165 (1986); text with note 15, chapter 4; Zykan v. Warsaw Community School Corp., 631 F.2d 1300, 1306–1307 (7th Cir. 1980).
85. Presidents Council, Dist. 25 v. Community School Bd. No. 25, 457 F.2d 289 (2d Cir. 1972), *cert. denied*, 409 U.S. 998 (1972). *See* chapter 8 for a discussion of teachers' rights to academic freedom.
86. Bicknell v. Vergennes Union High School Bd. of Directors, 638 F.2d 438 (2d Cir. 1980).
87. Zykan v. Warsaw Community School Corp., 631 F.2d 1300, 1303 (7th Cir. 1980). The students also alleged that the contracts of two teachers were not renewed for improper motives. Finding such allegations "creative," the appellate court concluded that such claims are properly initiated by employees who have allegedly suffered the harm and not by students. *See also* Cary v. Board of Educ. of Adams-Arapahoe School Dist., 598 F.2d 535 (10th Cir. 1979).

88. Zykan, *id.* at 1306.
89. Seyfried v. Walton, 668 F.2d 214 (3d Cir. 1981). *See also* Bell v. U-32 Bd. of Educ., 630 F. Supp. 939 (D. Vt. 1986).
90. Minarcini v. Strongsville City School Dist., 541 F.2d 577 (6th Cir. 1976).
91. *See also* Right to Read Defense Comm. v. School Comm. of the City of Chelsea, 454 F. Supp. 703 (D. Mass. 1978) (removal of an anthology from the high school library violated first amendment rights of students and faculty).
92. Salvail v. Nashua Bd. of Educ., 469 F. Supp. 1269 (D.N.H. 1979).
93. Pratt v. Independent School Dist., 670 F.2d 771, 777 (8th Cir. 1982).
94. Loewen v. Turnipseed, 488 F. Supp. 1138 (N.D. Miss. 1980).
95. 474 F. Supp. 387 (E.D. N.Y. 1979), *rev'd and remanded*, 638 F.2d 404 (2d Cir. 1980), *aff'd*, 457 U.S. 853 (1982).
96. Several board members received a list of "objectionable" books from a conservative parents' organization. Subsequently, the board ordered eleven books removed from the library despite the superintendent's objection to the directive. The superintendent urged the board to follow its policy for handling such problems and thus appoint a committee to study the materials and make recommendations. The board did eventually appoint a review committee, but disregarded the committee's recommendations by ordering the removal of nine books from the school libraries. Only one of the books originally questioned was returned to the school library without restriction, and another book was made available to students with parental permission.
97. Justices Brennan, Marshall, and Stevens supported this contention. Justices Blackmun and White also agreed that the case warranted a trial, but they did not endorse the plurality opinion's treatment of the first amendment issue. *See* David Schimmel, "The Limits on School Board Discretion: Board of Education v. Pico," *Education Law Reporter,* vol. 6 (1983), pp. 296–298.
98. Seyfried v. Walton, 668 F.2d 214, 219 (3d Cir. 1981) (Rosenn, J., concurring).
99. *See* Daniel Callison and Cynthia Kittleson, "Due Process Principles Applied to the Development of Reconsideration Policies," *Collection Building*, vol. 6, no. 4 (1985), pp. 3–9.
100. Board of Curators of the Univ. of Missouri v. Horowitz, 435 U.S. 78, 89–90 (1978). *See also* Mauriello v. University of Medicine and Dentistry of New Jersey, 781 F.2d 46 (3d Cir. 1986); Greenhill v. Bailey, 519 F.2d 5 (8th Cir. 1975); Connelly v. University of Vermont and State Agricultural College, 244 F. Supp. 156 (D. Vt. 1965).
101. Regents of the Univ. of Michigan v. Ewing, 106 S. Ct. 507, 513 (1985). The student was denied the opportunity to retake an examination (which was a prerequisite to completing the degree program) because of his singularly low score on the prior examination and the poor quality of his overall academic record. Despite the fact that other students had been allowed to retake the examination, the Court found no arbitrary or capricious behavior in dropping the student from the program without permitting reexamination.
102. Debra P. v. Turlington, 644 F.2d 397, 402 (5th Cir. 1981).
103. *See* Sandlin v. Johnson, 643 F.2d 1027 (4th Cir. 1981) (upholding the public school's authority to condition promotion to third grade on successful completion of the requisite level of the Ginn reading series); Student Doe v. Commonwealth of Pennsylvania, 593 F. Supp. 54 (E.D. Pa. 1984) (equal protection and due process rights were not implicated in the use of a stan-

dardized test as a criterion for admission to a special communications class for the gifted; text with note 110, *infra*.

104. Brookhart v. Illinois State Bd. of Educ., 534 F. Supp. 725, 728 (C.D. Ill. 1982).
105. *Education Week*, February 6, 1985, pp. 11–30; *Education Week*, September 18, 1985, p. 9. Most competency tests assess proficiency in communication and computation skills. *See* Chris Pipho, *State Activity—Minimal Competency Testing* (Denver, CO: Education Commission of the States, 1978); Fred Burke, *High School Graduation Requirements* (Trenton, NJ: New Jersey Department of Education, 1979), p. 23; Charles Thomas, "The Minimum Competencies of Minimum Competency Testing," *Viewpoints in Teaching and Learning*, vol. 56, no. 3 (1980), p. 30.
106. Goss v. Lopez, 419 U.S. 565 (1975).
107. Debra P. v. Turlington, 644 F.2d 397 (5th Cir. 1981).
108. *See* Anderson v. Banks, 540 F. Supp. 761 (S.D. Ga. 1982), *appeal dismissed sub nom.* Johnson v. Sikes, 730 F.2d 644 (11th Cir. 1984); Board of Educ. of Northport-East Northport Union Free School Dist. v. Ambach, 458 N.Y.S.2d 680 (App. Div. 1982), *aff'd*, 457 N.E.2d 775 (N.Y. 1983), *cert. denied*, 465 U.S. 1101 (1984).
109. Brookhart v. Illinois State Bd. of Educ., 697 F.2d 179 (7th Cir. 1983).
110. Bester v. Tuscaloosa City Bd. of Educ., 722 F. 2d 1514 (11th Cir. 1984). *See also* note 103, *supra*.
111. *See* Debra P. v. Turlington, 644 F.2d 397 (5th Cir. 1981); Anderson v. Banks, 540 F. Supp. 761 (S.D. Ga. 1982). *See also* text with note 72, chapter 5, for a discussion of racial discrimination claims in connection with ability-grouping schemes.
112. Debra P., *id.* at 406. This case also involved allegations that the test discriminated against minority students and that insufficient notice of the examination had been given. *See* notes 107 and 111, *supra*.
113. Debra P. v. Turlington, 564 F. Supp. 177 (M.D. Fla. 1983), *aff'd*, 730 F.2d 1405 (11th Cir. 1984). It should be noted that the fifth federal circuit was divided into the fifth and eleventh circuits while this case was in progress.
114. *See* Brookhart v. Illinois State Bd. of Educ., 697 F.2d 179 (7th Cir. 1983); Northport-East Northport Union Free School Dist. v. Ambach, 457 N.E.2d 775 (N.Y. 1983); Anderson v. Banks, 540 F. Supp. 761 (S.D. Ga. 1982).
115. Section 504 of the Rehabilitation Act of 1973, 29 U.S.C. § 794, protects otherwise qualified handicapped individuals against discrimination.
116. *See* Martha McCarthy, "The Application of Competency Testing Mandates to Handicapped Children," *Harvard Educational Review*, vol. 53 (1983), pp. 148–150.
117. Brookhart v. Illinois State Bd. of Educ., 697 F.2d 179, 187 (7th Cir. 1983).
118. 34 C.F.R. §§ 104.35(b)(3) and 300.532(c). *See* chapter 5 for a discussion of handicapped students' rights under this law.
119. Litigation involving claims of instructional negligence is addressed in the next section of this chapter.
120. *See* chapter 12 for an overview of tort law pertaining to negligence suits.
121. 131 Cal. Rptr. 854 (Cal. App. 1976).
122. *Id.* at 861.
123. Donohue v. Copiague Union Free Schools, 407 N.Y.S.2d 874 (App. Div. 1978), *aff'd*, 391 N.E.2d 1352 (N.Y. 1979).

124. Hoffman v. Board of Educ., 410 N.Y.S.2d 99 (App. Div. 1978), *rev'd*, 424 N.Y.S.2d 376 (Ct. App. 1979).
125. Keech v. Berkeley Unified School Dist., 210 Cal. Rptr. 7 (Cal. App. 1984).
126. *Id.* at 11. *See also* Smith v. Alameda County Social Services Agency, 153 Cal. Rptr. 712 (Cal. App. 1979) (rejecting a damages claim for alleged inappropriate placement in a class for the mentally retarded).
127. D.S.W. v. Fairbanks North Star Borough School Dist., 628 P.2d 554 (Alas. 1981). *See also* Aubrey v. School Dist. of Philadelphia, 437 A.2d 1306 (Pa. Commw. 1981) (rejecting a claim of educational negligence initiated by a student who failed a health education class containing material dealing with human sexuality; disputes over the inclusion of sex education in the curriculum or over a student's grades in a specific course are not matters that should be settled in judicial forums).
128. Doe v. Board of Educ. of Montgomery County, 453 A.2d 814 (Md. 1982). *See also* Tubell v. Dade County Public Schools, 419 So. 2d 388 (Fla. App. 1982).
129. Myers v. Medford Lakes Bd. of Educ., 489 A.2d 1240 (N.J. Super. 1985).
130. Hunter v. Board of Educ. of Montgomery County, 439 A.2d 582 (Md. 1982).
131. B.M. v. State, 649 P.2d 425 (Mont. 1982), *after remand*, 698 P.2d 399 (Mont. 1985).
132. Torres v. Little Flower Children's Services, 485 N.Y.S.2d 15 (Ct. App. 1984), *cert. denied*, 106 S. Ct. 181 (1985).
133. Snow v. State, 469 N.Y.S.2d 959 (App. Div. 1983), *aff'd*, 485 N.Y.S.2d 987 (Ct. App. 1984).
134. *Id.* at 964. The dissenting justices in *Torres* asserted that both cases involved "custodial malpractice" for failure to provide appropriate care for children placed in the institutions' custody, 485 N.Y.S.2d at 22–23 (Meyer, J., dissenting).
135. *See* Perry A. Zirkel, "Educational Malpractice: Cracks in the Door?" *Education Law Reporter*, vol. 23 (1985), pp. 453–460.
136. *See* Julie O'Hara, "The Fate of Educational Malpractice," *Education Law Reporter*, vol. 14 (1984), pp. 887–895.
137. *See* Griswold v. Connecticut, 381 U.S. 479 (1965); text with note 137, chapter 8.
138. Dawkins v. Billingsley, 172 P. 69 (Okla. 1918).
139. *See* Elder v. Anderson, 23 Cal. Rptr. 48 (Cal. App. 1962). *See also* chapter 12 for a discussion of tort law.
140. 20 U.S.C. § 1232(g); 34 C.F.R. § 99 *et seq.*
141. 34 C.F.R. § 99.5.
142. Page v. Rotterdam-Mohanasen Cent. School Dist., 441 N.Y.S.2d 323 (Sup. Ct., Albany County, 1981).
143. Over 700 schools were represented in the sample; fewer than 8 percent were in total compliance with FERPA, and 15 to 20 percent were in substantial violation. Gail Sorenson and David Chapman, "School Compliance with Federal Law Concerning the Release of Student Records," *Educational Evaluation and Policy Analysis*, vol. 7, no. 1 (1985), pp. 9–18.
144. Most courts have ruled that the Department of Education has enforcement authority, and individuals are not authorized to bring a private suit to compel compliance with FERPA. *See* Girardier v. Webster College, 563 F.2d 1267, 1276–1277 (8th Cir. 1977).

145. *See* text with note 98, chapter 5 for a more detailed discussion of this law.
146. Ind. Code Ann. §§ 4–1–6–2 to 4–1–6–5.
147. Klipa v. Board of Educ. of Anne Arundel County, 460 A.2d 601 (Md. App. 1983).
148. Laplante v. Stewart, 470 So. 2d 1018 (La. App. 1985). The court reasoned that the study was intended to identify factors that affect learning and not to determine the proficiency of individual students or to evaluate the performance of individual teachers or administrators. Thus, the results of the study were considered public records and were not included within the scope of exclusions from the state's public records law.
149. Red Bank Register v. Board of Educ. of Long Branch, 501 A.2d 985 (N.J. Super. 1985).
150. Rios v. Read, 480 F. Supp. 14 (E.D. N.Y. 1977).
151. Board of Educ., Island Trees Union Free School Dist. v. Butcher, 402 N.Y.S.2d 626, 627 (App. Div. 1978).
152. Einhorn v. Maus, 300 F. Supp. 1169 (E.D. Pa. 1969). *See also* Price v. Young, 580 F. Supp. 1 (E.D. Ark. 1983) (a parent could not use FERPA to challenge his son's rejection for the National Honor Society based on anonymous faculty recommendations).
153. Merriken v. Cressman, 364 F. Supp. 913 (E.D. Pa. 1973). For a discussion of legal issues associated with drug-testing among students, *see* text with note 149, chapter 6.
154. *See* 42 U.S.C. § 218(f)(1).
155. 20 U.S.C. § 1232h; 34 C.F.R., Parts 75, 76, and 98. The sensitive areas specified in the law are political affiliations, potentially embarrassing mental or psychological problems; sexual behavior and attitudes; illegal, antisocial, self-incriminating, and demeaning behavior; critical appraisals of family members; legally recognized, privileged relationships; or income (other than that required to determine eligibility for financial assistance programs).
156. *Education Daily*, February 20, 1985, p. 3. The National School Boards Association has urged the Department of Education to repeal the Amendment's regulations. *Education Daily*, June 21, 1985, p. 1. Senator Hatch has asserted that the amendment and regulations have been misinterpreted by conservative parents' groups in that they were not intended to erode local school boards' authority to determine the content of the curriculum, but rather were directed toward "nonscholastic" activities supported by federal funds. *Education Week*, February 27, 1985, p. 1.
157. Hatch Amendment Coalition and American Educational Research Association, *The Hatch Amendment Regulations: A Guidelines Document* (Washington, DC: AERA, 1985).
158. For a discussion of state legislation, *see Education Week*, May 29, 1985, pp. 1, 19.
159. *See* Anne Lewis, "Little-Used Amendment Becomes Divisive, Disruptive Issue," *Phi Delta Kappan*, vol. 66 (1985), p. 668.
160. The one notable exception to compulsory attendance pertains to Amish children who have successfully completed eighth grade. *See* Wisconsin v. Yoder, 406 U.S. 205 (1972); text with note 6, chapter 2.

4

Students' Rights in Noninstructional Matters

This chapter addresses students' rights in connection with selected noninstructional issues. The first two sections focus on first amendment freedoms of speech and press and closely related association rights. In the final two sections, the law governing student appearance and participation in extracurricular activities is examined.

FREEDOM OF EXPRESSION

Traditionally, it was accepted that public school authorities could restrict student expression for almost any reason. Since the mid-twentieth century, however, the Supreme Court has recognized that students do not shed their constitutional rights as a condition of public school attendance and that the public school is an appropriate setting in which to instill a respect for these rights, especially first amendment freedoms. The Court has noted that first amendment rights must receive "scrupulous protection" in schools "if we are not to strangle the free mind at its source and teach youth to discount important principles of our government as mere platitudes."[1] The Court also has recognized that schools function as "a marketplace of ideas" and that the "robust exchange of ideas" is "a special concern of the First Amendment."[2]

The first amendment and its fourteenth amendment application to the states restrict *governmental*—in contrast to private—interference with citizens' free expression rights. The government cannot curtail protected expression (e.g., political or philosophical viewpoints) or punish the speakers for such expression. Also protected by the first amendment is the individual's right to remain silent when confronted with an illegitimate governmental demand for expression, such as mandatory participation in the salute to the American flag in public schools.[3]

Free expression rights are perhaps the most preciously guarded of individual liberties, but they are not without limits. As Justice Oliver Holmes aptly noted, freedom of speech does not allow an individual to yell "fire" in a crowded theater if there is no fire.[4] While public school students enjoy free speech rights, the Supreme Court has recognized that "the constitutional rights of students in public school are not automatically coextensive with the rights of adults in other settings."[5] Free expression rights may be restricted by policies that are reasonably designed to take into account the special circumstances of the educational environment.

Unprotected Conduct and Expression

Before assessing whether specific expression enjoys first amendment protection, a threshold determination is whether the conduct constitutes expression *at all.* Only where conduct is intended to communicate an idea is it considered expression for first amendment purposes.[6] In discussing the limits of protected speech, an Oregon appellate court held that while college students had a first amendment right to distribute leaflets and collect petitions, the erection of a tentlike structure on the school lawn was not protected expression and could be the basis for the students' conviction for criminal trespass.[7] More recently, the Eighth Circuit Court of Appeals reasoned that social and recreational dancing in public schools is not a form of expression that enjoys first amendment protection.[8] Accordingly, the court upheld a school board's denial of permission for parents to rent the school gymnasium to hold dances for high school students.

Even if student expression is found to be at issue, the judiciary has recognized that certain types of expression are outside the protective arm of the first amendment. The following categories of student expression are considered unprotected in the public school context.

Defamatory Expression. Unprotected defamatory statements include "slander," which is spoken defamation, and "libel," which is defamation in print.[9] For statements to be slanderous, they must be false, expose another to public shame or ridicule, and be spoken in the presence of someone other than the person slandered. Fair comment on the actions of public figures, unlike defamatory expression, is constitutionally protected. Public officials can establish that they have been defamed only with evidence that the speaker acted recklessly and with actual malice. To be considered a public official, one must have substantial responsibility for or control over the conduct of governmental affairs; the mere fact that a matter attracts public attention does not transform a private individual into a public figure. While school board members and superintendents are generally considered public officials for defamation purposes,[10] courts have rendered conflicting opinions regarding whether teachers and coaches have assumed the risk of nonmalicious defamation.[11]

In some cases, courts must assess whether expression is a defamatory assertion of fact or an opinion that is protected by the first amendment. Courts evaluate the totality of circumstances surrounding an allegedly defamatory statement to decide whether it merits constitutional protection as an opinion. The common meaning of the specific language is considered as well as whether the statement is capable of being proven false empirically. Also considered are the statement's specific content and the broader context or setting in which the statement is made.[12]

Obscene and Vulgar Expression. The judiciary has held that individuals cannot claim a first amendment right to air obscenities, but there is no precise definition of what constitutes obscene expression. In *Miller v. California,* which did not involve a school situation, the United States Supreme Court attempted to distinguish obscene material from material that would receive first amendment protection by using the following test:

> (a) whether "the average person, applying contemporary community standards" would find that the work, taken as a whole, appeals to the prurient interests; . . . (b) whether the work depicts or describes, in a patently offensive way, sexual conduct specifically defined by the applicable state law; and (c) whether the work, taken as a whole, lacks serious literary, artistic, political or scientific value.[13] (Citations omitted.)

The *Miller* standard, however, has not clarified the concept of obscenity as applied to student expression in public schools. On several occasions, the Supreme Court has recognized that the government has the authority to adjust the definition of obscenity as appplied to minors because the power of the state to control the conduct of children reaches beyond its authority to regulate adult behavior. For example, the Court upheld a state law prohibiting the sale to minors of magazines depicting female nudity. Recognizing that the material in question was not obscene for adults, the Court ruled that the statute did not impair minors' free expression rights. The Court declared that because of the state's significant "interest in preventing distribution to children of objectionable material," it can accord minors "a more restricted right than that assured to adults to judge and determine for themselves what sex material they may read or see."[14]

In a significant 1986 decision, *Bethel School District No. 403 v. Fraser,* the Supreme Court endorsed the authority of public school personnel to restrict vulgar, lewd expression among students. Overturning the lower courts, the Supreme Court upheld disciplinary action imposed on a student for using a sexual metaphor in a nominating speech during a student government assembly.[15] Concluding that the sexual inuendos were plainly offensive to both teachers and students, the majority held that the school's legitimate interest in protecting minors from exposure to vulgar and offensive speech justified the disciplinary action. The Court reiterated that speech protected by the first amendment for adults is not necessarily protected for children, reasoning that in the public school context the sensibilities of fellow students must be considered in assessing the constitutional protection afforded to expression. The majority, however, distinguished the vulgar remarks at issue in this case from protected political expression, noting that the student's speech was not intended to convey a political message. The majority found it proper for school authorities to protect the captive student audience from exposure to sexually explicit, indecent, or lewd speech, recognizing that the inculcation of fundamental values of civility is a major objective of public schools and that it is a "highly appropriate function of public education to prohibit the use of vulgar and offensive terms in public discourse."[16] Moreover, the majority declared that the school board has the authority to determine what manner of speech is inappropriate in classes or assemblies. The majority also rejected the contention that the student had no way of knowing that his expression would subject him to disciplinary action, concluding that the school rule proscribing obscene and disruptive expression and the admonitions of teachers that his planned speech was inappropriate provided adequate warning of the consequences of the expression.

Inflammatory Expression. The judiciary has sanctioned regulations banning the use of "fighting words" or other types of inflammatory expression. Courts have differentiated expression that agitates and exhorts from speech that "is a mere doctrinal justification of a thought or idea," leaving an opportunity for calm and reasonable discussion.[17] To illustrate, the Sixth Circuit Court of Appeals upheld the suspension of a student for refusing to remove a Confederate flag sleeve patch which he persisted in wearing in a racially tense Tennessee school that had recently been integrated.[18] Also, where high school students conspired and threatened to assault a teacher, a Louisiana appeals court ruled that the first amendment did not shield the students from expulsion.[19]

A Pennsylvania court upheld disciplinary action against a student for insulting a teacher in a public place with indecent language. Even though the remark was made in a shopping center, the court reasoned that it affected school discipline because other students witnessed the incident. Noting that "speech including fighting words, the lewd and obscene, the profane and libelous, is not safeguarded by the Constitution," the court found that the disciplinary action did not impair the student's first amendment rights.[20]

Protected Expression

In contrast to defamatory, obscene, lewd, or inflammatory expression, verbal or symbolic expression of political or ideological viewpoints is protected by the first amendment.[21] In 1969 the Supreme Court rendered the landmark decision, *Tinker v. Des Moines Independent School District,* issuing in a new era in the protection of students' political expression in public schools. The Court declared that "students in school as well as out of school are 'persons' under our Constitution. They are possessed of fundamental rights which the state must respect."[22] In *Tinker,* three students were suspended from school for wearing armbands to protest the Vietnam War. School officials did not attempt to prohibit the wearing of all symbols, but instead prohibited the expression of one particular opinion. Concluding that school authorities punished the students for expression that was not accompanied by any disorder or disturbance, the Supreme Court ruled that "undifferentiated fear or apprehension of disturbance is not enough to overcome the right to freedom of expression."[23] Furthermore, the court declared that school officials must have "more than a mere desire to avoid discomfort and unpleasantness that always accompany an unpopular viewpoint" in order to justify the curtailment of student expression.[24]

In rendering the *Tinker* decision, the Supreme Court reiterated statements made in an earlier federal appellate ruling, in which the appeals court held that a student may express opinions on controversial issues in the classroom, cafeteria, playing field, or any other place, as long as the exercise of such rights does "not materially and substantially interfere with the requirements of appropriate discipline in the operation of the school" or collide with the rights of others.[25] In both cases, the courts emphasized that educators have the authority and *duty* to maintain discipline in schools. School officials simply must consider students' constitutional rights as they exert control.

If determined that protected speech is at issue, courts are then faced with the difficult task of assessing whether school authorities have justification to restrict students' freedom of verbal and symbolic expression. Under the *Tinker* principle, school authorities must establish that a disruption of the educational process reasonably can be predicted as a result of the protected expression. The law is clear in allowing students to be punished *after the fact* if their behavior interferes with the educational process, but the issuance of *prior restraints* on expression places a greater burden of justification on school authorities.

Courts have recognized that when protected expression is involved, the expectation of disruption must be based on "fact, not intuition" to justify restrictions.[26] The imposition of a prior restraint on speech must bear a substantial relationship to a "weighty governmental interest" and cannot be justified merely by a showing of some legitimate governmental interest,[27] "lest students' imaginations, intellects, and wills be unduly stifled or chilled."[28] In addition, any regulation must be drawn with narrow specificity. Regulations banning "misconduct" or "crimes of a serious nature" have been invalidated as overbroad and thus not capable of supporting the punishment of students engaged in a silent protest.[29] Furthermore, the assertion that a peaceful demonstration hampered school officials in performing their regular duties because they had to keep an eye on "potentially disruptive conditions" was found to be an inadequate basis for disciplining students involved in the protest.[30]

When a school policy has the effect of favoring a particular viewpoint or barring the expression of opposing views, the first amendment is plainly offended. For example, students prevailed in challenging the denial of an opportunity for anti-war activists to have access to the student body since the board of education allowed military recruiters access to the schools.[31] The federal district court reasoned that free speech and equal protection rights were impaired by the school board's practice of opening the school forum only to one point of view. A federal district court also ruled that a homosexual student had a free expression right to select another male as his escort to the senior prom.[32] The court reasoned that the student's choice of an escort of the same sex was intended to convey an ideological message that constituted protected speech.

In addition, students cannot be disciplined for nondisruptive expression that is critical of school personnel or policies. To illustrate, in 1985 an Arkansas federal district court ruled that two football players could not be disciplined for their symbolic protest against the coach whom they alleged had manipulated the homecoming queen election to preclude a black student from serving as queen.[33] The students were suspended from the high school football team for walking out of a pep rally and refusing to participate in a scheduled game to protest the election. The court declared:

> While it is well settled that public education in our country is the responsibility of school administrators and courts are reluctant to intervene in conflicts which develop in the day to day operation of a school system, this does not mean either that free expression, as enunciated under the Federal Constitution, must exist in a vacuum as opposed to a living reality on the school campus, or that school officials, as agents of the state, may stifle free expression, whether by written or unwritten policies . . .[34]

Concluding that the students' free expression rights were impaired by the disciplinary action, the court assessed punitive damages against the coach.

Similarly, expression that is merely offensive to the tastes of school authorities cannot be prohibited or serve as the basis for disciplinary action if the expression is intended to convey an ideological viewpoint. For example, the Maine Federal District Court ruled that a high school's yearbook constituted a forum for student expression and enjoined school officials from rejecting a student's choice of a quotation to appear with her picture in the yearbook.[35] The student selected a particular quotation to express an ideological position, and despite the fact that school authorities considered the quotation inappropriate, the court ruled that the student had a free expression right to make the selection. If expression is lewd or indecent, however, school boards may restrict it.[36]

Also, even expression intended to convey a political or ideological message can be curtailed if it is sufficiently linked to a disruption of the educational process. Prior restraint on expression was upheld in a recent Maine case based on the school board's legitimate concern for the safety and security of the school.[37] After receiving telephoned bomb threats, the school board cancelled a proposed Tolerance Day program in which a homosexual was scheduled to speak. The court noted that the school board did not restrict the discussion of tolerance or of prejudice against homosexuals within the school; only the program was prohibited because of the threat of disruption.

Other courts have applied similar reasoning in endorsing restrictions on disruptive expression. The Sixth Circuit Court of Appeals concluded that a rule banning the wearing of freedom buttons was lawful in a situation where the learning environment would be disrupted if pupils were allowed to wear the "badges of their respective disagreements, and provoke confrontations with their fellows and their teachers."[38] Also, where student button-wearers have created disturbances within the school by harassing students not participating in the form of expression, restrictions on such conduct have been upheld.[39]

In addition, courts have recognized that walkouts or boycotts[40] and sit-ins[41] can—under certain circumstances—constitute a material or substantial disruption, and thus can justifiably be curtailed. In 1972 the Eighth Circuit Court of Appeals held that students who disrupted a school assembly by walking out were properly suspended.[42] More recently, an Indiana federal district court upheld the suspension and subsequent expulsion of several students who attempted to incite a student walkout by distributing leaflets.[43] Recognizing that the students' action fell within the protective arm of the first amendment, the court nonetheless held that disciplinary action was justified because the school officials could reasonably forecast a serious disruption of the school environment. The fact that no disruption actually occurred did not negate the legitimate threat.

The Ninth Circuit Court of Appeals reasoned that school authorities were justified in confiscating signs (protesting the nonrenewal of a teacher's contract) which were brought to school by students who intended to distribute them.[44] While concluding that the signs posed a threat of disruption and thus could be confiscated, the court held that school authorities were not justified in suspending a student who initially refused to turn over his signs. The court declared that "the balancing necessary to enable school officials to maintain discipline and order allows curtailment but not necessarily punishment."[45] However, the court recognized that if the suspension had been based on the fact that the student violated a school rule by going to the parking lot to get the signs, rather than based on the exercise of pure speech, the disciplinary action would have been condoned.

School authorities have been upheld in disciplining students for protests involving conduct such as blocking hallways or damaging property. Courts have recognized that where demonstrations have caused students to miss class or disrupted the progress of classes, protestors could be punished for interfering with essential school activities.[46] Policies governing demonstrations, however, should convey to students that they have the right to gather, distribute petitions, and express their ideas under *nondisruptive* circumstances. Although restrictions can be placed on the *manner* of expression, such restrictions should be content-neutral and leave open alternative channels for the communication of ideas.[47] Vague wording of a regulation pertaining to demonstrations may result in a judicial declaration that the conduct cannot be punished because the demonstrators did not know in advance precisely what behavior was prohibited.[48]

In general, commercial speech, where the speaker has economic motives, has not been afforded the same protection under the first amendment as speech intended to convey a particular point of view.[49] However, unlike obscene, inflammatory, or defamatory expression, commercial speech does enjoy some measure of constitutional protection. To regulate lawful commercial speech, there must be a substantial governmental interest and the regulations must directly advance that interest and be no more extensive than necessary to achieve the government's objective.[50] In a higher education case, the Third Circuit Court of Appeals distinguished restrictions on group political expression from group commercial expression in upholding a university's ban on group sales demonstrations in individual rooms in the residence halls. The court reasoned that such commercial activity could interfere with the university's substantial interest in maintaining residence halls for their intended educational purpose and in ensuring that dormitories do not become rent-free merchandise marts.[51]

In public schools, regulations prohibiting sales and fund-raising activities on campus have generally been upheld as justified to preserve schools for their educational function. For example, the Second Circuit Court of Appeals declined to enjoin the implementation of a public school rule prohibiting students from soliciting funds from their classmates.[52] The students sought the injunction so that they could distribute leaflets to solicit funds for the legal defense of persons on trial for anti-war demonstrations. In denying the injunction, the court reasoned that it was unlikely that a court would find the school's rule overbroad.

It seems inevitable that courts will continue to be called upon to balance the interests involved when students' rights to express views and receive information collide with educators' duty to maintain an appropriate educational environment. Courts are protective of students' rights, given the length of time they spend in school and the fact that most individuals are first introduced to free expression rights and responsibilities in the public school setting. The Supreme Court has noted that "teachers and students must always remain free to inquire, to study and to evaluate, [and] to gain new maturity and understanding."[53] While school authorities have substantial latitude to prescribe and control activities in the schools to maintain an environment conducive to learning and to transmit fundamental values,[54] they should be careful not to restrict the expression of *particularly ideological viewpoints*. Once determined that protected speech is involved, the *Tinker* decision provides the basic guideline for educators to follow. Under this mandate, students' first amendment rights are subject to certain constraints; expression that threatens a substantial disruption of the educational process or interference with the rights of others can be the basis for disciplinary action against students.

Student-Initiated Clubs

Free expression and related association rights have been at issue in connection with the formation of student clubs and the recognition of such clubs in public schools. Freedom of association is not specifically included among first amendment protections, but the Supreme Court has recognized that associational rights are "implicit in the freedoms of speech, assembly, and petition."[55] The term "association" refers to the medium through which individuals seek to join with others to make the expression of their own views more effective.[56] This section focuses specifically on legal principles governing secret societies and student-initiated clubs with open membership.

Secret Societies. Adults have received consistent judicial protection in organizing social and political groups that promote unpopular and undemocratic causes. However, student clubs with exclusive membership traditionally have not been afforded similar protection in public schools. Pupils have unsuccessfully asserted that free expression and association rights shield student-initiated social organizations or secret societies.[57] Courts have upheld school officials' rights to deny recognition to such clubs and to prohibit student membership in secret societies. Some states, by statute, forbid student participation in a club that sustains itself by selecting new members "on the basis of the decision of its membership rather than upon the free choice of any pupil in the school who is qualified by the rules of the school to fill the special aims of the organization."[58] The judiciary has endorsed the notion that secret societies "tend to engender an undemocratic spirit of caste, to promote cliques, and to foster a contempt for school authority."[59] While there are limitations on the discretion of public school officials to restrict students' out-of-class behavior,[60] public schools can prohibit students from participating in exclusive clubs that have a detrimental impact on the school environment. Various punishments, ranging from suspension to denial of participation in extracurricular activities, have been upheld as penalties for membership in secret societies.[61]

In an illustrative case, a regulation of a California school district prohibited student membership in any fraternity, sorority, or nonschool club perpetuating its membership by the decision of its own members.[62] A student challenged the rule, claiming that a specific club was created to meet the objectives of "literature, charity and scholarship." However, the appeals court concluded that despite its stated objectives, the club was a secret society in that new members were "rushed" each semester and then chosen through a secret voting process. Thus, the board's prohibition was considered reasonable to advance the school's educational mission.

Student Organizations with Open Membership. In contrast to bans pertaining to secret societies, prohibitions against student-initiated organizations that have open membership may be more vulnerable to first amendment challenges. In 1972 the United States Supreme Court ruled that college authorities could not deny recognition to a student political organization merely because they disagreed with the group's philosophy.[63] The Court majority declared that "denial of official recognition, without justification, to college organizations" abridges students' first amendment rights.[64] The Court concluded that the proposed student organization did not present a substantial threat of disruption to the educational process, and that school officials did not carry their "heavy burden" of justifying the refusal of recognition, which was in effect "a form of prior restraint."[65] In several cases, courts also have recognized that student gay rights groups must be afforded similar recognition as available to other student organizations on college campuses.[66]

Of course, there are differences between the recognition of student groups in higher education and the recognition of student clubs in public high schools. The Supreme Court has acknowledged that state-supported institutions of higher education have created an open forum for student groups to use campus facilities for expressive purposes; content restrictions imposed on such meetings must be justified by a compelling governmental interest.[67] In contrast, school authorities in public high schools are not obligated to create such a forum for student groups to meet during noninstructional time. Public school access for student organizations can be restricted to those that are an extension of the curriculum, such as drama groups, language clubs, and athletic teams. If a limited forum for noncurriculum student groups is created, however, a school access policy must not discriminate against specific viewpoints.

A recent case focused on a Pennsylvania school district's denial of a request for a student group, the Student Coalition for Peace, to use school facilities for an anti-nuclear/peace exposition. Reasoning that the state may reserve school property for its intended purpose, as long as restrictions are not unreasonable or motivated by a desire to suppress particular ideas, the federal district court initially held that school officials could deny access for events that threatened political controversy and were not related to the school's educational function.[68] On appeal, the Third Circuit Court of Appeals affirmed the district court's disposition of the first amendment issue, reasoning that the school board's desire "to keep the 'podium of politics off school grounds' " was a rational basis for barring the peace exposition, even though other "noncontroversial" events were allowed to be held on public school property.[69] Recognizing that viewpoint discrimination is impermissible, the appeals court found no evidence of an attempt to censor particular views.

The appellate court, however, remanded the case to give the students an opportunity to prove that the school board violated their rights under the federal Equal Access Act (EAA) which became effective in 1984. As noted in chapter 2, this act stipulates that if public secondary schools provide a limited forum for noncurriculum student groups to meet during noninstructional time, access cannot be denied to specific groups based on the religious, philosophical, or political content of the groups' meetings.[70] Acknowledging a private right to bring suit to compel compliance with the EAA, the appeals court reasoned that the students should be given the opportunity to prove that school officials had established a limited forum for noncurriculum groups to use school property for expressive purposes since the effective date of the EAA and thus violated the federal law by barring the peace exposition.[71] On remand, the federal district court concluded that the school district had not created a limited forum for student-initiated noncurriculum groups to use the school athletic fields, but such a limited forum had been created in the high school gymnasium. Thus, under the EAA, the school district was prohibited from denying the Student Coalition for Peace use of the gymnasium during noninstructional time.[72]

Even before Congress enacted the Equal Access Act, several courts had recognized that if a public high school creates a limited forum for student groups to meet during noninstructional time, particular organizations cannot be discriminated against because of the content of their meetings. For example, a Michigan federal district court ruled that school authorities would have to present clear evidence that particular clubs would produce a disruption to the educational process in order to deny recognition to *selected* student organizations.[73]

Student-initiated religious clubs have presented particular problems for the judiciary because individuals' rights protected by the establishment clause often are pitted against free speech claims. As discussed in chapter 2, the Supreme Court in 1981 found no establishment clause violation in allowing all student groups to have equal access to state-supported college campus facilities for expressive purposes, including religious expression.[74] In contrast, however, several federal appellate courts have ruled that a content distinction among types of student expression is *required* by the establishment clause in public high schools; thus, free expression rights do not extend to student-initiated devotional meetings during noninstructional time because such expression infers public school endorsement of religion.[75] In essence, these courts have reasoned that compliance with the establishment clause is a compelling governmental interest that justifies restrictions on students' religious expression in the public school context. Whether the EAA violates the establishment clause by extending free speech protections to student religious groups has not been clarified by the judiciary. Of course, under the EAA, school authorities still retain a choice; they can restrict school access to groups that are an extension of the curriculum, thus declining to establish a limited forum for any noncurriculum student-initiated meetings. If such a forum is created, however, all student groups, with the possible exception of religious groups, must have access on equal terms.

FREEDOM OF PRESS: STUDENT PUBLICATIONS

Courts often have been called on to assess first amendment claims in connection with student publications. Do constitutional standards differ for school-sponsored versus nonschool publications? Can school officials impose prior restraints on student publications? Can student literature be suppressed and its distributors punished on the basis of the publication's content? These and related questions are addressed in this section.

School Sponsorship of Student Publications

School authorities often have claimed that they exert more control over school-sponsored publications than over nonschool material, but the judiciary has recognized that consitutional protections apply to both types of student literature. Mere school affiliation does not remove student literature from first amendment protection. The judiciary has reasoned that a governmental body "is not necessarily the unfettered master of all it creates."[76] Thus, the content of a school-sponsored paper that is established as a medium for student expression cannot be regulated more closely than a nonsponsored paper. For example, the Second Circuit Court of Appeals affirmed a decision in which the federal district court held that a principal could not prohibit the distribution of a school-sponsored newspaper in which students placed a four-page supplement with information about contraception and abortion.[77] The court noted that the articles in the supplement were intended to convey information and that the subjects were treated in a serious manner. While recognizing that the supplement might create some controversy, the court reasoned that it did not threaten a disruption of the educational environment.

Although school boards are not obligated to support student papers, if a given publication was originally created as a free speech forum, removal of financial or other school board support can be construed as an unlawful effort to stifle free expression. In essence, school authorities cannot withdraw support from a student publication simply because of displeasure with the content. In an illustrative case, the Eighth Circuit Court of Appeals ruled that a university could not change its funding policy for a student paper based on the "hue and cry" of the public objecting to a particular issue.[78] The court noted, however, that a policy could be established allowing students a refund of the portion of their activity fee that supports a student paper they oppose. The judiciary also has recognized that school officials have the right to stamp copies of student publications to disclaim responsibility for the content.

Boards of education are not totally powerless to regulate school-sponsored literature; they can determine the goals of a school paper, its advertising policies, and criteria for staff selection. If a student paper is published as part of a journalism class taken for credit, school authorities may even be able to justify restricting articles to assigned topics. But school personnel must bear the burden of proving that the publication is solely an instructional tool and not a free speech forum for students.

The Eighth Circuit Court of Appeals recently reversed a federal district court's conclusion that Missouri school officials met this burden of substantiating that a school-sponsored newspaper was an integral part of the school's curriculum and not a vehicle for students to express their views.[79] Even though the paper was part of the school's journalism curriculum, the appeals court concluded that it was a forum for student expression, and thus school authorities could not censor several articles pertaining to pregnant students and divorce. There was no evidence that the articles would disrupt school discipline or infringe upon the privacy rights of students.

Prior Review Regulations

Publications that are created as a forum for student expression have generated controversies over school policies requiring official approval prior to their distribution. The Supreme Court has stated that any "system of prior restraints of expression comes to this Court bearing a heavy presumption against its constitutional validity."[80] The burden of proof is placed on those who wish to suppress free expression, not on those who seek to exercise that right. Consequently, courts have been extremely sensitive to any prior administrative review of student publications that serves to curtail first amendment freedoms.

A few courts have invalidated all types of prior review of student literature as an unconstitutional restraint on free expression. In 1972 the Seventh Circuit Court of Appeals held that Chicago school officials could not require prior approval of the content of student publications or prevent distribution of the material.[81] The court recognized, however, that school authorities could regulate the *manner* of distribution and could punish students if the distributed materials were obscene, libelous, or caused a disruption. More recently, the California Supreme Court interpreted the state law pertaining to free expression rights of students as preventing school districts from: (1) establishing systems of prior restraint with respect to prohibited categories of expression, or (2) interfering with the distribution of student literature through administrative censorship of its content.[82] The court did acknowledge that once distribution had begun, school officials could intervene if the contents were obscene, libelous, or inflammatory, and they could discipline the students responsible for distributing such literature.

In contrast to the preceding opinions, most courts, including several federal appellate courts, have approved the principle of prior review applied to school-sponsored and nonschool student publications, but they have placed the burden of justifying such policies on school officials.[83] Many rules pertaining to prior approval have been successfully challenged because of defects in the policies or their application. Any policy governing the content of student publications must have "narrow, objective and reasonable standards"[84] and procedures that permit a speedy determination of whether the materials meet those standards. The regulations must provide unambiguous criteria and specific examples regarding what material is proscribed. Courts have invalidated school regulations if the procedures for the prior review have not been clearly stated, and have noted that "where the boundaries between prohibited and permissible conduct are ambiguous, we cannot assume that the curtailment of free expression is minimized."[85] Also, the regulations must provide an opportunity for the students to appear before the decisionmaker to argue why distribution of the material should be allowed.

The Second Circuit Court of Appeals invalidated procedures for prior submission of student literature because the policy failed to specify when review was to take place and to whom and how the material was to be submitted.[86] Similarly, the Fourth Circuit Court of Appeals struck down regulations requiring prior review of student publications because written criteria were not available for judging the material.[87] In a West Virginia case, a federal court invalidated a publication policy because the words "decency, taste, obscenity, and libelous" were not precisely defined. Calling the publication policy "a monument to vagueness," the court concluded that the regulation provided "no guidelines or criteria by which such levels of accuracy, taste and decency can be ascertained by either the author of the literature or the reviewing principal."[88]

It should be noted, however, that in 1986 the Supreme Court upheld a school's policy stipulating that "conduct which materially and substantially interferes with the educational process is prohibited, including the use of obscene, profane language or gestures." The Court declared: "Given the school's need to be able to impose disciplinary sanctions for a wide range of unanticipated conduct disruptive of the educational process, the school disciplinary rules need not be detailed as a criminal code which imposes criminal sanctions."[89] Although this case involved the restriction of "vulgar" student speech, rather than content in a publication, the Court's conclusion that the regulation provided adequate warning of proscribed expression may have implications for prior review regulations in connection with student literature.

Courts have found many prior review guidelines to be constitutionally defective, but a few schemes have been upheld. For example, a tightly controlled scheme for prior submission of literature was upheld by the Fifth Circuit Court of Appeals because the regulations were specific and consistently applied.[90] Subsequently, the same court reiterated that if a student flagrantly and consciously disregards a well-defined system of prior submission, such conduct is not protected by the first amendment.[91]

The Ninth Circuit Court of Appeals endorsed a school district's policy of prepublication administrative review of student newspaper articles on sensitive topics. A high school journalism teacher alleged that the policy violated students' first amendment rights, but the appeals court ruled that the high school environment necessitates supervision by faculty and administrators. Since the review was for accuracy rather than for possible censorship, the court concluded that students' first amendment rights were not implicated.[92]

A New York federal district court also upheld a high school principal's authority to prevent distribution of an issue of the school newspaper because its content would create a substantial risk of disruption of school activities.[93] The controversial publication contained a libelous attack on a student government officer and a threat of violence to the players on the school lacrosse team. The court concluded that the principal's interest in protecting students from harm provided a justifiable basis for barring distribution of the literature. Moreover, the court noted that the school board's authority to prevent distribution of material that is libelous, obscene, disruptive of school activities, or violative of the rights of others is not lessened simply because the board has not adopted written policies requiring prior review of student publications.

In another New York case, the Second Circuit Court of Appeals upheld school officials in prohibiting the high school newspaper editor from questioning students on their feelings about sex, contraception, homosexuality, masturbation, and the extent of their sexual experience.[94] The federal district court had concluded that school officials could prevent distribution of the survey to ninth- and tenth-grade students, but not to high school juniors and seniors. The appeals court, however, deferred to school officials' judgment that the survey should be prohibited for *all* high school students because of the risk of endangering the emotional health of some immature students. The court distinguished this factual situation from an earlier Virginia case in which the Fourth Circuit Court of Appeals ruled that students' constitutional rights were violated by the censorship of a school newspaper article dealing with student attitudes toward contraception.[95] The Fourth Circuit Appellate Court concluded that the paper was created as a vehicle for student expression, and thus articles could not be censored merely because they offended school officials. Since the survey of student attitudes toward birth control had already been completed in the Virginia case, only the exercise of expression was at issue. In contrast, the activity of conducting the survey itself was being prohibited in the New York case. The Second Circuit Appellate Court emphasized that the first amendment does not protect the "right to importune others to respond to questions when there is reason to believe that such importuning may result in harmful consequences."[96]

Permissible and Impermissible Content

While courts are reluctant to endorse prior restraints on the content of student publications, they are more inclined to support disciplinary action after distribution has begun. Students can be punished and publications confiscated if the material distributed fosters a disruption of the educational process, is libelous or obscene, or encourages others to engage in dangerous or unlawful activity. For example, the Fourth Circuit Court of Appeals ruled that school administrators acted within their authority when they banned further distribution on school property of a student publication that contained an advertisement for drug paraphernalia.[97] The appeals court emphasized that the literature was not subjected to predistribution approval; copies were impounded *after* distribution began. The school regulation authorizing the principal to halt the distribution of any publication encouraging actions that endanger the health or safety of students was not found to be unconstitutionally vague. Noting that commercial speech is not entitled to the same protection as other types of speech, the court held that school officials were not required to demonstrate that the harmful activity would lead to substantial disruption. The court further ruled that the school district's appeals procedures for students to contest the confiscation of literature were adequate and not unduly lengthy.[98]

The California Supreme Court also recognized that once distribution of a student publication has begun, school officials can curtail dissemination of libelous content and impose sanctions on students responsible for the material.[99] In this case, however, regulations *preventing* the distribution of libelous material were voided as vague and overbroad; the court reasoned that school authorities were not empowered to prevent the distribution of "potentially libelous" material by imposing prior restraints.[100]

Judicial ambiguity has surrounded the regulation of obscene content in student publications. As discussed previously, there is no precise definition of what constitutes obscene material. Since "the concept of obscenity or of unprotected matter may vary according to the group to whom the questionable material is directed or from whom it is quarantined,"[101] one would assume that student literature should be subject to more stringent standards than applied to literature distributed to adults. In several cases, however, the use of profanity and vulgarisms in student publications has *not* been considered obscene.[102] In a New York case, students challenged the authority of the school principal to impound copies of a school-affiliated literary magazine based on his judgment that some of the content was obscene because one article used four-letter words and referred to a movie scene where a couple "fell into bed."[103] The federal district court concluded that the content of the magazine was protected by first amendment guarantees because it contained "no extended narrative . . . constituting a predominant appeal to prurient interest" and because it was not "patently offensive . . . as evidenced by comparable material appearing in respected national periodicals and literature contained in the high school library."[104] Therefore, the court ruled that nondisruptive distribution of the magazine on school property must be allowed.

The Seventh Circuit Court of Appeals also ruled that a student publication, which contained a few earthy words relating to bodily functions and sexual intercourse, was not obscene to high school pupils.[105] In addition, the court found the school board's policy allowing suppression of literature that produces or is likely to produce "a significant disruption of the normal educational processes" to be unconstitutionally vague. On appeal, however, the United States Supreme Court vacated the appellate court's decision, noting that all of the students involved in the case had graduated from high school and therefore the issue had become moot as far as the original plaintiffs were concerned.

As discussed previously, the Supreme Court recently ruled that vulgar, lewd expression, although not considered obscene for adults, can be restricted among students in the public school context.[106] The Court further noted that the school board is the proper body to determine what language should be considered inappropriate for students. Although this decision did not involve student literature, it will likely be relied on by school authorities in future efforts to bar vulgar language from student publications.

While obscene, libelous, inflammatory, or importuning content in student publications can be the basis for disciplinary action, the fact that articles criticize school officials has been deemed an unjustifiable reason to suppress student literature. In an illustrative case, the Seventh Circuit

Court of Appeals upheld students' rights to criticize school personnel and policies in a mimeographed paper containing editorials, poetry, and reviews pertaining to the school administration and urging students to reject "propaganda."[107] The content included charges against the principal and an attack on the school's attendance requirements. Relying on *Tinker,* the court held that disciplinary action against the students responsible for the material unconstitutionally impaired protected rights because there was no evidence that the publication would create a disruption. Other courts have reiterated that school authorities cannot ban student literature simply to stifle criticism of themselves or school policies.[108]

Courts also have ruled that the mere discussion of controversial issues cannot be barred from student publications.[109] The judiciary has recognized that material dealing with war, drugs, abortion, and birth control information is not too controversial for high school students.[110] For example, a Georgia federal district court ruled that a principal impaired first amendment rights by censoring articles in the school newspaper and ultimately suspending its publication because of its controversial content pertaining to topics such as race relations, the Vietnam War, and censorship of prior issues of the newspaper.[111] The court found no evidence that the censored articles would have engendered a material and substantial disruption of school activities or interfered with the rights of others.

More recently, the Ninth Circuit Court of Appeals held that a school board violated students' first amendment rights by excluding an antidraft organization's advertisement from the school newspaper in the absence of a compelling justification.[112] Since military recruitment advertisements were allowed in the paper, the court found that the board was guilty of viewpoint-based discrimination. The board argued that it allowed nonstudents to engage only in nonpolitical, commercial expression in the paper, contending that military service advertisements fell within this category, whereas the antidraft material did not. The appeals court disagreed, noting the substantial political controversy surrounding military service and distinguishing such advertisements from commercial speech intended primarily to advance economic interests. Finding that the board had created the school paper as a limited public forum for expression, the court stated that even if the paper was considered a nonpublic forum, the viewpoint discrimination found here would not be permissible. The court further rejected the school board's contention that the antidraft advertisement would result in unlawful conduct (i.e., nonregistration for the draft) as purely speculative and not a reasonable basis to restrict free expression rights.

Time, Place, and Manner Regulations

Even though courts often have invalidated policies involving prior censorship of student publications, the judiciary has endorsed reasonable policies regulating the time, place, and manner of distribution.[113] Courts have concluded that such restrictions are justified in order to ensure that the distribution of student publications does not impinge upon other school activities. Accordingly, courts have upheld bans on literature distribution near the doors of classrooms while class is in session, near building exits during fire drills, and on stairways when classes are changing.[114]

Time, place, and manner regulations, however, must be reasonable, content-neutral, and uniformly applied to all forms of literature. School officials must inform students specifically as to when, how, and where they may distribute materials.[115] Moreover, literature distribution cannot be relegated to remote times or places either inside or outside the school building. Also, the regulations must not inhibit any person's right to accept or reject literature that is distributed in accordance with the rules. School officials must be able to substantiate the reasonableness of any time, place, and manner restrictions, because vague or ambiguous regulations threaten student expression as much as a blanket policy prohibiting literature distribution.

Although the distribution of student publications at school can be reasonably regulated, restrictions cannot be placed on the distribution of such literature off school grounds unless such off-campus activity threatens the educational process. The Second Circuit Court of Appeals concluded that school officials overstepped their authority by disciplining high school students who published a satirical magazine in their homes and sold it at a local store.[116] While not addressing the question of whether distribution of the "vulgar" publication at school was permissible, the court enjoined school officials from punishing the student publishers for off-campus distribution of the publication in the absence of evidence that the activity had an adverse impact on the school. The court concluded that to rule otherwise could subject students to school-imposed punishments for such behavior as watching X-rated movies on cable television in their own homes.

Since the Supreme Court has declined to deliver an opinion in a case involving student publications, school authorities must seek guidance from decisions rendered by their respective federal circuit courts of appeal. Although school authorities may control the content of publications that are an integral part of the instructional program, courts are protective of students' rights in connection with publications that are created as a forum for student expression. In general, educators would be wise to ensure that any restriction placed on the distribution of student literature is necessary to maintain a proper learning environment.

STUDENT APPEARANCE

Fads and fashions in hairstyles and clothing regularly have evoked litigation as educators have attempted to exert some control over pupil appearance. Courts have been called upon to balance students' interests in selecting their attire and hair length against school authorities' interests in preventing disruptions to the school environment.

Pupil Hairstyle

Substantial judicial activity has focused on school regulations governing the length of male students' hair. The United States Supreme Court, however, has refused to hear appeals of these cases, and federal circuit courts of appeal have reached different conclusions in assessing the legality of policies governing student hairstyle.

In the first, fourth, seventh, and eighth circuits, appellate courts have declared that hairstyle regulations impair students' constitutional rights. These courts have based their conclusions on the first amendment freedom of symbolic expression, the fourteenth amendment right to personal liberty, or the right to privacy included in the ninth amendment's unenumerated rights."[117] For example, in 1969 the Seventh Circuit Court of Appeals ruled that school personnel failed to produce evidence of an overriding interest that would justify impairing students' rights to select their hairstyle, which "is an ingredient of personal freedom protected by the United States Constitution."[118] It was not established that any distraction occurred as a result of male students wearing long hair, or that academic performance of male students with long hair was inferior to that of their short-haired peers. The following year, the First Circuit Court of Appeals held that a male student's right to wear shoulder-length hair was a protected "liberty" right under the fourteenth amendment.[119]

In contrast, appeals courts in the third, fifth, sixth, ninth, and tenth circuits have upheld grooming policies pertaining to pupil hairstyle.[120] In sanctioning a hair length restriction, the Fifth Circuit Court of Appeals concluded from testimony that the wearing of long hair by male students created some disturbances during school hours. Therefore, the requirement that hair be trimmed as a prerequisite to enrollment was not considered arbitrary or unreasonable.[121] In a subsequent case, the same court noted that grooming restrictions constitute a "reasonable means of furthering the school board's undeniable interest in teaching hygiene, instilling discipline, asserting authority, and compelling uniformity."[122] Relying on the fifth circuit precedent, in 1978 a Florida appeals court upheld the suspension of a male student because he refused to conform to the school board policy requiring students to be clean-shaven.[123] Concluding that no fundamental freedom was implicated, the court held that the school policy must simply be reasonably related to the accomplishment of a permissible objective.

If school officials have offered health or safety reasons for grooming regulations, usually the policies have been upheld. In an illustrative case, the Third Circuit Court of Appeals concluded that a school board acted properly in requiring a student to cut his hair because the student's long, unclean hair was a health hazard in the school cafeteria.[124] Similarly, regulations requiring hair nets, shower caps, and other hair restraints designed to protect students from injury or to promote sanitation have been upheld, as long as such regulations have been narrowly drawn.[125]

In a Maine case, a federal district court concluded that school authorities had the right to regulate student appearance where hairstyle or other unusual appearance interfered with the rights of others.[126] Accordingly, a vocational school's regulation barring beards and long hair on students was upheld as being necessary to create a positive image for potential employers visiting the school for recruitment purposes. The court reasoned that the legitimate goal of enhancing job opportunities for graduates justified the restrictions placed on student appearance. A Massachusetts federal district court similarly upheld a hair code at a vocational school based on the rationale that neat appearance among the student body enhances employment prospects for its students.[127]

Special grooming regulations as conditions of participation in extracurricular activites have usually been upheld if based on legitimate health or safety considerations. In an Illinois case, Jewish basketball players unsuccessfully challenged the state high school association rule forbidding basketball players from wearing hats or other headwear while playing. The Seventh Circuit Court of Appeals held that the players had no first amendment right to wear yarmulkes insecurely fastened by bobby pins and that the association's safety concerns, while not great, were not trivial either. The appeals court instructed the federal district court to retain jurisdiction in the case to give the students an opportunity to propose to the association a form of secure headcovering that could satisfy their faith and the association's safety concerns.[128]

Courts have not ruled in unison regarding whether grooming restrictions can be tied to extracurricular participation for school "image" reasons. The Eleventh Circuit Court of Appeals held that a school board's endorsement of a coach's clean-shaven requirement for students to participate in athletics was within the school board's power to regulate grooming and was not arbitrary or unreasonable.[129] Similarly, a California federal district court upheld the legality of a hair regulation for student athletes, noting that the regulation had been devised by a committee of students, coaches, community members, and administrators.[130] Other courts, however, have ruled that students have a right to govern their appearance in all school activities, not merely academic programs. For example, the Fourth Circuit Court of Appeals held that it was unconstitutional for a public school to force compliance with a "hair code" by withholding extracurricular awards.[131] The Vermont Federal District Court also struck down a hair regulation for high school athletes that was designed to "enhance esprit de corps, prevent adverse public reaction, prevent dissension on teams," and foster the general welfare of the teams and participants.[132] The court concluded that the regulation had no legitimate relationship to team performance, discipline, or conformity and could not be justified in terms of the school's educational mission.

A controversial issue has been whether different hair length restrictions can be applied to male and female students. A federal court in Ohio reasoned that long-haired male students could not be denied band participation if long-haired female students were not excluded.[133] Also, federal regulations promulgated to enforce Title IX of the Education Amendments of 1972 bar sex discrimination in grooming codes in educational programs receiving federal funds.[134] However, a Mississippi federal district court ruled that a hair length restriction applied only to male students did not violate prohibitions against sex discrimination in the administration of federally assisted education programs.[135] Thus, the legal status of grooming standards applied only to one sex remains somewhat unclear.

Pupil Attire

Although hairstyle continues to elicit some litigation, the issue of public school students' hair length has generally subsided as a major educational concern. Undoubtedly, other fads pertaining to student grooming will generate legal challenges as students continue to assert a right to govern their own appearance. Possibly, cases involving pupil attire (or lack thereof) will replace the haircut controversies during the next decade. Some courts have concluded that the decision to wear clothes of one's own choosing is, like the hairstyle decision, a constitutional right guaranteed by the fourteenth amendment.[136] Courts have invalidated school rules prohibiting female students from wearing slacks, barring tie-dyed clothing and blue jeans, and requiring male students to wear socks.[137]

In some jurisdictions, courts have distinguished dress codes from hair regulations because clothes, unlike hair length, can be changed after school. Even in situations where students' rights to govern their appearance have been upheld, the judiciary has noted that attire can be regulated if immodest and/or disruptive. The New Hampshire Federal District Court elaborated on the school's authority to exclude students who are unsanitary or scantily clad.

> Good hygiene and the health of the other pupils require that dirty clothes of any nature, whether they be dress clothes or dungarees, should be prohibited. Nor does the Court see anything unconstitutional in a school board prohibiting scantily clad students because it is obvious that the lack of proper covering, particularly with female students, might tend to distract other pupils and be disruptive of the educational process and school discipline.[138]

Although circuit appellate courts have differed in their interpretations of constitutional protections regarding grooming regulations, school officials would be wise to ensure that there is an overriding state interest before instituting a restrictive grooming or dress code. If specific hairstyles or attire are vulgar or can be related to a disruption of the educational process, restrictions will be upheld by courts. In addition, policies designed to protect the health and safety of students will usually be endorsed.

EXTRACURRICULAR ACTIVITIES

There has been substantial litigation pertaining to requirements and rights associated with extracurricular activities. Extracurricular activities are usually defined as those that are school-sponsored, but are not part of regular class activities or the basis for academic credit.[139] It is clear that once a state provides public education, students cannot be denied attendance without due process of law,[140] but there is less agreement regarding students' rights to participate in school-related activities.

Historically, school officials successfully asserted that extracurricular activities were additional benefits bestowed at the will of the school board, and courts endorsed the notion that the right to attend school did not include the right to participate in school-related activities.[141] A few courts in the early 1970s ruled that extracurricular activities are an integral part of the total school program, and thus the right to attend school encompasses the right to participate in such activities.[142] However, the prevailing view is that conditions can be attached to extracurricular participation that cannot be attached to school attendance. In essence, participation in extracurricular activities—unlike school attendance—is not assured.

Courts have generally allowed school authorities great flexibility in formulating rules governing extracurricular activities; regulations have not been invalidated unless clearly arbitrary. Conditions such as skill prerequisites for athletic teams, academic qualifications for honor societies, and musical proficiency for band and choral groups can be imposed. Members of athletic teams and other extracurricular groups often are selected through a competitive process, and students have no inherent right to be chosen.[143] Selection can be based on subjective judgments, and as long as fair procedures are uniformly applied, courts will not disturb such decisions.

Courts, however, have not agreed regarding procedural protections that must be provided when students face suspension or expulsion from extracurricular activities. In 1976 the Tenth Circuit Court of Appeals recognized that school attendance could not be denied without procedural safeguards, but concluded that similar constitutional protections did not extend to extracurricular components of the school program.[144] More recently, the Fifth Circuit Court of Appeals held that a student's interest in participating in interscholastic athletics is not an interest protected by the due process clause of the fourteenth amendment.[145] In contrast, the New Hampshire Supreme Court ruled that extracurricular participation is more than a privilege and is entitled to due process protection as a property right.[146] An Arkansas federal district court also held that students could not be suspended from the high school football team without due process because of their property interest in participating on the team.[147]

While school authorities may not be constitutionally required to provide due process under all circumstances involving the denial of extracurricular participation, a hearing for the affected students to explain their version of the situation is always advisable; school authorities will not be faulted for providing too much due process. If school boards have established their own rules for suspending or expelling students from extracurricular activities, courts will require such rules to be followed.

The remainder of this section focuses on various aspects of extracurricular activities that have generated legal activity. Allegations of discrimination based on sex and marital status in connection with such activities are discussed in chapter 5.

Attendance and Training Regulations

It is common for extracurricular participation to be conditioned on regular attendance at practice sessions and games/performances; students have been suspended from extracurricular activities for not complying with such requirements. An Illinois federal district court rejected a challenge to a coach's rule prohibiting elementary school basketball players who miss practice (except for illness or death in the family) from participating in the next scheduled game.[148] The plaintiff student had been denied an excused absence from practice to attend a catechism class once each week at a Catholic church. Noting that the student could make arrangements to attend catechism classes that would not conflict with basketball practice, the court concluded that the school had a legitimate interest in ensuring participation in practice sessions prior to games. The court further observed that a school cannot be expected to arrange practice schedules to accommodate the religious education classes of all team members. The Fourth Circuit Court of Appeals also upheld the removal of a student from the high school band for missing a required band trip. The student was not allowed to play in the band for a school game for disciplinary reasons, and, as a result, his mother refused to let him participate in the required trip. Finding the band director's conduct reasonable, the court held that the lawsuit was frivolous and awarded attorneys' fees to the defendant school district.[149]

However, in a case discussed previously, Arkansas students prevailed in challenging their suspension from the high school football team for walking out of a pep rally and refusing to participate in a scheduled game in protest of the coach's alleged manipulation of the homecoming queen election.[150] The coach defended his action as based on a policy under which any player is automatically suspended for missing a practice or game "without good cause." The court held that due process was required before a student's property right to participate on the team could be impaired and further held that the students could not be suspended from the team for exercising their first amendment rights.

In addition to attendance requirements, reasonable training rules and conduct restrictions have been judicially endorsed as conditions of participation on public school athletic teams. Courts have held that school officials should be given latitude in establishing training standards for high school athletes in order to foster discipline on competitive teams.[151] The judiciary has upheld the suspension of students from interscholastic athletic competition for violating training regulations prohibiting smoking and drinking among athletes, reasoning that such regulations clearly serve "a legitimate rational interest" to deter "the use of alcoholic liquor by student athletes."[152] A New York trial court upheld the denial of a high school football letter to a student who violated such a training regulation after the football season was over.[153]

More recently, an Illinois appeals court upheld a student's suspension from playing on the high school softball team because she violated the athletic code proscribing anti-social behavior considered detrimental to the team and to school spirit. The student was suspended for attending a party where minors were drinking beer; there was no allegation that the student herself was drinking. The court recognized that the coach had only advised students to avoid such parties and had not clearly defined what types of conduct were considered "anti-social behavior" under the policy. Nonetheless, the court reasoned that the disciplinary action was not "sufficiently egregious to come within the narrow concept of arbitrary or capricious official conduct which justifies the extraordinary intervention by the court in the operation of the public schools of the state."[154]

In general, courts will not interfere with attendance requirements or training regulations simply because they appear harsh.[155] The judiciary also is reluctant to invalidate disciplinary action for rule violations unless clearly arbitrary or excessive.

Residency Requirements

In addition to attendance and training regulations, courts have usually approved residency requirements as conditions of participation on extracurricular athletic teams. High school athletic association rules that prohibit involvement in extracurricular activities for one year after a change in a student's school without a change in the parents' address are intended to prevent high schools, including private schools,[156] from recruiting student athletes. The Fifth Circuit Court of Appeals held that such a residency requirement did not place an impermissible burden on students' rights to travel or their freedom of family association.[157] The Eighth Circuit Court of Appeals similarly rejected equal protection and due process challenges to a rule barring interscholastic athletic competition for one year following a transfer, concluding that the rule was rationally related to legitimate governmental interests.[158]

Most residency disputes have focused on transfers between schools, but some controversies have involved high school athletic association rules that bar nonresident students from participating in interscholastic sports. In 1985 the United States Supreme Court declined to review a decision in which the Sixth Circuit Court of Appeals upheld the Ohio High School Athletic Association's rule barring from interscholastic competition those students whose parents live in another state. The court reasoned that the rule did not infringe upon protected rights of Michigan residents who attended private high schools in the Toledo area.[159]

Although residency requirements have generally been upheld, courts have ordered exceptions to be made in some situations where a student's physical or mental welfare has necessitated the move. In a Texas case, a student with severe psychiatric difficulties was taken out of his family home and placed with his maternal grandparents on his therapist's recommendation.[160] The therapist felt that the student's participation on the football team would be therapeutically beneficial, but the request was denied because of the interscholastic league's transfer policy. The federal court granted an injunction concluding that atheletic considerations did not prompt the student's move and that there were compelling medical and psychiatric reasons necessitating the change of residence and supporting the need for the student to play on the football team.

A few courts have questioned whether residency requirements pertaining to student transfers serve their asserted purpose. For example, in 1981 the Supreme Court of Texas struck down a rule providing that students who had represented a high school other than their present school in either football or basketball were ineligible to participate in the same sport for one calendar year after moving to another district. A student, who moved with his family because his father was transferred, challenged the constitutionality of the regulation. Noting that there was no allegation that the student's move was athletically motivated, the court found that the rule was not rationally related to the objective of deterring the recruitment of high school athletes and thus violated equal protection rights.[161] While challenges to residency requirements seem likely to continue, it remains to be seen whether other courts will question the logic underlying such regulations.

Restrictions Pertaining to Age and Length of Eligibility

Several courts have endorsed age restrictions on extracurricular participation in order to equalize competitive conditions. In a typical case, the

Supreme Court of Oklahoma upheld a rule barring students who reach their nineteenth birthday by September 1 from participating in interscholastic athletics, as fair and reasonably related to legitimate state interests. The court agreed with the state defendants that older and more mature athletes could pose a threat to the health and safety of younger students and that the rule eliminated the possibility of "red shirting" athletes.[162]

In addition, courts have endorsed time limitations on a student's eligibility for interscholastic teams. The Supreme Court of Georgia, for example, upheld a rule specifying that eligibility for interscholastic competition would be for eight consecutive semesters, or four consecutive years, from the date of initial entrance into the ninth grade.[163] While noting that the rule appeared "harsh," the court concluded that the regulation was justified in order to equalize competition among teams. The Alabama Supreme Court upheld a similar rule limiting athletic eligibility to eight semesters after successful completion of eighth grade. Applying the rule, a student who received passing marks in eighth grade, but voluntarily repeated the year, was denied athletic eligibility during his senior year in high school.[164]

However, in 1984 a Pennsylvania commonwealth court issued a preliminary injunction barring the state athletic association from interfering with the participation of students in interscholastic contests because of alleged violations of an eight-semester rule. In this case, evidence indicated that the students in question were required to repeat courses because of extensive illnesses.[165] The Supreme Court of New Hampshire also held that a student, who had withdrawn from school during his sophomore year because of his health, was entitled to procedural due process before being denied team membership for violating the state athletic association's rule limiting elgibility to a specified number of days beyond eighth grade.[166]

Academic Conditions

A nationwide trend among school districts is to condition extracurricular participation on satisfactory academic performance. For example, in 1984 the Delaware Board of Education established a standard requiring ninth- and tenth-grade students to maintain passing grades in at least four classes (two of which must be academic subjects) to participate in extracurricular activities, and seniors must be passing all remaining courses required for graduation.[167]

Some of these academic conditions have generated litigation. In 1986 the United States Supreme Court dismissed an appeal of a decision in which the Texas Supreme Court upheld a state law requiring students, with some exceptions, to maintain a 70 average in all classes to be eligible for extracurricular participation.[168] The Texas high court reasoned that the law is rationally related to the state's legitimate interest in providing quality education to all students. Despite the law's exemption for handicapped students and students enrolled in honors or advanced courses, the court found no equal protection violation. Rejecting the due process claim as well, the court held that the regulation does not violate the principles of fundamental fairness. Recognizing that there is no property right to participate in extracurricular activities, the court held that fourteenth amendment due process rights are not impaired by the state authorizing local school officials to determine which courses qualify for the "honors" exemption.

In 1985 the West Virginia Supreme Court also endorsed academic standards for extracurricular participation. In this case, the state high court held that the state board of education's rule requiring students to maintain a 2.0 grade point average to participate in extracurricular activities was a legitimate exercise of its supervisory power and furthered the goal of educational excellence. The court also upheld a county school board's regulation that went beyond the state policy in requiring students to maintain a passing grade in all classes as a prerequisite to extracurricular participation.[169]

With the current concern for educational excellence, it seems likely that school boards and state legislatures will place additional academic conditions on extracurricular participation. Unless such policies are applied in a discriminatory manner, they will probably survive judicial challenges.

Fees for Participation

An increasingly controversial issue is whether extracurricular participation can be conditioned on the payment of fees. In the early 1970s, several courts upheld practices whereby students were charged fees to participate in extracurricular activities. For example, in 1970 the Supreme Court of Idaho rejected a state constitutional challenge to a school district's policy requiring students to pay fees for extracurricular participation, reasoning that such activities "are not necessary elements of a high school career."[170] The Wisconsin and Montana Supreme Courts reached similar conclusions regarding the legality of charging fees for activities that are optional or elective.[171]

In more recent cases, however, courts have rendered conflicting opinions on this issue. In 1984 the California Supreme Court struck down a school district's decision to adapt to its reduced budget by charging students fees for participation in dramatic productions, musical performances, and athletic competition. The court reasoned that extracurricular programs are an "integral fundamental part" of the educational program and thus encompassed within the state constitution's guarantee of a free public education.[172] The court was not persuaded that the fiscal crisis of the school district justified the fees or that the constitutional defect was mitigated by school district waivers for indigent students. The court further held that the fee violated the state administrative code stipulating that students shall not be required to pay "any fee, deposit, or other charge not specifically authorized by law." Finding this regulation a valid exercise of the general regulatory authority of the state board of education, the court concluded that it precludes the imposition of fees for extracurricular activities.

In contrast, a Michigan appeals court upheld the imposition of fees for participation on interscholastic athletic teams, noting the confidential waiver process available for students who could not afford the fees. The court recognized that no student had been denied participation because of inability to pay and further declared that interscholastic athletics are not considered an integral, fundamental part of the educational program that would necessitate providing them at no cost to students.[173]

Given the fiscal strains on school district budgets, fees for extracurricular activities are likely to be considered by an increasing number of school districts. In a survey conducted by the American Sports Education Institute in 1983, 16 percent of over 4,000 schools responding had "pay-for-play" programs.[174] Such programs seem destined to generate additional legal challenges that will be resolved primarily on the basis of interpretations of state law.

Other Conditions

A number of other conditions have been attached to extracurricular participation. Some courts have upheld limitations on student participation in out-of-school athletics as a condition of varsity participation in order to protect students from overtaxing themselves and to make interscholastic athletics more competitive and fair.[175] Restrictions on the number of team members allowed to participate in championship games also have been upheld as rationally related to legitimate state objectives of reducing costs of play-off contests, promoting fair play in championship games, and preventing violence during such games.[176]

Students can be required to have physical examinations and to be in good physical health to participate on athletic teams. However, restrictions imposed on the participation of handicapped students have been controversial. Although in 1977 the Second Circuit Court of Appeals rejected a federal challenge to a school board policy barring students with defective vision from participating in contact sports,[177] a partially sighted student subjected to the policy subsequently brought suit under state law and was granted relief.[178] The New York appeals court enjoined the school district from barring the student from contact teams, noting the availability of protective eyewear to minimize the risk of injury. The court concluded that it was in the best interest of the student to participate in the athletic program, and that such an opportunity could not be denied simply because of a physical impairment. More recently, a student with one kidney was successful in securing a court order enjoining the school district from barring him from the high school football team. The Pennsylvania federal district court reasoned that the student was likely to prevail in establishing that his exclusion from the team based on his handicap violated Section 504 of the Rehabilitation Act of 1973, which bars discrimination against otherwise qualified handicapped individuals in federally assisted programs.[179] Given recent rulings, school authorities would be wise to have evidence of legitimate risks to health or safety before excluding specific handicapped children from athletic teams.

While extracurricular activities remain a heavily contested aspect of public school offerings, courts have generally allowed school authorities latitude in attaching conditions (e.g., academic standards, skill criteria, residency rules, attendance and training regulations, and other requirements) to student participation in school-related activities. Educators should ensure, however, that all policies pertaining to extracurricular activities are reasonable, related to an educational purpose, clearly stated, publicized to parents and students, and applied without discrimination.

CONCLUSION

Noninstructional issues have generated a steady stream of school litigation. Many of the cases have focused on students' first amendment freedoms of speech and press, but other constitutional rights, such as due process and equal protection guarantees, also have been asserted in challenging restrictions on students' noninstructional activities. In the latter 1960s and early 1970s, the federal judiciary expanded constitutional protections afforded to students in noninstructional matters. More recently, however, courts have emphasized that public school students' rights are not coextensive with the rights of adults and have upheld the authority of school officials to restrict student behavior that interferes with the school's basic educational mission. Although judicial criteria applied in weighing the competing interests of students and school authorities are still being refined, the following generalizations accurately portray the current posture of the courts.

1. Public schools are not traditional open forums for expression; however, once school authorities create a limited forum for student expression, all students must have access to the forum on equal terms.
2. Student expression intended to convey an ideological point of view, including criticism of school policies and practices, cannot be curtailed by school authorities unless a material interference with or substantial disruption of the educational process can reasonably be forecast from the expression.

3. Students cannot assert a first amendment right to engage in defamatory, obscene, lewd, or inflammatory expression in public schools.
4. The establishment clause justifies restrictions on student religious expression that implies public school endorsement of a particular creed.
5. School authorities can restrict solicitation on public school premises.
6. Any regulation prohibiting a certain form of student expression or imposing time, place, and manner restrictions on expression must be specific, publicized to students and parents, and applied without discrimination.
7. School authorities can forbid student membership in secret societies and punish students for joining such clubs.
8. Public school authorities are not required to provide school access for student clubs that are not an extension of the curriculum; however, if the school provides a limited forum for student-initiated clubs to meet during noninstructional time, selected student organizations cannot be denied access simply because of the content of their meetings.
9. School authorities cannot bar controversial or critical content from nonschool student literature or school-sponsored publications created as a forum for student expression; even if a school paper is considered a nonpublic forum, school authorities cannot bar particular viewpoints.
10. While most courts have approved in principle the concept of prior administrative review of student publications, specific policies often have been struck down as unconstitutionally vague or overbroad; such prior review schemes must clearly specify the procedures for review and the types of material that are prohibited.
11. Distribution of student literature at school can be curtailed if the material is obscene, lewd, libelous, or inflammatory, or if it encourages dangerous or unlawful activity.
12. The time, place, and manner of student literature distribution at school can be regulated by reasonable policies to ensure that such distribution does not interfere with school activities.
13. School authorities cannot punish students for the content of literature that is published and distributed off school grounds unless such distribution substantially interferes with the educational process.
14. Grooming standards for students can be imposed for health and safety reasons and to prevent a disruption of the educational process.
15. Students do not have an inherent right to participate in extracurricular activities.

16. School authorities have considerable latitude in attaching reasonable conditions to extracurricular participation (e.g., attendance and training regulations, residency requirements, academic standards, requirements pertaining to age and length of eligibility, etc.).
17. Restrictions can be imposed on student participation in extracurricular activities based on legitimate health and safety considerations.
18. Whether fees can be charged for extracurricular participation hinges on an interpretation of an individual state's constitutional and statutory provisions.

NOTES

1. West Virginia Bd. of Educ. v. Barnette, 319 U.S. 624, 637 (1943).
2. Keyishian v. Board of Regents, 385 U.S. 589, 603 (1967), quoting in part, United States v. Associated Press, 52 F. Supp. 362, 372 (S.D.N.Y. 1943), *aff'd*, 326 U.S. 1 (1945).
3. *See* West Virginia State Bd. of Educ. v. Barnette, 319 U.S. 624 (1943); text with note 67, chapter 2.
4. Schenck v. United States, 249 U.S. 47, 52 (1919).
5. Bethel School Dist. No. 403 v. Fraser, 106 S. Ct. 3159, 3164 (1986).
6. *See* Jarman v. Williams, 753 F.2d 76, 78 (8th Cir. 1985); Justice v. National Collegiate Athletic Ass'n, 577 F. Supp. 356, 374 (D. Ariz. 1983).
7. State v. Ybarra, 550 P.2d 763 (Ore. App. 1976).
8. The court further recognized that the public school was not a public forum and that school facilities had previously been rented only to groups engaged in activities related to the school's educational function. Jarman v. Williams, 753 F.2d 76 (8th Cir. 1985). However, social dancing might enjoy first amendment protection under different circumstances. *See* Gay Students Organization of the Univ. of New Hampshire v. Bonner, 509 F.2d 652 (1st Cir. 1974) (request of a gay students' organization to hold social functions, including dances, on a state-supported college campus was part of the group's efforts to organize and convey an ideological message to the public; therefore, protected expression was involved).
9. *See* chapter 12 for a discussion of the principles of tort law governing personal damages suits for defamation.
10. *See* Garcia v. Board of Educ. of Socorro Consol. School Dist., 777 F.2d 1403 (10th Cir. 1985), *cert. denied*, 107 S. Ct. 66 (1986) (school board member); Scott v. News-Herald, 496 N.E.2d 699 (Ohio 1986) (school superintendent). For a discussion of defamation charges against public officials, *see* Gertz v. Robert Welch, 418 U.S. 323 (1974); Curtis Publishing Co. v. Butts, 388 U.S. 130 (1967); Rosenblatt v. Baer, 383 U.S. 75 (1966); New York Times Co. v. Sullivan, 376 U.S. 254 (1964).

11. Finding that public school teachers and coaches are not public figures, *see* True v. Ladner, 513 A.2d 257 (Me. 1986); Franklin v. Lodge 1108, 159 Cal. Rptr. 131 (Cal. App. 1979). Finding such individuals to be public figures, *see* Scott v. News-Herald, 496 N.E.2d 699 (Ohio 1986); Johnston v. Corinthian Television Corp., 583 P.2d 1101 (Okla. 1978); Basarich v. Rodeghero, 321 N.E.2d 739 (Ill. App. 1974).
12. *See* Ollman v. Evans, 750 F.2d 970 (D.C. Cir. 1984), *cert. denied*, 105 S. Ct. 2662 (1985).
13. 413 U.S. 15, 24 (1973).
14. Ginsberg v. New York, 390 U.S. 629, 636–637 (1968). *See also* New York v. Ferber, 458 U.S. 747 (1982).
15. Fraser v. Bethel School Dist. No. 403, 755 F.2d 1356 (9th Cir. 1985), *rev'd*, 106 S. Ct. 3159 (1986).
16. *Id.*, 106 S. Ct. at 3165. *See also* Hinze v. The Superior Court of Marin County, 174 Cal. Rptr. 403 (Cal. App. 1981) (badge containing the statement, "Fuck the Draft," was vulgar and not protected expression; thus, a student who persistently refused to remove the button could be disciplined).
17. Stacy v. Williams, 306 F. Supp. 963, 972 (N.D. Miss. 1969), *aff'd*, 446 F.2d 1366 (5th Cir. 1971).
18. Melton v. Young, 465 F.2d 1332 (6th Cir. 1972), *cert. denied*, 411 U.S. 951 (1973).
19. Williams v. Turner, 382 So. 2d 1040 (La. App. 1980).
20. Fenton v. Stear, 423 F. Supp. 767, 771 (W.D. Pa. 1976).
21. The Supreme Court has recognized that constitutional protection afforded expression differs based on the nature of the forum and the type of expression involved. Public places (e.g., streets and parks) that are reserved for assembly and communication, are considered *traditional public forums* where content-based restrictions cannot be imposed unless justified by a compelling governmental interest. At the other end of the continuum is a *nonpublic forum* where expression can be confined to the governmental purpose of the property. Content distinctions may be permissible in nonpublic forums to assure that activities are compatible with the intended governmental purpose as long as regulations are reasonable and not an effort to suppress particular views. Whereas a compelling governmental interest is required to justify restrictions on speakers in a traditional open forum, only a rational basis is necessary for such restrictions in a nonpublic forum. In some situations, the government has created a *limited open forum* for expression on public property that is otherwise considered a nonpublic forum and reserved for its governmental function. Such limited or designated open forums are subject to the same standards as applied to traditional public forums, but the government is not required indefinitely to retain the open character of a designated forum. In such a forum, viewpoint discrimination is not allowed, but the government can designate a limited forum for a certain class of speakers (e.g., students in public schools) to discuss any topic or for the public to discuss certain topics or for some combination of the two. For a discussion of types of forums, *see* Cornelius v. NAACP Legal Defense and Educational Fund, 105 S. Ct. 3439, 3446–3455 (1985); Perry Educ. Ass'n v. Perry Local Educators' Ass'n, 460 U.S. 37, 45–49 (1983); San Diego Comm. Against Registration and the Draft v. Governing Bd. of

Grossmont Union High School Dist., 790 F.2d 1471, 1474–1476 (9th Cir. 1986); Student Coalition for Peace v. Lower Merion School Dist., 776 F.2d 431, 436–437 (3d Cir. 1985); Jarman v. Williams, 753 F.2d 76, 79 (8th Cir. 1985).

22. 393 U.S. 503, 511 (1969).
23. *Id.* at 508.
24. *Id.* at 509.
25. Burnside v. Byars, 363 F.2d 744, 749 (5th Cir. 1966). *Compare* with Blackwell v. Issaquena County Bd. of Educ., 363 F.2d 749 (5th Cir. 1966); text with note 39, *infra*.
26. *See* Butts v. Dallas Independent School Dist., 306 F. Supp. 488 (N.D. Tex. 1969), *rev'd*, 436 F.2d 728 (5th Cir. 1971).
27. Anderson v. Central Point School Dist. No. 6, 554 F. Supp. 600 (D. Ore. 1982), *aff'd*, 746 F.2d 505 (9th Cir. 1984).
28. Scoville v. Board of Educ. of Joliet, 425 F.2d 10, 14 (7th Cir. 1970), *cert. denied*, 400 U.S. 826 (1970).
29. *See* Rasche v. Board of Trustees of Univ. of Illinois, 353 F. Supp. 973 (N.D. Ill. 1972). However, the Supreme Court recently upheld a school rule prohibiting "conduct which materially and substantially interferes with the educational process. . . ." Bethel School Dist. No. 403 v. Fraser, 106 S. Ct. 3159 (1986). *See* text with notes 15, *supra*; 89, *infra*.
30. Gebert v. Hoffman, 336 F. Supp. 694, 697 (E.D. Pa. 1972).
31. Clergy and Laity Concerned v. Chicago Bd. of Educ., 586 F. Supp. 1408 (N.D. Ill. 1984). The court rejected the contention that access to draft counselors who were members of the clergy violated the establishment clause, noting that their message was secular and not religious in nature. *See also* Searcey v. Crim, 642 F. Supp. 313 (N.D. Ga. 1986).
32. Fricke v. Lynch, 491 F. Supp. 381 (D.R.I. 1980).
33. Boyd v. Board of Directors of McGehee School Dist. No. 17, 612 F. Supp. 86, (E.D. Ark. 1985).
34. *Id.* at 92.
35. Stanton v. Brunswick School Dep't, 577 F. Supp. 1560 (D. Me. 1984).
36. The Supreme Court recently held that the first amendment does not entitle a student to engage in vulgar, lewd speech in a public school assembly and endorsed the authority of school boards to determine what expression is inappropriately vulgar, Bethel School Dist. No. 403 v. Fraser, 106 S. Ct. 3159, 3163 (1986). Although the Court emphasized that the expression at issue in *Fraser* did not involve a political message, the Court's conclusion that lewd speech in public schools interferes with the rights of others suggests that such expression could be restricted even though intended to convey a political position.
37. Solmitz v. Maine School Administrative Dist. No. 59, 495 A.2d 812 (Me. 1985). *See also* Coalition for Peace v. Lower Merion School Dist., 776 F.2d 431 (3d Cir. 1985) (school authorities' legitimate interest in keeping politics out of the public school can justify a distinction among types of speakers as long as viewpoint discrimination is not involved); text with note 68, *infra*. *But see* Wilson v. Chancellor, 418 F. Supp. 1358, 1364 (D. Ore. 1976) (invalidating a school board's order barring political speakers from the high school because of community objections to an invited Communist speaker in a class lecture series on political views); text with notes 81, 90, chapter 8.

38. Guzick v. Drebus, 431 F.2d 594, 600 (6th Cir. 1970), *cert. denied*, 401 U.S. 948 (1971).
39. *See* Blackwell v. Issaquena County Bd. of Educ., 363 F.2d 749 (5th Cir. 1966).
40. *See* Tate v. Board of Educ., 453 F.2d 975 (8th Cir. 1972).
41. *See* Herman v. University of South Carolina, 457 F.2d 902 (4th Cir. 1972); Farrell v. Joel, 437 F.2d 160 (2d Cir. 1971); Gebert v. Hoffman, 336 F. Supp. 694 (E.D. Pa. 1972).
42. Tate v. Board of Educ., 453 F.2d 975 (8th Cir. 1972).
43. Dodd v. Rambis, 535 F. Supp. 23 (S.D. Ind. 1981).
44. Karp v. Becken, 477 F.2d 171 (9th Cir. 1973).
45. *Id.* at 176.
46. *See* Gebert v. Hoffman, 336 F. Supp. 694, 697 (E.D. Pa. 1972); Buttny v. Smiley, 281 F. Supp. 280, 286–87 (D. Colo. 1968).
47. *See* Godwin v. East Baton Rouge Parish School Bd., 408 So. 2d 1214 (La. 1981), *appeal dismissed*, 459 U.S. 807 (1982); text with note 60, chapter 8.
48. In 1985 an Arkansas federal district court noted that students had not been adequately warned regarding what constituted "good cause" in connection with their suspension from the high school football team. Boyd v. Board of Directors of McGehee School Dist. No. 17, 612 F. Supp. 86 (E.D. Ark. 1985). *See* text with note 33, *supra*.
49. *See* Bolger v. Young Drug Products Corp., 463 U.S. 60, 64–75 (1983); Central Hudson Gas & Electric Corp. v. Public Service Comm'n of New York, 447 U.S. 557, 562–563 (1980); Ohralik v. Ohio State Bar Ass'n, 436 U.S. 447, 455–456 (1978).
50. Central Hudson, *id.* at 566.
51. American Future Systems, Inc. v. Pennsylvania State Univ., 752 F.2d 854 (3d Cir. 1984), *cert. denied sub nom.* Johnson v. Pennsylvania State Univ., 105 S. Ct. 3537 (1985). *See also* Glover v. Cole, 762 F.2d 1197 (4th Cir. 1985); Chapman v. Thomas, 743 F.2d 1056 (4th Cir. 1984), *cert. denied*, 105 S. Ct. 1866 (1985).
52. Katz v. McAulay, 438 F.2d 1058 (2d Cir. 1971), *cert. denied*, 405 U.S. 933 (1972). It should be noted, however, that some courts have distinguished expression with political *and* commercial elements from expression primarily intended to advance economic interests. *See* text with note 112, *infra*.
53. Sweezy v. New Hampshire, 354 U.S. 234, 250 (1957). *See* Shelton v. Tucker, 364 U.S. 479, 487 (1960); West Virginia Bd. of Educ. v. Barnette, 319 U.S. 624, 637 (1943). *See also* chapter 3 for a discussion of curriculum censorship cases in which students have asserted a first amendment right to receive information and have access to controversial materials.
54. *See* Bethel School Dist. No. 403 v. Fraser, 106 S. Ct. 3159, 3164 (1986); Tinker v. Des Moines Independent School Dist., 393 U.S. 503, 507 (1969).
55. Healy v. James, 408 U.S. 169, 181 (1972).
56. State Bd. for Community Colleges and Occupational Educ. v. Olson, 687 P.2d 429, 439 (Colo. 1984).
57. *See* notes 59–61, *infra*. *But see* Wright v. Board of Educ., 246 S.W. 43 (Mo. App. 1922) (school board regulation forbidding student membership in secret organizations was not authorized by the state legislature, and student conduct during out-of-school hours could not be regulated unless it was substantiated that it would clearly interfere with school discipline).

58. Ill. Rev. Stat., ch. 122, § 31–1.
59. Bradford v. Board of Educ., 121 P. 929, 931 (Cal. App. 1912). *See also* Burkitt v. School Dist. No. 1, Multnomah County, 246 P.2d 566 (Ore. 1952).
60. *See* Thomas v. Board of Educ., Granville Cent. School Dist., 607 F.2d 1043 (2d Cir. 1979), *cert. denied,* 444 U.S. 1081 (1980), text with note 116, *infra.*
61. *See* Passel v. Fort Worth Independent School Dist., 453 S.W.2d 888 (Tex. Civ. App. 1970); Holroyd v. Eibling, 188 N.E.2d 797 (Ohio App. 1962).
62. Robinson v. Sacramento Unified School Dist., 53 Cal. Rptr. 781 (Cal. App. 1966). A Texas court even upheld a school board's policy requiring parents to certify that their children attending secondary schools would not join or participate in the activities of fraternities, sororities, or secret societies. The court reasoned that the policy did not interfere with parental rights to direct the upbringing of their children. Passel, *id.*
63. Healy v. James, 408 U.S. 169 (1972).
64. *Id.* at 181.
65. *Id.* at 184.
66. *See, e.g.*, Gay Students Services v. Texas A & M Univ., 737 F.2d 1317 (5th Cir. 1984), *cert. denied*, 105 S. Ct. 1860 (1985); Gay Students Organization of the Univ. of New Hampshire v. Bonner, 509 F.2d 652 (1st Cir. 1974). It should be noted that students cannot be forced to support, through their activity fee, organizations which espouse political and ideological philosophies that the students oppose. *See* Galda v. Rutgers, 772 F.2d 1060 (3d Cir. 1985), *cert. denied*, 106 S. Ct. 1375 (1986) (first amendment precludes the university from compelling students to pay a fee to support a state public interest research group).
67. *See* Widmar v. Vincent, 454 U.S. 263 (1981); note 74, *infra.*
68. Student Coalition for Peace v. Lower Merion School Dist., 596 F. Supp. 169 (E.D. Pa. 1984), *aff'd in part, vacated and remanded in part*, 776 F.2d 431 (3d Cir. 1985).
69. *Id.*, 776 F.2d at 437.
70. *See* 20 U.S.C. § 4071. *See* text with note 28, chapter 2.
71. The court further held that the involvement of nonstudents in the meeting in question did not preclude finding a violation of the act as long as the group was neither controlled nor directed by nonstudents.
72. Student Coalition for Peace v. Lower Merion School Dist., 633 F. Supp. 1040 (E.D. Pa. 1986).
73. Dixon v. Beresh, 361 F. Supp. 253 (E.D. Mich. 1973).
74. Widmar v. Vincent, 454 U.S. 263 (1981). *See* text with note 25, chapter 2.
75. For a discussion of these cases, *see* text with note 24, chapter 2.
76. Trujillo v. Love, 322 F. Supp. 1266, 1270 (D. Colo. 1971). *See also* Reineke v. Cobb County School Dist., 484 F. Supp. 1252 (N. D. Ga. 1980); Antonelli v. Hammond, 308 F. Supp. 1329 (D. Mass. 1970); Zucker v. Panitz, 299 F. Supp. 102 (S.D.N.Y. 1969).
77. Bayer v. Kinzler, 383 F. Supp. 1164 (E.D.N.Y. 1974), *aff'd*, 515 F.2d 504 (2d Cir. 1975).
78. Stanley v. Magrath, 719 F.2d 279, 282–283 (8th Cir. 1983). Although holding that a refund policy can be established, the court noted that such a policy cannot be initiated in response to public criticism of the publication.
79. Kuhlmeier v. Hazelwood School Dist., 607 F. Supp. 1450 (E.D. Mo. 1985), *rev'd,* 795 F.2d 1368 (8th Cir. 1986).

80. Bantam Books v. Sullivan, 372 U.S. 58, 70 (1963). *See also* New York Times Co. v. United States, 403 U.S. 713 (1971); Carroll v. President and Comm'rs of Princess Anne, 393 U.S. 175, 181 (1968).
81. Fujishima v. Board of Educ., 460 F.2d 1355 (7th Cir. 1972).
82. Bright v. Los Angeles Unified School Dist., 134 Cal. Rptr. 639 (Cal. 1976).
83. *See* Nicholson v. Board of Educ., 682 F.2d 858 (9th Cir. 1982); Trachtman v. Anker, 563 F.2d 512 (2d Cir. 1977), *cert. denied*, 435 U.S. 925 (1978); Sullivan v. Houston Independent School Dist., 475 F.2d 1071 (5th Cir. 1973), *cert. denied*, 414 U.S. 1032 (1973); Speake v. Grantham, 440 F.2d 1351 (5th Cir. 1971).
84. *See* Baughman v. Freienmuth, 478 F.2d 1345, 1350 (4th Cir. 1973).
85. Jacobs v. Board of School Comm'rs, 490 F.2d 601, 606 (7th Cir. 1973), *vacated as moot*, 420 U.S. 128 (1975). *See also* Nitzberg v. Parks, 525 F.2d 378, 383–384 (4th Cir. 1975); Baughman, *id.* at 1348; Shanley v. Northeast Independent School Dist., 462 F.2d 960, 969 (5th Cir. 1972); Quarterman v. Byrd, 453 F.2d 54, 57–59 (4th Cir. 1971).
86. Eisner v. Stamford Bd. of Educ., 440 F.2d 803 (2d Cir. 1971).
87. Quarterman v. Byrd, 453 F.2d 54 (4th Cir. 1971).
88. Liebner v. Sharbaugh, 429 F. Supp. 744, 748 (E.D. Va. 1977).
89. Bethel School Dist. No. 403 v. Fraser, 106 S. Ct. 3159, 3166 (1986). *See* text with note 15, *supra.*
90. Speake v. Grantham, 317 F. Supp. 1253 (S.D. Miss. 1970), *aff'd per curiam*, 440 F.2d 1351 (5th Cir. 1971).
91. Sullivan v. Houston Independent School Dist., 475 F.2d 1071 (5th Cir. 1973), *cert. denied*, 414 U.S. 1032 (1973).
92. Nicholson v. Board of Educ., 682 F.2d 858 (9th Cir. 1982). The teacher, who sometimes failed to comply with the principal's request for review of the student literature, was not re-employed at the end of his probationary period and claimed wrongful discharge. However, the court reasoned that the contract nonrenewal was not predicated on the exercise of protected rights.
93. Frasca v. Andrews, 463 F. Supp. 1043 (E.D.N.Y. 1979).
94. Trachtman v. Anker, 563 F.2d 512 (2d Cir. 1977), *cert. denied*, 435 U.S. 925 (1978).
95. Gambino v. Fairfax County School Bd., 564 F.2d 157 (4th Cir. 1977).
96. Trachtman v. Anker, 563 F.2d at 520.
97. Williams v. Spencer, 622 F.2d 1200 (4th Cir. 1980). The newspaper also contained a potentially racially offensive cartoon, but the appeals court focused only on the health and safety issue, leaving open the question of libel.
98. *See also* Norton v. Discipline Comm. of East Tennessee State Univ., 419 F.2d 195, 197 (6th Cir. 1969), *cert. denied*, 399 U.S. 906 (1970) (disciplinary action was upheld against college students who distributed a publication that encouraged classmates to participate in a demonstration).
99. Bright v. Los Angeles Unified School Dist., 134 Cal. Rptr. 639, 646–648 (Cal. 1976).
100. *Id. But see* Frasca v. Andrews, 463 F. Supp. 1043 (E.D.N.Y. 1979); text with note 93, *supra.*
101. Bookcase, Inc. v. Broderick, 218 N.E.2d 668, 671 (N.Y. 1966), *dismissed*, 358 U.S. 12 (1966). *See* text with note 14, *supra.*
102. *See* Papish v. Board of Curators, 410 U.S. 667 (1973); Vail v. Board of Educ.

of Portsmouth School Dist., 354 F. Supp. 592, 599 (D.N.H. 1973), *vacated and remanded*, 502 F.2d 1159 (1973).

103. Koppel v. Levine, 347 F. Supp. 456, 458 (E.D.N.Y. 1972).
104. *Id.* at 459.
105. Jacobs v. Board of School Comm'rs, 490 F.2d 601, 604, 609 (7th Cir. 1973), *vacated as moot*, 420 U.S. 128 (1975).
106. Bethel School Dist. No. 403 v. Fraser, 106 S. Ct. 3159 (1986). *See* text with notes 15, 89, *supra*.
107. Scoville v. Board of Educ. of Joliet, 425 F.2d 10, 12 (7th Cir. 1970), *cert. denied*, 400 U.S. 826 (1970).
108. *See* Baughman v. Freienmuth, 478 F.2d 1345 (4th Cir. 1973); Pliscou v. Holtville Unified School Dist., 411 F. Supp. 842 (S.D. Cal. 1976).
109. *See* Shanley v. Northeast Independent School Dist., 462 F.2d 960 (5th Cir. 1972).
110. *See* Gambino v. Fairfax County School Bd., 429 F. Supp. 731 (E.D. Va. 1977), *aff'd*, 564 F.2d 157 (4th Cir. 1977); Jacobs v. Board of School Comm'rs, 490 F.2d 601 (7th Cir. 1973), *vacated*, 420 U.S. 128 (1975); Koppell v. Levine, 347 F. Supp. 456 (E.D.N.Y. 1972).
111. Reineke v. Cobb County School Dist., 484 F. Supp. 1252 (N.D. Ga. 1980).
112. San Diego Comm. Against Registration and the Draft v. Governing Bd. of Grossmont Union High School Dist., 790 F.2d 1471 (9th Cir. 1986). *See also* Zucker v. Panitz, 299 F. Supp. 102 (S.D.N.Y. 1969) (school authorities could not bar publication of an advertisement opposing the Vietnam War in a school newspaper because the paper was a forum for the dissemination of ideas).
113. *See* Shanley v. Northeast Independent School Dist., 462 F.2d 960 (5th Cir. 1972); Riseman v. School Comm. of Quincy, 439 F.2d 148 (1st Cir. 1971). *See also* Heffron v. International Society for Krishna Consciousness, 452 U.S. 640 (1981) (upholding a restriction on literature distribution at a fairgrounds to maintain orderly movement of the fair crowd and protect citizens from fraudulent solicitation).
114. *See* Fujishima v. Board of Educ., 460 F.2d 1355 (7th Cir. 1972).
115. *See* Nicholson v. Board of Educ., Torance Unified School Dist., 682 F.2d 858 (9th Cir. 1982); Vail v. Board of Educ. of Portsmouth School Dist., 354 F. Supp. 592 (D.N.H. 1973), *vacated and remanded*, 502 F.2d 1159 (1st Cir. 1973).
116. Thomas v. Board of Educ., Granville Cent. School Dist., 607 F.2d 1043 (2d Cir. 1979), *cert. denied*, 444 U.S. 1081 (1980). The publication's only connection with the public school was that some copies were temporarily stored in a closet in a classroom. *But see* Baker v. Downey City Bd. of Educ., 307 F. Supp. 517 (C.D. Cal. 1969) (upholding suspension of students for use of profane and vulgar language in publication distributed immediately outside of school's main campus gate).
117. *See* Bishop v. Colaw, 450 F.2d 1069 (8th Cir. 1971); Richards v. Thurston, 424 F.2d 1281 (1st Cir. 1970); Massie v. Henry, 455 F.2d 779 (4th Cir. 1972); Breen v. Kahl, 419 F.2d 1034 (7th Cir. 1969), *cert. denied*, 398 U.S. 937 (1970).
118. Breen, *id.* at 1036.
119. Richards v. Thurston, 424 F.2d 1281, 1286 (1st Cir. 1970). *See also* Graber v.

Kniola, 216 N.W.2d 925 (Mich. App. 1974); Wallace v. Ford, 346 F. Supp. 156 (E.D. Ark. 1972).

120. *See* Zeller v. Donegal School Dist., 517 F.2d 600 (3d Cir. 1975), *overruling*, Stull v. School Bd. of Western Beaver Jr.-Sr. High School, 459 F.2d 339 (3d Cir. 1972); Olff v. East Side Union High School Dist., 445 F.2d 932 (9th Cir. 1971), *cert. denied*, 404 U.S. 1042 (1972); Freeman v. Flake, 448 F.2d 258 (10th Cir. 1971), *cert. denied*, 405 U.S. 1032 (1972); Jackson v. Dorrier, 424 F.2d 213 (6th Cir. 1970), *cert. denied*, 400 U.S. 850 (1970); Ferrell v. Dallas Independent School Dist., 392 F.2d 697 (5th Cir. 1968), *cert. denied*, 393 U.S. 856 (1968).
121. Ferrell, *id.* at 703. *See also* Karr v. Schmidt, 460 F.2d 609 (5th Cir. 1972), *cert. denied*, 409 U.S. 989 (1972).
122. Domico v. Rapides Parish School Bd., 675 F.2d 100, 102 (5th Cir. 1982).
123. Ferrara v. Hendry County School Bd., 362 So. 2d 371 (Fla. App. 1978), *cert. denied*, 444 U.S. 856 (1979). *See also* Stevenson v. Board of Educ. of Wheeler County, Georgia, 426 F.2d 1154 (5th Cir. 1970), *cert. denied*, 400 U.S. 957 (1970) (upholding a school policy requiring students to be clean-shaven in the interest of maintaining school discipline).
124. Gere v. Stanley, 453 F.2d 205 (3d Cir. 1971).
125. *See* text with note 128, *infra*.
126. Farrell v. Smith, 310 F. Supp. 732 (D. Maine 1970).
127. Bishop v. Cermenaro, 355 F. Supp. 1269 (D. Mass. 1973). *See also* Christmas v. El Reno Bd. of Educ., Independent School Dist. No. 34, 313 F. Supp. 618 (W.D. Okla. 1970), *aff'd*, 449 F.2d 153 (10th Cir. 1971) (student could be barred from an optional post-graduation diploma ceremony because of violating hair length regulation).
128. Menora v. Illinois High School Ass'n, 683 F.2d 1030 (7th Cir. 1982), *cert. denied*, 459 U.S. 1156 (1983).
129. Davenport v. Randolph County Bd. of Educ., 730 F.2d 1395 (11th Cir. 1984). *See also* Zeller v. Donegal School Dist., 517 F.2d 600 (3d Cir. 1975); Humphries v. Lincoln Parish School Bd., 467 So. 2d 870 (La. App. 1985). Courts have rendered conflicting opinions regarding whether participation in the high school band can be conditioned on adherence to a hair length code. *Compare* Dostert v. Berthold Public School Dist. No. 54, 391 F. Supp. 876 (D.N.D. 1975) (school's interest in requiring uniformity in hair length to secure high marks in band competition was not a sufficiently compelling reason to interfere with students' constitutionally protected interest in determining their hair length) *with* Corley v. Daunhauer, 312 F. Supp. 811 (E.D. Ark. 1970) (public school system has the right to require students in the school band to conform to reasonable hair length regulations).
130. Neuhaus v. Torrey, 310 F. Supp. 192 (N.D. Cal. 1970).
131. Long v. Zopp, 476 F.2d 180 (4th Cir. 1973) (recognizing that legitimate health and safety concerns might justify a hair restriction during football season, the court found no justification for denying a letter to a student who violated a hair restriction after football season ended).
132. Dunham v. Pulsifer, 312 F. Supp. 411 (D. Vt. 1970).
133. Cordova v. Chonko, 315 F. Supp. 953 (N.D. Ohio 1970).
134. *See* 45 C.F.R. § 86.31(b)(5); *Education Daily*, November 21, 1979, p. 1.

135. Trent v. Perritt, 391 F. Supp. 171 (S.D. Miss. 1975) (claim focused on federal aid under the Emergency School Aid Act).
136. *See* Bannister v. Paradis, 316 F. Supp. 185 (D.N.H. 1970).
137. *See* Johnson v. Joint School Dist. No. 60, Bingham County, 508 P.2d 547 (Idaho 1973); Wallace v. Ford, 346 F. Supp. 156 (E.D. Ark. 1972); Press v. Pasadena Independent School Dist., 326 F. Supp. 550 (S.D. Tex. 1971); Bannister, *id.*; Scott v. Board of Educ., Union Free School Dist. No. 17, 305 N.Y.S.2d 601 (Sup. Ct., Nassau County, 1969). *But see* Dunkerson v. Russell, 502 S.W.2d 64 (Ky. 1973) (upholding a dress code provision forbidding female students from wearing jeans).
138. Bannister, *id.* at 189. *See also* Westley v. Rossi, 305 F. Supp. 706, 714 (D. Minn. 1969).
139. Edward L. Winn, "Legal Control of Student Extracurricular Activities," *School Law Bulletin*, vol. 3, no. 3 (1976), p. 2.
140. *See* Goss v. Lopez, 419 U.S. 565 (1975); text with note 42, chapter 6.
141. *See* State *ex rel.* Indiana High School Athletic Ass'n v. Lawrence Circuit Court, 162 N.E.2d 250 (Ind. 1959).
142. *See* Davis v. Meek, 344 F. Supp. 298 (N.D. Ohio 1972); Moran v. School Dist. No. 7, 350 F. Supp. 1180 (D. Mont. 1972); Kelley v. Metropolitan County Bd. of Educ. of Nashville, 293 F. Supp. 485 (M.D. Tenn. 1968).
143. *See* Karnstein v. Pewaukee School Bd., 557 F. Supp. 565 (E.D. Wis. 1983); Price v. Young, 580 F. Supp. 1 (E.D. Ark. 1983) (students do not have a property right at stake in connection with selection to the National Honor Society).
144. Albach v. Odle, 531 F.2d 983 (10th Cir. 1976). *See also* Pegram v. Nelson, 469 F. Supp. 1134 (M.D.N.C. 1979).
145. Niles v. University Interscholastic League, 715 F.2d 1027 (5th Cir. 1983), *cert. denied*, 465 U.S. 1028 (1984). *See also* Hardy v. University Interscholastic League, 759 F.2d 1233 (5th Cir. 1985).
146. Duffley v. New Hampshire Interscholastic Athletic Ass'n, 446 A.2d 462 (N.H. 1982).
147. Boyd v. Board of Directors of the McGehee School Dist. No. 17, 612 F. Supp. 86 (E.D. Ark. 1985).
148. Keller v. Gardner Community Consol. Grade School Dist. 72C, 552 F. Supp. 512 (N.D. Ill. 1982).
149. Bernstein v. Menard, 728 F.2d 252 (4th Cir. 1984).
150. Boyd v. Board of Directors of the McGehee School Dist. No. 17, 612 F. Supp. 86 (E.D. Ark. 1985). *See* text with note 33, *supra*.
151. *See* Hasson v. Boothby, 318 F. Supp. 1183 (D. Mass. 1970); Stevenson v. Wheeler County Bd. of Educ., 306 F. Supp. 97 (S.D. Ga. 1969), *aff'd*, 426 F.2d 1154 (5th Cir. 1970), *cert. denied*, 400 U.S. 957 (1970).
152. Braesch v. DePasquale, 265 N.W.2d 842, 846 (Neb. 1978), *cert. denied*, 439 U.S. 1068 (1979). *See also* French v. Cornwall, 276 N.W.2d 216 (Neb. 1979).
153. O'Connor v. Board of Educ., 316 N.Y.S.2d 799 (Sup. Ct., Herkimer County, 1970).
154. Clements v. Board of Educ. of Decatur Public School Dist. No. 61, 478 N.E.2d 1209, 1213 (Ill. App. 1985).
155. However, the Iowa Supreme Court invalidated a student's suspension from interscholastic competition for violating the association's rule prohibiting

the use of alcoholic beverages among student athletes, reasoning that the school board unlawfully delegated its rule-making authority regarding student discipline to the athletic association. Bunger v. Iowa High School Athletic Ass'n, 197 N.W.2d 555 (Iowa 1972).

156. *See* Steffes v. California Interscholastic Fed'n, 222 Cal. Rptr. 355 (Cal. App. 1986).
157. Niles v. University Interscholastic League, 715 F.2d 1027 (5th Cir. 1983), *cert. denied*, 465 U.S. 1023 (1984). *See also* Walsh v. Louisiana High School Athletic Ass'n, 616 F.2d 152 (5th Cir. 1980), *cert. denied*, 449 U.S. 1124 (1981); Albach v. Odle, 531 F.2d 983 (10th Cir. 1976); Kulovitz v. Illinois High School Ass'n, 462 F. Supp. 875 (N.D. Ill. 1978); Herbert v. Ventetuolo, 480 A.2d 403 (R.I. 1984); Pennsylvania Interscholastic Athletic Ass'n v. Greater Johnstown School Dist., 463 A.2d 1198 (Pa. Commw. 1983); Cooper v. Oregon School Activities Ass'n, 629 P.2d 386 (Ore. App. 1981); Menke v. Ohio High School Athletic Ass'n, 441 N.E.2d 620 (Ohio App. 1981); Kriss v. Brown, 390 N.E.2d 193 (Ind. App. 1979); Florida High School Activities Ass'n v. Bradshaw, 369 So. 2d 398 (Fla. App. 1979); Mozingo v. Oklahoma Secondary High School Activities Ass'n, 575 P.2d 1379 (Okla. App. 1978).
158. In re United States *ex rel.* Missouri State High School Activities Ass'n, 682 F.2d 147, 152 (8th Cir. 1982).
159. Zeiler v. Ohio High School Athletic Ass'n, 755 F.2d 934 (6th Cir. 1985), *cert. denied*, 106 S. Ct. 63 (1985). *See also* Alerding v. Ohio High School Athletic Ass'n, 779 F.2d 315 (6th Cir. 1985).
160. Doe v. Marshall, 459 F. Supp. 1190 (S.D. Tex. 1978), *vacated*, 622 F.2d 118 (5th Cir. 1980) (appeals court ruled that the case was moot because the student, who had continued to play football throughout high school, had graduated; however, attorneys' fees were awarded to the student). *See also* Doe v. Marshall, 694 F.2d 1038 (5th Cir. 1983), *cert. denied*, 462 U.S. 1119 (1983).
161. Sullivan v. University Interscholastic League, 616 S.W.2d 170 (Tex. 1981).
162. Mahan v. Agee, 652 P.2d 765 (Okla. 1982). *See also* Cavallaro v. Ambach, 575 F. Supp. 171 (W.D.N.Y. 1983) (exceptions are not required for handicapped athletes); Blue v. University Interscholastic League, 503 F. Supp. 1030 (N.D. Tex. 1980); Missouri State High School Activities Ass'n v. Schoenlaub, 507 S.W. 2d 354 (Mo. 1974).
163. Smith v. Crim, 240 S.E.2d 884 (Ga. 1977). *See also* DeKalb County School System v. White, 260 S.E.2d 853 (Ga. 1979).
164. Alabama High School Athletic Ass'n v. Medders, 456 So. 2d 284 (Ala. 1984).
165. Pennsylvania Interscholastic Athletic Ass'n v. Geisinger, 474 A.2d 62 (Pa. Commw. 1984).
166. Duffley v. New Hampshire Interscholastic Athletic Ass'n, 446 A.2d 462 (N.H. 1982).
167. *See Education Daily*, August 31, 1984, pp. 5–6.
168. Spring Branch Independent School Dist. v. Stamos, 695 S.W.2d 556 (Tex. 1985), *appeal dismissed*, 106 S. Ct. 1170 (1986).
169. Truby v. Broadwater, 332 S.E.2d 284 (W.Va. 1985). *See also* Parish v. NCAA, 506 F.2d 1028 (5th Cir. 1975).
170. Paulson v. Minidoka County School Dist. No. 331, 463 P.2d 935, 938 (Idaho 1970).

171. Board of Educ. v. Sinclair, 222 N.W.2d 143 (Wis. 1974); Granger v. Cascade County School Dist., 499 P.2d 780 (Mont. 1972).
172. Hartzell v. Connell, 679 P.2d 35 (Cal. 1984).
173. Attorney General v. East Jackson Public Schools, 372 N.W.2d 638 (Mich. App. 1985).
174. *Education Week*, May 2, 1984, p. 17.
175. *See* Kite v. Marshall, 661 F.2d 1027 (5th Cir. 1981), *cert. denied*, 457 U.S. 1120 (1982); Eastern New York Youth Soccer Ass'n v. New York State Public High School Athletic Ass'n, 490 N.E.2d 538 (N.Y. 1986); University Interscholastic League v. North Dallas Chamber of Commerce Soccer Ass'n, 693 S.W.2d 513 (Tex. App. 1985); Kubiszyn v. Alabama High School Athletic Ass'n, 374 So. 2d 256 (Ala. 1979).
176. *See* The Florida High School Activities Ass'n v. Thomas, 434 So. 2d 306 (Fla. 1983).
177. Kampmeier v. Nyquist, 553 F.2d 296 (2d Cir. 1977). *See also* Rettig v. Kent City School Dist., 788 F.2d 328 (6th Cir. 1986) (handicapped student does not have a federal statutory right to be provided with an hour of extracurricular activities each week).
178. Kampmeier v. Harris, 411 N.Y.S.2d 744 (App. Div. 1978). *See also* Wright v. Columbia Univ., 520 F. Supp. 789 (E.D. Pa. 1981); Swiderski v. Board of Educ., City School Dist. of Albany, 408 N.Y.S.2d 744 (Sup. Ct., Albany County, 1978).
179. Grube v. Bethlehem Area School Dist., 550 F. Supp. 418 (E.D. Pa. 1982).

5

Student Classification Practices

"Equal opportunity" is an exalted principle in our democratic heritage, but one that has not been easily translated into concrete school policies and practices. Although twentieth-century educators have asserted that all children should have an equal chance to develop their capabilities, only recently have judicial and legislative bodies addressed the scope of the public school's obligation to realize this goal. Various classification practices have been scrutinized to determine if they have impeded students' access to appropriate instructional programs. After a brief discussion of equal protection mandates in general, this chapter focuses on student classifications based on sex, marriage and pregnancy, age, ability or achievement, handicaps, and native language. Racial classifications in connection with school desegregation are discussed in chapter 13.

EQUAL PROTECTION GUARANTEES

The fourteenth amendment to the United States Constitution provides in part that "no State shall . . . deny to any person within its jurisdiction, the equal protection of the laws."[1] Historically, courts have allowed differential treatment of individuals, as long as the bases for the distinctions were reasonably related to legitimate governmental goals. Since challenged state action usually prevailed under this *rational basis* test, the Warren Supreme Court developed a second equal protection standard to afford greater protection to individuals. If the classification of individuals for differential treatment is considered "suspect" or affects a fundamental interest, evidence of a compelling governmental objective is required to justify the state action. As legislation rarely has withstood analysis under this *strict scrutiny* standard of review, the decision as to which test to apply often has determined the outcome of equal protection cases. In essence, the identification of either a suspect classification or fundamental interest has been the critical factor in shifting the burden of proof to the state to justify its policies.

The Supreme Court has defined fundamental interests as those specifically mentioned in the Constitution, such as freedom of speech, as well as rights that are closely related to constitutional guarantees (i.e., "fundamental" by implication), such as the rights to vote, procreate, and travel.[2] While many lower courts assumed that education was a fundamental interest by implication, in 1973 the Supreme Court delivered a landmark decision, *San Antonio Independent School District v. Rodriguez,* declining to hold that education is among the implied fundamental rights under the Federal Constitution.[3] In this case, plaintiffs alleged that resource inequities across Texas school districts impaired the fundamental right to an education, but the Court majority disagreed. The majority reasoned that challenged state action involving *relative* deprivations in education would trigger only the rational basis equal protection test, unless a suspect classification (e.g., race, alienage, or national origin[4]) was implicated. Finding that Texas's scheme for funding education did not create a suspect classification, the Court held that as long as a minimally adequate education was provided for all children, the equal protection clause was satisfied.[5]

In identifying suspect classifications, the Supreme Court has considered factors such as whether the classification is based on an immutable characteristic, whether members of the class are stigmatized, whether there has been a history of discrimination against the class, and whether the class is politically powerless. To date, the judiciary has not declared that classifications based on gender, handicaps, or wealth are "suspect"; thus, state action based on such distinctions has not been subject to the strict scrutiny standard of review.[6]

Because of dissatisfaction with having to choose between the lenient rational basis and the strict scrutiny standards, an intermediate test for evaluating equal protection claims emerged during the Burger Supreme Court era. While declining to expand the category of suspect classes and fundamental interests, the Court has invalidated state action that traditionally would have withstood analysis under the rational basis test. The Court has required classifications affecting important individual interests to be substantially related to advancing significant governmental objectives.[7] Under this intermediate standard, state-imposed classifications must be necessary, not merely convenient, to achieve important governmental goals, and the Court has invalidated classification schemes if there have been reasonable, less restrictive means of reaching the same goal.[8]

In 1982 the Supreme Court in *Plyler v. Doe* invoked the intermediate standard in reviewing a Texas law that allowed school systems to deny undocumented alien children public schooling.[9] Unlike the *Rodriguez* case, which involved relative deprivations of education, *Plyler* involved the total exclusion of a class of students. Because of the vital role of education to individuals and to the maintenance of society, the Court ruled that such a discriminatory classification could be upheld only if it furthered a substantial goal of the state. The state advanced several objectives for denying schooling to illegal alien children, such as preserving the state's financial resources, protecting the state from an influx of unlawful immigrants, maintaining high quality education for resident children, and excluding children unlikely to remain in the state and contribute to its productivity. The Court found no evidence that the contested law would be an effective method to advance these objectives. Furthermore, any monetary savings that might be realized by denying free schooling to children of illegal aliens were insignificant compared to the costs to these children, the state, and the nation. Accordingly, the Court concluded that the state was unable to meet its burden of demonstrating that the classification advanced a substantial public interest.

In addition to constitutional protections, equal opportunity rights are guaranteed through various federal and state laws. These laws focus on classifications based on race, sex, national origin, age, religion, handicaps, and alienage. In many instances the laws create new substantive rights that are more extensive than constitutional guarantees. Among the significant laws discussed in this chapter are Title VI of the Civil Rights Act of 1964 (barring discrimination on the basis of race, color, or national origin in federally assisted programs), the Equal Educational Opportunities Act (guaranteeing all children equal educational opportunity without regard to race, color, sex, or national origin), Title IX of the Education Amendments of 1972 (prohibiting sex discrimination in federally assisted educational programs), Section 504 of the Rehabilitation Act (prohibiting discrimination against otherwise qualified handicapped individuals in programs receiving federal financial assistance), and the Education for All Handicapped Children Act (providing funds to ensure a free appropriate public education for handicapped children).

How are these equal protection guarantees applied to public education? It might appear from a literal translation of "equality" that once a state establishes an educational system, all students must be treated in the same manner. Courts, however, have recognized that individuals are different and that equal treatment of unequals can have negative consequences. Accordingly, valid classification practices, designed to enhance the educational experiences of children by recognizing their unique needs, generally have been accepted as a legitimate prerogative of educators. Indeed, all schools classify students in some fashion, and state laws often specifically authorize school boards to set criteria for student classification schemes. Children are grouped by academic levels, social maturity, athletic ability, sex, age, and many other distinguishing traits. It has been asserted that without these various classifications, the business of public education could not proceed.

While the authority of educators to classify students has not been contested, the bases for certain classifications and the procedures used to make distinctions among students recently have been the focus of substantial litigation. To the extent that school classifications determine a student's access to various types of educational resources, courts and legislatures have looked closely at the practices, particularly if they have an adverse impact on vulnerable minority groups. In some instances, courts have interpreted "equal educational opportunity" as requiring more than neutral treatment of students and have ordered school officials to take affirmative steps to overcome the deficiencies of certain groups of students.[10]

CLASSIFICATIONS BASED ON SEX

The judiciary has been called upon to review a growing number of claims of sex discrimination in public schools, but the applicable principles of law in this area are less settled than are those pertaining to racial discrimination.[11] Sex, like race, is "an immutable characteristic determined solely by the accident of birth,"[12] but the Supreme Court has been reluctant to apply strict judicial scrutiny to sex-based distinctions. In 1973 four justices on the high court argued that sex should be elevated to the status of a suspect class:

> . . . the imposition of special disabilities upon the members of a particular sex because of their sex would seem to violate "the basic concept of our system that legal burdens should bear some relationship to individual responsibility. . . ."[13]

A majority of the Supreme Court, however, has not been persuaded to apply the rigorous equal protection test to sex-based classifications. Hence, the arguments that have been so persuasive in desegregation litigation have been less effective when applied to claims of sex discrimination. Courts, nonetheless, have invalidated gender-based classifications that have not been sufficiently related to the achievement of a valid governmental objective.[14] This section focuses on legal developments pertaining to allegations of sex discrimination in high school athletics and academic programs.

High School Athletics

In the school context, the most publicized sex discrimination litigation has focused on the denial of sports opportunities for female students and sex segregation on interscholastic teams in noncontact and contact sports. Courts have generally ordered school districts to allow female athletes to compete with males in *noncontact* sports if no comparable programs have been available for female students. In one of the first notable cases, the Eighth Circuit Court of Appeals invalidated a policy restricting participation on the interscholastic tennis, track, and cross-country ski teams to male students.[15] The court concluded that the lack of alternative competitive programs for females raised a valid equal protection claim. The court rejected the high school athletic league's contention that relief was inappropriate because participation in interscholastic sports was a privilege and not a right. The court reasoned that whether or not there was an absolute right to engage in interscholastic athletics, female students were denied equal protection of the laws because benefits provided by the state to male students were denied to females. While there have been a few cases to the contrary,[16] most courts have echoed the rationale espoused by the Eighth Circuit Appellate Court in mandating that qualified female students be allowed to participate on interscholastic tennis, track, and other noncontact teams that have traditionally been reserved for male students.[17]

Without question, the most controversial issue involving high school athletics is the participation of males and females together in *contact* sports. Public schools traditionally have not provided teams for each sex in contact sports and thus have denied female students the opportunity to participate on various interscholastic teams in sports such as football and basketball. In recent years, however, plaintiffs have challenged (1) the exclusion of females from varsity contact teams and (2) the provision of sex-segregated teams in certain contact sports.

Several courts have applied the intermediate level equal protection test in determining whether the denial of interscholastic participation on the basis of gender violates the Federal Constitution and have ruled that female students must be provided the opportunity to participate in contact sports either through sex-segregated or coeducational teams. In a recent case, a New York federal district court reviewed a female student's request to try out for the junior varsity football squad.[18] The school district was unable to show that its policy of prohibiting mixed competition served an "important governmental objective." In rejecting the school district's assertion that its policy was necessary to ensure the health and safety of female students, the court noted that no female student was given the opportunity to show that she was as fit, or more fit, than the weakest male member of the team. Such a regulation was found to have no reasonable relation to the achievement of the school's objective of protecting the health of students.[19] A Missouri federal district court also found the objective of ensuring safety to be inadequate to justify exclusion of all female students from the school's football team, especially when all males were eligible regardless of safety considerations.[20] The court further rejected the school district's claim that the goal of maximizing equal athletic opportunities for all students supported denying female students the right to participate in selected sports. Facts of the case did not substantiate the board's concern that coeducational teams would result in male domination of all sports.

A Wisconsin federal district court similarly ruled that female students have the right to compete for positions on traditionally male contact teams.[21] The Wisconsin court declared that once a state undertakes to provide interscholastic competition, such opportunities must be provided to all students on equal terms. The court reasoned that the objective of preventing injury to female athletes was not sufficient to justify the prohibition of coeducational teams in contact sports. In preventing the school district from absolutely denying female students the opportunity to participate in varsity interscholastic competition in certain contact sports, the court noted that school officials had options available other than establishing coeducational teams: Interscholastic competition in these sports could be eliminated for all students, or separate teams for females could be established. The court also recognized that if comparable sex-segregated programs were provided, female athletes could not assert the right to try out for the male team simply because of its higher level of competition arising from the abilities of team members themselves.

Although policies excluding female students from varsity competition in specific sports have been struck down, the provision of sex-segregated contact teams has usually received judicial endorsement. An Illinois federal district court upheld a school district's policy of maintaining separate teams for male and female students in order to maximize the participation of all students in interscholastic sports.[22] The plaintiff student challenged the policy because it did not permit her to engage in the level of competition she needed to fully develop her athletic potential. Based on the fact that most males are better athletes than females, the court found that the maintenance of separate teams was a legitimate means of ensuring female students the opportunity to participate in interscholastic sports. Denying a stay for a preliminary injunction in this case, Justice Stevens noted: "If the classification is reasonable in substantially all of its applications, I do not believe that the general rule can be said to be unconstitutional simply because it appears arbitrary in an individual case."[23] In this case, all parties agreed that male and female teams were equal in most respects (i.e., in terms of funding, facilities, personnel, time, etc.).

Title IX regulations require schools to allow coeducational *noncontact* teams if sex-segregated teams are not provided, but contact sports are excluded from this mandate.[24] Under the regulations, contact sports include "boxing, wrestling, rugby, ice hockey, football, basketball and other sports the purpose or major activity of which involves bodily contact."[25] There is general agreement that the regulation's exclusion of contact sports does not proscribe female participation but merely allows each school the flexibility of determining whether to meet the goal of equal athletic opportunity through single-sex or coeducational teams. In several instances, athletic association rules have limited the options available to school districts by prohibiting coeducational teams. The Sixth Circuit Court of Appeals reviewed a rule of the Ohio High School Athletic Association that prohibited coeducational participation in all contact sports in grades seven through twelve.[26] In this case, a school system that desired to establish coeducational interscholastic basketball teams at the middle school level challenged the athletic association's rule. The appeals court, noting that compliance with Title IX rests with individual schools and not with athletic associations, concluded that the rule impermissibly restricted the discretion of school systems to provide equal athletic opportunities for female students. The court, however, emphasized that its ruling did not mean that all teams must be coeducational or that Title IX's regulations were unconstitutional because they permitted separate teams.[27]

While most courts have reasoned that school districts can satisfy their legal obligations by providing comparable, sex-segregated contact teams, a few courts have ruled that *all* teams must be open to both sexes. The Supreme Court of Pennsylvania relied on the state's equal rights amendment in ruling that females must be allowed to compete with males in all contact sports, including football and wrestling.[28] The court noted that even if women's teams are available, female athletes are denied the opportunity to reach their full potential when they are limited to playing on such teams, which usually offer a lower level of competition.

In addition to challenging their exclusion from varsity contact teams, female athletes have contested the use of sex-based modifications in sports. The Sixth Circuit Court of Appeals addressed the legality of split-court rules for women's basketball, finding that the different rules were legitimate because of the differences between the sexes in physical characteristics and capabilities.[29] The court found that there was no equal protection violation simply because basketball rules were tailored to accommodate differences between male and female athletes. An Oklahoma federal court followed the Sixth Circuit Appellate Court's reasoning,[30] but an Arkansas federal district court invalidated the use of separate rules for males and females as lacking a rational basis.[31] Noting that tradition was the only justification offered for the differential treatment, the Arkansas court concluded that the practice violated equal protection rights. According to a policy statement issued by the Department of Health, Education, and Welfare (now the Department of Education), Title IX allows split-court rules for women's basketball. The law requires schools to offer *comparable* athletic opportunities, but *not identical versions* of a single sport.[32] It follows that the provision of a softball team for females and a baseball team for males would be legally permissible under Title IX.

Separate playing seasons for women's and men's teams were challenged as a violation of the equal protection clause in a Minnesota case. The state supreme court found the scheduling decision permissible based on the fact that the school districts lacked adequate tennis and swimming facilities to accommodate both teams and that one season was not substantially better than the other. While upholding the separation of playing seasons, the court emphasized that treatment of both teams must be "as nearly equal as possible";[33] a practice that benefited males at the expense of females would not be condoned. Furthermore, the court noted that it was not ruling on the constitutionality of separate seasons where adequate facilities were available. Similarly, a Montana federal district court held that the state athletic association's scheduling of girls' basketball and volleyball seasons contrary to national norms did not violate the equal protection clause or Title IX.[34] Scheduling of the seasons was found to be substantially related to maximizing student participation and availability of coaches, officials, and facilities.

The majority of the suits alleging sex discrimination in high school athletics have been initiated by women, but a few male students have asserted their right to compete for positions on all-female teams. While conflicting opinions have been rendered on this issue, it appears that males may be barred from these teams if their participation impedes athletic opportunities of females. The Ninth Circuit Court of Appeals upheld an Arizona interscholastic association policy prohibiting males from playing on women's teams even though females were permitted to play on men's teams.[35] The court concluded that the policy was related to the important governmental objectives of achieving equal athletic opportunities for women and redressing past discrimination against them. According to the court, permitting males to participate on women's teams would thwart the realization of these legitimate goals; males would dominate women's teams because of their physiological advantage.

Academic Programs

Allegations of sex bias in public schools have not been confined to athletic programs. Differential treatment of males and females in academic courses and schools also has generated litigation. While the "separate but equal" principle has been applied in this area, as it has in athletics, recent litigation indicates that public school officials must bear the burden of showing exceedingly persuasive justification for classifications based on sex in academic programs.

In a significant 1976 case, *Vorchheimer v. School District of Philadelphia,* the Third Circuit Court of Appeals held that the operation of sex-segregated public high schools, in which enrollment is voluntary and educational offerings are essentially equal, is permissible under the equal protection clause of the fourteenth amendment and the Equal Educational Opportunities Act of 1974.[36] The court distinguished *Vorchheimer* from prior decisions in which sex-based classifications had been invalidated because of the absence of a rational basis for differential treatment disadvantaging one sex. Noting that Philadelphia's sex-segregated college preparatory schools offered functionally equivalent programs, the court concluded that the separation of the sexes was justified because adolescents may study more effectively in single-sex high schools. The appellate court reiterated that "gender has never been rejected as an impermissible classification in all instances."[37] The court also emphasized that the female plaintiff was not compelled to attend the sex-segregated academic school; she had the option of enrolling in a coeducational school within her attendance zone. Furthermore, the court stated that her petition to attend the male academic high school was based on personal preference rather than on an objective evaluation of the offerings available in the two schools.[38] Subsequently, the United States Supreme Court, equally divided, affirmed this decision without delivering an opinion.

In 1982, however, the Supreme Court struck down a nursing school's admission policy that limited admission in degree programs to women.[39] In this situation, there were not comparable sex-segregated programs, but rather the denial of opportunities to members of one sex. While the Court acknowledged that sex-based classifications may be justified in limited circumstances when a particular sex has been disproportionately burdened, it rejected the university's contention that its admission policy was to compensate for past discrimination against women. The Court found no evidence that women had ever been denied opportunities in the field of nursing that would justify remedial action by the state.

Like sex-segregated programs and schools, sex-based *criteria for admission* have been challenged, and courts have used constitutional grounds in voiding standards that blatantly disadvantage either sex.[40] For example, the admission practices of the Boston Latin Schools were invalidated because they discriminated against female applicants.[41] Because of the different seating capacities of the two schools, the Latin School for males required a lower score on the entrance examination than did the school for females. While sanctioning the operation of sex-segregated schools, the federal district court was unsympathetic to the physical plant problems and ruled that the same entrance requirements had to be applied to both sexes. Similarly, the Ninth Circuit Court of Appeals concluded that a school district's plan to admit an equal number of male and female students to a high school with an advanced college preparatory curriculum violated equal protection guarantees because it resulted in stricter admission criteria for female applicants.[42] The appellate court rejected the assertion that the school district's admission policy was a legitimate means of reaching its admittedly desirable goal of balancing the number of male and female students enrolled in the school.

Courts have not sanctioned *unequal* educational opportunities for males and females. Female students have been successful in gaining admission to specific courses that have traditionally been offered only to males. For example, the exclusion of female students from auto mechanics classes, wood shop, and metal shop has been invalidated as a denial of equal protection guarantees.[43] Also, courts have required industrial arts and home economics classes to be made available to male and female students on equal terms.[44]

While most cases challenging the exclusion of one sex from specific curricular offerings have been settled on constitutional grounds, Title IX regulations prohibit sex-segregated health, industrial arts, business, vocational-technical, home economics, and music classes in educational programs that receive federal funds. These regulations also ban sex discrimination in counseling and sex-based course requirements for graduation (e.g., home economics for females and industrial arts for males). Separate physical education classes also are prohibited under Title IX, although students may be grouped by skill levels.[45]

Sex-segregated student clubs also may be subject to challenge. The Fifth Circuit Court of Appeals found that a prestigious all-male honor society at a university violated Title IX because it had a pervasive discriminatory effect upon women.[46] Since the honor society represented the "best" in achievement and commanded respect campus-wide, the appellate court found any continued association with the university to be impermissible. Although sex-segregated honoraries have not been prevalent at the high school level, some schools have maintained sex-segregated extracurricular clubs, and the legality of the practice seems doubtful.

Unresolved Questions

Many diverse issues have been raised in these sex-bias suits, and claims of sex discrimination in academic as well as athletic programs seem destined to generate additional litigation. While the doctrine of "separate but equal" remains viable in a number of areas, courts are not in agreement as to the *type* of equality required under constitutional or statutory provisions. Questions such as the following persist: Are sex-segregated varsity teams in noncontact and contact sports comparable if they have different levels of competition? What criteria should be used to gauge the equality between sex-segregated academic programs and/or schools? Under what circumstances is sex segregation unjustified, even if comparable opportunities are provided for both sexes? In the absence of a federal equal rights amendment, it appears that the Supreme Court will eventually have to address these questions and take a stand on the nature of sex equality required in public education.

CLASSIFICATIONS BASED ON MARRIAGE AND PREGNANCY

Legal principles governing the rights of married and pregnant students have changed dramatically since 1960. The evolution of the law in this area is indicative of the increasing judicial commitment to protect students from unjustified classifications that limit educational opportunities.

Married Students

Historically, courts have sanctioned differential treatment of married students in public education. In 1957 the Supreme Court of Tennessee upheld a school regulation requiring students to withdraw from school for the remainder of the term following their marriage.[47] In the early 1960s, an Ohio regulation barring married students from participation in extracurricular activities was upheld by a common pleas court, because school officials demonstrated that married athletes were often in a position to be idolized and copied by other students.[48] The court concluded that the school's purpose of attempting to curtail underage marriages justified the policy.

During the past decade, however, most courts have rejected the traditional view that students can be denied school attendance or participation in extracurricular activities because of their marital status. The United States Supreme Court has held that the right to marry is "one of the vital personal rights," thereby requiring classifications affecting this right to be justified by a compelling state interest.[49] A Kentucky appeals court declared that a policy excluding married students from school was arbitrary, unrelated to the school's asserted purpose, and a denial of the students' right to obtain an education.[50] In 1972 an Ohio federal court held that married students were entitled to equal treatment in all aspects of public education, including school-related activities. The court recognized extracurricular functions as "an integral part" of the total school program and declared that the Federal Constitution prohibited discrimination against married students in any school offerings.[51] Similarly, a Tennessee federal district court held that school regulations preventing married students from participating in extracurricular activities unconstitutionally infringed upon the students' right to marry and right to attend school.[52] Other courts have invalidated the exclusion of married students from extracurricular activities on the rationale that once a state establishes such programs, it cannot exclude a certain class of students without showing a compelling state interest.[53]

Pregnant Students

School regulations that deny pregnant students an education or discriminate against such students have been questioned by litigation grounded in the fourteenth amendment, Title IX, and state laws.[54] Since the latter part of the 1960s, courts have generally placed the burden on school officials to demonstrate that any differential treatment of pregnant students is absolutely necessary for health reasons. In an illustrative Massachusetts case, the federal district court held that school authorities could not exclude a pregnant, unmarried student from regular high school classes.[55] School officials had proposed that the pregnant student be allowed to use all school facilities, attend school functions, participate in senior activities, and receive assistance from teachers in continuing her studies. However, she was not to attend school during regular school hours. Since there was no evidence of any educational or medical reason for this special treatment, the court held that the pregnant student had a constitutional right to attend classes with other pupils. Similarly, a Texas civil appeals court invalidated a public school rule that prohibited married mothers from attending regular classes.[56] The only alternative available to the excluded students was to attend adult education classes, for which one had to be at least twenty-one years of age. The appeals court ruled that such a policy violated pregnant students' entitlement to free public schooling.

While most litigation has involved constitutional claims, the Supreme Court has held that classifications based on pregnancy do not constitute sex discrimination under the equal protection clause.[57] Accordingly, Title IX may afford greater protection to pregnant students in curricular as well as extracurricular activities.[58] Title IX's regulations specifically provide that recipients of federal funds cannot condition program admission or participation on parental status. Enforcement of Title IX, however, is restricted to specific programs receiving federal financial assistance.[59]

It would appear that any denial of equal opportunities to married and pregnant students must be justified by an overriding educational objective. While school districts may offer special courses designed to address pregnant students' unique needs (e.g., instruction in child care), such students should not be forced to enroll in special classes that segregate them from other pupils. In addition, courts have held that pregnant students cannot be relegated to evening programs that offer limited instruction or require fees for academic courses.[60] Restrictions placed on pregnant, unwed students for reasons that are not grounded in valid health or safety considerations (e.g., alleged lack of moral character) will no longer be tolerated by courts.[61]

CLASSIFICATIONS BASED ON AGE

Age is one of the factors most commonly used to classify individuals, not only in schools but also in society in general. A specified age is used as a prerequisite to obtaining a driver's license, buying alcoholic beverages, and voting in state and national elections. Age is also used to classify individuals for employment eligibility (e.g., child labor laws) and for mandatory retirement. Discrimination based on age has generated more litigation in connection with employees[62] than with elementary and secondary pupils, but a few public school situations have evoked legal challenges.

It is generally accepted that a specified age can be used as a school entrance requirement, as a criterion for compulsory education, and as a condition for participation in certain extracurricular activities. Students below or above state-established age limits for school enrollment do not have a constitutional right to school attendance, but most states allow attendance outside the specified statutory ages. For example, under Pennsylvania law, students between the ages of six and twenty-one must be provided a free public education, and school systems *may* provide kindergarten programs for children between the ages of four and six. A Pennsylvania commonwealth court recently held that since education is not mandated for children below the age of six, no constitutionally protected property interest exists, and a child under six can thus be excluded from kindergarten without a formal hearing.[63] In an earlier Pennsylvania case, a school district refused to admit a potential kindergarten student who did not meet the school district's minimum-age requirement.[64] The student's birthday was in October, and the policy stipulated that all students had to be five years old by September 1 to enroll in kindergarten. The state court upheld the board's age classification as rationally related to a legitimate educational purpose.

In a Maine case, the controversy focused on a state law rather than a school board policy. Parents contested a statute that required all children entering first grade to be six years old by October 15.[65] It was asserted that the student, whose birthday fell short of the deadline by over two months, was academically ready for first grade and that he would lose interest in school if denied admission. Nonetheless, the federal court upheld the school board in enforcing the state's minimum-age law. The court relied on evidence that substantiated a correlation between chronological age and school readiness in concluding that the law had a reasonable educational basis and, therefore, was constitutionally sound. Furthermore, the court noted the prohibitive costs that would be involved in making such a determination of readiness for each individual child.

Not all controversies over age restrictions have focused on policies pertaining to school entrance. In New York City, parents challenged the refusal of school authorities to admit their son to a two-year special progress class conducted at his junior high school.[66] The student had completed elementary school and was academically qualified for the program, but was denied admission because he was six months younger than the required age. The special progress classes were accelerated to cover the regular three-year junior high school curriculum in two years. The board asserted that the age requirement for admission to the special class was justified because younger students needed an additional year at the junior high school level in order to develop emotionally, socially, and physiologically. The New York court upheld the requirement, concluding that "to thrust a youngster into an environment where all his classmates are older may result in the consequent impairment of the necessary social integration of the child with his classmates."[67] The court further emphasized that actions of school officials, taken in the best interests of students, should not be disturbed by the judiciary as long as such administrative determinations are reasonable.

Age also is one of the criteria used to determine entitlement to special services and programs under the Education for All Handicapped Children Act. The federal law mandates that services must be available for all children between the ages of three and twenty-one, but does not require a school district to provide programs for handicapped children under the state's minimum school age unless programs are being provided for nonhandicapped children in this age group.[68] Concomitantly, if services are provided for nonhandicapped students beyond eighteen years of age, handicapped students are entitled to similar opportunities. The Tenth Circuit Court of Appeals recently held that services to handicapped children could not be limited to twelve years when nonhandicapped children routinely were allowed to repeat grades.[69] Generally, handicapped students cannot demand tuition-free services beyond the statutory limit of twenty-one years of age.[70]

Courts have not concluded that the Federal Constitution requires governmental action to reflect an "age blind" society. The judiciary has recognized the unique characteristics of childhood in sanctioning reasonable age restrictions on students' acitivities, as long as age-based classifications are related to valid educational objectives.

CLASSIFICATIONS BASED ON ABILITY OR ACHIEVEMENT

Courts have upheld decisions related to grade placement, denial of promotion, and assignment to instructional groups as rationally related to providing students instruction that is most appropriate to their abilities and needs.[71] It is claimed that ability grouping permits more effective and efficient teaching by allowing teachers to concentrate their efforts on students with similar needs. While ability grouping is clearly permissible, some legal challenges have focused on the use of standardized intelligence and achievement tests for determining pupil placements in regular classes and special education programs. These suits have alleged that such tests are racially and culturally biased, and that their use to classify pupils often results in erroneous placements that stigmatize the children involved. Other challenges have arisen regarding the rights of gifted and talented students to an appropriate education. Advocates for gifted and talented students have maintained that the needs of these students have not been addressed by state and federal governments.

Tracking Schemes

In the most widely publicized case pertaining to ability grouping, *Hobson v. Hansen,* the use of standardized intelligence test scores to place students in various ability tracks in Washington, D.C., was attacked as unconstitutional.[72] Plaintiffs contended that some children were erroneously assigned to lower tracks and had very little chance of advancing to higher tracks because of the limited curriculum and the absence of remedial instruction. The federal district court closely examined the test scores used to assign students to the various tracks, analyzed the accuracy of the test measurements, and concluded that mistakes often resulted from assigning pupils to instructional programs on this basis. For the first time, a federal court evaluated testing methods and concluded that they discriminated against minority children. In prohibiting the continuation of ability-grouping schemes that resulted in segregation, the court emphasized that it was *not* abolishing the use of track systems *per se*: "[W]hat is at issue here is not whether defendants are entitled to provide different kinds of students with different kinds of education."[73] The court noted that classifications reasonably related to educational purposes are constitutionally permissible unless they result in discrimination against identifiable groups of children.

Ability grouping also has been invalidated in school systems with a history of purposeful segregation. Two years after *Hobson,* the Fifth Circuit Court of Appeals reviewed the legality of a Jackson, Mississippi tracking scheme.[74] The court struck down the plan and held that students could not be placed in classes on the basis of standardized test scores until a desegregated school district had been established to the court's satisfaction. In a later case, the court emphasized that ability grouping in a school system that has not fully erased a history of segregation may perpetuate the effects of past discrimination. The court noted, however, that "as a general rule, school systems are free to employ ability grouping, even when such a policy has a segregative effect, so long, of course, as such a practice is genuinely motivated by educational concerns and not discriminatory motives."[75]

Based on evidence indicating that ability grouping provided better educational opportunities for black students, the Eleventh Circuit Appellate Court in 1985 upheld grouping practices in several Georgia school districts even though they had not achieved fully unitary systems.[76] Ability grouping allowed targeting of resources for low-achieving students, and its effectiveness was demonstrated by students achieving higher scores on statewide tests and by their reassignment to higher-level achievement groups.[77] The court did note that, unlike students in earlier cases, these students had not attended inferior segregated schools.

Grouping schemes designed to enhance educational opportunities for students are not only permissible, but indeed desirable. While school systems undergoing desegregation may be subjected to closer judicial review when implementing such schemes, ability-grouping plans will be prohibited only if found to be a ploy to resegregate students.[78]

Although ability grouping is permissible, the assessment procedures used in placing students in instructional programs may be vulnerable to legal challenge if racial or cultural bias is shown. Courts have paid particular attention to the use of test scores in assigning students to special education programs because of the adverse effects that an incorrect placement can have on a child's future. Two cases provide the background for the debate on the use of standardized intelligence tests for determining placement of students. In both cases, plaintiffs alleged that standardized intelligence tests used for placement purposes were culturally biased against black children. In a California case, the Ninth Circuit Court of Appeals upheld a federal district court's decision enjoining school authorities from using the results of intelligence tests to place minority students in educable mentally retarded (EMR) classes.[79] The federal district court had concluded that the testimony overwhelmingly demonstrated that the intelligence tests, which were the central element in the placement decisions, were biased against black students and as a result contributed to the disproportionate placement of these students in EMR classes. Since the tests had been standardized for white, middle-class students, school officials were unable to show that they were valid for the placement of black students.

In contrast to the California case, an Illinois federal district court, hearing many of the same expert witnesses, found little evidence of cultural bias in standardized intelligence tests.[80] Instead of reacting to the general issue of cultural bias, the Illinois federal judge reviewed each question on the tests to determine whether test bias existed. The judge concluded that the few instances of cultural bias found in the test items would not significantly affect an individual's score and that the use of these test results in conjunction with other criteria for determining appropriate pupil placements did not discriminate against black students.

While the conclusions reached in these cases were quite different, both courts emphasized that nonbiased assessment procedures must be used.[81] The Ninth Circuit Court of Appeals prohibited intelligence tests as the single criterion for placement in special education programs; the Illinois court upheld the use of intelligence tests but as only one element in the assessment process for placement. State and federal laws regarding the rights of handicapped children reinforce that screening procedures for special education placements must be culturally and racially nondiscriminatory.[82] These laws stipulate that tests must be administered in the child's native language, validated for the specific purpose for which they are used, administered by trained personnel, and used only in conjunction with other criteria.

Other types of tests used for instructional placement purposes also have generated claims that the instruments are culturally and racially biased, or that they have not been properly validated. As discussed in chapter 3, minimum competency tests have been challenged as violating due process and equal protection rights. While the state's authority to assess student proficiency has been upheld, in some situations the implementation of testing programs has been enjoined because the effects of prior racial discrimination have not been eliminated or students have not been provided adequate notice or preparation for the tests.[83]

Gifted and Talented Students

Often overlooked in assessing the appropriateness of educational programs are students labeled as "gifted and talented." Congress has defined such students as those "possessing demonstrated or potential abilities that give evidence of high performance capability in areas such as intellectual, creative, specific academic, or leadership ability, or in the performing and visual arts, and who by reason thereof, require services or activities not ordinarily provided by the school."[84] While advocates for gifted students assert that the needs of this group require special attention similar to that of other groups such as the handicapped, few state or local education agencies have mandated the identification of these students or the establishment of special education programs for them.

Most of the legal activity in this area has taken place in legislative forums and has focused primarily on the need to provide services. Through the Gifted and Talented Children's Education Act of 1978, the federal government provided limited financial assistance to states attempting to serve these students, but this law was repealed in 1982.[85] Most states have allocated some special categorical funds for the gifted and talented, but in the early 1980s, less than 3 percent of the student population were receiving special services designed for the gifted.[86] This is modest considering estimates that indicate in excess of 10 percent of the school-age population may qualify for special programs for the gifted.

Specific rights of gifted and talented students and the adequacy of programs provided must be interpreted under state laws. In Pennsylvania, for example, the statutory definition of exceptional children includes gifted and talented students who require special education facilities and services. A Pennsylvania commonwealth court interpreted this law as placing a mandatory obligation on school districts to establish appropriate educational programs for gifted students.[87] Furthermore, the court recognized that this duty was not contingent upon state reimbursement for such programs. In a later case, a Pennsylvania court found a school district's weekly enrichment program inadequate to meet the needs of a sixth-grade gifted student and ordered the development of an individualized education program in all areas of the curriculum.[88] Acccording to the court, the appropriateness of a program depends upon whether it meets the identified needs of the child. In this case, the "pull-out" program was not considered sufficient because a significant disparity existed between the child's intellectual ability and his classroom performance.

Similar to Pennsylvania's law, gifted students in Connecticut also are covered by statutory protections pertaining to other categories of exceptional children and are entitled to private school placements if appropriate programs are not available in the public education system.[89] New York law specifically provides that school districts *should* develop programs to assist gifted students in achieving their full potential. An appellate court, however, found that the use of the word "should" indicated that the development of gifted programs was optional, not mandatory.[90] Consequently, the court held that a school district was permitted to serve only a portion of the students identified as gifted and to select those students through a lottery system.

Although litigation has focused primarily on the adequacy of programs under state mandates, students who have not qualified for gifted programs have challenged their exclusion as a violation of the equal protection clause of the fourteenth amendment. For a classification scheme to pass equal protection review, school officials need only show that selection procedures for gifted programs have a rational relationship to their objective of identifying gifted students since a suspect classification or a fundamental right is not affected. In two cases, a Pennsylvania federal district court held that the use of a standardized test or high IQ scores to identify gifted students did not infringe on students' constitutional rights.[91] While weaknesses can be noted in the two methods, the court found both procedures reasonably related to the school district's objective of providing special opportunities to develop the abilities of gifted students.

There have been few lawsuits asserting the rights of gifted pupils, but such litigation seems destined to escalate in light of the legal activity pertaining to other types of exceptional children. In an unsuccessful Illinois suit, parents asked for injunctive relief and $1 million dollars in damages because of the school district's alleged failure to meet the needs of their son, who had a measured intelligence of 170.[92] Noting the discrepancy in state funds supplied to local school districts for handicapped pupils and for gifted students ($162 million compared with $3.6 million), the parents alleged that gifted students were being denied their right to be educated to the maximum level of their ability. Although the state court dismissed the case, it appears that other suits will be initiated challenging the disproportionate appropriation of funds to serve handicapped versus gifted students.

CLASSIFICATIONS BASED ON HANDICAPS

Since handicapped children represent a vulnerable minority group, the treatment of these children has aroused much judicial and legislative concern. Courts have addressed the constitutional rights of handicapped children to attend school and to be classified accurately and instructed appropriately. Federal and state laws have further clarified the rights of handicapped students and have provided funds to assist school districts in meeting the special needs of these children.

Legal Framework

No firm precedent has been established by the United States Supreme Court regarding handicapped children's constitutional right to a public education, but several lower courts have addressed the question. Two decisions rendered in the early 1970s define the basic contours of the constitutional protections afforded such children. The first case was initiated in Pennsylvania, challenging the constitutionality of a state law that allowed school systems to exclude handicapped children from school.[93] The case resulted in a consent agreement stating that handicapped children could not be denied admission to public school programs or have their educational status changed without procedural due process. The agreement further stipulated that each mentally retarded child must be placed in a free public program of education and training appropriate to the child's capacity.

A District of Columbia case followed the principle established in the Pennsylvania agreement and expanded the right to an appropriate public education beyond the mentally retarded to all other children alleged to be suffering from mental, behavioral, emotional, or physical deficiencies.[94] Moreover, the court held that public interest in conserving funds could not justify the denial of an education to a certain class of students. The court also ordered school officials to adhere to stringent due process procedures in pupil assignments, and stated that any change affecting a student's instructional program for as much as two days had to be accompanied by some type of hearing to give parents an opportunity to contest the placement.

Litigation similar to the Pennsylvania and District of Columbia cases was initiated in many states during the 1970s, and the basic right of each handicapped child to receive a public education was consistently upheld by courts. The Supreme Court's 1973 *Rodriguez* decision lent support to the contention that the total exclusion of selected children, such as the handicapped, from public schools would not withstand constitutional scrutiny. Although stating that the right to an education is not an inherent fundamental right, the Court conceded that "some identifiable quantum of education'' may be constitutionally protected.[95] Subsequently, in the *Plyler* decision, the Court refused to raise education to a fundamental right but did apply a higher level of scrutiny in determining that a class of students (undocumented alien children) could not be excluded from public schools.[96] The judiciary, however, to date has not found that handicapped children are a ''suspect class'' or that they have any ''fundamental right'' to a particular level of education. The basic legal principle that has evolved from constitutional challenges is that handicapped children must have access to a public education; school systems cannot exclude them.

As often happens, legislation has paralleled court decisions regarding the rights of handicapped children. While constitutional suits have been instrumental in focusing attention on the plight of handicapped students, state and federal laws have defined the specific rights of such students and the responsibilities and duties of public schools and have provided a basis for relief. Two pieces of federal legislation, in particular, have altered the role of public school personnel. Section 504 of the Rehabilitation Act of 1973 prohibits the recipients of any federal financial assistance from discriminating against an otherwise qualified handicapped person solely because of the handicap.[97] Public Law 94–142, the Education for All Handicapped Children Act (EAHCA) of 1975, provides federal funds to assist state and local education agencies in offering appropriate educational programs for handicapped children.[98] In essence, Section 504 is a civil rights law that stipulates what *cannot* be done in the treatment of handicapped individuals; the EAHCA contains a blueprint of what *can* be done to upgrade educational opportunities for handicapped children.

Under Section 504, a handicapped individual is one ''who has a physical or mental impairment which substantially limits one or more of such person's major life activities.''[99] For employment purposes, alcohol and drug addiction are specifically excluded from the definition of ''handicapped,'' but under a recent Office for Civil Rights ruling, such student addictions are considered physical or mental impairments.[100] While the law is not explicit on chronic diseases, several courts have ruled that students with acquired immune deficiency syndrome (AIDS) and hepatitus B are handicapped and thus are protected against discriminatory treatment by Section 504.[101]

Section 504 is more global than the EAHCA and applies to educational and noneducational agencies receiving any type of federal assistance. It prohibits discrimination against handicapped persons in postsecondary education and requires public school agencies to provide appropriate educational services for all handicapped children. It also bars recipients of federal funds from discriminating against otherwise qualified handicapped persons in recruitment, selection, compensation, job assignment and classification, and fringe benefits. Where rights are guaranteed by both Section 504 and the EAHCA, an individual initiating a claim under Section 504 must exhaust the administrative procedures required under the EAHCA prior to filing court action.[102]

States have the option of declining to participate in the EAHCA funding program, but they still must comply with Section 504's antidiscrimination mandate, which has been interpreted as requiring school districts to provide appropriate educational programs for handicapped children.[103] Consequently, all states currently participate in the EAHCA assistance program and must adhere to the law's regulations as a condition of receiving aid. Among the major provisions of the law are the following:

- States must institute a comprehensive program to identify all handicapped children within the state. Under the act, handicapped children include those who are "mentally retarded, hard of hearing, deaf, speech impaired, visually impaired, or other health impaired children, or children with specific learning disabilities, who by reason thereof require special education and related services."[104]
- No handicapped child is to be excluded from an appropriate public education (zero reject).
- Individualized education programs must be developed for all handicapped children.
- Policies and procedures must be established to safeguard due process rights of parents and children.
- Handicapped children must be placed in the least restrictive educational setting, which means educating handicapped children with nonhandicapped children to the extent appropriate.
- Nondiscriminatory tests and other materials must be used in evaluating a child's level of achievement for placement purposes.
- Parents must have access to their child's records, and the confidentiality of such information must be respected.
- Comprehensive personnel development programs, which include in-service training for regular and special education teachers and ancillary personnel, must be established.
- One state agency must be accountable for ensuring that all provisions of the law are properly implemented by other agencies in the state serving handicapped children.

Federal handicapped persons' laws have generated substantial litigation, and the rights guaranteed under these laws continue to be clarified. The following sections address specific statutory rights related to a free appropriate education, procedural safeguards, least restrictive environment, private placements, related services, extended school year, discipline of handicapped children, and legal remedies for violations of protected rights.

Free Appropriate Public Education

Under the EAHCA, states must assure that all handicapped children have the right to a free appropriate public education (FAPE). An appropriate education is one that is designed to meet the unique needs of each child and includes special education and related services. In the law, "special education" refers to "specially designed instruction, at no cost to parents or guardians, to meet the unique needs of a handicapped child, including classroom instruction, instruction in physical education, home instruction, and instruction in hospitals and institutions." [105] These services must be provided for handicapped children between the ages of three and twenty-one, unless services are not provided for nonhandicapped children under or over regular school age.[106]

The central element of a free appropriate public education is the development of a written individualized education program (IEP) identifying the child's needs, annual instructional goals and objectives, specific educational services to be provided, and evaluation procedures. This program must be jointly prepared by school officials and the child's parents and must be reviewed at least annually. Lack of agreement between school officials and parents in the development or revision of the program is resolved through impartial due process hearings.

A continuing issue before the judiciary has been what level of educational services meets the FAPE requirement. Is it an optimum program to maximize a child's learning potential or a minimum program to assure equal educational opportunity? The United States Supreme Court's interpretation of this provision in 1982 has been significant in shaping handicapped students' rights.

In *Board of Education of the Hendrick Hudson Central School District v. Rowley,* the parents of Amy Rowley, a deaf student with minimal residual hearing, had requested that the school district provide a sign language interpreter for the child in her academic classes.[107] Amy's IEP specified a regular first-grade placement with special instruction from a tutor for the deaf one hour per day and a speech therapist three hours per week. Based on the advice of the IEP committee and others familiar with Amy's program, school officials concluded that an interpreter was unnecessary since Amy was achieving at an above-average level. Upon judicial review, the federal district court and appellate court concluded that Amy had been denied a free appropriate public education because of the disparity between her academic potential and her achievement level. According to the lower courts, an appropriate educational program is one that maximizes the potential of handicapped children "commensurate with the opportunity provided to other children." [108]

In rejecting the lower courts' definition of "appropriate," the Supreme Court did not provide a specific substantive educational standard but rather noted that access should be meaningful. The Court reasoned that "the intent of the Act was more to open the door of public education to handicapped children on appropriate terms than to guarantee any particular level of education once inside." [109] The Court concluded that there was a "basic floor of opportunity" guaranteed by the EAHCA. In the Court's words, that floor would consist of an education "sufficient to confer some educational benefits," that is, "access to specialized instruction and related services which are individually designed to provide educational benefit to the handicapped child." [110] Applying these principles, the Court held that Amy was receiving an appropriate education. She was receiving educational benefit from personalized instruction and related services, as evidenced by her better-than-average performance in class.

The standard of judicial review established in *Rowley* has been controlling in subsequent litigation. According to the Supreme Court, the role of courts in reviewing the appropriateness of educational programs under the EAHCA is not to define what is an appropriate education. Rather, the review is limited to a twofold inquiry: Has the state complied with procedures identified in the EAHCA, and is the IEP developed through these procedures "reasonably calculated to enable the child to receive educational benefits"? [111] If school systems satisfy these requirements, "courts can require no more." [112]

Following *Rowley,* courts have been reluctant to respond to parental demands for optimum programs where school systems are providing individualized programs resulting in educational benefits. For example, New York parents were unsuccessful in demanding that their educable mentally retarded child be taught in a class with a teacher/pupil ratio of six-to-one or less to assure maximum achievement.[113] The Second Circuit Appellate Court held that the central issue was whether educational benefits would be received in a placement with a ratio of twelve-to-one, not whether a ratio of six-to-one provided a better education.

The Rhode Island Federal District Court concluded that while a residential placement might be the most effective placement for a specific handicapped child, the program proposed by the school district met the EAHCA's FAPE requirement.[114] Similarly, Maryland parents were unsuccessful in asserting that a private placement was more appropriate than the proposed public school placement because it involved less commuting time and greater opportunity to associate with nonhandicapped children.[115] Relying on *Rowley,* the appellate court concluded that parents must specifically allege that the proposed program is inadequate. The court noted that because the requested program is *more* appropriate, it does not follow that the recommended program is inappropriate.

In addition to federal laws, all states have statutes or administrative regulations granting handicapped children specific rights. While most state mandates parallel federal requirements, some place additional obligations on school districts in connection with ensuring a free appropriate education. When legal challenges to state laws have been filed in federal courts, questions have arisen regarding the authority of the federal judiciary to enforce state requirements. In 1984 the Supreme Court ruled that under the eleventh amendment federal courts cannot enforce state law claims.[116] Specifically, the Court held that if a federal court granted relief on the basis of state law, it would constitute a significant intrusion on state sovereignty in direct conflict with the eleventh amendment.

Following this decision, uncertainty has existed as to whether state mandates that exceed the EAHCA requirements can be enforced in federal courts. Two federal appellate courts have ruled that the EAHCA obligates districts to comply with state standards that go beyond the EAHCA requirements pertaining to appropriate services for handicapped students. In reviewing enforcement of state claims, these courts have avoided the eleventh amendment strictures by concluding that the federal language and legislative history of the EAHCA "intertwined federal and state standards into one body of law."[117] The First Circuit Court of Appeals noted that "Congress explicitly defined a free appropriate education as an education which 'meets the standards of the state education agency' and expressly authorized review of the question whether the education actually provided (or proposed) met those standards."[118] The Third Circuit Court of Appeals noted the incongruity that would result if Congress allowed the level of a child's education to depend on whether parents challenged a district's program in state or federal courts.[119]

Handicapped children's entitlement to a free appropriate public education also has been controversial in connection with state-mandated minimum competency testing (MCT) programs. As discussed in chapter 3, several courts have rejected the assertion that conditioning the receipt of a high school diploma on passage of a competency test denies handicapped students their right to a FAPE.[120] Relying on *Rowley,* courts have concluded that the intent of the EAHCA is to guarantee access to specialized educational services, not to require "specific results." Courts have not been persuaded that handicapped students are entitled to a high school diploma based on completion of their IEP objectives if nonhandicapped students must satisfy other requirements such as passage of an MCT. Since the students in these cases had been receiving the special education and related services required under the EAHCA, the use of an MCT as a prerequisite to receipt of a regular high school diploma has not been considered a denial of an appropriate educational program. Similarly, claims that an MCT requirement is unlawful discrimination under Section 504 have been rejected; Section 504 entitles the individual to equal opportunities (e.g., accommodations in test administration), but not to equal results.

Procedural Safeguards

Extensive procedural safeguards are identified in the EAHCA to ensure appropriate identification, evaluation, and placement of handicapped children. Prior to the evaluation of a child, parents must be informed of their procedural rights, including a description of the process and procedures. This includes the opportunity to examine the child's records and to obtain an independent educational evaluation of the child. If parents are dissatisfied with the classification of their child or the proposed IEP, they have the right to an impartial due process hearing to present complaints at the local and state levels. After exhausting administrative review, parents may seek judicial review of the state administrative decision. The elaborate procedural safeguards mandated in the EAHCA are central to the goal of assuring handicapped children a free appropriate education through open communication between parents and school officials. Courts have frequently been called upon to interpret these procedural rights and to assess school officials' compliance.

Prior to placement of a handicapped child in a special education program, the EAHCA requires a full evaluation. Federal regulations specify that no single criterion can be used to determine a handicapped child's placement. Pupil assignments must be based on a composite analysis of such data as teacher recommendations, the child's cultural background and adaptive behavior, and test scores. Issues often arise regarding the validity of tests used to evaluate and place students.[121] The EAHCA requires that tests must be validated for the purposes for which they are used, administered in a child's native language by trained personnel, and must consider limitations posed by the child's handicap.

A school district's proposed program for a given child can be rejected solely on the ground that the district failed to comply with mandated evaluation procedures. For example, a New Jersey federal court invalidated a district's proposed IEP for a hearing-impaired child because of serious procedural violations related to the methodology used to formulate the program.[122] The recommendation was based upon simple observations; no validated instrument was used to test the child's aptitude; tests focused only on a narrow range of behaviors; procedures used tended to be biased against deaf children; and no member of the evaluation team was an expert in the education of hearing-impaired children.

Extensive procedural safeguards surround any change in a child's placement. The "stay put" or "status quo" provision of the EAHCA provides that "[d]uring the pendency of any proceedings . . . unless the state or local educational agency and the parents or guardian otherwise agree, the child shall remain in the current educational placement of such child. . . ."[123] The purpose of maintaining the current placement is to provide stability and continuity in a child's educational program. While school authorities are prohibited from changing a child's placement for educational reasons during review proceedings, they may be able to alter it without parental consent if the child poses a danger to others or threatens disruption of the educational environment. Relying upon the EAHCA regulations, in 1985 the Fifth Circuit Court of Appeals reasoned that emergency disciplinary procedures could be used where a threat of danger existed.[124] The Ninth Circuit Appellate Court also agreed that emergency or temporary suspensions could be invoked but the "stay-put" provision would be violated if the child is suspended for an indefinite period pending re-evaluation.[125]

Least Restrictive Environment

After agreement has been reached on an individual education program, an appropriate placement must be made at public expense. Alternative placements may include a regular classroom with various support services, a regular classroom supplemented with resource room instruction, self-contained special classes, home instruction, and hospital or institutional instruction. Within this continuum of placements, the child must be educated in the least restrictive environment (LRE). That is, a placement must meet the special needs of the handicapped child and at the same time allow for maximum integration with nonhandicapped children. The EAHCA requires that "to the maximum extent appropriate, handicapped children, including children in public or private institutions or other care facilities, are educated with children who are not handicapped." [126] While this provision does not require that every child be educated in a regular classroom, the judiciary has noted that the term "to the maximum extent appropriate" does indicate a strong congressional preference for mainstreaming.

The Ninth Circuit Court of Appeals noted, however, that mainstreaming "must be balanced with the primary objective of providing handicapped children with an 'appropriate' education." [127] In this case, the court supported the school officials' decision that the neighborhood school was not appropriate because the severity of the child's handicap required instruction by a specially certified teacher. Earlier, the same court held that a proposed homebound program for a child suffering from cystic fibrosis and tracheomalacia did not satisfy the LRE concept.[128] The court found that the child's previous participation and progress in a regular classroom at a private school demonstrated that similar services could be provided in the public school.

In 1983 the Sixth Circuit Court of Appeals advanced guidelines strongly supporting mainstreaming for most handicapped children. In this case, parents of a severely mentally retarded child rejected school officials' recommended placement of their son in a school exclusively for mentally retarded children because it would not allow for contact with nonhandicapped children. According to the appellate court:

> [W]here the segregated facility is considered superior, the court should determine whether the services which make that placement superior could be feasibly provided in a non-segregated setting. If they can, the placement in the segregated school would be inappropriate under the Act.[129]

While favoring mainstreaming, the court stated that the cost of providing such a program is a legitimate consideration; "excessive spending on one handicapped child deprives other handicapped children."[130]

In contrast to the prevailing endorsement of assuring a placement in the LRE, a federal district court, later supported by the Eighth Circuit Court of Appeals, ruled that Missouri's system of separate schools for the severely handicapped does not *per se* violate the EAHCA.[131] While the courts found that the EAHCA procedural placement requirements had been met by the state, the issue of whether an LRE placement is available to each child in the state who might benefit from such a placement was not addressed.

Private Placement

In addition to specifying that placement must be in the LRE, the federal law requires public school districts to place handicapped children in private facilities if an appropriate public placement is unavailable. Conflicting rulings have been rendered as to whether the federal mandate requires school systems to incur all *noneducational* costs, such as medical and custodial expenses, associated with a private residential placement. Although the fiscal obligation placed on school systems can be substantial, courts have generally held that where educational needs necessitate residential placement, a school district or state must cover all costs.[132] The First Circuit Court of Appeals ordered payment of residential costs in a Massachusetts case because twenty-four-hour care, training, and reinforcement were essential for the child to make *any* educational progress.[133] The EAHCA provision for residential care, however, is not intended to compensate for a poor home environment or to serve as a means of delivering other social services; a residential placement is required only when the minimal educational benefits to which a child is entitled cannot be delivered through a day program.

The Seventh Circuit Court of Appeals recently reviewed an Illinois law that required parents on the basis of their incomes to contribute up to $100 a month for living expenses if students were placed in a private facility because of a developmental disability rather than special educational needs.[134] The appellate court noted that living expenses are implied in the EAHCA's authorization of institutional placements and specifically required by the act's regulations. In this instance, the court concluded that the state had carved out a class of handicapped children and had denied them entitlement to full rights under the EAHCA. Developmental disability as defined by Illinois law paralleled the definition of mental retardation in the EAHCA regulations.

In some situations where parents and school authorities have disagreed as to what is an appropriate placement, parents have unilaterally placed their children in private schools prior to exhaustion of the review process. School systems have maintained that violation of the "status quo" principle forecloses later reimbursement to parents for tuition costs. Until 1985 most federal courts held that the EAHCA barred recovery of costs for unilateral changes in placement during pendency of due process proceedings unless exceptional circumstances existed. Such circumstances have included: (1) the current placement posed a danger to the child's health; (2) the school system acted in bad faith by failing to provide procedural safeguards; or (3) the school system failed to provide private placement when clearly warranted.[135]

In 1985 the Supreme Court addressed parental rights in connection with unilateral placement changes in *Burlington School Committee v. Department of Education.*[136] A parent disagreed with the school district's proposed educational placement of his learning-disabled child and, after seeking an independent evaluation from medical experts, enrolled the child in a private school. The Court rejected the school district's argument that a change in placement without the district's consent waived all rights to reimbursement. In the Court's opinion, denying relief would defeat the EAHCA's major objective of providing a free appropriate education. The Court found reimbursement to be necessary relief because the review process can be quite lengthy (eight years in this case); children should not be educationally disadvantaged by an inappropriate placement, nor should parents be economically penalized by removing their children. In rejecting the school board's argument that reimbursement was "damages," which generally are not awarded under the EAHCA, the Court stated that an award of reimbursement of private tuition simply required the school "to belatedly pay expenses that it should have paid all along and would have borne in the first instance had it developed a proper IEP."[137]

One caveat, however, was issued by the Court: Parents who unilaterally seek private placement do so at their own financial risk. If the public school placement is found to be proper, reimbursement would be barred.[138] Parents cannot demand the "best" program; the EAHCA requires only that a program be appropriate.

In the wake of *Burlington,* lower courts have addressed the appropriateness of public school placements and whether reimbursements for private placements are justified. Tuition costs have been awarded when school officials have failed to comply with procedural requirements of the EAHCA or to consider carefully the handicapped student's unique, individual needs.[139] Parents, however, have been denied relief if school systems have followed all procedures set forth in the EAHCA and have designed a program to enable the child to receive educational benefits.[140] The Tenth Circuit Court of Appeals recognized that a private placement selected by parents was superior but relied on *Rowley* in reiterating that the EAHCA does not require an education that maximizes a child's potential.[141] Accordingly, the court upheld the child's placement in the individual multi-handicapped program proposed by the school since it was designed to enable the child to receive educational benefits.

While private placements may not necessarily be required under the EAHCA, several courts have held that they may be mandated under state laws that exceed federal standards. The Third Circuit Court of Appeals held that continuation of a residential placement was required to provide a handicapped student with the "best" opportunity for educational success as required by New Jersey legislation.[142] Substantial evidence supported the private placement: The student regressed when he returned home for more than a week; he was unable to adjust to a less structured school environment; and his communication skills were enhanced where peers used sign language. Similarly, the First Circuit Court of Appeals interpreted a Massachusetts law as requiring a private placement "to assure the maximum possible development of a child with special needs." [143]

Related Services

As noted previously, a free appropriate education under the EAHCA includes both "special education and related services." Related services are defined as:

> transportation, and such developmental, corrective, and other supportive services (including speech pathology and audiology, psychological services, physical and occupational therapy, recreation, and medical and counseling services, except that such medical services shall be for diagnostic and evaluation purposes only) as may be required to assist a handicapped child to benefit from special education . . .[144]

Few controversies have arisen in areas specifically identified in the law, such as transportation, occupational therapy, physical therapy, recreation, and counseling. Transportation must be provided, and as the First Circuit Appellate Court noted, this includes door-to-door transportation.[145] In addition, extracurricular and summer enrichment activities may be required for a child to obtain an appropriate education.[146] Reasonable modifications also must be made in school facilities; in one instance this required that a classroom be air-conditioned.[147]

The most difficult question, however, has involved distinctions between medical and school health services. The EAHCA excludes medical services except for diagnostic and evaluative purposes.[148] Parents, however, have asserted that certain "medical" needs must be addressed to enable handicapped children to benefit from special education.

In 1984 the Supreme Court in *Irving Independent School District v. Tatro* provided some clarification regarding the state's obligation to provide related services to address medical needs.[149] This case involved an eight-year-old handicapped child with spina bifida and a neurogenic bladder, requiring clean intermittent catheterization (CIC) every three to four hours. The federal district court supported the school officials' decision to exclude CIC from the child's IEP because life-support services are not required; only services that arise from the effort to educate a child are mandatory. The Fifth Circuit Court of Appeals, however, disagreed, finding that CIC was required to enable the child to attend school and to benefit from the education she was guaranteed. On appeal, the Supreme Court affirmed the order requiring the school district to provide CIC.

In assessing whether CIC was a related service, the Supreme Court reasoned that "[a] service that enables a handicapped child to remain at school during the day is an important means of providing the child with the meaningful access to education that Congress envisioned."[150] Furthermore, the Court emphasized that such services are "no less related to the effort to educate than are services that enable the child to reach, enter, or exit the school."[151]

In determining whether CIC was a medical service, the Court relied upon the definition of medical and school health services in the EAHCA regulations. Under the regulations, medical services are defined as "services provided by a licensed physician," while health services are categorized as "services provided by a qualified school nurse or other qualified person."[152] Since CIC is a procedure that can be performed by a nurse or a trained layperson, the Court concluded that it was not a medical service qualifying for exclusion under the act.[153]

The Court in *Tatro,* however, recognized specific limitations on the school district's responsibility to provide related services. In addition to specifying that school districts are not required to provide services that must be performed by a physician, the Court stated that students must be classified as handicapped to be entitled to related services, and only services necessary for a child to benefit from special education must be provided. Furthermore, the Court limited its decision to personnel services, implying that services requiring specialized equipment would not be required under the EAHCA.

While the *Tatro* decision provides significant guidance in assessing whether various parental requests are required "related services," psychotherapy is not easily classified. Generally, psychotherapy is provided only by licensed physicians. Yet, the EAHCA specifically includes psychological and counseling services that could be considered part of psychotherapy. Several courts have concluded that psychotherapy is a related service when it is shown to be an integral part of the child's educational program.[154] For example, the New Jersey Federal District Court found that therapeutic services provided to a child in a specialized treatment program could not be separated from his educational program and thus were "an essential service" to enable the child to benefit from the educational program.[155] In contrast, an Illinois federal court classified psychiatric services as medical treatment and refused to require the placement of a handicapped child in a psychiatric hospital.[156] In a later decision, however, the same court held that if psychotherapy and similar psychological services *can* be provided by professionals other than physicians, the mere fact that such services are performed by a psychiatrist does not render them nonreimbursable.[157]

In assessing what related services must be provided by public schools, it appears that the crucial question is not the type of service requested but who provides the service. Services that *must* be performed by licensed physicians are excluded from the services mandated by the EAHCA. In view of the range of medically related services that can be provided by nurses and other paraprofessionals, however, the scope of related services remains extensive.

Extended School Year

Although the Supreme Court has not ruled on parental requests for extended school year programs, four federal appellate courts have held that states cannot restrict available services to the number of days provided nonhandicapped students. These courts have not required year-round instruction for all handicapped children but merely flexibility in state and local policies to permit consideration of a longer school program if needed by a child to attain reasonable education goals. In the first case involving this issue, the Third Circuit Court of Appeals examined a Pennsylvania state education agency policy that limited publicly supported education for all students to 180 days.[158] The court found that this rigid restriction violated the EAHCA because, regardless of a student's unique needs, a longer educational program could not be considered. The Eleventh Circuit Court of Appeals applied similar reasoning, holding that a Georgia statewide policy of limiting instruction to 180 days for handicapped children did not allow for adequate consideration of an individual student's needs.[159] The court stated that its ruling required "no more than that the state *consider* the need for continuous education, along with a range of other concerns, when developing a plan of education . . ." [160] Likewise, the Fifth and Eighth Circuit Appellate Courts held that restrictions precluding consideration of individual needs are impermissible under the EAHCA.[161]

Discipline of Handicapped Children

Disciplinary practices may impair the rights guaranteed to handicapped children under the EAHCA. Specifically, several courts have found expulsions to be changes in placement and thus have prohibited such disciplinary actions for behavior related to handicapping conditions.[162] In 1981 the Fifth Circuit Court of Appeals reviewed a disciplinary matter in which nine mentally retarded students sued state and local school officials in

Florida for improper expulsion.[163] The students were expelled for a portion of the 1977–78 school year and the entire 1978–79 school year for disruptive behavior ranging from sexual acts against other students to insubordination, vandalism, and use of profane language. The appellate court held that an expulsion constituted a change in placement requiring the full change-of-placement proceedings under the EAHCA.

According to the Fifth Circuit Appellate Court, the critical aspect in this process is determining whether the misconduct is related to the handicap. School officials asserted that expulsion was appropriate because the students did not have behavioral handicaps and knew right from wrong. In rejecting the school officials' position, the court concluded that a child does not have to be classified as seriously emotionally disturbed for a relationship to exist between the behavior and the handicap. Testifying that there may have been such a relationship in this case, a psychologist noted that students "with low intellectual functions and perhaps the lessening of control would respond to stress or respond to a threat in the only way that they feel adequate, which may be verbal aggressive behavior."[164] Since stress and frustration associated with any handicap could result in disruptive behavior, the court held that school officials must meet the substantial burden of proving a lack of a causal connection between the handicapping condition and the behavior before expelling a handicapped child. Furthermore, the court noted that the responsibility for this determination resides with a knowledgeable, professional team charged with determining appropriate student placements.

Similar cases have been decided by the Fourth, Sixth, and Ninth Circuit Appellate Courts.[165] These courts agreed that expulsion is a change of placement which triggers the EAHCA procedural protections. The Fourth Circuit Court of Appeals reviewed an expulsion case in which a committee of professionals in a school system had conducted a special hearing and found no causal relationship between a student's learning disability and his involvement in distributing drugs.[166] The appellate court disagreed, concurring with the federal district court's conclusion that the student's learning disability resulted in a loss of self-image and susceptibility to peer pressure that led to drug trafficking.

If school officials find that the misbehavior is not a manifestation of the child's handicap, is expulsion a disciplinary alternative? The Ninth Circuit Appellate Court held that expulsions can be imposed if proper procedures are followed and, as in the expulsion of any student, all services can be terminated.[167] The Fifth and Sixth Circuit Courts of Appeal agreed that handicapped students can be expelled, but they declined to permit complete cessation of educational services during the expulsion period.[168] An examination of the EAHCA and its regulations lends support to the assertion that all services cannot be terminated for the handicapped. It appears that the appropriate discipline would not be expulsion, but removal of the student to a more restrictive placement on the continuum of alternative placements. Current practice indicates that few handicapped children are expelled; they are simply moved from a less restrictive environment to a more restrictive one.[169]

Most of the litigation involving discipline of handicapped students has focused on expulsion rather than suspension. Generally, courts have noted that temporary suspensions do not require the special safeguards of the EAHCA. In an Illinois case, a federal district court ruled directly on the question of suspensions in a case involving a five-day suspension of an eleventh-grade, learning-disabled student for verbal abuse of a teacher.[170] School officials had provided a standard disciplinary hearing at which it was determined that the misconduct was unrelated to the learning disability and suspension was warranted under school policy. Upholding the school system, the court noted that special education services were not terminated as in an expulsion but rather there was simply a five-day disciplinary interruption for a serious offense. Such a brief suspension was not found to be a change in placement necessitating procedural protection under the EAHCA. Furthermore, the court emphasized that handicapped students are not excused from compliance with reasonable conduct regulations. The Ninth Circuit Appellate Court held that a five-day suspension for conduct *related* to a student's handicap did not violate the EAHCA.[171] The court further noted that the California law authorizing suspensions had been changed since the commencement of the student's legal challenge; the permissible suspension period was extended from five to twenty days. In the opinion of the court, even this longer suspension would not constitute a change in placement or loss of an appropriate education.

It appears that courts will continue to mandate extensive procedural safeguards in the discipline of handicapped students. At a minimum, a school system's discipline policy should contain procedures to ensure that a handicapped student is not expelled for misbehavior resulting from the handicap. This entails a special assessment and review by individuals who are knowledgeable of the student's handicapping condition and program. If expulsion is an option for handicapped students in the school's policies, provision for continuation of educational services should be addressed since it is unlikely that complete termination of the educational program is legally permissible. While short-term suspensions can generally be employed, frequent suspensions may indicate a need to examine the appropriateness of the student's placement. Furthermore, suspensions should not be overutilized as a means to avoid expulsion proceedings.

Remedies for the Denial of an Appropriate Education

In the absence of exceptional circumstances, courts have generally agreed that damages are unavailable under the EAHCA. The Supreme Court in *Burlington* drew a sharp distinction between awarding damages and requiring tuition reimbursement; the latter is simply recovery of justified costs which should have initially been incurred by the school district.[172]

The EAHCA originally did not provide courts the discretion to award attorneys' fees but was amended in 1986 to permit "reasonable attorneys' fees" to parents who prevail in any hearing or court action.[173] Impetus for the amendment came from the Supreme Court's 1984 decision in *Smith v. Robinson* interpreting the EAHCA as the exclusive means for enforcing handicapped children's comprehensive rights to a free appropriate education.[174] In this case, the Court concluded that where rights were guaranteed by the EAHCA, parents could not allege violations under either Section 1983 of the Civil Rights Act of 1871 or Section 504 of the Rehabilitation Act to enlarge available remedies, such as attorneys' fees.

Because Congress feared that the lack of redress for costly attorneys' fees might impede enforcement of the rights of handicapped children to appropriate educational programs, legislation was introduced immediately following *Smith* to amend the law, but substantial debate ensued prior to the passage of the amendment two years later. Controversy arose primarily over the provision that permitted courts to award attorneys' fees to parents for due process hearings or reviews. Although the provision was approved as part of the law, it resulted in specifications designed to limit the amount of attorneys' fees that are recoverable under the amendment as well as a requirement that a study must be conducted to assess the impact of the legislation.

CLASSIFICATIONS BASED ON NATIVE LANGUAGE

As indicated in the preceding section, courts and legislatures have directed attention to the *absence* of needed student classifications as well as to the existence of discriminatory classifications. In other words, the lack of special instruction for certain groups of children who cannot benefit from the mainstream educational program has been critically reviewed. Some of the legal activity dealing with such "functional exclusion" has focused on the right of linguistic minority students, who allegedly have been denied an adequate education because of the absence of remedial English instruction. Title VI, the Equal Educational Opportunities Act, and the Bilingual Education Act have been invoked to ensure the provision of special services for these students.

In the only United States Supreme Court decision involving English-deficient students, *Lau v. Nichols,* Chinese students asserted that the San Francisco public school program failed to provide for the needs of non-English-speaking students in violation of the equal protection clause of the Federal Constitution and Title VI of the Civil Rights Act of 1964.[175]

Both the federal district court and the Ninth Circuit Court of Appeals rejected the pupils' claim. The appellate court acknowledged that each student brought to school different advantages and disadvantages "caused in part by social, economic and cultural backgrounds," and that some of these disadvantages could be overcome by special instructional programs.[176] Nonetheless, the court reasoned that the provision of such special services, although desirable, was not constitutionally required.

The Supreme Court, however, reversed the appellate court's ruling and held that the lack of sufficient remedial English instruction violated Section 601 of the Civil Rights Act of 1964. The Court concluded that equality of treatment was not realized merely by providing students with the same facilities, textbooks, teachers, and curriculum, and that requiring children to acquire English skills on their own before they could hope to make any progress in school made "a mockery of public education." [177] The Court emphasized that "basic English skills are at the very core of what these public schools teach," and, therefore, "students who do not understand English are effectively foreclosed from any meaningful education." [178]

While the Supreme Court declined to address the constitutional issue in *Lau,* several lower courts have relied on equal protection guarantees in ordering bilingual-bicultural education programs in school districts where discrimination against linguistic minority students has been uncovered. For example, in 1972 the Fifth Circuit Court of Appeals affirmed the lower court's conclusion that the segregation of Mexican-American students in a Texas school district was unconstitutional.[179] As part of the remedial decree, the federal court ordered a comprehensive bilingual program. In another Texas case, a federal district court similarly mandated the expansion of bilingual programs in order to provide equal educational opportunities for Mexican-American students.[180] It is noteworthy that in the latter case the court did not find the existence of unconstitutional segregation, but still declared that the absence of an appropriate curriculum for bilingual students created an "inherently unequal" situation that placed a constitutional duty on school officials to provide for the unique needs of students with language deficiencies. Other federal courts have ordered school districts to provide special services for limited-English proficiency (LEP) students, even if only a few students within the district have needed such assistance[181] and have required school officials to upgrade bilingual programs considered to be insufficient.[182] In 1975 the Fifth Circuit Court of Appeals stated that "it is now an unlawful education practice to fail to take appropriate action to overcome language barriers." [183]

The Ninth Circuit Court of Appeals concluded, however, that school districts do not have a duty under the Federal Constitution or civil rights laws to ensure that all courses, instructors, testing procedures, and instructional materials for LEP students are bicultural and bilingual.[184] The appellate court reasoned that the provision of compensatory programs to cure language deficiencies of these students satisfies the mandate in *Lau v. Nichols*. Courts have agreed that LEP students are entitled to special assistance, but consensus has not been reached as to whether they are entitled only to remedial English instruction or instruction in their native language as well.

Plaintiffs have a heavy burden of proof in establishing intentional discrimination under the equal protection clause and Title VI; however, such suits are not the only means to ensure that the language needs of linguistic minorities are met. The federal Equal Educational Opportunities Act (EEOA) of 1974 requires school systems to develop appropriate programs for LEP students. The act provides in part that:

> No state shall deny equal educational opportunity to an individual on account of his or her race, color, sex, or national origin, by . . . the failure by an educational agency to take appropriate action to overcome language barriers that impede equal participation by its students in its instructional program.[185]

The EEOA does not impose a specific program of bilingual education on state and local education agencies, but rather requires "appropriate action." The Fifth Circuit Court of Appeals noted that Congress left state and local educational agencies "a substantial amount of latitude" in developing programs to meet their obligations under the EEOA.[186] The court found, however, that the legislative history of the EEOA provided almost no guidance in interpreting when a district's efforts are "appropriate." To assess the appropriateness of remediation programs and at the same time avoid prescribing educational standards, the court posed three questions:

1. Is the district's program based upon recognized, sound educational theory or principles?
2. Is the school system's program or practice designed to implement the adopted theory?
3. Has the program produced satisfactory results?[187]

Implicit in the first question is the recognition that several legitimate, competing strategies exist for meeting language deficiencies. Courts simply determine if a selected strategy is one recognized by education experts. Under the remaining questions, courts examine the level of resources committed to programs, language competency of bilingual teachers, efforts to assess competency of teachers, methods of classifying students for instruction, and procedures for evaluating student progress.[188]

The Colorado Federal District Court, in assessing the compliance of the Denver Public Schools with the EEOA, concluded that the law does not require a full bilingual education program for every single LEP student but that the district has a duty to take action to eliminate barriers that prevent many Denver children from participating in the system's educational program.[189] According to the court, "good faith effort" is inadequate: "What is required is an effort which will be reasonably effective in producing intended results . . ."[190]

Under the Bilingual Education Act of 1968, Congress provided supplemental funding for school districts to establish programs to meet the special educational needs of low-income students with limited-English proficiency.[191] The Bilingual Education Act of 1974 removed the criterion that children receiving such assistance had to be from low-income families and provided a more explicit definition of bilingual education as instruction in English and the child's native language to the extent necessary for the child to make effective progress.[192] Subsequently, in response to the *Lau* decision, the former Department of Health, Education, and Welfare issued advisory guidelines, known as the *Lau Remedies,* to assist school districts in designing programs to meet the needs of LEP students. In 1980, the Department of Education proposed formal regulations under Title VI of the Civil Rights Act of 1964 to prevent discrimination based on national origin in elementary and secondary education. The rules were withdrawn in 1981 because school districts and professional organizations objected to the proposed constraints on local prerogatives to design bilingual programs. Many states, however, have enacted legislation and/or administrative regulations pertaining to bilingual education. For example, Indiana law specifies that non-English-dominant students must be provided with bilingual-bicultural instruction designed to meet their language skill needs.[193]

With reauthorization of the Bilingual Education Act in 1984, the debate has continued as to the "best" method for meeting the needs of LEP students.[194] Unless mandated by state law, districts are not required to offer bilingual-bicultural programs in which students are instructed in their native language and English throughout their school years. Widely adopted alternatives to this approach include English as a second language, where students are placed in regular classrooms with special English instruction several hours a week, and transitional bilingual education, where students are provided special instruction in English but taught the basic curriculum in their native language until they have gained English proficiency. The latter alternatives have sparked considerable political discussion because the federal administration has favored greater flexibility for school districts serving LEP students. The Department of Education has indicated a strong preference for increasing the English language component in bilingual education programs and more rapid mainstreaming of program participants. Critics argue that these proposals will be detrimental to the acquisition of English skills as well as subject area knowledge. The proposals are particularly controversial since recent research studies indicate that these programs are not as effective as other alternatives.[195]

While most legal activity has focused on LEP students, a federal court in Michigan addressed the special needs of students who speak various English dialects. The court ruled that school districts must offer students who speak "black English" assistance in learning to use standard English.[196] The court reasoned that the dialect used by many black children constituted a language barrier necessitating special consideration from teachers in order to enable the students to participate equally in instructional programs. Although dismissing the constitutional challenges, the court held that the students' rights under the EEOA were violated because the education agencies failed to take appropriate action to overcome the students' language deficiencies. School officials were ordered to submit a plan for identifying children speaking black English and to design a program to offer special assistance to the students in acquiring standard English skills.

The legal mandates pertaining to English-deficient students, in conjunction with directives on behalf of handicapped children, raise several crucial issues regarding individual rights and the corresponding state duty to provide appropriate educational opportunities for all pupils. The mandates go beyond the mere right of every child to attend school. They address the suitability of the programs to the unique characteristics of pupils. Possibly, other classes of children who cannot benefit from the mainstream instructional program, such as the culturally disadvantaged or the gifted, may begin capitalizing on the protections afforded to handicapped and LEP students in asserting their rights to a public school program designed to meet their unique needs.

CONCLUSION

A basic purpose of public education is to enhance adult opportunities for all students, regardless of their innate characteristics. Accordingly, courts and legislatures have become increasingly assertive in guaranteeing that pupils have the chance to realize their capabilities while in school. Arbitrary classification practices that disadvantage certain groups of children no longer will be tolerated. On the other hand, valid classifications, applied in the best interests of students, are not being questioned. Indeed, legal mandates *require* the classification of certain pupils to ensure that they receive instruction appropriate to their needs. In exercising professional judgment pertaining to the classification of pupils, educators should be cognizant of the following generalizations drawn from recent judicial and legislative mandates.

1. Students cannot be segregated by sex in academic programs or schools unless there is a legitimate educational reason for main-

taining sex segregation, and then only if comparable courses/schools are available to both sexes.

2. Criteria for admission to programs or schools cannot be sex-based.
3. If a school district establishes an interscholastic athletic program, such opportunities must be made available to male and female athletes on an equal basis (i.e., either mixed-gender teams or comparable sex-segregated teams).
4. Students cannot be disadvantaged based on their marital status.
5. Any differential treatment of pregnant students must be justified by valid health or safety considerations.
6. Students can be classified by age, but such classifications must be substantiated as necessary to advance legitimate educational objectives.
7. Ability-tracking schemes are permissible; however, any such schemes that result in the segregation of minority children will be carefully scrutinized by courts to ensure that such practices are not a ploy to perpetuate discrimination.
8. If ability grouping is used, pupil assignments should be based on multiple criteria such as tests, teacher recommendations, and the socioeconomic background and adaptive behavior of the child.
9. Handicapped children are entitled to a free appropriate education in the least restrictive environment.
10. A free appropriate public education for a handicapped child is one that provides meaningful access to an education program that confers some educational benefit; the best program or one that maximizes the child's potential is not required.
11. An individual education program (including goals and objectives, specification of the services to be provided, and an education plan) must be developed for each handicapped child.
12. Due process procedures must be followed in identifying, evaluating, or changing a handicapped child's educational placement.
13. A parent may recover tuition costs for a unilateral private placement of a handicapped child if the placement is later determined to be appropriate and the public school placement is found to be inappropriate.
14. Related services necessary to support the specially designed instruction for handicapped children are required; school districts are not obligated to provide services that must be performed by a physician.
15. Disciplinary expulsion of handicapped children is a change in placement and triggers the procedural safeguards of the EAHCA; misconduct related to a handicapping condition cannot be the basis for expulsion.
16. The EAHCA provides the exclusive remedy for the denial of an

appropriate education for handicapped children; attorneys' fees are available for violations of the EAHCA.

17. English-deficient children are entitled to compensatory instruction designed to overcome English language barriers.

NOTES

1. Most states have similar antidiscrimination provisions. Connecticut law, for example, stipulates that "public schools shall be open to all children over five years or age without discrimination on account of race, color, sex, religion, or national origin . . . ," Conn. Gen. Stat. § 10–15.
2. *See* Dunn v. Blumstein, 405 U.S. 330 (1972) (right to vote in state elections); Shapiro v. Thompson, 394 U.S. 618 (1969) (right to interstate travel); Skinner v. Oklahoma, 316 U.S. 535, 541 (1942) (right to procreation).
3. 411 U.S. 1 (1973).
4. Graham v. Richardson, 403 U.S. 365 (1971) (alienage); Brown v. Board of Educ. of Topeka, 347 U.S. 483 (1954) (race); Oyama v. California, 332 U.S. 633 (1948) (national origin).
5. The Supreme Court recently recognized that *Rodriguez* does not foreclose the possibility of an equal protection violation where a state has decided to divide resources unequally among school districts. Papasan v. Allain, 106 S. Ct. 2932 (1986).
6. *See* San Antonio Independent School Dist. v. Rodriguez, 411 U.S. 1 (1973) (wealth); Frontiero v. Richardson, 411 U.S. 677 (1973) (sex); Gurmankin v. Costanzo, 556 F.2d 184 (3d Cir. 1977), *cert. denied,* 450 U.S. 923 (1981) (handicaps).
7. Dunn v. Blumstein, 405 U.S. 330 (1972).
8. *See* Bullock v. Carter, 405 U.S. 134, 145 (1972); Eisenstadt v. Baird, 405 U.S. 438, 452 (1972).
9. 457 U.S. 202 (1982).
10. *See* Lau v. Nichols, 414 U.S. 563 (1974), text with note 175, *infra;* Mills v. Board of Educ. 348 F. Supp. 866 (D.D.C. 1972), text with note 93, *infra.*
11. *See* chapters 9 and 13 for a discussion of legal principles pertaining to race discrimination.
12. Frontiero v. Richardson, 411 U.S. 677, 686 (1973).
13. *Id.,* quoting from Weber v. Aetna Casualty & Surety Co., 406 U.S. 164, 175 (1972).
14. *See* chapter 9 for further discussion of gender-based classifications.
15. Brenden v. Independent School Dist., 477 F.2d 1292 (8th Cir. 1973).
16. *See* Bucha v. Illinois High School Ass'n, 351 F. Supp. 69 (N.D. Ill. 1972), in which the federal court upheld the exclusion of two girls from the school's interscholastic swim team on the basis of the state athletic association regulation barring coeducational competition. The court reasoned that the physical and psychological differences between the sexes were constitutionally sufficient reasons for prohibiting coeducational interscholastic competition among high school students.
17. *See* Morris v. Michigan State Bd. of Educ., 472 F.2d 1207 (6th Cir. 1973); Gilpin v. Kansas State High School Activities Ass'n, 377 F. Supp. 1233 (D.

Kan. 1973); Reed v. Nebraska School Activities Ass'n, 341 F. Supp. 258 (D. Neb. 1972); Haas v. South Bend Community School Corp., 289 N.E.2d 495 (Ind. 1972).

18. Lantz by Lantz v. Ambach, 620 F. Supp. 663 (S.D.N.Y. 1985).
19. *Id.* at 665.
20. Force by Force v. Pierce City R-VI School Dist., 570 F. Supp. 1020 (W.D. Mo. 1983).
21. Leffel v. Wisconsin Interscholastic Athletic Ass'n, 444 F. Supp. 1117 (E.D. Wis. 1978).
22. O'Connor v. Board of Educ. of School Dist. 23, 545 F. Supp. 376 (N.D. Ill. 1982).
23. O'Connor v. Board of Educ. of School Dist. 23, 449 U.S. 1301, 1306 (1980). (Stevens, J., on application to vacate stay).
24. 34 C.F.R. § 106.41(b). Under Title IX, the Department of Education is empowered to terminate federal funds to institutions if charges of sex bias are substantiated. Application of Title IX, however, may be severely restricted because of the requirements that sex discrimination must occur in specific programs receiving federal financial assistance. *See* Grove City College v. Bell, 465 U.S. 555 (1984); Bennett v. West Texas State Univ., 799 F.2d 155 (5th Cir. 1986). For discussion of the application of Title IX to employees, *see* text with note 134, chapter 9.
25. *Id.*
26. Yellow Springs Exempted Village School Dist. Bd. of Educ. v. Ohio High School Athletic Ass'n, 647 F.2d 651 (6th Cir. 1981).
27. *See* Force by Force v. Pierce City R-VI School Dist., 570 F. Supp. 1020 (W.D. Mo. 1983) (a similar prohibition against female participation was found unconstitutional under the equal protection clause of the fourteenth amendment).
28. Pennsylvania v. Pennsylvania Interscholastic Athletic Ass'n, 334 A.2d 839 (Pa. 1975). The Pennsylvania ERA states: "Equality of rights under the law shall not be denied or abridged in the Commonwealth of Pennsylvania because of the sex of the individual," Pa. Const., art. 1, § 28.
29. Cape v. Tennessee Secondary School Athletic Ass'n, 563 F.2d 793 (6th Cir. 1977).
30. Jones v. Oklahoma Secondary School Activities Ass'n, 453 F. Supp. 150 (W.D. Okla. 1977).
31. Dodson v. Arkansas Activities Ass'n, 468 F. Supp. 394 (E.D. Ark. 1979).
32. *Education Daily,* January 2, 1979, p. 1.
33. Striebel v. Minnesota State High School League, 321 N.W.2d 400, 402 (Minn. 1982).
34. Ridgeway v. Montana High School Ass'n, 633 F. Supp. 1564 (D. Mont. 1986).
35. Clark v. Arizona Interscholastic Ass'n, 695 F.2d 1126 (9th Cir. 1982). *cert. denied,* 464 U.S. 818 (1983). *See also* Mularadelis v. Haldane Cent. School Bd., 427 N.Y.S.2d 458 (App. Div. 1980); Petrie v. Illinois High School Ass'n, 394 N.E.2d 855 (Ill. App. 1979); Hoover v. Meiklejohn, 430 F. Supp. 164 (D. Colo. 1977). *But see* Gomes v. Rhode Island Interscholastic League, 469 F. Supp. 659 (D.R.I. 1979), *vacated as moot,* 604 F.2d 733 (1st Cir. 1979); Attorney General v. Massachusetts Interscholastic Athletic Ass'n,

393 N.E.2d 284 (Mass. 1979) (sex-based discrimination against males could not be justified by health or safety considerations or by the assertion that the rule was necessary to shield the emergent women's sports program from inundation by male athletes).

36. 532 F.2d 880 (3d Cir. 1976), *aff'd by an equally divided court,* 430 U.S. 703 (1977).
37. *Id.*, 532 F.2d at 886, quoting from Kahn v. Shevin, 416 U.S. 351, 356 (1974).
38. In a later state case, a trial court declared that the two Philadelphia sex-segregated schools in *Vorchheimer* violated the fourteenth amendment and Pennsylvania's Equal Rights Amendment. The court did not reverse the Third Circuit Appellate Court's decision but rather found on a complete evidentiary record that the opportunities provided were *not equal.* Newberg v. Board of Public Educ., 478 A.2d 1352 (Pa. Super. 1984). *See* William D. Valente, *Education Law: Public and Private,* vol. 2 (St. Paul, MN: West Publishing Co., 1985), p. 73.
39. Mississippi Univ. for Women v. Hogan, 458 U.S. 718 (1982).
40. Title IX regulations also stipulate that differential admission criteria cannot be applied to male and female students. 45 C.F.R. § 86.35(b).
41. Bray v. Lee, 337 F. Supp. 934 (D. Mass. 1972).
42. Berkelman v. San Francisco Unified School Dist., 501 F.2d 1264 (9th Cir. 1974).
43. *See* Della Casa v. Gaffney, No. 171673 (Cal. Super. Ct. 1973); Seward v. Della, No. 134173 (Cal. Super. Ct. 1973); Sanchez v. Baron, No. 69–C–1615 (E.D.N.Y. 1971).
44. *See* Hickey v. Black River Bd. of Educ., No. 73–889 (N.D. Ohio 1973).
45. *See* 45 C.F.R. § 86.34–36.
46. Iron Arrow Honor Society v. Heckler, 702 F.2d 549 (5th Cir. 1983), *vacated as moot,* 464 U.S. 67 (1983).
47. State v. Marion County Bd. of Educ., 302 S.W.2d 57 (Tenn. 1957).
48. State *ex rel.* Baker v. Stevenson, 189 N.E.2d 181 (Ohio C.P. 1962). *See also* Board of Directors of Independent School Dist. of Waterloo v. Green, 147 N.W.2d 854 (Iowa 1967); Starkey v. Board of Educ. of Davis County School Dist., 381 P.2d 718 (Utah 1963).
49. Loving v. Virginia, 388 U.S. 1, 12 (1967).
50. Board of Educ. of Harrodsburg v. Bentley, 383 S.W.2d 677, 680 (Ky. App. 1964). *See also* Anderson v. Canyon Independent School Dist., 412 S.W.2d 387 (Tex. Civ. App. 1967).
51. Davis v. Meek, 344 F. Supp. 298, 301 (N.D. Ohio 1972). *See also* Moran v. School Dist. No. 7, 350 F. Supp. 1180, 1186–87 (D. Mont. 1972).
52. Holt v. Shelton, 341 F. Supp. 821 (M.D. Tenn. 1972).
53. *See* Beeson v. Kiowa County School Dist. RE–1, 567 P.2d 801 (Colo. App. 1977); Bell v. Lone Oak Independent School Dist., 507 S.W.2d 636, 641–642 (Tex. Civ. App. 1974). *See also* Hollon v. Mathis Independent School Dist., 358 F. Supp. 1269 (S.D. Tex. 1973), *vacated for mootness,* 491 F.2d 92 (5th Cir. 1974).
54. *See* Grace Belsches-Simmons, "Teenage Pregnancy and Schooling: Legal Considerations," *Education Law Reporter,* vol. 24 (1985), pp. 1–11.
55. Ordway v. Hargraves, 323 F. Supp. 1155 (D. Mass. 1971).
56. Alvin Independent School Dist. v. Cooper, 404 S.W.2d 76 (Tex. Civ. App.

1966). *See also* Perry v. Grenada Mun. Separate School Dist., 300 F. Supp. 748, 753 (N.D. Miss. 1969).

57. *See* Geduldig v. Aiello, 417 U.S. 484 (1974). *See also* discussion of sex discrimination in chapter 9.
58. 20 U.S.C. § 1681(a); 45 C.F.R. § 86.21(c)(2).
59. *See* discussion at note 24, *supra.*
60. *See* Houston v. Prosser, 361 F. Supp. 295 (N.D. Ga. 1973), in which the federal district court sanctioned a school policy requiring teenage mothers to complete high school by enrolling in evening classes (comparable to the regular daytime program), but prohibited school officials from charging such students fees for textbooks and tuition. It should be noted that this ruling does not follow the prevailing precedent in so far as the court sanctioned the segregation of pregnant students in special programs based on the conclusion that married and pregnant students were more promiscuous.
61. Courts have held that school officials cannot expel students from the National Honor Society based on their pregnant, unwed status. *See* Wort v. Vierline, No. 82–3169 (C.D. Ill. 1984); James A. Rapp, ed., *Education Law,* vol. 2 (New York: Matthew Bender, 1984), chapter 8, p. 164.
62. *See* Gault v. Garrison, 569 F.2d 993 (7th Cir. 1977), *cert. denied,* 440 U.S. 945 (1979).
63. Goldsmith v. Lower Moreland School Dist., 461 A.2d 1341 (Pa. Commw. 1983).
64. O'Leary v. Wisecup, 364 A.2d 770 (Pa. Commw. 1976). *See also* Zweifel v. Joint Dist. No. 1, Belleville, 251 N.W.2d 822 (Wis. 1977).
65. Hammond v. Marx, 406 F. Supp. 853 (D. Me. 1975).
66. Ackerman v. Rubin, 231 N.Y.S.2d 112 (Sup. Ct., Bronx County, 1962).
67. *Id.* at 114.
68. *See* Stewart by Stewart v. Salem School Dist. 24J, 670 P.2d 1048 (Ore. App. 1983). *See also* P.L. 99–457, Education of the Handicapped Amendments Act of 1986. The act included strong incentives for states to serve three- to five-year-old handicapped children by 1991 and to create programs for handicapped infants. If states do not serve these children, they will lose funds appropriated for the preschool programs and will not be allowed to count three- to five-year-old handicapped children under the basic grant.
69. Helms v. Independent School Dist. No. 3 of Broken Arrow, Tulsa County, 750 F.2d 820 (10th Cir. 1984), *cert. denied,* 105 S. Ct. 2024 (1985).
70. *See* Adams County v. Deist, 334 N.W.2d 775 (Neb. 1983) (no authority under federal or state law to order educational services beyond twenty-one years of age). *But see* Max M. v. Thompson, 592 F. Supp. 1450 (N.D. Ill. 1984) (services required beyond twenty-one years of age where child was denied earlier compensatory education).
71. *See* Sandlin v. Johnson, 643 F.2d 1027 (4th Cir. 1981) (upheld denial of promotion for twenty-one second-grade students in a class of twenty-two for failure to pass Ginn Reading series test).
72. 269 F. Supp. 401, 492 (D.D.C. 1967), *aff'd sub nom.,* Smuck v. Hobson, 408 F.2d 175 (D.C. Cir. 1969).
73. *Id.*, 269 F. Supp. at 511.
74. Singleton v. Jackson Mun. Separate School Dist., 419 F.2d 1211 (5th Cir. 1969). *See also* United States v. Gadsden County School Dist., 572 F.2d

1049 (5th Cir. 1978); Moore v. Tangipahoa Parish School Bd., 304 F. Supp. 244 (E.D. La. 1969).

75. Castaneda v. Pickard, 648 F.2d 989, 996 (5th Cir. 1981). On remand, the court subsequently affirmed the district court's finding that ability grouping did not discriminate on the basis of race, 781 F.2d 456 (5th Cir. 1986).
76. Georgia State Conference of Branches of NAACP v. State of Georgia, 775 F.2d 1403 (11th Cir. 1985).
77. *See* Bond v. Keck, 616 F. Supp. 565 (E.D. Mo. 1985) (black student's reassignment from highest ability math group to second highest group was appropriate based on her short attention span and poor time on task); Bond v. Keck, 629 F. Supp. 225 (E.D. Mo. 1986) (defendants were awarded attorneys' fees because suit was found to be frivolous and without foundation).
78. *See* Bester v. Tuscaloosa City Bd. of Educ., 722 F.2d 1514 (11th Cir. 1984).
79. Larry P. v. Riles, 495 F. Supp. 926 (N.D. Cal. 1979), *aff'd*, 793 F.2d 969 (9th Cir. 1984) (violations of Title VI, the Rehabilitation Act, and the Education for All Handicapped Children Act were found).
80. Parents in Action on Special Educ. v. Hannon, 506 F. Supp. 831 (N.D. Ill. 1980).
81. *See* Ernest Rose and Dixie S. Huefner, "Cultural Bias in Special Education Assessment and Placement," in *School Law Update: Preventive School Law,* Thomas Jones and Darel Semler, eds. (Topeka, KS: National Organization on Legal Problems of Education, 1984).
82. *See* P.L. 94–142, The Education for All Handicapped Children Act of 1975, 20 U.S.C. § 1401 *et seq.;* discussion with text at note 121, *infra.*
83. *See* Debra P. v. Turlington, 730 F.2d 1405 (11th Cir. 1984); Brookhart v. Illinois State Bd. of Educ., 697 F.2d 179 (7th Cir. 1983).
84. Gifted and Talented Children's Education Act, 20 U.S.C. § 3311 (1978) (repealed 1982).
85. *Id.*
86. *The Condition of Education,* Valena W. Plisko, ed. (Washington, DC: National Center for Education Statistics, 1983).
87. Central York School Dist. v. Pennsylvania, 399 A.2d 167 (Pa. Commw. 1979). *See also* Lisa H. v. State Bd. of Educ., 447 A.2d 669 (Pa. Commw. 1982) (all students are not entitled to special individualized education, only those who deviate from the norm).
88. Centennial School Dist. v. Commonwealth of Pennsylvania, Dep't of Educ., 503 A.2d 1090 (Pa. Commw. 1986). *See* Scott v. Commonwealth of Pennsylvania, Dep't of Educ., 512 A.2d 790 (Pa. Commw. 1986) (calculus course was not required when evidence showed that special activities and services provided in the IEP were appropriate).
89. Conn. Gen. Stat. §§ 10–76a, 10–76d(d).
90. Bennett v. City School Dist. of New Rochelle, 497 N.Y.S.2d 72 (App. Div. 1985).
91. Student Roe v. Commonwealth of Pennsylvania, 638 F. Supp. 929 (E.D. Pa. 1986); Student Doe v. Commonwealth of Pennsylvania, 593 F. Supp. 54 (E.D. Pa. 1984).
92. Irwin v. Board of Educ., Community Consol. School Dist. No. 15, No. 79L49 (Ill. Cir. Ct., McKindry County, dismissed, June 1980).

93. Pennsylvania Ass'n for Retarded Children v. Commonwealth, 343 F. Supp. 279 (E.D. Pa. 1972).
94. Mills v. Board of Educ., 348 F. Supp. 866 (D.D.C. 1972).
95. San Antonio Independent School Dist. v. Rodriguez, 411 U.S. 1, 36 (1973).
96. Plyler v. Doe, 457 U.S. 202 (1982).
97. 29 U.S.C. § 794.
98. 20 U.S.C. § 1401. *See generally* T. Page Johnson, *The Principal's Guide to the Educational Rights of Handicapped Students* (Reston, VA: National Association of Secondary Principals, 1986); Stephen B. Thomas, *Legal Issues in Special Education* (Topeka, KS: National Organization on Legal Problems of Education, 1985).
99. 29 U.S.C. § 706(7)(B).
100. Lake Washington School Dist. No. 414, Case No. 10841039, Office for Civil Rights, June 28, 1985.
101. *See* In re Ryan White, No. 86–144 (Ind. Cir. Ct., Clinton County, 1986); District 27 Community School Bd. v. Board of Educ. of City of New York, 502 N.Y.S.2d 325 (Sup. Ct., Queens County, 1986).
102. P.L. 99–372, Handicapped Children's Protection Act of 1986.
103. For several years New Mexico did not participate in the EAHCA funding, but after the Tenth Circuit Court of Appeals ruled that the state was obligated under Section 504 to provide appropriate educational programs for handicapped children, the state decided to participate in the assistance program. *See* New Mexico Ass'n for Retarded Citizens v. State of New Mexico, 678 F.2d 847 (10th Cir. 1982).
104. 29 U.S.C. § 1401.
105. 20 U.S.C. § 1401(16).
106. Helms v. Independent School Dist. No. 3 of Broken Arrow, Tulsa County, 750 F.2d 820 (10th Cir. 1984), *cert. denied,* 105 S. Ct. 2024 (1985). Stewart by Stewart v. Salem School Dist., 670 P.2d 1048 (Ore. App. 1983). *See* note 68, *supra.*
107. 458 U.S. 176 (1982).
108. 483 F. Supp. 528, 534 (S.D.N.Y. 1980).
109. Rowley, 458 U.S. at 192.
110. *Id.* at 200. While the Supreme Court in *Rowley* held that the EAHCA does create substantive rights, a year earlier the Court declared that the Developmental Disabled Act did not. That act was designed to *encourage,* but not to *mandate,* better services for the developmentally disabled. *See* Pennhurst v. Halderman, 451 U.S. 1 (1981).
111. Rowley, *id.* at 207.
112. *Id.*
113. Karl v. Board of Educ. of Geneseo Cent. School Dist., 736 F.2d 873 (2d Cir. 1984).
114. Scituate School Comm. v. Robert B., 620 F. Supp. 1224 (D.R.I. 1985).
115. Hessler v. State Bd. of Educ. of Maryland, 700 F.2d 134 (4th Cir. 1983).
116. Pennhurst State School and Hosp. v. Halderman, 465 U.S. 89 (1984).
117. David D. v. Dartmouth School Comm., 775 F.2d 411, 419 (1st Cir. 1985), *cert. denied,* 106 S. Ct. 1790 (1986). *See also* Geis v. Board of Educ. of Parsippany-Troy Hills, 774 F.2d 575 (3d Cir. 1985); Students of California

School for the Blind v. Honig, 736 F.2d 538 (9th cir. 1984), *vacated on other grounds,* 465 U.S. 1016 (1985).

118. David D., *id.* at 420.
119. Geis v. Board of Educ. of Parsippany-Troy Hills, 774 F.2d 575 (3d Cir. 1985).
120. *See* Brookhart v. Illinois State Bd. of Educ., 697 F.2d 179 (7th Cir. 1983); Board of Educ. of Northport-East Northport Union Free School Dist. v. Ambach, 458 N.Y.S.2d 680 (App. Div. 1982), *aff'd,* 469 N.Y.S.2d 669 (1983), *cert. denied,* 465 U.S. 401 (1984).
121. Particularly troublesome issues are raised by the participation of handicapped children in mandatory proficiency testing programs, since most competency tests have been validated with the nonhandicapped. Handicapped students would be unfairly disadvantaged without modifications in the test instrument and administration, but school authorities must ensure that such accommodations allow for the child's actual knowledge to be assessed and do not unfairly disadvantage handicapped children. The Seventh Circuit Appellate Court has indicated that a competency test used as a prerequisite to receipt of a high school diploma would be subject to EAHCA's "no single criterion" requirement. In this case, the requirement was satisfied as the test was used in conjunction with other criteria in awarding diplomas. Brookhart, *id.*
122. Bonadonna v. Cooperman, 619 F. Supp. 401 (D.N.J. 1985).
123. 20 U.S.C. § 1415(e)(3). *See* Stock v. Massachusetts Hosp. School, 467 N.E.2d 448 (Mass. 1984). In this case, the Massachusetts Supreme Court held that graduation is a change in placement requiring the full procedural protections of the EAHCA. Under the requirement that a student remain in his or her current educational placement during review proceedings, special education services could not be discontinued if parents objected to this change in their child's status.
124. Jackson v. Franklin County School Bd., 765 F.2d 535 (5th Cir. 1985); *see* 45 C.F.R. § 300.513.
125. Doe by Gonzales v. Maher, 793 F.2d 1470 (9th Cir. 1986).
126. 20 U.S.C. § 1412 (5).
127. Wilson v. Marana Unified School Dist. No. 6 of Pima County, 735 F.2d 1178, 1183 (9th Cir. 1984).
128. Department of Educ., State of Hawaii v. Katherine D., 727 F.2d 809 (9th Cir. 1983), *cert. denied,* 105 S. Ct. 2360 (1985).
129. Roncker v. Walter, 700 F.2d 1058, 1063 (6th Cir. 1983), *cert. denied,* 464 U.S. 864 (1983).
130. *Id.*
131. St. Louis Developmental Disabilities Treatment Center Parents' Ass'n v. Mallory, 591 F. Supp. 1416 (W.D. Mo. 1984), *aff'd,* 767 F.2d 518 (8th Cir. 1985).
132. *See* Abrahamson v. Hershman, 701 F.2d 223 (1st Cir. 1983); Kruelle v. New Castle County School Dist., 642 F.2d 687 (3d Cir. 1981); North v. District of Columbia Bd. of Educ., 471 F. Supp. 136 (D.D.C. 1979).
133. Abrahamson, *id.*
134. Parks v. Pavkovic, 753 F.2d 1397 (7th Cir. 1985), *cert. denied,* 105 S. Ct. 3529 (1985).

135. *See, e.g.*, Department of Educ., State of Hawaii v. Katherine D., 727 F.2d 809 (9th Cir. 1983); *cert. denied,* 105 S. Ct. 2360 (1985); Zvi D. v. Ambach, 694 F.2d 904 (2d Cir. 1982); Stemple v. Board of Educ., Prince George's County, 623 F.2d 893 (4th Cir. 1980), *cert. denied,* 450 U.S. 911 (1981).
136. 105 S. Ct. 1996 (1985).
137. *Id.* at 2003.
138. *Id.*
139. *See* Hall by Hall v. Vance County Bd. of Educ., 774 F.2d 629 (4th Cir. 1985); McKenzie v. Smith, 771 F.2d 1527 (D.C. Cir. 1985), *aff'd,* 795 F.2d 77 (1st Cir. 1986).
140. *See* Cain v. Yukon Public Schools, 775 F.2d 15 (10th Cir. 1985); Scituate School Comm. v. Robert B., 620 F. Supp. 1224 (D.R.I. 1985).
141. Cain, *id.*
142. Geis v. Board of Educ. of Parsippany-Troy Hills, 774 F.2d 575 (3d Cir. 1985).
143. David D. v. Dartmouth School Comm., 775 F.2d 411, 423 (1st Cir. 1985), *cert. denied,* 106 S. Ct. 1790 (1986).
144. 20 U.S.C. § 1401(17).
145. Hurry v. Jones, 734 F.2d 879 (1st Cir. 1984).
146. *See* Birmingham and Lamphere School Dists. v. Superintendent of Public Instruction, State of Michigan, 328 N.W.2d 59 (Mich. App. 1982). *But see* Rettig v. Kent City School Dist., 788 F.2d 328 (6th Cir. 1986), *cert. denied,* 106 S. Ct. 3297 (1986) (extracurricular activities are not required if a student would not receive a significant educational benefit from participation).
147. Espino v. Besteiro, 520 F. Supp. 905 (S.D. Tex. 1981).
148. *See* Seals v. Loftis, 614 F. Supp. 302 (E.D. Tenn. 1985) (parents could not be required to reduce their available lifetime insurance benefits to cover neurological and psychological examinations requested by the school system during the evaluation process).
149. 468 U.S. 883 (1984).
150. *Id.* at 891.
151. *Id.*
152. *Id.* at 892, citing 34 C.F.R. § 300.13(b).
153. Detsel by Detsel v. Board of Educ. of the Auburn Enlarged City School Dist., 637 F. Supp. 1022 (N.D.N.Y. 1986) (constant in-school nursing care that must be performed by a skilled, trained health professional is not required); Department of Educ., State of Hawaii v. Katherine D., 727 F.2d 809 (9th Cir. 1984), *cert. denied,* 105 S. Ct. 2360 (1985) (periodic replacement of a tracheostomy tube, which could be performed by a nurse or trained layperson, is a related service under the EAHCA).
154. *See* Papacoda v. State of Connecticut, 528 F. Supp. 68 (D. Conn. 1981); In the Matter of the "A" Family, 602 P.2d 157 (Mont. 1979).
155. T. G. v. Board of Educ. of Piscataway, 576 F. Supp. 420 (D.N.J. 1983), *aff'd,* 738 F.2d 420 (1984), *cert. denied,* 469 U.S. 1086 (1984).
156. Darlene L. v. Illinois State Bd. of Educ., 568 F. Supp. 1340 (N.D. Ill. 1983). *See also* McKenzie v. Jefferson, 566 F. Supp. 404 (D.D.C. 1983).
157. M. v. Thompson, 592 F. Supp. 1437 (N.D. Ill. 1984).
158. Battle v. Commonwealth of Pennsylvania, 629 F.2d 269 (3d Cir. 1980), *cert. denied,* 452 U.S. 968 (1981).

159. Georgia Ass'n of Retarded Citizens v. McDaniel, 716 F.2d 1565 (11th Cir. 1983), *cert. denied,* 469 U.S. 1228 (1985).
160. *Id.*, 716 F.2d at 1576.
161. Yaris v. Special School Dist. of St. Louis, 728 F.2d 1055 (8th Cir. 1984); Crawford v. Pittman, 708 F.2d 1028 (5th Cir. 1983).
162. Stuart v. Nappi, 443 F. Supp. 1235 (D. Conn. 1978); Doe v. Koger, 480 F. Supp. 225 (N.D. Ind. 1979).
163. S–1 v. Turlington, 635 F.2d 342 (5th Cir. 1981), *cert. denied,* 454 U.S. 1030 (1981).
164. *Id.* at 347.
165. Doe by Gonzales v. Maher, 793 F.2d 1470 (9th Cir. 1986); School Bd. of the County of Prince William, Virginia v. Malone, 762 F.2d 1210 (4th Cir. 1985); Kaelin v. Grubbs, 682 F.2d 595 (6th Cir. 1982).
166. School Bd. of the County of Prince William, Virginia, *id.*
167. Doe by Gonzales v. Maher, 793 F.2d 1470 (9th Cir. 1986).
168. Kaelin v. Grubbs, 682 F.2d 595 (6th Cir. 1982); S–1 v. Turlington, 635 F.2d 342 (5th Cir. 1981), *cert. denied,* 454 U.S. 1030 (1981). In 1985 the Michigan Attorney General ruled that under virtually no expulsion circumstances could there be a complete termination of educational services to handicapped students. Mich. Att'y Gen., Opinion No. 6271 (1985).
169. Thomas, *Legal Issues in Special Education,* p. 44. Any change in placement, however, must be preceded by due process. An Ohio school district violated the procedural terms of the EAHCA by unilaterally moving two students from a classroom to home instruction for disciplinary reasons. Lamont X. v. Quisenberry, 606 F. Supp. 809 (S.D. Ohio 1984).
170. Board of Educ. of the City of Peoria v. Illinois State Bd. of Educ., 531 F. Supp. 148 (C.D. Ill. 1982).
171. Doe by Gonzales v. Maher, 793 F.2d 1470 (9th Cir. 1986).
172. Burlington School Comm. v. Department of Educ., 105 S. Ct. 1996 (1985).
173. P.L. 99–372, Handicapped Children's Protection Act of 1986. The amended law provides that a *court* may award reasonable attorneys' fees. A recent decision of the Supreme Court indicates that parents prevailing in administrative proceedings may have difficulty in recovering attorneys' fees in legal actions initiated solely to recover fees. *See* North Carolina Dep't of Transp. v. Crest Street Community Council, 107 S. Ct. 336 (1986).
174. 468 U.S. 992 (1984).
175. 483 F.2d 791 (9th Cir. 1973), *rev'd,* 414 U.S. 563 (1974).
176. *Id.,* 483 F.2d at 798.
177. Lau, 414 U.S. at 566.
178. *Id.* Following the Supreme Court's decision in Regents of the Univ. of California v. Bakke, 438 U.S. 265 (1978), substantial doubt has been raised regarding the viability of Title VI to challenge the adequacy of programs for language-deficient students. While the Supreme Court in *Bakke* did not specifically overrule *Lau*, it appears that Title VI, like the equal protection clause, is violated with evidence of intentional discrimination. *But see* Guardians Ass'n v. Civil Service Comm'n of the City of New York, 463 U.S. 582 (1983) (intent not required for *equitable* relief). Several lower courts have rejected claims of alleged Title VI violations in the absence of proof of

purposeful discrimination in structuring bilingual education programs. *See* Castaneda v. Pickard, 648 F.2d 989 (5th Cir. 1981); Gomez v. Illinois State Bd. of Educ., 614 F. Supp. 342 (N.D. Ill. 1985); Keyes v. School Dist. No. 1, Denver, Colo., 576 F. Supp. 1503 (D. Colo. 1983).

179. United States v. Texas, 342 F. Supp. 24 (E.D. Tex. 1971), *aff'd*, 466 F.2d 518 (5th Cir. 1972).
180. Arvizu v. Waco Independent School Dist., 373 F. Supp. 1264 (W.D. Tex. 1973).
181. Otero v. Mesa County School Dist. No. 51, 408 F. Supp. 162 (D. Colo. 1975).
182. Rios v. Read, 73 F.R.D. 589 (E.D.N.Y. 1977).
183. Morales v. Shannon, 516 F.2d 411, 414–415 (5th Cir. 1975), *cert. denied,* 423 U.S. 1034 (1975).
184. Guadalupe Organization, Inc. v. Tempe Elementary School Dist. No. 3, 587 F.2d 1022 (9th Cir. 1978). *See also* Serna v. Portales Mun. Schools, 351 F. Supp. 1279 (D.N.M. 1972), *aff'd*, 499 F.2d 1147 (10th Cir. 1974).
185. 20 U.S.C. § 1703(f).
186. Castaneda v. Pickard, 648 F.2d 989, 1009 (5th Cir. 1981) (bilingual programs found to be nondiscriminatory); Castaneda II, 781 F.2d 456 (5th Cir. 1986) (affirmed district court's decision on remand that ability grouping did not discriminate against Mexican-American students).
187. *Id.*, 648 F.2d at 1009–1010.
188. *See* Castaneda, *id.*; Keyes v. School Dist. No. 1, Denver, Colo., 576 F. Supp. 1503 (D. Colo. 1983).
189. Keyes, *id.*
190. *Id.* at 1520.
191. 20 U.S.C. § 880b et seq.
192. 20 U.S.C. § 880b–1(a)(4)(A).
193. Ind. Code Ann. § 20–10.1–5.5–1.
194. *See, e.g., Education Week,* February 12, 1986, pp. 1, 22; *Education Week,* November 27, 1985, pp. 1, 16; *Education Week,* October 23, 1985, pp. 1, 12.
195. *See Education Week,* April 23, 1986, pp. 1, 10.
196. Martin Luther King Junior Elementary School Children v. Ann Arbor School Dist. Bd., 473 F. Supp. 1371 (E.D. Mich. 1979).

6

Student Discipline

One of the most persistent and troublesome problems confronting educators is student misconduct. According to the annual Gallup Poll of public attitudes toward education, the lack of appropriate school discipline has been the primary concern among citizens for sixteen of the past eighteen years.[1] In this chapter, the various strategies employed to address such disciplinary problems are examined from a legal perspective. The analysis focuses on the development of conduct regulations, the imposition of sanctions for noncompliance, and the procedures required in the administration of pupil punishments.

The law is clear in authorizing the state and its agencies to establish and enforce reasonable conduct codes to protect the rights of students and school districts and to ensure school environments conducive to learning. Historically, courts exercised limited review of student disciplinary regulations, and pupils were seldom successful in challenging policies governing their behavior. In 1923 the Arkansas Supreme Court upheld the expulsion of a student who wore talcum powder on her face in violation of a school rule forbidding pupils to wear transparent hosiery, low-necked dresses, face paint, or cosmetics.[2] In another early case, the Michigan Supreme Court endorsed the suspension of a female high school student for smoking and riding in a car with a young man.[3] In these and similar cases, courts were reluctant to interfere with the judgment of school officials because public education was considered to be a privilege bestowed by the state.

While there has been a quantum leap from the posture espoused during the first third of the twentieth century to the active protection of students' rights characterized by cases such as *Tinker v. Des Moines.*,[4] the judicial developments of the past several decades have not eroded educators' rights or their responsibilities.[5] Reasonable disciplinary regulations, even those infringing students' protected liberties, have been upheld if justified by a "legitimate state interest." Educators have not only the authority but also the *duty* to maintain discipline in public schools. While rules made at any level cannot conflict with higher authorities (e.g., constitutional and statutory provisions), building administrators and teachers retain a great deal of latitude in establishing and enforcing conduct codes that are necessary for instructional activities to take place. In the subsequent sections of this chapter, educators' prerogatives and students' rights are explored in connection with conduct regulations, expulsions and suspensions, disciplinary transfers, corporal punishment, academic sanctions, search and seizure, and remedies for lawful disciplinary actions.

CONDUCT REGULATIONS

In determining the legality of specific disciplinary measures, courts initially assess the validity of the conduct regulation that allegedly has been breached. In 1885 the Wisconsin Supreme Court discussed the criteria by which such conduct rules should be judged.

> The rules and regulations made must be reasonable and proper . . . for the government, good order, and efficiency of the schools, such as will best advance the pupils in their studies, tend to their educational and mental improvement, and promote their interest and welfare. But the rules and regulations must relate to these objects.[6]

School boards are granted considerable latitude in establishing and interpreting their own disciplinary rules and regulations.[7] The Supreme Court has held that the interpretation of a school regulation resides with the body that adopted it and that is charged with its enforcement.[8] Disciplinary policies, however, have been struck down if unconstitutionally vague. Policies prohibiting "improper conduct" and behavior "inimical to the best interests of the school" have been invalidated because they have not specified the nature of the impermissible conduct.[9] Courts have recognized, however, that disciplinary regulations do not have to satisfy the stringent criteria or specificity required in criminal statutes.[10] Less detail has been required in regulations dealing with activities that are clearly disruptive, such as behavior interfering with the right of access to school buildings.[11]

In addition to reviewing the validity of the conduct regulation upon which a specific punishment is based, courts evaluate the nature and extent of the penalty imposed in relation to the gravity of the offense. In deciding whether a given punishment is appropriate, courts also consider the age, sex, mental condition, and past behavior of the student. Punishments such as the denial of privileges, suspension, expulsion, corporal punishment, and detention after school have been judicially sanctioned. Any of these punishments, however, could be considered unreasonable under a specific set of circumstances. Consequently, courts study each unique factual situation; they do not evaluate the validity of student punishments in the abstract.

Lawsuits challenging disciplinary practices often have focused on the procedures followed in administering punishments, rather than on the substance of disciplinary rules or the nature of the sanctions imposed. Implicit in all judicial declarations regarding school discipline is the notion that severe penalties require more formal procedures while minor punishments necessitate only minimal due process. Nonetheless, any disciplinary action should be accompanied by some procedure to ensure the rudiments of fundamental fairness and to prevent mistakes in the disciplinary process. The Fifth Circuit Court of Appeals has recognized that "the quantum and quality of procedural due process to be afforded a student varies with the seriousness of the punishment to be imposed."[12]

Although school boards have discretionary authority pertaining to student disciplinary matters, they cannot place students' protected rights at the mercy of the collective bargaining process. In an illustrative case, the Erie, Pennsylvania teachers' organization secured a contract that provided an inadequate procedure for student disciplinary cases.[13] Teachers were authorized to remove any disruptive child from the classroom and send the student to another teacher. The receiving teacher also had the right to reject the disruptive student, and in such instances the child was not to be readmitted to school until a special committee had met and determined what action should be taken. In a consent agreement, this procedure was invalidated as depriving students of their constitutional right to due process.

In addition to prohibiting boards of education from bargaining away students' protected rights, courts have prohibited school authorities from punishing students because of the acts of others, such as their parents. In 1974, for example, the Fifth Circuit Court of Appeals held that two children could not be suspended indefinitely from school simply because their mother struck the assistant principal.[14] In reaching its conclusion, the appellate court noted that a fundamental principle of justice is that personal guilt must be present before an individual can be punished. Similarly, an Indiana federal district court held that a student could not be suspended for the parent's failure to pay textbook fees.[15]

The judiciary also has recognized that punishments imposed for student conduct *off school grounds* must be supported by evidence that the student behavior outside of school has a detrimental impact on the well-being of other pupils, teachers, or school activities. In an early case, the Connecticut Supreme Court held that student conduct outside of school hours and school property could be regulated by school officials if such conduct affected the management of the school.[16] Courts have upheld sanctions imposed on students for fighting after school,[17] using insulting language to a teacher on the way home from school,[18] and making an offensive remark about a teacher to a group of students at a shopping center.[19] Courts, however, have prohibited school authorities from punishing students for misbehavior off school grounds if pupils have not been informed that such conduct would result in sanctions[20] or if the misbehavior has had no direct relationship to the welfare of the school.[21]

School personnel should be careful not to place *unnecessary* constraints on student behavior. In developing disciplinary policies, all possible means of achieving the desired outcomes should be explored, and means that are least restrictive of students' personal freedoms should be selected. Once it is ascertained that a certain conduct regulation is necessary, the rule should be clearly written so that it is not open to multiple interpretations. Each regulation should include the rationale for enacting the rule as well as penalties for infractions. It may be advisable to require students to sign a form indicating that they have read the conduct regulations. With such documentation, pupils would be unable to plead ignorance of the rules as a defense for their misconduct.

In general, educators would be wise to adhere to the following guidelines:

- Any conduct regulation adopted should be necessary in order to carry out the school's educational mission; rules should not be designed merely to satisfy the preferences of school board members, administrators, or teachers.
- The rules should be publicized to students and their parents.
- The rules should be specific and clearly stated so that students know which behaviors are prohibited.
- The regulations should not infringe constitutionally protected rights unless there is an overriding public interest to justify the infringement, such as a threat to the safety of other students.
- A rule should not be "ex post facto"; it should not be adopted to prevent a specific activity that school officials know is being planned or has already occurred.
- The regulations should be consistently enforced and uniformly applied to all students without discrimination.
- Punishments should be appropriate to the offense, taking into consideration the child's age, sex, mental condition, and past behavior.
- Some procedural safeguards should accompany the administration of all punishments; the formality of the procedures should be in accord with the severity of the punishment.

In designing and enforcing pupil conduct codes, it is important for school personnel to keep in mind the distinction between students' substantive and procedural rights. If a disciplinary regulation or the administration of punishment violates substantive rights (e.g., restricts protected speech), the regulation cannot be enforced nor the punishment imposed. If only procedural rights are impaired, however, the punishment eventually can be administered after the student has been provided an appropriate hearing.

EXPULSIONS AND SUSPENSIONS

Expulsions and suspensions are among the disciplinary measures most widely used to control student behavior. Uniformly, courts have upheld educators' authority to use expulsions and suspensions as punishments, but due process is required to ensure that students are afforded fair and impartial treatment. This section focuses on disciplinary action in which students are removed from the instructional program; suspensions and expulsions from extracurricular activities are addressed in chapter 4.

EXPULSIONS

State laws and/or school board regulations are usually quite specific regarding the grounds for expulsions, that is, the removal of students from school for a lengthy period of time (usually in excess of ten days[22]). Such grounds are not limited to occurrences during school hours, but generally include infractions on school property immediately before or after school or at any time the school is being used for a school-related activity. Also, expulsions can result from infractions occurring en route to or from school or during school functions held off school premises. While specific grounds vary from state to state, the following infractions are typically considered legitimate grounds for expulsion, as long as the offense occurs while the student is under the jurisdiction of the school:

- using or encouraging others to use violence, force, noise, coercion, or comparable conduct that interferes with school purposes;
- stealing or vandalizing valuable school or private property or repeatedly damaging or stealing school or private property of small value;
- causing or attempting to cause physical injury to a school employee or student;
- possessing a weapon;
- knowingly possessing, using, or transmitting intoxicants of any kind (with the exception of prescriptions from authorized physicians);
- failing repeatedly to comply with reasonable directives of school personnel; and
- engaging in criminal activity or other behavior forbidden by the laws of the state.[23]

State statutes specify limitations on the length of student expulsions. Generally, a student cannot be expelled beyond the end of the current academic year unless the expulsion takes place near the close of the term. A teacher or administrator may initiate expulsion proceedings, but usually only the school board itself can expel a pupil. Although the details of required procedures must be gleaned from state statutes and school board regulations, courts have held that students facing expulsion from school are guaranteed at least minimum due process under the fourteenth amendment. The judiciary has recognized that the following safeguards are advisable:

- written notice of the charges, the intention to expel, and the place, time, and circumstances of the hearing, with sufficient time for a defense to be prepared;[24]
- a full and fair hearing before an impartial adjudicator;[25]
- the right to legal counsel or some other adult representation;[26]
- the opportunity to present witnesses or evidence;[27]
- the opportunity to cross-examine opposing witnesses;[28] and
- some type of written record demonstrating that the decision was based on the evidence presented at the hearing.[29]

Procedural safeguards required may vary depending upon the circumstances of a particular situation. In a Mississippi case, a student and his parents claimed that prior to an expulsion hearing they should have been given a list of the witnesses and a summary of their testimony.[30] While the Fifth Circuit Court of Appeals recognized that these procedural protections should generally be afforded prior to a long-term expulsion, the court held that they were not requisite in the context of this case. The parents had been fully apprised of the charges, the facts supporting the charges, and the nature of the hearing. Consequently, the court concluded that the student suffered no material prejudice from the school board's omission; the witnesses provided no surprises or interference with the student's ability to present his case. In a later case of expulsion for possession of drugs, the same court held that a student's rights were not infringed because he was not provided an opportunity to confront and rebut witnesses who accused him of selling drugs.[31] The names of student witnesses had been withheld to prevent retribution against them. While the contested testimony related to *drug dealing,* the court did not find an error in school officials' considering it in assessing the maximum length of punishment for *possession of drugs.*

State laws and school board regulations often provide students facing expulsion with more elaborate procedural safeguards than the constitutional protections noted above. Once such expulsion procedures are established, courts will require that they be followed.[32] In a 1979 Texas case, an expulsion decision was invalidated because the student did not have proper notice that his behavior would result in expulsion and the applicable school policy was not followed in making the expulsion decision.[33] The student was expelled for possession of marijuana in his car (parked off school grounds), but the school regulation did not stipulate that such behavior off school property would constitute grounds for expulsion. Furthermore, the school district policy on expulsion specified that other means of correcting a student's misbehavior had to be employed before expulsion could be recommended. Since there was no evidence that any other disciplinary measures were used, the Texas civil appeals court ordered reinstatement of the student. More recently, a Louisiana appeals court ruled that a student's possession of marijuana off school property did not justify expulsion under a state law that proscribed only the possession of controlled substances on school property.[34]

Often, expulsions are challenged as excessive for certain offenses. Unless actions are arbitrary, capricious, or oppressive, school officials have broad discretionary powers in establishing disciplinary penalties. An Illinois student protested an expulsion for the remainder of the school year for possession of caffeine pills as too harsh for a first offense.[35] While the trial court agreed that the punishment far outweighed the crime, the appellate court found the action reasonable and justified in light of the dangers posed by unauthorized drugs in the schools. A Pennsylvania commonwealth court held that a ten-day suspension followed by a twenty-four-calendar-day expulsion for drinking on school property after a football game may have been "harsh" but was supported by substantial evidence.[36] Several months later, however, the same court in another case confirmed a trial court's modification of a three-month expulsion of two students who had a couple of sips of a soft drink mixed with whiskey at a football game.[37] The punishment was found to be excessive for students with no prior history of discipline problems.

Recently, federal courts have addressed the special considerations involved in the expulsion of handicapped children. In addition to constitutional procedural safeguards, the Education for All Handicapped Children Act (EAHCA) has been invoked to protect the rights of the handicapped.[38] As discussed in chapter 5, the EAHCA assures every handicapped child a free appropriate education in the least restrictive environment. While the EAHCA is silent on the issue of expulsion, federal courts have found such action to be a change in placement where handicapped children are involved.[39] Prior to any change in the student's program, a special review committee must determine if a student's misconduct is related to the handicap. If a relationship is found, expulsion is prohibited, and the appropriate disciplinary measure would be placement of the student in a more restrictive setting. Even if no connection is found between behavior and handicap, it appears that all educational services cannot be terminated.[40]

Suspensions

Suspensions are frequently used to punish students for violating school rules and standards of behavior when the infractions are not of sufficient magnitude to warrant expulsion. Suspensions include the short-term denial of school attendance as well as the denial of participation in regular courses and activities (in-school suspensions). Most legal controversies have focused on out-of-school suspensions, but the same principles of law appear to apply to any disciplinary action that separates the student from the regular instructional program even for a short period of time.

In contrast to the detailed statutory provisions pertaining to expulsions, state laws have traditionally been silent concerning procedures that must be followed in suspending students from a class or school. As a result, there has been little consistency in standards from one jurisdiction to the next. Prior to 1975, lower courts differed widely in interpreting whether fourteenth amendment procedural protections applied to student suspensions. One federal district court upheld a thirty-day suspension of a student without a hearing, while another court declared that a student's educational status could not be changed for even two days without procedural due process.[41] Standards across the nation ranged on a continuum between these extremes. Finally, in 1975 the United States Supreme Court provided substantial clarification regarding the constitutional rights of students confronting short-term suspensions.

In this case, *Goss v. Lopez,* the Supreme Court majority held that minimum due process must be provided before a student is suspended for even a short period of time.[42] Recognizing that a student's state-created property right to an education is protected by the fourteenth amendment, the Court ruled that such a right cannot be impaired unless the student is afforded notice of the charges and an opportunity to refute them. The Supreme Court also emphasized that suspensions implicate students' constitutionally protected liberty interests because of the potentially damaging effects that the disciplinary process can have on a student's reputation and permanent record:

> School authorities here suspended appellees from school for periods of up to ten days based on charges of misconduct. If sustained and recorded, those charges could seriously damage the students' standing with their fellow pupils and their teachers as well as interfere with later opportunities for higher education and employment.[43]

The Court majority strongly suggested, but did not make explicit, that its holding applied to *all* short-term suspensions, including those of only one class period. Consequently, many school boards have instituted policies that require informal procedures for every brief suspension and more formal procedures for longer suspensions. In the absence of greater specificity in state statutes or administrative regulations, students facing short-term suspensions have a constitutional right to the following protections prior to suspension:

- oral or written notification of the nature of the violation and the intended punishment;
- an opportunity to refute the charges before an objective decision maker (such a discussion may immediately follow the alleged rule infraction); and
- an explanation of the evidence upon which the disciplinarian is relying.

The requirement of an impartial decision maker does not infer that an administrator or teacher who is familiar with the facts cannot serve in this capacity. The decision maker simply must judge the situation fairly and on the basis of valid evidence.

While the Supreme Courts' decision in *Goss* established the rudimentary procedural requirements for short-term suspensions, efforts continue on the part of students to expand their procedural rights. The Supreme Court specifically noted that such formal procedures as the right to secure counsel, to confront and cross-examine witnesses, and to call witnesses were not required. Recently, the Supreme Court reiterated this stance by noting that a two-day suspension "does not rise to the level of a penal sanction calling for the full panoply of procedural due process protections applicable to a criminal prosecution."[44] Decisions by lower state and federal courts indicate a reluctance to impose these additional requirements unless mandated by state law. A Maine case illustrates the types of procedural safeguards which have been advanced in an effort to extend the *Goss* ruling.[45] In that case, the student claimed a violation of procedural due process because the school administrator denied him permission to leave during questioning and failed to advise him of his right to remain silent or to have his parents present during the interrogation. The court rejected all claims, noting that there was no legal authority to substantiate any of the asserted rights. The court reasoned that to rule otherwise would, in fact, contradict the informal procedures outlined in *Goss* allowing for immediate questioning and disciplinary action.

The "right to remain silent" also has been advanced in other disciplinary cases. Students have argued that the principle established by the Supreme Court in *Miranda v. Arizona* (persons subjected to custodial interrogation must be advised of their right to remain silent, that any statement made may be used against them, and that they have the right of legal counsel[46]) applies in school disciplinary proceedings. Courts have readily dismissed these claims, finding that discussions with school administrators are noncustodial.[47] Clearly, in the *Miranda* decision, the Supreme Court was interpreting an individual's fifth amendment right against self-incrimination when first subjected to police questioning in connection with criminal charges.

Although the Supreme Court in *Goss* recognized the possibility of "unusual situations" that would require more formal procedures than those outlined, little guidance was given as to what these circumstances might be. The only suggestion offered in *Goss* was that a disciplinarian should adopt more extensive procedures in instances involving factual disputes "and arguments about cause and effect."[48] It has been suggested that suspensions involving loss of course credit or occurring during exam periods might entail greater due process. The Fifth Circuit Court of Appeals, however, did not find persuasive the argument that the loss incurred for a ten-day suspension during final examinations required more than a mere give-and-take discussion between the principal and student.[49] In refusing to require more formal proceedings, the court noted that *Goss* makes no distinctions as to when a short-term suspension occurs and a contrary ruling would "significantly undermine, if not nullify, its definitive holding."[50]

Suspensions, however, may require additional procedural protections under state laws. For example, the Ohio statute, earlier found to be constitutionally defective in *Goss*, now requires that prior to suspension each student must be provided written notice of the intent to suspend and the reasons for the intended suspension.[51] For suspensions in excess of three days, Pennsylvania law mandates written notification to parents prior to the informal hearing.[52] Recently, a Pennsylvania commonwealth court declared that a seven-day suspension violated a student's due process rights because the parents received only oral notification of the reasons for suspension.[53]

For the past decade, courts have resisted attempts to elaborate or formalize the minimal due process requirements outlined in *Goss* for short-term suspensions. As the Supreme Court noted, "further formalizing the suspension process and escalating its formality and adversary nature may not only make it too costly as a regular discipline tool but also destroy its effectiveness as part of the teaching process."[54]

DISCIPLINARY TRANSFERS

Closely related to suspensions are involuntary student transfers for disciplinary reasons. Legal challenges to the use of disciplinary transfers have primarily focused on the adequacy of the procedures followed. Recognizing that students do not have an inherent right to attend a given school, courts nonetheless have held that pupils facing involuntary reassignment are entitled to a hearing if such transfers are occasioned by alleged misbehavior.

For example, a New Jersey superior court ruled that a hearing was required before a pupil could be assigned to home instruction because of misconduct occurring off school premises after school hours.[55] The court noted that school officials had the authority to suspend the student, and to place him in homebound instruction, if it were determined at a proper hearing that he was dangerous to himself or others. The court declared, however, that the student could not be denied the right to attend school without first being given an opportunity to present a full defense regarding the incident precipitating the disciplinary action. Similarly, a New York court held that a pupil could not be assigned to homebound instruction for disruptive behavior and truancy without procedural due process.[56] The court rejected the assertion that the student was merely being afforded alternative education, and equated the assignment to homebound instruction with a suspension from school.

Courts also have held that disciplinary transfers to special schools or programs necessitate some type of procedural safeguards to ensure that the students are not being relegated to inferior programs. The judiciary has required due process prior to reassigning a student to a school for habitual truants or to a program for pupils with behavior problems.[57] Transfer policies allowing the receiving program or school to refuse to admit the child also have been disallowed.[58]

In 1977 a Pennsylvania federal district court ruled that "lateral transfers" for disciplinary reasons affected personal interests of sufficient magnitude to require due process procedures.[59] Even though such transfers involved comparable schools, the court reasoned that a disciplinary transfer carried with it a stigma, and thus implicated a protected liberty right. Noting that a transfer of a pupil "during a school year from a familiar school to a strange and possibly more distant school would be a terrifying experience for many children of normal sensibilities," the court concluded that such transfers were more drastic punishments than suspensions, and thus necessitated due process.[60] As to the nature of the procedures required, the court held that the student and parents must be given notice of the proposed transfer and that a prompt informal hearing before the school principal must be provided. The court stipulated that if parents were still dissatisfied with the arrangement after the informal meeting, they had to be given the opportunity to contest the transfer recommendation at a more formal hearing, with the option of being represented by legal counsel.

CORPORAL PUNISHMENT

Corporal punishment is defined as chastisement inflicted on the body to modify behavior. Corporal punishment in American public schools has evoked litigation for several decades, and historically it has been the most frequently challenged student punishment. Courts generally have assumed that teachers acted reasonably in using corporal punishment and have placed the burden on the aggrieved students to prove otherwise. In evaluating the reasonableness of a teacher's actions in a given situation, courts have assessed the child's age, maturity, and past behavior; the nature of the offense; the instrument used; whether there was evidence of lasting harm to the child; and the motivation of the person inflicting the punishment.[61] Corporal punishment accompanied by malice or anger has been deemed unlawful.[62]

Constitutional Issues

In *Baker v. Owen,* a North Carolina federal court addressed a constitutional challenge to a teacher's use of corporal punishment over parental objections.[63] The federal district court concluded that the use of reasonable corporal punishment did not constitute "cruel and unusual punishment" under the eighth amendment, and that parental consent was not necessary before using this disciplinary technique. The court, however, stipulated that the following procedural safeguards must accompany the administration of corporal punishment:

- Students must be informed as to what behaviors will occasion a spanking.
- School officials must try other disciplinary measures before resorting to corporal punishment.
- The use of corporal punishment must be witnessed by another staff member.
- Written reasons for the punishment must be provided to parents upon request.

The United States Supreme Court affirmed the district court's decision in *Baker* without delivering a written opinion. Thus, the high court left some ambiguity as to the constitutional status of corporal punishment until two years later, when it again reviewed a case pertaining to this issue. In *Ingraham v. Wright,* the Supreme Court majority stated that the use of corporal punishment in schools does not violate the eighth amendment, nor does it violate fourteenth amendment procedural due process guarantees.[64] While recognizing that corporal punishment implicates students' constitutionally protected liberty interests, the Court emphasized that state remedies are available, such as suits in assault and battery, if students are excessively or arbitrarily punished by school personnel. In essence, the Court majority concluded that cases dealing with corporal punishment should be handled by state courts under provisions of state laws. The majority distinguished corporal punishment from a suspension by noting that the denial of school attendance is a more severe penalty, and thus deprives students of a property right which necessitates procedural requisites. Furthermore, the majority reasoned that the purpose of corporal punishment would be diluted if elaborate procedures had to be followed prior to using this disciplinary measure. The Court concluded that the procedures outlined by the federal court in *Baker v. Owen,* although desirable, are not required under the Federal Constitution.

Constitutional issues have continued to be raised in the wake of *Ingraham.* In 1980 the Fourth Circuit Court of Appeals held that students' substantive due process right to be free of brutal and harmful state intrusions into realms of personal privacy and bodily security might be impaired by the use of excessive corporal punishment.[65] The court concluded that *Ingraham* bars federal litigation on procedural due process issues, but "there may be circumstances under which specific corporal punishment administered by state school officials gives rise to an independent federal course of action to vindicate substantive due process rights."[66] According to the court, the standard for determining if such a violation has occurred is "whether the force applied caused injury so severe, was so disproportionate to the need presented, and was so inspired by malice or sadism rather than a merely careless or unwise excess of zeal that it amounted to a brutal and inhumane abuse of official power literally shocking to the conscience."[67] While *Ingraham* does not foreclose a successful federal constitutional challenge to the use of unreasonable corporal punishment, most courts have declined to find substantive due process violations.[68]

State Law

While the Supreme Court has ruled that corporal punishment in public schools is not prohibited under the Federal Constitution, the use of such punishment may conflict with state constitutional provisions or statutes or local administrative regulations. In West Virginia, the doctrine of *in loco parentis* (in place of parent), insofar as it permitted corporal punishment, was challenged under the state constitution.[69] While declining to address the constitutionality of *in loco parentis,* the state high court concluded that the doctrine did not permit corporal punishment by mechanical devices (e.g., paddles, whips, sticks) but did permit spanking by hand or physical restraint and removal of unruly students. The court reasoned that because a liberty interest is implicated when the state attempts to use even manual corporal punishment, some minimal due process must be provided. The court noted that this would include at least an opportunity for the student to explain his or her version of the disruptive event and the administration of the punishment in the presence of another adult.

Several states prohibit corporal punishment by law,[70] and many school boards have regulations that place explicit conditions on the use of this form of discipline. In contrast, a few states by law empower school personnel to use corporal punishment. Local school boards cannot prohibit corporal punishment if a state law specifically authorizes educators to use this disciplinary technique.[71] In states without statutory language to the contrary, corporal punishment is permissible, but local boards may develop policies restricting or banning its use.

Teachers can be discharged for violating state laws or board policies regulating corporal punishment. Several courts have upheld dismissals based on insubordination for failure to comply with reasonable school board requirements in administering corporal punishment.[72] In a typical case, a New York teacher was dismissed because he violated board policy by using corporal punishment after having been warned repeatedly to cease.[73] Teachers also have been dismissed under the statutory cause of "cruelty" for improper use of physical force with students. In Illinois, a tenured teacher was dismissed on this ground for using a cattle prod in punishing students.[74] A Pennsylvania teacher was dismissed for "cruelty" because she threw a student against a blackboard and then pulled him upright by his hair.[75]

In the absence of statutory or board restrictions, there are other legal means available to challenge the use of unreasonable corporal punishment in public schools. Teachers can be charged with criminal assault and battery which might result in the imposition of a fine and/or imprisonment. Civil assault and battery suits for monetary damages also can be initiated against school personnel. For example, a Louisiana appeals court awarded a student $1,000 for pain, suffering, and humiliation associated with an excessive and unreasonable whipping administered by a teacher.[76]

Educators should use caution in administering corporal punishment since improper administration can result in dismissal, monetary damages, and even imprisonment.[77] Corporal punishment should never be administered with malice, and the use of excessive force should be avoided. Teachers would be wise to keep a record of incidents involving corporal punishment and to adhere to the minimum procedures outlined by the federal court in *Baker v. Owen*[78] as legal safeguards in the event that their actions are challenged. Moreover, teachers should become familiar with relevant state laws and school board policies before attempting to use corporal punishment in their classrooms.

ACADEMIC SANCTIONS

It is indisputable that school authorities have the right to use academic sanctions for poor academic performance. Consistently, courts have been reluctant to substitute their own judgment for that of educators in assessing students' academic accomplishments. Failing grades, denial of credit, academic probation, retention, and expulsion from particular programs have been upheld as legitimate means of dealing with poor academic performance.[79] In 1965 the Vermont Federal District Court stated:

> In matters of scholarship, the school authorities are uniquely qualified by training and experience to judge the qualifications of a student, and efficiency of instruction depends in no small degree upon the school faculty's freedom from interference from other noneducational tribunals. It is only when the school authorities abuse this discretion that a court may interfere with their decision. . . .[80]

While courts usually have granted broad discretionary powers to school personnel in establishing academic standards,[81] there has been less agreement regarding the use of grade reductions or academic sanctions as punishments for student misbehavior and/or absences.[82] More complex legal issues are raised when academic penalties are imposed for *nonacademic* reasons. These issues are explored below in connection with grade reductions for unexcused absences and misconduct.

Unexcused Absences

Excessive student absenteeism is a growing concern and has led many school boards to the use of academic sanctions for unexcused absences. These practices have generated legal challenges related to students' substantive due process rights. To meet the due process requirements the sanctions must be reasonable—that is, rationally related to a valid educational purpose. Since students must attend class to benefit from the educational program, most courts have found that academic penalties for absenteeism serve a valid educational goal.

In a 1976 Illinois case, a student claimed that protected rights were impaired by a school regulation stipulating that grades would be lowered one letter grade per class for an unexcused absence.[83] In defending the rule, school officials asserted that it was the most appropriate punishment for the serious problem of truancy. It also was argued that students could not perform satisfactorily in their classwork if they were absent, as grades reflected class participation in addition to other standards of performance. The appeals court was not persuaded by the student's argument that grades should reflect only scholastic achievement, and therefore concluded that the regulation was reasonable.

The Supreme Court of Connecticut in a recent case upheld a schoolwide policy that provided for a five-point reduction in the course grade for each unapproved absence and denied course credit for absences in excess of twenty-four.[84] The court drew a sharp distinction between academic and disciplinary sanctions, noting that the school board's policy was academic in intent and effect rather than disciplinary. Specifically, the court found that a board's determination that academic grades should reflect more than examinations and papers "constitutes an academic judgment about academic requirements."[85]

To ensure procedural fairness, however, students must be informed that unexcused absences will result in academic penalties. In a Missouri case, a student received a failing grade for half of a semester in a music course for failure to attend the last two performances of the semester.[86] The court upheld the grade reduction because the students were informed the first day of class that all performances were required to complete the course and that unexcused absences would result in a failing grade. Where grade reductions are part of academic evaluation, courts do not generally require additional procedural safeguards beyond notice.

While courts usually have supported sanctions that link attendance and scholastic achievement, state laws may limit the use of academic penalties or require other responses to the problem of truancy. For example, a Colorado appeals court found that academic sanctions for absenteeism were impermissible under state statutory provisions.[87] The contested school board policy stipulated that any student who missed more than seven days during a semester would not receive academic credit for the courses taken. Under the regulation, it was irrelevant whether the absences were because of illness, family problems, or any other reasons. Two students, who were denied academic credit because of the accumulation of more than seven absences in a semester, filed suit challenging the policy as inconsistent with state law that required attendance for 172 days excluding absences for illness and disciplinary suspensions. The court invalidated the school board's regulation, holding that the board had exceeded its authority in enacting such a policy. In contrast, the Supreme Court of Arkansas upheld a board policy that disallowed course credit and permitted expulsion of students who accumulated more than twelve absences.[88] The court, in refusing to substitute its judgment for the school board, concluded that under state law this action was within the board's power to make reasonable rules and regulations for the administration of the schools.

Given the serious truancy problem confronting many school districts, it seems likely that the imposition of academic sanctions will continue to be considered. The legality of such policies will depend primarily on judicial interpretation of applicable state law.

Misconduct

Academic sanctions imposed for student misconduct also have been challenged. It is generally accepted that students can be denied credit for work missed while they are suspended from school. In fact, if students could make up such work without penalty, a suspension might be viewed as a vacation rather than a punishment. More controversy has surrounded policies that impose an additional grade reduction for suspension days, and courts have not agreed regarding the legality of this practice.

For example, a Kentucky appeals court voided a regulation whereby grades were reduced because of unexcused absences resulting from student suspensions.[89] The school board policy stated that work missed because of unexcused absences could not be made up, and that five points would be deducted for every unexcused absence from each class during the grading period. The court held that the use of suspensions or expulsions for misconduct was permissible, but the lowering of grades as a punitive measure was not. Similarly, a Pennsylvania court found grade reductions for suspensions to be beyond a school board's authority.[90] In the court's opinion, it was a clear misrepresentation of students' scholastic achievement; the penalty went beyond the five-day suspension and downgraded achievement for a full grading period.

A Texas appellate court, however, upheld a school system's right to impose scholastic penalties for suspension days.[91] Relying on a state attorney general's opinion approving grade reductions, the court found the pivotal question to be whether the board had actually adopted a policy that would authorize grade reductions. According to the court, oral announcements in school assemblies explaining grade penalties constituted a valid policy. Further, the court noted that the grade reductions did not impair constitutionally protected property or liberty rights. Since the penalized students had already been admitted to universities of their choice, the court concluded that no adverse impact was shown on their educational, professional, or personal interests.

Generally, courts have ruled that academic course credit or high school diplomas cannot be withheld solely for disciplinary reasons. As early as 1921, the Supreme Court of Iowa held that students who had completed all academic requirements had the right to receive a high school diploma even though they refused to wear graduation caps during the ceremony.[92] The court ruled that the school board was obligated to issue a diploma to a pupil who had satisfactorily completed the prescribed course of study and who was otherwise qualified to graduate from high school.[93]

Courts have issued conflicting decisions regarding the legality of denying a student the right to participate in graduation ceremonies as a disciplinary measure. A New York appeals court held that a student could not be denied such participation on disciplinary grounds,[94] whereas a North Carolina federal district court held that a student could be denied the privilege of participating in the graduation ceremony as a penalty for misconduct.[95] In the latter case, the federal court concluded that the student was not deprived of any property right, since he did receive his high school diploma even though he was not allowed to take part in the ceremony.

While the use of grade reductions as sanctions for student misconduct, as well as truancy, is prevalent, students seem likely to continue to challenge such practices. Even if the Supreme Court should declare that grades need not reflect only academic performance, any regulation stipulating that grades will be lowered for nonacademic reasons should be reasonable, related to absences from class, and serve a legitimate school purpose. Furthermore, the rules should be made known to all students through the school's official student handbook or some similar means.

SEARCH AND SEIZURE

Search and seizure cases involving public schools have increased in recent years, with the majority of these cases resulting from the confiscation of illegal drugs. Students have asserted that warrantless searches conducted by school officials impair their fourth amendment rights guaranteed by the Federal Constitution. Through an extensive line of decisions, the United States Supreme Court has affirmed that the basic purpose of the amendment is to "safeguard the privacy and security of individuals against arbitrary invasions by governmental officials."[96] This amendment protects individuals against unreasonable searches by requiring state agents to obtain a warrant based on probable cause prior to conducting a search. Under the probable cause standard, a governmental official must have reasonable grounds of suspicion, supported by sufficient evidence, to warrant a cautious person to believe that the suspected individual is guilty of the charged offense and that the search will produce evidence of the crime committed. Governmental officials violating fourth amendment rights are subject to criminal or civil liability, but the most important remedy for the aggrieved individual is the exclusionary rule.[97] This rule renders evidence of an illegal search inadmissible in criminal prosecutions.[98]

Significant fourth amendment questions have been raised in the public school setting.[99] Since fourth amendment protections apply only to searches conducted by agents of the state, a fundamental issue in education cases is whether school authorities function as private individuals or as state agents. While most courts have found the fourth amendment applicable to the public schools, it was not until 1985 in *New Jersey v. T.L.O.* that the United States Supreme Court finally held that the amendment's prohibition on unreasonable searches applies to school officials.[100] The Court concluded that school officials are state agents, and all governmental actions come within the constraints of the fourth amendment.[101] Strictures of the law are not limited to law enforcement officers.

Although finding the fourth amendment applicable, the Court in *T.L.O.* concluded that school officials' substantial interest in maintaining discipline required "easing" the warrant and probable cause requirements imposed on public authorities. In rejecting these restrictions, the Court reasoned that "requiring a teacher to obtain a warrant before searching a child suspected of an infraction of school rules (or of the criminal law) would unduly interfere with the maintenance of the swift and informal disciplinary procedures needed in the schools."[102] In modifying the level of suspicion required to conduct a search, the Court found the public interest was best served in the school setting with a standard less than probable cause. Accordingly, the Court held that the legality of a search should depend "simply on the reasonableness, under all the circumstances, of the search."[103]

Two tests were advanced for determining reasonableness. First, is the search justified at its inception? That is, are there "reasonable grounds for suspecting that the search will turn up evidence that the student has violated or is violating either the law or the rules of the school?"[104] Second, is the scope of the search reasonable? In the Court's words, are "the measures adopted reasonably related to the objectives of the search and not excessively intrusive in light of the age and sex of the student and the nature of the infraction?"[105]

The "reasonableness" standard allows for substantial latitude among courts in interpreting fourth amendment rights.[106] Among the factors courts have considered in assessing reasonable grounds are the child's age, history, and record in the school; prevalence and seriousness of the problem in the school to which the search is directed; exigency to make the search without delay and further investigation; probative value and reliability of the information used as a justification for the search; the school officials' experience with the student and with the type of problem to which the search was directed; and the type of search.[107] Courts have differed, however, in the rigor applied in making these assessments.[108] While some courts have essentially imposed the stringency of the probable cause standard in connection with student searches, others have accepted a mere hunch as substantiating reasonable grounds for such searches.

Clearly, reasonable suspicion requires more than a hunch, good intentions, or good faith. The Supreme Court, in upholding an exception of the warrant requirement for a "stop and frisk" search for weapons by police officers, concluded that to justify the intrusion the police officer must be able to point to "specific and articulable facts."[109] In recognizing school searches also as special exceptions, it appears that, at a minimum, the judiciary will require searches to be supported by objective facts.[110]

In assessing the constitutionality of searches in the public schools two questions are central: What constitutes a search, and what types of searches are reasonable? What constitutes a search must be appraised in the context of the Supreme Court's statement that:

> the Fourth Amendment protects people, not places. What a person knowingly exposes to the public, even in his own home or office, is not a subject of Fourth Amendment protection. But what he seeks to preserve as private, even in an area accessible to the public, may be constitutionally protected.[111]

According to the Court's rulings, essential considerations in determining whether an action is a search are an individual's reasonable expectation of privacy (reasonable in the sense that society is prepared to recognize the privacy)[112] and the extent of governmental intrusion.[113] The reasonableness of a specific type of search must be evaluated in terms of all the circumstances surrounding the search.[114] This would include variables such as who initiated the search, who conducted the search, need for the search, purpose of the search, information or factors prompting the search, what or who was searched, and use of the evidence.[115] In the following sections, various types of school searches are examined within this framework.

Lockers and Other Property

Although the Supreme Court has held that the fourth amendment applies to people and not places, school lockers have been singled out as generating a lower expectation of privacy. Courts have usually distinguished locker searches on the basis that the locker is school property, and the student does not retain exclusive possession. Under the view of joint control, school officials have been allowed to inspect lockers or even to consent to searches by law enforcement officers. The judiciary, however, has not given school personnel blanket approval to make indiscriminate locker searches; any search must be based on reasonable suspicion that contraband disruptive to the educational process will be uncovered. If the purpose of the search is to gather criminal evidence, a search warrant is required.

A Kansas case illustrates the prevalent judicial view toward locker searches. The Supreme Court of Kansas held that the right of inspection is inherent in the authority granted school officials to manage the schools.[116] The court maintained that it is a proper function of school personnel to inspect the lockers under their control and to prevent the use of lockers in illicit ways or for illegal purposes. Earlier, the New York high court proclaimed that "[n]ot only have the school authorities a right to inspect but this right becomes a duty when suspicion arises that something of an illegal nature may be secreted there."[117] The Tenth Circuit Court of Appeals also concluded that "school authorities have, on behalf of the public, an interest in these lockers and a duty to police the school, particularly where possible serious violations of the criminal laws exist."[118] All three courts noted that school officials had a list of the combinations and had occasionally inspected the lockers. These points have been emphasized in other cases to support the nonexclusive nature of lockers.[119]

Applying the *T.L.O.* standards for reasonableness, the West Virginia Supreme Court upheld a search of a locker that produced evidence of drug use.[120] The search of the student's locker for alcohol was initiated by an administrator based on information that a friend of the student had consumed alcohol at the suspected student's home that morning. Finding that this was reasonable grounds for conducting the search, the court concluded that discovery of drugs in the pocket of a jacket in the locker was reasonably related to the search for alcoholic beverages.

A recent decision of the New Jersey high court, however, departed from the general judicial view of locker privacy.[121] In this situation, the court held that the student did have an expectation of privacy in the contents of his locker. The locker was characterized as a home away from home, a place to store personal "effects." Although the existence of a master key did not lower the expectation of privacy, the court noted in its discussion that a policy of regularly inspecting the students' lockers might have that effect.

In some cases students have contested locker searches on the basis of state constitutional provisions or state statutes. A Washington appeals court interpreted the state constitution as affording students no greater protection from searches of their lockers by school officials than is guaranteed by the fourth amendment.[122] Although the Washington high court has found that state law is almost a complete bar to warrantless searches and arrests, the appellate court declined to extend this holding to school searches, concluding that a prior decision of the state supreme court on school searches controlled and was similar to fourth amendment protections.[123]

Statutes in some states address students' rights in connection with locker searches. Indiana law, for example, indicates that a student's locker is property of the school district and that a student is presumed to have no expectation of privacy in the locker or its contents. The law, however, also stipulates that other than a general search of all lockers, "where possible," locker searches will be conducted in the presence of the affected students.[124] If a state law provides greater privacy protections than the Federal Constitution, school authorities are expected to adhere to the statutory mandates.

Personal property or effects of students usually entail a greater expectation of privacy than school lockers. The constitutionality of searches of personal effects is determined by assessing the grounds for the search and the circumstances surrounding it. A Florida district court upheld the search of a student's car when a school aide observed a waterpipe in plain view.[125] In this instance, the aide regularly patrolled the school parking lot to ensure enforcement of school regulations and to supervise students during their lunch break. In the court's opinion, patrolling of the lot fell within the school's duty to maintain order and discipline. Moreover, patrolling itself was not a search. A Texas federal district court, however, declined to uphold a general dragnet search of a school parking lot.[126] The school's interest in the contents of the cars was viewed as minimal since students did not have access to their cars during the school day. Furthermore, the search was indiscriminate, lacking any evidence of individualized suspicion.

Personal Searches

Warrantless searches of a student's person raise significant legal questions. Unlike locker searches, it cannot be asserted that there is a lower expectation of privacy. The Fifth Circuit Appellate Court noted that "the fourth amendment applies with its fullest vigor against any intrusion on the human body." [127] In personal searches not only is it necessary to have reasonable cause to search, but also the search itself must be reasonable. Reasonableness is assessed in terms of the specific facts and circumstances of a case.

In the Supreme Court's *T.L.O.* decision, a teacher had reported that a student was smoking in the restroom. Upon questioning by the assistant principal, she denied smoking and, in fact, denied that she even smoked. The assistant principal then opened the student's purse seeking evidence to substantiate that she did smoke. In the process of removing a package of cigarettes, he spotted rolling papers, and subsequently found marijuana and other evidence implicating her in drug dealing. The state brought delinquency charges against the student, and she moved to suppress the evidence from the search.

Using the "reasonable suspicion" test, the Supreme Court found that the search in *T.L.O.* was reasonable. The school official had a basis for suspecting that the student had cigarettes in her purse. Although possession was not a violation of a school rule, it was not irrelevant; discovery of cigarettes provided evidence to corroborate that she had been smoking and challenged her credibility. No direct evidence existed that the student's purse contained cigarettes, but, based on a teacher's report that the student had been smoking, it was logical to suspect that she might have cigarettes in her purse. Characterizing this as a "common-sense" conclusion, the Court noted that "the requirement of reasonable suspicion is not a requirement of absolute certainty: 'sufficient probability, not certainty, is the touchstone of reasonableness under the fourth amendment.' " [128]

In a recent California case, an appellate court found the search of a student's pockets reasonable under the *T.L.O.* standard.[129] In this case, a school official found a student in a restroom without a pass during class time. Because the student appeared to be nervous and was acting suspiciously, the administrator requested that he empty his pockets which led to the discovery of drugs. The court found that the search was justified on the basis of suspicious behavior and that the scope of the search was not excessive or intrusive.

An individual may waive entitlement to fourth amendment protection by consenting to a search or volunteering requested evidence. The consent, however, is valid only if voluntarily given in the absence of coercion. Serious questions arise as to whether a student's consent is actually voluntary. Did the student have a free choice? Was the student aware of his or her fourth amendment rights? A Texas federal district court argued that the very nature of the school setting diminishes the assumption of consent.[130] Students are accustomed to receiving and following orders of school officials; refusal to obey a request is insubordination. In this case, the threat to call the students' parents and the police if they did not cooperate further substantiated a coercive atmosphere. In another case, the Sixth Circuit Court of Appeals stated that there is "a presumption against the waiver of constitutional rights," placing the burden on school officials to show that students knowingly and intelligently waived their constitutional rights.[131] Although some courts have found student consent valid,[132] the inherent pitfalls of pursuing such a search in the absence of reasonable cause must be duly considered.

Strip Searches

It is problematic as to whether a strip search can ever be justified on the basis of reasonable suspicion. The Second Circuit Court of Appeals noted that "as the intrusiveness of the search intensifies, the standard of fourth amendment 'reasonableness' approaches probable cause, even in the school context."[133] The Seventh Circuit Appellate Court, in a strongly worded statement, proclaimed in an Indiana case:

> [I]t does not require a constitutional scholar to conclude that a nude search of a thirteen-year-old child is an invasion of constitutional rights of some magnitude. More than that: it is a violation of any known principle of human decency.[134]

Litigation indicates that substantial evidence must exist to conduct strip searches. The Ninth Circuit Court of Appeals found a "pat-down" search and subsequent strip search to be unlawful.[135] Such an invasion of privacy could not be justified on the basis that a bus driver saw the student exchange "what appeared to be money" for an unidentified object. Similarly, a New York federal district court held that a strip search of a fifth-grade class to find three dollars that had been stolen was unreasonable.[136] Factors considered by the court were the lack of danger in the situation, the intrusiveness of the search, and the age of the students. The court did imply that a more dangerous situation, such as drug possession, might support a strip search. The New York high court indicated a similar position in supressing evidence obtained from the search of a student's wallet and follow-up strip search for lack of reasonable grounds for the action.[137] The court noted, however, that if there had been a reasonable basis to conduct the search, the discovery of drugs in the wallet would have warranted a strip search.

In contrast to the general trend in judicial decisions, a Kentucky appeals court recently found the strip search of a student reasonable because it was based on sufficient evidence.[138] Such evidence included the student's passing of prescription drugs and marijuana to other students and his admission that he had grown marijuana and smoked it frequently. Other influential facts in this case were that no criminal charges were filed; law enforcement officers were not involved; and the search was initiated for a specific reason, that is, it was not a systematic search of the entire student body.

Although courts have not prohibited strip searches of students, enough caveats exist to alert school officials of the inherent risks of such intrusive searches. The judicial trend indicates that reasonable suspicion alone may be inadequate to justify strip searches; rather, the required standard approaches probable cause. Except for emergency situations, few circumstances appear to warrant such intrusions.

Use of Canines

The use of drug-detecting dogs in searches raises a number of controversial questions regarding fourth amendment rights. Does the presence of a dog sniffing students constitute a search? Must reasonable suspicion exist to justify the use of the dogs? Does the alert of a dog establish reasonable suspicion? A few courts have addressed these issues.

The Tenth Circuit Court of Appeals upheld the use of trained police dogs in the sniffing of lockers but did not directly address the issues presented by the use of the dogs.[139] Rather, the court discussed generally the school administrator's duty to inspect, even to the point that an inspection may violate fourth amendment rights. Under this broad grant of authority, the alert of a dog three times at a locker established reasonable suspicion to conduct a search.

The Fifth Circuit Court of Appeals, on the other hand, confronted the question of whether sniffing by a dog is a search in terms of an individual's reasonable expectation of privacy.[140] The appellate court noted that the vast majority of courts have held that law enforcement use of canines for the sniffing of objects is not a search. Specifically, the court referenced cases involving checked luggage, shipped packages, public lockers, and cars parked on public streets.[141] According to the court, a reasonable expectation of privacy does not extend to the airspace surrounding these objects. The court maintained that what has evolved is a doctrine of "public smell," equivalent to the "plain view" theory (that is, an object in plain view can be seized). This point was illustrated by the example of a police officer detecting the odor of marijuana from an object or property. No search is involved because the odor is considered to be in public view and thus unprotected.

From this line of reasoning, the court noted that the use of canines has been viewed as merely enhancing the ability to detect an odor, as the use of a flashlight improves vision. Accordingly, the court concluded that sniffing of student lockers and cars in public view was not a search, and, therefore, the fourth amendment did not apply.[142] While permitting the use of dogs to detect drugs, the court held that reasonable suspicion is required for a further search of a locker or car by school officials, and that such suspicion can be established only upon showing that the dogs are reasonably reliable in detecting the actual presence of contraband.[143]

In most instances, judicial support for the use of dogs has been limited to the sniffing of objects. The Seventh Circuit Court of Appeals, however, concluded in an Indiana case that the presence of dogs in the classroom was not a search.[144] In this well-publicized case, school officials, with the assistance of police officers, conducted a school-wide inspection for drugs in which trained dogs were brought into each classroom for approximately five minutes. When a dog alerted beside a student, the student was requested to remove the contents of his or her pockets or purse. A continued alert by the dog resulted in a strip search. The appellate court, in weighing the minimal intrusion of the dogs against the school's desire to eliminate a significant drug problem, concluded that sniffing of the students by the dogs did not constitute a search invoking fourth amendment protections. Search of pockets and purses, however, did involve an invasion of privacy, but was justified on the basis that the dog's alert constituted reasonable cause to believe that the student possessed drugs. However, as discussed previously, the court drew the line at conducting a strip search based on a dog's alert.

In contrast to the reasoning of the Seventh Circuit Court of Appeals, a Texas federal district court concluded that the use of dogs in a blanket "sniffing" (or inspection) of students did constitute a search.[145] In examining sophisticated surveillance devices, the court noted that drug-detecting dogs posed a greater intrusion upon personal privacy than electronic devices that have been found to be searches. According to the court, "[t]he dog's inspection was virtually equivalent to a physical entry into the students' pockets and personal possessions."[146] In finding the dog's sniffing to be a search, the court further held that for school authorities to use dogs in a search they must have *prior* individualized suspicion that a student possesses contraband that will disrupt the educational process.[147] In essence, a dog alert cannot be used to establish such suspicion.

Similarly, the Fifth Circuit Court of Appeals held that sniffing of students by dogs significantly intrudes on an individual's privacy, thereby constituting a search.[148] While recognizing that the sniffing of a person is a search, the court did not prohibit such searches, but held that the intrusiveness of the search must be weighed against the school's need to search. The court concluded that even a significant need to search requires individualized suspicion prior to the use of dogs because of the degree of intrusion on personal dignity and security.

Given the scope of the drug problem in public schools, it seems likely that other school districts will consider the use of drug-detecting canine units. Until the Supreme Court addresses whether such a practice constitutes a search (requiring individualized suspicion) or whether a dog alert can establish reasonable grounds for a personal search, different interpretations among lower courts seem destined to persist.

Drug Testing

In an effort to control drug use among students, some districts have considered adopting school-wide drug testing programs. Such programs raise serious questions about students' privacy rights under the fourth amendment. These issues were highlighted in a 1985 New Jersey case in which the constitutionality of a school district's plan to require urinalysis of all students was reviewed.[149]

As part of a comprehensive medical examination, the board's policy required high school students to submit to urine testing to detect the use of twenty-six illegal drugs. School officials argued that the fourth amendment was inapplicable because drug abuse is an illness and urine testing is a medical procedure. In rejecting the school district's argument, the state judge held that urinalysis did not meet the "reasonableness" test advanced by the Supreme Court in *T.L.O.* The scope of the test was not reasonable since all students were required to be tested without individualized suspicion of drug use, and the few instances of drug-related problems in the district did not justify the substantial interference. Further, the judge found that constitutional safeguards were violated because students who refused to submit to the test were excluded from school for "medical reasons" without due process.

Police Involvement

While a "reasonable suspicion" or "reasonable cause to believe" standard is generally invoked in assessing the reasonableness of school searches, it appears that a higher standard may be required when police officers are involved. The nature and extent of such involvement are important considerations in determining whether a search is reasonable. If the police role is one of finding evidence of a crime, probable cause would be required.[150] If, on the other hand, it is simply providing school officials assistance in a disciplinary action, reasonable suspicion may be adequate.[151] While early decisions generally supported police participation in searches initiated and conducted by school officials,[152] more recent decisions have tended to draw a sharp distinction between searches with and without police assistance.[153]

The more stringent judicial posture is represented in an Illinois decision.[154] In that case, the school principal received a call that led him to suspect that three girls possessed illegal drugs. Upon the superintendent's advice, he called the police to assist in the investigation. After the police arrived, each girl was searched by the school nurse and the school psychologist, but no drugs were discovered. Subsequently, suit was brought alleging that the civil rights of the students had been violated. The court found that the police were not called merely to assist in maintaining school discipline but to search for evidence of a crime. Under the circumstances, the court concluded that the students had a constitutional right not to be searched unless the police had a warrant based on probable cause.

In contrast, the same Illinois court held that a police officer's involvement in persuading a student to relinquish the contents of his pockets did not violate fourth amendment rights under the *T.L.O.* standard.[155] The police officer's role was quite limited in this case. He was in the school building on another matter, and his role in the search was restricted simply to requesting that the student empty his pockets. There was no police involvement in the investigation that led to detaining the student nor was the evidence used for criminal prosecution. Furthermore, the facts did not indicate that the school and the police officer were attempting to avoid the warrant and probable cause requirements.

Similarly, an Indiana federal district court held that the assistance of police did not subject a search for drugs to the fourth amendment's probable cause standard.[156] The court stated that "[t]he officers were merely aiding in the inspection, at the request of the school administrators."[157] This role was supported by a prior agreement with the police that students possessing drugs would not be prosecuted. Accordingly, the court concluded that their presence did not alter the *in loco parentis* supervision status of the school officials. The court implied that a search to discover evidence of criminal activity would have required probable cause.

The Washington Supreme Court ruled that a call from the chief of police informing a principal that two high school students were selling speed did not constitute "police action" or "joint action."[158] The court emphasized that the chief of police did not initiate the search or request that the principal search the students. Furthermore, the court noted that there would have been a duty to search the students and to report the results to the police regardless of the source of the information. In a strongly worded dissent, one justice argued that the standard in this case should have been probable cause since the search was used for criminal prosecution, not for school disciplinary action.

In a number of recent decisions applying the reasonable suspicion standard to school searches, courts have specifically noted or implied that this lower standard is not applicable if law enforcement officials are involved. A Florida district court stated: "The reasonable suspicion standard does not apply in cases involving a search directed or participated in by a police officer."[159] Similarly, a Kentucky appellate court found the lower standard appropriate for searches in school settings *in the absence* of police participation.[160] Implicit in an Alaska decision was the assumption that police involvement would require probable cause.[161] The court in that instance declined to suppress evidence found in searching a student for stolen money in the absence of police instigation or involvement.

Police involvement in school searches raises serious questions as to the viability of students' fourth amendment guarantees.[162] At what point is the reasonable suspicion standard insufficient to ensure constitutional rights? Classifying searches on the basis of who conducts the search and what happens to the fruits of the search is inadequate. Searches cannot be discretely classified as either administrative or criminal. A search may be clearly criminal when the purpose is to find evidence of a crime, thereby necessitating probable cause prior to the search. But administrative searches undertaken strictly for disciplinary or safety purposes may result in prosecution of students if evidence of a crime is uncovered and reported to the police. In fact, school authorities have a duty to alert the police if evidence of a crime is discovered, even though the search was initiated for school purposes. Whether the exclusionary rule applies in searches undertaken for school, but not criminal, purposes remains to be clarified by courts.

While many legal issues involving search and seizure in schools are still evolving, school personnel can generally protect themselves from a successful legal challenge by adhering to a few basic guidelines. First, students and parents should be informed at the beginning of the school term of the procedures for conducting locker and personal searches. Any search conducted should be based on "reasonable suspicion" that the student is in possession of contraband that may be disruptive to the educational process. Further, the authorized person conducting a search should have another staff member present who can verify the procedures used in the search. School personnel should refrain from using strip searches or mass searches of groups of students. And, finally, if police officials are conducting a search in the school, either with or without the school's involvement, school authorities should ensure that a search warrant is obtained.

REMEDIES FOR UNLAWFUL DISCIPLINARY ACTIONS

There are several remedies available to students who are unlawfully disciplined by school authorities. Where physical punishment is involved, students can seek damages through assault and battery suits against those who inflicted the harm.[163] For unwarranted suspensions or expulsions, students are entitled to reinstatement without penalty to grades and to have their school records expunged of any reference to the illegal disciplinary action.[164] If academic penalties are unlawfully imposed, grades must be restored and transcripts altered accordingly.[165] For unconstitutional searches, illegally seized evidence may be suppressed, and damages may be awarded if the unlawful search results in substantial injury to the student.[166]

In *Wood v. Strickland,* the Supreme Court stated that school officials could be held liable for monetary damages under the Civil Rights Act of 1871 if they arbitrarily violated students' federally protected rights in disciplinary proceedings.[167] The Court declared that ignorance of the law could not be used as a valid defense to shield school officials from liability if they should have known that their actions would impair "clearly established" federal rights of students. Under the *Wood* proclamation, a showing of malice is not always required in order to prove that the actions of school officials were taken in bad faith. However, a mere mistake in carrying out duties does not render school authorities liable. The Court also recognized in *Wood* that educators are not charged with predicting the future direction of constitutional law.

Other courts have reiterated the potential liability of school officials in connection with student disciplinary proceedings, but to date students have not been as successful as teachers in obtaining actual monetary awards for constitutional violations. Courts have been reluctant to delineate students' "clearly established" rights, the impairment of which would warrant compensatory damages. In an illustrative case involving the exclusion of students from a soccer team because of their hair length, the Third Circuit Court of Appeals dismissed the claim for damages, concluding that the right of students to wear their hair at a chosen length was not "clearly established law," since circuit courts were almost evenly divided on the question and the Supreme Court had not addressed the issue.[168]

In 1978 the Supreme Court placed restrictions on the amount of damages that could be awarded to students in instances involving the impairment of procedural due process rights. In *Carey v. Piphus,* the Court declared that students who were suspended without a hearing, but were not otherwise injured, could recover only nominal damages (not to exceed one dollar).[169] This case involved two Chicago students who had been suspended without hearings for violating school regulations. They brought suit against the school district for a total of $8,000 in damages for the alleged abridgment of their constitutional rights. While the Seventh Circuit Court of Appeals held that the students were entitled to monetary damages, the United States Supreme Court disagreed, ruling that substantial damages could be recovered only if the suspensions were unjustified. Accordingly, the case was remanded for the district court to determine whether the students would have been suspended if correct procedures had been followed.

While this decision may appear to have strengthened the position of school boards in exercising discretion in disciplinary proceedings, the Supreme Court indicated that students *might* be entitled to substantial damages if suspensions are proven to be unwarranted. To illustrate, an Arkansas federal district court assessed punitive damages against a high school coach for intentionally impairing students' free speech rights in a disciplinary action.[170] Also, students have received damages when subjected to unlawful searches. For example, the Seventh Circuit Court of Appeals assessed damages against school officials for an intrusive body search.[171]

Educators should take every precaution to afford fair and impartial treatment to students. School personnel would be wise to provide at least an informal hearing if in doubt as to whether a particular situation necessitates due process. Liability never results from the provision of too much due process, whereas punitive damages possibly could be assessed in situations involving willful violations of procedural rights that result in unjustified suspensions, expulsions or other disciplinary actions. Although constitutional and statutory due process requirements do not mandate that a specific procedure be followed in every situation, courts will carefully study the record to ensure that any procedural deficiencies do not impede the student's efforts to present a full defense.

Also, school authorities should ensure that constraints placed on student conduct are necessary for the proper functioning of the school. Educators have considerable latitude in controlling student behavior to maintain an appropriate educational environment, but courts will award students relief where restrictions are clearly unreasonable. School personnel, however, should not feel that their authority to discipline students has been curtailed by the judiciary. As noted in *Goss,* courts "have imposed requirements which are, if anything, less than a fairminded principal would impose upon himself. . . ."[172]

CONCLUSION

In 1969, Justice Black noted that "school discipline, like parental discipline, is an integral and important part of training our children to be good citizens—to be better citizens."[173] Accordingly, school personnel have been empowered with the authority and duty to regulate pupil behavior in order to protect the interests of the student body and the school. Reasonable sanctions can be imposed if students do not adhere to legitimate conduct regulations. Courts, however, will intervene if disciplinary procedures are arbitrary or impair students' protected rights. Although the law pertaining to certain aspects of student discipline remains in a state of flux, judicial decisions support the following generalizations.

1. School authorities must be able to substantiate that any disciplinary regulation enacted is reasonable and necessary for the management of the school or for the welfare of pupils and school employees.

2. All regulations should be stated in precise terms and disseminated to students and parents.
3. Punishments for rule infractions should be appropriate for the offense and the characteristics of the offender (i.e., age, mental condition, prior behavior).
4. Students cannot be punished for the acts of others (such as their parents).
5. Some type of due process should be afforded to students prior to the imposition of punishments. For minor penalties, an informal hearing suffices; for serious punishments, more formal procedures are required (e.g., notification of parents, representation by counsel, opportunity to cross-examine witnesses).
6. Students can be punished for misbehavior occurring off school grounds if the conduct directly relates to the welfare of the school.
7. Suspensions and expulsions are legitimate punishments if accompanied by appropriate procedural safeguards and not arbitrarily imposed.
8. The transfer of students to different classes, programs, or schools for disciplinary reasons must be accompanied by due process procedures.
9. Reasonable corporal punishment can be used as a disciplinary technique as long as state laws and school board regulations are followed.
10. Academic sanctions for nonacademic reasons should be reasonable, related to absences from class, and serve a legitimate school purpose.
11. School personnel can search students' lockers or personal effects for educational purposes upon reasonable suspicion that the students are in possession of contraband that will disrupt the school.
12. Strip searches should be avoided unless evidence substantiates that there is probable cause to search or an emergency exists.
13. While the use of canines to sniff objects is generally not viewed as a search, courts are not in agreement regarding whether their use with students is a search and requires reasonable and individualized suspicion.
14. Chemical screening of students comes within the purview of the fourth amendment and requires reasonable suspicion that an individual student is using drugs.
15. If students are unlawfully punished, they are entitled to be restored (without penalty) to their status prior to the imposition of the punishment and to have their records expunged of any reference to the illegal punishment.
16. School officials can be held liable for compensatory damages if

unlawful punishments result in substantial injury to the students involved (e.g., unwarranted suspensions from school); however, only nominal damages, not to exceed one dollar, can be assessed against school officials for the abridgment of students' procedural rights (e.g., the denial of an adequate hearing).

NOTES

1. *See* George Gallup, "The Seventeenth Annual Gallup Poll of the Public's Attitudes Toward the Public Schools," *Phi Delta Kappan*, vol. 68 (1986), p. 44.
2. Pugsley v. Sellmeyer, 250 S.W. 538 (Ark. 1923). *See also* Jones v. Day, 89 So. 906 (Miss. 1921).
3. Tanton v. McKenney, 197 N.W. 510 (Mich. 1924).
4. 393 U.S. 503 (1969). *See* text with note 22, chapter 4.
5. Bethel School Dist. No. 403 v. Fraser, 106 S. Ct. 3159 (1986); New Jersey v. T.L.O., 469 U.S. 325 (1985).
6. State *ex rel.* Bowe v. Board of Educ. of City of Fond du Lac, 23 N.W. 102, 104 (Wis. 1885).
7. *See, e.g.*, Craig by Craig v. Buncombe County Bd. of Educ., 343 S.E.2d 222 (N.C. App. 1986) (ban on student smoking found to be valid exercise of school board authority).
8. *See* Board of Educ. of Rogers, Arkansas v. McCluskey, 458 U.S. 966 (1982); Wood v. Strickland, 420 U.S. 308 (1975).
9. *See* Mitchell v. King, 363 A.2d 68 (Conn. 1975); Soglin v. Kauffman, 418 F.2d 163 (7th Cir. 1969).
10. Bethel School Dist. No. 403 v. Fraser, 106 S. Ct. 3159 (1986).
11. *See* Sill v. Pennsylvania State Univ., 462 F.2d 463 (3d Cir. 1972).
12. Pervis v. LaMarque Independent Dist., 466 F.2d 1054, 1057 (5th Cir. 1972).
13. Jordan v. School Dist. of the City of Erie, Pennsylvania (Jordan I), 548 F.2d 117 (3d Cir. 1977); Jordan II, 583 F.2d 91 (3d Cir. 1978); Jordan III, 615 F.2d 85 (3d Cir. 1980).
14. St. Ann v. Palisi, 495 F.2d 423, 426 (5th Cir. 1974).
15. Carder v. Michigan City School Corp., 552 F. Supp. 869 (N.D. Ind. 1982).
16. O'Rourke v. Walker, 102 Conn. 130 (1925).
17. Hutton v. State, 5 S.W. 122 (Tex. App. 1887).
18. Lander v. Seaver, 32 Vt. 114 (1859).
19. Fenton v. Stear, 423 F. Supp. 767 (W.D. Pa. 1976).
20. *See* Galveston Independent School Dist. v. Boothe, 590 S.W.2d 553 (Tex. Civ. App. 1979).
21. *See* Thomas v. Board of Educ., Granville Cent. School Dist., 607 F.2d 1043 (2d Cir. 1979), *cert. denied*, 444 U.S. 1081 (1980); Klein v. Smith, 635 F. Supp. 1440 (D. Me. 1986).
22. The definition of an expulsion varies from state to state. While expulsions are generally considered the denial of school attendance in excess of ten days, in some states, such as Indiana, an expulsion is defined as the denial of school attendance in excess of five days. Ind. Code Ann. § 20–8.1–1–10.

23. *See* Ind. Code Ann. § 20–8.1–5–5.
24. *See* Pervis v. LaMarque Independent School Dist., 466 F.2d 1054 (5th Cir. 1972); Dunn v. Tyler Independent School Dist., 460 F.2d 137, 144 (5th Cir. 1972); Wasson v. Trowbridge, 382 F.2d 807, 812 (2d Cir. 1967).
25. *See* Andrews v. Knowlton, 509 F.2d 898 (2d Cir. 1975); Murray v. West Baton Rouge Parish School Bd., 472 F.2d 438, 443 (5th Cir. 1973); Sill v. Pennsylvania State Univ., 462 F.2d 463, 469–470 (3d Cir. 1972); Lance v. Thompson, 432 F.2d 767 (5th Cir. 1970).
26. *See* Black Coalition v. Portland School Dist. No. 1, 484 F.2d 1040, 1045 (9th Cir. 1973); Fielder v. Board of Educ. of Winnebago, 346 F. Supp. 722, 724, n. 1 (D. Neb. 1972).
27. *See* Jones v. State Bd. of Educ., 279 F. Supp. 190 (M.D. Tenn. 1968), *aff'd*, 407 F.2d 834 (6th Cir. 1969), *cert. dismissed as improvidently granted*, 397 U.S. 31 (1970); Esteban v. Central Missouri State College, 277 F. Supp. 649 (W.D. Mo. 1967), *approved*, 415 F.2d 1077 (8th Cir. 1969), *cert. denied*, 398 U.S. 965 (1970).
28. *See* Dillon v. Pulaski County Special School Dist., 594 F.2d 699 (8th Cir. 1979); DeJesus v. Penberthy, 344 F. Supp. 70 (D. Conn. 1972).
29. *See* Marzette v. McPhee, 294 F. Supp. 562, 567 (W.D. Wis. 1968).
30. Keough v. Tate County Bd. of Educ., 748 F.2d 1077 (5th Cir. 1984).
31. Brewer v. Austin Independent School Dist., 779 F.2d 260 (5th Cir. 1985).
32. The failure to enact required state rules or to follow them would violate state rather than constitutional law. *See* White v. Salisbury Township School, 588 F. Supp. 608 (E.D. Pa. 1984); Rutz v. Essex Junction Prudential Comm., 457 A.2d 1368 (Vt. 1983).
33. Galveston Independent School Dist. v. Boothe, 590 S.W.2d 553 (Tex. Civ. App. 1979).
34. Labrosse v. St. Bernard Parish School Bd., 483 So. 2d 1253 (La. App. 1986).
35. Wilson v. Collinsville Community Unit School Dist., 451 N.E.2d 939 (Ill. App. 1983). *See also* McEntire v. Brevard County School Bd., 470 So. 2d 1287 (Fla. App. 1985) (expulsion of student for selling caffeine pills was overturned because evidence did not support that the student represented the pills as speed; school board policy prohibited the selling of counterfeit pills only if represented as speed).
36. In re McClellan, 475 A.2d 867 (Pa. Commw. 1984).
37. Tomlinson v. Pleasant Valley School Dist., 479 A.2d 1169 (Pa. Commw. 1984).
38. 20 U.S.C. § 1401.
39. S–1 v. Turlington, 635 F.2d 342 (5th Cir. 1981), *cert. denied*, 454 U.S. 1030 (1981); School Bd. of the County of Prince William, Va. v. Malone, 762 F.2d 1210 (4th Cir. 1985); Kaelin v. Grubbs, 682 F.2d 595 (6th Cir. 1982).
40. *See* S–1, *id.*
41. *Compare* Hernandez v. School Dist. No. 1, Denver, 315 F. Supp. 289 (D. Colo. 1970) with Mills v. Board of Educ. of Dist. of Columbia, 348 F. Supp. 866 (D.D.C. 1972).
42. 419 U.S. 565 (1975).
43. *Id.* at 574–575.
44. Bethel School Dist. No. 403 v. Fraser, 106 S. Ct. 3159, 3166 (1986).
45. Boynton v. Casey, 543 F. Supp. 995 (D. Me. 1982).

46. 384 U.S. 436 (1966).
47. *See* Pollnow v. Glennon, 594 F. Supp 220 (S.D. N.Y. 1984), *aff'd*, 757 F.2d 496 (2d Cir. 1985); In re Drolshagen, 310 S.E.2d 927 (S.C. 1984); State v. Wolfer, 693 P.2d 154 (Wash. App. 1984).
48. 419 U.S. at 583–584.
49. Keough v. Tate County Bd. of Educ., 748 F.2d 1077 (5th Cir. 1984).
50. *Id.* at 1081.
51. Ohio Revised Code § 3313.661.
52. 22 Pa. Code § 12.8(c)(2)(i).
53. Mifflin County School Dist. v. Stewart, 503 A.2d 1012 (Pa. Commw. 1986). *See* Underwood v. Board of Educ. of City School Dist. of the City of Kingston, 498 N.Y.S.2d 907 (App. Div. 1986) (suspension by principal unlawful when board had not delegated authority to principal).
54. 419 U.S. at 583.
55. R.R. v. Board of Educ. of Shore Regional High School Dist., 263 A.2d 180 (N.J. Super. 1970).
56. Johnson v. Board of Educ., Union Free School Dist. No. 6, Manhasset, 393 N.Y.S.2d 510 (Sup. Ct., Nassau County, 1977).
57. *See* Chicago Bd. of Educ. v. Terrile, 361 N.E.2d 778 (Ill. App. 1977); Betts v. Board of Educ. of Chicago, 466 F.2d 629, 633 (7th Cir. 1972).
58. *See* Jordan v. School Dist. of the City of Erie, Pa., 615 F.2d 85 (3d Cir. 1980); text with note 13, *supra*.
59. Everett v. Marcase, 426 F. Supp. 397 (E.D. Pa. 1977). *See also* Hobson v. Bailey, 309 F. Supp. 1393 (W.D. Tenn. 1970).
60. Everett, *id.* at 400.
61. *See* Suits v. Glover, 71 So. 2d 49 (Ala. 1954); Calway v. Williamson, 36 A.2d 377 (Conn. 1944); People v. Mummert, 50 N.Y.S.2d 699 (Sup. Ct., Nassau County, 1944).
62. *See* People *ex rel.* Hogan v. Newton, 56 N.Y.S.2d 779 (White Plains City Ct. 1945); Berry v. Arnold School Dist., 137 S.W.2d 256 (Ark. 1940).
63. 395 F. Supp. 294 (M.D.N.C. 1975), *aff'd*, 423 U.S. 907 (1975).
64. 525 F.2d 909 (5th Cir. 1976), *aff'd*, 430 U.S. 651 (1977).
65. Hall v. Tawney, 621 F.2d 607 (4th Cir. 1980). *See* Monique Weston Clague, "Hall v. Tawney: Corporal Punishment and Judicial Activism," *Education Law Reporter*, vol. 8 (1983), pp. 909–925.
66. Hall, *id.* at 611.
67. *Id.* at 613.
68. *See* Woodard v. Los Fresnos Independent School Dist., 732 F.2d 1243 (5th Cir. 1984); Hale v. Pringle, 562 F. Supp. 598 (M.D. Ala. 1983). A Virginia federal district court held that the piercing of a student's upper arm with a straight pin did not involve brutal, inhumane, conscious-shocking treatment required to establish a substantive due process violation. Furthermore, the court concluded that the student must allege and prove that the teacher intended to deprive him or her of a specific constitutional right. Brooks v. School Bd. of City of Richmond, Va., 569 F. Supp. 1534 (E.D. Va. 1983).
69. Smith v. West Virginia State Bd. of Educ., 295 S.E.2d 680 (W. Va. 1982).
70. For example, California, New Jersey, and Massachusetts prohibit corporal punishment by statute, and Maryland prohibits its use by action of the state board of education.

71. *See* Eugene Connors, *Student Discipline and the Law* (Bloomington, IN: Phi Delta Kappa, 1979), p. 11.
72. *See* Harris v. Commonwealth, 372 A.2d 953 (Pa. Commw. 1977); Welch v. Board of Educ. of Bement Community School Dist. No. 5, 358 N.E.2d 1364 (Ill. App. 1977).
73. Jerry v. Board of Educ. of the City School Dist. of the City of Syracuse, 376 N.Y.S.2d 737 (App. Div. 1975).
74. Rolando v. School Directors of Dist. No. 125, 358 N.E.2d 945 (Ill. App. 1976).
75. Landi v. West Chester Area School Dist., 353 A.2d 895 (Pa. Commw. 1976).
76. Johnson v. Horace Mann Mutual Ins. Co., 241 So. 2d 588 (La. App. 1970).
77. For a discussion of recommended guidelines, *see* Robert Simpson and Paul O. Dee, "Usual But Not Cruel: Policy Guidelines on Corporal Punishment," *NOLPE School Law Journal*, vol. 7 (1977), pp. 183–193.
78. 395 F. Supp. 294 (M.D.N.C. 1975), *aff'd*, 423 U.S. 907 (1975).
79. *See* Fiacco v. Santee, 421 N.Y.S.2d 431 (App. Div. 1979); Barnard v. Inhabitants of Shelburne, 102 N.E. 1095 (Mass. 1913).
80. Connelly v. University of Vermont and State Agricultural College, 244 F. Supp. 156, 160 (D. Vt. 1965).
81. In Horowitz v. Board of Curators of the Univ. of Missouri, 435 U.S. 78 (1978), the United States Supreme Court reiterated that school authorities can establish and enforce academic standards. In this case, a medical student who was dismissed without notice of the charges or a formal hearing alleged that her constitutional rights were violated. The high court, however, concluded that neither the student's liberty nor property interests were impaired by the academic dismissal without a hearing. *See also* Regents of the Univ. of Michigan v. Ewing, 106 S. Ct. 507 (1985); Spencer v. New York City Bd. of Higher Educ., 502 N.Y.S.2d 358 (Sup. Ct., New York County, 1986).
82. *See* Emily Bernheim, "Academic Penalties for Misconduct and Nonattendance," *School Law Bulletin*, vol. 16 (1985), pp. 18–28.
83. Knight v. Board of Educ. of Tri-Point Community Unit School Dist., 348 N.E.2d 299 (Ill. App. 1976).
84. Campbell v. Board of Educ. of New Milford, 475 A.2d 289 (Conn. 1984).
85. *Id.* at 294.
86. R.J.J. by Johnson v. Shineman, 658 S.W.2d 910 (Mo. App. 1983).
87. Gutierrez v. School Dist. R–1, Otero County, 585 P.2d 935 (Colo. 1978).
88. Williams v. Board of Educ. for the Marianna School Dist., 626 S.W.2d 361 (Ark. 1982).
89. Dorsey v. Bale, 521 S.W.2d 76 (Ky. App. 1975).
90. Katzman v. Cumberland Valley School Dist., 479 A.2d 671 (Pa. Commw. 1984). *See also* In re Angela, 340 S.E.2d 544 (S.C. 1986) (under state law, absences for suspension could not be counted as unexcused absences for determining delinquency).
91. New Braunfels Independent School Dist. v. Armke, 658 S.W.2d 330 (Tex. App. 1983).
92. Valentine v. Independent School Dist. of Casey, 183 N.W. 434 (Iowa 1921).
93. *See also* Spence v. Bailey, 465 F.2d 797 (6th Cir. 1972) (school board's denial of a diploma to a student who refused to take a required officer's training course impaired his rights protected by the first amendment).

94. Ladson v. Board of Educ. of Union Free School Dist. No. 9, 323 N.Y.S.2d 545 (Sup. Ct., Nassau County, 1971).
95. Fowler v. Williamson, 448 F. Supp. 497 (W.D.N.C. 1978). There have also been a few challenges to school board policies prohibiting students from participating in graduation activites if they have completed graduation requirements in less than the normal four years. *See* Clark v. Board of Educ., Hamilton Local School Dist., 367 N.E.2d 69 (Ohio 1977) (public school officials could not deny an early graduate the right to participate in graduation ceremonies).
96. Camara v. Municipal Court of the City and County of San Francisco, 387 U.S. 523, 528 (1967). *See generally* Louis Trosch, Robert Williams, and Fred Devore, "Public School Searches and the Fourth Amendment," *Journal of Law and Education*, vol. 11 (1982), pp. 41–63.
97. *See* Mapp v. Ohio, 367 U.S. 643 (1961).
98. Evidence seized by a private person, however, is admissible since the exclusionary rule does not apply. *See, e.g.*, People v. Stewart, 313 N.Y.S.2d 253 (N.Y. 1970).
99. Search and seizure issues are not problematic solely in the educational setting. These issues in the law enforcement area pose perplexing dilemmas for police officers and consume a tremendous amount of the United States Supreme Court's time. In the 1983 term alone, the Court rendered opinions in seven law enforcement cases.
100. 469 U.S. 325 (1985).
101. *Id.* at 336.
102. *Id.* at 340.
103. *Id.* at 341.
104. *Id.* at 342.
105. *Id.*
106. As Justice Brennan noted in his dissent in *T.L.O.*, the "only definite content [of reasonableness] is that it is *not* the same test as the 'probable cause' standard. . . ." He argued that the departure from probable cause was unclear and unnecessary, creating an "amorphous" standard that will promote more litigation and uncertainty among school officials, *id.* at 354.
107. *See* State v. D.T.W., 425 So. 2d 1383, 1387 (Fla. App. 1983); State v. McKinnon, 558 P.2d 781, 784 (Wash. 1977); People v. D., 315 N.E.2d 466, 470 (N.Y. 1974); In the Interest of L.L., 280 N.W.2d 343, 351 (Wis. App. 1979).
108. *See, e.g.*, M. v. Board of Educ. Ball-Chatham, 429 F. Supp. 288 (S.D. Ill. 1977); State v. Baccino, 282 A.2d 869 (Del. Super. 1971).
109. Terry v. Ohio, 392 U.S. 1, 21 (1968).
110. *See* Tarter v. Raybuck, 742 F.2d 977 (6th Cir. 1984), *cert. denied*, 105 S. Ct. 1749 (1985); State v. McKinnon, 558 P.2d 781 (Wash. 1977); State v. D.T.W., 425 So. 2d 1383 (Fla. App. 1983).
111. Katz v. United States, 389 U.S. 347, 351–352 (1967).
112. *Id.* at 361 (Mr. Justice Harlan, concurring).
113. United States v. Chadwick, 433 U.S. 1, 7 (1977).
114. Terry v. Ohio, 392 U.S. 1, 9 (1968).
115. *See* David Kirp and Mark Yudof, *Educational Policy and the Law* (Berkeley, CA: McCutchan, 1982), p. 231.
116. State v. Stein, 456 P.2d 1, 2 (Kan. 1969), *cert. denied*, 397 U.S. 947 (1970).

117. People v. Overton, 229 N.E.2d 596, 598 (N.Y. 1967).
118. Zamora v. Pomeroy, 639 F.2d 662, 670 (10th Cir. 1981).
119. *See* In re Donaldson, 75 Cal. Rptr. 220 (Cal. App. 1969).
120. State v. Joseph T., 336 S.E.2d 728 (W. Va. 1985). *See also* State v. Brooks, 718 P.2d 837 (Wash. App. 1986) (reasonable grounds for search was established by tip from a student informant; search was further supported by previous teachers' reports of suspected drug use and observations of administrator).
121. State in the Interest of T.L.O., 463 A.2d 934 (N.J. 1983).
122. State v. Brooks, 718 P.2d 837 (Wash. App. 1986).
123. *See* State v. McKinnon, 558 P.2d 781 (Wash. 1977). *See also* text with note 158, *infra,* for a discussion of this case.
124. Indiana Code § 20–8.1–5–7.
125. State v. D.T.W., 425 So. 2d 1383 (Fla. App. 1983).
126. Jones v. Latexo Independent School Dist., 499 F. Supp. 223 (E.D. Tex. 1980).
127. Horton v. Goose Creek Independent School Dist., 690 F.2d 470, 478 (5th Cir. 1982), *cert. denied,* 463 U.S. 1207 (1983).
128. New Jersey v. T.L.O., 105 S. Ct. 733, 746 (1985).
129. In re Bobby B., 218 Cal. Rptr. 253 (Cal. App. 1985).
130. Jones v. Latexo Independent School Dist., 499 F. Supp. 223 (E.D. Tex. 1980).
131. Tarter v. Raybuck, 742 F.2d 977, 980 (6th Cir. 1984), *cert. denied,* 105 S. Ct. 1749 (1985).
132. *See* Rone v. Daviess County Bd. of Educ., 655 S.W.2d 28 (Ky. App. 1983); State in the Interest of Feazell, 360 So. 2d 907 (La. App. 1978).
133. M.M. v. Anker, 607 F.2d 588, 589 (2d Cir. 1979).
134. Doe v. Renfrow, 631 F.2d 91, 92–93 (7th Cir. 1980), *cert. denied,* 451 U.S. 1022 (1981).
135. Bilbrey v. Brown, 738 F.2d 1462 (9th Cir. 1984).
136. Bellnier v. Lund, 438 F. Supp. 47 (N.D.N.Y. 1977).
137. People v. D., 315 N.E.2d 466 (N.Y. 1974). *See* Cales v. Howell Public Schools, 635 F. Supp. 454 (E.D. Mich. 1985) (required reasonable suspicion that a *specific* rule or law has been violated).
138. Rone v. Daviess County Bd. of Educ., 655 S.W.2d 28 (Ky. App. 1983).
139. Zamora v. Pomeroy, 639 F.2d 662, 670 (10th Cir. 1981). *See generally* Martin Gardner, "Sniffing for Drugs in the Classroom," *Northwestern University Law Review*, vol. 74 (1980), pp. 803–853.
140. Horton v. Goose Creek Independent School Dist., 690 F.2d 470 (5th Cir. 1982), *cert. denied,* 463 U.S. 1207 (1983). *See also* Jones v. Latexo Independent School Dist., 499 F. Supp. 223 (E.D. Tex. 1980).
141. *See* Horton, *id.* at 477 for listing of case cites.
142. The Fifth Circuit Appellate Court's position is bolstered by a recent Supreme Court decision in a law enforcement case, United States v. Place, 462 U.S. 696 (1983). The Court concluded that the brief detention of a passenger's luggage at an airport for the purpose of subjecting it to a "sniff" test by a trained narcotics detection dog did not constitute a search under the fourth amendment. Use of canines was characterized as unique, involving a very limited investigation and minimal disclosure.
143. Subsequently, in denying a rehearing, the court clarified the issue of the

dogs' reliability. According to the court, a school district does not have to establish with "*reasonable certainty* that contraband is present . . . or even that there is *probable cause* to believe that contraband will be found." Rather, there must be some evidence to indicate that the dogs' performance is reliable enough to give rise to a reasonable suspicion. Horton, 693 F.2d 524, 525 (5th Cir. 1982).

144. Doe v. Renfrow, 631 F.2d 91 (7th Cir. 1980), *cert. denied,* 451 U.S. 1022 (1981).
145. Jones v. Latexo Independent School Dist., 499 F. Supp. 223 (E.D. Tex. 1980).
146. *Id.* at 233.
147. *See also* Kuehn v. Renton School Dist. No. 403, 694 P.2d 1078, 1081 (Wash. 1985), in which the state high court declared: "The fourth amendment demands more than a generalized probability; it requires that the suspicion be particularized with respect to each individual searched."
148. Horton, 690 F.2d 470 (5th Cir. 1982).
149. Odenheim v. Carlstadt-East Rutherford Regional School Dist., No. 4305–85E, December 9, 1985. *See* Anable v. Ford, No. 84-6033 (W.D. Ark., 1985); text with note 148, chapter 8 for discussion of drug testing of employees.
150. *See* Picha v. Wielgos, 410 F. Supp 1214 (N.D. Ill. 1976).
151. *See* Doe v. Renfrow, 475 F. Supp. 1012 (N.D. Ind. 1979).
152. *See* J. W. Shaw, *Admissibility, in Criminal Cases, of Evidence Obtained by Search Conducted by School Official or Teacher,* 49 A.L.R.3d 978.
153. *See* M. v. Board of Educ. Ball-Chatham Community Unit School Dist. No. 5, 429 F. Supp. 288 (S.D. Ill. 1977); State v. D.T.W., 425 So. 2d 1383 (Fla. App. 1983); D.R.C. v. State of Alaska, 646 P.2d 252 (Alas. App. 1982).
154. Picha v. Wielgos, 410 F. Supp. 1214 (N.D. Ill. 1976).
155. Martens v. District No. 220, Bd. of Educ., 620 F. Supp. 29 (N.D. Ill. 1985).
156. Doe v. Renfrow, 475 F. Supp. 1012 (N.D. Ind. 1979).
157. *Id.* at 1020.
158. State v. McKinnon, 558 P.2d 781 (Wash. 1977).
159. State v. D.T.W., 425 So. 2d 1383, 1385 (Fla. App. 1983). *See also* M.J. v. State, 399 So. 2d 996 (Fla. App. 1981).
160. Rone v. Daviess County Bd. of Educ., 655 S.W.2d 28 (Ky. App. 1983).
161. D.R.C. v. State of Alaska, 646 P.2d 252 (Alas. App. 1982).
162. Other constitutional questions also may be raised. In some public schools, undercover police have been placed in classes to investigate drug trafficking. In a case before the Sixth Circuit Court of Appeals, teachers, students, and parents alleged that such action constituted an impairment of first amendment rights. Rejecting this claim, the court held that the surveillance did not disrupt classroom activities, and even though the investigation allegedly focused on classes involving students and teachers with "liberal" sociopolitical views, there was no indication that the investigation had any tangible and concrete inhibitory effect on classroom expression. Gordon v. Warren Consol. Bd. of Educ., 706 F.2d 778 (6th Cir. 1983). *See also* Labrosse v. St. Bernard Parish School Bd., 483 So. 2d 1253 (La. App. 1986).
163. *See* Ingraham v. Wright, 430 U.S. 651 (1977).
164. *See, e.g.*, McEntire v. Brevard County School Bd., 471 So. 2d 1287 (Fla. App. 1985); Quinlan v. University Place School Dist., 660 P.2d 329 (Wash.

App. 1983); John A. v. San Bernardino City Unified School Dist., 654 P.2d 242 (Cal. 1982).

165. *See, e.g.*, Katzman v. Cumberland Valley School Dist., 479 A.2d 671 (Pa. Commw. 1984).
166. *See, e.g.*, Jones v. Latexo Independent School Dist., 499 F. Supp. 223 (E.D. Tex. 1980); People v. D., 315 N.E.2d 466 (N.Y. 1974).
167. 420 U.S. 308 (1975). Section 1983 of the Civil Rights Act of 1871, 42 U.S.C. § 1983, provides a damages remedy for deprivations of federally protected rights under color of state law. *See* text with note 168, chapter 8.
168. Zeller v. Donegal School Dist. Bd. of Educ., 517 F.2d 600, 609 (3d Cir. 1975).
169. 545 F.2d 30 (7th Cir. 1976), *rev'd and remanded*, 435 U.S. 247 (1978).
170. *See* Boyd v. Board of Directors of McGehee School Dist., No. 17, 612 F. Supp. 86 (E.D. Ark. 1985). *See* text with note 33, chapter 4.
171. Doe v. Renfrow, 631 F.2d 91 (7th Cir. 1980), *cert. denied*, 451 U.S. 1022 (1981).
172. Goss v. Lopez, 419 U.S. 565, 583 (1975).
173. Tinker v. Des Moines Independent School Dist., 393 U.S. 503, 524 (1969) (Black, J., dissenting).

7

Terms and Conditions of Employment

As noted in chapter 1, the control of public education resides with the states. The judiciary has clearly recognized the plenary power of the state legislature in establishing, conducting, and regulating all public education functions. The legislature, through statutory law, establishes the boundaries within which the educational system operates; however, the actual administration of school systems is delegated to state boards of education, state departments of education, and local boards of education. These agencies promulgate rules and regulations pursuant to legislative policy for the operation of public schools.

While state statutory provisions are prominent in defining teachers' employment rights, they cannot be viewed in isolation of state and federal constitutional provisions, state and federal civil rights laws, and negotiated agreements between school boards and teacher unions. These laws may restrict or modify alternatives available under the state school code. For example, the authority to transfer teachers may be vested in the school board, but the board cannot use this power to discipline a teacher for exercising protected constitutional rights. The board's discretion may be further limited if it has agreed in the master contract to follow certain procedures prior to transferring an employee.

Among the areas affected by state statutory and regulatory provisions are the terms and conditions of a public school teacher's employment. This chapter presents an overview of state requirements pertaining to teacher certification, employment, contracts, tenure, and related conditions of employment. Specific job requirements that implicate constitutional rights or antidiscrimination mandates are addressed in subsequent chapters.

CERTIFICATION

To qualify for a teaching position in public schools, prospective teachers must acquire a valid certificate or license.[1] Certification is a state responsibility, and certificates are issued according to the statutory provisions of each state. Although the responsibility for licensing resides with the legislature, administration of the process has been delegated to state boards of education and state departments of education. It is recognized that states have not only the right but also the duty to establish certain minimum qualifications and to ensure that teachers meet these standards.[2]

Certificates are granted primarily on the basis of professional preparation. In most states, educational requirements include a college degree, with minimum credit hours or courses identified in various curricular areas. In addition to professional preparation, other prerequisites to certification may include good personal character, a specified age, United States citizenship, signing of a loyalty oath, and passage of an academic examination. The following is a representative statutory requirement.

> The Department of Public Instruction shall have the power, and its duty shall be—
>
> (a) To provide for and to regulate the certificates and the registration of persons qualified to teach in such schools;
>
> (b) To certify as qualified to practice the art of teaching in such schools any applicant eighteen (18) years of age, of good moral character, not addicted to the use of intoxicating liquor or narcotic drugs and who has graduated from a college, university or institution of learning approved as herein provided, and who has completed such professional preparation for teaching as may be prescribed by the State Board of Education, and to register such person upon such proof as the State Board of Education may require that applicant possess such qualifications.[3]

As noted in the above statutory requirement, an applicant for teacher certification may be required to possess "good moral character." The definition of what constitutes good character is often elusive, with a number of factors entering into the determination. The Supreme Court of Oregon found that conviction for burglary eight years prior to application for a teaching certificate was pertinent in assessing character for certification purposes. The court noted that character embraced all "qualities and deficiencies regarding traits of personality, behavior, integrity, temperament, consideration, sportsmanship, altruism, etc."[4] Courts generally will not rule on the wisdom of a certifying agency's assessment of character; they will intervene only if statutory or constitutional rights are abridged.

Certification of teachers by examination was common prior to the expansion of teacher education programs in colleges and universities. Then, for many years, only a few southern states required passage of an exam. With the emphasis on improving the quality of schools and teachers in the early 1980s, the trend has been toward the reinstatement of examinations as a prerequisite to certification. By 1986, forty-four states required some type of standardized test for entry into teacher education programs, program completion, or initial teacher certification.[5] Most of the states have employed the National Teachers Examination, and its use has been upheld by the United States Supreme Court even though the test has been shown to disproportionately disqualify black applicants.[6] Constitutional and statutory challenges to employment tests are discussed in chapter 9.

The signing of a loyalty oath often is included as a condition of obtaining a teaching certificate, but such oaths cannot be used to restrict association rights guaranteed under the Constitution. The Supreme Court has invalidated oaths that require teacher applicants to swear that they are not members of subversive organizations;[7] however, teachers can be required to sign an oath pledging faithful performance of duties and support for the Federal Constitution and an individual state's constitution.[8] According to the Supreme Court, these oaths must be narrowly limited to affirmation of support to the government and a pledge not to act forcibly to overthrow the government.[9]

As a condition of certification, a teacher may be required to be a citizen of the United States. In 1979 the Supreme Court addressed the question of whether such a requirement in New York violated the equal protection clause of the fourteenth amendment.[10] Under the New York education laws, a teacher who is eligible for citizenship but refuses to apply for naturalization cannot be certified. Although the Supreme Court has placed restrictions on the states' ability to exclude aliens from governmental employment, it has recognized that certain functions are "so bound up with the operation of the state as a governmental entity as to permit the exclusion from those functions of all persons who have not become part of the process of self-government."[11] Following this principle, the Court held that teaching is an integral "governmental function;" thus, a state must show only a rational relationship between a citizenship requirement and a legitimate state interest. Accordingly, the Court concluded that New York's interest in furthering its educational goals justified the citizenship stipulation for teachers.

A teacher who has met all of the legal qualifications for certification must be issued a certificate. Because legislatures periodically alter certification standards by imposing new or additional requirements, a certified teacher may be required later to meet other qualifications to maintain or renew a certificate. A Texas appellate court held that teachers possessing life certificates could be required to pass an examination as a condition of continued employment.[12] While the certifying agency has broad authority in establishing qualifications, restrictions on licensing that violate statutory or constitutional rights are prohibited. A New York court held that the denial of a teaching license to one classified as legally blind was "arbitrary, capricious, and contrary" to state law.[13]

Certificates are issued for designated periods of time, including various classifications such as emergency, temporary, provisional, professional, and permanent. Renewal or upgrading of a certificate may require additional academic coursework, other continuing education work, or passage of an examination. Certificates also specify professional position (e.g., teacher, administrator, librarian), subject areas (e.g., history, English, math), and grade levels (e.g., elementary, high school). Where certification subject areas have been established, a teacher must possess a valid certificate to teach a specific subject.[14] Failure of a school district to employ certified teachers may result in the loss of state accreditation and financial support.[15]

A certificate to teach is a license, not an absolute right to acquire a position. Certification indicates only that a teacher has satisfied minimum qualification requirements of the state. It does not entitle an individual to employment in a particular district or guarantee employment in the state,[16] nor does it prevent a local school board from attaching additional qualifications or conditions for employment.[17] If a local board imposes additional standards for employment, however, the requirements must be uniformly applied to all teachers in the district.[18]

Teaching credentials must be in proper order to ensure full employment rights. Where a state law required a teacher's certificate to be on file in the district of employment, the failure to file the certificate rendered the teacher's contract voidable.[19] Failure to renew a certificate prior to expiration[20] or to meet educational requirements necessary to maintain or acquire a higher grade certification[21] can result in loss of employment. Lack of proper credentials can also invalidate a claim for compensation.[22] Teaching services provided without certification are viewed by courts as voluntary and, as such, require no compensation.

The state is empowered not only to certify teachers but also to revoke certification. Although a local board may initiate charges against a teacher, only the state can revoke a teacher's certificate. Revocation of a certificate is a harsh penalty, generally interpreted as foreclosing all future employment as a teacher in the state.[23] In most states, it must be based on statutory cause with full procedural rights provided to the teacher.[24] The most frequently cited causes for revoking certification are immorality, incompetency, contract violation, and neglect of duty.[25]

When revocation of a certificate is being considered, determination of a teacher's competency encompasses not only classroom performance but also actions outside of the school setting that may impair the teacher's effectiveness. The California Supreme Court found that a teacher's participation in a "swingers" club and disguised appearance on television discussing nonconventional sexual behavior justified revocation of certification on grounds of unfitness to teach.[26] In an earlier case, however, the same court held that an isolated incident of private homosexuality did not justify license revocation; no connection was shown between the teacher's activity and effectiveness to teach.[27] Similarly, the Supreme Court of Iowa found an extramarital affair insufficient to justify revoking the certificate of an effective, highly respected teacher.[28] A Florida appellate court, however, ruled that the possession of marijuana plants by two teachers established "moral turpitude" justifying revocation of their certificates.[29] The conduct, which received widespread publicity, was found to have impaired the effectiveness of the teachers.

EMPLOYMENT BY LOCAL SCHOOL BOARDS

As noted, certification does not guarantee employment in a state; it attests only to the fact that the teacher has met minimum state requirements. The decision to employ or not to employ a certified teacher is among the discretionary powers of local school boards. While such powers are broad, school board actions cannot be arbitrary or capricious or in violation of an individual's statutory or constitutional rights.[30] Employment decisions must be neutral as to race, religion, national origin, and sex.[31] Unless individually protected rights are abridged, courts will not review the wisdom of a local school board's judgment in employment decisions made in good faith.

The duty to hire teachers is vested in the school board and cannot be delegated.[32] Employment decisions cannot be made by the superintendent or board members individually but must be made by the board as a collective body. In most states, binding employment agreements between a teacher and school board must be approved at legally scheduled board meetings. Procedurally, a number of state laws specify that the superintendent must make employment recommendations to the board;[33] however, the board is not compelled to follow these recommendations unless mandated to do so by law.

School boards possess broad authority in establishing job requirements and conditions of employment for school personnel. In the following sections, the school board's power to impose specific conditions on teacher employment and to assign personnel is examined.

Employment Requirements

Although the state prescribes the minimum certification standards for teachers, this does not preclude the local school board from requiring higher professional or academic standards as long as they are applied in a uniform and nondiscriminatory manner. For example, school boards often establish continuing education requirements for teachers. The right of a board to dismiss teachers for failure to satisfy such requirements has been upheld by the United States Supreme Court.[34] The Court concluded that school officials merely had to establish that the requirement was rationally related to a legitimate state objective, which in this case was to provide competent well-trained teachers.

School boards also may require teachers to live within the school district as a condition of employment. Such residency requirements have been challenged as impairing equal protection rights by interfering with interstate and intrastate travel. Generally, as long as the board has a rational basis for adopting the rule, courts will uphold a residency requirement as constitutionally acceptable. A Sixth Circuit Court of Appeals case is illustrative of this genre of cases.[35] The case involved a Cincinnati school board policy that required all new employees to establish residency in the school district within ninety days of employment. The rule was challenged by a teacher on equal protection grounds. Declining to extend constitutional protection to intrastate travel, the court required the district to show only a rational basis for the regulation. Among the reasons advanced by the school system for establishing the residency requirement were that teachers living in the community are more likely to be involved in community affairs, have a commitment to urban education, and support district tax increases.

Shortly after the Sixth Circuit Appellate Court decision, the United States Supreme Court also upheld a municipal regulation requiring all employees hired after a certain date in the city of Philadelphia to be residents of the city.[36] The requirement was challenged as a violation of interstate travel by a fire department employee who was terminated when he moved to New Jersey. In upholding the regulation, the Court distinguished a requirement of residency of a given duration *prior to employment* (which violates the right to interstate travel) from a continuing residency requirement applied *after employment*. The Court concluded that a continuing residency requirement, if "appropriately defined and uniformly applied," does not violate an individual's constitutional rights.[37]

Although residency requirements after employment have been upheld at the federal level, individual states may have statutory provisions prohibiting such requirements. For example, Indiana school boards, by statute, are not permitted to adopt any requirements pertaining to employee residence.[38] In states with such statutory provisions, the laws would have to be repealed or amended to enable school boards to establish residency regulations.

While school board residency requirements have been upheld, requirements that employees must send their children to public schools have been declared unconstitutional. As discussed in chapter 8, education of one's children is a basic fundamental right under the Federal Constitution and cannot be restricted unless there is a compelling state interest. The Eleventh Circuit Appellate Court held that a school board policy requiring employees to enroll their children in public schools could not be justified to promote an integrated public school system and good relationships among teachers when weighed against the right of parents to direct the education of their children.[39]

School boards can adopt reasonable health and physical requirements for teachers. Courts have recognized that such standards are necessary to safeguard the health and welfare of students and other employees. Requirements, however, must not be applied in an arbitrary manner. The Second Circuit Court of Appeals found arbitrary and unreasonable a New York school board's insistence that a teacher on extended sick leave for a back ailment be examined by the district's male physician rather than a female physician (to be selected by the board).[40] School board standards for physical fitness also must be rationally related to ability to perform teaching duties. A New York appellate court found that obesity *per se* was not reasonably related to ability to teach or to maintain discipline.[41]

In addition, regulations must not contravene various state and federal laws designed to protect the rights of the handicapped. For example, in a Pennsylvania case the Third Circuit Court of Appeals ruled that school officials cannot refuse to consider blind individuals as teachers for sighted students.[42] A New York trial court similarly held that blindness *per se* cannot disqualify one as a teacher.[43] The Eleventh Circuit Court of Appeals concluded that a contagious disease is a handicap under federal antidiscrimination provisions that protect otherwise qualified handicapped individuals from adverse employment consequences. Accordingly, a school district could not dismiss a teacher for chronic recurrences of tuberculosis without evidence that the teacher was otherwise unqualified to perform her job or that accommodations would place undue hardships on the school district.[44]

A school board's authority in employment also extends to prohibiting employees from engaging in outside employment during the school year. The Fifth Circuit Court of Appeals reviewed the constitutionality of a board policy, incorporated into employment contracts, providing that employees "shall not engage in any other business or profession directly or indirectly, for full time or part time, but shall devote his or her entire working time to the performance of . . . duties under this contract."[45] In this case, the school board relied on the outside employment policy in declining to renew the contracts of a principal and his wife, an elementary teacher, after they purchased a dry goods store. Prior to that time the couple had operated a substantial cattle ranch, but the school board based its decision entirely on the purchase of the dry goods store. While the court upheld the policy, finding that it was related to a legitimate state purpose—"assuring that public school employees devote their professional energies to the education of children"—the court concluded that the rule was arbitrarily and discriminatorily applied to the plaintiffs.[46] Although a number of employees in the district were involved in outside employment, the policy had never been applied to anyone else. The court held that a restriction must be applied equally to all who are similarly situated. The appellate court noted the "wide latitude" a school board has in adopting policies necessary for effective administration of the schools but emphasized that such policies must be uniformly applied.

Assignment of Personnel

The authority to assign teachers to schools within the district resides with the board of education.[47] As with employment in general, these decisions can be challenged only if arbitrary or made in bad faith.[48] Within the limits of certification, a teacher can be assigned to teach in any school at any grade level.[49] Assignments, designated within the teacher's contract, however, cannot be changed during a contractual period without the consent of the teacher. That is, a board cannot reassign a teacher to a first-grade class if the contract specifies a fifth-grade assignment. If the contract designates only a teaching assignment within the district, the assignment still must be in the teacher's area of certification. Additionally, objective, nondiscriminatory standards must be used in any employment or assignment decision pertaining to teachers.[50] Assignments to achieve racial balance may be permitted in school districts that have not eliminated the effects of prior school segregation; however, any racial classification must be temporary and necessary to eradicate the effects of prior discrimination.[51]

While school boards retain the authority to assign or transfer teachers, such decisions often are challenged as demotions requiring procedural due process. Depending on statutory law, factors considered in determining whether a reassignment is a demotion may include reduction in salary, responsibility, and stature of position.[52] A Pennsylvania teacher contested a transfer from a ninth-grade class to a sixth-grade class as a demotion.[53] The court, noting the equivalency of the positions, stated that "there is no less importance, dignity, responsibility, authority, prestige, or compensation in the elementary grades than in secondary."[54] In another instance, however, the reassignment of a Montana band instructor to a teaching position in an ungraded rural school without a band was held to be a demotion.[55] Similarly, the reassignment of an Ohio regular classroom teacher as a permanent substitute or floating teacher was found to be a demotion in contravention of the state tenure law.[56] The court recognized the pervasive authority of the superintendent and board to make teaching assignments, but noted that this power may be limited by other statutory provisions, such as the state tenure law. This reduction in status without a notice and hearing was found to deprive the teacher of due process guarantees.

Administrative reassignments are frequently challenged as demotions because of reductions in salary, responsibility, and stature of position. An Alabama high school principal asserted that his transfer to an elementary principalship and a $4,000 reduction in salary violated state law that prohibited transfers involving a "loss of status."[57] According to a state appellate court, the only factor to be considered in determining "status" is tenure status. Since the principal's tenure was not affected, there was no loss in status. A Michigan principal was unsuccessful in challenging a salary freeze as a demotion.[58] Although other administrators were given raises each year, the court found that under state law compensation must be actually reduced for an action to be considered a demotion. A reassignment from an administrative to a teaching position because of financial constraints or good faith reorganization does not constitute a demotion requiring due process unless specified by state law.[59]

Statutory procedures and agency regulations established for transferring or demoting employees must be strictly followed.[60] For example, under a West Virginia State Board of Education policy, school boards cannot initiate a disciplinary transfer unless there has been a prior evaluation informing the individual that specific conduct can result in a transfer.[61] Furthermore, there must be an opportunity for the employee to improve his or her performance. Under Pennsylvania law, demotions related to declining enrollment involve a realignment of staff, and to assure proper realignment of positions, procedural protections are required.[62]

The assignment of noninstructional duties often is defined in a teacher's contract; in the absence of such specification, it is generally held that boards can make reasonable and appropriate assignments.[63] Assignments are usually restricted by courts to activities that are an integral part of the school program and, in some situations, to duties that are related to the employee's teaching responsibilities. A California teacher claimed that being required to supervise six athletic events during the school year was both beyond the scope of his duties and unprofessional.[64] The court determined that the assignment was within the scope of the contract and reasonable, since it was impartially distributed and did not place an onerous burden on the teacher in terms of time. An Illinois appellate court concluded that requiring teachers to submit typed copies of class examinations for duplication was not demeaning or detrimental to a teacher's professional standing; an incidental power of the board is the right to assign nonclassroom duties.[65] A New Jersey appellate court stated that reasonableness of an assignment should be evaluated in terms of time involvement, teachers' interests and abilities, benefits to students, and the professional nature of the duty.[66] Refusal to accept assigned duties can result in dismissal.[67]

CONTRACTS

The employment contract defines the rights and responsibilities of the teacher and the school board in the employment relationship. The general principles of contract law apply to this contractual relationship.[68] Like all other legal contracts, it must contain the basic elements of (1) offer and acceptance, (2) competent parties, (3) consideration, (4) legal subject matter, and (5) proper form.[69] Beyond these basic elements, it also must meet the requirements specified in state law and administrative regulations.

The authority to contract with teachers is an exclusive right of the board. The school board's offer of a position to a teacher, including (1) designated salary, (2) specified period of time, and (3) identified duties and responsibilities, creates a binding contract when accepted by the teacher. In most states, only the board can make an offer, and this action must be approved by a majority of the board members in a properly called meeting. In a South Dakota case, a teacher was extended an employment offer at the beginning of the school year by the superintendent and chairperson of the school board pending approval of the board two weeks later.[70] Because of classroom teaching problems encountered by the teacher during that brief period of time, the board refused to approve the contract. The Supreme Court of South Dakota concluded that no contract existed between the teacher and the district because the statutorily mandated procedure for contract approval had not been met.

Contracts also can be invalidated for lack of competent parties. To form a valid, binding contract, both parties must have the legal capacity to enter into an agreement. The school board has been recognized as a legally competent party with the capacity to contract. A teacher who lacks certification or is under the statutorily required age for certification is not a competent party for contractual purposes. Consequently, a contract formed with such an individual is not enforceable.[71]

Consideration is another essential element of a valid contract. Consideration is something of value that one party pays in return for the performance by the other party. Also, the contract must pertain to a legal subject matter and follow the proper form required by law. Most states prescribe that a teacher's contract must be in writing to be enforceable. If there is no statutory specification, an oral agreement is legally binding on both parties.

While a teacher's legal rights of employment are derived from the contract, additional rights accrue from any collective bargaining agreement in effect at the time of employment. Also, statutory provisions and rules and regulations of the school board may be considered as part of the terms and conditions of the contract. If not included directly, the provisions existing at the time of the contract may be implied. Moreover, the contract cannot be used as a means of waiving a teacher's statutory rights.[72]

Two basic types of employment contracts are issued to teachers: term contracts and tenure contracts. Term contracts are valid for a fixed period of time (i.e., one or two years). At the end of the contract period, renewal of the contract is at the discretion of the school board, and nonrenewal requires no explanation, unless one is statutorily mandated. Generally, a school board is required only to provide notice prior to the expiration of the contract that employment will not be renewed. Tenure contracts, created through state legislative action, ensure a teacher that employment will be terminated only for adequate cause and that procedural due process will be provided. After the award of tenure or *during* a term contract, the school board cannot unilaterally abrogate a teacher's contract. At a minimum, the teacher must be provided with notice of charges on which the dismissal is based and a hearing.[73]

Since tenure contracts involve statutory rights, specific procedures and protections vary among the states. Consequently, judicial interpretations from other states provide little guidance in understanding one's own state law. Most tenure statutes specify requirements and procedures for obtaining tenure and identify causes and procedures for dismissal of a tenured teacher. In interpreting tenure laws, courts have attempted to protect teachers' rights while simultaneously maintaining flexibility for school officials in personnel management.[74]

Prior to a school board awarding a tenure contract to a teacher, most states require a probationary period of approximately three years to allow time to assess a teacher's ability and competence. During the probationary period, teachers receive term contracts, and there is no guarantee of employment beyond each contract. Tenure statutes generally require regular and continuous service to complete the probationary period. For example, the Massachusetts tenure law requires teaching service of three consecutive school years immediately prior to the award of tenure.[75] Interpreting this mandate, a Massachusetts appellate court held that a teacher who taught for approximately three-fourths of a school term could not count such teaching service toward tenure because it was less than a year.[76] On the other hand, part-time employment of a continuous and regular nature was interpreted as meeting probationary requirements under the Massachusetts statute, because the law required only continuous service and did not designate a separate classification for part-time service.[77]

The authority to grant a tenure contract is a discretionary power of the local school board which cannot be delegated.[78] Although the school board confers tenure, it cannot alter the tenure terms established by the legislature. Thus, if the statute requires a probationary period, this term of service must be completed prior to acquisition of tenure, or if areas in which school personnel may accrue tenure are identified, school boards can grant tenure only in those areas.[79] While a tenure contract provides a certain amount of job security, it does not guarantee permanent employment, nor does it convey the right to teach in a particular school or grade.[80] Teachers may be dismissed for the causes specified in the tenure law, and may be reassigned to positions for which they are certified.

In establishing tenure, a legislature may create a contractual relationship that cannot be altered without violating constitutional guarantees. The Federal Constitution, Article I, Section 10, provides that the obligation of a contract may not be impaired. The United States Supreme Court found such a contractual relationship in the 1927 Indiana Teacher Tenure Act, which prevented the state legislature from subsequently depriving teachers of rights conveyed under the act.[81] However, a statutory relationship that does not have the elements of a contract can be altered or repealed at the legislature's discretion.[82] Some state tenure laws are clearly noncontractual, containing provisos that the law may be altered, while other state laws are silent on revisions. If a tenure law is asserted to be contractual, the language of the act is critical in the judicial interpretation of legislative intent.

A number of states limit the award of tenure to teaching positions, thereby excluding administrative and supervisory positions. Where tenure is available for administrative positions, probationary service and other specified statutory terms must be met.[83] While tenure as a teacher usually does not imply tenure as an administrator, most courts have concluded that continued service as a certified professional employee, albeit as an administrator, does not alter tenure rights acquired as a teacher.[84] The Supreme Court of Wyoming noted: "It is desirable—and even important—to have people with extensive classroom teaching experience in administrative positions. It would be difficult to fill administrative positions with experienced teachers if the teachers would have to give up tenure upon accepting administrative positions."[85] In contrast to the prevailing view, the Supreme Court of New Mexico held that an individual who voluntarily resigned a teaching position for advancement to an administrative position forfeited tenure rights.[86] According to the court, tenure rights attach to a position rather than to an individual.

Supplementary service contracts are usually considered to be outside the scope of tenure protections. Coaches, in particular, have asserted that supplemental contracts are an integral part of the teaching position and thereby must be afforded the procedural and substantive protections of state tenure laws. Several courts have noted that tenure rights apply only to employment in certified areas and that the lack of certification requirements for coaches in a state negates tenure claims for such positions.[87] The Supreme Court of Iowa held that even a requirement that coaches must be certified did not confer teachers' tenure rights on coaching positions.[88] In this case, the coaching assignment was found to be clearly extra duty, requiring a separate contract and compensation based on an extra duty pay scale. Other courts also have distinguished coaching and various extra duties from teaching duties based on the extracurricular nature of the assignment and supplemental compensation.[89]

Because coaching assignments generally require execution of a supplemental contract, a teacher can usually resign a coaching position and maintain the primary teaching position.[90] School districts experiencing difficulties in filling coaching positions, however, may tender an offer to teach on the condition that an individual assume certain coaching responsibilities. If a single teaching and coaching contract is found to be indivisible, a teacher cannot unilaterally resign the coaching duties without relinquishing the teaching position.[91] Individual state laws must be consulted to determine the status of such contracts.

Where teaching and coaching positions are combined, a qualified teaching applicant who cannot assume the coaching duties may be rejected. This practice, however, may be vulnerable to legal challenge if certain classes of applicants, such as women, are excluded from consideration. In an Arizona case, female plaintiffs successfully established that a school district was guilty of sex discrimination by coupling a high school biology teaching position with a football coaching position. The school board was unable to demonstrate a business necessity for the practice that resulted in the twenty female applicants for the teaching position being eliminated from consideration.[92]

If one-year limited supplemental contracts are used for duties such as coaching, school boards may be required to issue timely notification of intent of nonrenewal. In Ohio, teachers with supplemental contracts are automatically reemployed for the following year if written notice is not given before the statutory deadline.[93] If the regular teaching contract has been terminated, however, a supplemental contract is not enforceable.

Contracts may specify various types of leaves of absence. Within the parameters of state law, school boards have discretion in establishing requirements for these leaves. This topic often is the subject of collective negotiations, with leave provisions specified in bargained agreements. School boards, however, cannot negotiate leave policies that impair rights guaranteed by the Federal Constitution and various federal and state antidiscrimination laws.[94] Similarly, where state law confers specific rights, local boards do not have the discretion to deny or alter these rights. Generally, statutes identify employees' rights related to various kinds of leaves such as sick leave, personal leave, sabbatical leave, disability leave, and military leave. State laws pertaining to leaves of absence usually specify eligibility for benefits, minimum days that must be provided, whether leave must be granted with or without pay, and restrictions that may be imposed by local school boards. If a teacher meets all statutory and procedural requirements for a specific leave, a school board cannot deny the request.[95]

PERSONNEL EVALUATION

To ensure a quality teaching staff, many states have enacted laws requiring periodic appraisal of teaching performance. Beyond the purposes of faculty improvement and remediation, results of evaluations may be used in a variety of employment decisions including retention, tenure, dismissal, promotion, salary, reassignment, and reduction in force. When adverse personnel decisions are based on the outcome of evaluations, legal concerns arise regarding issues of procedural fairness. Were established state and local procedures followed? Did school officials employ equitable standards? Was sufficient evidence collected to support the staffing decision? Were evaluations conducted in a uniform and consistent manner?

While school systems have broad discretionary powers to establish teacher performance criteria, state statutes may impose specific evaluation requirements. Over half of the states have enacted laws governing the evaluation of teachers. Content and requirements vary substantially from state to state with some states merely mandating the establishment of an appraisal system and others specifying procedures and criteria to be employed. Iowa law notes only that the local board must establish an evaluation system.[96] California, on the other hand, specifies the intent of evaluations, areas to be assessed, frequency of evaluations, notice to employees of deficiencies, and an opportunity to improve performance.[97] Florida requires the superintendent of schools to establish criteria and procedures for appraisal including evaluation at least once a year by the principal, written record of assessment, prior notice to teachers of criteria and procedures, and a meeting with the principal to discuss the results of the evaluation.[98] While a few evaluation systems are established at the state level,[99] state laws usually require local officials to develop evaluation criteria, often in conjunction with teachers or other professionals.[100]

Teacher evaluation also may be required by state administrative regulations rather than by statute. For example, a West Virginia Board of Education policy entitles a teacher to an "open and honest evaluation of his performance on a regular basis."[101] Failure of school officials to follow the state board procedures will nullify demotion, promotion, transfer, or dismissal of a teacher.[102] Under this policy, the West Virginia Supreme Court overturned the discharge of a teacher who was not afforded an opportunity to improve his performance[103] and ordered reinstatement of two teachers in the absence of honest and open evaluations.[104]

When evaluation procedures are identified in statutes, board policies, or employment contracts, courts generally require strict compliance with these provisions. A California appeals court found that the nonrenewal of a teacher's contract violated the statutory notification deadline and requirement for a written evaluation; the court held that school officials must strictly adhere to the evaluation statute.[105] A Washington appellate court required the reinstatement of a principal because the school board had not adopted evaluation criteria and procedures as required by law.[106] The court noted that in the absence of evaluation criteria the principal would serve at the whim of the superintendent and would be deprived of guidelines to improve his performance. The West Virginia Supreme Court held that a school system could not transfer an individual because the decision was not based on performance evaluations as required by state board policy.[107] A Pennsylvania school system was unable to reassign a principal to a teaching position based on performance evaluations when the action involved realignment of staff because another statutory provision required that realignments must be based solely on seniority.[108]

Where school boards have been attentive to evaluation requirements, challenged employment decisions have been upheld by courts.[109] A California appellate court found that a teacher's dismissal comported with state evaluation requirements because he received periodic appraisals noting specific instances of unsatisfactory performance.[110] The evaluation reports informed the teacher of the system's expectations, his specific teaching failures, and actions needed to correct deficiencies. An Iowa court found a school district's policy requiring a formal evaluation every three years for nonprobationary teachers to be adequate under a statutory requirement that "[t]he board shall establish evaluation criteria and shall implement evaluation procedures."[111] The court denied a teacher's claim that the law required an additional evaluation whenever termination of employment was contemplated. According to the Supreme Court of South Dakota, violation of an evaluation procedure *per se* does not require reinstatement of a teacher.[112] Reinstatement is justified only if a teacher can show that the violation substantially interfered with his or her ability to improve deficiencies.

Courts are reluctant to interject their judgment into the teacher evaluation process. Judicial review is generally limited to procedural issues of fairness and reasonableness. Several principles emerge from case law to guide educators in developing equitable systems: Standards for assessing the adequacy of teaching must be defined and communicated to teachers; criteria must be applied uniformly and consistently; an opportunity and direction for improvement must be provided; and procedures specified in state laws and school board policies must be followed.

PERSONNEL RECORDS

State laws and employment contracts govern access to and disclosure of information in teachers' personnel records. Because several or more statutes in each state relate to school records, it is difficult to generalize as to the specific nature of teachers' privacy rights regarding personnel files. Personnel information is generally protected by state privacy laws that place restrictions on maintenance and access to the records. Among other provisions, the laws may require school boards to maintain necessary and relevant information, provide individual employees access to their files, inform employees of the various uses of the files, and provide a procedure for challenging the accuracy of information. Collective bargaining contracts may impose additional and more stringent requirements regarding access and dissemination of personnel information.

A central issue in the confidentiality of personnel files is whether the information constitutes a public record that must be reasonably accessible to the general public. Public record, or right-to-know, laws that grant broad access to school records may directly conflict with privacy laws, requiring courts to balance the interests of the teacher, the school officials, and the public. For example, the Ohio Supreme Court has held that in such instances three factors must be weighed prior to the disclosure of information: (1) Is there an invasion of the individual's privacy and, if so, how serious is that invasion? (2) What is the nature of the public interest in obtaining the information? and (3) Is the information available from other sources?[113] Under Ohio law, the court concluded that any doubt as to the appropriateness of disclosure should be decided in favor of public disclosure. Because of the numerous statutes affecting records, in most states the law is unsettled as to what personnel information is confidential and what information is public record.

Access to personnel files also has been controversial in situations involving allegations of employment discrimination. Personnel files must be relinquished if subpoenaed by a court. In several cases, courts have ruled that the Equal Employment Opportunity Commission (EEOC) is authorized to subpoena *relevant* personnel files of university faculty members to enable the Commission to investigate thoroughly allegations that a particular faculty member has been the victim of discriminatory treatment.[114] The concept of relevancy has been construed broadly by courts to provide the EEOC access "to virtually any material that might cast light on the allegations against the employer."[115] In other situations where individuals rather than federal investigatory agencies have requested access to the personnel files of colleagues to substantiate discrimination charges, courts have denied the requests.[116]

Regarding maintenance of records, information clearly cannot be placed in personnel files in retaliation for the exercise of constitutional rights. Courts have ordered letters of reprimand expunged from files when they have been predicated on protected speech and association activities. Reprimands, while not a direct prohibition on protected activities, may present a constitutional violation because of their potentially chilling effect on the exercise of constitutional rights.[117]

OTHER EMPLOYMENT ISSUES

In addition to the terms and conditions of employment discussed in the previous sections of this chapter, other reasonable requirements can be attached to public employment as long as civil rights laws are respected and constitutional rights are not impaired without a compelling governmental justification. Public educators are expected to comply with such reasonable requirements as a condition of maintaining their jobs. Some requirements such as those pertaining to the instructional program and prohibitions against proselytizing students are discussed in other chapters of this book. Requirements pertaining to two topics—using copyrighted materials and reporting child abuse—warrant discussion here. These topics have received substantial attention in the 1980s.

Use of Copyrighted Material

Educators' extensive use of published materials and various media in the classroom raises issues related to the federal copyright law. As a condition of employment, educators are expected to comply with restrictions on the use of copyrighted materials. While the law grants the owner of a copyright exclusive control over the protected material, courts since the 1800s have recognized exceptions to this control under the doctrine of "fair use." The fair use doctrine cannot be precisely defined, but a common definition frequently used is the "privilege in others than the owner of the copyright to use the copyrighted material in a reasonable manner without his consent, notwithstanding the monopoly granted to the owner. . . ."[118]

Congress incorporated the judicially created fair use concept into the 1976 revisions of the Copyright Act.[119] In identifying the purposes of the fair use exception, Congress specifically noted teaching. The exception provides needed flexibility for teachers but by no interpretation grants them exemption from copyright infringement. Four factors were stipulated in the law for assessing whether the use of specific material constitutes fair use or an infringement:

> (1) the purpose and character of the use, including whether such use is of a commercial nature or is for non-profit educational purposes; (2) the nature of the copyrighted work; (3) the amount and substantiality of the portion used in relation to the copyrighted work as a whole; and (4) the effect of the use upon the potential market for or value of the copyrighted work.[120]

To clarify fair use pertaining to photocopying from books and periodicals, Congress incorporated into the committees' conference report a set of guidelines developed by a group representing educators, authors, and publishers. While the guidelines are only part of the legislative history of the act and do not have the force of law, they have been widely used in assessing the legality of reproducing printed materials in the educational environment. These guidelines permit the making of single copies of copyrighted material for teaching or research but are quite restrictive on the use of multiple copies. To use multiple copies of a work, the tests of brevity, spontaneity, and cumulative effect must be met. *Brevity* is precisely defined according to type of publication. For example, reproduction of a poem cannot exceed 250 words; copying from longer works cannot exceed 1,000 words or 10 percent of the work (whichever is less); only one chart, or drawing can be reproduced from a book or an article. *Spontaneity* requires that the copying be initiated by the individual teacher (not an administrator or supervisor) and occurs in such a manner that does not reasonably permit a timely request for permission. *Cumulative effect* restricts use of the copies to one course; limits material reproduced from the same author, book, and journal during the term; and sets a limit of nine instances of multiple copying for each course during one class term. Furthermore, the guidelines do not permit copying to substitute for anthologies or collective works or to replace consumable materials such as workbooks.

Publishers have taken legal action to ensure compliance with these guidelines. For example, in 1982 nine publishers filed a suit against New York University (NYU), several professors, and an off-campus copying facility, charging that copies of materials were made without permission of the publisher. The suit was settled out of court with NYU agreeing to adopt the 1976 copyright guidelines as part of university policy.[121] Under the agreement, faculty also must file copies of requests for permission to use copyrighted works and responses to requests with the university's legal counsel.

It appears that the fair use factors and congressional guidelines will be strictly construed in educational settings. In 1983 the Ninth Circuit Court of Appeals held that a teacher's use of a copyrighted booklet to make a learning activity packet was an infringement of the copyright law.[122] The court concluded that fair use was not met in this case because the learning packet was used for the same purpose as the protected booklet, the nature of the work reproduced was a "creative" effort rather than "information," and one-half of the packet was verbatim copy of the copyrighted material. Furthermore, the copying was found to violate the guideline of spontaneity in that it was reproduced several times over two school years. It is significant to note that the appeals court did not find the absence of personal profit on the part of the teacher to lessen the violation.

Rapid developments in instructional technology pose a new set of legal questions regarding use of videotapes and computer software. Recognizing the need for guidance related to videotaping, Congress issued guidelines for educational use in 1981.[123] These guidelines specify that taping must be made at the request of the teacher. The taped material must be used only once by the teacher within the first ten days of taping for relevant classroom activities. Additional use is limited to instructional reinforcement or evaluation purposes. After forty-five calendar days the tape must be erased. A New York federal district court held that a school system violated the fair use standards by extensive off-the-air taping and replaying of entire television programs.[124] The taping interfered with the producers' ability to market the tapes and films. In a subsequent appeal, the school system sought permission for temporary taping. Because of the availability of these programs for rental or lease, even temporary recording and use was held to violate fair use by interfering with the marketability of the films.[125]

Taping television broadcasts on home video recorders for later classroom use may constitute copyright infringement if off-the-air taping guidelines are not followed. Under the legal principles advanced by the Supreme Court in *Sony Corporation v. Universal City Studios,* "[e]ven copying for noncommercial purposes may impair the copyright holder's ability to obtain the rewards that Congress intended him to have."[126] In this case, the Court found that personal video recording for the purpose of "time shifting" was a legitimate, unobjectionable purpose, posing minimal harm to marketability. Home taping for broader viewing by students in the classroom would be beyond the purposes envisioned by the Court in *Sony* and would necessitate careful adherence to the guidelines for limited use discussed above.

Illegal copying of computer software in the school environment has generated significant concern among software publishers. Limited school budgets and the high cost of software have led to abuse of copyrighted software. In 1980 the copyright law was amended to include software.[127] While there are no legal cases interpreting the law for educational use, established copyright principles provide guidance in analyzing fair use. It is clear from the amended law that only one duplicate or backup copy can be made by the owner of the master computer program. This is to ensure a working copy of the program if the master copy is damaged. Application of the fair use exception does not alter this restriction for educators. While duplicating multiple copies would be clearly for educational purposes, other factors of fair use would be violated: The software is readily accessible for purchase (not impossible to obtain), programs can only be duplicated in their entirety, and copying substantially reduces the potential market.

A question not answered by the copyright law but plaguing schools is the legality of multiple use of a master program. That is, can a program be loaded in a number of computers in a laboratory for simultaneous use, or can a program by modified for use in a network of microcomputers? Again, application of the fair use concept would indicate that this is impermissible.[128] The most significant factor is that the market for the educational software would be greatly diminished. A number of students using the master program one at a time (serial use), however, would appear not to violate the copyright law. School boards are being urged to adopt guidelines or policies to prohibit illegal duplication of software. A survey in 1985 showed that 78 percent of 300 large school districts surveyed had developed such policies.[129]

Reporting Child Abuse

Child abuse and neglect are recognized as national problems. Reports indicate that the number of abused or neglected children each year is approaching one million.[130] Because the majority of these children are school age, teachers are in a unique role to detect signs of potential abuse. States, recognizing the daily contact teachers have with students, have imposed certain *duties* for reporting suspected abuse.

All states have enacted some type of child abuse law, and with few exceptions, teachers are identified among the professionals required to report signs of abuse. Most state laws impose criminal liability for failure to report child abuse. Penalties may include fines ranging from $500 to $1,000, prison terms up to one year, or both. Civil suits also may be initiated against teachers for negligence in failing to report suspected abuse.[131]

While specific aspects and coverage of the laws may vary from one state to another, definitions of abuse and neglect often are similar to that included in the federal Child Abuse Prevention and Treatment Act of 1974. That definition identifies child abuse and neglect as:

> the physical or mental injury, sexual abuse or exploitation, negligent treatment, or maltreatment of a child under the age of eighteen, or the age specified by the child protection law of the State in question, by a person who is responsible for the child's welfare under the circumstances which indicate that the child's health or welfare is harmed or threatened thereby . . .[132]

Several common elements are found in state child abuse statutes. The laws mandate that certain professionals such as doctors, nurses, and teachers report suspected abuse. Statutes do not require that reporters have absolute knowledge that a child has been abused or neglected but rather have "reasonable cause to believe" or "reason to believe."[133] Once abuse is suspected, the report must be made immediately to the designated child protection agency, department of welfare, or law enforcement unit. All states grant immunity from civil and criminal liability to individuals if reports are made in good faith.[134] In Ohio, absolute immunity exists even for reports made in bad faith.[135]

Although state laws are explicit as to reporting requirements for suspected child abuse, it is difficult to prove that a teacher had sufficient knowledge of child abuse to trigger legal liability for failure to report. Therefore, it is desirable for school officials to establish policies and procedures to encourage effective reporting. The pervasiveness of the problem and the lack of reporting by teachers[136] also indicate a need for in-service programs to assist teachers in recognizing signs of abused and neglected children.

Given the substantial national publicity focusing on child abuse, many school boards also are enacting policies to ensure that teachers and other school employees do not become the targets of child abuse charges. It is becoming increasingly common for school boards to prohibit physical contact between teachers and students in the absence of another adult and to place restrictions on private meetings between students and teachers before or after school. Employees can face disciplinary action for failing to comply with such directives, even if they are not found guilty of actual child abuse.

CONCLUSION

Except for certain limitations imposed by constitutional provisions and federal civil rights laws, the employment of teachers is governed by state statutes. The state prescribes general requirements for certification, contracts, tenure, and employment. Local school boards must follow state mandates and, in addition, may impose other requirements. In general, the following terms and conditions govern teacher employment.

1. The state establishes minimum qualifications for certification, which may include professional preparation, a specified age, United States citizenship, good moral character, signing of a loyalty oath, and passage of an academic examination.
2. A teacher must acquire a valid certificate to teach in public school systems.
3. Certification does not assure employment in a state.
4. Certification may be revoked for cause, generally identified in state law.
5. School boards are vested with the power to appoint teachers and to establish professional and academic employment standards above the state minimums.
6. Courts have generally upheld school board residency requirements, reasonable health and physical standards, and limitations on outside employment if formulated on a reasonable basis.
7. A teacher may be assigned or transferred to any school or grade at the board's discretion, as long as the assignment is within the teacher's certification area and not circumscribed by contract terms.
8. School officials can make reasonable and appropriate extracurricular assignments.
9. Contracts of teachers must satisfy the general principles of contract law, as well as conform to any additional specifications contained in state law.
10. Tenure is a statutory right that ensures that dismissal must be based on adequate cause and accompanied by procedural due process.

11. Tenure must be conferred in accordance with statutory provisions.
12. Supplemental contracts for extra duty assignments are generally outside the scope of tenure laws.
13. A school board's broad authority to determine teacher performance standards may be restricted by state imposed evaluation requirements.
14. Maintenance, access, and dissemination of personnel information must conform to state law and contractual agreements.
15. Educators must comply with the federal copyright law; copyrighted materials may be used for instructional purposes without the publisher's permission if "fair use" guidelines are followed.
16. Most states have laws requiring teachers to report suspected child abuse and granting immunity from liability if reports are made in good faith.

NOTES

1. *See, e.g.*, Bradford Cent. School Dist. v. Ambach, 451 N.Y.S.2d 654 (N.Y. 1982); Johnson v. Central Valley School Dist., 645 P.2d 1088 (Wash. 1982).
2. *See* Georgia Ass'n of Educators v. Nix, 407 F. Supp. 1102 (D. Ga. 1976).
3. Pa. Stat. Ann. 24 § 1225.
4. Bay v. State Bd. of Educ., 378 P.2d 558, 561 (Ore. 1963).
5. *Education Daily*, vol. 19, no. 129 (July 7, 1986), p. 1. *See* Patricia M. Lines, "Teacher Competency Testing: A Review of Legal Considerations," *Education Law Reporter*, vol. 23 (1985), pp. 811–833.
6. *See* United States v. South Carolina, National Educ. Ass'n v. South Carolina, 445 F. Supp. 1094 (D.S.C. 1977), *aff'd*, 434 U.S. 1026 (1978); text with note 17, chapter 9.
7. Keyishian v. Board of Educ., 385 U.S. 589 (1967).
8. *See* Ohlson v. Phillips, 397 U.S. 317 (1970).
9. *See* Cole v. Richardson, 405 U.S. 676 (1972); Connell v. Higginbotham, 403 U.S. 207 (1971).
10. Ambach v. Norwick, 441 U.S. 68 (1979).
11. *Id.* at 73–74.
12. Texas State Teachers Ass'n v. State, 711 S.W.2d 421 (Tex. App. 1986).
13. Chavich v. Board of Examiners of Bd. of Educ., 252 N.Y.S.2d 718, 723 (Sup. Ct., Kings County, 1964).
14. *See* Tate v. Livingston Parish School Bd., 444 So. 2d 219 (La. App. 1983).
15. *See* Wagenblast v. Crook County School Dist., 707 P.2d 69 (Ore. App. 1985).
16. *See* Richards v. Board of Educ. of Township High School Dist. No. 201, 171 N.E.2d 37 (Ill. 1960).
17. *See, e.g.*, Steiner v. Independent School Dist., 262 N.W.2d 173 (Minn.

1978); Wardwell v. Board of Educ. of the City School Dist. of Cincinnati, 529 F.2d 625, 629 (6th Cir. 1976).

18. *See* Moore v. Board of Educ. of Chidester School Dist. No. 59, 448 F.2d 709 (8th Cir. 1971).
19. Johnson v. School Dist. No. 3, Clay County, 96 N.W.2d 623 (Neb. 1959). *But see* Woodrum v. Rolling Hills Bd., 421 N.E.2d 859 (Ohio 1981) (failure to file a renewal certificate with the board did not result in a loss of tenure rights where the board had been notified by the state of the renewal).
20. *See* Wagenblast v. Crook County School Dist., 707 P.2d 69 (Ore. App. 1985).
21. *See* Smith v. Board of Educ. of the Wallkill Cent. School Dist., 482 N.E.2d 910 (N.Y. 1985); Occhipinti v. Board of School Directors, 464 A.2d 631 (Pa. Commw. 1983).
22. *See* Floyd County Bd. of Educ. v. Slone, 307 S.W.2d 912 (Ky. 1957).
23. *See* Longenecker v. Turlington, 464 So. 2d 1249 (Fla. App. 1985).
24. *See* Greenwald v. Community School Bd. No. 27, 329 N.Y.S.2d 203 (Sup. Ct., Queens County, 1972); Stone v. Fritts, 82 N.E. 792 (Ind. 1907); text with note 48, chapter 10, for details of procedural due process. *See also* Couch v. Turlington, 465 So. 2d 557 (Fla. App. 1985) (state education practices commission has the power to reject a teacher's voluntary surrender of teaching certificate to avoid revocation).
25. *See* Floyd G. Delon, *Legal Controls on Teacher Conduct: Teacher Discipline* (Topeka, KS: National Organization on Legal Problems in Education, 1977).
26. Pettit v. State Bd. of Educ., 513 P.2d 889 (Cal. 1973).
27. Morrison v. State Bd. of Educ., 461 P.2d 375 (Cal. 1969).
28. Erb v. Iowa State Bd. of Public Instruction, 216 N.W.2d 339 (Iowa 1974).
29. Adams v. State Professional Practices Council, 406 So. 2d 1170 (Fla. App. 1981).
30. *See generally* chapter 8 for a discussion of teachers' constitutional rights.
31. *See generally* chapter 9 for a discussion of discriminatory employment practices.
32. *See* Crawford v. Board of Educ., 453 N.E.2d 627 (Ohio 1983); Fortney v. School Dist. of West Salem, 321 N.W.2d 225 (Wis. 1982); Walter v. Independent School Dist., 323 N.W.2d 37 (Minn. 1982).
33. *See* Bonar v. City of Boston, 341 N.E.2d 684 (Mass. 1976); Armstead v. Starkville Mun. Separate School Dist., 331 F. Supp. 567 (D. Miss. 1971).
34. Harrah Independent School Dist. v. Martin, 440 U.S. 194 (1979) (policy required teachers to earn an additional five semester hours of college credit every three years while employed).
35. Wardwell v. Board of Educ. of the City School Dist. of Cincinnati, 529 F.2d 625 (6th Cir. 1976). *See also* Meyers v. Newport Consol. Joint School Dist., 639 P.2d 853 (Wash. App. 1982). *But see* Angwin v. City of Manchester, 386 A.2d 1272, 1273 (N.H. 1978) (invalidating a school district's residency requirement, finding no "public interest which is important enough to justify the restriction on the private right").
36. McCarthy v. Philadelphia Civil Service Comm'n, 424 U.S. 645 (1976).
37. *Id.* at 647. In several recent cases, the Supreme Court has confirmed that *prior resident requirements* for conferring certain benefits or employment

preference violate the equal protection clause and the constitutional right to travel. *See* Attorney General of New York v. Soto-Lopez, 106 S.Ct. 2317 (1986); Hooper v. Bernalillo County Assessor, 105 S.Ct. 2862 (1985); Zobel v. Williams, 457 U.S. 55 (1982).

38. Ind. Code Ann. 20 § 6.1–6–12. *See also* Pa. Stat. 24 § 11–1106.
39. Stough v. Crenshaw County Bd. of Educ., 579 F. Supp. 1091 (M.D. Ala. 1983) *aff'd*, 744 F.2d 1479 (11th Cir. 1984). *See also* Brantley v. Surles, 765 F.2d 478 (5th Cir. 1985).
40. Gargiul v. Tompkins, 704 F.2d 661 (2d Cir. 1983). The teacher, however, was not ultimately successful in obtaining back pay for the period in which she was suspended for failing to submit to the exam because she had not appealed the commissioner of education's decision in state legal proceedings. *See* Gargiul v. Tomkins, 790 F.2d 265 (2d Cir. 1986), text with note 139, chapter 8. *See also* Jones v. McKenzie, 628 F. Supp. 1500 (D.D.C. 1986) (board requirement that employees submit to mandatory screening for drugs may impair privacy rights).
41. Parolisi v. Board of Examiners of City of New York, 285 N.Y.S.2d 936 (Sup. Ct., Kings County, 1967).
42. Gurmankin v. Costanzo, 556 F.2d 184 (3d Cir. 1977).
43. Bevan v. New York State Teachers' Retirement System, 345 N.Y.S.2d 921 (Sup. Ct., Albany County, 1973).
44. Arline v. School Bd. of Nassau County, 772 F.2d 759 (11th Cir. 1985), *cert. granted,* 106 S. Ct. 1633 (1986). *See* chapter 9 for discussion of discrimination based on handicaps.
45. Gosney v. Sonora Independent School Dist., 603 F.2d 522, 523 (5th Cir. 1979).
46. *Id.* at 526.
47. *See* Stevenson v. Lower Marion County School Dist., 327 S.E.2d 656 (S.C. 1985).
48. *See* Alabama State Tenure Comm'n v. Phenix City Bd. of Educ., 467 So. 2d 263 (Ala. App. 1985) (under state law, transfers must not be personal, political, or arbitrarily unjust); Glanville v. Hickory County Reorganized School Dist., 637 S.W.2d 328 (Mo. App. 1982) (teachers cannot be transferred for exercising constitutional rights).
49. *See* Adlerstein v. Board of Educ. of New York City, 485 N.Y.S.2d 1 (N.Y. 1984); Olson v. Board of School Directors, 478 A.2d 954 (Pa. Commw. 1984). *See also* Jett v. Dallas Independent School Dist., 798 F.2d 748 (5th Cir. 1986) (coaching responsibilities could be changed); Kelleher v. Flawn, 761 F.2d 1079 (5th Cir. 1985) (no entitlement to teach specific courses).
50. *See* Moore v. Board of Educ. of Chidester School Dist. No. 59, 448 F.2d 709 (8th Cir. 1971); Singleton v. Jackson Mun. Separate School Dist., 419 F.2d 1211 (5th Cir. 1969); Bolin v. San Bernardino City Unified School Dist., 202 Cal. Rptr. 416 (Cal. App. 1984).
51. *See* Wygant v. Jackson Bd. of Educ., 106 S. Ct. 1842 (1986).
52. *See* Jett v. Dallas Independent School Dist., 798 F.2d 748 (5th Cir. 1986) (change in coaching duties and responsibilities without an economic loss did not require due process); Glanville v. Hickory County Reorganized School Dist., 637 S.W.2d 328 (Mo. App. 1982) (only factor to be considered under state law is reduction in salary); Rockdale County School Dist. v. Weil, 266

S.E.2d 919 (Ga. 1980) (individual must claim reduction in salary, responsibility level, and prestige of position—one factor alone is insufficient); Elam v. Waynesville R-VI School Dist., 676 S.W.2d 880 (Mo. App. 1984) (reduction in longevity salary increments to all teachers in a classification—nonresidents of districts—is not a demotion); Wagner v. West Perry School Dist., 480 A.2d 1336 (Pa. Commw. 1984) (salary loss from discontinuance of summer programs is not a demotion).

53. In re Santee Appeal, 156 A.2d 830 (Pa. 1959). *See also* Hood v. Alabama State Tenure Comm'n, 418 So. 2d 131 (Ala. App. 1982).
54. In re Santee, *id.* at 832.
55. Smith v. School Dist. No. 18, Pondera County, 139 P.2d 518 (Mont. 1943).
56. Mroczek v. Board of Educ. of the Beachwood City School Dist., 400 N.E.2d 1362 (Ohio C.P. 1979).
57. Alabama State Tenure Comm'n v. Shelby County Bd. of Educ., 474 So. 2d 723 (Ala. App. 1985). *See also* Williams v. Plainfield Bd. of Educ., 422 A.2d 461 (N.J. Super. 1980).
58. LeGalley v. Bronson Community Schools, 339 N.W.2d 223 (Mich. App. 1983). *But see* Vilelle v. Reorganized School Dist. No. R–1, Benton County, 689 S.W.2d 72 (Mo. App. 1985) (under state law, teacher's salary could not be frozen if other teachers received raises).
59. *See* Breslin v. School Comm. of Quincy, 478 N.E.2d 149 (Mass. App. 1985); Philadelphia Ass'n of School Administrators v. School Dist. of Philadelphia, 471 A.2d 581 (Pa. Commw. 1984) (*temporary* reassignment of administrators to teaching assignments during a teachers' strike was not a demotion in rank or salary requiring due process).
60. *See* Powers v. Freetown-Lakeville Regional School Dist. Comm., 467 N.E.2d 203 (Mass. 1984); Chester Upland School Dist. v. Brown, 447 A.2d 1068 (Pa. Commw. 1982).
61. Holland v. Board of Educ. of Raleigh County, 327 S.E.2d 155 (W.Va. 1985).
62. Fry v. Commonwealth, 485 A.2d 508 (Pa. Commw. 1984).
63. *See* Ballard v. Board of Educ. of Goshen, 469 N.E.2d 951 (Ohio App. 1984) (additional duties can be assigned to teachers without providing supplemental pay).
64. McGrath v. Burkhard, 280 P.2d 864 (Cal. App. 1955).
65. Thomas v. Board of Educ. of Community Unit School Dist., 453 N.E.2d 150 (Ill. App. 1983). *See* Penns Grove-Carneys Point Educ. Ass'n v. Board of Educ. of Penns Grove-Carneys Point Regional School Dist., 506 A.2d 1289 (N.J. Super. 1986) (band instructor could be assigned extra duties on weekends).
66. Board of Educ. v. Asbury Park Educ. Ass'n, 368 A.2d 396 (N.J. Super. 1976).
67. *See* Howell v. Alabama State Tenure Comm'n, 402 So. 2d 1041 (Ala. 1981) (teacher refused to participate in a program to improve classroom management); Jones v. Alabama State Tenure Comm'n, 408 So. 2d 145 (Ala. 1981) (counselor refused to supervise students before school hours).
68. *See, e.g.*, Gillespie v. Board of Educ. of the North Little Rock School Dist., 528 F. Supp. 433 (E.D. Ark. 1981), *aff'd*, 692 F.2d 529 (8th Cir. 1982); Maddox v. St. Paul School Dist., 697 S.W.2d 130 (Ark. App. 1985); Board of Educ. of Alamogordo Public Schools v. Jennings, 651 P.2d 1037 (N.M. App. 1982).

69. *See* Kern Alexander and David Alexander, *American Public School Law* (St. Paul, MN: West Publishing Co., 1985), pp. 551–553, for a discussion of contract elements.
70. Minor v. Sully Buttes School Dist., 345 N.W.2d 48 (S.D. 1984). *See also* Ogbunugafor v. St. Christopher's Union Free School Dist., 473 N.Y.S.2d 517 (App. Div. 1984) (promise of superintendent to recommend a teacher to the board does not create a contract).
71. *See* Nelson v. Doland Bd. of Educ., 380 N.W.2d 665 (S.D. 1986); Floyd County Bd. of Educ. v. Slone, 307 S.W.2d 912 (Ky. 1957).
72. *See* Bruton v. Ames Community School Dist., 291 N.W.2d 351 (Iowa 1980).
73. *See* text with note 48, chapter 10, for discussion of procedural due process requirements.
74. Virginia Nordin, "Employees," *The Yearbook of School Law 1977*, Philip Piele, ed. (Topeka, KS: National Organization on Legal Problems in Education, 1977), p. 177.
75. Brodie v. School Community of Easton, 324 N.E.2d 922 (Mass. App. 1975).
76. *Id. See* Schmidt v. Unified School Dist., 644 P.2d 396 (Kan. 1982) (a one-month gap in employment due to uncertainty of federal funding rendered a teacher ineligible for tenure under statutory requirement of two consecutive years of employment).
77. *See* State *ex rel.* Rogers v. Hubbard Local School Dist., 461 N.E.2d 1308 (Ohio 1984) (regular and substantial part-time employment rendered teacher eligible for tenure); Stafford v. Valley Community School Dist., 328 N.W.2d 323 (Iowa 1982) (part-time tutoring of one student did not qualify for employment as a teacher for probationary purposes).
78. *See, e.g.*, Board of Educ. v. Carroll County Educ. Ass'n, 452 A.2d 1316 (Md. App. 1982) (cannot enter a negotiated agreement delegating authority to another party).
79. In New York, for example, tenure may be acquired by special area, general area, vertical (subject area junior and senior high) or horizontal (junior or senior high only). *See* Cole v. Board of Educ., 457 N.Y.S.2d 547 (App. Div. 1982), *aff'd*, 471 N.Y.S.2d 84 (N.Y. 1983).
80. See text with note 47, *supra*.
81. Indiana *ex rel.* Anderson v. Brand, 303 U.S. 95 (1938). Under such legislation, the status of teachers who have received tenure cannot be altered, but the legislature is not prohibited from changing the law for future employees.
82. *See* Gullett v. Sparks, 444 S.W.2d 901 (Ky. 1969).
83. *See, e.g.*, Wooten v. Alabama State Tenure Comm'n, 421 So. 2d 1277 (Ala. App. 1982).
84. *See, e.g.*, Berry v. Pike County Bd. of Educ., 448 So. 2d 315 (Ala. 1984); Burke v. Lead-Deadwood School Dist., 347 N.W.2d 343 (S.D. 1984); Wolfe v. Sierra Vista Unified School Dist., 722 P.2d 389 (Ariz. App. 1986); Wahlquist v. School Bd. of Liberty County, 423 So. 2d 471 (Fla. App. 1982).
85. Spurlock v. Board of Trustees, 699 P.2d 270, 272 (Wyo. 1985).
86. Atencio v. Board of Educ., 655 P.2d 1012 (N.M. 1982).
87. Smith v. Board of Educ. of Urbana School Dist., 708 F.2d 258 (7th Cir. 1983); Bryan v. Alabama State Tenure Comm'n, 472 So. 2d 1052 (Ala. App. 1985); Neal v. School Dist. of York, 288 N.W.2d 725 (Neb. 1980).
88. Slockett v. Iowa Valley Community School Dist., 359 N.W.2d 446 (Iowa 1984).

89. *See* Issaquah Educ. Ass'n v. Issaquah School Dist., 706 P.2d 618 (Wash. 1985); Lexington County School Dist. v. Bost, 316 S.E.2d 677 (S.C. 1984). *But see* Smith v. Board of Educ. of County of Logan, 341 S.E.2d 685 (W. Va. 1985) (failure of a school board to renew a coaching contract was considered a transfer, which under state law required procedural due process).
90. *See* Swager v. Board of Educ., 688 P.2d 270 (Kan. 1984); Babitzke v. Silverton Union High School, 695 P.2d 93 (Ore. App. 1985).
91. *See* Munger v. Jesup Community School Dist., 325 N.W.2d 377 (Iowa 1982).
92. Civil Rights Div. of the Arizona Dep't of Law v. Amphitheater Unified School Dist., 680 P.2d 517 (Ariz. App. 1983).
93. Tate v. Westerville City Bd. of Educ., 448 N.E.2d 144 (Ohio 1983).
94. Charges of discrimination in connection with leave policies pertaining to pregnancy-related absences and the observance of religious holidays are discussed in chapter 9.
95. *See* Bristol Township School Dist. v. Karafin, 478 A.2d 539 (Pa. Commw. 1984); Collins v. Orleans Parish School Bd., 384 So. 2d 236 (La. 1980).
96. Iowa Code Ann. § 279.14. *See also* Ark. Stat. Ann. 80-1266.6.
97. Cal. Educ. Code §§ 44660, 44662, 44664.
98. Fla. Stat. § 231.29.
99. *See, e.g.*, La. Rev. Stat. Ann. § 17.391.5; Pa. Stat. Ann. tit. 24, § 11–1123.
100. *See, e.g.*, Ariz. Rev. Stat. § 15–537; Or. Rev. Stat. § 342.850; Conn. Gen. Stat. Ann. § 10–151(b).
101. West Virginia Bd. of Educ. Policy No. 5300 (6) (a).
102. Trimboli v. Board of Educ., 280 S.E.2d 686 (W. Va. 1981).
103. Wren v. McDowell County Bd. of Educ., 327 S.E.2d 464 (W. Va. 1985).
104. Lipan v. Board of Educ., County of Hancock, 295 S.E.2d 44 (W. Va. 1982); Wilt v. Flanigan, 294 S.E.2d 189 (W. Va. 1982).
105. Anderson v. San Mateo Community College Dist., 151 Cal. Rptr. 111 (Cal. App. 1978).
106. Hyde v. Wellpinit School Dist. 49, 611 P.2d 1388 (Wash. App. 1980).
107. Holland v. Board of Educ. of Raleigh County, 327 S.E.2d 155 (W. Va. 1985).
108. In re Cowden, 486 A.2d 1014 (Pa. Commw. 1985).
109. *See, e.g.*, Kudasik v. Board of Directors, Port Allegany School Dist., 455 A.2d 261 (Pa. 1983).
110. Perez v. Commission on Professional Competence, 197 Cal. Rptr. 390 (Cal. App. 1983).
111. Johnson v. Board of Educ. of the Woden-Crystal Lake Community School Dist., 353 N.W.2d 883, 887 (Iowa App. 1984).
112. Schaub v. Chamberlain Bd. of Educ., 339 N.W.2d 307 (S.D. 1983). It must be emphasized that failure to follow established evaluation procedures does not necessarily result in a denial of *constitutional due process* rights in termination actions if the minimum of notice, specification of charges, and an opportunity for a hearing are provided. *See* Goodrich v. Newport News School Bd., 743 F.2d 225 (4th Cir. 1984). *See also* text with note 50, chapter 10.
113. Wooster Republican Printing Company v. City of Wooster, 383 N.E.2d 124 (Ohio 1978). Amendments in 1980 and 1981 to the state privacy act, Ohio Rev. Code § 1347, and the public records act, Ohio Rev. Code § 149.43, however, clearly expand the right to disclose personnel information and may limit the applicability of the state high court's balancing test.

114. Equal Employment Opportunity Comm'n v. Franklin and Marshall College, 775 F.2d 110 (3d Cir. 1985), *cert. denied,* 106 S. Ct. 2288 (1986). *But see* Equal Employment Opportunity Comm'n v. University of Notre Dame Du Lac, 715 F.2d 331 (7th Cir. 1983) (compelling necessity and particularized need must be shown before disclosure is required).
115. Equal Employment Opportunity Comm'n v. Shell, 466 U.S. 54, 68-69 (1984). *See also* Equal Employment Opportunity Comm'n v. Maryland Cup Corp., 785 F.2d 471 (4th Cir. 1986), *cert. denied,* 107 S.Ct. 68 (1986).
116. *See* Keyes v. Lenoir Rhyne College, 552 F.2d 579 (4th Cir. 1977), *cert. denied,* 434 U.S. 904 (1977); McKillop v. Regents of the University of Calif., 386 F. Supp. 1270 (N.D. Cal. 1975).
117. *See* Aebisher v. Ryan, 622 F.2d 651 (2d Cir. 1980); Columbus Educ. Ass'n v. Columbus City School Dist., 623 F.2d 1155 (6th Cir. 1980); Swilley v. Alexander, 629 F.2d 1018 (5th Cir. 1980).
118. Marcus v. Rowley, 695 F.2d 1171, 1174 (9th Cir. 1983).
119. 17 U.S.C. § 101 *et seq. See* Virginia M. Helm, *What Educators Should Know About Copyright,* Fastback 233 (Bloomington, IN: Phi Delta Kappa, 1986).
120. *Id.* at § 107.
121. Agreement between Addison-Wesley Pub. Co., et al. and New York University, April 7, 1983. The off-campus copying facility also entered into a consent decree to require proof of compliance with the copyright law from NYU faculty. Addison-Wesley Pub. Co. v. New York University, No. 82–Civ–8333–S, consent decree, May 31, 1983.
122. Marcus v. Rowley, 695 F.2d 1171 (9th Cir. 1983).
123. Guidelines for Off-The-Air Recording of Broadcast Programming for Educational Purposes, Cong. Rec. § E4751, October 14, 1981.
124. Encyclopedia Britannica Educational Corp. v. Crooks, 542 F. Supp. 1156 (W.D.N.Y. 1982).
125. Encyclopedia Brittanica Educational Corp. v. Crooks, 558 F. Supp. 1247 (W.D.N.Y. 1983).
126. 464 U.S. 417, 450 (1984).
127. 17 U.S.C. § 117.
128. *See* Virginia M. Helms, "Copyright Issues in Computer-Assisted Instruction," *School Law Update 1985,* Thomas Jones and Darel Semler, eds. (Topeka, KS: National Organization on Legal Problems of Education, 1985); John T. Soma and Dwight L. Pringle, "Computer Software in the Public Schools," *Education Law Reporter,* vol. 28 (1985), pp. 315–324.
129. *Education Daily,* May 31, 1985, p. 1.
130. U.S. Department of Health and Human Services, Report of the National Center on Child Abuse and Neglect, 1983.
131. While there are no legal suits where educators have been prosecuted for failure to report, the California Supreme Court, finding liability against a physician, commented that other professionals identified as mandated reporters by law, such as teachers, also could be held liable. Landeros v. Flood, 551 P.2d 389, 392, n. 5 (Cal. 1976). *See also* chapter 12 for discussion of the elements of negligence.
132. 42 U.S.C. § 5102.
133. *See* Roman v. Appleby, 558 F. Supp. 449, 459 (E.D. Pa. 1983).

134. *See* McDonald v. Children's Services Division, 694 P.2d 569 (Ore. App. 1985) (immunity existed for good faith reporting).
135. ORC § 2151.421. Bishop v. Ezzone, No. WD–80–63 (Wood County AP, June 26, 1981).
136. Various reports show that less than 10 percent of child abuse reports are made by teachers. *See* Eric S. Mondschein, "Legal Responsibilities of Educators in Child Abuse," *School Law Update: Preventive School Law,* Thomas N. Jones and Darel P. Semler, eds. (Topeka, KS: National Organization on Legal Problems of Education, 1984); Janet Mason and L. Poindexter Watts, "The Duty of School Personnel to Report Abuse and Neglect," *School Law Bulletin,* vol. 17, no. 2 (1986), pp. 28–38.

8

Teachers' Substantive Constitutional Rights

While statutory law is prominent in defining specific rights and responsibilities of public school teachers in terms of certification, contracts, tenure, and many other aspects of teaching, significant substantive rights also are conferred on public employees by the Federal Constitution. These guaranteed rights cannot be abridged by state or local action without an overriding governmental interest, nor can employment be conditioned on their relinquishment. The exercise of these protected rights often results in a conflict of interests between school officials and teachers. In balancing these interests, courts have cautiously guarded teachers' rights against undue governmental encroachment.

This chapter provides an overview of the scope of teachers' constitutional rights as defined by the judiciary in connection with free expression, academic freedom, freedom of association, freedom of choice in appearance, and privacy rights. The concluding section focuses on remedies available to aggrieved individuals when their constitutional rights have been violated by school officials or school boards. Constitutional rights pertaining to equal protection, due process, and religious guarantees are discussed in other chapters.

FREEDOM OF EXPRESSION

Until the mid-twentieth century, it was generally accepted that public school teachers could be dismissed or disciplined for expressing views considered objectionable by the school board. The private sector practice of firing the critical employee was assumed to apply to public employment as well. During the past few decades, however, the Supreme Court has recognized that the first amendment places restrictions on public employers' discretion to condition employment on the expression of certain views, including those that are critical of governmental policies and actions. Although it is now clearly established that the right to free expression is not relinquished by accepting public school employment, courts have recognized that this right must be weighed against the school district's interest in operating public schools. The federal judiciary is continually refining the applicable principles of law in an attempt to achieve the appropriate balance between these interests. In this section, the evolution of these legal principles and their application to specific school situations are reviewed.

Legal Principles: From *Pickering* to *Connick*

In the landmark 1968 case, *Pickering v. Board of Education,* the Supreme Court recognized that teachers have a first amendment right to air their views on matters of public concern.[1] The controversy in *Pickering* focused on a letter written to a local newspaper in which the teacher criticized the school board's expenditure of funds, especially the allocation of funds between the educational and athletic programs. The school board dismissed Pickering because of this letter, which included false statements that were allegedly damaging to the reputation of the school board members and district administrators, and the Illinois courts upheld the dismissal.

Reversing the state courts, the Supreme Court first identified expression pertaining to matters of public concern as constitutionally protected, and reasoned that the funding and allocation issues raised by Pickering were clearly questions of public interest requiring free and open debate. The Court then applied a balancing test, weighing the teacher's interest in expressing his views on public issues against the school board's interest in operating the school system. The Court recognized that if the expression jeopardized Pickering's relationship with his immediate supervisor, harmony with coworkers, classroom performance, or the operation of the school system, the school district's interest in curtailing the expression would prevail. Finding that Pickering's letter did not have a detrimental effect in any of these areas, the Court concluded that there was no justification for limiting the teacher's contribution to public debate. Indeed, the Court noted that a teacher's role provides a special vantage point from which to formulate an "informed and definite opinion" on the allocation of school district funds, thus making it essential for teachers to be able to speak freely without fear of reprisal.[2] Furthermore, the Court held that false statements, in the absence of proof that they were "knowingly or recklessly" made, cannot be the basis for dismissal.

Since *Pickering,* teachers often have challenged dismissals or other disciplinary actions as unconstitutional because the exercise of protected expression in part precipitated the adverse employment consequences. In 1977, however, the Supreme Court established the principle that even if a teacher's expression is constitutionally protected, school officials are not prevented from discharging the employee if sufficient cause exists independently of the protected conduct. In *Mt. Healthy City School District v. Doyle,* the school board voted not to renew the contract of a nontenured teacher who had made a telephone call to a local radio station concerning a proposed teacher dress and appearance code. The teacher had been involved in several previous incidents; however, in not renewing his contract the board cited "lack of tact in handling professional matters" with reference only to the radio station call and obscene gestures made to several female students.[3] Both the trial court and Sixth Circuit Court of Appeals concluded that reinstatement was warranted because the telephone call was protected speech and was a substantial reason for the adverse personnel action.

Reversing and remanding the decision, the Supreme Court instructed the lower court to assess whether the school board would have reached the same decision in the absence of the teacher's exercise of protected speech. The Court reasoned that protected expression should not place an employee in a better or worse position with regard to continued employment:

> A borderline or marginal candidate should not have the employment question resolved against him because of constitutionally protected conduct. But that same candidate ought not to be able, by engaging in such conduct, to prevent his employer from assessing his performance record and reaching a decision not to rehire on the basis of that record, simply because the protected conduct makes the employer more certain of the correctness of its decision.[4]

On remand for a determination of whether the school board would have released the teacher in the absence of his radio station call, the board clearly established that there were other grounds justifying his nonrenewal.[5]

Under the *Mt. Healthy* test, the burden is on the employee to show that the conduct was constitutionally protected and was a "substantial or motivating" factor in the school board's adverse employment decision. If this is established, the burden then shifts to the board to show by a preponderance of evidence that it would have reached the same decision if the protected expression had not occurred. Of course, even if proven that the school board's decision was predicated on the exercise of protected speech, the decision might still be upheld if established that the expression interfered with working relationships or disrupted school operations.

For over a decade after the *Pickering* decision, it was unclear whether private communication of public employees enjoyed first amendment protection. In 1979 the Supreme Court addressed this issue in *Givhan v. Western Line Consolidated School District,* concluding that as long as the expression pertains to issues of public concern (in contrast to a personal grievance), statements made in private or through a public medium enjoy the same constitutional protection.[6] The Court reasoned that the forum where the expression occurs does not determine whether it is of public or personal interest. In this case, the teacher made critical comments to her principal regarding race relations in the school. Finding these private comments to be constitutionally protected, the Court did note, however, that the balancing process may involve additional considerations when private speech is at issue. Whereas public expression is generally evaluated on its content and impact, private expression (because of the nature of the employer-employee relationship) should also be assessed based on the time, place, and manner of the remarks.

A significant Supreme Court decision involving public employees' free speech rights was rendered in 1983. In this case, *Connick v. Myers,* the Court added a new dimension to the *Pickering* balancing test, one that tends to narrow the categories of protected speech for public employees.[7] The Court noted that the threshold inquiry in free speech cases is whether the expression involves matters of public concern since *only* such expression enjoys first amendment protection. Of particular significance was the Court's conclusion that the form and context as well as the content of the expression should be considered in assessing whether the expression relates to public interests. Thus, the Court indicated that the factors used under the *Pickering* balancing test to determine whether speech adversely affects governmental interests can be considered in the initial determination of whether the expression informs public debate or is simply part of a personal employment grievance.

In *Connick,* an assistant district attorney was dissatisfied with her proposed transfer and circulated within the district attorney's office a questionnaire concerning transfer policy, office morale, need for a grievance committee, level of confidence in supervisors, and existence of pressure to work in political campaigns. Following this action, she was terminated, and she challenged the action as violating her first amendment rights. Both the federal district court and Fifth Circuit Court of Appeals ruled in favor of the employee, reasoning that the primary reason for the discharge was the survey involving matters of public policy and that the state had not "clearly demonstrated" that the questionnaire "substantially interfered" with the operations of the district attorney's office.[8]

Reversing the courts below, the Supreme Court ruled five-to-four that the questionnaire related primarily to a personal employment grievance rather than matters of public interest. Only one question (regarding pressure to participate in political campaigns) was found to involve an issue of public concern. Weighing the various factors—the importance of close working relationships to fulfill public responsibilities, the employee's attempt to precipitate a vote of no confidence in the district attorney, the distribution of the questionnaire during office hours, and the district attorney's conclusion that the functioning of his office was endangered—the Court concluded that the employee's expression was not constitutionally protected and could be the basis for dismissal.

The *Connick* majority reasoned that the state's burden of justifying a given discharge varies according to the nature of the employee's expression; the employer's burden of proof increases as the employee's speech more directly involves public issues and decreases as the expression interferes with close working relationships that are essential to fulfilling public responsibilities. The majority did concede, however, that this "particularized balancing" of competing interests is a difficult task.[9]

Application of the Legal Principles

During the 1970s and early 1980s, courts relied on the *Pickering* guidelines in striking down a variety of restrictions on teachers' rights to express views on matters of public interest. For example, courts ordered reinstatement or nullified transfers when evidence substantiated that the dismissal or other disciplinary action was based on the exercise of protected expression, such as wearing black armbands as a symbolic protest against the Vietnam War;[10] expressing views publicly (to the school board, city council, and news media) regarding school violence and the inability of the school staff to deal with multiracial student bodies and communities;[11] criticizing school policies in a school-sponsored open forum;[12] making public comments favoring a collective bargaining contract;[13] and criticizing the instructional program.[14] While most of these cases involved challenges to terminations or involuntary transfers, courts also have ordered letters of reprimand to be expunged from personnel files if predicated on employees' exercise of protected speech.[15]

The first amendment has been interpreted as affording considerable protection to educators in expressing their views on matters of public interest, but courts have concluded that constitutional protection does not extend to personal attacks on superiors. For example, the Supreme Court of Missouri upheld the transfer of a teacher who called two assistant principals "scabs" during a teachers' strike, reasoning that the transfer was justified for "legitimate managerial reasons" because of the detrimental impact of the speech on the close working relationship between the teacher and immediate supervisors.[16] Similarly, the Sixth Circuit Court of Appeals ruled that racially derogatory comments made by a teacher to the principal and assistant principal were not constitutionally protected,[17] and a New Jersey teacher's attacks on the superintendent and school district at an orientation meeting for new teachers were found not to be shielded by the first amendment.[18] A federal district court also upheld the dismissal of a Connecticut teacher who distributed in the school parking lot leaflets containing false allegations against the principal,[19] and a California appeals court held that a varsity coach's strongly worded attacks on his principal (contained in a letter distributed to several other people) justified nonreassignment as a coach because of the letter's substantial threat to discipline and harmony in working relationships.[20]

Courts have reasoned that speech intended to disrupt the normal operation of the school system, like personal attacks on superiors, is not constitutionally protected. For example, the Eighth Circuit Court of Appeals upheld the dismissal of a teacher who opposed the presence of R.O.T.C. recruiters at the school, harassed the recruiters, and urged his students to force the military out of the school. The court reasoned that the teacher's statements, which threatened disruption of the educational process, were not constitutionally protected.[21]

Even if protected speech is involved, courts have relied on the principle enunciated in *Mt. Healthy* to uphold terminations or transfers if other legitimate reasons justify the personnel actions. In an illustrative case, the Fifth Circuit Court of Appeals upheld the dismissal of a teacher based on a confrontation with the assistant coach during a basketball game and repeated threats toward the athletic director. The fact that the teacher also had criticized the athletic program and voiced disagreement with an unsatisfactory evaluation did not negate the legitimate grounds for dismissal.[22] Similarly, the Supreme Court of Mississippi upheld the nonrenewal of a teacher because of insubordination for taking unauthorized personal leave, even though the teacher's exercise of protected speech in criticizing the school board and participating in teacher organization activities and grand jury investigations was a substantial factor in the board's decision not to reemploy her.[23]

Mt. Healthy, however, cannot be relied on to justify termination or other adverse employment action if the school officials' stated reasons for personnel decisions are merely a pretext to restrict protected expression. For example, the Tenth Circuit Court of Appeals ruled that a Wyoming teacher, who was terminated for alleged lack of satisfactory progress and enthusiasm and failure to cooperate with other teachers, was in fact impermissibly terminated for protected speech involving public criticism of the new superintendent's recommendations for changes in teaching methods.[24] Similarly, the Fifth Circuit Court of Appeals in two cases concluded that school boards would not have initiated dismissal actions in the absence of the employees' exercise of protected expression in connection with support of unsuccessful candidates for the school board and criticism of the administration of a special reading program.[25]

In recent cases involving free speech claims of employees, courts have relied on the *Connick* decision in determining whether the expression is constitutionally protected. Considering the context and form as well as the content of the expression, courts seem more inclined than they were a decade ago to conclude that a public employee's expression relates to private employment disputes rather than to matters of public concern. To illustrate, the Sixth Circuit Court of Appeals found no first or fourteenth amendment violation in the suspension, transfer, and ultimate nonrenewal of a guidance counselor after she revealed her bisexuality to various school employees. Relying on *Connick,* the appellate court concluded that the counselor's statements did not enjoy first amendment protection as they were not about a matter of public concern.[26] The court did not require evidence that the remarks had some disruptive effect on the school or on working relationships in concluding that the expression pertained to a personal interest and was unprotected. Also rejecting the equal protection claim, the appeals court noted that to establish discrimination, the counselor would have to prove that she had performed her job properly and was released for no apparent legitimate reason. However, evidence indicated improper job performance as she had breached the confidence of two advisees by disclosing their homosexuality to a third party. Furthermore, no evidence was presented indicating that heterosexual employees would be treated differently for making their personal sexual preference the topic of discussion in the high school community. The Supreme Court declined to review this decision, but Justices Brennan and Marshall wrote a strong dissent to the denial of review, arguing that the Court should have addressed these serious, unsettled issues. They also admonished the appellate court for condoning the dismissal of a teacher for merely speaking about her bisexuality when no adverse consequences resulted from the expression: "Speech that 'touches upon' this explosive issue is no less deserving of constitutional attention than speech relating to more widely condemned forms of discrimination."[27]

The Supreme Court also declined to review a case in which the Eleventh Circuit Court of Appeals upheld the dismissal of a teacher who had filed a grievance after being offered a job-sharing position that meant part-time employment. The court concluded that the teacher's speech was personal in nature, and that her reference to the negative impact of the job-sharing assignment on students' welfare was "not sufficient to bring her grievance within the rubric of matters of 'public concern.' "[28] In essence, the court reasoned that the teacher's grievance focused on personal dissatisfaction over her assignment rather than on the impact of the employment arrangement on the instructional program.

In 1986 the Tenth Circuit Court of Appeals concluded that the nonrenewal of a teacher's contract, in part because of discussing her allocation of teacher aide time with two parents, did not implicate first amendment rights.[29] The court reasoned that the expression did not concern a matter of public importance, but rather a personal dispute with her superior. Even assuming that it touched on public interest, the court relied on *Connick* in concluding that the speech was not entitled to constitutional protection because the *manner* in which the subject was raised had an adverse impact on working relationships and the school's ability to carry out its teaching responsibilities. The court reached a different conclusion, however, on the teacher's second claim—that her nonrenewal was in retaliation for union activities as a faculty representative. Finding such activities constitutionally protected, the court ruled that a jury must address whether the teacher's union activity was a motivating factor in the adverse employment decision.

Other courts have relied on *Connick* in finding that specific expression primarily pertains to a private grievance rather than public issues. For example, the Eighth Circuit Court of Appeals concluded that a teacher's "frequent, lengthy, and uncompromising criticisms of the administration, faculty, and students" was generally not protected by the first amendment "when balanced against the needs of the Board for efficient operation and internal harmony in its schools."[30] The First Circuit Court of Appeals upheld disciplinary action against a teacher who posted in her classroom on parents' night letters of reprimand that she received for refusing to give her principal a case history she had written on one of her students for a college course.[31] The following also have been found to involve personal employment disputes about internal school policies, rather than expression on matters of public interest: a grievance concerning the amount of advance notice required in connection with termination of employment;[32] complaints about class assignments, a policy allowing students to select their own courses (and thus their teachers), and the hiring of coaches to teach social studies;[33] a grievance regarding the training schedule for a new statewide reading program and criticism of the superintendent in a newsletter article;[34] statements accusing the superintendent of inciting student disturbances;[35] and a teacher's protest over the principal's unfavorable evaluation of her performance.[36]

Although the *Connick* test makes it more difficult for public employees to establish that their expression pertains to public issues and is, therefore, constitutionally protected, this burden can be satisfied. For example, within a month after the *Connick* decision, both the Ninth Circuit Court of Appeals and the Eleventh Circuit Court of Appeals overturned dismissals of police officers, concluding that their expression regarding pay raises and race relations was protected speech and could not be the basis for dismissals.[37]

Also, in several school cases federal appellate courts have overturned personnel actions, finding the school boards' reliance on *Connick* misguided. The Eighth Circuit Court of Appeals invalidated a teacher's discharge for writing a letter to the newspaper protesting the school board's decision to drop junior high school track which he coached.[38] Noting that the fate of the junior high track program was of public interest, the court rejected the school board's contention that the letter was not constitutionally protected expression. The same court held that plaintiff coaches, who made public statements about the severity of the head coach's disciplinary practices, could not be transferred to undesirable coaching assignments based on their exercise of protected speech. The court reasoned that the corporal punishment administered by the head coach was a matter of public concern, and indeed of public debate, and that the right to free expression outweighed any interest of the school board in maintaining harmonious and loyal working relationships among the coaching staff.[39] Applying similar reasoning, the Third Circuit Court of Appeals ordered reinstatement of a school district employee who was dismissed for speaking at two county school board meetings, where he charged that the Division of Motor Vehicles was engaged in inefficient, wasteful, and possibly fraudulent practices. The appeals court concluded that unlike the situation in *Connick,* the employee here "spoke as a concerned citizen and taxpayer and not as a grieved employee."[40]

The Supreme Court dismissed an appeal of a case in which the Seventh Circuit Court of Appeals discussed *Connick* at length in reviewing a teacher's claim that he was harrassed, given negative evaluations, denied a personal leave day, removed as an assistant baseball coach, and transferred to a grade school assignment for exercising protected speech.[41] The appellate court concluded that the teacher's speech pertaining to classroom assignment and the content of his evaluations was clearly personal and not constitutionally protected. However, his expression of views regarding inequities in mileage allowances and liability insurance coverage for coaches (and volunteer parents who transported students to athletic events) was of public concern. Applying *Connick,* the defendant school district argued that if any of the employee's speech pertained to personal grievances, then all of the expression was unprotected. Rejecting this interpretation, the appeals court held that if any of the speech was found to be protected, the court "must move to the next stage of the *Connick* test and balance the interest of the school district in the efficient operation of its system with the plaintiff's right to speak on matters of public concern."[42] Finding that the teacher's speech was a substantial factor in the adverse employment decisions and that the school district's interests did not justify the disciplinary action, the district was ordered to reinstate the teacher to his former position and pay him compensatory damages.

The First Circuit Court of Appeals also ruled that a school principal and superintendent were liable for compensatory and punitive damages for actions taken in retaliation for a teacher's exercise of protected speech in criticizing a cutback in the district's high school reading program and in filing several grievances with the teachers' union. The defendants had ordered the teacher's termination (although not authorized to do so), had threatened another firing after the school board reinstated the teacher, and had deprived her of a job to which she was entitled.[43] The jury concluded from the evidence that the principal and superintendent were guilty of "extraordinary misconduct" for retaliating against the teacher for her exercise of constitutionally protected rights.

Dismissals predicated on political expression or union activities are clearly impermissible. A New Jersey federal district court overturned a tenured teacher's dismissal, reasoning that the action was intended to retaliate for the teacher's exercise of protected expression at a political rally, where the teacher criticized the board's decision to transfer another teacher as being politically motivated.[44] The Eighth Circuit Court of Appeals also affirmed a jury's verdict that a teacher had been improperly dismissed because of her labor union activities. The board asserted that the teacher had used improper, indecent language with a student, but the jury concluded that the dismissal was for protected conduct.[45] Espousing similar logic, the Sixth Circuit Court of Appeals rejected the discharge of a probationary teacher for the asserted decline in teaching evaluations and a personality conflict with the principal, finding that the dismissal was closely linked to protected speech and union activities.[46]

In applying the principles articulated by the Supreme Court, the threshold question is whether the speech pertains to a public issue. Considering the content, form, and context of the expression in making this determination, courts in general have concluded that comments related to political advocacy, collective bargaining, and policies governing the welfare of the school and student body are of public interest. However, complaints about individual work assignments or conditions of employment and personal attacks on superiors have not been considered public issues. Until recently, it was generally assumed that even educators' expression involving matters of personal rather than public interest could not be the basis for adverse personnel action unless the expression posed some threat of disrupting the educational process. But some recent cases indicate that sanctions can be imposed for such expression regarding personal concerns in the absence of any disruptive effect.[47] Thus, the threshold determination of whether the speech pertains to public or private issues may become increasingly important.

If determined that expression pertains to public issues, the employee has the burden of demonstrating that the expression was a substantial or motivating factor in the adverse employment decision. The employer can rebut the free speech claim by showing by a preponderance of evidence that the same decision would have been reached in the absence of the protected speech. Even if established that the expression on matters of public concern was the sole basis for adverse action, the public employer may still prevail by showing that its interests in protecting the efficiency of the public agency outweigh the individual's interest in exercising protected speech. Under *Connick,* the employer's burden varies according to the nature of the employee's expression. This balancing process is destined to generate a steady stream of first amendment litigation, with state and individual interests weighed in light of the circumstances of each case.

Prior Restraint and Channel Rules

While reprisals for the exercise of views have been the focus of most of the litigation, courts also have addressed prior restraints on public employees' expression and restrictions on the channels through which views may be aired. The judiciary has been more reluctant to condone such prior restraint on expression than it has to uphold disciplinary action after the expression has occurred.

For example, the Supreme Court recently divided evenly in a case, thus affirming a decision in which the Tenth Circuit Court of Appeals struck down a portion of an Oklahoma law authorizing the termination of teachers for "advocating, soliciting, imposing, encouraging or promoting public or private homosexual activity in a manner that creates a substantial risk that such conduct will come to the attention of school children or school employees."[48] The appellate court held that such restrictions on teachers' expression could not be imposed unless shown to be necessary to prevent disruption of the educational process. Recognizing "that a state has interests in regulating the speech of teachers that differ from its interests in regulating the speech of the general citizenry," the court reasoned that "a state's interests outweigh a teacher's interests only when the expression results in a material or substantial interference or disruption in the normal activities of the school."[49]

In 1982 the Fifth Circuit Court of Appeals also struck down a school board policy requiring prior approval of all political, sectarian, or special interest materials distributed in the schools. The board had invoked the policy to prevent distribution of documents prepared by the teachers' association which were critical of a proposed teacher competency testing program. Literature written by the school board supporting the program had been distributed in the schools. The court reasoned that "school administrators and principals may not permit one side to promote its position while denying the other side the same opportunity."[50] The court noted, however, that the policies were not invalidated simply because they required prior approval; rather, they were unconstitutional because they did not "furnish sufficient guidance" to prohibit school administrators from exercising "unbridled discretion" in curtailing communication within the schools.[51]

More recently, the United States Supreme Court affirmed a decision in which the Fifth Circuit Court of Appeals invalidated school policies that denied teachers the right to discuss employee organizations during nonclass time and preventing teachers from using school mail facilities for communications including any mention of employee organizations.[52]

However, the appeals court distinguished restrictions on speech among the school's employees from the regulation of nonemployees' expression. Concluding that the public school was not a public forum, the court held that representatives of the teachers' organization who were not employees of the school had no right to visit the school to confer with teachers during nonclass time or to use school mail facilities.

In a significant 1983 decision, *Perry Education Association v. Perry Local Educators' Association,* the Supreme Court ruled that a school district is not constitutionally obligated to allow a rival teachers' union access to internal school mailboxes although the exclusive bargaining agent is granted such access. Concluding that a public school's internal mail system is not an open forum for expression, the Court declared that "the state may reserve the forum for its intended purposes, communicative or otherwise, as long as the regulation on speech is reasonable and not an effort to suppress expression merely because public officials oppose the speaker's view."[53] The Court reasoned that alternative channels of communication were available for use by the rival union to conduct its business.

Under certain circumstances, however, a school's mail system might be considered an open forum because it has been designated as such by school officials. Applying the principle articulated by the Supreme Court in *Perry,* the Fifth Circuit Court of Appeals reasoned that although a school was not obligated to open its internal mail system to the general public or to employee organizations, in this case the school had designated its mail system as a forum for communication by employee organizations and thus was bound by constitutional standards governing access to traditional public forums.[54] The court also found the school district's guidelines, requiring prior clearance of material distributed through the mail system, to be unconstitutionally vague.

While controversies often have focused on the use of school facilities and mail systems by teacher organizations, other prior restraints on expression have been challenged. An Indiana case involved a school board's denial of a request for a group of teachers to hold religious meetings in the public school before students arrived in the morning. Rejecting a teacher's challenge to the board's action, the Seventh Circuit Court of Appeals reasoned that employees cannot assert an inherent free speech right to use public school facilities for expressive purposes unrelated to school business.[55] Distinguishing private conversations during noninstructional time from group meetings, the court concluded that the public school is not a public forum for employees to hold meetings on matters of personal concern. The court did note, however, that if the school had created a forum for such employee meetings and barred only religious meetings, there might be a justiciable issue regarding whether such action discriminates against religious speech and if so, whether the establishment clause requires such discrimination.

In addition to controversies over restrictions on employees' rights to distribute literature and hold meetings in public schools, policies limiting teachers' access to the school board also have generated legal disputes. Several courts have struck down policies prohibiting individual teachers from communicating with the school board. In 1976 the Supreme Court held that a nonunion teacher has a free speech right to comment on a bargaining issue at a public school board meeting.[56] More recently, an Oregon federal district court found that a requirement of advance notice to the superintendent of any direct messages to the school board constituted impermissible prior restraint.[57] Similarly, the Seventh Circuit Court of Appeals struck down a policy requiring all communication to the school board to be directed through the superintendent and ordered removed from a teacher's personnel file a reprimand for communicating directly with board members.[58] The Kansas Supreme Court also found a school board guilty of unconstitutional prior restraint on expression by forbidding teachers from speaking at school board meetings or holding press conferences in school buildings.[59]

While prior restraints on teachers' expression rights are vulnerable to legal attack, courts have recognized school districts' discretion to impose reasonable time, place, and manner restrictions on such expression. For example, the Supreme Court of Louisiana recognized that restrictions may be placed on expression as long as they: (1) are not based on the content of speech, (2) serve significant governmental interests, and (3) leave open alternative channels for communication. Accordingly, the court upheld a ban on hand-held signs in the school board office building or any of its rooms.[60] The court reasoned that the regulation served the legitimate governmental interest of ensuring that school board meetings were conducted in an orderly manner. In general, time, place, and manner restrictions will be upheld if justified to prevent a disruption of the educational environment and if other avenues are available for employees to express their views.

ACADEMIC FREEDOM

Historically, the concept of academic freedom was applied to post-secondary education and embodied the principle that faculty members should be free from governmental controls in conducting research and imparting new knowledge to students. The notion of academic freedom came from German universities and applied to internal, not external, activities of faculty members. The concept has undergone substantial change in American universities and has been expanded to encompass conduct away from the classroom as well as freedom in research and teaching.[61]

While public school teachers have asserted a similar right to academic freedom, courts have not concluded that the breadth of academic freedom found in higher education is appropriate for public elementary and secondary schools. Teachers possess judicially recognized academic interests, but courts have refrained from establishing general legal principles in this domain. Rather, controversies have been resolved on a case-by-case basis and have involved the delicate process of balancing the teacher's interest in academic freedom against the school board's interest in assuring an appropriate instructional program and the efficient operation of the school. Since controversies pertaining to curriculum censorship have been addressed in chapter 3, this section concentrates specifically on public educators' academic freedom within the classroom setting. Can a teacher determine the most appropriate materials for classroom use? Does the first amendment protect a teacher's expression of personal ideas and philosophies? Is a teacher free to determine teaching methodologies? What topics or issues can a teacher discuss in a course?

Course Content

In contrast to the discretion enjoyed by university faculty in curriculum matters, public school teachers in elementary and secondary schools do not have a right to determine the content of the instructional program. Legislatures in all states have granted local school boards considerable discretionary authority to establish programs of study and prescribe course content, including the scope and sequence of materials. Several courts have declared that school boards are not legally obligated to accept teachers' curricular recommendations in the absence of a board policy to that effect. For example, in 1975 the Tenth Circuit Court of Appeals recognized the authority of the school board to determine the curriculum and rejected the notion that teachers "have an unlimited liberty as to structure and content of the courses."[62] In a subsequent decision, the same court upheld the school board's authority to reject a proposal from teachers for books to use in the English curriculum, "even though the decision was a political one influenced by the personal views of the [board] members."[63]

In addition, teachers are not permitted to ignore or omit prescribed course content under the guise of academic freedom. For example, the Seventh Circuit Court of Appeals upheld a school board's dismissal of a kindergarten teacher who refused to teach patriotic topics for religious reasons, and the United States Supreme Court declined to review the decision.[64] The Supreme Court of Washington similarly reasoned that "course content is manifestly a matter within the board's discretion," and requiring teachers to cover this content in a conventional manner does not violate academic freedom protections.[65] In this case, two teachers claimed their first amendment rights had been abridged because the school board would not allow them to team-teach a history course. The teachers characterized the dispute as one involving freedom to select teaching methodology; however, the board focused on the significant loss of course content between the traditional teaching mode and the proposed alternative delivery method.

Other courts have rendered similar decisions regarding school board requirements for conformity in content coverage. For example, the Eighth Circuit Court of Appeals upheld the dismissal of a teacher who ignored the warning of her principal to cover prescribed course content in a conventional manner. The teacher had structured her economics course to allow substantial student input in the selection of topics for class discussion, resulting in considerable instructional time devoted to internal school disputes. According to the appellate court, academic freedom does not include the right to disregard a superior's valid instructional directives regarding appropriate course content.[66]

The Supreme Court of Alaska upheld a rule requiring the superintendent's approval of supplementary materials used in the classroom. The court reasoned that the school board, not teachers, is authorized to make decisions regarding the use of instructional materials.[67] In this case, a teacher did not comply with this rule in selecting materials to teach about homosexual rights in a unit of his course on American minorities. The principal advised the teacher on two occasions to comply with the prior approval rule, but the teacher did not, asserting that the rule abridged his first amendment rights. Noting that the issue was not whether the materials selected by the teacher were appropriate, but rather where the authority to make such a determination resides, the court concluded that the school board has the authority to control the curriculum.

Teaching Strategies

While teachers are not empowered to determine the public school curriculum, courts have been receptive to teachers' assertions that they retain some discretion in choosing *strategies* to convey the prescribed content. State laws and school board policies establish the basic contours of the curriculum, but in the past two decades, courts have confirmed that teachers clearly possess some measure of academic freedom in the classroom setting. In reviewing school board restrictions on teachers' classroom behavior, the judiciary considers a number of factors, such as whether teachers have been provided adequate notice that use of specific teaching methodologies or materials will result in disciplinary action, the relevance of the method to the course of study, the threat of disruption posed by the method, and the impact of the strategy on community mores. These factors and related issues are discussed below.

Prior Notice. Courts in general have recognized the substantive right of teachers to select appropriate teaching methods that serve a demonstrated educational purpose. If a particular method is supported by professional educators, the teacher has no reason to anticipate that its use might result in discipline or discharge unless there is a regulation proscribing its use. This procedural right of notice that specific methods are prohibited often is the decisive factor in academic freedom cases.

In an early case acknowledging the teacher's right to exercise academic discretion, one of the central issues was the board's failure to notify the teacher that certain conduct was forbidden. The controversy involved the use of an article from the *Atlantic Monthly* by a senior high school English teacher.[68] Parents complained of its use because of its vulgar terms. Subsequently, the teacher was suspended and sought an injunction to bar dismissal, alleging that his right to academic freedom was impaired. The First Circuit Court of Appeals conceded that some regulation of classroom speech is inherent in public education but found the "rigorous censorship" in this situation to have a chilling effect on the teacher's constitutional rights. The potential due process violation coupled with the academic freedom claim convinced the appeals court that the teacher would likely prevail when the case was heard by the trial court on remand.

In a Massachusetts case, a high school English teacher was dismissed for the illustrative use of a slang term for sexual intercourse in a discussion of taboo words.[69] The federal district court concluded that the use of the word could be the basis for dismissal because it did not have the "support of the preponderant opinion of the teaching profession."[70] However, since no regulation existed prohibiting the teaching method, the teacher's reinstatement was ordered. The court noted that a teacher should not be placed in a position of guessing whether certain conduct will result in dismissal. Subsequently, the district court's decision was affirmed by the First Circuit Court of Appeals.

The failure to provide notice also was an issue in a Texas case.[71] A high school civics teacher was dismissed for discussing controversial issues such as interracial marriages and antiwar protests in his classes. The court upheld the right of the teacher to select valid teaching methods and found that the lack of notice regarding prohibited behavior denied the teacher procedural due process. The school board had not adopted regulations or issued a statement to forewarn the teacher that the method in question was considered inappropriate.

Courts addressing the procedural due process issue have indicated that teachers enjoy some academic prerogatives, but have held that certain classroom behavior may be restricted by the school board if proper notice of proscribed methods is given. Behavior which does not have strong support from the education profession would certainly be more susceptible to restrictions.

Relevance. A primary consideration in reviewing the legitimacy of classroom activities is whether instructional strategies are related to course objectives. If no relationship can be established, the teacher's behavior is not constitutionally protected. Relevancy applies not only to the instructional objectives but also to the age and maturity of the students. A controversial topic that would be appropriate for high school students would not necessarily be appropriate for elementary and junior high students. Even though the relevancy of a certain method may be established, if it lacks the general support of the profession, a school board may still prevail in barring its use.[72]

The Seventh Circuit Court of Appeals found that the distribution by several teachers of a brochure on the pleasures of drug use and sex to an eighth-grade class lacked a legitimate educational purpose.[73] In upholding the board's dismissal of the teachers, the court reasoned that the materials, which were distributed without any explanation or discussion, were unrelated to the courses taught by the teachers and were totally inappropriate for eighth-grade students. Similarly, a Louisiana appeals court found that a teacher's statements regarding the sexual behavior of blacks lacked instructional relevancy.[74] Since the statements served no educational purpose, they were considered outside the scope of protected academic freedom. More recently, relevance was found to be lacking in the decision of a photography teacher to show a pornographic film to high school students.[75]

In contrast, the Fifth Circuit Court of Appeals ruled that a teacher's use of a simulation to teach about post-Civil War American history was related to legitimate educational objectives and therefore could not be the basis for dismissal.[76] Parents had complained that the simulation aroused racial feelings, and the school board subsequently instructed the teacher to eliminate its use in the classroom. Upon refusal to comply with the directive, the teacher was discharged. Ruling that the board's action violated the teacher's academic rights, the appellate court recognized that teachers cannot be forced to eliminate instructionally relevant activities simply because of parental displeasure.

Similarly, the Sixth Circuit Court of Appeals ordered reinstatement of a teacher who had been effectively discharged when citizens complained to the school board regarding the teacher's instruction in a life science course. The teacher was suspended and told that he would be terminated unless he accepted a letter of reprimand which he refused. Noting that the films and text used by the teacher had been approved by the school board and used for several years, the court reasoned that the teacher's classroom behavior was appropriate and relevant to the course objectives. Although the appeals court affirmed awards of compensatory and punitive damages, the Supreme Court reversed the decision regarding the compensatory damages award because faulty instructions had been given to the jury. The case was remanded to determine the amount of damages necessary to compensate the teacher for the injury he suffered.[77]

Threat of Disruption. Among the factors courts examine in assessing restrictions in classroom instruction is whether a teacher's action poses a threat of disruption to the operation of the school. An Alabama federal district court singled out this factor and the appropriateness of instructional strategies for the age of students in reviewing the dismissal of an eleventh-grade English teacher.[78] The teacher was dismissed for the use of a Kurt Vonnegut story because it encouraged "the killing off of elderly people and free sex."[79] The court found the dismissal of the teacher unwarranted since the story was not considered inappropriate for high school students and did not pose "a material and substantial threat of disruption."[80]

In an Oregon case, a school board policy banning all political speakers from the high school was challenged. The federal district court found the order unreasonable for several reasons, one being that no disruptions had occurred from political discussions in the past nor were disruptions expected in the future.[81] More recently, the Fifth Circuit Court of Appeals concluded that numerous complaints from parents and students about a particular teaching method did not constitute a sufficient disruption to destroy the teacher's effectiveness in the classroom.[82] The court noted that the "test is not whether substantial disruption occurs but whether such disruption overbalances the teacher's usefulness as an instructor."[83] Similarly, a Texas federal court reasoned that community objections to a teacher's administration of a survey regarding sex roles did not equate to disruption of the school system.[84]

In contrast, the Supreme Court of Maine held that a school board's decision to cancel a Tolerance Day program was based on a legitimate concern for safety, order, and security at school due to bomb threats that had been received.[85] The court found no impairment of teachers' academic freedom or students' free speech rights in cancelling the program at which a homosexual was scheduled to speak. The court noted that teachers and students were not precluded from discussing tolerance and prejudice against homosexuals in classes.

Community Standards. Courts have been protective of school boards' authority to design the curriculum to reflect community values. In 1980 the Seventh Circuit Court of Appeals recognized that school board members represent the community which "has a legitimate, even a vital and compelling, interest in the choice [of] and adherence to a suitable curriculum for the benefit of our young citizens."[86] Similarly, the Tenth Circuit Court of Appeals acknowledged that community standards can be considered in determining the appropriateness of teaching materials and methods.[87]

However, the judiciary also has recognized that school boards cannot suppress first amendment rights simply to placate angry citizens. In a case discussed previously, the Sixth Circuit Court of Appeals held that parental complaints regarding a teacher's instruction in a life science course did not warrant an impairment of the academic rights of the teacher who was teaching the course in conformance with board directives.[88] In this case, a parent mobilized a community protest against the teacher, and neither the administrators who had approved the course materials nor the school board came to the support of the teacher. Concluding that the teacher's "exercise of 'academic freedom' had followed rather than violated his superior's instructions," the court held that a community uproar does not justify school board action that stigmatizes a teacher and inflicts pain and suffering for impermissible reasons.[89]

In the Oregon case also referenced previously, a civics teacher had invited political speakers representing four viewpoints to address his class.[90] Severe community objection to the invited Communist speaker resulted in the school board's ban on all political speakers. Citizens had exerted pressure for this action through petitions and threats to vote down the school budget and to defeat incumbent board members at the polls. The court noted that first amendment rights of teachers may be restricted in light of the special circumstances of the school environment if the restrictions are reasonable. In this case, however, the suppression of selected viewpoints was not considered reasonable; the only basis for the board's action appeared to be fear of taxpayer reaction.

Because of the school board's legitimate interest in advancing community mores, the judiciary has considered community standards in evaluating challenges to various teaching methods. However, if a particular strategy is instructionally relevant and supported by the profession, it will probably survive judicial review even though it might disturb some school patrons.

FREEDOM OF ASSOCIATION

Although freedom of association is not specifically addressed in the first amendment, the Supreme Court has recognized that associational rights are "implicit in the freedoms of speech, assembly, and petition."[91] Accordingly, public educators cannot be disciplined for forming or joining political, labor, religious, or social organizations. However, limitations may be placed on associational activities that disrupt the operation of the school system or interfere with the professional duties of the teacher. This section encompasses an overview of teachers' association rights with specific attention to political affiliations and activities. Public educators' rights in connection with labor unions are addressed in chapter 11.

Political Affiliations

States have made frequent attempts to prohibit or limit teachers' affiliations with subversive political organizations. These restrictions have been imposed to protect the public educational system from treasonable and seditious acts. In early cases, the Supreme Court held that associational rights could be restricted when a public employee was fully knowledgeable of an organization's subversive purpose.[92] In the mid-1960s, however, this stance was rejected, and the Supreme Court struck down loyalty oaths requiring individuals to deny membership in subversive organizations as unduly vague or imposing sanctions for "guilt by association."[93] Although courts have recognized the state's legitimate interest in protecting the schools from subversion, they have not allowed this interest to infringe on fundamental associational rights. The Supreme Court in *Keyishian v. Board of Regents* firmly established that *mere membership* in an organization such as the Communist Party, without the specific intent to further the unlawful aims of the organization, could not disqualify an individual for public school employment.[94]

Thus, state statutes specifically barring members of subversive or controversial organizations from public employment are clearly unconstitutional.[95] Neither can a school system impose restrictions, directly or indirectly, on teachers' memberships in certain organizations or on their activities in those organizations. As with protected speech, dismissal of a teacher will not be supported if the motivating factor behind the decision is the teacher's exercise of freedom of association. For example, in a Texas case, a nontenured teacher was reinstated because evidence indicated that nonrenewal was based on active membership in the American Civil Liberties Union.[96]

Governmental action does not have to proscribe organizational membership to impair associational rights. Courts are reluctant to sanction any law that *inhibits* the free exercise of constitutional guarantees unless the state can show that the measure is substantially related to a compelling governmental interest. The Supreme Court overturned an Arkansas law that required all teachers each year to submit a list of every organization to which they had belonged or regularly contributed to for five years.[97] The Court found that this law went well beyond the state's interest in determining the fitness and competence of teachers and constituted "comprehensive interference with associational freedom."[98] Similarly, teachers relied on first amendment associational rights to challenge a Texas statute that allowed county judges to compel disclosure of membership lists by certain organizations engaged in activities designed to disrupt public schools.[99] As in the Arkansas case, this law also was found to sweep too broadly; the required disclosure exposed to public recrimination those members who did not participate in disruptive activities.

The fact that associational rights are ensured by the first amendment, however, does not preclude school administrators from legitimately questioning a teacher about activities that may adversely affect classroom teaching. In *Beilan v. Board of Public Education of Philadelphia,* the Supreme Court held that questions regarding a teacher's activities in the Communist Party were relevant to an assessment of his classroom teaching, and that refusal to answer the superintendent's inquiries could result in dismissal.[100] Although organizational membership *per se* is protected, if the impact of associational activities on classroom performance is questioned, a teacher must respond to queries related to fitness to teach.

Membership in controversial political organizations has not been the only source of litigation; partisan political affiliations have been at issue in some cases. Historically, public employment was characterized by the patronage system; that is, with a change in the controlling political party, non-civil service employees belonging to the defeated party lost their jobs. In 1976 the Supreme Court examined the constitutionality of a patronage system under which Republican employees of an Illinois sheriff's office would be replaced by Democrats, the new controlling party, unless they pledged support for the Democratic Party, campaigned for Democratic candidates, or contributed financial support to the party.[101] The Supreme Court viewed this practice as a severe restriction on political association and belief. The justifications advanced for the patronage system were that it promoted effectiveness and efficiency in government and ensured representative government. The Court rejected both arguments noting that, if anything, the threat of replacement was detrimental to governmental effectiveness and efficiency. Furthermore, nonpolicy-making, nonconfidential individuals were not found to be in a position to undermine policies of the new administration. The Court concluded that the democratic process would be preserved by limiting patronage dismissals to policy-making positions. In 1980 the Supreme Court reiterated that the employment of nonpolicy-making public employees cannot be conditioned on affiliation with a political party.[102]

Unlike non-civil service public employees, teachers are substantially insulated from partisan politics because of extensive state statutory provisions safeguarding their employment rights. When school board employment actions have been based solely on partisan affiliation, however, the principle of freedom of political association enunciated by the Supreme Court has been applied. In such cases, the burden has been placed on the school employee to substantiate that protected political affiliation was the motivating factor in the board's employment decision.[103] If an employee has met this burden, then the board must demonstrate by a preponderance of evidence that it would have reached the same decision in the absence of the political association.

POLITICAL ACTIVITY

Teachers, like all citizens, are guaranteed the right to participate in the political process. However, active participation often has prompted school officials to place limitations on the exercise of this right. Many questions arise: Can teachers run for partisan political offices? What types of political activities are permitted in the school setting? Can certain political activities outside the school be restricted? These questions and others are addressed in this section.

Campaigning for Issues and Candidates. First amendment association as well as free speech rights have been invoked to protect teachers in expressing opinions on political issues and campaigning for candidates. While such political activity is constitutionally protected, restrictions can be placed on the teacher's activities in the school setting. Proscribed activities would include making campaign speeches in the classroom. Teachers cannot take advantage of their position of authority with a captive audience to impose their political views on students.[104] However, if campaign issues are related to the class topic, a teacher can objectively present election issues and candidates in a nonpartisan manner.

In general, political activity in the schools that would cause divisiveness in the faculty also can be restricted. But school officials must not impose unnecessary constraints; there must be a threat that the activity will interfere with the operation of the school. In a California case, a school board refused to allow teachers to circulate a petition in the school lounge regarding the financing of the schools, asserting that the issue would create dissension in the faculty. The California Supreme Court rejected the board's claim, noting that "in order to justify a restraint on the political activities of its teachers, [school] officials must demonstrate that the restraint is a practical necessity in order to meet a 'compelling public need to protect efficiency and integrity of the public service.' "[105]

Although limitations may be placed on specific political activities of teachers in the schools, courts have tended to reject restrictions affecting such activity outside the school. Public employees are constitutionally protected from retaliation for their participation in political affairs at the local, state, and federal levels.[106] For example, in a recent case the New Jersey Federal District Court prevented dismissal of a tenured teacher based on clear evidence that the charges were brought only for the purpose of harassment and retaliation for the teacher's statements at a political rally and his activities supporting a political faction that was opposed by the current school board majority.[107] The Fifth Circuit Court of Appeals also held that political activities constituted the motivating factor in dismissing a deputy tax assessor-collector appointed by a school district. The employee was dismissed immediately following the school board election in which the party she supported was defeated.[108] Other courts also have overturned dismissals, transfers, or demotions predicated on the support or nonsupport of particular candidates in school board elections where protected political activity was a motivating or substantial factor in the adverse employment action.[109]

Holding Public Office. In general, a teacher has the right to run for and hold public office, but restrictions may be imposed to promote efficiency in the provision of public services. For example, courts have recognized that certain offices are incompatible with public school employment, especially if they involve an employer-employee relationship. Common law has established that an incompatibility exists when a teacher seeks a position on the school board in the employing district. A New Jersey appellate court found such board membership to be "patently incompatible" with employment as a teacher.[110] The Supreme Court of Wyoming similarly concluded that if the teacher is both employer and employee, it is "inimical to the public interest."[111] Moreover, the Wyoming court noted that this infirmity cannot be remedied by the teacher's abstention from voting on certain financial and personnel issues. According to the court, for the teacher "to hold office as trustee while acting as teacher would deprive the citizens of the school district of independent judgment of a full and impartial board of trustees elected to represent the entire public interest."[112] These decisions, of course, would not prevent a teacher from serving on the school board of another school district.[113]

The Supreme Court of Virginia held that a city council member who also was employed as a principal was disqualified from voting on appointments to the school board because of the personal interest involved.[114] The court noted that the state statutory prohibition on conflicts of interests does not require proof that the individual's decisions on specific issues are affected by personal considerations; individuals are disqualified from voting on matters where there is a *danger* that judgments may be compromised for personal reasons.

Although many school districts allow employees considerable political freedom in partisan politics, it appears that districts can prohibit or place restrictions on teachers running for a political position if justified by an overriding public interest. The Supreme Court has not rendered a decision pertaining to teachers, but the Court has upheld a federal law (the Hatch Act) that prevents federal employees from holding formal positions in political parties, playing substantial roles in partisan campaigns, and running for partisan office.[115] In upholding the act, the Court recognized that there are legitimate reasons for curtailing political activities of public employees, such as the need to ensure impartial government, promote effective and fair government, remove employees from political pressure, and prevent employee selection based on political factors. In a companion case, the Court upheld an Oklahoma law forbidding classified civil servants from running for paid political offices.[116]

In 1977 the Georgia Supreme Court reasoned that a state law, prohibiting legislators from being employed by a state agency, was necessary to ensure the provision of efficient governmental services.[117] A professor at a state college challenged this law after she was elected to the legislature and was denied a leave of absence from her teaching position. The court concluded that the law was reasonably constructed to avoid a conflict of interests where an individual is employed by two branches of state government. Accordingly, the court held that it would be necessary for the professor to give up her position in the state college to serve in the legislature.

More recently, the Rhode Island Supreme Court upheld a state law restricting municipal employees from holding elective public office in the city or town where they are employed. Ruling that a city employee could not hold an elected office as a school committee member, the court reasoned that the "government has a strong interest in protecting its employees from entanglements caused by dual positions or even the appearance of such entanglements."[118] But the court struck down the portion of the city charter prohibiting all elected officers from holding any other local, state, or federal partisan or nonpartisan office. The court found this restriction unconstitutionally overbroad because it foreclosed access to numerous offices that posed no threat to the promotion of governmental efficiency and integrity. Similarly, an Oregon court overturned a state law prohibiting all public employees from running for political office.[119] The court acknowledged that it might be necessary to restrict the political campaigning of some employees but found this law to be overly broad.

Individual states may impose restrictions on certain types of political activities of teachers, such as requiring a leave of absence or resignation before running for a public office, if campaigning would interfere with teaching responsibilities. However, some restrictions on political activity have been judicially struck down where there has been insufficient justification for the policies. For example, a Kentucky appellate court overturned a school board regulation requiring all employees who were political candidates to take a one-month leave of absence prior to the election.[120] This policy was found to violate teachers' free association and speech rights since there was no showing that the political activities would hinder performance of their duties. The court further noted that an individual determination should be made to assess whether certain types of political participation would have an adverse effect on teaching duties.

The United States Supreme Court affirmed a lower court's decision striking down a Georgia school board's policy requiring any school employee who became a candidate for public office to take a leave of absence without pay for the duration of the candidacy. Finding this policy to be a violation of the federal Voting Rights Act, the Court reasoned that it imposed a substantial economic disincentive on seeking elective public office and had the potential for discrimination since it was adopted after a black employee announced his candidacy for the state legislature.[121] However, the school board's revised policy was subsequently upheld by the federal district court, and the Supreme Court affirmed this decision without an opinion.[122] The revised policy denied leaves of absence for political purposes and required employees holding elective office to abide by the same leave policies applicable to all employees. The federal district court reasoned that the revised policy was a legitimate reaffirmation of the board's authority to require employees to fulfill their contracts and did not impair federally protected rights.

Although school boards must respect associational rights of their staff members, they also have an obligation to ensure that the political activities of public school personnel do not have an adverse impact on the school. If educators neglect instructional duties to campaign for issues or candidates, use the classroom as a political forum, or disrupt the operation of the school because of their political activities, disciplinary actions would be warranted. But school boards must be certain that constraints imposed on employees' freedom of association are not predicated on mere disagreement with the political orientation of the activities. Personnel actions must be justified as necessary to protect the interests of the students and the school.

PERSONAL APPEARANCE

Historically, school boards often imposed rigid grooming restrictions on teachers.[123] In the 1970s, such attempts to regulate the appearance of teachers generated extensive litigation, as did grooming regulations applied to students. Although the intense controversy has subsided, the issue continues to plague school officials who enact regulations governing appearance. The various efforts to control teacher appearance have been predicated on the necessity of setting an appropriate tone in the classroom and enforcing similar appearance and dress codes for students. Teachers have challenged these requirements as abridgements of their constitutionally protected rights of privacy, liberty, and free expression.

Most courts have recognized that personal appearance involves a constitutional interest, but there has not been judicial consensus regarding whether hair and dress restrictions imposed on school employees violate this freedom. A few courts have declared that the right to govern one's own appearance is a fundamental constitutional right requiring close judicial review of governmental action that might impair its exercise. A Mississippi federal district court held that prescribing the personal appearance of adults as a condition of employment must be viewed with "close judicial scrutiny."[124] The court found no legitimate state interest to justify applying a school board's student grooming policy to teachers in the absence of evidence that a certain manner of grooming would disrupt the educational process. A California appeals court also found that beards could not be constitutionally banned without evidence that they would have an adverse effect on the learning environment,[125] and a Florida federal district court ordered reinstatement of a teacher whose contract was not renewed because he failed to comply with the principal's request to remove his goatee.[126]

In contrast to the above cases, the majority of courts have supported school officials' authority to impose grooming and dress restrictions on teachers. A 1974 decision rendered by the Seventh Circuit Court of Appeals is illustrative of the judicial view. The court recognized that appearance is a liberty interest but emphasized that all restrictions on the interest are not unconstitutional. A rule prohibiting teachers from wearing beards and sideburns was found to be, at best, a "relatively minor deprivation of protected rights."[127]

The United States Supreme Court provided significant clarification of public employers' authority regarding regulation of employee appearance in a 1976 decision upholding a hair grooming regulation for police officers. The Court acknowledged that personal appearance does involve a constitutional right but "implicates only the more general contours of the substantive liberty interest protected by the Fourteenth Amendment."[128] According to the Court, the protected interest would be impaired only if a regulation were "so irrational that it [could] be branded 'arbitrary.' "[129] The Court did not place the burden on the public employer to justify a grooming restriction, but rather the burden of proof was placed on the individual to demonstrate that there is no rational connection between the regulation and the accomplishment of a legitimate public purpose.

The rationale advanced by the Supreme Court in upholding the grooming regulation for police officers has been followed by other courts assessing dress and appearance restrictions for teachers. For example, the Second Circuit Court of Appeals held that a Connecticut school board was justified in imposing a dress regulation requiring all male teachers to wear a tie.[130] The court did not find the dress code arbitrary but accepted it as a rational means of promoting respect for authority, traditional values, and classroom discipline. Because of the uniquely influential role of teachers, the court noted that they may be subjected to restrictions in their professional lives which otherwise would not be acceptable.[131] The Fifth Circuit Court of Appeals also found a Louisiana school board's prohibition against beards to be rationally related to the board's "undeniable interest in teaching hygiene, instilling discipline, asserting authority, and compelling uniformity."[132] Applying similar reasoning, the First Circuit Appellate Court upheld a school board's dismissal of a teacher for wearing short skirts.[133]

The judicial trend is toward upholding the school board's authority to regulate employee appearance, but restrictions will not be supported if they are arbitrary or void of a legitimate school concern.[134] To illustrate, the Seventh Circuit Court of Appeals found that a regulation prohibiting school bus drivers from wearing mustaches lacked a valid school purpose, and accordingly, overturned the school board's suspension of a driver for violating the rule.[135] The only justification the school board offered for the policy was conservative community attitudes. There was no indication in this case that the bus driver's mustache affected his ability to perform his job. The court noted that the arbitrariness and irrationality of this policy were exemplified by the fact that the bus driver was also a full-time teacher but was not suspended from his teaching position.

Although courts generally acknowledge that the right to govern personal appearance is a protected interest, it has not been declared a fundamental right requiring heightened judicial scrutiny of regulations that might impair its exercise. School officials can thus restrict appearance as long as there is a rational basis for the regulation. Arbitrary rules, however, are vulnerable to challenge as a violation of personal liberty.

PRIVACY RIGHTS

Public employees have asserted the right to be free from unwarranted governmental intrusions in their personal affairs. Protections of personal privacy flow from both constitutional and statutory provisions.[136] Litigation covered in this section focuses on constitutional privacy claims initiated under the fourth amendment (protection against unreasonable searches and seizures), the ninth amendment (personal privacy as an unenumerated right reserved to the people), and the fourteenth amendment (protection against state action impairing personal liberties without due process of law).

Although the Federal Constitution does not explicitly address personal privacy rights, the Supreme Court has recognized that certain *implied* fundamental rights warrant constitutional protection because of their close relationship to explicit constitutional guarantees. Protected privacy rights have been interpreted as encompassing personal choices in matters such as marriage, contraception, abortion, procreation, family relations, and child rearing.[137]

Interpreting teachers' privacy rights, the Fifth Circuit Court of Appeals held that a teacher has a constitutionally protected interest in breast-feeding her child at school during noninstructional time. The court reasoned that such conduct is sufficiently close to fundamental rights regarding family relationships to trigger constitutional privacy protection. However, the court recognized that, if necessary, fundamental liberties can be restricted to further compelling state interests. Thus, the case was remanded for a trial to ascertain if the school board's interests in avoiding disruption of the educational process, ensuring that teachers perform their duties without distraction, and avoiding liability for potential injuries were strong enough to justify the restriction imposed on the teacher's privacy interests.[138]

More recently, the Second Circuit Court of Appeals upheld a teacher's privacy claim in her refusal to submit to a physical examination by the school district's male physician. Finding it unnecessary to determine whether there is a fundamental constitutional right to be examined by a physician of the same sex, the court reasoned that the school board's action was so unreasonable that it was unconstitutionally arbitrary. Since the teacher offered to go at her own expense to any female physician selected by the board, rather than to be examined by the school district's male physician, the court found an impairment of substantive due process rights.[139] However, the teacher was subsequently dismissed on other grounds and denied pay for the period of suspension for refusing to submit to the examination because she had not appealed the Commissioner of Education's adverse decision in state legal proceedings involving the same injury. Thus, a federal civil rights action for back pay was barred.

Public school teachers also have asserted personal privacy rights in connection with the decision to send their own children to private schools. Such decisions have been controversial in school districts involved in desegregation; some school boards have tried to restrict teachers' prerogatives to send their children to private, segregated academies. In 1975 the Fifth Circuit Court of Appeals found no impairment of rights protected by the first or fourteenth amendments in connection with a school board's decision not to rehire nontenured teachers who elected to send their own children to racially segregated private schools after the public school district was judicially ordered to desegregate.[140] A decade later, however, the same court invalidated a dismissal as impairing protected privacy rights because the employee's enrollment of her son in a private academy played a substantial part in the decision.[141] The Eleventh Circuit Court of Appeals also struck down a school board's requirement that employees' children must attend public schools in the counties of their residence to promote public education and desegregation.[142] The court found that the requirement violated fundamental rights of parents to decide where their children were to be educated. Despite the policy's well-meaning goals, the court held that its interference with the individual's decision-making prerogatives was excessive.

Although courts have exhibited sensitivity toward educators' claims involving matters of personal privacy, the judiciary also has recognized that the school board's interest in maintaining an appropriate educational environment provides justification for some constraints on teachers' personal freedoms. School officials have defended such restrictions on the grounds that teachers serve as role models for students and therefore should conform to community norms. While regulations are far less restrictive today than they were in the early 1900s, when some school districts prohibited female teachers from marrying or even dating, school boards still attempt to proscribe aspects of teachers' personal lives that are inimical to community values. The remainder of this section focuses on litigation in which courts have assessed the competing interests of employees and employers in connection with search and seizure and lifestyle choices.

Search and Seizure

Public educators, like all citizens, are shielded against unreasonable governmental invasions of their personal property by the fourth amendment. This amendment requires police officers and other agents of the state to secure a search warrant (based on probable cause that a crime has been committed and that the person or place is likely to yield evidence of the crime) before conducting a search of an individual's person, house, papers, or effects. As discussed in chapter 6, most search and seizure controversies in the public school setting have focused on whether warrantless searches of students are justified to maintain a proper educational environment. The Supreme Court has ruled that although school authorities are considered agents of the state, subject to the fourth amendment, they can conduct personal searches of students without a warrant as long as they have reasonable suspicion that contraband disruptive to the educational process is secreted.[143]

The Supreme Court has not addressed teachers' rights in connection with searches initiated by school authorities, but a few lower courts have rendered decisions involving fourth amendment claims of teachers and other public employees. For example, the Third Circuit Court of Appeals held that a search by a school board member of a public school guidance counselor's desk violated the fourth amendment.[144] The search was conducted to find evidence that the counselor had submitted to the local newspaper a cartoon ridiculing the financial and personnel policies of the school board. The court reasoned that teachers and counselors have a legitimate expectation of privacy in the contents of their school desks, which have been assigned to them for personal use. The court rejected the assertion that the counselor could not rely on the fourth amendment because the desk belonged to the school system. The court declared that an employer can conduct searches only in accordance with a regulation or practice dispelling in advance any expectation of privacy. No such policy had been established in this case.

Applying similar reasoning in a nonschool case, the Ninth Circuit Court of Appeals held that a search of an employee's office conducted by state hospital staff members impaired fourth amendment rights.[145] Concluding that the employee had a reasonable expectation of privacy in the contents of his office, the appeals court noted that private offices at the hospital were not routinely inspected and that the search in question was undertaken to find evidence to substantiate charges against the employee.

The judiciary, however, has recognized that in assessing the reasonableness of a job-related search or seizure by a supervisor, the role of the supervisor in overseeing performance must be considered.[146] In some instances, educational interests can override the individual employee's privacy interest. In a recent case, the First Circuit Court of Appeals rejected a teacher's fourth amendment claim, reasoning that the teacher had no expectation of privacy in withtholding from the school administration a term paper she had written about a handicapped child in her class. Although the paper was written for a college course, the court reasoned that the teacher extinguished any expectation of privacy in connection with the paper when she shared it with the professor of the course and offered to share it with the school official in charge of the committee convened to design an educational program for the child in question. Concluding that the school principal had a legitimate interest in the contents of the paper as it pertained to a student under his charge, the court held that disciplinary action resulting from the teacher's initial refusal to turn the paper over to her principal did not violate fourth amendment rights.[147] While public school teachers are constitutionally protected against arbitrary invasions of their personal effects by school officials, in some situations, such as this one, courts have reasoned that educational interests can justify interference with the individual's expectation of privacy.

Public school employees' fourth amendment rights also have been asserted in connection with drug screening programs. School boards can require employees to have physical examinations as a condition of employment, but mandatory screening for drugs has been challenged as impairing protected privacy rights. Teachers in a New York school district secured a restraining order prohibiting the school board from forcing probationary teachers to submit urine samples for purposes of determining whether they were using controlled substances. The school district defended its policy as part of an effort to reduce substance abuse, but the state appeals court affirmed the trial court's conclusion that the "compulsory extraction of bodily fluids is a search and seizure within the meaning of the fourth amendment."[148] Noting that the school board would *not* have to secure a search warrant (based on probable cause that a crime had been committed) in order to search employees, the appeals court concluded that the drug testing program did not satisfy the more lenient standard that requires reasonable suspicion of conduct detrimental to the school environment. Since there was no individualized suspicion of wrongdoing, the drug testing program was found to violate the teachers' privacy rights. The District of Columbia Federal District Court also ruled that a school board impaired a bus attendant's fourth amendment rights by forcing her to submit to urinalysis without individualized suspicion of substance abuse.[149] While school boards have a significant interest in ensuring that school employees are not drug users and protecting the safety of students, blanket drug testing programs are not likely to survive legal challenges.

Lifestyle Choices

In recent years, teachers have frequently challenged school officials' authority to restrict personal lifestyle choices. Although the right to such personal freedom is not an enumerated constitutional guarantee, it is a right implied in the concept of personal liberty embodied in the fourteenth amendment. Constitutional protection afforded to teachers' privacy rights is determined not only by the *location* of the conduct, but also by the *nature* of the activity.[150] The judiciary has attempted to balance the teacher's privacy interests against the school board's legitimate interests in safeguarding the welfare of students and the management of the school. Litigation to date indicates that sanctions cannot be imposed solely because school officials disapprove of the personal and private conduct of the teacher. Concomitantly, the recognition of teachers' privacy rights does not prevent school officials from restricting unconventional behavior that is detrimental to teaching effectiveness or harmful to students.

The precise contours of public educators' privacy rights that command constitutional protection have not been clearly delineated, and constitutional claims involving pregnancies out of wedlock, unconventional living arrangements, homosexuality, and other alleged sexual improprieties have usually been decided on a case-by-case basis according to the particular circumstances involved. Since many of these cases also are discussed in chapter 10 in connection with dismissals based on charges of immorality, the following discussion is confined to an overview of the constitutional issues involved.

Because the judiciary has recognized that decisions pertaining to marriage and parenthood are within the realm of constitutionally protected privacy, courts have been reluctant to support dismissal actions based on a teacher's unwed, pregnant status in the absence of evidence that the teacher's condition impairs fitness to teach. In a Mississippi case, the Fifth Circuit Court of Appeals invalidated a school district's rule prohibiting the employment of unwed parents to promote a "properly moral scholastic environment."[151] Finding the policy unconstitutional, the court rejected the school district's contention that unwed parenthood was proof of immorality. According to the court, the policy equating birth of an illegitimate child with immoral conduct precluded an individual determination of each applicant's qualifications, thereby violating equal protection and due process guarantees. More recently, the same court reiterated that the discharge of a teacher because of pregnancy out of wedlock is unconstitutional.[152] Pregnant, unmarried teachers also have relied on constitutionally protected privacy rights in challenging school boards' attempts to force them to take a leave of absence during the pregnancy.[153]

Most courts have similarly reasoned that public employees, including educators, have a protected privacy right to engage in consenting sexual relationships out of wedlock, and that such relationships cannot be the basis for dismissal unless teaching effectiveness is impaired. For example, the Supreme Court of Iowa held that a teacher's isolated adulterous relationship was insufficient to justify revocation of his teaching certificate, since it was not substantiated that the teacher's private conduct had a harmful impact on his teaching.[154] Likewise, a Florida court overturned a school board's termination of a teacher for lacking good moral character based on her relationship with a member of the opposite sex.[155] The Sixth Circuit Court of Appeals also found that the dismissal of a married police officer for cohabitating with a married woman who was not his wife impaired fundamental privacy and associational rights.[156]

In 1986 the Supreme Court declined to review a case in which the Sixth Circuit Court of Appeals ruled that a school board's nonrenewal of a nontenured teacher because of her involvement in a divorce abridged the teacher's privacy rights. Relying on Supreme Court precedent clearly establishing that matters relating to marriage and marital status are constitutionally protected against unwarranted governmental interference, the court emphasized that school officials could not, "without sufficient justification, deny public employment because of involvement in constitutionally protected activity." [157] The court further held that the superintendent was personally liable for refusing to recommend the teacher's reemployment based on impermissible reasons.

Some courts, however, have upheld dismissals or other disciplinary actions based on public employees' lifestyle choices, finding no impairment of protected privacy rights. The Supreme Court declined to review two nonschool decisions in which appellate courts upheld dismissals of public employees for engaging in adulterous relationships that allegedly impaired job performance. In one case, the Third Circuit Court of Appeals upheld the firing of two public librarians for living in "open adultery.' Although the pair had been living together for some time, their employment was terminated after it became public knowledge that they were expecting a child.[158] In the second case, the Fifth Circuit Court of Appeals upheld disciplinary action against two members of a police department for their off-duty cohabitation which allegedly violated departmental regulations proscribing conduct that, if brought to the attention of the public, could result in justified, unfavorable criticism of the department.[159] The Eighth Circuit Court of Appeals also upheld the dismissal of an unmarried female teacher who was living with a male friend in a mobile home close to the school, reasoning that the arrangement offended community norms and had an adverse effect on students. The court rejected the teacher's claim that the dismissal violated her association and privacy rights.[160]

The homosexual teacher's right to privacy has become increasingly controversial, and the scope of constitutional protections afforded to teachers who select a homosexual lifestyle has not yet been clarified by the courts. Among factors considered by courts are the nature of the homosexual conduct (public or private), the notoriety surrounding the conduct, and its impact on teaching effectiveness.

In 1984 the Tenth Circuit Court of Appeals upheld an Oklahoma statutory provision permitting a teacher to be discharged for engaging in public homosexual activity, finding that this provision was neither vague nor a violation of equal protection rights.[161] However, as discussed previously, the Court struck down the portion of the law authorizing the dismissal or nonrenewal of teachers for *advocating* public or private homosexual activity. The court found that this section of the law was overbroad in restricting teachers' free speech rights and declared that the first amendment protects advocacy of legal as well as illegal conduct as long as such advocacy does not incite imminent, lawless action. Since the United States Supreme Court divided evenly in this case, the appellate ruling was affirmed, but it does not establish a precedent that is binding on courts outside the jurisdiction of the tenth federal circuit.

A Georgia law attaching criminal penalties to public *or private* consensual sodomy resulted in a widely publicized Supreme Court decision in 1986. An individual challenged the law's constitutionality after he was charged with violating the statute by committing sodomy with another adult male in the bedroom of his home. The Court by a narrow margin upheld the law, reasoning that legislation reflecting the citizenry's view that sodomy is immoral and unacceptable has a rational basis.[162] Declaring that homosexuals do not have a fundamental constitutional right to engage in sodomy, the Court majority focused its opinion on the homosexual nature of the conduct at issue. However, the prohibition in the Georgia law is not limited to homosexual activity, and there is some sentiment that the Court's decision may have implications for the scope of constitutional privacy rights in connection with private heterosexual activity as well. A number of other states currently have laws similar to the contested Georgia statute, although criminal sanctions for private sodomy have not generally been enforced.

While educators can be dismissed for convictions under state antisodomy laws, dismissals based solely on an individual's homosexual orientation, in the absence of criminal charges, have generated a range of judicial interpretations. According to the Supreme Court of California, mere disapproval of private conduct does not constitute adequate grounds for dismissal of a teacher. In several decisions, the California high court has suggested that evidence of impaired teaching effectiveness must accompany a teacher's discharge for private homosexuality.[163] Other courts, however, have not universally adopted this reasoning.

The Ninth Circuit Court of Appeals affirmed a trial court's conclusion that a teacher who was unconstitutionally dismissed for being a homosexual was entitled only to damages and attorneys' fees, but not to reinstatement.[164] Although finding the dismissal for immorality to be unconstitutionally vague, the court reasoned that the nature of the constitutional right to be vindicated can be considered in determining whether reinstatement is required. Concluding that unconstitutional dismissals predicated on the exercise of protected speech or racial considerations would necessitate reinstatement, the appellate court majority held that choice of a nonconventional lifestyle does not trigger such a remedy. A dissenting justice, however, argued that reinstatement is the appropriate remedy for an individual who has been unconstitutionally dismissed, regardless of the personal right impaired, and he asserted that any disruption that might result from such reinstatement should not be a consideration.[165]

Some courts have upheld dismissals based on mere knowledge of a teacher's homosexuality, reasoning that such knowledge is sufficient to establish an impairment of teaching effectiveness which overrides any protected privacy interest. For example, the Washington Supreme Court upheld a teacher's dismissal after he admitted to a school administrator that he was a homosexual, and the United States Supreme Court declined to review the case.[166] In a case referenced previously, the Supreme Court also declined to review a decision in which the Sixth Circuit Court of Appeals upheld the nonrenewal of a guidance counselor who communicated to other school personnel about her bisexuality.[167] Since the Supreme Court has not recognized a constitutional privacy right to engage in homosexual conduct, a range of interpretations among lower courts regarding homosexual teachers' rights seems likely to persist.

REMEDIES FOR VIOLATIONS OF SUBSTANTIVE CONSTITUTIONAL RIGHTS

When established that school officials or school districts have violated employees' constitutional rights, several remedies are available to the aggrieved individuals. In some situations, the employee may seek a court injunction that orders the unconstitutional action to cease. For example, this remedy might be sought if a school board has unconstitutionally imposed prior restraints on teachers' expression. As discussed in chapter 10, where terminations, transfers, or other adverse employment consequences have been unconstitutionally imposed, courts will order school districts to return the affected employees to their original status with back pay.

In addition to the above remedies, educators are increasingly bringing suits to recover damages for actions that violate their constitutional rights. These suits are usually based on Section 1983 of the Civil Rights

Act of 1871—a federal law rarely invoked until the 1960s. Section 1983 provides that any person who acts under color of state law to deprive another individual of rights secured by the Federal Constitution or laws is subject to personal liability.[168] This law, which was originally enacted to prevent discrimination against black citizens, has been broadly interpreted as conferring liability upon school officials and school districts, not only for racial discrimination, but also for actions that may result in the impairment of other federally protected rights.[169] Exhaustion of state administrative remedies is not required before initiating a federal suit under Section 1983.[170] However, where a federal law authorizes an exclusive non-damages remedy, a Section 1983 suit is precluded.[171] The remainder of this section focuses on the liability of school officials and school districts under Section 1983 and the types of damages available to aggrieved employees. Awards of attorneys' fees in connection with civil rights violations are discussed in chapter 10.

Liability of School Officials

Under Section 1983, school officials can be held personally liable for actions that impair a student's or teacher's federal rights. However, the Supreme Court has recognized that individual governmental officials cannot be held liable under Section 1983 for the actions of their subordinates, thus rejecting the doctrine of *respondeat superior,* even where school officials have general supervisory authority over the employment-related activities of the wrongdoers. In order to be held liable, the officials must have personally participated in, or had personal knowledge of, the unlawful conduct.[172]

In some circumstances, school officials may be protected by qualified immunity. The burden of establishing immunity clearly resides with the official claiming the protection; the plaintiff does not have to prove that immunity is not applicable.[173] The Supreme Court has recognized that individual school officials do not enjoy absolute immunity, but they can claim qualified immunity to shield themselves from liability when they have acted in good faith. In a 1975 student discipline case, *Wood v. Strickland,* the Court addressed good faith immunity and the conditions that must be satisfied.

> A school board member is not immune from liability for damages under Section 1983 if he knew or reasonably should have known that the action he took within his sphere of official responsibility would violate the constitutional rights of the student affected, or if he took the action with the malicious intention to cause a deprivation of constitutional rights or other injury to the student.[174]

For the next several years, federal courts interpreted *Wood* as creating a two-part test, involving both objective and subjective components.

The objective test involves an assessment of whether the defendants acted with disregard for clearly established law; this question is a matter of law which is decided by a judge. The subjective test involves an assessment of whether the defendants acted with malicious intention to impair federally protected rights; this question involves factual issues which must be addressed by a jury.

However, in a significant 1982 decision, *Harlow v. Fitzgerald,* the Supreme Court eliminated the subjective good-faith requirement from the qualified immunity standard. The court reasoned that the subjective standard requiring a factual judgment virtually foreclosed determining immunity status without a trial. Under the *Harlow* standard, "government officials performing discretionary functions generally are shielded from liability for civil damages insofar as their conduct does not violate clearly established statutory or constitutional rights of which a reasonable person would have known."[175] Public officials are not expected to predict the future course of constitutional law, but they are expected to adhere to principles of law that were well established at the time of the violation.[176]

For example, school officials were not entitled to qualified immunity where they reasonably should have known that retaliating against a teacher for using her union's grievance procedure violated constitutional rights.[177] Similarly, a superintendent was not protected by qualified immunity in his official capacity for refusing to recommend a teacher's reemployment based on constitutionally impermissible reasons pertaining to her involvement in a divorce.[178] Where a school official claims qualified immunity, this objective test is to be applied by a judge prior to the trial.

Liability of School Districts

Although school board members and administrators can be held personally liable for their actions under Section 1983, prior to the latter 1970s, school boards and school districts as entities were generally not viewed as "persons" subject to suit under the act.[179] However, in 1978 the Supreme Court departed from precedent and ruled that local governments are "persons" under Section 1983.[180] In essence, school districts can now be assessed damages when action taken pursuant to official policy violates federally protected rights. The Court reiterated that the governmental unit (like the individual official) cannot be held liable for the wrongful acts committed solely by its employees. Liability against the agency can be imposed only when execution of official policy causes infringement of a federally protected right.

In a subsequent decision, the Supreme Court ruled that governmental subdivisions, which include school districts, cannot claim qualified immunity based on the good faith actions of their officials. The Court acknowledged that under certain circumstances sovereign immunity can shield municipal corporations from state tort suits.[181] However, the Court concluded that governmental immunity had been abrogated in situations involving the impairment of federally protected rights by the enactment of Section 1983, which "abolished whatever vestige of the State's sovereign immunity the municipality possessed" in this regard.[182] Consequently, while individual school officials can plead good faith immunity, the school district cannot.

To avoid liability for the abridgment of constitutional rights, school districts have introduced claims of eleventh amendment immunity. The eleventh amendment, prohibiting citizens of one state from bringing suit against another state without its consent, has been interpreted as also precluding federal lawsuits against a state by its own citizens.[183] A state can waive this immunity by specifically consenting to be sued, and Congress can abrogate state immunity through legislation enacted to enforce the fourteenth amendment. However, such congressional intent must be explicit in the federal legislation. In 1985 the Supreme Court held that Congress did not intend to abrogate the state's eleventh amendment immunity in connection with claims brought under the Rehabilitation Act of 1973 because the act does not specify such an intent.[184]

School districts have asserted eleventh amendment protection based on the fact that they perform a state function. Admittedly, education is a state function, but it does not necessarily follow that school districts gain eleventh amendment immunity against claims of constitutional abridgments. For the eleventh amendment to be invoked in a suit against a school district, the state must be the "real party in interest." The Third Circuit Court of Appeals identified the following factors in determining if a governmental agency, such as a school district, is entitled to eleventh amendment protection: (1) whether payment of the judgment will be from the state treasury; (2) whether a governmental or proprietary function is being performed; (3) whether the agency has autonomy over its operation; (4) whether it has the power to sue and be sued; (5) whether it can enter into contracts; (6) and whether the agency's property is immune from state taxation.[185] The most significant of these factors in determining if a district is shielded by eleventh amendment immunity has been whether or not the judgment will be recovered from state funds. If funds are to be paid from the state treasury, courts have declared the state to be the real party in interest, and thus school districts have been entitled to immunity.[186]

For many states, the eleventh amendment question with respect to school district immunity was resolved in the *Mt. Healthy* case.[187] The Supreme Court concluded that the issue in this case turned on whether the Ohio school district was an arm of the state as opposed to that of a municipality or other political subdivision. This determination was dependent in part upon the "nature of the entity created by state law."[188] According to Ohio law, political subdivisions, including school districts, are not part of the "state." Considering as well the taxing power and autonomy of school district operations, the Supreme Court found school districts to be more like counties or cities than an extension of the state. Since the *Mt. Healthy* ruling, other state/local relationships have been similarly interpreted as excluding school districts from eleventh amendment immunity.

However, in 1984 the Tenth Circuit Court of Appeals found that the eleventh amendment precluded a suit against school districts in New Mexico.[189] The court reasoned that this state has such extensive administrative and financial control over local school districts that the local systems are mere arms of the state. The court noted that New Mexico has the power to bar all local school districts' spending unless their budgets are state-certified and that the state provides 96 percent of local school funds. Because of New Mexico's unique role in local school financing and the unusual existence of a state agency to pay awards of damages, the applicability of this decision to other states appears quite limited.[190]

Damages

When the individual school official or school district is found liable for violating an individual's federally protected rights, an award of damages will be assessed to compensate the claimant for the injury received. However, actual injury must be shown for the aggrieved person to recover damages; without evidence of monetary or mental injury, the plaintiff will be entitled only to nominal damages (not to exceed one dollar), even though an impairment of federal rights is established. In 1978 the Supreme Court held that pupils who were denied procedural due process in a disciplinary proceeding would be entitled only to nominal damages unless established that the lack of proper procedures resulted in actual injury to the students.[191]

In 1986 the Supreme Court emphasized that compensatory damages are not to be based on a jury's perception of the value or importance of constitutional rights.[192] In this case, involving the award of compensatory damages to a teacher for his unconstitutional dismissal, the Supreme Court reiterated that such damages are available *only* to compensate for proven harm. Individuals are entitled to full compensation for the injury suffered, but they are not entitled to supplementary damages based on the perceived value of the constitutional rights that have been abridged.

In some instances, plaintiffs have sought punitive in addition to compensatory damages. The judiciary has ruled that school officials can be liable for punitive damages (to punish the wrongdoer) if a jury concludes that the individual's conduct is willful or in reckless and callous disregard of federally protected rights.[193] For example, punitive damages were assessed against a principal and superintendent who, without authority, discharged a teacher in retaliation for her exercise of protected speech.[194] Punitive damages, however, must be assessed on an individual basis against each defendant and cannot be imposed jointly against several officials.[195]

In 1981 the Supreme Court ruled that Section 1983 does not authorize the award of punitive damages against a municipality.[196] Reasoning that compensation for injuries is an obligation of a municipality, the Court held that punitive damages were appropriate only for the individual wrongdoers and not for the municipality itself. The Court also noted that punitive damages constitute punishment against individuals to deter similar conduct in the future, but they are not intended to be punishment for innocent taxpayers. This ruling does not bar claims for punitive damages for violations of federal rights in school cases, but such claims must be brought against individuals rather than against the school district itself.

CONCLUSION

While clearly established that public educators do not shed their constitutional rights as a condition of public employment, under certain conditions impairments of these freedoms are justified by overriding governmental interests. Protections afforded to educators' constitutional rights continue to be delineated by the judiciary; the following generalizations reflect the present status of the law in the substantive areas discussed in this chapter.

1. Public educators have a first amendment right to express their views on public issues related to the welfare of the school and students; dismissal or other retaliatory personnel action, such as transfers, demotions, or written reprimands, cannot be predicated solely on protected speech.
2. Expression pertaining to personal employment disputes, attacks on supervisors, or speech intended to disrupt the school is not constitutionally protected.
3. The exercise of protected speech will not invalidate a dismissal action if the school board can show by a preponderance of evidence that it would have reached the same decision had the protected speech not occurred.
4. Even if protected speech is the sole basis for adverse employment action, the school board might still prevail if established that its interests in maintaining the efficiency of the public agency outweigh the individual's interest in expressing views.
5. A school's internal mail system is not a traditional open forum for expression, and unless designated as such a forum, access to the mail system can be restricted to business that relates to the school's educational function as long as restrictions are not viewpoint-based.

6. Reasonable time, place, and manner restrictions can be imposed on educators' expression, but arbitrary prior restraints on the content and channel of communication violate the first amendment.
7. Public school teachers do not have the right to determine the content of the instructional program, but they do have some latitude in selecting strategies to convey the prescribed content.
8. In evaluating the appropriateness of teaching materials and strategies, courts consider relevance to course objectives, threat of disruption, age and maturity of students, and community standards.
9. Public employees cannot be retaliated against because of their membership in labor unions, political groups, or organizations with unlawful purposes.
10. Educators' participation in political activities outside the classroom cannot be the basis for employment decisions related to promotion, transfer, or dismissal.
11. By state law, restrictions may be placed on the types of elected offices that may be held by public educators (e.g., two incompatible positions cannot be held).
12. Employees can be required to take temporary leave from their positions to campaign for office if it is established that campaign demands would interfere with job responsibilities.
13. School officials can impose reasonable restrictions on educators' personal appearance as long as there is a rational basis for such regulations.
14. School policies that interfere with recognized privacy rights in connection with marriage, procreation, and child rearing must be justified by a compelling governmental interest.
15. Educators have a legitimate expectation of privacy in their persons, school desks, and other personal effects at school; school authorities cannot impair such privacy rights without an overriding educational justification.
16. Public educators have protected privacy rights in their lifestyle choices; however, adverse employment consequences may be justified if private choices have a detrimental effect on job performance.
17. School officials and school districts can be held liable for compensatory damages in connection with actions that impair educators' constitutional rights.
18. An individual can recover only nominal damages for the impairment of constitutional rights unless monetary, emotional, or mental injury can be established.
19. School officials can plead immunity to protect themselves from liability if their actions were taken in good faith; ignorance of clearly established principles of law is evidence of bad faith.

20. School districts cannot plead good faith as a defense against liability for the impairment of federally protected civil rights.
21. Punitive damages to punish the wrongdoer can be assessed against individual school officials but not against school districts.
22. The eleventh amendment can shield school districts from liability in civil rights cases if established that the state is the real party in interest.

NOTES

1. 391 U.S. 563 (1968).
2. *Id.* at 572. *See also* Perry v. Sinderman, 408 U.S. 593 (1972) (professor's lack of tenure, taken alone, did not defeat his claim that nonrenewal of his contract was in retaliation for his public criticism of the Board of Regents); text with note 19, chapter 10.
3. 429 U.S. 274, 282 (1977).
4. *Id.* at 286.
5. Doyle v. Mt. Healthy City School Dist., 670 F.2d 59 (6th Cir. 1982).
6. 439 U.S. 410 (1979).
7. 461 U.S. 138 (1983).
8. *Id.* at 142.
9. *Id.* at 150.
10. James v. Board of Educ. of Cent. Dist. No. 1, 461 F.2d 566 (2d Cir. 1972), *cert. denied,* 409 U.S. 1042 (1972).
11. Lusk v. Estes, 361 F. Supp. 653 (N.D. Tex. 1973).
12. Adcock v. Board of Educ. of San Diego Unified School Dist., 513 P.2d 900 (Cal. 1973).
13. McGill v. Board of Educ. of Pekin Elementary School Dist. No. 108, 602 F.2d 774 (7th Cir. 1979).
14. Wells v. Hico Independent School Dist., 736 F.2d 243 (5th Cir. 1984), *cert. dismissed,* 106 S. Ct. 11 (1985); Lemons v. Morgan, 629 F.2d 1389 (8th Cir. 1980); Bernasconi v. Tempe Elementary School Dist. No. 3, 548 F.2d 857 (9th Cir. 1977), *cert. denied,* 434 U.S. 825 (1977).
15. *See* Columbus Educ. Ass'n v. Columbus City School Dist., 623 F.2d 1155 (6th Cir. 1980); Swilley v. Alexander, 629 F.2d 1018, 1020 (5th Cir. 1980); Aebisher v. Ryan, 622 F.2d 651 (2d Cir. 1980); Gregory v. Durham County Bd. of Educ., 591 F. Supp. 145 (M.D.N.C. 1984).
16. Austin v. Mehlville R–9 School Dist., 564 S.W.2d 884 (Mo. 1978).
17. Anderson v. Evans, 660 F.2d 153 (6th Cir. 1981).
18. Pietrunti v. Board of Educ. of Brick Township, 319 A.2d 262 (N.J. Super. 1974).
19. Gilbertson v. McAlister, 403 F. Supp. 1 (D. Conn. 1975).
20. Shimoyama v. Board of Educ. of the Los Angeles Unified School Dist., 174 Cal. Rptr. 748 (Cal. App. 1981).
21. Birdwell v. Hazelwood School Dist., 491 F.2d 490 (8th Cir. 1974). *See also* Whitsell v. Southeast Local School Dist., 484 F.2d 1222 (6th Cir. 1973)

(upholding dismissal of a teacher because he addressed protesting students after the principal had ordered all students to return to class); Russ v. White, 680 F.2d 47 (8th Cir. 1982) (college dean's disruptive utterances did not constitute protected speech); Franklin v. Leland Stanford Junior Univ., 218 Cal. Rptr. 228 (Cal. App. 1985) (upholding dismissal of a professor who gave a speech calling for a strike to protest the Vietnam War and interfered with a police dispersal order).

22. White v. South Park Independent School Dist., 693 F.2d 1163 (5th Cir. 1982). *See also* Kelleher v. Flawn, 761 F.2d 1079 (5th Cir. 1985); Hughes v. Whitmer, 714 F.2d 1407 (8th Cir. 1983), *cert. denied,* 465 U.S. 1023 (1984); Landrum v. Eastern Kentucky Univ., 578 F. Supp. 241 (E.D. Ky. 1984).
23. Board of Trustees of the Hattiesburg Mun. Separate School Dist. v. Gates, 461 So. 2d 730 (Miss. 1984).
24. Simineo v. School Dist. No. 16, Park County, Wyoming, 594 F.2d 1353 (10th Cir. 1979). *See also* Abston v. Woodard, 437 So. 2d 1261 (Ala. 1983) (sufficient evidence was introduced to show that nonrenewal of a teacher's contract may have been based on his complaints against the principal regarding irregularities in football game gate receipts; case was remanded for a determination of whether the board would have reached the same decision in the absence of the teacher's allegations).
25. Solis v. Rio Grande City Independent School, 734 F.2d 243 (5th Cir. 1984); Wells v. Hico Independent School Dist., 736 F.2d 243 (5th Cir. 1984), *cert. dismissed,* 106 S. Ct. 11 (1985).
26. Rowland v. Mad River Local School Dist., Montgomery County, Ohio, 730 F.2d 444, 449 (6th Cir. 1984), *cert. denied,* 105 S. Ct. 1373 (1985).
27. *Id.*, 105 S. Ct. at 1375.
28. Renfroe v. Kirkpatrick, 722 F.2d 714, 715 (11th Cir. 1984), *cert. denied,* 469 U.S. 823 (1984). *See also* Reichert v. Draud, 511 F. Supp. 679 (E.D. Ky. 1981) (teacher was denied relief for a single course change in her schedule, even though the personnel action was in retaliation for the exercise of protected speech; there was no monetary or other loss or evidence that the schedule change would have a chilling effect on free expression among teachers).
29. Saye v. St. Vrain Valley School Dist., 785 F.2d 862 (10th Cir. 1986).
30. Derrickson v. Board of Educ. of the City of St. Louis, 738 F.2d 351, 352–353 (8th Cir. 1984) (the first amendment did not shield the teacher from adverse personnel action based on his inability to work harmoniously with superiors, peers, and students, even assuming that some of his criticisms pertaining to personnel reductions touched upon matters of public concern). *But see* Lewis v. Harrison School Dist. No. 1, 805 F.2d 310 (8th Cir. 1986) (principal's criticism of superintendent before school board was protected speech).
31. Alinovi v. Worchester School Comm., 766 F.2d 660 (1st Cir. 1985), *cert. denied,* 107 S. Ct. 72 (1986). *See* text with note 147, *infra*, for a discussion of the privacy issue raised in this case.
32. Cook v. Ashmore, 579 F. Supp. 78 (N.D. Ga. 1984). *See also* Ballard v. Blount, 581 F. Supp. 160 (N.D. Ga. 1983), *aff'd*, 734 F.2d 1480 (11th Cir. 1984), *cert. denied,* 105 S. Ct. 590 (1984) (professor's speech concerning colleague's denial of tenure, course assignment procedures, salary in-

creases, and proposed course syllabus did not involve matters of public interest).

33. Ferrara v. Mills, 781 F.2d 1508 (11th Cir. 1986) (teacher asserted that his comments had public significance because his dismissal had been covered by the press, but the court distinguished between coverage of his discharge and coverage of the issues he raised). *See also* Callaway v. Hafeman, 628 F. Supp. 1478 (W.D. Wis. 1986) (teacher's complaints of sexual harassment were not protected speech).
34. Gregory v. Durham County Bd. of Educ., 591 F. Supp. 145 (M.D. N.C. 1984). *See also* Patterson v. Masem, 774 F.2d 251 (8th Cir. 1985) (teacher's denial of a promotion to a supervisory role was not in retaliation for recommending that a play not be performed because she found it racially offensive).
35. Stevenson v. Lower Marion County School Dist. No. 3, 327 S.E.2d 656 (S.C. 1985). *See also* Rabon v. Bryan County Bd. of Educ., 326 S.E.2d 577 (Ga. App. 1985), *cert. denied,* 106 S. Ct. 160 (1985) (termination based on a principal's sexual remarks that intimidated teachers and reduced his competency did not impair free speech rights).
36. Day v. South Park Independent School Dist., 768 F.2d 696 (5th Cir. 1985), *cert. denied,* 106 S. Ct. 883 (1986). *See also* Roberts v. Van Buren Public Schools, 773 F.2d 949 (8th Cir. 1985) (a grievance, expressing elementary teachers' dissatisfaction with the way parental complaints concerning a field trip had been handled, pertained more to the teacher/principal relationship than to the discharge of the public function of education).
37. McKinley v. City of Eloy, 705 F.2d 1110 (9th Cir. 1983); Leonard v. City of Columbus, 705 F.2d 1299 (11th Cir. 1983), *cert. denied,* 468 U.S. 1204 (1984).
38. McGee v. South Pemiscot School Dist. R–V, 712 F.2d 339 (8th Cir. 1983).
39. Bowman v. Pulaski County Special School Dist., 723 F.2d 640 (8th Cir. 1983). *See also* Cox v. Dardanelle Public School Dist., 790 F.2d 668 (8th Cir. 1986) (nonrenewal of teacher's contract for criticizing the principal's administrative style of discouraging teacher input, inhibiting creativity, and adversely affecting morale, violated the teacher's first amendment rights).
40. Czurlanis v. Albanese, 721 F.2d 98, 104 (3d Cir. 1983).
41. Knapp v. Whitaker, 757 F.2d 827 (7th Cir. 1985), *appeal dismissed,* 106 S. Ct. 36 (1985). The case was remanded to reconsider the award of compensatory damages (limited to between $200,000 and $400,000) and evidence regarding the teacher's certification status for a high school science position.
42. *Id.*, 757 F.2d at 839, citing 577 F. Supp. 1265, 1271 (C.D. Ill. 1984).
43. Fishman v. Clancy, 763 F.2d 485 (1st Cir. 1985).
44. Wichert v. Walter, 606 F. Supp. 1516 (D.N.J. 1985). *See also* Thomas v. Farmer, 573 F. Supp. 128 (S.D. Ohio 1983) (speech made at school board meeting was protected expression).
45. Hinkle v. Christensen, 733 F.2d 74 (8th Cir. 1984).
46. Hickman v. Valley Local School Dist. Bd. of Educ., 619 F.2d 606 (6th Cir. 1980). *See also* text with note 29, *supra.*
47. Prior to *Connick,* courts had relied on the principle that undifferentiated fear of disruption was not sufficient to curtail free expression rights. *See* Tinker

v. Des Moines Independent Community School Dist., 393 U.S. 503 (1969); text with note 22, chapter 4.

48. National Gay Task Force v. Board of Educ. of City of Oklahoma City, 729 F.2d 1270, 1274 (10th Cir. 1984), *aff'd by an equally divided court,* 105 S. Ct. 1858 (1985).
49. *Id.*, 729 F.2d at 1274, citing in part, Pickering v. Board of Educ., 391 U.S. 563, 568 (1968) and Tinker v. Des Moines Independent Community School Dist., 393 U.S. 503, 513 (1969).
50. Hall v. Board of School Comm'rs of Mobile County, Alabama, 681 F.2d 965, 968 (5th Cir. 1982). *See also* Substitutes United for Better Schools v. Rohter, 496 F. Supp. 1017 (N.D. Ill. 1980) (teachers had a first amendment right to sell their organization's newspaper in the school where employed, since the activity was not disruptive or for commercial gain).
51. Hall, *id.* at 969.
52. Texas State Teachers Ass'n v. Garland Independent School Dist., 777 F.2d 1046 (5th Cir. 1985), *aff'd mem.*, 107 S. Ct. 41 (1986).
53. Perry Educ. Ass'n v. Perry Local Educators' Ass'n, 460 U.S. 37, 46 (1983).
54. Ysleta Fed'n of Teachers v. Ysleta Independent School Dist., 720 F.2d 1429 (5th Cir. 1983). The court further held that the school board had not produced evidence of a compelling interest for limiting employee organizations to one distribution of recruitment literature per year through the school mail system. The case was remanded for development of the record on this issue.
55. May v. Evansville-Vanderburgh School Corp., 787 F.2d 1105 (7th Cir. 1986).
56. City of Madison Joint School Dist. No. 8 v. Wisconsin Employment Relations Comm'n, 429 U.S. 167 (1976).
57. Anderson v. Central Point School Dist., 554 F. Supp. 600 (D. Ore. 1982).
58. Knapp v. Whitaker, 757 F.2d 827 (7th Cir. 1985), *appeal dismissed,* 106 S. Ct. 36 (1985).
59. Unified School Dist. No. 503 v. McKinney, 689 P.2d 860 (Kan. 1984).
60. Godwin v. East Baton Rouge Parish School Bd., 408 So. 2d 1214, 1216 (La. 1982). *See also* Heffron v. International Society of Krishna Consciousness, 452 U.S. 640 (1981) (upholding restriction on literature distribution at a fairgrounds to ensure order).
61. For a discussion of the historical evolution of the concept of academic freedom, *see* Ralph F. Fuchs, "Academic Freedom—Its Basic Philosophy, Function, and History," *Law and Contemporary Problems,* vol. 28 (1968), pp. 431–446.
62. Adams v. Campbell County School Dist., 511 F.2d 1242, 1247 (10th Cir. 1975).
63. Cary v. Board of Educ. of the Adams-Arapahoe School Dist. 28–J, 598 F.2d 535, 544 (10th Cir. 1979).
64. Palmer v. Board of Educ. of the City of Chicago, 603 F.2d 1271, 1274 (7th Cir. 1979), *cert. denied,* 444 U.S. 1026 (1980).
65. Millikan v. Board of Directors of Everett School Dist. No. 2, 611 P.2d 414, 418 (Wash. 1980).
66. Ahern v. Board of Educ. of School Dist. of Grand Island, 456 F.2d 399 (8th Cir. 1972). *See also* Moore v. School Bd. of Gulf County, Florida, 364 F. Supp. 355 (N.D. Fla. 1973).

67. Fisher v. Fairbanks North Star Borough School Dist., 704 P.2d 213 (Alas. 1985).
68. Keefe v. Geanakos, 418 F.2d 359 (1st Cir. 1969).
69. Mailloux v. Kiley, 323 F. Supp. 1387 (D. Mass. 1971), *aff'd*, 448 F.2d 1242 (1st Cir. 1971).
70. *Id.*, 323 F. Supp. at 1392.
71. Sterzing v. Fort Bend Independent School Dist., 376 F. Supp. 657 (S.D. Tex. 1972), *vacated* (regarding denial of reinstatement) *and remanded,* 496 F.2d 92 (5th Cir. 1974). *See also* Dean v. Timpson Independent School Dist., 486 F. Supp. 302 (E.D. Tex. 1979); Lindros v. Governing Bd. of the Torrance Unified School Dist., 510 P.2d 361 (Cal. 1973), *cert. denied,* 414 U.S. 1112 (1973).
72. *See* Mailloux v. Kiley, 323 F. Supp. 1387 (D. Mass. 1971), *aff'd*, 448 F.2d 1242 (1st Cir. 1971).
73. Brubaker v. Board of Educ., School Dist. 149, 502 F.2d 973 (7th Cir. 1974), *cert. denied,* 421 U.S. 965 (1975).
74. Simon v. Jefferson Davis Parish School Bd., 289 So. 2d 511 (La. App. 1974).
75. Shurgin v. Ambach, 436 N.E.2d 1324 (N.Y. 1982).
76. Kingsville Independent School Dist. v. Cooper, 611 F.2d 1109 (5th Cir. 1980).
77. Stachura v. Memphis Community School Dist., 763 F.2d 211 (6th Cir. 1985), *rev'd and remanded* regarding award of compensatory damages, 106 S. Ct. 2537 (1986). *See* text with notes 88, 192, *infra.*
78. Parducci v. Rutland, 316 F. Supp. 352 (M.D. Ala. 1970).
79. *Id.* at 353–354.
80. *Id.,* citing the standard adopted by the Supreme Court in Tinker v. Des Moines Independent Community School Dist., 393 U.S. 503 (1969). *See* text with note 23, chapter 4.
81. Wilson v. Chancellor, 418 F. Supp. 1358 (D. Ore. 1976).
82. Kingsville Independent School Dist. v. Cooper, 611 F.2d 1109 (5th Cir. 1980).
83. *Id.* at 1113.
84. Dean v. Timpson Independent School Dist., 486 F. Supp. 302 (E.D. Tex. 1979).
85. Solmitz v. Maine School Administrative Dist. No. 59, 495 A.2d 812 (Me. 1985).
86. Zykan v. Warsaw Community School Corp., 631 F.2d 1300, 1304 (7th Cir. 1980), citing Palmer v. Board of Educ. of the City of Chicago, 603 F.2d 1271, 1274 (7th Cir. 1979).
87. Adams v. Campbell County School Dist., 511 F.2d 1242 (10th Cir. 1975).
88. Stachura v. Memphis Community School Dist., 763 F.2d 211 (6th Cir. 1985).
89. *Id.* at 215. In a related suit, combined on appeal, the teacher sued the parent who initiated the protests, but the court concluded that the parent's expression was made to the public body charged with administering the schools, and thus, the action was protected by the right to petition encompassed in the first amendment. Stachura v. Truszkowski, 763 F.2d 211 (6th Cir. 1985).
90. Wilson v. Chancellor, 418 F. Supp. 1358 (D. Ore. 1976). *See also* Vail v.

Board of Educ. of Portsmouth School Dist., 354 F. Supp. 592, 596 (D.N.H. 1973), *vacated and remanded,* 502 F.2d 1159 (1st Cir. 1973).

91. Healy v. James, 408 U.S. 169, 181 (1972).
92. *See* Adler v. Board of Educ. of City of New York, 342 U.S. 485 (1952); Wieman v. Updegraff, 344 U.S. 183 (1952).
93. *See* Keyishian v. Board of Regents of the Univ. of the State of New York, 385 U.S. 589, 606 (1967); Elfbrandt v. Russell, 384 U.S. 11, 19 (1966); Baggett v. Bullitt, 377 U.S. 360 (1964). However, employees can be required to pledge that they will uphold and defend the Constitution and oppose the overthrow of the government. *See* Cole v. Richardson, 405 U.S. 676 (1972); Connell v. Higginbotham, 403 U.S. 207 (1971); text with note 7, chapter 7.
94. Keyishian, *id.*
95. *See* National Ass'n for the Advancement of Colored People v. Alabama, 357 U.S. 449 (1958).
96. Woodward v. Hereford Independent School Dist., 421 F. Supp. 93 (N.D. Tex. 1976).
97. Shelton v. Tucker, 364 U.S. 479 (1960).
98. *Id.* at 490.
99. Familias Unidas v. Briscoe, 619 F.2d 391 (5th Cir. 1980).
100. 357 U.S. 399 (1958).
101. Elrod v. Burns, 427 U.S. 347 (1976).
102. Branti v. Finkel, 445 U.S. 507 (1980).
103. *See* Burris v. Willis Independent School Dist., 713 F.2d 1087 (5th Cir. 1983) (nonrenewal of an administrator's contract was predicated on his association with previous "old-line" board members and thereby violated his protected associational rights). *But see* Smith v. Harris, 560 F. Supp. 677 (D.R.I. 1983) (prospective teacher failed to show that partisan politics was a motivating factor in the board's decision not to hire her).
104. *See* Goldsmith v. Board of Educ., 225 P. 783 (Cal. App. 1924).
105. Los Angeles Teachers Union v. Los Angeles City Bd. of Educ., 455 P.2d 827, 832 (Cal. 1969). *But see* Connick v. Myers, 461 U.S. 138 (1983) (questionnaire that did not relate to matters of public concern was not protected expression); text with note 7, *supra.*
106. In some states, constitutional protections are buttressed by laws that specifically protect public employees from retaliation for political activities. Relying on such a Texas law and the first amendment, a federal district court struck down a school board policy prohibiting all political activity except voting. Montgomery v. White, 320 F. Supp. 303 (E.D. Tex. 1969).
107. Wichert v. Walter, 606 F. Supp. 1516 (D.N.J. 1985).
108. Alaniz v. San Isidro Independent School Dist., 742 F.2d 207 (5th Cir. 1984).
109. *See, e.g.,* Childers v. Independent School Dist. No. 1 of Bryan County, 676 F.2d 1338 (10th Cir. 1982); Melendez v. Aponte Roque, 641 F. Supp. 1326 (D. Puerto Rico 1986). Miller v. Board of Educ. of the County of Lincoln, 450 F. Supp. 106 (S.D.W.V. 1978); Guerra v. Roma Independent School Dist., 444 F. Supp. 812 (S.D. Tex. 1977); Calhoun v. Cassady, 534 S.W.2d 806 (Ky. 1976).
110. Visotcky v. City Council of the City of Garfield, 273 A.2d 597 (N.J. Super. 1971).
111. Haskins v. State *ex rel.* Harrington, 516 P.2d 1171, 1178 (Wyo. 1973).
112. *Id.* at 1179.

113. In addition to proscriptions on individuals holding two incompatible roles, courts have ruled that states can prohibit the practice of more than one member of a family serving concurrently on a school board. *See* Rosenstock v. Scaringe, 357 N.E.2d 347 (N.Y. 1976).
114. West v. Jones, 323 S.E.2d 96 (Va. 1984).
115. United States Civil Service Comm'n v. National Ass'n of Letter Carriers, 413 U.S. 548 (1973). *See* 5 U.S.C. § 7324.
116. Broadrick v. Oklahoma, 413 U.S. 601 (1973).
117. Galer v. Board of Regents of the Univ. System, 236 S.E.2d 617 (Ga. 1977).
118. Cranston Teachers Alliance v. Miele, 495 A.2d 233, 237 (R.I. 1985).
119. Minielly v. State, 411 P.2d 69 (Ore. 1966).
120. Allen v. Board of Educ. of Jefferson County, 584 S.W.2d 408 (Ky. App. 1979).
121. White v. Dougherty County Bd. of Educ., 431 F. Supp. 919 (M.D. Ga. 1977), *aff'd*, 439 U.S. 32 (1978).
122. White v. Dougherty County Bd. of Educ., 579 F. Supp. 1480 (M.D. Ga. 1984), *aff'd*, 105 S. Ct. 1824 (1985).
123. One district went so far as to require female teachers to wear at least two petticoats and dresses no shorter than two inches above the ankle. *See* Michael W. LaMorte, *School Law: Cases and Concepts* (Englewood Cliffs, NJ: Prentice-Hall, 1982), p. 216.
124. Conard v. Goolsby, 350 F. Supp. 713 (N.D. Miss, 1972).
125. Finot v. Pasadena City Bd. of Educ., 58 Cal. Rptr. 520 (Cal. App. 1967).
126. Braxton v. Board of Public Instruction of Duval County, Florida, 303 F. Supp. 958 (M.D. Fla. 1969). The court held that the wearing of a beard is a constitutionally protected liberty interest under the fourteenth amendment's due process clause, and, in this case, it also implicated first amendment rights because it was worn as an expression of the teacher's heritage, culture, and racial pride.
127. Miller v. School Dist. No. 167, Cook County, Illinois, 495 F.2d 658, 666 (7th Cir. 1974).
128. Kelley v. Johnson, 425 U.S. 238, 245 (1976).
129. *Id.* at 248.
130. East Hartford Educ. Ass'n v. Board of Educ. of the Town of East Hartford, 562 F.2d 838 (2d Cir. 1977).
131. Although the teacher asserted that his refusal to wear a tie involved "symbolic speech," the court reasoned that "as conduct becomes less and less like 'pure speech' the showing of governmental interest required for its regulation is progressively lessened," *id.* at 858.
132. Domico v. Rapides Parish School Bd., 675 F.2d 100, 102 (5th Cir. 1982). *See also* Ball v. Board of Trustees of the Kerrville Independent School Dist., 584 F.2d 684 (5th Cir. 1978), *cert. denied,* 440 U.S. 972 (1979).
133. Tardif v. Quinn, 545 F.2d 761 (1st Cir. 1976).
134. Whereas restrictions on teachers' appearance are assessed in terms of whether school officials are motivated by a legitimate educational concern, some courts have applied a more stringent standard in assessing restrictions on students' appearance, requiring evidence that the hair length or attire poses a threat of disruption to the educational process. *See* text with notes 117, 136, chapter 4.
135. Pence v. Rosenquist, 573 F.2d 395 (7th Cir. 1978).

136. Most states have laws providing employees with access to their personnel files and safeguarding the confidentiality of such records. Courts can require the contents of personnel files to be revealed, if necessary to investigate discrimination charges. *See* Equal Employment Opportunity Comm'n v. Maryland Cup Corp., 785 F.2d 471 (4th Cir. 1986), *cert. denied,* 107 S. Ct. 68 (1986); Equal Employment Opportunity Comm'n v. Franklin and Marshall College, 775 F.2d 110 (3d Cir. 1985), *cert. denied,* 106 S. Ct. 2288 (1986); Duke v. University of Texas at El Paso, 729 F.2d 994 (5th Cir. 1984), *cert. denied,* 105 S. Ct. 386 (1984); Equal Employment Opportunity Comm'n v. University of New Mexico, 504 F.2d 1296 (10th Cir. 1974). For a discussion of personnel records, *see* text with note 114, chapter 7.
137. *See* Thornburgh v. American College of Obstetricians and Gynecologists, 106 S. Ct. 2169 (1986); Roe v. Wade, 410 U.S. 113 (1973); Loving v. Virginia, 388 U.S. 1 (1967); Griswold v. Connecticut, 381 U.S. 479 (1965); Skinner v. Oklahoma, 316 U.S. 535 (1942); Pierce v. Society of Sisters, 268 U.S. 510 (1925).
138. Dike v. School Bd. of Orange County, Florida, 650 F.2d 783 (5th Cir. 1981).
139. Gargiul v. Tompkins, 704 F.2d 661 (2d Cir. 1983), *vacated and remanded,* 104 S. Ct. 1263 (1984). *See also* Gargiul v. Tompkins, 790 F.2d 265 (2d Cir. 1986); note 190, *infra.*
140. Cook v. Hudson, 511 F.2d 744 (5th Cir. 1975), *cert. dismissed,* 429 U.S. 165 (1976).
141. Brantley v. Surles, 765 F.2d 478 (5th Cir. 1985).
142. Stough v. Crenshaw County Bd. of Educ., 744 F.2d 1479 (11th Cir. 1984).
143. New Jersey v. T.L.O., 105 S. Ct. 733 (1984). *See* text with note 100, chapter 6.
144. Gillard v. Schmidt, 579 F.2d 825 (3d Cir. 1978).
145. Ortega v. O'Connor, 764 F.2d 703 (9th Cir. 1985), *cert. granted in part,* 106 S. Ct. 565 (1985).
146. *See* United States v. Collins, 349 F.2d 863, 867–868 (2d Cir. 1965), *cert. denied,* 383 U.S. 960 (1966).
147. Alinovi v. Worcester School Comm., 766 F.2d 660 (1st Cir. 1985), *cert. denied,* 107 S. Ct. 72 (1986). *See* text with note 31, *supra,* regarding the free expression claim in this case.
148. Patchogue-Medford Congress of Teachers v. Board of Educ. of Patchogue-Medford Union Free School Dist., No. 85–8759 (Sup. Ct., Suffolk County, N.Y. 1985), slip opinion, p. 5, *aff'd,* 505 N.Y.S.2d 888 (App. Div. 1986).
149. Jones v. McKenzie, 628 F. Supp. 1500 (D.D.C. 1986). The court further held that termination of the bus attendant based on a single, unconfirmed positive urinalysis drug test was arbitrary, capricious, and in violation of school board requirements. It should be noted that drug testing without individualized suspicion has been upheld for military personnel and prisoners. *See* Committee for G.I. Rights v. Callaway, 518 F.2d 466 (D.C. Cir. 1975); Storms v. Coughlin, 600 F. Supp. 1214 (S.D.N.Y. 1984). There is some sentiment that blanket drug testing would be justified for certain categories of employees, e.g., bus drivers, where overriding safety considerations are involved. *See* Janet M. White and Stephen B. Thomas, "Drug Testing in Public Schools," *Journal of Educational Equity and Leadership* (forthcoming 1987).

150. *See* Lile v. Hancock Place School Dist., 701 S.W.2d 500, 508 (Mo. App. 1986).
151. Andrews v. Drew Mun. Separate School Dist., 507 F.2d 611, 614 (5th Cir. 1975), *cert. dismissed,* 425 U.S. 559 (1976). *See also* Eckmann v. Board of Educ. of Hawthorn School Dist. No. 17, 636 F. Supp. 1214 (N.D. Ill. 1986).
152. Avery v. Homewood City Bd. of Educ., 674 F.2d 337 (5th Cir. 1982), *cert. denied,* 461 U.S. 943 (1983). *See also* Cochran v. Chidester School Dist., 456 F. Supp. 390 (W.D. Ark. 1978); Reinhardt v. Board of Educ., 311 N.E.2d 710 (Ill. App. 1974), *vacated,* 329 N.E.2d 218 (Ill. 1975); New Mexico State Bd. of Educ. v. Stoudt, 571 P.2d 1186 (N.M. 1977); Drake v. Covington County Bd. of Educ., 371 F. Supp. 974 (M.D. Ala. 1974).
153. *See* Ponton v. Newport News School Bd., 632 F. Supp. 1056 (E.D. Va. 1986).
154. Erb v. Iowa State Bd. of Public Instruction, 216 N.W.2d 339 (Iowa 1974).
155. Sherburne v. School Bd. of Suwannee County, 455 So. 2d 1057 (Fla. App. 1984).
156. Briggs v. North Muskegon Police Dep't, 563 F. Supp. 585 (W.D. Mich. 1983), *aff'd,* 746 F.2d 1475 (6th Cir. 1984), *cert. denied,* 105 S. Ct. 3535 (1985).
157. Littlejohn v. Rose, 768 F.2d 765, 769 (6th Cir. 1985), *cert. denied,* 106 S. Ct. 1260 (1986). *See* text with note 178, *infra.*
158. Hollenbaugh v. Carnegie Free Library, 578 F.2d 1374 (3d Cir. 1978), *cert. denied,* 439 U.S. 1052 (1979). Justice Marshall disagreed with the denial of review, contending that there was no evidence presented by the employer to substantiate that the employees' private conduct was related to job performance.
159. Shawgo v. Spradlin, 701 F.2d 470 (5th Cir. 1983), *cert. denied, sub nom.* Whisenhunt v. Spradlin, 464 U.S. 965 (1983).
160. Sullivan v. Meade Independent School Dist. No. 101, 530 F.2d 799 (8th Cir. 1976).
161. Okla. Stat. Title 70, § 6–103.15(A)(1). National Gay Task Force v. Board of Educ., 729 F.2d 1270 (10th Cir. 1984), *aff'd by an equally divided court,* 105 S. Ct. 1853 (1985). *See* text with note 48, *supra.*
162. Bowers v. Hardwick, 106 S. Ct. 2841 (1986).
163. *See* Board of Educ. of Long Beach Unified School Dist. v. Jack M., 566 P.2d 602 (Cal. 1977); Morrison v. State Bd. of Educ., 461 P.2d 375 (Cal. 1969); Sarac v. State Bd. of Educ., 57 Cal. Rptr. 69 (Cal. App. 1967); text with note 137, chapter 10.
164. Burton v. Cascade School Dist., Union High School No. 5, 512 F.2d 850 (9th Cir. 1975), *cert. denied,* 423 U.S. 839 (1975).
165. *Id.*, 512 F.2d at 854–856 (Lumbard, J., dissenting).
166. Gaylord v. Tacoma School Dist. No. 10, 559 P.2d 1340 (Wash. 1977), *cert. denied,* 434 U.S. 879 (1977).
167. Rowland v. Mad River Local School Dist., 730 F.2d 444 (6th Cir. 1984), *cert. denied,* 105 S. Ct. 1373 (1985). *See* text with note 26, *supra.*
168. 42 U.S.C. § 1983.
169. *See* Maine v. Thiboutot, 448 U.S. 1 (1980).
170. *See* Patsy v. Board of Regents of the State of Florida, 457 U.S. 496 (1982).

171. *See* Middlesex County Sewerage Auth. v. National Sea Clammers Ass'n, 453 U.S. 1 (1981).
172. Rizzo v. Goode, 423 U.S. 362 (1976). *See* chapter 12, for a discussion of the application of *respondeat superior* in state tort cases.
173. Gomez v. Toledo, 446 U.S. 635 (1980).
174. 420 U.S. 308, 322 (1975).
175. 457 U.S. 800, 818 (1982).
176. *See* Davis v. Scherer, 468 U.S. 183 (1984).
177. Gavrilles v. O'Connor, 611 F. Supp. 210 (D. Mass. 1985).
178. Littlejohn v. Rose, 768 F.2d 765 (6th Cir. 1985), *cert. denied,* 106 S. Ct. 1260 (1986). The court held that any qualified immunity enjoyed by the superintendent in his individual capacity would not absolve him of liability in his official capacity.
179. *See* Monroe v. Pape, 365 U.S. 167 (1961).
180. Monell v. Department of Social Services of the City of New York, 436 U.S. 658 (1978).
181. Owen v. City of Independence, Missouri, 445 U.S. 622 (1980). *See* chapter 12 for a discussion of tort law.
182. *Id.* at 647–648.
183. *See* Hans v. Louisiana, 134 U.S. 1 (1890).
184. Atascadero State Hosp. v. Scanlon, 105 S. Ct. 3142 (1985).
185. Urbano v. Board of Managers of the New Jersey State Prison, 415 F.2d 247, 250–251 (3d Cir. 1969), *cert. denied,* 397 U.S. 948 (1970). *See* Blake v. Kline, 612 F.2d 718 (3d Cir. 1979), *cert. denied,* 447 U.S. 921 (1980), for an application of the *Urbano* criteria to the Public School Employees' Retirement Board of Pennsylvania.
186. Eleventh amendment immunity covers only federal suits; it does not have any bearing on immunity in state tort actions. *See* chapter 12.
187. Mt. Healthy City School Dist. v. Doyle, 429 U.S. 274 (1977).
188. *Id.* at 280.
189. Martinez v. Board of Educ. of Taos Mun. School Dist., 748 F.2d 1393, 1394 (10th Cir. 1984). *See also* Garcia v. Board of Educ., Socorro Consol. School Dist., 777 F.2d 1403 (10th Cir. 1985), *cert. denied,* 107 S. Ct. 66 (1986).
190. Under certain circumstances, school districts may be able to use other defenses to preclude liability in a Section 1983 suit. If the plaintiff has previously litigated in a state court any claims relating to the factual situation on which the Section 1983 suit is brought, the individual may be barred from litigating constitutional issues even though those issues were not directly raised or decided in the prior action. Basically, all claims which have already been decided (res judicata) or could have been litigated between the same parties in a prior action (collateral estoppel) may be barred in a federal suit under Section 1983. Migra v. Warren City School Dist., 465 U.S. 75 (1984). However, the application of res judicata or collateral estoppel does not extend to the decision of an arbitrator under a collective bargaining agreement; arbitration is not a judicial proceeding and would not preclude court action under Section 1983. *See* McDonald v. City of West Branch, Michigan, 466 U.S. 284 (1984).
191. Cary v. Piphus, 435 U.S. 247 (1978). *See* text with note 169, chapter 6.
192. Memphis Community School Dist. v. Stachura, 106 S. Ct. 2537 (1986).

193. *See* Smith v. Wade, 461 U.S. 30 (1983). *See also* text with note 242, chapter 10, for examples of damages awards for unlawful terminations.
194. Fishman v. Clancy, 763 F.2d 485 (1st Cir. 1985). *See* text with note 43, *supra*.
195. *See* McFadden v. Sanchez, 710 F.2d 907 (2d Cir. 1983), *cert. denied*, 464 U.S. 961 (1983).
196. City of Newport v. Fact Concerts, 453 U.S. 247 (1981).

9

Discrimination in Employment

Since the 1960s, legislative bodies have enacted numerous protections against bias in hiring, promotion, compensation, and other employment practices. Courts also have been active in reviewing claims of employment discrimination and requests for remedies to compensate discrimination victims. This chapter focuses on litigation involving discrimination in employment under both the Federal Constitution and civil rights statutes. Following a brief discussion of constitutional and statutory standards of review, legal protections that shield educational personnel from discrimination based on race and national origin, sex, age, handicaps, and religion are examined.[1]

CONSTITUTIONAL AND STATUTORY STANDARDS OF REVIEW

The federal judiciary has applied several tests in assessing claims of discrimination in public employment. These judicially created standards vary depending on the type of discrimination alleged, the nature of the contested policies or practices, and whether constitutional or statutory grounds are used to challenge the governmental action.

Constitutional Standards

Most constitutional suits involving discrimination in public employment are initiated under the fourteenth amendment's guarantee that states must provide each person equal protection of the laws. Governmental action that facially discriminates against individuals on the basis of a suspect classification, such as race or national origin, cannot be justified under the equal protection clause of the fourteenth amendment unless evidence substantiates that a compelling state interest is being served. Rarely have legislative bodies been able to justify the creation of a suspect class.[2] However, if legislation does not involve a suspect classification or affect a fundamental interest (i.e., an explicit or implicit constitutional right), courts have traditionally required only that governmental classifications have a rational relationship to a legitimate goal, a standard most legislation can satisfy. This lenient rational basis test has generally been used to evaluate the constitutionality of challenged governmental classifications based on traits such as age and handicaps.[3]

As discussed in chapter 5, dissatisfaction with having to choose between the stringent and lenient equal protection tests has caused the Supreme Court since the 1970s to apply an intermediate standard in some cases where neither a suspect class nor a fundamental right is involved. This test requires that the challenged classification serve "important governmental objectives" and be "subtantially related to the achievement of those objectives."[4] The Court has applied this middle tier standard in assessing equal protection claims involving sex-based classifications.[5]

While the equal protection clause offers significant protections to citizens who are victims of invidious governmental discrimination, most allegations of discrimination in public employment do not involve *overt* classifications based on race, sex, or other inherent traits. Rather, suits usually involve claims that an individual has been treated less favorably than others solely because of an inherent characteristic or that facially neutral employment policies adversely affect certain classes of employees. To establish a constitutional violation in such suits, aggrieved individuals must prove that they have been victims of *purposeful* governmental discrimination. In 1979 the Supreme Court held that mere awareness of a policy's adverse impact on a protected class does not constitute proof of unlawful motive. The Court stated that a discriminatory purpose "implies that the decision maker . . . selected or reaffirmed a particular course of action at least in part 'because of,' not merely 'in spite of,' its adverse effects upon an identifiable group."[6] The Court, however, has recognized that the foreseeable discriminatory consequences of acts can be considered by courts in assessing intent, even though foreseeable consequences alone cannot substantiate unlawful motive.[7] In addition, the judiciary has noted that evidence of a pattern or practice of employment discrimination can be used in conjunction with other evidence to substantiate a plaintiff's charge of discriminatory intent.[8]

Statutory Standards

Because of the difficulty in proving discriminatory intent in constitutional cases, plaintiffs have recently relied primarily on federal civil rights statutes to challenge allegedly biased employment practices; some civil rights laws apply to private as well as public employers, so they have broader application than the equal protection clause. A substantial amount of litigation has been based on Title VII of the Civil Rights Act of 1964, which prohibits employers with fifteen or more employees, employment agencies, and labor organizations from discriminating against employees on the basis of race, color, religion, sex, or national origin. Title VII covers hiring, promotion, and compensation practices as well as fringe benefits and other terms and conditions of employment.[9] The law allows employers to impose hiring restrictions based on sex, national origin, or religion (but not on race), if such characteristics are bona fide occupational qualifications.

Assuming that a plaintiff satisfies the procedural requisites to file a Title VII suit,[10] there remains the difficult substantive task of proving that specific employment practices have violated the act. The plaintiff has the burden of establishing an initial or prima facie case of discrimination. A prima facie case raises an inference of discrimination, which if unexplained, is "more likely than not based on the consideration of impermissible factors."[11] The judiciary often has been called on to interpret the nature of proof required to establish and rebut claims of unlawful discrimination under Title VII and to determine the appropriate remedy when Title VII violations have been substantiated.

Two legal doctrines have been developed for assessing the merits of claims of employment discrimination under Title VII, and these doctrines also have been applied under civil rights laws prohibiting discrimination based on age and handicaps. The first pertains to allegations of *discriminatory treatment* predicated on a protected characteristic (e.g., race or sex). In such cases, proof of the employer's discriminatory motive is required, which is similar to the constitutional standard of proof under the equal protection clause. Once a prima facie case of disparate treatment is established, the employer can rebut the inference of discrimination by articulating a nondiscriminatory reason for the action. If the employer is successful in producing such a nondiscriminatory reason, the plaintiff then must prove that the asserted legitimate reason is a mere pretext for discrimination. The Supreme Court has recognized that the employer is not required to accord preference to minorities and women among equally qualified applicants or to persuade the judiciary that it had convincing, objective reasons for selecting a certain applicant. Instead, the employer bears only the burden of explaining clearly and specifically the nondiscriminatory reasons for the action.[12] The burden of persuasion remains with the plaintiff to prove intentional discrimination by a preponderance of evidence. In 1982 the Supreme Court declared that discriminatory intent means actual motive and is not a legal presumption to be drawn from a factual showing of something less than motive.[13]

The second Title VII doctrine pertains to cases involving *neutral* employment policies that have a *disparate impact* on a protected group. In these cases, proof of discriminatory intent is *not* necessary. After a prima facie case of disparate impact is established, the burden shifts to the employer to prove that the policy has a "manifest relationship" to the job.[14] Assuming that the employer demonstrates such a business necessity for a practice with a disparate impact on a protected group, the plaintiff might still prevail by showing that the employer's legitimate interest can be served through less discriminatory means.[15]

Because it is more difficult to prove discrimination in disparate *treatment* than in disparate *impact* cases, the court's assessment of the nature of the charge presented often is important in determining the outcome of the case. Yet, the distinction between the two types of discrimination is not always clear, and legal principles pertaining to the burden of proof in disparate treatment cases are still evolving. The remainder of this chapter focuses on judicial interpretations of both constitutional and statutory standards in assessing specific types of alleged discrimination in employment.

DISCRIMINATION BASED ON RACE OR NATIONAL ORIGIN

The criteria discussed in the preceding section have been applied in assessing a variety of claims of racial or national origin discrimination in public employment. Cases have been initiated by minorities challenging prerequisites to employment; hiring, promotion, and dismissal decisions; compensation practices; or the application of seniority systems. In addition, the operation of affirmative action programs has resulted in claims of discrimination against the racial majority, often referred to as "reverse discrimination." While most of the cases have involved alleged discrimination against blacks, the legal principles apply to other racial and ethnic minorities as well.[16]

Test Requirements as a Condition of Employment

Controversies involving prerequisites to employment have focused primarily on the use of examinations that eliminate a disproportionate percentage of minorities from the applicant pool. Challenges to such practices on equal protection grounds have been rejected if substantiated that the use of the test is rationally related to a legitimate objective and not accompanied by discriminatory motive. In the leading case, the Supreme Court in 1976 endorsed the use of a written skills test as an entrance requirement for the Washington, D.C., police training program, even though the test had a disparate adverse impact on black applicants. The Court reasoned that the test was directly related to requirements of the training program; a positive relationship between test results and training school performance was sufficient to validate the test. Finding no intentional discrimination, the Court held that the practice did not violate the Federal Constitution.[17]

More recently, the Supreme Court affirmed a lower court's conclusion that South Carolina's use of the National Teachers Examination (NTE) for teacher certification and salary purposes satisfied fourteenth amendment equal protection guarantees since the test had a rational relationship to the legitimate purpose of improving the effectiveness of the state's teaching force and was not administered with any intent to discriminate against minority applicants for teacher certification.[18] The trial court was satisfied that the test was valid in that it measured knowledge of course content in teacher preparation programs. The court further reasoned that there was sufficient evidence to establish a relationship between the use of the test scores in determining teachers' placement on the pay scale and legitimate employment objectives such as encouraging teachers to upgrade their skills.

In 1986 the Fifth Circuit Court of Appeals overturned a preliminary injunction against using a basic skills competency test as a prerequisite to enrollment in teacher education programs in Texas.[19] The lower court had reasoned that the minority plaintiffs were likely to prevail on their claim that use of the competency test (which disproportionately disqualifies black and Hispanic applicants to teacher education programs) violates a 1971 desegregation order in that it unconstitutionally deprives minority elementary and secondary school pupils of access to minority teachers. Ruling that the district court abused its discretion in issuing the injunction, the appeals court reasoned that a state is not obligated to educate or certify teachers who cannot pass a valid test of basic skills necessary for professional training. Noting that the state presented considerable evidence to establish the test's validity, the court concluded that plaintiffs would have to prove intentional discrimination to substantiate a constitutional violation.

Since employers can rebut an inference of purposeful discrimination under the equal protection clause by showing that the challenged test is rationally related to the attainment of a legitimate governmental objective, the plaintiff's burden of proving unlawful motive is difficult to satisfy. Some employment testing programs, however, have been invalidated under the equal protection clause as lacking the requisite rational relationship. The Fifth Circuit Court of Appeals found that the use of a specified score on the Graduate Record Examination (GRE) as a prerequisite to employment in a Mississippi school district was not rationally related to the objective of ensuring competent teachers. Noting that the GRE is not a reliable or valid measure of teacher effectiveness, the court held that the test "has no reasonable function in the teacher selection process."[20] Subsequently, a Georgia federal district court struck down the use of a minimum NTE score as an alternate criterion for attaining an advanced certification level, reasoning that the practice was arbitrary and not rationally related to its intended purpose.[21]

While plaintiffs in relatively few cases have established that prerequisites to employment impair rights protected by the Federal Constitution,[22] they have been more successful in proving a Title VII violation in connection with facially neutral requirements with a *disparate impact* on minorities. In *Griggs v. Duke Power Company,* the Supreme Court found that the use of a test of general intelligence as a prerequisite to employment violated Title VII because the requirement disproportionately eliminated minority applicants and was not proven to be a business necessity. The Court held that "the consequences of employment practices, not simply motivation," must be considered in assessing the legality of such requirements having an adverse impact on minorities.[23] In this 1971 case, the Court did not prohibit the use of tests *per se,* but concluded that the employer must substantiate that tests used as a condition of employment are related to job performance in order to satisfy Title VII.

In a subsequent case, the Court elaborated on the Title VII requirement that tests must be validated for the specific jobs for which they are used. The Court concluded that a company's test validation study, which used experienced, white workers, could not be used to validate a test designed for job applicants who were primarily inexperienced and nonwhite. Also, the Court noted that a test cannot be used for jobs other than those for which it has been professionally validated unless there are "no significant differences" between the jobs.[24] The Court further held that if employee rankings by supervisors are compared with employees' test scores in validating the test, there must be clear job performance criteria applied by all supervisors.

In a significant 1982 decision, the Supreme Court ruled that if prerequisites to employment or promotion (e.g., tests) have a disparate impact on minorities and are not substantiated as job-related, they abridge Title VII even though the "bottom line" of the hiring or promotion process results in an appropriate racial balance.[25] While acknowledging that evidence of a nondiscriminatory work force might in some instances assist an employer in rebutting a charge of unconstitutional motive, the Court majority reasoned that the "bottom line" makeup of the work force is immaterial in a disparate impact case. The Court declared that where "an identifiable pass-fail barrier denies an employment opportunity to a disproportionately large number of minorities and prevents them from proceeding to the next step in the selection process," that barrier must be shown to be job-related to satisfy Title VII.[26] The majority noted that Congress did not intend to give an employer license to discriminate against some employees on the basis of race or sex merely because other members of the protected group are favorably treated.[27]

In several school cases, courts have relied on Title VII in concluding that specific tests with an adverse racial impact cannot be used in making employment decisions without proof of the business necessity for the practice. For example, the Second Circuit Court of Appeals upheld a district court's ruling that examinations for supervisory positions in the New York City School District had a disparate impact on minorities and were not empirically substantiated as job-related.[28] The Fourth Circuit Court of Appeals also enjoined a school district's use of a specified score on the NTE in making hiring and retention decisions in the absence of proper validation studies and job analyses.[29]

Similarly, a federal district court granted a preliminary injunction against the use of the NTE by the Mobile County, Alabama School Board to determine whether untenured teachers would be retained.[30] The plaintiff teachers, whose contracts were not renewed based on their low NTE scores (despite positive ratings from their principals), alleged racial discrimination because the test requirement resulted in more black than white teachers being released. The court found that the cutoff score for hiring and retaining teachers had not been properly validated in that no evidence was presented to substantiate that those scoring higher on the test performed better than those with low scores. Thus, the school district was ordered to reemploy the nontenured teachers who would have been retained except for their low test scores. Subsequently, in 1986 the court approved a consent decree enjoining the school district from ever using the NTE or any other written examination in the hiring, reemployment, or promotion of teachers if the test has an adverse racial impact and has not been properly validated.[31]

Recently, a class action suit was also initiated in Alabama, charging that the state's use of standardized tests as a prerequisite to teacher certification impermissibly discriminates against minorities. The district court initially upheld a settlement agreement, but subsequently ruled that the agreement was not enforceable because it did not have the written consent of the state board of education.[32] On appeal, the Eleventh Circuit Court of Appeals reinstated the settlement, concluding that the state board had agreed to its terms, even though not in writing.[33] Among other things, the agreement requires the state to develop new subject area tests, discontinue use of its professional knowledge test, appoint a panel of experts to oversee the test development process, and assess the racial impact of test items. The agreement also requires the state to set lower passing scores on the current tests until the new examinations are developed and to award certificates and monetary damages to black applicants who have been denied certification because they failed the professional knowledge test.

Although aggrieved employees have a greater likelihood of prevailing in disparate impact cases because proof of intentional discrimination is not required (as it is in disparate treatment claims), an employer's burden of establishing a business necessity for policies with a disparate racial impact is not impossible to satisfy. For example, in the South Carolina case discussed previously, the Supreme Court affirmed the trial court's holding that Title VII as well as the equal protection clause did not preclude the use of the NTE for certification and salary purposes to further the legitimate objective of assuring more competent teachers.[34] Subsequently, in a similar case, the Fourth Circuit Court of Appeals found no constitutional or Title VII violation in connection with a school district's use of certification levels based on scores on the NTE to determine teachers' salaries.[35] Despite the fact that the use of certification grades resulted in the denial of pay raises to a disproportionate number of black teachers, the appellate court reasoned that the practice was justified by the job necessity of attracting the most qualified teachers and encouraging self-improvement among low-rated instructional personnel. Rejecting the contention that there were less discriminatory means available to attain the employer's objectives, the court observed that the use of test scores to make decisions regarding certification grades posed less potential for bias than did the use of subjective ratings by principals.

With the increasing legislative interest in assuring teacher competence, it seems likely that additional state and local education agencies will consider test requirements as a prerequisite to certification and admission to teacher education programs, as a criterion for the award of merit pay, and as a condition of recertification. Such mandates, particularly the required passage of examinations by practicing teachers to determine whether they will retain their jobs, seem destined to generate future discrimination claims.[36] Public employers would be wise to ensure that any tests used to determine job opportunities or benefits have been properly validated and serve legitimate objectives.

Screening, Dismissal, and Compensation Practices

In addition to alleged discriminatory prerequisites to employment, individuals often have claimed that employment decisions have been racially motivated. Discrimination charges in hiring and promotion processes have been particularly troublesome for the judiciary because of the subjective judgments involved. Courts have been reluctant to strip employers of their prerogatives to base decisions on personality and other subjective factors, but, the judiciary also has recognized that "greater possibilities for abuse . . . are inherent in subjective definitions of employment selection and promotion criteria" because of the potential for masking racial discrimination.[37]

In a 1973 decision, *McDonnell Douglas v. Green,* the Supreme Court provided criteria for establishing a prima facie case of disparate treatment in hiring: A plaintiff must show membership in a racial minority, rejection for a position for which he or she is qualified, and that the employer continued to seek similarly qualified applicants after rejecting the plaintiff.[38] Once the plaintiff establishes a prima facie case of discrimination, the burden shifts to the employer. This prima facie showing under *McDonnell Douglas* criteria does not mean that discrimination under Title VII ultimately will be established. It only raises an inference of discriminatory hiring practices that, if unexplained by the employer, can be used to substantiate discrimination. To rebut a claim, the Supreme Court has held that the employer must "articulate some legitimate, nondiscriminatory reason for the employee's rejection."[39] The plaintiff is then provided with an opportunity to refute the employer's evidence. The judiciary has recognized that the employer's burden is "merely a burden of production," and "the burden of persuasion remains at all times with the plaintiff."[40]

Courts have accepted employers' asserted nondiscriminatory reasons for denying employment or promotion to racial and ethnic minorities and for other differential treatment if the individuals have not been qualified for the positions sought or if the decisions have been based on quality of performance or other considerations unrelated to race and ethnic background. In an illustrative case, the Ninth Circuit Court of Appeals ruled that even if a Mexican-American curriculum supervisor had been able to establish an inference of discrimination, the school board's evidence that the supervisor was not able to work well with other employees was sufficient to satisfy its burden of articulating a legitimate nondiscriminatory reason for nonrenewal of her contract.[41] Similarly, the Fifth Circuit Court of Appeals found no discrimination in a school board's demotion of a black principal to a teaching position at a reduced salary for willful neglect of duty and incompetence. The principal had instructed teachers to keep certain students from participating in a mandatory proficiency testing program.[42]

Plaintiffs, however, have prevailed upon a proper showing that an avowed nondiscriminatory reason was merely pretextual to mask a discriminatory motive. For example, the Eleventh Circuit Court of Appeals affirmed a lower court's finding that a school board's nondiscriminatory reasons for its employment practices were pretextual. The courts reasoned that over a period of years the school board appointed less qualified white persons to administrative positions and refused to consider seriously the minority plaintiff for any such positions. The plaintiff was awarded back pay and compensatory damages; in addition, punitive damages were assessed against the superintendent for intentional racial discrimination.[43] Employees need not be racial minorities to invoke Title VII's protection against discrimination; in several school cases, white employees have gained relief where they have substantiated that personnel actions were racially motivated.[44] In addition, individuals have substantiated national origin discrimination where they have suffered adverse employment consequences because of their foreign language accents in the absence of evidence that such accents impede job performance.[45]

Compensation discrepancies based on race clearly offend Title VII.

In 1986 the Supreme Court ruled in a nonschool case that a public employer was guilty of violating Title VII by paying black employees less than whites occupying the same positions. Even though the salary disparity originated before Title VII became applicable to public employment, the Court reasoned that the discriminatory practice was perpetuated after this date in that the employer did not remedy the disparity.[46] In essence, the Court concluded that preact salary discrimination must be eradicated for employers to be in compliance with Title VII. The Court further noted that the plaintiff's regression analyses need not include *all* measurable variables that have an effect on salary level to be admissible as evidence to establish compensation discrimination. If a regression analysis includes major factors, it may serve to prove a plaintiff's case when considered in conjunction with other evidence.

Statistical analyses also have played an important role for both plaintiffs and defendants in hiring discrimination cases. Minority employees have used statistics pertaining to the racial composition of the labor market in establishing either a pattern of discrimination or a prima facie case, and employers have rebutted discrimination charges by substantiating that the racial mix of their employees reflects the composition of the work force. The Supreme Court has noted that the usefulness of statistics depends on the circumstances of each case, and it is commonly known that statistics can be used selectively to prove almost any point. This has been demonstrated in cases where the plaintiffs and defendants, by comparing different population groups and time periods, have used the same data to support claims of both discriminatory and nondiscriminatory practices.

Title VII does not require that a work force mirror the racial composition of the local labor market, but a substantial discrepancy may be a strong indicator of the existence of employment discrimination. For example, the Supreme Court held that the discrepancy between the racial composition of the teaching staff and the composition of the teacher applicant pool in the area established a pattern and practice of discriminatory hiring practices in the Hazelwood, Missouri School District. The Court held that a comparison between the black teaching force and the black pupils in the district was irrelevant in establishing a Title VII violation.[47] More recently, the Court has reiterated that minority representation in the student body is not the standard by which to assess employment discrimination; the appropriate comparison is with the relevant labor pool.[48]

Seniority Adjustments for Discrimination Victims

Seniority credit is increasingly important to employees because it frequently is the basis for determining fringe benefits, priority lists for promotions and other job opportunities, and the order of personnel layoffs and recall privileges. Seniority rights often have become the focus of controversy after an employer has been found guilty of employment discrimination under Title VII. Plaintiffs, who have been victims of discriminatory hiring and promotion practices, have sought retroactive or constructive seniority to restore them to their proper place in relation to other employees.

Title VII insulates seniority systems from disparate impact suits to the extent that employers are allowed to "apply different standards of compensation, or different terms, conditions, or privileges of employment pursuant to a bona fide seniority or merit system" as long as *intentional discrimination* is not involved.[49] Substantial Title VII litigation has focused on the scope of immunity provided to seniority systems under Title VII and whether equitable relief to compensate for prior discrimination can include seniority adjustments.

In a significant 1976 decision, the Supreme Court held that minority plaintiffs who were denied employment because of race after the effective date of Title VII were entitled to priority hiring with retroactive seniority to the date of their rejected applications.[50] The Court did not order the employer to modify its negotiated seniority system, but rather to award seniority that the plaintiffs would have earned in the absence of the discriminatory practice to make them "whole." Without retroactive seniority for the hiring discrimination, the Court reasoned that the plaintiffs could never obtain their rightful place in the seniority hierarchy. The burden was placed on the company to prove that individuals who reapplied for the jobs in question had not been victims of the discriminatory hiring practice.

In the latter 1960s and early 1970s, several federal appellate courts awarded retroactive seniority to individuals where neutral seniority systems perpetuated discrimination, even though the discriminatory practices occurred *prior* to the effective date of Title VII. However, in 1977 the Supreme Court ruled that a bona fide seniority system does not become unlawful simply because it operates to "freeze" the adverse impact of pre-Title VII discrimination.[51] The Court reasoned that the seniority system at issue was negotiated and maintained free from any discriminatory intent, even though it perpetuated an advantage given to white employees who had accumulated greater seniority than minority employees who were victims of pre-Title VII discrimination in a particular job category. While barring relief for minority applicants who suffered only preact discrimination, the Court held that victims of postact discrimination in a specific job category were entitled to seniority adjustments to restore them to their rightful place in the seniority hierarchy.[52]

More recently, the Supreme Court recognized that proof of discriminatory intent is necessary to invalidate seniority systems established before or *after* the effective date of Title VII. The majority noted that if postact seniority systems were subjected to disparate impact suits, employers would be discouraged from modifying preact systems to make them more equitable.[53] Although courts seem increasingly inclined to give deference to negotiated collective bargaining agreements in concluding that challenged seniority systems are bona fide, it is not impossible for plaintiffs to establish a Title VII violation where a given seniority system was established with the intent and effect of having a disparate impact on minority workers.[54]

Since legal proceedings in discrimination suits often are quite lengthy, some employers charged with hiring discrimination have attempted to reduce their potential liability by remedying the alleged discriminatory practice before being judicially ordered to do so. Whether such job offers must include retroactive seniority has been controversial. In 1982 the Supreme Court resolved the controversy by ruling that an employer can toll the continuing accrual of back pay liability under Title VII by unconditionally offering the claimant the job previously denied, and the offer need not include retroactive seniority to the date of the alleged refusal to hire.[55] The Court majority reasoned that without such an opportunity to reduce back pay liability, employers charged with engaging in discrimination have no incentive to initiate corrective action before the suit is resolved. Declaring that Title VII does not entitle a claimant to be "catapulted" into a better position simply because of alleged discrimination, the Court stated that to require job offers to include retroactive seniority would have the "perverse result of requiring the employer in effect to insure the claimant against the risk that the employer might win at trial."[56] Of course, if the claimant accepts the unconditional job offer and ultimately wins a favorable judicial ruling, the court may award retroactive seniority and back pay to the date of the unlawful refusal to hire.

Affirmative Action Plans

Affirmative action is a concept that has been embodied in presidential executive orders, legislation, and court rulings. The United States Commission on Civil Rights has defined affirmative action as "steps taken to remedy the grossly disparate staffing and recruitment patterns that are the present consequences of past discrimination and to prevent the occurrence of employment discrimination in the future."[57] The term "affirmative action" is most often used to refer to the development of a systematic plan with goals and timetables designed to eliminate employment discrimination.

The initial federal executive orders were general pronouncements prohibiting discrimination in federal employment and in companies and institutions holding federal contracts, but, by the 1960s, it was clear that employment discrimination would not be curbed without *affirmative steps* to recruit and retain employees from underrepresented groups. Executive orders signed by Presidents Kennedy and Johnson strengthened affirmative action requirements and penalties for noncompliance. Executive Order 11246 of 1965, which has subsequently been revised several times, requires institutions with federal contracts of $50,000 or more and fifty or more employees to develop written affirmative action plans with numerical goals and timetables.

In addition to the federal executive orders, federal antidiscrimination laws and funding provisions have furthered the concept of affirmative action. Some federal laws specifically require affirmative action, such as the Education for All Handicapped Children Act (EAHCA), which places a duty on education agencies receiving funds under the act to take positive steps to employ qualified handicapped persons in programs assisted with EAHCA funds.[58] Often, affirmative action plans have been developed by school boards as a result of a judicial finding of unconstitutional school segregation or prior intentional discrimination in personnel practices. In other instances, employers have voluntarily adopted such plans or agreed to affirmative action goals and timetables in collective bargaining agreements in the absence of a judicial finding of legal liability for prior discrimination. Affirmative action plans designed to expand employment opportunities for underrepresented groups have not been controversial; disputes have focused on plans entailing preferential treatment that results in the denial of employment opportunities to individuals who are not members of the protected classes.[59]

In a number of cases, nonminorities have relied on the Federal Constitution and Title VII in contesting affirmative action plans that call for modifications in seniority systems to give preference to minorities in eligibility for promotion and other job benefits or in protection from personnel reductions. Such affirmative action plans, similar to awards of retroactive seniority, have an impact on the competitive status of employees. However, in contrast to seniority adjustments for *individual* discrimination victims, *class* remedies benefit certain class members who have not personally suffered discrimination. Such preferential treatment of minorities has been challenged as resulting in "reverse" discrimination, that is, discrimination against nonminorities that occurs in the process of attempting to remedy the effects of prior bias against minorities.[60]

These claims raise complex issues that do not lend themselves to simple solutions. Can employers voluntarily adopt affirmative action plans that would not be permissible for courts to impose? Is there a legal distinction between preferential treatment of racial minorities in hiring practices in contrast to personnel reduction plans? Can employment quotas in school settings be defended as necessary to guarantee *students'* rights to equal educational opportunities? To date, only partial answers to these and related questions have been provided by the Supreme Court.

Preferential Treatment in Hiring and Promotion Practices. In 1979 the Supreme Court confronted the issue of "reverse" discrimination under Title VII in connection with a company's *voluntary* affirmative action program imposing racial quotas in an on-the-job training program. In this case, *Kaiser Aluminum and Chemical Corporation v. Weber,* the Court did not address what Title VII requires or what a court might order, but "whether Title VII *forbids* private employers and unions from voluntarily agreeing upon bona fide affirmative action plans that accord racial preference."[61] The Court held that Title VII's prohibition against racial discrimination does not condemn all private, voluntary, race-conscious affirmative action plans to correct a racial imbalance in traditionally segregated jobs. Although Title VII stipulates that nothing contained in the law shall be interpreted to "require" employers to grant preferential treatment based on race to remedy a de facto racial imbalance among employees, the Court concluded that if Congress had intended to *prohibit* all race-conscious affirmative action, it would have substituted the phrase "require or permit" for the word "require in the law."[62] While not defining precisely the line of demarcation between permissible and impermissible affirmative action plans under Title VII, the Court ruled that the company's challenged plan was on the permissible side of the line. The purposes of the plan mirrored those of Title VII and did not "unnecessarily trammel" the interests of white employees. It neither required white workers to be discharged and replaced with new black hirees, nor created an absolute bar to the advancement of white employees because half of those trained in the program were white. Moreover, the plan was a temporary measure, not intended to maintain a specific racial balance, but simply to eliminate a manifest racial imbalance.[63]

Although *Weber* involved a private company, in numerous subsequent cases federal appellate courts have upheld voluntary affirmative action plans entailing minority preferences in hiring, promotion, and assignment of *public* employees.[64] The courts have reasoned that such plans are permissible as long as they are necessary to remedy *chronic* and *substantial* minority underrepresentation in the work force even though the employer has not been found legally liable for prior discrimination. The plans, however, must be fair and reasonable to nonminorities in that they are temporary, do not require the discharge of nonminorities, or bar the advancement of nonminorities.

In two 1986 decisions of first impression, the Supreme Court endorsed the concept of voluntary and court-ordered, race-conscious remedies in hiring and promotion practices. In one case, a labor union, joined by the United States Solicitor General, contested a consent decree that had been agreed to by the city of Cleveland and an organization of black and Hispanic firefighters (Vanguards).[65] The decree, adopted by the federal district court, called for the creation of additional promotion opportunities for all firefighters and specified promotion goals in terms of racial percentages for each rank of firefighters. Affirming the Sixth Circuit Court of Appeals' conclusion that the decree was reasonable, the Supreme Court held that, regardless of whether Title VII precludes a court from imposing certain forms of race-conscious relief after a trial, such relief is not precluded in a consent decree. The court further rejected the contention that the consent decree between the city and Vanguards was invalid because it was entered without the union's consent. Noting that the intervenor union was entitled to present evidence and have its objections aired at the hearings on whether to approve the consent decree, the Supreme Court held that the intervenor did not have the power to block a decree that imposed no legal duties or obligations on the union.

In the companion case, the Supreme Court held that federal courts can *order* affirmative race-conscious relief (that benefits individuals who may not have been discrimination victims) to vindicate Title VII rights. The federal district court had found a labor union guilty of a pattern of discrimination against nonwhite workers in recruitment, selection, training, and admission to the union. The court ordered the union to cease its discriminatory practices and admit a certain percentage (29 percent) of nonminorities. After the union was found in contempt of the court's order for numerous violations, the district court imposed a $150,000 fine to be placed in a fund designed to increase minority membership in the apprenticeship program and in the union. The court also entered an amended affirmative action plan, extending the time for the union to meet the 29 percent minority membership goal, abolishing the apprenticeship examination, and requiring the union to assign one apprentice for every four journeymen and to select one minority apprentice for each white apprentice. The Second Circuit Court of Appeals, and subsequently the Supreme Court, affirmed the contempt order and amended affirmative action plan with one modification (removing the requirement that one minority apprentice be identified for every white apprentice). Noting that the plan did not conflict with a bona fide seniority system and was imposed to remedy egregious, intentional discrimination, the Supreme Court majority declared that "the use of numerical goals provides a compromise between two unacceptable alternatives: an outright ban on hiring or promotions, or continued use of a discriminatory selection procedure."[66] The Court recognized that an employer or union would not violate Title VII by having a racially imbalanced work force and that a court could not order an employer to adopt racial preferences merely to correct such an imbalance. However, the majority reasoned that Congress did not intend to limit a court from exercising its remedial authority where an employer or union has engaged in egregious, intentional discrimination or where such a remedy is necessary to dissipate the effects of pervasive discrimination.[67] Also rejecting the contention that the affirmative action plan violated federal constitutional guarantees, the Court observed that the plan in question was narrowly tailored to further the compelling governmental interest in remedying past discrimination.

In both of these cases, the Supreme Court noted that the challenged affirmative action plans were temporary, did not require unqualified minorities to be hired or nonminorities to be fired, and did not bar advancement opportunities for nonminorities. The Court also recognized that the purpose of affirmative action is to dismantle prior patterns of employment discrimination and prevent such discrimination in the future rather than to make identified discrimination victims "whole." It thus rejected the Justice Department's position that race-conscious remedies should be available only to individual victims of discriminatory practices.

Several lower courts have reasoned that temporary employment quotas also can be justified in some situations to remedy school segregation. Racial preferences in hiring and assigning staff have been upheld as part of school desegregation plans to achieve integrated faculties and assure students' constitutional rights to equal educational opportunities. Both court-ordered and voluntary affirmative action plans have survived legal attacks with evidence that the plans were necessary to eliminate the effects of school segregation.[68]

Layoff Quotas. Until recently, the use of quotas in affirmative action plans was usually confined to hiring, promotion, and assignment practices, but provisions addressing personnel layoffs have become increasingly common. Plans that disregard seniority rights to *preserve* a designated percentage of minority employees are particularly troublesome because such preferential treatment can result in nonminorities losing their jobs.

In a significant 1984 decision, the Supreme Court placed restrictions on the authority of federal courts to *impose* racial quotas in personnel layoffs. In this case, *Firefighters Local Union No. 1784 v. Stotts,* the Court held that the federal district court had exceeded its powers in entering an injunction and modifying a consent decree, which required the city to disregard its negotiated seniority system and release white employees with greater seniority than black employees who were retained.[69] The Court majority reasoned that the express terms of the decree agreed to by both parties did not contemplate such an abrogation of seniority rights; the majority rejected the contention that the court order was justified by the unanticipated fiscal exigency requiring layoffs that threatened gains made under the negotiated affirmative action plan. The Court declared that "Title VII precludes a district court from displacing a nonminority employee with seniority under the contractually-established seniority system absent either a finding that the seniority system was adopted with discriminatory intent or a determination that such a remedy was necessary to make whole a proven victim of discrimination."[70]

Recognizing that *individual* discrimination victims can be awarded competitive seniority to restore them to their rightful place, the *Stotts* majority held that a trial court cannot disregard a seniority system in fashioning a *class* remedy where an employer has been found guilty of a pattern or practice of racial discrimination. However, the Court specifically limited its ruling to court-imposed layoff quotas, declining to address whether the city would have run afoul of Title VII if it had *voluntarily* adopted an affirmative action program abrogating seniority rights in reducing personnel.

The *Stotts* decision also did not clarify whether employment layoff quotas can be justified in the school desegregation context where students rather than employees are the identified discrimination victims. In several desegregation cases, courts have reasoned that neither Title VII nor the equal protection clause bars the use of employment quotas in reducing personnel to remedy unconstitutional school segregation. As discussed in chapter 13, the Supreme Court has declined to review two federal appellate rulings in which racial quotas in layoff as well as hiring practices were upheld in desegregation decrees to assure students' constitutional rights to equal educational opportunities.[71] The Second Circuit Court of Appeals declared that Title VII's immunity for seniority systems that are established and maintained without discriminatory intent does not preclude the federal judiciary from ordering modifications in the application of seniority rights to correct unconstitutional school segregation.[72]

In several cases prior to 1986, federal appellate courts also upheld school districts' *voluntary* adoption of racial quotas in layoff policies to advance legitimate interests in "eliminating historic discrimination, promoting racial harmony in the community, and providing role models for minority students."[73] In 1986, however, the Supreme Court in a five-to-four decision struck down a Michigan school district's collective bargaining agreement that protected minority teachers from layoffs to preserve the percentage of minority personnel employed prior to any reductions in force. Five opinions were written in *Wygant v. Jackson Board of Education*–a plurality endorsed by three justices, two concurrences, and two dissenting opinions.[74] The *Wygant* plurality reasoned that the layoff quota system, resulting in the release of some white teachers with greater seniority than black teachers who were retained, violated the equal protection clause. "Societal discrimination" alone was found to be insufficient to justify the class preferential treatment. Recognizing that racial classifications in employment must be justified by a compelling governmental purpose and means must be narrowly tailored to accomplish that purpose, the plurality concluded that the layoff provision in question did not satisfy either of these conditions. The plurality further rejected the lower courts' reliance on the "role model" theory–tying the percentage of minority teachers to the percentage of minority students to ensure appropriate role models.[75] Noting that the proper comparison for determining employment discrimination is between the racial composition of the teaching staff and the relevant labor market, the plurality reasoned that use of the role model theory would allow school boards to go far beyond legitimate remedial purposes.

Concluding that employment quotas cannot be adopted in the absence of convincing evidence of prior discrimination, the plurality recognized, however, that certain circumstances may necessitate race-conscious remedies. The plurality also made a distinction between layoff quotas and hiring goals, indicating that the latter would be easier to justify in the absence of liability for past discrimination. Observing that the Jackson School Board had "less intrusive means" available to further its desegregation objectives, the plurality declared that hiring goals do not impose the substantial injury associated with layoff quotas: "Denial of a future employment opportunity is not as intrusive as loss of an existing job."[76]

Although the Supreme Court has endorsed temporary class remedies in hiring and promotion practices, the *Wygant* decision coupled with the *Stotts* ruling suggests that racial quotas in layoff policies will be carefully scrutinized by the federal judiciary. Given the *Wygant* plurality's clear preference for less burdensome means to achieve affirmative action goals, it is likely that employers will be reluctant to adopt layoff quotas. The Supreme Court, however, has not foreclosed the legitimacy of class preferences in staff reduction practices. Conceivably, a majority of the justices would have upheld the Jackson School Board's affirmative action plan if the racial quotas had been imposed to remedy prior employment discrimination, measured by a statistical discrepancy between the teaching staff and the available labor market.[77] Also, the Court has not clarified whether the necessary predicate for layoff quotas in employment can be established where a school district is operating under a court-ordered desegregation plan to eliminate unconstitutional school segregation. The Supreme Court seems destined to be called on to provide further clarification regarding the conditions under which class remedies might be justified in reducing personnel, and until it does, the legality of racial quotas in layoff policies will remain in doubt.

SEX DISCRIMINATION

Until the 1970s, unequal treatment in employment based on sex was legally sanctioned, reflected in sex-based differences in working conditions, compensation, prerequisites to employment, and work-related benefits. A statement from an 1873 case is illustrative of the prevailing judicial attitude through much of the twentieth century toward differential treatment of men and women.

> Man is, or should be, woman's protector and defender. The natural and proper timidity and delicacy which belong to the female sex evidently unfits it for many of the occupations of civil life. The constitution of the family organization, which is founded in the divine ordinance, as well as in the nature of things, indicates the domestic sphere as that which properly belongs to the domain and functions of womanhood. The harmony, not to say

> identity, of interest and views which belong, or should belong, to the family institution is repugnant to the idea of a woman adopting a distinct and independent career from that of her husband. . . .[78]

Along with gains in securing equal rights for minorities, the earlier status of women has given way to a recognition of greater equality in employment. Extensive litigation based on constitutional and statutory guarantees has challenged sex-based classifications that impose unequal employment burdens on female employees.

Although many discriminatory practices have been invalidated under the fourteenth amendment, sex has not been designated a "suspect class," as has race, and thus does not trigger strict judicial scrutiny under the equal protection clause. This distinction is critical in judicial review, for if sex were elevated to a "suspect class," a compelling justification would be required for any governmental classifications based on gender. In recent sex discrimination cases, the Supreme Court has not reverted to the lenient equal protection standard of review which requires the government to show only a rational relationship between classifications and a legitimate governmental purpose. Instead, the Court has applied an intermediate standard, requiring classifications based on sex to bear a "close and substantial relationship to important governmental objectives."[79]

For example, in 1982 the Supreme Court struck down a state university's policy that restricted enrollment in its nursing school to women. Noting that the policy was not substantially related to important governmental objectives, the Court majority declared that there must be "an exceedingly persuasive justification" for such classifications. The majority rejected the contention that the single-sex admission policy was a justifiable affirmative action effort to compensate for past discrimination against women, finding instead that the policy "tends to perpetuate the stereotyped view of nursing as an exclusively woman's job."[80]

While discriminatory sex-based classifications have been struck down under the intermediate equal protection standard, the mere disparate impact of a facially neutral law on men or women is not sufficient to abridge equal protection guarantees. To illustrate, in 1979 the Supreme Court ruled that the Massachusetts Veterans Preference Statute, which has a disparate impact on women, satisfies the equal protection clause.[81] The statute, giving absolute preference to veterans (98% are males) in civil service positions, was found to be gender neutral because it classifies individuals on veteran status and not on sex. Recognizing that the adverse impact of the law on women was foreseeable when the statute was written, the Court nonetheless concluded that the legislation was not *designed* to exclude women from civil service positions. In the absence of discriminatory motive, the Court found no violation of the equal protection clause.

As with claims of racial discrimination, the difficult burden of establishing unconstitutional motive has caused most plaintiffs in sex-bias suits to rely on federal statutory guarantees, specifically the Equal Pay Act of 1963, Title VII of the Civil Rights Act of 1964, and Title IX of the Education Amendments of 1972. Numerous employment concerns have generated statutory sex-bias suits, and several topics of particular importance to educators are discussed in this section.

Hiring and Promotion Practices

Charges of sex bias in hiring, promotion, job assignment, and other conditions of employment have generally been initiated under Title VII. As mentioned previously, employers can defend a facially discriminatory hiring policy under Title VII with proof that gender is a bona fide occupational qualification (BFOQ) necessary to the normal operation of the business. While this type of sex discrimination is usually not at issue in public employment, the BFOQ exception to Title VII has generated some litigation. For example, in 1971 the Supreme Court ruled that an employer could not deny employment to women with preschool-age children while hiring men with such children without establishing that the policy was justified as a legitimate BFOQ.[82] More recently, however, the Supreme Court of Montana held that gender was a bona fide occupational qualification for a second guidance counselor position because of the compelling need to give students an opportunity to discuss very private and personal matters with either a male or female counselor.[83]

Only a few cases have involved sex-based challenges to facially *neutral* prerequisites to employment, and these cases have not focused on examinations—the central target in racial discrimination suits. Such sex-bias suits have primarily entailed allegations that physical requirements (e.g., height and weight specifications) adversely affect women. Courts have struck down such physical prerequisites under Title VII if employers have not substantiated a legitimate business necessity for the requirements.[84]

Most sex-bias suits in public employment have involved allegations that women have been treated unfairly solely because of their sex, thus requiring proof of intentional discrimination. In these cases, plaintiffs often have attempted to establish a prima facie case of disparate treatment by presenting both specific and general statistical data. Specific data relate to the individual's qualifications for the job or promotion that was allegedly denied for discriminatory reasons. General data are presented to establish that a prevalent pattern or practice of sex bias exists in the institution. Female plaintiffs have not been able to substantiate a prima facie case of sex discrimination if the labor market data presented do not reflect the number of women actually qualified for the specific jobs in question. Also, statistical disparity data have been rejected where factors other than sex that might account for the employment decision have not been considered.[85]

Public employers have successfully rebutted a prima facie case of sex discrimination by showing that positions were filled by males who were better qualified or as qualified as females who were rejected. The Supreme Court declared in 1981 that employers are not legally obligated under Title VII to give preference to a female applicant when choosing between a male and female with similar credentials.[86] Also, employers have prevailed by showing that hiring or promotion decisions were based on factors other than sex, such as inability to get along with coworkers or inadequate experience, scholarship, or performance.[87]

Plaintiffs, however, have obtained relief where employers have been unable to articulate a nondiscriminatory reason for their actions. Title VII violations have been found with evidence that female applicants were better qualified for specific jobs but were rejected in favor of males because of stereotypic attitudes toward the capabilities of women.[88] Courts have similarly awarded equitable relief where job advertisements have included the phrase, "prefer male," or job descriptions have been specifically drafted to exclude qualified women.[89] In addition, where women have been barred from specific positions, such as coaching boys' sports, courts have intervened.[90]

Even if the employer does produce a nondiscriminatory reason for the employment decision, it is not impossible for the employee to prove that the nondiscriminatory reason is merely pretextual. For example, in 1979 the First Circuit Court of Appeals ruled that a female university professor established that the legitimate reasons offered for her denial of promotion were a pretext for sex bias. Evidence indicated that the plaintiff had been compared to a "school marm" and in other ways judged on her sex rather than merit. Moreover, the court found that evidence of a general atmosphere of sex bias in the institution, although not proof *per se* of disparate treatment, could be considered "along with any other evidence bearing on motive" in assessing whether the defendant's reasons were pretexts for discrimination.[91] More recently, the Seventh Circuit Court of Appeals vacated a trial court's ruling and remanded a case for a determination of whether an employee was discharged in retaliation for contesting the school board's salary policy. The appeals court rejected the trial court's position that *any* reason offered by the employer would suffice to discharge its burden of articulating a nondiscriminatory reason for its personnel action.[92]

Pregnancy-Related Policies

Since pregnancy affects only women, disadvantages in employment that accrue because of this condition have generated numerous charges of sex bias under federal and state constitutional and statutory provisions. Courts have been called upon to address dismissals based on employees' pregnant status and the treatment of pregnancy in disability benefits programs and leave policies.

Pregnancy *per se* cannot be the basis for refusing to hire applicants or for terminating employees. The Fourth Circuit Court of Appeals invalidated a school board's practice of not renewing teachers' contracts where a foreseeable period of absence could be predicted for the ensuing year. The policy had only been applied to pregnant employees who were required to notify school administrators of their pregnancy and anticipated delivery date. This policy was found to impose a disproportionate burden on female teachers.[93]

The exclusion of pregnancy-related disabilities from employee disability benefits programs elicited two Supreme Court rulings and stimulated congressional action in the mid-1970s. The Supreme Court ruled that the differential treatment of pregnancy in disability benefits packages does not constitute sex discrimination and thus satisfies both the Federal Constitution and Title VII.[94] The Court held that the classification involved was based on pregnancy, not on sex, noting that nonpregnant employees included both men and women. In reaction to the Supreme Court's interpretation of Title VII, Congress amended the law in 1978 specifically to prohibit employers from excluding pregnancy benefits in comprehensive medical and disability insurance plans.[95] Under the Pregnancy Discrimination Act (PDA), it is discriminatory for employers to treat pregnancy-related conditions less favorably than other medical conditions. For example, employees are entitled to use sick leave for pregnancy-related illnesses. An Ohio appeals court held that a school board could not require a physician's statement from an employee desiring to use sick leave for pregnancy-related absences but not for other types of illnesses.[96]

Applying the principle that employment policies with a disparate impact on women must be justified as a business necessity to satisfy Title VII, the Supreme Court has ruled that the denial of accumulated seniority upon return from maternity leave violates Title VII.[97] In this case, employees retained seniority rights when on leave for all disabilities except pregnancy. The Court concluded that the policy respecting pregnancy was not on its face discriminatory, but that the impact on employment opportunities for women was discriminatory. The employer failed to establish that the policy was justified by an overriding business need. More recently, the Massachusetts Supreme Court held that maternity leave cannot be considered an interruption in employment for the purposes of accumulating credit toward tenure.[98] However, Title VII cannot be applied retroactively in that individuals who were denied credit toward tenure for maternity leave taken prior to the effective date of Title VII are not entitled to relief.[99]

Prior to 1987 it was unclear whether the PDA required employers to treat pregnancy-related illness the *same* as other illnesses. Some courts reasoned that special leave could not be offered *only* to pregnant workers; employees were entitled to the same treatment for pregnancy as for other prolonged disabilities.[100] However, in 1987 the Supreme Court affirmed a decision in which the Ninth Circuit Court of Appeals interpreted the PDA as allowing a state to enact a law requiring employers to grant employees up to four months of unpaid pregnancy leave. The Court reasoned that the PDA's prohibition against less favorable treatment of pregnancy-related conditions does not preclude a state from affording greater protections than required by Title VII. According to the appeals court, the PDA was intended "to construct a floor beneath which pregnancy disability benefits may not drop" rather than "a ceiling above which they may not rise."[101]

Like benefits for pregnancy-related absences, mandatory pregnancy leave policies have been the subject of litigation. The Supreme Court in *Cleveland Board of Education v. LaFleur* ruled that a compulsory maternity leave policy violated due process rights.[102] At issue in this case was a school board rule requiring every pregnant teacher to take a leave of absence five months prior to the birth of her child and specifying a return date of the next semester after the child reached three months of age. The Court recognized the need for continuity in the classroom instruction but found the arbitrary five-month date to have no relationship to that purpose. The Court concluded that this need could be met by requiring teachers to give "substantial advance notice of their condition."[103] The second ground concerning physical incapacity was invalidated because there was an "irrebuttable presumption" that all pregnant teachers were physically incompetent as of a specified date. Similarly, the Court found the three-month return date following the birth of the child to suffer the same deficiencies.

The Court in *LaFleur* did not prohibit school boards from establishing maternity leave policies but prevented the establishment of arbitrary cutoff dates unrelated to a legitimate state interest. The Ninth Circuit Court of Appeals upheld as reasonable a leave policy that required all teachers to take maternity leave at the beginning of the ninth month of pregnancy.[104] The board adequately demonstrated that the business necessity of obtaining a replacement teacher justified the policy, given the unpredictability of childbirth.

School boards are not required to *ignore* pregnancy in designing personnel policies, but they should insure that pregnancy is not singled out for *less favorable* treatment in leave policies, disability benefits programs, or other conditions of employment. Only if justified by a valid business necessity will courts uphold policies that disadvantage pregnant employees.

Retirement Benefits Programs

Unlike stereotypic assumptions on which many personnel policies have been designed in the past, longevity is a true generalization of women as a class; women live longer than men. Recognition of women's longevity has traditionally resulted in differential treatment of women as a class with respect to retirement benefits. Employers have required women either to make a higher contribution as they pay into a system or to receive lower benefits upon retirement. Such differential treatment has been defended as based on longevity rather than sex.

Recently, this justification has not been persuasive; on two occasions the United States Supreme Court has struck down the use of sex-segregated actuarial tables in retirement benefits programs as constituting sex discrimination in violation of Title VII. In 1978 the Court invalidated a retirement program requiring women to make a higher contribution to receive equal benefits upon retirement, noting that sex was the only factor considered in predicting life expectancy. The Court held that discrimination exists when individuals are treated as "simply components of a racial, religious, sexual, or national class." [105] The Court, however, specifically limited its ruling to retirement plans requiring unequal contributions to an employer-operated pension plan.

In a subsequent decision, the Court invalidated an Arizona retirement program that used sex-segregated actuarial tables in a deferred compensation plan.[106] The Court majority reasoned that the plan violated Title VII because upon retirement, female employees received lower monthly annuity payments than male employees who contributed the same amount. Rejecting the argument that relief was barred because Title VII cannot be used to regulate insurance companies, the majority emphasized that it was not prohibiting companies from using sex-segregated annuity tables. Rather, it was enjoining an employer from contracting with a company to offer a fringe benefit that treats individuals differently because of their sex. The majority concluded that it is as discriminatory "to pay a woman lower benefits when she has made the same contributions as a man as it is to make her pay larger contributions to obtain the same benefits." [107] However, a majority of the justices concluded that relief should not be retroactive in that contributions already made to the fund could be subjected to sex-segregated tables in determining benefits.

Given these two Supreme Court rulings and substantial activity in lower courts,[108] employers would be wise to contract with companies that have eliminated the use of sex-segregated actuarial tables in retirement plans. Responding to judicial pressure,[109] in 1985 the Teachers Insurance and Annuity Association and the College Retirement Equities Fund (TIAA-CREF), which represents 450,000 teachers at more than 3,000 colleges and schools, announced that it would calculate all retirement benefits (retroactive to May 1980) on unisex mortality tables. It seems likely that the judicial reasoning pertaining to retirement benefits may ultimately affect other arenas where sex distinctions have been made in calculating premiums and benefits, such as life insurance programs.

Compensation Practices

Claims of sex discrimination in compensation have been litigated under the Equal Pay Act of 1963 (EPA) and Title VII. The EPA stipulates that all employees are entitled to equal pay for equal work; jobs performed do not have to be identical but must be substantially equal with regard to skills, effort, and responsibilities. Employers can defend compensation differentials under the EPA on the basis of "a seniority system, a merit system, a system which measures earnings by quantity or quality of production, or a differential based on any factor other than sex."[110] Relying on the EPA, courts have invalidated pay differentials between male and female coaches who perform substantially equivalent duties[111] and have struck down other sex-based differentials such as male public school teachers receiving a "head of household" supplement.[112]

In the latter 1970s, federal appellate courts rendered conflicting opinions regarding whether Title VII protections against sex-based discrimination in compensation controversies were limited to the EPA's "equal pay for equal work" standard. In 1981 the Supreme Court rendered an opinion on this issue, ruling that the application of Title VII in compensation controversies is not confined by the Equal Pay Act. In this case, *Gunther v. County of Washington,* female prison matrons challenged the pay discrepancy between matrons and male guards, even though their duties were not equivalent.[113] The employer had conducted a job evaluation study, assessing the responsibilities and working conditions of various positions, and concluded that female guards should be paid 95 percent as much as male guards. Since the matrons were actually paid only 70 percent as much as their male counterparts, the appellate court and subsequently the Supreme Court found evidence of intentional sex discrimination under Title VII.

While the Supreme Court in *Gunther* cautioned that its decision was not based on the controversial notion of "comparable worth," the decision left the door ajar for subsequent Title VII claims of sex-based compensation discrimination beyond claims of unequal pay for equivalent work. A basic premise of the "comparable worth" concept is that the marketplace alone should not govern compensation practices. Instead, jobs should be evaluated and compensation assigned based on the training and skills required, responsibilities, and working conditions. Proponents of the comparable worth theory claim that wage differentials among job classifications reflect sex discrimination rather than an objective assessment of the positions.[114]

To date, however, the judiciary has not found the "comparable worth" doctrine persuasive. The Ninth Circuit Court of Appeals has rendered two decisions specifically rejecting claims of sex discrimination grounded in this theory. In the first case, female faculty members in the School of Nursing at the University of Washington claimed that their lower salaries compared to faculty in other units of the university constituted a Title VII violation.[115] Reasoning that the evidence of a pay disparity between jobs that are only "comparable" does not infer a Title VII violation, the court concluded that intentional discrimination must be proven. The court also rejected the Equal Pay Act claim because the plaintiffs failed to establish that they performed work substantially equal to that performed by male faculty members in other units of the university.

In 1985 the same court reversed a decision in which the federal district court had ordered the state of Washington to implement pay adjustments for civil service positions based on a comparable worth study of 121 job classifications. The study indicated that salaries were less for jobs dominated by women than for jobs of comparable value dominated by men. In spite of this evidence, the Ninth Circuit Court of Appeals ruled that Title VII does not require an employer to provide equal pay for different jobs, even if the employer's own study indicates that the jobs are comparable based on objective criteria.[116] The court reasoned that in the absence of proof of intentional sex discrimination, the state is not obligated to eliminate an economic disparity caused by market factors.

Other courts also have rejected the notion of comparable worth in holding that employers do not have to disregard market considerations in establishing wage rates for different work classifications. For example, the Eighth Circuit Court of Appeals declared that mere evidence that "employees of different sexes receive disparate compensation for work of differing skills that may, subjectively, be of equal value to the employer, but does not command an equal price in the labor market" is not sufficient to establish a prima facie violation of Title VII.[117]

Despite the judiciary's reluctance to accept the comparable worth theory, this concept seems likely to generate additional litigation. In addition, women's groups have pressed for state legislation requiring compensation adjustments for public employees based on an objective analysis of the worth of positions.[118] Even without statutory requirements, many employers, including educational institutions, are voluntarily implementing pay equity studies involving an evaluation of positions according to level of training and skills required, responsibilities, and working conditions. Thus, the notion that comparable jobs should be compensated equally is having an impact on employment practices, even though compensation based on the doctrine of comparable worth has not been required under Title VII.

Sexual Harassment

An emerging area of legal activity under Title VII pertains to claims of sexual harassment in employment. The term sexual harassment is generally used to refer to "repeated and unwelcomed sexual advances, derogatory statements based on . . . sex, or sexually demeaning gestures or acts."[119] Both men and women have been victims of sexual harassment, inflicted by members of the opposite as well as their own sex. While sexual harassment is not a new phenomenon, only recently have claims of such harassment generated litigation.

Initially, courts concluded that claims of sexual harassment were beyond the purview of Title VII,[120] but in the mid-1970s, courts began interpreting Title VII as providing a remedy to victims of sexual harassment that results in adverse employment consequences such as termination, demotion, or denial of other job benefits. Back pay and accompanying employment benefits have been awarded where employers have not successfully rebutted charges that an employee has been terminated or otherwise disadvantaged because of rejection of sexual advances.[121] Employers also have been found in violation of Title VII when they have failed to investigate employee complaints of adverse employment consequences stemming from sexual harassment by individuals in supervisory positions. For example, in 1979 the Ninth Circuit Court of Appeals found a Title VII violation "where the action complained of was that of a supervisor authorized to hire, fire, discipline or promote, or at least to participate in or recommend such actions, even though what the supervisor is said to have done violates company policy."[122] More recently, a Michigan federal district court held that an employer could not plead good faith to foreclose liability if the employer "knowingly acquiesced" in action that clearly violated well-established law prohibiting sexual harassment.[123]

In 1986 the Supreme Court delivered its first decision involving a claim of sexual harassment, recognizing that a Title VII violation can be predicated on either (1) harassment that involves conditioning concrete employment benefits (e.g., promotions) on sexual favors or (2) harassment that creates a hostile or offensive working environment.[124] Rejecting the employer's claim that Title VII's prohibition of sex discrimination is intended to prevent only tangible losses of an economic character, rather than injury from psychological aspects of the working environment, the Court found nothing in Title VII to suggest that a hostile environment based on discriminatory sexual harassment would be permissible under the act. The Court noted that the 1980 guidelines issued by the Equal Employment Opportunity Commission (EEOC) stipulate that conduct with "the purpose or effect of unreasonably interfering with an individual's work performance or creating an intimidating, hostile or offensive working environment" is actionable under Title VII.[125] The Court concluded that the EEOC guidelines allowing redress for noneconomic injuries are fully consistent with existing case law. However, the Court cautioned that "for sexual harassment to be actionable, it must be sufficiently severe or pervasive 'to alter the conditions of [the victim's] employment and create an abusive working environment.' "[126]

The Supreme Court further agreed with the appellate court that the employer could not use as a defense "the fact that sex-related conduct was 'voluntary,' in the sense that the complainant was not forced to participate against her will."[127] However, it rejected the appeals court's conclusion that evidence regarding the victim's sexual fantasies and provocative dress was inadmissible. Finding the crucial consideration to be whether the alleged sexual advances were "unwelcome," the Supreme Court reasoned that evidence regarding the victim's conduct could be relevant in making this determination on remand.

The Court left some ambiguity regarding the employer's liability for the acts of supervisors, declining to endorse the appellate court's position that an employer is *automatically* liable for a hostile environment created by a supervisor's sexual advances, even though the employer could not have reasonably been aware of the alleged misconduct.[128] The Supreme Court noted that Congress surely intended to place some limits on the acts of employees for which employers are liable under Title VII. However, the Court also recognized that the absence of notice to an employer in that the aggrieved employee has not invoked an available grievance procedure would not preclude liability in all circumstances. For example, in this case the company's nondiscriminatory policy did not specifically address sexual harassment, and more importantly, the grievance procedure apparently required employees to complain first to their supervisors, which in this situation was the alleged perpetrator. The case was remanded for further proceedings since the district court's findings were insufficient to dispose of the merits of the hostile environment claim and the employer's liability.

While most sexual harassment litigation has been based on Title VII, other grounds have been used to challenge such behavior. In 1985 a Michigan federal district court recognized that sexual harassment can violate the equal protection clause as well as Title VII. The court reasoned that sexual harassment is the "sort of invidious gender discrimination" that the equal protection clause forbids.[129] In addition, several courts have relied on state human rights provisions in providing remedies for sexual harassment. For example, in 1980 the Minnesota Supreme Court interpreted state law as placing an obligation on employers to curb sexual harassment among co-workers (which is not covered by Title VII).[130] In a subsequent case, a Minnesota appeals court upheld the dismissal of a guidance counselor for sexual harassment of students and female staff members, noting that the counselor was not entitled to be warned of his deficiencies where his conduct violated professional ethics.[131] A Louisiana court also relied on state law in upholding the discharge of a principal for incompetence based on evidence of his sexual harassment of a former teacher and an applicant for a position.[132]

Although charges of sexual harassment are problematic, administrative agencies and courts have become more inclined to address this subject than was true a decade ago. The judiciary has interpreted civil rights mandates as placing an obligation on employers to assure that employees are not subjected to harassment based on sex as well as on race, religion, or national origin.[133] Stakes are particularly high in sexual harassment cases because, in addition to the threat of legal sanctions, reputations and sometimes family harmony can be jeopardized.

Title IX and Employment Discrimination

Title IX of the Education Amendments of 1972 provides:

> No person in the United States shall, on the basis of sex, be excluded from participation in, be denied the benefits of, or be subjected to discrimination under any educational program or activity receiving Federal financial assistance . . .[134]

Individuals have a private right to bring suit to force institutions to comply with Title IX,[135] but the law does not provide personal remedies. The sanction for a Title IX violation is withdrawal of federal funds from the program in noncompliance. Without question, Title IX has provided the impetus for many schools and colleges to reassess institutional policies and take steps to curb sex bias. However, the imposition of federal sanctions for Title IX violations has been impeded by disputes over the reach of the law. Since its enactment, the scope of Title IX coverage has been debated in legislative, judicial, and administrative forums.

Two of the most controversial issues have involved Title IX's application to educational employees and the program-specific nature of the law. During the first decade after Title IX's enactment, federal courts rendered conflicting rulings regarding whether "participants in and beneficiaries of" educational programs include employees or only students. Finally, in 1982 the United States Supreme Court resolved the controversy by ruling in *North Haven Board of Education v. Bell* that Congress intended for the law to cover employees as well as students in federally assisted educational programs.[136] The Court reasoned that because the drafters did not specify "employment" among the list of Title IX exceptions, the law was meant to prohibit gender-based discrimination against employees. The Court also pointed out that Congress did not adopt a resolution disapproving the employment regulations promulgated by the former Department of Health, Education and Welfare and that bills to amend Title IX specifically to exclude employees from its coverage had not received congressional support.

Two years after the *North Haven* decision, the Court addressed the program-specific nature of Title IX. Lower courts had disagreed as to whether federal financial assistance to an educational program brought the entire institution or only the specific program receiving funds under the purview of Title IX. In *Grove City College v. Bell,* the Supreme Court held that Title IX is narrowly program-specific in that it applies *only* to programs or activities receiving direct federal assistance. In this case, the college's only federal financial assistance was aid that flowed directly to students.[137] The Court majority concluded that the college was subject to Title IX compliance even if its students—rather than the institution—received federal financial assistance. However, the majority reasoned that the receipt of federal student aid did *not* bring the entire college under the purview of Title IX; accordingly, the college was instructed to assure Title IX compliance *only* in its student financial aid program.

Immediately following this decision, legislation was proposed in Congress to nullify the Supreme Court's interpretation of Title IX as being narrowly program-specific and to clarify that Title IX and other civil rights laws with similar language were intended to apply to "recipients" of federal funds (rather than only to programs or activities within institutions). The bill, called the "omnibus civil rights act of 1984," received support from over forty civil rights, education, and women's groups.[138] In 1984 the House overwhelmingly passed the bill, but the measure was stalled in the Senate. Unless such congressional action is taken, Title IX seems destined to remain embroiled in enforcement disputes.

AGE DISCRIMINATION

Unlike other characteristics that generate charges of discrimination, age is unique in that all individuals are subject to the aging process. The mean age of the American population has climbed steadily in recent years, and this phenomenon has been accompanied by an increase in legal activity pertaining to age discrimination. Although legislative enactments that classify individuals on the basis of age can satisfy the equal protection clause if rationally related to a legitimate governmental objective,[139] in recent years plaintiffs have not had to rely on constitutional protections in challenging age-based employment discrimination.

In 1967 Congress enacted the Age Discrimination in Employment Act (ADEA), prohibiting age-based discrimination against employees aged forty to sixty-five in hiring, promotion, and compensation.[140] The upper limit on the protected group was extended to seventy in 1978 and completely removed in 1986.[141] Thus, employees over forty are now protected under ADEA. Remedies for violations of ADEA include: (1) injunctive relief, (2) offer of employment or reinstatement, (3) back pay, and (4) liquidated damages (equal to the back pay award) where established that age discrimination was unlawfully motivated.[142] If reinstatement is impossible or impractical, courts can award "front pay" to compensate for the loss of future earnings. Successful plaintiffs also can be awarded attorneys' fees.

There has been considerable litigation over the constitutionality of the 1974 amendments to ADEA, which extended the act's protections to state and local government employees. In 1983 the Supreme Court resolved the controversy by ruling that the amendments constitute a valid exercise of congressional power under the commerce clause of the Federal Constitution.[143] Reversing the Wyoming federal district court's conclusion that ADEA imposes an encroachment on state authority preserved by the tenth amendment, the Supreme Court concluded that ADEA does not involve an attribute of state sovereignty essential for carrying out traditional governmental functions. Noting that the state retains the authority to assess the fitness of employees and to dismiss those considered unfit, the majority reasoned that "the Act requires the State to achieve its goals in a more individualized and careful manner than would otherwise be the case, but it does not require the State to abandon those goals, or to abandon the public policy decisions underlying them."[144]

The substantive provisions of ADEA are almost identical to those of Title VII of the Civil Rights Act of 1964, and the judicial criteria developed in Title VII cases often are adapted to evaluate age discrimination charges under ADEA.[145] In disparate treatment claims, which require proof of intentional discrimination, employers have been able to rebut a prima facie ADEA violation by articulating nondiscriminatory reasons for dismissals, such as excessive tardiness, poor performance, or inability to relate to a supervisor.[146]

For example, in 1986 the Ninth Circuit Court of Appeals affirmed a federal district court's conclusion that a former school administrator did not carry his burden of proving disparate treatment based on age.[147] The fifty-seven-year-old plaintiff's position as assistant superintendent had been eliminated, and he asserted that his age was a major factor in the personnel action. Finding that unlawful intent was not established, the trial court reasoned that the school district articulated a nondiscriminatory basis for its action. Even though one of the school district's defenses—that administrative reorganization was necessitated by a fiscal crisis—was not considered credible, the court found that the district's desire to create a new administrative team provided a legitimate justification for eliminating the plaintiff's position. Since age did not play a central role in the personnel action, the ADEA claim was dismissed.

While most courts have adopted the disparate treatment standard of review in ADEA cases, in 1980 the Second Circuit Court of Appeals recognized that plaintiffs could establish a violation of ADEA by establishing that employment practices, regardless of motive, have a disparate impact on older employees.[148] In this case, the defendant school board adopted a cost-cutting policy of preferentially hiring teachers with fewer than five years experience. Evidence substantiated that over 92 percent of the state's teachers over forty years of age had at least five years of experience, whereas only 62 percent of teachers under forty had this much experience. The court concluded that the policy, with a disparate impact on teachers over forty, had to be justified as a job necessity to satisfy ADEA. A Missouri federal district court applied similar logic in evaluating a prima facie case of age discrimination in connection with a university's policy reserving a certain portion of faculty positions for nontenured professors.[149] The court rejected the economic rationale offered in defense of this practice as an insufficient business necessity to justify the adverse impact of the policy on older professors.

The United States Department of Labor and several courts have interpreted ADEA as prohibiting age discrimination among employees *within* the protected age group in that an employer cannot discriminate against employees who are sixty years old by preferring those who are forty-five. To illustrate, the First Circuit Court of Appeals ruled that an employee need not show that he or she was replaced by a person under forty years of age to establish a prima facie case of discrimination under ADEA.[150] An employee may not even need to show replacement by a younger person to substantiate an inference of age discrimination; the Seventh Circuit Court of Appeals recognized that evidence that a termination is based on age would be sufficient to establish an ADEA violation.[151]

In addition to federal protections, most states have enacted legislation protecting employees from age discrimination. For example, the Montana Human Rights Act has been interpreted as prohibiting age-based employment decisions unless age is directly related to job performance.[152] This act was held to prevail over a school board's mandatory retirement policy in the absence of evidence that the policy was necessitated by the nature of the job. The Nevada Supreme Court similarly ruled that a state university could not make hiring and retention decisions on the basis of age because of the state statute requiring all personnel actions taken by state, county, or municipal departments, agencies, boards, or appointing officers to be based solely on merit and fitness.[153] The Iowa Supreme Court also struck down a school board's attempt to dismiss a teacher who had attained age sixty-five and refused to retire in compliance with the school board's policy. The court reasoned that "age has nothing to do with fault," and therefore the discharge was not based on good cause.[154] The court declared that the "legislature did not vest school boards with the power to designate or change what might constitute good cause by mere process of adopting local school board policies."[155]

Although federal and state statutes have removed mandatory retirement ages, exceptions may be permissible for certain job categories.[156] Employers, however, must be able to produce a legitimate rationale for such exceptions. With the graying of American society, it seems likely that legal protections for older employees and incentives for voluntary early retirement will receive increasing attention.

DISCRIMINATION BASED ON HANDICAPS

During the past decade, substantial attention has been directed toward protecting the employment rights of handicapped individuals. Federal legislation, as well as some state statutory provisions, have sought to eliminate handicaps as a barrier to the employment of qualified individuals and have provided financial assistance for the rehabilitation of disabled individuals.[157] The most significant legislation in this area has been Section 504 of the Rehabilitation Act of 1973. Section 504 provides in part that "no otherwise qualified handicapped individual" shall be excluded from participation in a program receiving federal financial assistance "solely by reason of his handicap."[158]

Discriminatory practices occurring prior to the implementation of the Rehabilitation Act of 1973 were litigated on constitutional grounds. For example, a blind teacher successfully challenged the Philadelphia School District's policy barring applicants with "chronic or acute physical defects" from taking the examination used as a prerequisite to employment.[159] The appellate court reasoned that the school district's refusal to permit the teacher to take the exam constituted an irrebuttable presumption that blindness *per se* was evidence of incompetence; the school district violated the teacher's due process rights by refusing to give her an opportunity to demonstrate competence. The teacher, who passed the test when finally allowed to take it, was awarded retroactive seniority from the date of her original petition to take the exam. In a subsequent appeal, the court also awarded back pay for the same time period.[160] However, the court refused to order the award of tenure, reasoning that tenure must be based on the school's evaluation of the teacher's performance.[161]

In 1979, the first case involving an interpretation of Section 504 requirements reached the United States Supreme Court. *Southeastern Community College v. Davis* was initiated by a licensed practical nurse who was denied admission to a college program to train registered nurses because of her serious hearing disability.[162] The college rejected her application based on her inability to participate in all aspects of the program and the danger she might pose to future patients. The Court, interpreting Section 504, concluded that the language of the statute does not compel an institution to ignore the disabilities of an individual or to substantially modify its program to enable a handicapped person to participate. Rather, the law provides that a qualified individual cannot be excluded solely on the basis of a particular disability. The Court interpreted an "otherwise qualified" person as "one who is able to meet all of a program's requirements in spite of his handicap."[163] In this case, effective oral communication was considered critical to full participation in the program. The applicant's inability to communicate would have necessitated close supervision and substantial alteration in the curriculum to accommodate her disability. The Court determined that Section 504 does not require such modifications; institutions do not have to lower or substantially modify their standards to accommodate handicapped individuals.

However, *reasonable* accommodations must be made for handicapped individuals who are otherwise qualified to participate in federally assisted programs or activities. A deaf graduate student, who claimed that the University of Texas violated Section 504 by failing to provide him a sign language interpreter, was granted a preliminary injunction because of his likelihood of prevailing on the merits of his claim.[164] The Fifth Circuit Appellate Court affirmed the injunction, which was conditioned on the student posting a security bond pending the outcome of the litigation. On appeal, the Supreme Court ruled that the correctness of the decision to grant a preliminary injunction was moot (since the student had graduated), but the case was remanded for a trial regarding who should bear the cost of the interpreter.

In employment cases, courts have reiterated that Section 504 protects *otherwise qualified* handicapped persons and does not require special accommodations for individuals who are not qualified for the positions sought.[165] In a California case, a blind teacher was unsuccessful in challenging the school board's failure to appoint him to an administrative position because the board produced evidence that the plaintiff did not possess the requisite administrative skills or leadership experience for an administrative job.[166] The court rejected both equal protection and Section 504 claims, finding that the individual was not otherwise qualified for an administrative position and that there was a rational basis for the board's decision. In addition, the court rejected the assertion that the board's action violated due process guarantees by creating an irrebuttable presumption that blind persons were unqualified to serve as administrators; the board did not impose a blanket ban on hiring blind employees in leadership roles. More recently, the Eighth Circuit Court of Appeals found that a legally blind applicant who was rejected for a librarian position was not the victim of unlawful discrimination because the school board articulated a legitimate nondiscriminatory reason for its action. Concluding that the applicant was not rejected solely because of her blindness, the court accepted the evidence that the candidate selected by the board had better qualifications.[167]

However, handicapped individuals have successfully challenged employment decisions by establishing that they were qualified for the job and disadvantaged solely because of their handicaps or that they were not provided an individual assessment of their ability to perform the job being sought.[168] For example, a rejected applicant for a position teaching handicapped preschool children was awarded attorneys' fees and damages for mental anguish and loss of earnings because of the school board's violation of Section 504. Evidence showed that the multiply handicapped applicant was better qualified for the job than the individual subsequently hired and was denied employment solely because of his handicap.[169] In an earlier case, a New York federal district court ruled that a school district's preemployment inquiries about an applicant's prior mental problems were impermissible under Section 504 because the questions were not related to his present fitness for the position of teacher's aid.[170]

The definition of "handicapped" under Section 504 continues to generate controversy. An amendment to the law specifically excludes from coverage individuals suffering from drug or alchohol addictions, but some courts have reasoned that current disabilities resulting from *prior* addictions should be considered handicapping conditions under the federal law and similar state anti-discrimination provisions.[171] Also, the status of disabling conditions associated with certain diseases has not been clarified under Section 504. In 1985 the Supreme Court reversed a decision in which the Ninth Circuit Court of Appeals had ruled that an individual with Crohn's Disease was an otherwise qualified handicapped person under the act and had been unlawfully denied admission to a nursing school.[172] Since no opinion accompanied the Supreme Court's reversal, it is unclear whether the Court reasoned that Crohn's Disease is not a handicap under the Rehabilitation Act or that the individual was not otherwise qualified because of her academic deficiencies.

In a widely publicized 1985 decision, the Eleventh Circuit Court of Appeals held that a teacher with a communicable disease, tuberculosis, was "handicapped" within the meaning of Section 504 and thus could not be summarily dismissed because of the disease.[173] Reversing the lower court's decision that Congress did not intend to include contagious diseases within the definition of handicapping conditions, the appeals court held that neither the statutory language nor regulations indicate that chronic, contagious diseases are to be excluded from Section 504 coverage. The case was remanded for a determination of whether risks of infection precluded the teacher from being considered "otherwise qualified" for her job and whether her condition could be reasonably accommodated without undue burdens on the school district.

There is some sentiment that individuals infected with other diseases, such as acquired immune deficiency syndrome (AIDS), would similarly be considered handicapped under Section 504. Although no court has yet addressed the legal protections afforded to AIDS victims under the act, in 1986 the Justice Department issued a forty-nine-page opinion on AIDS in the workplace.[174] Recognizing that Section 504 might be violated by discrimination based on physical disabilities resulting from AIDS, the Justice

Department reasoned that the ability to transmit the disease cannot itself be considered a handicap. Thus, according to the opinion, an AIDS carrier would not qualify as "handicapped" and could not rely on Section 504 in challenging a dismissal intended to protect other employees from a perceived threat of transmission of the disease. The Justice Department's opinion does not have the force of a court ruling; thus, the judiciary will likely be called on to clarify the extent to which antidiscrimination mandates protect AIDS victims who suffer adverse employment consequences because of the disease.

Given the similarity in language between Section 504 and Title IX, the Supreme Court's interpretation of Title IX as applying *only* to programs directly receiving federal aid is generally assumed to affect Section 504 as well. Several lower courts endorsed this position even before the Supreme Court's decision interpreting Title IX as being program specific.[175] Unless Congress acts to change the wording of Section 504 and similar civil rights laws, enforcement of the antidiscrimination provisions will be restricted to federally assisted programs.

RELIGIOUS DISCRIMINATION

Individuals enjoy explicit constitutional protection against governmental interference with their religious freedom. As discussed in chapter 2, the first amendment in part prohibits Congress from enacting any law *respecting an establishment* of religion or interfering with the *free exercise* of religious beliefs. These provisions have been made applicable to the states through the fourteenth amendment.

The Supreme Court has recognized on numerous occasions that while the freedom to believe is absolute, the freedom to act on those beliefs is subject to reasonable governmental regulations.[176] For example, public educators cannot assert a free exercise right to conduct devotional activities in public schools or to proselytize students; the establishment clause prohibits such activities.[177] Similarly, the free exercise clause does not entitle teachers to disregard a portion of the state-prescribed curriculum that conflicts with their religious views.[178]

Although public employees cannot use their governmental positions to spread their faith, neither must they relinquish their religious beliefs as a condition of employment. Prerequisites to public employment that entail a profession of sectarian faith abridge the first amendment. For example, the Supreme Court invalidated a Maryland law requiring notary publics to sign an oath affirming their belief in God.[179] Public employees also have a free exercise right to abstain from certain observances and activities that conflict with their religious beliefs as long as such abstention does not impede their work performance. To illustrate, public school teachers have a first amendment right to refrain from saluting the American flag and pledging their allegiance, even though they cannot deny students the opportunity to engage in these observances.[180]

In addition to constitutional guarantees, employees are protected from religious discrimination under Title VII. In the 1972 amendments to Title VII, Congress stipulated that the protection against religious discrimination includes "all aspects of religious observance and practice, as well as belief, unless an employer demonstrates that he is unable to reasonably accommodate an employee's or prospective employee's religious observance or practice without undue hardship on the conduct of the employer's business."[181] The Equal Employment Opportunity Commission has promulgated guidelines with suggested religious accommodations such as accepting voluntary substitutes and assignment exchanges, using flexible scheduling, and changing job assignments.

Many controversies have arisen over the degree of religious accommodations required in work schedules to satisfy Title VII. In a significant 1977 case, a plaintiff challenged his dismissal for refusing to work on Saturdays in contravention of his religious beliefs.[182] The employer, Trans World Airlines (TWA), asserted that a Saturday schedule could not be avoided because shift assignments were based on seniority in conformance with the collective bargaining agreement. Evidence also showed that TWA had taken appropriate steps in meeting with the plaintiff and attempting to find someone to exchange shifts. The United States Supreme Court found no Title VII violation, reasoning that an employer need not bear more than minimal costs in making religious accommodations. The Court further noted that the employer is not required to disregard a bona fide seniority system in the absence of proof of intentional discrimination.

In a more recent school case, the Supreme Court ruled that while an employer is obligated to offer reasonable accommodations to enable employees to practice their religious beliefs, a school board is not required to prove that an employee's proposal for religious accommodations would create an undue business hardship.[183] In this case a Connecticut school board argued that its negotiated agreement allowing three days of paid leave for religious ceremonies and unpaid leave for additional religious absences constituted a reasonable accommodation. The plaintiff teacher asserted that the agreement violated Title VII by permitting employees to use three days of paid personal business leave for secular, but not religious, activities. The plaintiff proposed either to take personal leave for additional religious observances required by his faith or to receive full pay and hire a substitute for his religious absences beyond the three days allowed. The Second Circuit Court of Appeals ruled that the teacher established a prima facie case of religious discrimination and that Title VII requires employers to accept the employee's proposal for religious accommodation unless it would create an undue hardship. The Supreme Court, however, held that the appeals court applied an erroneous principle of law in that once the employer fulfills its obligation of providing a reasonable religious accommodation, it is not required to prove that the employee's proposal would entail a business hardship. Agreeing with the appellate court that the record was incomplete regarding whether the leave policy in this case constituted a reasonable accommodation, the Supreme Court remanded the case for additional proceedings.

Although employers are not obligated to make costly religious accommodations, in several school cases plaintiffs have proven that they suffered adverse employment consequences for unauthorized religious absences that should have been accommodated by unpaid leave. For example, in 1981 the Fourth Circuit Court of Appeals affirmed a federal district court's conclusion that the discharge of a teacher's aide for unauthorized absences to observe the seven-day convocation of the World Church of God violated Title VII.[184] However, the appellate court disagreed with the district court's holding that the aide was entitled only to back pay from the time of her discharge to the end of her one-year contract. Reasoning that Title VII creates a substantive right to nondiscriminatory treatment, the appeals court held that the plaintiff was entitled to back pay (mitigated by interim earnings) from the time of the discharge until a valid offer of reinstatement was made.

In 1980 a New Jersey federal district court also concluded that religious absences were a "substantial motivating factor" in the dismissal of a teacher in violation of Title VII.[185] Finding that the absences created no hardship for the school or students, the court ordered the teacher's reinstatement with back pay. However, the court denied the teacher's request for compensatory and punitive damages. The court was not persuaded that the teacher suffered mental and emotional distress or that the superintendent and board acted with malicious and wanton disregard for his constitutional rights.

In addition to federal requirements, most states also have constitutional or statutory provisions protecting individuals from religious discrimination. Interpreting such a provision, the California Supreme Court ordered reinstatement of a teacher who had been terminated for unauthorized absences for religious reasons.[186] The court held that the teacher was entitled to unpaid leave for religious observances since no evidence was presented that the teacher's absences had a detrimental effect on the educational program. In contrast, a Colorado appeals court upheld the dismissal of a tenured teacher for similar unauthorized religious absences, reasoning that his teaching duties had been neglected.[187] The court ruled that the termination was justified and did not violate Colorado's antidiscrimination law because testimony indicated that the teacher's four unauthorized absences interfered with the academic progress of his students and disrupted the management of the school.

While public employers generally attempt to accommodate reasonable absences for religious reasons, most courts have ruled that paid leave need not be provided for this purpose. In 1984 the Tenth Circuit Court of Appeals upheld a Colorado school district's leave policy allowing teachers two days of paid leave ("special leave") that could be used for religious observances and other purposes.[188] The court rejected a Jewish teacher's claim that the policy violated Title VII and burdened his free exercise of religion because he had to take unpaid leave occasionally to observe Jewish holidays. The court reasoned that the availability of *unpaid* leave for religious purposes constituted a reasonable accommodation under Title VII and did not place a substantial burden on free exercise rights.

Whether paid leave tied specifically to religious observances implicates the establishment clause has not been clarified. Some decisions suggest that such leave would unconstitutionally advance religion. For example, in a New Jersey case, public school teachers were allowed to use personal leave days for religious as well as other purposes, but the teachers' association sought paid leave specifically for religious observances.[189] The state supreme court ruled that the establishment clause prohibits the school board from granting such religious leave and, therefore, negotiations over this item would be unconstitutional. Similarly, in 1976 a California appeals court found unconstitutional a proposed order of the governor that granted state employees paid leave on Good Friday for religious worship.[190]

However, the Supreme Court has not ruled that school boards are *precluded* from providing paid religious leave. In the Connecticut case discussed previously, the Court did not invalidate the school board's provision of three days of paid leave for religious ceremonies. While noting that a policy requiring employees to take unpaid leave for religious observances would satisfy Title VII, the Court declared that it would not be a reasonable accommodation if paid leave were provided "for all purposes *except* religious ones."[191]

Public employees, like all citizens, enjoy constitutional and statutory protection of their religious freedoms. Employers are expected to make reasonable accommodations to enable individuals to practice their faith. However, a minimal infringement on the practice of sectarian beliefs may be required in public school settings to ensure that religion is not being advanced under the auspices of the state.

CONCLUSION

Equal employment opportunity has been an elusive concept, continually refined through legislative enactments and judicial opinions. In general, it means that employment decisions should be based on qualifications, merit, seniority, and similar factors rather than on an individual's characteristics such as race, sex, age, or handicaps. Courts have applied varying standards in assessing discriminatory employment practices. The standard of judicial review depends on the classification challenged (e.g., race or sex), the basis for the litigation (i.e., constitutional or statutory grounds), and the nature of the claim (i.e., disparate treatment or impact). Broad generalizations pertaining to discrimination in employment are enumerated below.

1. The Federal Constitution and various civil rights laws protect employees from discrimination in employment based on race, national origin, sex, age, handicaps, and religion.
2. Facially discriminatory classifications based on race can never be justified; overt discrimination based on other characteristics, such as sex or age, can be justified only if the characteristic is a bona fide occupational qualification.
3. The foreseeable adverse impact of a facially *neutral* employment practice on a protected group does not establish a federal constitutional violation unless the practice lacks a rational basis or is accompanied by unlawful intent; however, such disparate impact can violate Title VII of the Civil Rights Act of 1964 if the employment practice is not justified as a business necessity.
4. A standardized test can be used to screen teacher applicants, even though it has a disproportionate impact on minorities, as long as the test is job-related and used to advance legitimate job objectives.
5. In challenging disparate treatment under Title VII, plaintiffs must establish discriminatory intent; employers can rebut an inference of discrimination by articulating a legitimate, nondiscriminatory basis for the practice.
6. Employers can *voluntarily* establish temporary affirmative action plans involving racial preferences in hiring and promotion practices to overcome chronic and substantial patterns of discrimination, even though the past discrimination has not resulted in legal liability; however, such affirmative action plans cannot foreclose employment opportunities for nonminorities.
7. Courts can *order* hiring and promotion preferences based on race to remedy intentional discrimination or to dissipate the lingering effects of prior discrimination.
8. Layoff quotas based on race that abrogate seniority rights cannot be judicially imposed or voluntarily adopted unless justified by a compelling governmental purpose and less intrusive means are not available to accomplish that purpose.
9. Pregnancy-related conditions cannot be treated less favorably than other temporary disabilities in medical and disability insurance plans or leave policies.

10. Individuals cannot be required to take maternity leave at a specified date during pregnancy unless the policy is justified as a business necessity.
11. Employers cannot make a distinction between men and women in retirement contributions and benefits.
12. Employees can gain relief under Title VII for sexual harassment that results in the loss of tangible benefits or creates a hostile working environment; the fact that an individual has submitted to sexual advances cannot be used as a defense if the advances were unwelcomed.
13. Title VII provides remedies for sex discrimination in compensation that extend beyond the Equal Pay Act's guarantee of equal pay for substantially equivalent work; however, the judiciary has not endorsed the controversial theory of "comparable worth."
14. The antidiscrimination provisions contained in Title IX of the Educational Amendments of 1972, Title VI of the Civil Rights Act of 1964, and Section 504 of the Rehabilitation Act of 1973 protect individuals *only* in programs or activities *directly* receiving federal funds.
15. School boards can establish bona fide retirement benefits programs, but the Age Discrimination in Employment Act precludes mandatory retirement based on age.
16. An otherwise qualified handicapped individual cannot be excluded from employment solely on the basis of a disability, but employers are not obligated to make substantial adjustments in working conditions to accommodate handicapped employees or to hire handicapped persons who are not qualified.
17. Employers must make reasonable accommodations to enable employees to practice their religious beliefs as long as an undue business hardship is not created; however, accommodations that advance religion are barred by the establishment clause.

NOTES

1. Part of this chapter is adapted with permission from Martha McCarthy, *Discrimination on Employment: The Evolving Law* (Topeka, KS: National Organization of Legal Problems of Education, 1983). For a discussion of remedies in the form of damages for impairments of federally protected rights, see chapter 8.
2. *See* Hirabayashi v. United States, 320 U.S. 81 (1943) (a wartime restriction on citizens of Japanese descent served a sufficiently compelling governmental interest).

3. *See* Massachusetts Bd. of Retirement v. Murgia, 427 U.S. 307 (1976); Gurmankin v. Costanzo, 411 F. Supp. 982, 992, n. 8 (E.D. Pa. 1976), *aff'd*, 556 F.2d 184 (3d Cir. 1977).
4. Craig v. Boren, 429 U.S. 190, 197 (1976).
5. *See* Mississippi Univ. for Women v. Hogan, 458 U.S. 718 (1982); Craig, *id.*
6. Personnel Administrator of Massachusetts v. Feeney, 442 U.S. 256, 279 (1979). *See also* Washington v. Davis, 426 U.S. 229 (1976).
7. *See* Dayton Bd. of Educ. v. Brinkman, 443 U.S. 526, 536, n. 9 (1979).
8. *See* Hazelwood School Dist. v. United States, 433 U.S. 299 (1977); Evans v. Harnett, 684 F.2d 304 (4th Cir. 1982); Sweeney v. Board of Trustees of Keene State College, 604 F.2d 106 (1st Cir. 1979), *cert. denied,* 444 U.S. 1045 (1980).
9. 42 U.S.C. § 2000e *et seq.* Originally, Title VII did not apply to educational institutions, but in 1972 this exemption was substantially repealed. The only remaining exemption pertains to the employment by educational institutions of "individuals of a particular religion." 42 U.S.C. § 2000e–1.
10. Time limitations are specified for complaints to be filed with the Equal Employment Opportunity Commission, which investigates the complaint and attempts to conciliate an agreement if a violation is found. A lawsuit can be filed after applicable administrative remedies have been exhausted without relief. *See* 42 U.S.C. § 2000e–5 for procedural requirements in filing Title VII claims. In 1982 the Supreme Court ruled that a claimant does not have a right to a federal trial on a Title VII claim if the issue has already been litigated in a state court under state antidiscriminatory provisions, Alexander v. Gardner-Denver Co., 415 U.S. 36 (1974). However, an employee's right to trial under Title VII is not foreclosed by prior submission of the claim to arbitration under a nondiscrimination provision of a collective bargaining agreement. Federal antidiscrimination mandates are public policy considerations that cannot be subjected to the bargaining process, Kremer v. Chemical Construction Corp., 456 U.S. 461 (1982).
11. Furnco Construction Corp. v. Waters, 438 U.S. 567, 577 (1978).
12. *See* Texas Dep't of Community Affairs v. Burdine, 450 U.S. 248, 258–259 (1981).
13. Pullman-Standard v. Swint, 456 U.S. 273, 289–290 (1982).
14. *See* Griggs v. Duke Power Co., 401 U.S. 424, 432 (1971); New York City Transit Auth. v. Beazer, 440 U.S. 568, 587, n. 31 (1979).
15. *See* Dothard v. Rawlinson, 433 U.S. 321, 329 (1977).
16. Title VII explicitly prohibits employment discrimination based on national origin. However, some civil rights statutes enacted shortly after the War Between the States limit protections specifically to race, such as 42 U.S.C. § 1981 (affording nonwhites equal rights to make and enforce contracts, sue, and receive full and equal benefit of the laws) and 42 U.S.C. § 1982 (affording nonwhites equal rights to acquire and hold property). Whether "race" under these laws should be broadly defined has become controversial. *See* Al-Khazraji v. Saint Francis College, 784 F.2d 505 (3d Cir. 1986), *cert. granted,* 107 S. Ct. 62 (1986) (ethnic Arabs could claim race discrimination under § 1981 even though taxonomically classified as members of the Caucasian race); Shaare Tefila Congregation v. Cobb, 785 F.2d 523 (4th Cir. 1986), *cert. granted,* 107 S. Ct. 62 (1986) (Jewish congregation could not assert

claims of racial discrimination under §§ 1981 and 1982 based on defendants' perception of Jews as a racially distinct group); Manzanares v. Safeway Stores, 593 F.2d 968 (10th Cir. 1979) (plaintiff of Mexican-American descent could claim discrimination under § 1981).

17. Washington v. Davis, 426 U.S. 229 (1976). This case was brought under the fifth amendment, rather than the fourteenth, because the latter provision applies only to *state* action. Although the fifth amendment does not include an equal protection clause, the Supreme Court has interpreted its due process clause as prohibiting the federal government from denying citizens equal protection of the laws. *See* Bolling v. Sharpe, 347 U.S. 497 (1954).
18. National Educ. Ass'n v. South Carolina, 445 F. Supp. 1094 (D.S.C. 1977), *aff'd*, 434 U.S. 1026 (1978). *See* text with note 33, *infra*, for discussion of the Title VII claim. *See also* Moore v. Tangipahoa Parish School Bd., 594 F.2d 489 (5th Cir. 1979).
19. United States v. Texas, 628 F. Supp. 304 (E.D. Tex. 1985), *rev'd sub nom.* United States v. Lulac, 793 F.2d 636 (5th Cir. 1986).
20. Armstead v. Starkville Mun. Separate School Dist., 461 F.2d 276, 280 (5th Cir. 1972).
21. Georgia Ass'n of Educators v. Nix, 407 F. Supp. 1102 (N.D. Ga. 1976).
22. Most constitutional challenges to employment test requirements have focused on equal protection guarantees, whereas challenges to student competency testing programs have relied on due process protections as well. Students have successfully argued that they have a property interest in receiving a high school diploma, necessitating sufficient notice of test requirements, adequate preparation, and fundamentally fair examinations used as a diploma sanction. However, employees may find it more difficult to establish that testing programs implicate a property interest (i.e., a legitimate entitlement to employment). *See* Michael Rebell, "Disparate Impact of Teacher Competency Testing on Minorities: Don't Blame the Test-Takers or the Tests," *Yale Law & Policy Review,* vol. 4 (1986), pp. 384–391. For a discussion of legal challenges to student competency testing programs, *see* text with note 106, chapter 3.
23. 401 U.S. 424, 432 (1971).
24. Albemarle Paper Co. v. Moody, 422 U.S. 405, 432 (1975). In 1978 the Equal Employment Opportunity Commission (EEOC) issued *Uniform Guidelines on Employee Selection Procedures* designed to assure that employment practices with an adverse impact on a group protected by Title VII are justified by a business necessity. While the EEOC prefers test validation by correlating job performance with test scores, the agency will allow other types of validation that meet recognized standards of the American Psychological Association and standard textbooks and journals in the field of personnel selection. *See* 29 C.F.R. § 1607 *et seq.*
25. Connecticut v. Teal, 457 U.S. 440 (1982).
26. *Id.* at 445, *quoting* 645 F.2d 133, 138 (2d Cir. 1981).
27. In 1983 the Supreme Court also affirmed a decision in which the Second Circuit Court of Appeals ordered relief for victims of an employment practice that locked in a discriminatory method of making hiring decisions. New York City's practice of conditioning employment eligibility on tests, which had not been validated as job related and had a disparate impact on blacks

and Hispanics, was considered a continuing policy of discrimination that ended only when the last person was hired off the list. The appeals court held that minority employees who had suffered from the discriminatory hiring practice since the effective date of Title VII were entitled to back pay and retroactive seniority. Compensatory relief also was requested under Title VI of the Civil Rights Act of 1964 (which prohibits discrimination against persons on the basis of race, color, or national origin in programs receiving federal funds), but such relief was denied. The Supreme Court majority reasoned that while proof of discriminatory intent is not essential to establish a Title VI violation, an individual can recover only injunctive, noncompensatory relief for Title VI impairments in the absence of proof of unlawful motive. Guardians Ass'n v. Civil Service Comm'n of the City of New York, 633 F.2d 232 (2d Cir. 1980), *aff'd*, 463 U.S. 582 (1983).

28. Chance v. Board of Examiners, 458 F.2d 1167 (2d Cir. 1972).
29. Walston v. School Bd. of Suffolk, 566 F.2d 1201 (4th Cir. 1977).
30. York v. Alabama State Bd. of Educ., 581 F. Supp. 779 (M.D. Ala. 1983).
31. York v. Alabama State Bd. of Educ., 631 F. Supp. 78 (M.D. Ala. 1986). *See also* Ensley Branch, NAACP v. Seibels, 616 F.2d 812 (5th Cir. 1980), *cert. denied,* 449 U.S. 1061 (1980).
32. Allen v. Alabama State Bd. of Educ., 612 F. Supp. 1046 (M.D. Ala. 1985) supplemental memorandum, 636 F. Supp. 64 (M.D. Ala. 1986), *rev'd and remanded,* 804 F.2d 1227 (11th Cir. 1986).
33. *Id.*, 804 F.2d 1227.
34. National Educ. Ass'n v. South Carolina, 445 F. Supp. 1094 (D. S.C. 1977), *aff'd*, 434 U.S. 1026 (1978). *See* text with note 18, *supra.*
35. Newman v. Crews, 651 F.2d 222 (4th Cir. 1981).
36. While most discrimination claims in connection with employment testing programs have been based on constitutional or Title VII grounds, some testing programs to determine eligibility for recertification and job retention have been challenged under state law. Courts in Texas and Arkansas have rejected state challenges to the use of tests to determine whether educators will retain their certification. *See* Texas State Teachers Ass'n v. State of Texas, 711 S.W.2d 421 (Tex. App. 1986); Stanfield v. Turnbow, Chancery Ct., Pulaski County, Arkansas, March 22, 1985.
37. Rogers v. International Paper Co., 510 F.2d 1340, 1345 (8th Cir. 1975), *vacated,* 423 U.S. 809 (1975), *modified,* 526 F.2d 722 (8th Cir. 1975). *See also* Royal v. Missouri Highway and Transportation Comm'n, 655 F.2d 159, 164 (8th Cir. 1981); Barnett v. W.T. Grant Co., 518 F.2d 543, 550 (4th Cir. 1975). In addition to protecting employees against discrimination based on their class membership, the judiciary has recognized that Title VII prohibits discrimination based on an individual's *association* with people of a particular race or national origin. *See* Reiter v. Center Consol. School Dist., 618 F. Supp. 1458, 1460 (D. Colo. 1985).
38. 411 U.S. 792, 802 (1973). Once a prima facie case is established, questions of fact are to be resolved by a jury. *See* Equal Employment Opportunity Comm'n v. University of Oklahoma, 774 F.2d 999 (10th Cir. 1985).
39. *See* Sweeney v. Board of Trustees of Keene State College, 604 F.2d 106, 108 (1st Cir. 1979), *cert. denied,* 444 U.S. 1045 (1980).
40. *Id.*, 604 F.2d at 108.
41. Correa v. Nampa School Dist. No. 131, 645 F.2d 814 (9th Cir. 1981). *See*

also Morgan v. South Bend Community School Corp., 797 F.2d 471 (7th Cir. 1986) (black principal's demotion was because of his substandard performance rather than race); Simmons v. Camden County Bd. of Educ., 757 F.2d 1187 (11th Cir. 1985) (teachers were suspended and discharged for their pattern of disrespect and defiance toward supervisors and not in response to their filing of discrimination charges); Lujan v. Franklin County Bd. of Educ., 766 F.2d 917 (6th Cir. 1985) (school board articulated nondiscriminatory reason for hiring white head football coach over minority applicant); Patterson v. Masem, 774 F.2d 251 (8th Cir. 1985) (neither sex nor race was a significant factor in a school board's failure to promote a black female teacher to a supervisory position); McDaniel v. Temple Independent School Dist., 770 F.2d 1340 (5th Cir. 1985) (school district produced legitimate reasons for not promoting black female); Lewis v. Central Piedmont Community College, 689 F.2d 1207 (4th Cir. 1982), *cert. denied,* 460 U.S. 1040 (1983) (white applicant was better qualified than black applicant who was rejected); Torrence v. Oxford Mun. School Dist., 615 F. Supp. 321 (N.D. Miss. 1985) (black band director's discharge was based on declining band performance and failure to maintain discipline).

42. Hammond v. Rapides Parish School Bd., 757 F.2d 284 (5th Cir. 1985), *cert. denied,* 106 S. Ct. 91 (1985).
43. Stallworth v. Shuler, 777 F.2d 1431 (11th Cir. 1985). *See also* Webb v. Board of Educ. of Dyer County, 715 F.2d 254 (6th Cir. 1983), *aff'd,* 105 S. Ct. 1923 (1985) (damages were awarded to a black teacher whose discharge was racially motivated; however, attorneys' fees for services performed in administrative proceedings were denied); Lams v. General Water Works Corp., 766 F.2d 386 (8th Cir. 1985) (company's nondiscriminatory reasons for hiring whites in a particular department were found to be a pretext to maintain segregation and discrimination in promoting and transferring minority employees).
44. *See, e.g.,* Jett v. Dallas Independent School Dist., 798 F.2d 748 (5th Cir. 1986) (white athletic director's reassignment was racially motivated); Lincoln v. Board of Regents of Univ. System of Georgia, 697 F.2d 928 (11th Cir. 1983), *cert. denied,* 464 U.S. 826 (1983) (white professor established that she would have received a new contract, "but for" her race); Carter v. Community Action Agency of Chambers, Tallapoosa, and Coosa Counties, 625 F. Supp. 199 (M.D. Ala. 1985) (white former director of headstart program was dismissed because of racial considerations).
45. *See* Carino v. University of Oklahoma Bd. of Regents, 750 F.2d 815 (10th Cir. 1984); Berke v. Ohio Dep't of Public Welfare, 628 F.2d 980 (6th Cir. 1980). In Garcia v. Gloor, 618 F.2d 264 (5th Cir. 1980), the appeals court reasoned that for some foreign born individuals language may be an immutable characteristic, like skin color, sex, or place of birth. However, national origin discrimination was not found where a multilingual individual elected to speak his native language in violation of company policy.
46. Bazemore v. Friday, 106 S. Ct. 3000 (1986). *See also* Pittman v. Hattiesburg Mun. Separate School Dist., 644 F.2d 1071 (5th Cir. 1981) (black employee established that a pay differential was primarily based on racial considerations).
47. Hazelwood School Dist. v. United States, 433 U.S. 299 (1977). *See also* Castaneda v. Pickard, 648 F.2d 989 (5th Cir. 1981).

48. Wygant v. Jackson Bd. of Educ., 106 S. Ct. 1842, 1847–1848 (1986). *See* text with note 74, *infra*. *See also* Price v. Denison Independent School Dist., 694 F.2d 334 (5th Cir. 1982) (statistical measures comparing the racial composition of principals with that of student bodies could not be used in establishing a prima facie case of employment discrimination under the equal protection clause). However, some courts have considered the racial composition of student bodies in assessing specific types of employment discrimination claims. *See* Evans v. Harnett County Bd. of Educ., 684 F.2d 304 (4th Cir. 1982) (statistical evidence that black principals were placed primarily in schools that formerly had predominantly black student bodies established inference of a pattern of racial discrimination); Williams v. Colorado Springs School Dist. No. 11, 641 F.2d 835 (10th Cir. 1981) (concentration of black teachers in schools with predominantly black students and black principals established a prima facie case of discrimination).
49. 42 U.S.C. § 2000e–2(h).
50. Franks v. Bowman Transp. Co., 424 U.S. 747 (1976).
51. Teamsters v. United States, 431 U.S. 324 (1977). In a dissenting opinion, Justice Marshall cited over thirty federal appellate decisions supporting his conclusion that Congress did not intend to legalize seniority systems that perpetuate either pre- or post-Title VII discrimination, *id.* at 378–379 (Marshall, J., dissenting). While Title VII insulates race-neutral seniority systems even though they tend to freeze the effects of pre-Title VII discrimination, liability has been assessed against employers who have not eliminated a pre-Title VII salary disparity between black and white workers. *See* Bazemore v. Friday, 106 S. Ct. 3000 (1986); text with note 46, *supra*.
52. The Court further held that minority employees who had not submitted futile applications for the jobs in question since 1972 were not barred from an award of retroactive seniority if they could carry the difficult burden of proving that they would have applied for the positions *but for* the company's discriminatory policies, Teamsters, *id.* at 367–368.
53. American Tobacco Co. v. Patterson, 634 F.2d 744 (4th Cir. 1980), *vacated and remanded,* 456 U.S. 63 (1982). *See also* Pullman-Standard v. Swint, 456 U.S. 273 (1982) (federal appeals court cannot substitute its judgment for that of the trial court in determining whether a seniority system is bona fide; assessment of intentional discrimination based on the evidence is a finding of fact to be made by the trial court and not a question of law or mixed question of fact and law permitting independent assessment by the appeals court).
54. *See* Wattleton v. International Brotherhood of Boilermakers, 686 F.2d 586 (7th Cir. 1982).
55. Ford Motor Co. v. Equal Employment Opportunity Comm'n, 458 U.S. 219 (1982). Although this case involved alleged sex discrimination, the principle announced by the Court is applicable to charges of discrimination in hiring practices against other groups protected by Title VII.
56. *Id.* at 238.
57. United States Comm'n on Civil Rights, "Statement of Affirmative Action for Equal Employment Opportunities," 1973.
58. For an interpretation of this law's affirmative action requirements, *see* Fitzgerald v. Green Valley Area Educ. Agency, 589 F. Supp. 1130 (S.D. Iowa 1984).

59. *See* Arval Morris, "Affirmative Action and 'Quota Systems,' " *Education Law Reporter,* vol. 28 (1986), pp. 1203–1235.
60. The issue of "reverse" discrimination was first addressed by the Supreme Court in Regents of the Univ. of California v. Bakke, 438 U.S. 265 (1978). Six different opinions were written in this case, with five members of the Court concluding that the admissions policy of the University of California Medical School at Davis violated Title VI of the Civil Rights Act of 1964. The university reserved a designated number of openings in each class for minority students; thus, minority applicants were accepted while white applicants with higher scores were rejected. Although invalidating the rigid quota system, a majority of the Court also reasoned that race could be a consideration in making admissions decisions.
61. 443 U.S. 193, 200 (1979).
62. *Id.* at 205.
63. Subsequently, in Fullilove v. Klutznick, 448 U.S. 448 (1980), the Supreme Court upheld the Minority Business Enterprise provision of the Public Works Employment Act of 1977, which requires at least 10 percent of federal funds granted for local public works projects to be "set aside" to ensure participation by minority contractors. Finding no violation of the equal protection clause, the Court concluded that Congress was authorized to fashion a remedy with a racial factor in light of a history of prior discrimination.
64. *See* Bratton v. City of Detroit, 704 F.2d 878 (6th Cir. 1983), *modified on rehearing,* 712 F.2d 222 (6th Cir. 1983), *cert denied,* 464 U.S. 1040 (1984); Detroit Police Officers' Ass'n v. Young, 608 F.2d 671 (6th Cir. 1979), *cert. denied,* 452 U.S. 938 (1981); Valentine v. Smith, 654 F.2d 503 (8th Cir. 1981), *cert. denied,* 454 U.S. 1124 (1981); Zaslawsky v. Board of Educ. of Los Angeles, 610 F.2d 661 (9th Cir. 1979). *See also* Johnson v. Transportation Agency, 770 F.2d 752 (9th Cir. 1984), *cert. granted,* 106 S. Ct. 3331 (1986) (upheld affirmative action plan adopted to attain gender balance in agency's work force).
65. Local No. 93, International Ass'n of Firefighters, AFL-CIO v. City of Cleveland, 753 F.2d 479 (6th Cir. 1985), *aff'd,* 106 S. Ct. 3063 (1986).
66. Local 28 of the Sheet Metal Workers' International Ass'n and Local 28 Joint Apprenticeship Comm. v. Equal Employment Opportunity Comm'n, 753 F.2d 1172 (2d Cir. 1985), *aff'd,* 106 S. Ct. 3019, 3037 (1986). The Court distinguished this case from the circumstances in Firefighters Local Union No. 1784 v. Stotts, 467 U.S. 561 (1984). *See* text with note 69, *infra.*
67. *Id.,* 106 S. Ct. at 3049. *See also* Paradise v. Prescott, 767 F.2d 1514 (11th Cir. 1985), *cert. granted,* 106 S.Ct. 3331 (1986).
68. *See* Kromnick v. School Dist. of Philadelphia, 739 F.2d 894 (3d Cir. 1984), *cert. denied,* 105 S. Ct. 782 (1985); Zaslawsky v. Board of Educ. of Los Angeles, 610 F.2d 661 (9th Cir. 1979); note 71, *infra.*
69. 467 U.S. 561 (1984).
70. *Id.* at 576, n. 9.
71. Arthur v. Nyquist, 712 F.2d 816 (2d Cir. 1983), *cert. denied,* 104 S. Ct. 3555 (1984); Morgan v. O'Bryant, 671 F.2d 23 (1st Cir. 1982), *cert. denied sub nom.* Boston Ass'n of School Administrators and Supervisors v. Morgan, 459 U.S. 827 (1982). *See* text with note 89, chapter 13.
72. Arthur, *id.,* 712 F.2d at 822.
73. *See* Wygant v. Jackson Bd. of Educ., 746 F.2d 1152, 1157 (6th Cir. 1984),

rev'd, 106 S. Ct. 1842 (1986); Marsh v. Board of Educ. of City of Flint, 762 F.2d 1009 (6th Cir. 1985), *vacated,* 106 S. Ct. 2240 (1986); Britton v. South Bend Community School Corp., 775 F.2d 794 (7th Cir. 1985), *vacated,* 783 F.2d 105 (7th Cir. 1986).

74. Wygant, *id.,* 106 S. Ct. 1842. Chief Justice Burger and Justice Rehnquist joined in Justice Powell's plurality opinion, and Justice O'Connor joined in all but one part. Justice White concurred in the judgment, and Justices Marshall, Brennan, Blackmun, and Stevens dissented.
75. *Id.* at 1847–1848. In an earlier case, the Sixth Circuit Court of Appeals rejected the notion that students have a constitutional right to attend schools with faculties of a specified racial composition, Oliver v. Kalamazoo Bd. of Educ., 706 F.2d 757, 764 (6th Cir. 1983). *See* text with note 92, chapter 13.
76. Wygant, *id.*
77. *See id.* at 1852–1856 (O'Connor, J., concurring).
78. Bradwell v. Illinois, 83 U.S. 130, 141 (1873).
79. Craig v. Boren, 429 U.S. 190, 197 (1976).
80. Mississippi Univ. for Women v. Hogan, 458 U.S. 718, 729 (1982).
81. Personnel Administrator of Massachusetts v. Feeney, 442 U.S. 256, 273 (1979).
82. Phillips v. Martin Marietta Corp., 400 U.S. 542 (1971). *See also* Sprogis v. United Airlines, 444 F.2d 1194 (7th Cir. 1971), *cert. denied,* 404 U.S. 991 (1971) (airline's policy requiring only female flight attendants to be unmarried was not justified as a BFOQ).
83. Stone v. Belgrade School Dist. No. 44, 703 P.2d 136 (Mont. 1985).
84. *See* Martha McCarthy, "Recent Developments in Sex Discrimination Litigation," in *School Law Update—1977,* M. McGhehey, ed. (Topeka, KS: National Organization on Legal Problems of Education, 1978), pp. 53–56.
85. *See* Wilkins v. University of Houston, 654 F.2d 388 (5th Cir. 1981), *rehearing,* 662 F.2d 1156 (5th Cir. 1981), *vacated and remanded,* 459 U.S. 809 (1982), *vacated and remanded in part,* 695 F.2d 134 (5th Cir. 1983).
86. Texas Dep't of Community Affairs v. Burdine, 450 U.S. 248, 259 (1981). *See also* Eckroth v. Flasher Public School Dist. No. 39, 583 F.2d 415 (8th Cir. 1978); Lombard v. School Dist. of Erie, 463 F. Supp. 566 (W.D. Pa. 1978).
87. *See* McCarthney v. Griffin-Spalding County Bd. of Educ., 791 F.2d 1549 (11th Cir. 1986); Wardwell v. School Bd. of Palm Beach County, Florida, 786 F.2d 1554 (11th Cir. 1986); Sullivan v. School Bd. of Pinellas County, 773 F.2d 1182 (11th Cir. 1985); Trout v. Lehman, 702 F.2d 1094 (D.C. Cir. 1983), *vacated and remanded,* 465 U.S. 1056 (1984); Patterson v. Greenwood School Dist. 50, 696 F.2d 293 (4th Cir. 1982); Laborde v. Regents of the Univ. of Cal., 686 F.2d 715 (9th Cir. 1982); Cummings v. School Dist. of Lincoln, 638 F.2d 1168 (8th Cir. 1981); Danzl v. North St. Paul-Maplewood-Oakdale Independent School Dist., 663 F.2d 65 (8th Cir. 1981).
88. *See* Joshi v. Florida State Univ. Health Center, 763 F.2d 1227 (11th Cir. 1985); Rodriguez v. Board of Educ. of Eastchester Union Free School Dist., 620 F.2d 362 (2d Cir. 1980); Tyler v. Board of Educ. of New Castle County, 519 F. Supp. 834 (D. Del. 1981).
89. *See* Coble v. Hot Springs School Dist. No. 6, 682 F.2d 721 (8th Cir. 1982), Rodriguez, *id.;* Schoneberg v. Grundy County Special Educ. Coop., 385 N.E.2d 351 (Ill. App. 1979). *See also* Harrington v. Vandalia-Butler Bd. of Educ., 585 F.2d 192 (6th Cir. 1978), *cert. denied,* 441 U.S. 932 (1979) (pro-

viding female physical education teachers facilities inferior to facilities provided for male teachers violated Title VII; however, the appellate court interpreted Title VII as not authorizing compensatory damages, and since the plaintiff could not be considered the prevailing party, attorneys' fees were also denied).

90. *See* Burkey v. Marshall County Bd. of Educ., 513 F. Supp. 1084 (N.D. W.V. 1981).

91. Sweeney v. Board of Trustees of Keene State College, 604 F.2d 106, 113 (1st Cir. 1979), *cert. denied,* 444 U.S. 1045 (1980). *But see* Canham v. Oberlin College, 666 F.2d 1057 (6th Cir. 1981), *cert. denied,* 456 U.S. 977 (1982) (a college's asserted nondiscriminatory reasons for denying a permanent position to a male in favor of a female based on the male candidate's inadequate performance during a trial period were not mere pretexts for sex bias).

92. Jennings v. Tinley Park Community School Dist. No. 146, 796 F.2d 962 (7th Cir. 1986).

93. Mitchell v. Board of Trustees of Pickens County School Dist. A., 599 F.2d 582 (4th Cir. 1979), *cert. denied,* 444 U.S. 965 (1979). *See also* Zuniga v. Kleberg County Hospital, 692 F.2d 986 (5th Cir. 1982). In 1986 the Supreme Court ruled that the Ohio Civil Rights Commission was authorized to investigate a claim of sex discrimination (resulting from an employee's nonrenewal based on her pregnancy) against a private religious school. Ohio Civil Rights Comm'n v. Dayton Christian Schools, 106 S. Ct. 2718 (1986); text with note 113, chapter 2. Dismissals based on *unwed,* pregnant status are covered in chapters 8 and 10, as challenges to such terminations are usually based on asserted constitutional privacy rights.

94. Geduldig v. Aiello, 417 U.S. 484 (1974) (no constitutional violation under the equal protection clause); General Electric Co. v. Gilbert, 429 U.S. 125 (1976) (no Title VII violation).

95. Pregnancy Discrimination Act, 42 U.S.C. § 2000e(k) (1978). A health care plan that covered pregnancy for employees but limited spouses' coverage for pregnancy was struck down as violating this law. Newport News Shipbuilding and Dry Dock Co. v. Equal Employment Opportunity Comm'n, 667 F.2d 448 (4th Cir. 1982), *aff'd,* 462 U.S. 669 (1983).

96. Hoeflinger v. West Clermont Local Bd. of Educ., 478 N.E.2d 251 (Ohio App. 1984). School districts are not obligated to provide paid leave for employees to care for infants, Record v. Mill Neck Manor Lutheran School for the Deaf, 611 F. Supp. 905 (E.D.N.Y. 1985). If such childcare leave is provided, however, both men and women must be eligible.

97. Nashville Gas Co. v. Satty, 434 U.S. 136 (1977). However, a school district's policy disallowing unpaid leave and denying seniority credit for preresignation service was upheld where the policy was uniformly applied to male and female employees. Daly v. Three Village Cent. School Dist., 486 N.Y.S.2d 286 (App. Div. 1985). Also, employees who voluntarily quit their jobs because of pregnancy are not entitled to unemployment benefits. Wimberly v. Labor and Industrial Relations Comm'n of Missouri, 688 S.W.2d 344 (Mo. 1985), *cert. granted,* 106 S. Ct. 1633 (1986).

98. Solomon v. School Comm. of Boston, 478 N.E.2d 137 (Mass. 1985).

99. *See* Schwabenbauer v. Board of Educ. of City of Olean, 777 F.2d 837 (2d Cir. 1985).

100. For example, a New York appeals court found no Title VII violation in a

school board requiring a pregnant teacher to choose between taking unpaid maternity leave for an extended period of time or paid sick leave for the time pregnancy resulted in the inability to work; pregnant employees were treated the same as other employees facing a prolonged disability. West Hempstead Union Free School Dist. v. State Div. of Human Rights, 497 N.Y.S.2d 721 (App. Div. 1986).

101. California Federal Savings and Loan Ass'n v. Guerra, 758 F.2d 390, 396 (9th Cir. 1985), *aff'd,* 55 USLW 4077 (1987).
102. 414 U.S. 632 (1974). *See also* Ponton v. Newport News School Bd., 632 F. Supp. 1056 (E.D. Va. 1986) (school district and school officials were liable for damages under Title VII for forcing a married, pregnant teacher to take a leave of absence).
103. *Id.*, 414 U.S. at 643.
104. deLaurier v. San Diego Unified School Dist., 588 F.2d 674 (9th Cir. 1978).
105. City of Los Angeles Dep't of Water and Power v. Manhart, 435 U.S. 702, 708 (1978).
106. Arizona Governing Comm. v. Norris, 463 U.S. 1073 (1983).
107. *Id.* at 1086.
108. *See* Probe v. State Teachers' Retirement System, 780 F.2d 776 (9th Cir. 1986); Spirt v. TIAA-CREF, 691 F.2d 1054 (2d Cir. 1982), *vacated and remanded,* 463 U.S. 1223 (1983), *on remand,* 735 F.2d 23 (2d Cir. 1984), *cert. denied,* 105 S. Ct. 247 (1984).
109. Spirt, *id.*
110. 29 U.S.C. § 206(d)(1).
111. Burkey v. Marshall County Bd. of Educ., 513 F. Supp. 1084 (N.D.W.V. 1981). *See also* United Teachers of Seaford v. New York State Human Rights Appeal Bd., 414 N.Y.S.2d 207 (App. Div. 1979) (teacher's union violated Title VII because the union was aware that female coaches were paid less than male coaches and by failing to negotiate equitable salaries, did not represent its members fairly).
112. *See* Equal Employment Opportunity Comm'n v. Fremont Christian School, 609 F. Supp. 344 (N.D. Cal. 1984); Brennan v. Woodbridge School Dist., 74 Lab. Case (CCH) 33, 121 (D. Del. 1974). A willful violation of the EPA was found where a college could not justify the difference between the wages of male and female teachers in the same discipline who were performing substantially equivalent duties, Brock v. Georgia Southwestern College, 765 F.2d 1026 (11th Cir. 1985).
113. 452 U.S. 161 (1981). It should be noted that in a recent Title VII case involving compensation discrimination based on race, the Supreme Court ruled that an employer is obligated to eradicate the continuing impact of a pre-Title VII compensation disparity. Bazemore v. Friday, 106 S. Ct. 3000 (1986). *See* text with note 46, *supra. See also* Sobel v. Yeshiva Univ., 797 F.2d 1478 (2d Cir. 1986).
114. *See* Martha McCarthy, "Comparable Worth," *Educational Horizons,* vol. 64 (1986), pp. 109–111.
115. Spaulding v. University of Washington, 740 F.2d 686 (9th Cir. 1984), *cert. denied,* 105 S. Ct. 511 (1984).
116. American Fed'n of State, County, and Mun. Employees (AFSCME) v. Washington, 578 F. Supp. 846 (W.D. Wash. 1983), *rev'd,* 770 F.2d 1401 (9th Cir. 1985). In both cases, the appeals court rejected the assertion that mar-

ket-driven compensation practices could be challenged under the disparate impact model; plaintiffs were required to establish disparate treatment which necessitates proof of discriminatory intent.

117. Christensen v. State of Iowa, 563 F.2d 353, 356 (8th Cir. 1977). *See also* Lemons v. City and County of Denver, 620 F.2d 228 (10th Cir. 1980), *cert. denied,* 449 U.S. 888 (1980); American Nurses Ass'n v. State of Illinois, 606 F. Supp. 1313 (N.D. Ill. 1985), *rev'd and remanded,* 783 F.2d 716 (7th Cir. 1986) (while rejecting claim based on the state's failure to alter salaries according to its comparable worth study, allegations of *intentional* sex discrimination constituted cause of action).
118. For example, Minnesota and Washington have enacted such pay equity statutes. *See* "Comparable Worth in School Employment," *Title IX Line* (Center for Sex Equity in Schools, University of Michigan), vol. 5, no. 1 (1985), p. 10; *Education Week,* January 15, 1986, p. 8.
119. D. Nolan, "Sexual Harassment in Public and Private Employment," *Education Law Reporter,* vol. 3 (1982), p. 227.
120. *See* Corne v. Bausch & Lomb, Inc., 390 F. Supp. 161 (D. Ariz. 1975); Barnes v. Train, 13 FEP Cases 123 (D.D.C. 1974), *rev'd and remanded sub nom.* Barnes v. Costle, 561 F.2d 983 (D.C. Cir. 1977).
121. *See* Barnes v. Costle, *id.*; Tomkins v. Public Service Electric and Gas Co., 568 F.2d 1044 (3d Cir. 1977); Heelan v. Johns-Manville Corp., 451 F. Supp. 1382 (D. Colo. 1978).
122. Miller v. Bank of America, 600 F.2d 211, 213 (9th Cir. 1979).
123. Scott v. DeLeon, 603 F. Supp. 1328 (E.D. Mich. 1985).
124. Meritor Savings Bank v. Vinson, 106 S. Ct. 2399 (1986). *See also* Bundy v. Jackson, 641 F.2d 934 (D.C. Cir. 1981).
125. Meritor Savings Bank, *id.* at 2405. *See* 29 C.F.R. § 1604.11(a)(3).
126. *Id.* at 2406, *quoting* Henson v. City of Dundee, 682 F.2d 897, 904 (11th Cir. 1982).
127. *Id.* at 2406.
128. All justices agreed that harassment creating a hostile environment is actionable under Title VII and that the victim's consent in submitting to unwelcomed advances cannot be used as a defense. However, four justices argued that the Court should have resolved the liability issue by holding that "sexual harassment by a supervisor of an employee under his supervision, leading to a discriminatory work environment, should be imputed to the employer for Title VII purposes regardless of whether the employee gave 'notice' of the offense." *Id.* at 2411 (Marshall, J., concurring).
129. Scott v. DeLeon, 603 F. Supp. 1328, 1332 (E.D. Mich. 1985). The federal government also is authorized to investigate complaints of sexual harassment in federally funded educational programs under Title IX of the Education Amendments of 1972. *See* L. Berthel, "Sexual Harassment in Educational Institutions," *Capital University Law Review,* vol. 10 (1981), pp. 585–590.
130. Continental Can Co., Inc. v. Minnesota, 297 N.W.2d 241 (Minn. 1980). *See also* Board of Educ. of Alamogordo Public School Dist. No. 1 v. Jennings, 651 P.2d 1037 (N.M. App. 1982) (sexual harassment constitutes unsatisfactory work performance under New Mexico education law; accordingly, two work conferences and the opportunity to eliminate the unsatisfactory conduct are required before dismissal).

131. Downie v. Independent School Dist. No. 141, 367 N.W.2d 913 (Minn. App. 1985).
132. Philips v. Plaquemines Parish School Bd., 465 So. 2d 53 (La. App. 1985).
133. *See* Rogers v. Equal Employment Opportunity Comm'n, 454 F.2d 234, 238 (5th Cir. 1971) *cert. denied,* 406 U.S. 957 (1972); Brown v. City of Guthrie, 22 FEP Cases 1627, 1631 (W.D. Okla. 1980).
134. 20 U.S.C. § 1681(a).
135. *See* Cannon v. University of Chicago, 441 U.S. 677 (1979).
136. 456 U.S. 512 (1982).
137. 465 U.S. 555 (1984).
138. *See Education Week,* April 18, 1984, p. 13; *The Chronicle of Higher Education,* April 18, 1984, p. 21; *Education Daily,* April 13, 1984, pp. 1–2.
139. *See* Palmer v. Ticcione, 576 F.2d 459 (2d Cir. 1978), *cert. denied,* 440 U.S. 945 (1979). *But see* Gault v. Garrison, 569 F.2d 993 (7th Cir. 1977), *cert. denied,* 440 U.S. 945 (1979) (fitness to teach should be determined on an individual basis; mandatory retirement *per se* violates the employee's due process rights).
140. 29 U.S.C. § 621 *et seq.* This law applies to all employers, employment agencies, and labor unions. The Age Discrimination Act of 1975, 42 U.S.C. § 6101 *et seq.* also prohibits age discrimination in federally assisted programs or activities.
141. P. L. 99-592, Cong. Rec. H-11,280 (October 17, 1986). Among exceptions, this amendment allows employers to adhere to collective bargaining agreements in effect until January 1, 1990, and allows colleges and universities to compel tenured faculty members to retire at age seventy until December 31, 1993. A study is commissioned to analyze the potential consequences of eliminating mandatory retirement on institutions of higher education.
142. *See* Loeb v. Textron, Inc., 600 F.2d 1003 (1st Cir. 1979).
143. Equal Employment Opportunity Comm'n v. Wyoming, 514 F. Supp. 595 (D. Wyo. 1981), *rev'd and remanded,* 460 U.S. 226 (1983).
144. *Id.* at 239. Under ADEA, employers can observe the terms of a bona fide retirement benefit plan as long as such a plan is not a subterfuge to evade the purposes of the act. *See* United Air Lines v. McMann, 434 U.S. 192 (1977); Patterson v. Independent School Dist. No. 709, 742 F.2d 465 (8th Cir. 1984).
145. See text with notes 12–15, *supra.* For a discussion of the similarities between ADEA and Title VII, *see* Oscar Mayer Co. v. Evans, 441 U.S. 750 (1979); Lorillard v. Pons, 434 U.S. 575 (1978).
146. *See* Schwager v. Sun Oil Co., 591 F.2d 58 (10th Cir. 1979) (poor performance); Price v. Maryland Casualty Co., 561 F.2d 609 (5th Cir. 1977) (poor performance); Kerwood v. Mortgage Bankers Ass'n, 494 F. Supp. 1298 (D.D.C. 1980) (inability to relate to supervisor); Brennan v. Reynolds and Co., 367 F. Supp. 440 (N.D. Ill. 1973) (excessive tardiness).
147. Sherlock v. Merced Union High School Dist., 788 F.2d 1566 (9th Cir. 1986), *cert. denied,* 107 S. Ct. 250 (1986). For a discussion of the employee's burden of proving that age was a determinative factor in the employer's decision, *see* Equal Employment Opportunity Comm'n v. University of Oklahoma, 774 F.2d 999, 1002 (10th Cir. 1985) *cert. denied,* 106 S. Ct. 1637 (1986); Haring v. CPC International, 664 F.2d 1234, 1239 (5th Cir. 1981); Smithers v. Bailar, 629 F.2d 892, 897 (3d Cir. 1980); Loeb v. Textron, 600

F.2d 1003, 1019 (1st Cir. 1979); Laugesen v. Anaconda Co., 510 F.2d 307, 315 (6th Cir. 1975).

148. Geller v. Mackham, 635 F.2d 1027, 1032 (2d Cir. 1980), *cert. denied,* 451 U.S. 945 (1981).

149. Leftwich v. Harris-Stowe State College, 540 F. Supp. 37 (E.D. Mo. 1982), *modified,* 702 F.2d 686 (8th Cir. 1983).

150. Loeb v. Textron, 600 F.2d 1003, 1012–1013 (1st Cir. 1979). *See also* Polstorff v. Fletcher, 452 F. Supp. 17 (N.D. Ala. 1978); 29 C.F.R. 860.91(a).

151. Stumph v. Thomas and Skinner, Inc., 770 F.2d 93 (7th Cir. 1985).

152. Dolan v. School Dist. No. 10, 636 P.2d 825 (Mont. 1981). *See also* Wantagh Union Free School Dist. v. New York State Div. of Human Rights, 505 N.Y.S.2d 713 (App. Div. 1986) (Commissioner of Education was authorized to award compensatory damages where female applicant for director of pupil personnel services was discriminated against because of her sex and age).

153. Board of Regents of the Univ. of Nevada System v. Oakley, 637 P.2d 1199 (Nev. 1981).

154. Johnston v. Marion Independent School Dist., 275 N.W.2d 215, 216 (Iowa 1979).

155. *Id. See also* Selland v. Fargo Public School Dist. No. 1, 302 N.W.2d 391 (N.D. 1981).

156. *See* Vance v. Bradley, 440 U.S. 93 (1979) (federal government produced a rational basis for requiring foreign service employees to retire at age sixty); Ten Hoeve v. Board of Educ. of Dundee Cent. School Dist., 489 N.Y.S.2d 59 (Ct. App. 1985) (age restriction for school bus drivers was upheld).

157. The Developmentally Disabled Assistance and Bill of Rights Act, 42 U.S.C. § 601 *et seq.,* provides federal funds to participating states to create programs for the developmentally disabled. In 1981 the Supreme Court ruled that this law was enacted pursuant to congressional spending powers, rather than to enforce the fourteenth amendment. The court further held that the bill of rights section does not create substantive rights for the developmentally disabled, Pennhurst State School and Hosp. v. Halderman, 451 U.S. 1 (1981).

158. 29 U.S.C. § 794.

159. Gurmankin v. Costanzo, 411 F. Supp. 982 (E.D. Pa. 1976), *aff'd,* 556 F.2d 184 (3d Cir. 1977), *aff'd in part, vacated and remanded in part,* 626 F.2d 1115 (3d Cir. 1980), *cert. denied,* 450 U.S. 923 (1981).

160. *Id.,* 626 F.2d 1115 (3d Cir. 1980).

161. The court distinguished this case from Kunda v. Muhlenberg College, 621 F.2d 532 (3d Cir. 1980), in which it ordered the award of tenure to a professor who had been employed a sufficient length of time for performance to be assessed.

162. 442 U.S. 397 (1979).

163. *Id.,* 442 U.S. at 406. This conclusion is reinforced by Section 504's regulations pertaining to program admissions, which specify that an individual must meet academic *and* technical standards, with technical standards defined as all nonacademic criteria.

164. Camenisch v. University of Texas, 616 F.2d 127 (5th Cir. 1980), *vacated and remanded,* 451 U.S. 390 (1981).

165. The Supreme Court has recognized that claims of employment discrimina-

tion under Section 504 are not limited to situations "where a primary objective of the federal financial assistance is to provide employment;" as long as programs or activities receive federal funds, they must comply with the act. Consolidated Rail Corp. v. Darrone, 465 U.S. 624, 631–633 (1983).

166. Upshur v. Love, 474 F. Supp. 332 (N.D. Cal. 1979). *See also* Coleman v. Darden, 595 F.2d 533, 537 (10th Cir. 1979), *cert. denied,* 444 U.S. 927 (1979); Sabol v. Board of Educ. of Township of Willingboro County., 510 F. Supp. 892 (D.N.J. 1981).
167. Norcross v. Sneed, 755 F.2d 113 (8th Cir. 1985). *See also* School Dist. of Philadelphia v. Friedman, 507 A.2d 882 (Pa. Commw. 1986) (personality disorder causing an employee to be chronically late was not a mental disability under state law; and even if it was a disability, the employer was not required to accommodate chronic lateness).
168. Handicapped individuals also can establish disparate impact under Title VII by showing that an employer has created insurmountable barriers to employing the handicapped. For a discussion of disparate impact claims under Section 504, *see* Prewitt v. United States Postal Service, 662 F.2d 292 (5th Cir. 1981).
169. Fitzgerald v. Green Valley Area Educ. Agency, 589 F. Supp. 1130 (S.D. Iowa 1984). *See also* Board of Trustees of the Univ. of Illinois v. Human Rights Comm'n, 485 N.E.2d 33 (Ill. App. 1985).
170. Doe v. Syracuse School Dist., 508 F. Supp. 333 (N.D.N.Y. 1981). Physically handicapped plaintiffs also have prevailed in challenging their exclusion from employment as school bus drivers, if established that they can perform the job with reasonable accommodations. *See, e.g.,* Longoria v. Harris, 554 F. Supp. 102 (S.D. Tex. 1982); Coleman v. Casey County Bd. of Educ., 510 F. Supp. 301 (W.D. Ky. 1980); State Div. of Human Rights v. Averill Park Cent. School Dist., 388 N.E.2d 729 (N.Y. 1979). However, bus drivers can be required to meet standards considered necessary for the safety of students, Giampa v. Commonwealth, 492 A.2d 504 (Pa. Commw. 1985).
171. *See* Hazlett v. Martin Chevrolet, 25 Ohio St. 3d 279 (Ohio 1986); Consolidated Freightways v. Cedar Rapids Civil Rights Comm'n, 366 N.W.2d 522, 527 (Iowa 1985).
172. Kling v. County of Los Angeles, 769 F.2d 532 (9th Cir. 1985), *rev'd mem.,* 106 S. Ct. 300 (1985).
173. Arline v. School Bd. of Nassau County, 772 F.2d 759 (11th Cir. 1985), *cert. granted,* 106 S. Ct. 1633 (1986). The court reasoned that the school district's receipt of federal impact aid obligated the district to comply with Section 504. For a discussion of this case, *see* Joseph Beckham, "Arline v. School Board of Nassau County: Contagious Disease as a 'Handicap' Within the Meaning of Section 504 of the Rehabilitation Act," *Education Law Reporter,* vol. 28 (1985), pp. 325–332.
174. *See The Chronicle of Higher Education,* July 2, 1986, pp. 9, 11. The National Centers for Disease Control have issued guidelines indicating that AIDS is not transmitted through casual contact. For a discussion of students with AIDS attending school, *see* text with note 35, chapter 3.
175. *See* Doyle v. University of Alabama-Birmingham, 680 F.2d 1323, 1326 (11th Cir. 1982); Brown v. Sibley, 650 F.2d 760, 769 (5th Cir. 1981). State agencies also may be able to avoid liability under Section 504 by pleading immunity

under the eleventh amendment which bars federal suits against a state by its citizens. The Supreme Court has ruled that states do not waive eleventh amendment immunity by accepting funds under the Rehabilitation Act. Atascadero State Hosp. v. Scanlon, 105 S. Ct. 3142 (1985). For a discussion of the application of eleventh amendment immunity to school districts, *see* text with note 183, chapter 8.

176. *See* Torcaso v. Watkins, 367 U.S. 488 (1961); Cantwell v. Connecticut, 310 U.S. 296, 303–304 (1940).
177. *See* text with note 41, chapter 2.
178. Palmer v. Board of Educ. of City of Chicago, 603 F.2d 1271 (7th Cir. 1979), *cert. denied,* 444 U.S. 1026 (1980).
179. Torcaso v. Watkins, 367 U.S. 488 (1961). *See also* Beauregard v. City of St. Albans, 450 A.2d 1148 (Vt. 1982) (membership on the public school board of trustees could not be conditioned on religious preference).
180. *See* Russo v. Central School Dist. No. 1, 469 F.2d 623, 634 (2d Cir. 1972), *cert. denied,* 411 U.S. 932 (1973); Opinions of the Justices to the Governor, 363 N.E.2d 251 (Mass. 1977); Hanover v. Northrup, 325 F. Supp. 170 (D. Conn. 1970); text with note 71, chapter 2.
181. 42 U.S.C. § 2000e(j).
182. Trans World Airlines v. Hardison, 432 U.S. 63 (1977).
183. Philbrook v. Ansonia Bd. of Educ., 757 F.2d 476 (2d Cir. 1985), *remanded,* 107 S. Ct. 367 (1986).
184. Edwards v. School Bd. of Norton, Virginia, 483 F. Supp. 620 (W.D. Va. 1980), *vacated and remanded,* 658 F.2d 951 (4th Cir. 1981).
185. Niederhuber v. Camden County Voc.-Tech. School Dist., 495 F. Supp. 273 (D.N.J. 1980).
186. Rankins v. Commission on Professional Competence, 593 P.2d 852 (Cal. 1979), *appeal dismissed,* 444 U.S. 986 (1979).
187. School Dist. No. 11, Joint Counties of Archuleta and LaPlata v. Umberfield, 512 P.2d 1166 (Colo. App. 1973), *modified,* 522 P.2d 730 (Colo. 1974).
188. Pinsker v. Joint Dist. No. 28J of Adams and Arapahoe Counties, 735 F.2d 388 (10th Cir. 1984). *See also* Pasquale v. Board of Educ., Williamsville Cent. School Dist., 626 F. Supp. 457 (W.D.N.Y. 1985).
189. Hunterdon Cent. High School Bd. of Educ. v. Hunterdon Cent. High School Teachers' Ass'n, 429 A.2d 354 (N.J. 1981). A 1985 Supreme Court decision lends support to the contention that paid leave tied specifically to religious observances might unconstitutionally advance religion. The Court struck down a Connecticut law (giving employees the unqualified right not to work on their chosen sabbath) as entailing an absolute preference based on religious beliefs in violation of the establishment clause. Thorton v. Caldor, 105 S. Ct. 2914 (1985).
190. Mandel v. Hodges, 127 Cal. Rptr. 244 (Cal. App. 1976). However, the following year a California appeals court upheld a school district's collective bargaining agreement, designating Good Friday as a paid holiday for all employees. The court reasoned that the main purpose of the agreement was to afford teachers a longer spring vacation, and the paid holiday was not expressly tied to religious worship. California School Employment Ass'n v. Sequoia Union High School Dist., 136 Cal. Rptr. 594 (Cal. App. 1977).
191. Ansonia Bd. of Educ. v. Philbrook, 107 S. Ct. 367, 373 (1986).

10

Termination of Employment

State laws define the authority of school boards in terminating the employment of school personnel. Generally, these laws specify the causes for which a teacher may be terminated and the procedures that must be followed. The right of the school board to determine the fitness of teachers has been well established; in fact, courts have declared that school boards have a duty as well as a right to make such determinations. The United States Supreme Court has recognized that such authority is vested in school boards. According to the Court:

> A teacher works in a sensitive area in a schoolroom. There he shapes the attitude of young minds towards the society in which they live. In this, the state has a vital concern. It must preserve the integrity of the schools. That the school authorities have *the right and the duty to screen* the officials, teachers, and employees as to their fitness to maintain the integrity of the schools as a part of ordered society, cannot be doubted.[1] [emphasis added]

Numerous factors surround the screening process of the school board. This chapter addresses the procedures that must be followed in termination of a teacher's employment and the grounds for dismissal. First, an overview of due process is presented, exploring two basic questions: *When* is due process required? *What* process is due? Since due process is required only if a teacher is able to establish that a protected property or liberty interest is at stake, the initial section of the chapter focuses on the dimensions of teachers' property and liberty rights in the context of employment termination. In the next section, specific procedural requirements are identified and discussed. A survey of causes for dismissal is presented in the third section to provide a broad perspective on judicial interpretations of state laws. The concluding section provides an overview of remedies available to teachers for wrongful termination.

DUE PROCESS IN GENERAL

Basic due process rights are embodied in the fourteenth amendment, which guarantees that no state shall "deprive any person of life, liberty, or property without due process of law."[2] Due process safeguards apply not only in judicial proceedings but also to acts of governmental agencies such as school boards. As discussed in chapter 1, constitutional due process entails substantive protections against arbitrary governmental action and procedural protections when the government threatens an individual's life, liberty, or property interests. Most teacher termination cases have focused on procedural due process requirements.

The nature of procedural due process required is influenced by the individual and governmental interests at stake and the applicable state laws. Courts have established that a teacher's interest in public employment may entail significant "property" and "liberty" rights necessitating due process prior to employment termination. A property interest is a "legitimate claim of entitlement" to continued employment that is created by state law.[3] The granting of tenure conveys such a right to a teacher. Also, a contract establishes a property right to employment within the terms of the contract.

The judiciary has recognized that fourteenth amendment liberty rights encompass fundamental constitutional guarantees, such as freedom of speech. Procedural due process is always required when terminations implicate such fundamental liberties. A liberty interest also is involved when termination creates a stigma or damages an individual's reputation in a manner that forecloses future employment opportunities.[4] If protected liberty or property interests are implicated, due process entitles the teacher at least to notice of the reasons for the school board's action and an opportunity for a hearing.

Employment terminations can be classified as either dismissals or nonrenewals. The distinction between the two has significant implications for the procedural rights that must be accorded a teacher. Nonrenewal is the release of a probationary or nontenured teacher at the end of the contract period, and generally requires only notice that the teacher will not be reappointed. On the other hand, dismissal is the termination of a tenured teacher, or a nontenured teacher within the contract period, and necessitates full procedural protection. In this section, the procedural safeguards that must be provided the tenured teacher and the nontenured teacher are distinguished. Specific attention is given to the conditions that may give rise to a nontenured teacher acquiring a protected liberty or property interest in employment, and, thereby, establishing a claim to procedural due process.

Dismissal

The term "dismissal" refers to the termination for cause of any tenured teacher or a probationary teacher within the contract period. Both tenure statutes and employment contracts establish a property interest entitling teachers to full procedural protection. At a minimum, the Federal Constitution guarantees that an individual will not be deprived of a property right without notice and an opportunity to be heard. Beyond the basic constitutional requirements, state laws and school board policies contain detailed procedures that must be followed. However, failure to provide these procedures results in a violation of state law, rather than constitutional law.[5] Statutory procedures vary as to specificity, with some states enumerating detailed steps and others identifying only broad parameters. In each instance, the requirements are binding on the school board. Furthermore, a school district must comply with its own procedures, even if they exceed state law. For example, if school board policy provides for a preliminary notice of teaching inadequacies and an opportunity to correct remediable deficiences prior to dismissal, fairness dictates that a board comply with these steps.

A critical element in dismissal actions is a showing of justifiable cause for termination of employment. If causes are identified by state law, a school board must base dismissal on those grounds. Failure to relate the charges to statutory grounds can invalidate the termination decision. Because typical statutes list broad causes such as incompetency, insubordination, immorality, unprofessional conduct, neglect of duty, and other good and just cause, notice of discharge must clearly indicate conduct substantiating the legal charges. Procedural safeguards ensure that, not only will a teacher be informed of the specific reasons and grounds for dismissal, but also, the school board must prove the grounds and base its decision on those grounds. Detailed aspects of procedural due process requirements and dismissal for cause are addressed in subsequent sections of this chapter.

Nonrenewal

In most states, procedural protections are not accorded the probationary teacher when the employment contract is not renewed. At the end of the contract period, employment can be terminated simply for no reason or any reason, as long as the reason is not constitutionally impermissible (e.g., racial discrimination, denial of protected speech).[6] Generally, the only statutory requirement is notification of nonrenewal on or before a specified date prior to the expiration of the contract. Timeliness of nonrenewal notices is strictly construed by courts. When a deadline for nonrenewal is designated by statute, a school board *must* notify a teacher on or before the established date. The fact that the school board has set in motion notification (e.g., mailed the notice) generally does not satisfy the statutory requirement; actual receipt of the notice by the teacher is critical.[7] For example, in a situation where a statutory deadline was April 30 and the notice was mailed on April 29 but not received until May 2, notice was held to be inadequate.[8] A teacher, however, cannot purposively avoid or deliberately thwart delivery of notice and then claim insufficiency of notice.[9] Failure of school officials to observe the notice deadline may result in reinstatement of a teacher for an additional year or even the granting of tenure in some jurisdictions.[10]

In the nonrenewal of teachers, a few states require a written statement of reasons and, on the request of the teacher, an opportunity for a hearing; such provisions do not usually imply the right to an evidentiary hearing requiring the school board to show cause for termination.[11] A teacher is simply provided the reasons underlying the nonrenewal and an opportunity to address the school board.[12] Where state law establishes specific requirements and procedures for nonrenewal, however, failure to abide by these provisions may invalidate a termination. In West Virginia, for example, school officials' failure to follow the State Board of Education evaluation procedure requiring that probationary employees be informed of inadequate job performance and provided time for improvement resulted in reinstatement of teachers.[13] Likewise, the failure of a local school board to comply substantially with its own nonrenewal procedures will not be upheld by the judiciary.[14]

Although state laws may not provide the probationary teacher specific procedural protections, a teacher's interest in continued public employment may be constitutionally protected if established that a liberty or property right has been abridged. The scope of protected interests encompassed by the fourteenth amendment was addressed by the United States Supreme Court in two significant decisions in 1972, *Board of Regents v. Roth*[15] and *Perry v. Sindermann.*[16] According to these decisions, the infringement of a liberty or property interest entitles a probationary teacher to due process rights similar to the rights of tenured teachers. While these cases involved faculty members at the postsecondary level, the rulings are equally applicable to public elementary and secondary school teachers.

In *Roth,* the question presented to the Court was whether a nontenured teacher had a constitutional right to a statement of reasons and a hearing prior to nonreappointment. Roth was hired on a fixed contract for one academic year. The university elected not to rehire him for a second year. Since Roth did not have tenure, there was no entitlement under Wisconsin law to an explanation of charges or a hearing; the univeristy simply did not reemploy him for the succeeding year. Roth challenged the nonrenewal, alleging that failure to provide notice of reasons and an opportunity for a hearing infringed upon his due process rights.

The Supreme Court held that nonrenewal did not require procedural protection unless impairment of a protected liberty or property interest could be shown. To establish infringement of a liberty interest, the Court held that the teacher must show that the employer's action (1) resulted in damage to his or her reputation and standing in the community, or (2) imposed a stigma that foreclosed other employment opportunities. The evidence presented by Roth indicated that there was no such damage to his reputation or future employment. Accordingly, the Supreme Court concluded that "it stretches the concept too far to suggest that a person is deprived of 'liberty' when he simply is not rehired in one job but remains as free as before to seek another."[17]

The Court also rejected Roth's claim that he had a protected property interest to continued employment. The Court held that in order to establish a valid property right an individual must have more than an "abstract need or desire" for a position; there must be a "legitimate claim of entitlement."[18] Property interests are not defined by the Federal Constitution, but rather by state laws or employment contracts that secure specific benefits. An abstract desire or unilateral expectation of continued employment alone does not constitute a property right. The terms of Roth's one-year appointment and the state law precluded any claim of entitlement.

On the same day it rendered the *Roth* decision, the Supreme Court in the *Sindermann* case explained the circumstances that might create a legitimate expectancy of reemployment for a nontenured teacher.[19] Sindermann was a nontenured faculty member in his fourth year of teaching when he was notified, without a statement of reasons or an opportunity for a hearing, that his contract would not be renewed. He challenged the lack of procedural due process, alleging that nonrenewal deprived him of a property interest protected by the fourteenth amendment and violated his first amendment right to freedom of speech.

In advancing a protected property right, Sindermann claimed that the college, which lacked a formal tenure system, had created an informal or de facto tenure system through various practices and policies. Specifically, Sindermann cited a provision in the faculty guide stating that "the College wishes the faculty member to feel that he has permanent tenure as long as his teaching services are satisfactory."[20] The Supreme Court found that Sindermann's claim, unlike Roth's, may have been based on a legitimate expectancy of reemployment promulgated by the college. According to the Court, the lack of a formal tenure system did not foreclose the possibility of an institution fostering an entitlement to a position through its personnel policies.

In assessing Sindermann's free speech claim, the Supreme Court confirmed that a teacher's lack of tenure does not void a claim that nonrenewal was based on the exercise of constitutionally protected conduct. Procedural due process must be afforded when a substantive constitutional right is violated. According to a more recent Supreme Court decision, if a constitutional right is implicated in a nonrenewal, the burden is placed on the teacher to show that protected conduct was a substantial or motivating factor in the school board's decision.[21] The establishment of this inference of a constitutional violation then shifts the burden to the school board to show by a preponderance of evidence that it would have reached the same decision in the absence of the protected activity.

The *Roth* and *Sindermann* cases serve as the legal precedents for assessing the procedural rights of nontenured teachers. To summarize, the Supreme Court held that a nontenured teacher does not have a constitutionally protected property right in employment requiring procedural due process before denial of reappointment. However, certain actions of the school board may create conditions entitling a nontenured teacher to notice and a hearing similar to the tenured teacher. Such actions would include:

- nonrenewal decisions damaging an individual's reputation and integrity,
- nonrenewal decisions foreclosing other employment opportunities,
- policies and practices creating a valid claim to reemployment, and
- nonrenewal decisions violating fundamental constitutional guarantees.

Since the Supreme Court has held that impairment of a nontenured teacher's property or liberty interest triggers procedural protections, the question arises as to what constitutes a violation of these interests. Courts have purposely avoided precisely defining the concepts of liberty and property, preferring to allow experience and time to shape their meanings.[22] Since 1972 the Supreme Court and federal appellate courts have rendered a number of decisions that provide some guidance in understanding these concepts.

Property Interest. In general, a nontenured employee does not have a property claim to reappointment unless state or local governmental action has clearly established such a right.[23] A federal district court found that a Delaware school board created a reasonable expectancy of reemployment requiring procedural protection when it advised a principal that his contract would be renewed if his performance was satisfactory.[24] The court concluded that the principal was justified in believing that he would be reappointed after receiving a satisfactory rating. Similarly, the Fourth Circuit Court of Appeals found that a two-year employment promise to a coach/athletic director established a legitimate expectation of continued employment.[25] To persuade the athletic director to accept the position, the board had assured him that his one-year contract would be extended for a second year. Based on such an implied contract, the court found that unilateral termination of the contract after one year violated the individual's due process rights.

Protected property interests are not created by mere longevity in employment. Both the Fourth and Tenth Circuit Appellate Courts found that issuing an employee a series of contracts over a number of years did not constitute a valid claim to continued employment in the absence of a guarantee in state law, local policy, or an employment contract.[26] Similarly, a statute or collective bargaining agreement providing a teacher, upon request, a hearing and statement of reasons for nonrenewal does not confer a property interest in employment requiring legally sufficient cause for termination.[27] Such a provision simply gives the teacher an opportunity to present reasons why the contract should be renewed.[28]

Establishing a legitimate expectancy of reemployment in a school district with a formal tenure system is difficult.[29] If a tenure system exists, courts have refused to consider de facto tenure arguments except in "extraordinary circumstances."[30] An Arizona federal district court decision illustrates the unique conditions that must exist to present a valid property claim.[31] In that case, an individual was offered a faculty position with tenure, but because of personal considerations, he rejected the offer of tenure and secured assurance that it would be awarded at a later time. In fact, the dean of the college attached an addendum to the offer stating that "the initial appointment will not be with tenure, but you will receive tenure automatically beginning in [your third year], or sooner at our mutual convenience."[32] Prior to awarding the teacher tenure, the university decided, without a statement of reasons or a hearing, not to renew his contract. The teacher challenged the action as a violation of his property rights, and the federal court agreed. The court concluded that the offer of employment promising tenure was an exceptional situation that would lead the faculty member legitimately to expect continued employment. With such an expectation, the university was required to treat his termination in the same manner as that of a tenured teacher.

As noted, property rights are created by state laws or contracts but also may emanate from policies, regulations, or implied contracts. The sufficiency of the claim, however, must be interpreted in light of a state's laws, irrespective of the claim's origin. In some instances, reference to state law can narrowly restrict or limit alleged property interests. For example, the United States Supreme Court, in construing a North Carolina employee's property rights, relied on the state supreme court's opinion that "an enforceable expectation of continued public employment in that State can exist only if the employer, by *statute or contract,* has actually granted some form of guarantee"[33] [emphasis added]. Although in this case a city ordinance gave rise to an expectancy of reemployment after the successful completion of a six-month probationary period, the Supreme Court reasoned that, in the absence of a statutory or contractual obligation, the employee worked at the will and pleasure of the city. To determine a property right, then, it is necessary to establish not only that the employer's actions led to an expectancy of employment but also that state law does not limit the claim.

Liberty Interest. As noted previously, liberty interests encompass fundamental constitutional guarantees such as freedom of expression and privacy rights. If the reason given for a nonrenewal implicates such fundamental liberties, procedural due process must be afforded. Most nonrenewals, however, do not overtly implicate fundamental rights, and thus, the burden is on the aggrieved employee to prove that the proffered reason is pretextual to mask impermissible grounds.

A liberty interest also may be implicated if a nonrenewal damages the employee's reputation. The Supreme Court established in *Roth* that damage to a teacher's reputation or employability could infringe fourteenth amendment liberty rights. In subsequent decisions, the Supreme Court has identified other factors that are prerequisite to establishing that a constitutionally impermissible stigma has been imposed. According to the Court, procedural protections must be afforded only if stigma or damaging statements are:

- related to loss of employment,
- publicly disclosed, and
- alleged to be false.[34]

Governmental action damaging a teacher's reputation, standing alone, is insufficient to invoke the procedural safeguards of the fourteenth amendment. The Supreme Court has held that a liberty interest must be raised in connection with a loss of a governmental benefit such as employment. Generally, under this "stigma-plus" test, a teacher who has been defamed by reassignment or a transfer cannot claim violation of a liberty interest.[35] The Fifth Circuit Court of Appeals noted that "the internal transfer of an employee, unless it constitutes such a change of status as to be regarded essentially as a loss of employment, does not provide the additional loss of a tangible interest necessary to give rise to a liberty interest meriting protection under the due process clause of the fourteenth amendment."[36] Similarly, the suspension of a teacher for one week with pay for improper touching of a female student was not considered a tangible loss that would implicate a liberty interest.[37] While the charge was stigmatizing and affected the teacher's reputation, there was no deprivation of liberty.

Likewise, liberty is unaffected unless damaging reasons are publicly communicated.[38] The primary purpose of a hearing is to enable an individual to clear his or her name. Without public knowledge of the reasons for nonreappointment, such a hearing is not required. A school board is not constitutionally obligated to provide a hearing as long as reasons are conveyed in a confidential manner or at a closed meeting.[39] Neither is a protected liberty interest affected by statements that are disclosed in a public meeting requested by the teacher, since the board's action did not publicize the comments.[40] Further, rumors or hearsay remarks surfacing as a result of nonrenewal do not impair liberty interests. The First Circuit Court of Appeals noted that "in terms of likely stigmatizing effect, there is a world of difference between official charges (say, of excessive drinking) made publicly and a campus rumor based upon hearsay."[41] Even when a school board publicly announces stigmatizing reasons for its action, there must be a factual dispute regarding the truth of the allegations for a hearing to be required. If a teacher does not challenge the truth of the statements, a name-clearing hearing serves no purpose.[42]

The primary issue in these terminations is determining what charges constitute stigmatization. Nonrenewal alone is insufficient. As the Ninth Circuit Court of Appeals noted, "nearly any reason assigned for dismissal is likely to be to some extent a negative reflection on an individual's ability, temperament, or character," but circumstances giving rise to a liberty interest are narrow.[43] Charges must be serious implications against character, such as immorality and dishonesty, to create a stigma of constitutional magnitude. According to the Fifth Circuit Appellate Court, a charge must give rise to "a 'badge of infamy,' public scorn, or the like."[44] Such a liberty violation is clearly illustrated by the termination of a teacher of life science after public attacks on his teaching of human reproduction.[45] In this case, the appellate court found that the teacher was subjected to extensive, embarrassing publicity in the local as well as worldwide media (being referred to as a sex maniac), incurred substantial personal harassment, and suffered permanent damage to his professional career.

Among the accusations that lower federal courts have found to necessitate a hearing are: (1) a serious drinking problem, (2) apparent emotional instability, (3) mental illness, and (4) immoral conduct.[46] Reasons held to pose no threat to a liberty interest include: (1) job-related comments such as personality differences and difficulty in getting along with others, (2) hostility toward authority, (3) incompetence, (4) aggressive behavior, and (5) poor performance.[47] Charges relating to job performance may have an impact on future employment but do not create a stigma of constitutional magnitude.

PROCEDURAL DUE PROCESS REQUIREMENTS IN DISCHARGE PROCEEDINGS

Termination of a tenured teacher or a nontenured teacher during the contract period requires procedural due process. The central question is *what process is due.* Courts have noted that there is no fixed set of procedures applicable under all circumstances. Rather, due process entails a balancing of the individual and governmental interests affected in each situation. According to the Supreme Court, a determination of the specific aspects of due process requires consideration of:

> [f]irst, the private interest that will be affected by the official action; second, the risk of an erroneous deprivation of such interest through the procedures used, and the probable value, if any, of additional or substitute procedural safeguards; and finally, the Government's interest, including the function involved and the fiscal and administrative burdens that the additional or substitute procedural requirement would entail.[48]

Application of these standards would require only minimum procedures in the suspension of a student but a more extensive, formal process in the dismissal of a teacher.

Minimally, due process requires that dismissal proceedings be based on established rules or standards, and that the teacher be notified of the charges and provided an opportunity to be heard. Actual procedures will depend on state law and school board regulations. In assessing the adequacy of procedural safeguards, the judiciary looks for the provision of certain basic elements to meet constitutional guarantees. Courts have generally held that a teacher facing a severe loss such as termination of employment must be ensured procedures encompassing the following elements:[49]

- notification of charges,
- opportunity for a hearing,
- adequate time to prepare a rebuttal to the charges,
- access to evidence and names of witnesses,
- hearing before an impartial tribunal,
- representation by legal counsel,
- opportunity to present evidence and witnesses,
- opportunity to cross-examine adverse witnesses,
- decision based on evidence and findings of the hearing,
- transcript or record of the hearing, and
- opportunity to appeal an adverse decision.

Beyond these constitutional considerations, courts also enforce procedural protections conferred by state laws and local policies. The procedures often are more extensive than constitutional guarantees and must be strictly followed. Examples of such requirements might be providing detailed performance evaluations prior to termination, notifying teachers of weaknesses, and allowing an opportunity for improvement before dismissal. While failure to comply with these stipulations may invalidate the school board's action under state law, federal due process rights *per se* are not violated if minimal constitutional procedures are provided.[50]

Various elements of school board due process proceedings may be contested as inadequate. Questions arise regarding issues such as the sufficiency of notice, impartiality of the board members, and placement of the burden of proof. The aspects of procedural due process that courts frequently scrutinize in assessing the fundamental fairness of school board actions are examined below.

NOTICE

In general, a constitutionally adequate notice is timely, informs the teacher of specific charges, and allows the teacher sufficient time to prepare a response. Beyond the constitutional guarantees, state laws and school board policies (local and state) usually impose very specific requirements relating to form, timeliness, and content of notice. In legal challenges, the adequacy of a notice is assessed in terms of whether it meets constitutional as well as other requirements. Failure to comply substantially with mandated requisites will void school board action.

The form or substance of notice is usually stipulated in statutes. In determining appropriateness of notice, courts have generally held that substantial compliance with form requirements (as opposed to strict compliance required for notice deadlines) is sufficient. Under this standard, the decisive factor is whether the notice adequately informs the teacher of the pending action rather than the actual form of the notice.[51] For example, if a statute requires notification by certified mail and the notice is mailed by registered mail or is personally delivered, it substantially complies with the state requirement. Although adequacy is the primary consideration regarding form, oral notification will not satisfy the requirement of written notification.[52] If the form of the notice is not specified in statute, any timely notice that informs a teacher is adequate.[53]

While form and timeliness are important concerns in issuing a notice, the primary consideration is the statement of reasons or charges for an action. With termination of a tenured or nonprobationary teacher's contract, school boards must bring specific charges against the teacher. If the state law identifies grounds for dismissal, charges must be based on the statutory causes. A teacher, however, cannot be forced to defend against vague and indefinite statutory charges such as incompetency or neglect of duty. Notice must include specific accusations to enable the teacher to prepare a proper defense. To illustrate, the Supreme Court of Nebraska held that a listing of statutory causes and witnesses did not inform the teacher of the factual allegations underlying the charges.[54] Impermissible vagueness also was found by the Wyoming Supreme Court in a notice specifying that the teacher was using instructional methods that conflicted with the philosophy of the school board and administration.[55] Similarly, a federal district court found conclusory statements identifying the teacher's need to improve and ways to improve to be inadequate notice.[56] In some instances, state law may further require that the notice delineate the nexus between the teacher's conduct and responsibilities and duties as a teacher.[57] Finally, only charges identified in the notice can form the basis for dismissal.[58]

Hearing

In addition to notice, some type of hearing is required *before* an employer makes the initial termination decision; posttermination hearings do not satisfy constitutional due process requirements. Most state statutory provisions ensure this procedural protection for teachers. In a significant 1985 decision, *Cleveland Board of Education v. Loudermill,* the United States Supreme Court recognized the necessity for a pretermination hearing. While the Court emphasized that a full evidentiary hearing to resolve the propriety of the discharge is not required, an initial hearing must be provided to serve as a check against wrong decisions.[59] This would entail determining if there are reasonable grounds to believe that the charges are true and that they support the dismissal of an employee. Essentially, in such a pretermination hearing, an employee is entitled to notice of the charges and evidence and an opportunity to respond, orally or in writing, as to why the proposed action should not be taken. If only the minimal pretermination procedures outlined by the Supreme Court are provided, a full evidentiary posttermination hearing is required. Even extenuating circumstances involving severe disruption to the educational process cannot justify the omission of a preliminary determination. Under emergency conditions, however, teachers can be suspended with pay pending a termination hearing.

Courts have not prescribed in detail the procedures to be followed in administrative hearings. Basically, the fundamental constitutional requirement is fair play, that is, an opportunity to be heard at a meaningful time and in a meaningful manner.[60] Beyond this general requirement, the specific aspects of a hearing are influenced by the circumstances of the case, with the potential for grievous losses necessitating more extensive safeguards. According to the Missouri Supreme Court, a hearing generally should include a meaningful opportunity to be heard, to state one's position, to present witnesses, and to cross-examine witnesses; the accused also has the right to counsel and access to written reports in advance of the hearing.[61] Implicit in these rudimentary requirements are the assumptions that the hearing will be conducted by an impartial decision maker and that the decision will be based on the evidence presented. The following discussion examines issues that may arise in adversarial hearings before the school board.

Adequate Notice of Hearing. As noted, due process rights afford an individual the opportunity to be heard at a meaningful time. This implies that sufficient time is allowed between notice of the hearing and the scheduled meeting. Unless a time period is designated by state law, the school board can establish a reasonable time for the hearing. The length of time provided may vary from situation to situation, depending on the facts and circumstances. In a termination action, the school board would be expected to provide ample time for the teacher to prepare a defense. The burden, however, is placed on the teacher to request additional time if the length of notice is insufficient to prepare an adequate response. A notice as short as two days was upheld as satisfying due process requirements where the teacher participated in the hearing and did not object to the time or request a postponement.[62] Similarly, a one-day notice was found not to violate due process rights when the teacher did not attend the meeting to raise objections.[63] A teacher who participates fully in the hearing process or waives the right to a hearing by failure to attend cannot later raise lack of adequate time to invalidate the due process proceeding.

Waiver of Hearing. Although a hearing is an essential element of due process, a teacher can waive this right by refusing to attend a hearing or by walking out of a hearing.[64] If state law provides an opportunity for a hearing upon the request of a teacher, failure to request such a hearing also constitutes a waiver. In some states, a hearing before the school board may be waived by an employee's election of an alternative hearing procedure such as an impartial referee or a grievance mechanism. A Pennsylvania school board was not required to provide a school employee a hearing in addition to the arbitration proceeding he selected.[65] In this case, the Third Circuit Court of Appeals held that either a hearing before the school board or arbitration under the collective bargaining agreement met the constitutional requirements of due process. Similarly, an Ohio federal district court held that due process rights were not infringed by denying a teacher the right to be heard before the school board prior to a decision on an impartial referee's report.[66]

Impartiality of the School Board. One of the central questions raised regarding hearings is the impartiality of the school board as a hearing body. This issue arises because school boards often perform multiple functions in a hearing; they may investigate the allegations against a teacher, initiate the proceedings, and render the final judgment. Teachers have contended that such expansive involvement violates their right to an unbiased decision maker. Courts have generally rejected the idea that combining the adjudicative and investigative functions violates due process rights.[67] As such, prior knowledge of the facts does not disqualify school board members. In addition, the fact that the board makes the initial decision to terminate employment does not render subsequent review impermissibly biased. Neither is a hearing prejudiced by a limited, preliminary inquiry to determine if there is a basis for terminating a teacher. The Colorado Supreme Court noted that, since hearings are costly and time-consuming, a preliminary investigation to determine the need for school board action may save time as well as potential embarrassment.[68]

In *Hortonville Joint School District v. Hortonville Education Association,* the United States Supreme Court firmly established that the school board is a proper review body to conduct dismissal hearings.[69] In this case, the Supreme Court held that a school board's involvement in collective negotiations did not disqualify it as an impartial hearing board in the subsequent dismissal of striking teachers. The Court noted:

> A showing that the Board was "involved" in the events preceding this decision, in light of the important interest in leaving with the Board the power given by the state legislature, is not enough to overcome the presumption of honesty and integrity in policymakers with decisionmaking power.[70]

Although the school board is the proper hearing body, specific bias on the part of the board or its members is constitutionally unacceptable. A teacher challenging the impartiality of the board has the burden of proving actual, not merely potential, bias. This requires the teacher to show more than prior knowledge of the issues or views by board members. A high probability of bias, however, can be shown to exist if a board member has a personal interest in the outcome of the hearing or has suffered personal abuse or criticism from a teacher.

Several recent cases illustrate instances of unacceptable bias. For example, the Alabama Supreme Court invalidated a teacher termination hearing for "intolerably high bias" created by a school board member's son testifying against the teacher.[71] The son had been the target of personal abuse by the teacher. The Tenth Circuit Court of Appeals also ruled that bias was shown because one of the board members had campaigned to remove the superintendent from his position, and two other board members had made unfavorable statements to the effect that the superintendent "had to go."[72] The Iowa Supreme Court concluded that a school board's role of "investigation, instigation, prosecution, and verdict rendering" denied a teacher an impartial hearing, since the board used no witnesses and relied solely on its personal knowledge of the case in reaching a decision.[73] Other instances showing lack of impartiality include board members testifying as witnesses, prior announcements by board members of views and positions showing closed minds, and board members assuming adversarial or prosecutorial roles.[74]

An individual serving as prosecutor and also as advisor or counsel to the board may impair due process rights. The Supreme Court of Colorado cautioned that "[n]ot only is actual fairness mandated, but the integrity of the administrative process also requires that the appearance of fairness be preserved." [75] In this case, the presence of the superintendent and principal, both initiators of the charges and witnesses, during the board's closed deliberations, was found to undermine the appearance of impartiality. In addition, a school board's legal counsel serving both prosecutorial and advisory roles may create an unacceptable risk of bias or appearance of prejudice.[76]

Evidence. Under teacher tenure laws, the burden of proof is placed on the school board to show cause for dismissal. The standard of proof generally applied to administrative bodies is to produce a "preponderance of evidence."[77] Administrative hearings are not held to the more stringent standards applied in criminal proceedings (e.g., clear and convincing evidence beyond a reasonable doubt).[78] Proof by a preponderance of evidence simply indicates that the majority of the evidence supports the board's decision or, as several courts have stated, "such relevant evidence as a reasonable mind might accept as adequate to support a conclusion."[79] If the board fails to meet this burden of proof, the decision will not be upheld by the judiciary. For example, the Nebraska Supreme Court, in overturning a school board's dismissal decision, concluded that dissatisfaction of parents and school board members was not sufficient evidence to substantiate claims of incompetency against a teacher who had received above-average performance evaluations during her entire term of employment.[80]

The objective of school board hearings is to ascertain the relevant facts of the situation.[81] In the school setting, hearings are not encumbered by technical, judicial rules of evidence.[82] In some termination cases, charges also carry criminal liability, but termination proceedings are separate from the criminal proceedings. Dismissal might be warranted based on the evidence presented, even though such evidence would not satisfy the more stringent requirements to sustain a criminal conviction.

Evidence introduced, however, should be relevant to the charges[83] and well documented. Only evidence presented at the hearing can be the basis for the board's decision.[84] Unlike formal judicial proceedings, hearsay evidence is generally admissible in administrative hearings.[85] Courts have held that such evidence provides the background necessary for understanding the situation. While comments and complaints of parents have been considered relevant, hearsay statements of students have been given little weight.[86]

Findings and Decisions. At the conclusion of the hearing, the board must make specific findings of fact. A written report of the findings on which the board based its decision is essential. Without a report of the findings of fact, appropriate administrative or judicial review would be impeded. The Minnesota Supreme Court noted that "[i]f the trial court were to review the merits of the case without findings of fact, there would be no safeguard against judicial encroachment on the school board's function since the trial court might affirm on a charge rejected by the school board."[87] Similarly, the Oklahoma Supreme Court held that a probationary teacher's statutory entitlement to a hearing includes the right to be told why the board reached its decision.[88] The court admonished that "an absence of required findings is fatal to the validity of administrative decisions even if the record discloses evidence to support proper findings."[89] The findings of fact do not have to be issued in technical language but simply in a form that explains the reasons for the action.

DISMISSAL FOR CAUSE

Tenure laws are designed to provide competent teachers assurance of continued employment as long as their performance is satisfactory. With the protection of tenure, a teacher can be dismissed only for cause, and only in accordance with the procedures specified by law. Although acquiring tenure status gives a teacher a vested interest in continued employment that cannot be denied without due process of law, it does not guarantee permanent employment. The school district may discharge the teacher for cause or because of conditions within the district, such as financial exigencies or declining enrollment, that necessitate reductions in the teaching force. Tenure rights accrue under individual state laws and therefore must be interpreted in light of each state's provisions.

Dismissal safeguards generally emanate from tenure statutes and are not applicable to the nontenured teacher. Within a contract period, however, certain procedural rights are constitutionally guaranteed. That is, a probationary teacher with an annual contract cannot be dismissed during the term of the contract except for cause and with procedural due process. The contract itself establishes a property right to due process that extends throughout the contract period.

Where causes or grounds for dismissal of a permanent teacher are identified by statute, a school board cannot base the dismissal decision on reasons other than those contained in law.[90] To cover unexpected matters, statutes often include a catch-all phrase such as "other good and just cause." Causes included in statutes vary considerably among states and range from an extensive listing of individual grounds to a simple statement that dismissal must be based on cause. The most frequently cited causes are incompetency, neglect of duty, insubordination, and immorality.[91]

Since grounds for dismissal are statutorily determined, it is difficult to provide generalizations for all teachers. The causes are broad in scope and application; in fact, individual causes often have been attacked for impermissible vagueness. It is not unusual to find dismissal cases with similar factual situations based on different grounds. In addition, a number of grounds often are introduced and supported in a single termination case. Illustrative case law is examined below in relation to several of the more frequently cited grounds for dismissal. Claims that dismissals impair constitutional rights have been discussed in chapter 8.

INCOMPETENCY

Incompetency has been broadly defined by courts. Although it usually refers to classroom performance, it has been extended in some instances to a teacher's private life. The term is legally defined as "lack of ability, legal qualifications, or fitness to discharge the required duty."[92] While incompetency has been challenged as unconstitutionally vague, courts have found that it is sufficiently precise to give fair warning of prohibited conduct.[93] Incompetency cases often involve issues relating to teaching methods, grading procedures, classroom management, and professional relationships.

Two Pennsylvania cases illustrate the range of conduct that has been found to constitute incompetency. An early case dealt with a teacher working in her husband's "beer garden," where she occasionally had a drink of beer, served beer, and played a pinball machine with customers.[94] The Pennsylvania Supreme Court held that the loss of respect and good will of the community that resulted from her outside activities was evidence of incompetency. In a later Pennsylvania case, the United States Supreme Court reiterated that classroom performance alone was not the only basis for determining a teacher's fitness.[95] The superintendent in this case was seeking information concerning a teacher's loyalty as related to alleged prior activities in the Communist Party. Since the teacher refused to answer the superintendent's questions, he was dismissed on the ground of incompetency.[96] The Supreme Court, in upholding the dismissal, agreed with the Pennsylvania high court that incompetency included the teacher's "deliberate and insubordinate refusal to answer the questions of his administrative superior in a vitally important matter pertaining to his fitness."[97]

In general, dismissals for incompetency are based on a number of factors or a pattern of behavior rather than isolated incidents. A Louisiana appeals court noted that a teacher's repeated violations of rules in the administrative handbook, lack of control of students, and neglect of instructions of the principal as to grading procedures, lesson plans, and lunch counts constituted incompetence.[98] Similarly, in a Minnesota case, indicators of incompetency included poor rapport with students, inappropriate use of class time, irrational grading of students, and lack of student progress.[99] A Pennsylvania court interpreted incompetency as deficiencies in personality, composure, judgment, and attitude which have a detrimental effect on a teacher's performance.[100] Incompetency in this case was supported by evidence that the teacher was a disruptive influence in the school; could not maintain control of students; and failed to maintain her composure in dealing with students, other professionals, and parents.

Courts frequently examine dismissals based on incompetency to determine if the teacher received adequate notice of the need to improve performance. In Illinois, by law, the teacher must be given notice of deficiencies and provided an opportunity to correct them. The Supreme Court of Illinois invalidated a teacher's dismissal because of lack of warning of deficiencies.[101] The teacher had failed to submit lesson plans and attendance reports and to perform football duties adequately. In finding these causes remediable, the court held that the teacher should have been notified and given an opportunity to correct the problems. Where a school board provided notice and an opportunity for remediation, however, the dismissal of a teacher for incompetency was upheld by a Missouri appellate court.[102] The Washington Supreme Court found that a teacher's striking of students in the genitals did not constitute a remediable teaching deficiency and held that the conduct was "so patently unacceptable that the school district was entitled to discharge the teacher for his actions in this case regardless of prior warnings."[103]

A wide range of charges appears under dismissals for incompetency. To illustrate, dismissals were upheld in Louisiana cases based on findings of incompetency where a teacher required two eleven-year-old girls to write a vulgar word one thousand times,[104] where a teacher brandished a starter pistol in an attempt to gain control of a group of students,[105] and where a principal sexually harassed a job applicant.[106] In a Wyoming case, inadequate supervision of the school newspaper and general improper appearance and dress justified a dismissal based on incompetency.[107] Two Arkansas teachers, hired primarily as coaches, were dismissed from their positions for unsatisfactory performance because of their inability to field competitive teams.[108]

Frequently, school boards have based charges of incompetency on teachers' lack of proper classroom management and control. Such dismissals often have been contested on the grounds that the penalty of discharge is too severe for the offense. Courts have generally held that school boards have latitude in determining penalties[109] and their decisions will be vacated only if disproportionate to the offense.[110] As long as evidence is presented to substantiate the board's charge, poor classroom management can result in termination.[111]

An Iowa teacher was dismissed for incompetency, in part, because her students scored poorly on standardized basic skills tests.[112] The Eighth Circuit Court of Appeals noted that the school board has responsibility for evaluation of teachers and that such evaluations are not subject to judicial review. With the current emphasis on teacher accountability, the consideration of pupil performance in evaluating teacher competence may become increasingly controversial.

Immorality

Immorality, the most frequently cited cause for dismissal, is generally not defined in state laws.[113] In interpreting the term, the judiciary has tended to use a broad, subjective definition, defining "immorality" as unacceptable conduct that affects a teacher's fitness. Traditionally, the teacher was viewed as an exemplar whose conduct was influential in shaping the lives of young students. This high standard was noted by the Supreme Court of Pennsylvania:

> It has always been the recognized duty of the teacher to conduct himself in such a way as to command the respect and good will of the community, though one result of the choice of a teacher's vocation may be to deprive him of the same freedom of action enjoyed by persons in other vocations. Educators have always regarded the example set by the teacher as of great importance. . . .[114]

Sexually related conduct *per se* between a teacher and student has consistently been held to constitute sufficient cause for dismissal.[115] The Supreme Court of Colorado stated that "whenever a male teacher engages in sexually provocative or exploitative conduct with his minor female students, a strong presumption of unfitness arises against the teacher."[116] Similarly, a Washington appeals court found that a male teacher's sexual relationship with a minor student justified dismissal.[117] The court declined to hold that an adverse effect on fitness to teach must be shown. Rather, the court concluded that when a teacher and a minor student are involved, the board may reasonably decide that such conduct is harmful to the school district. A Michigan appellate court also held that school officials were not required to show that a female teacher's relationship with a male student had an adverse affect on the school or students; discharge was supported by the very existence of the unprofessional relationship.[118]

Teachers discharged for sexually related conduct have challenged the statutory grounds of "immorality" or "immoral conduct" as impermissibly vague. An Alabama teacher dismissed for sexual advances toward female students asserted that the term immorality did not adequately warn a teacher as to what behavior would constitute an offense.[119] The court acknowledged the lack of clarity in defining immorality but rejected the teacher's contention, reasoning that his behavior fell "squarely within the hard core of the statute's proscriptions."[120] The court noted that the teacher should have been aware that his conduct was improper, and the claim of vagueness or overbreadth could not invalidate his dismissal. A Missouri federal district court conceded that the term "immoral conduct" is abstract, but, when construed in the overall statutory scheme, can be precisely defined as conduct rendering a teacher unfit to teach.[121] The Supreme Court of Missouri concurred and upheld the dismissal of a teacher for sexual harassment of the only female member of his class and for permitting male members of the class also to harass the female student.[122]

Under the "role model" standard, conduct that sets a bad example for students may constitute adequate cause for dismissal. In recent years, however, courts have become more restrictive in construing immoral conduct and have required that school officials show that misconduct has an adverse impact on fitness to teach. Courts have recognized that allowing dismissal merely upon a showing of immoral behavior without consideration of the nexus between the conduct and fitness to teach would be an unwarranted intrusion upon a teacher's right to privacy.[123]

While constitutionally protected privacy rights may exist for a teacher's sexual conduct outside the school, the teacher does not have the freedom to select any desired lifestyle if there is a potential for adverse impact on students. An Eighth Circuit Court of Appeals decision exemplifies the judiciary's reasoning in circumscribing the teacher's freedom outside the classroom.[124] In this case, an unmarried teacher was living with a male friend in a mobile home in close proximity to the school. School officials gave her several opportunities to alter her living arrangements, but she declined, claiming that this demand violated her rights to privacy and free association. In upholding the teacher's dismissal, the appellate court found that the conduct offended community mores and had an adverse effect on students. A strong connection was established between the teacher's actions and her effectiveness as a teacher.[125] In contrast, a Florida appellate court found that school officials had not produced evidence to show that an off-campus sexual relationship between a teacher and an adult of the opposite sex adversely affected the teacher's ability to teach.[126]

Community disapproval of a teacher's sexual conduct outside of school is not sufficient to justify termination of employment. An Oregon court noted that "no amount of public opposition" can override an individual's tenure rights if statutory grounds for dismissal are not met.[127] In a Nebraska case, a middle-aged divorced teacher was occasionally visited by friends of her son.[128] Because of the lack of motel accommodations, these guests stayed in her apartment. One young man, who was a frequent visitor, spent one week with the teacher while he attended classes in the district to complete certain college-course requirements. Following his visit, the teacher was notified that her contract would not be renewed. The Eighth Circuit Court of Appeals, rejecting the board's assertion that the teacher's behavior exhibited a "strong potential for sexual misconduct," found the dismissal to be arbitrary and capricious.[129]

School boards have attempted to use the ground of immorality as the basis for dismissing unwed, pregnant employees. Whether such a pregnancy is sufficient to justify termination depends on the resulting harm to the pupils, other teachers, and the school itself.[130] If an adverse impact can be demonstrated, adequate cause for dismissal can be established. A Nebraska federal district court, in upholding the discharge of an unwed, pregnant teacher, concluded that there was "a rational connection between the plaintiff's pregnancy out of wedlock and the school board's interest in conserving marital values when acts probably destructive of those values are revealed, verbally or non-verbally, in the classroom. . . ."[131] In this instance, the teacher was popular with the students, and the court concluded that her effectiveness as a role model was diminished by her unwed, pregnant condition.

Most courts, however, have invalidated dismissals based on a teacher's unwed, pregnant status. In an Alabama case, an unmarried, pregnant teacher was reinstated when the board failed to establish a connection between the teacher's condition and her fitness to teach.[132] An Arkansas teacher also was successful in obtaining damages and reinstatement because the board had not informed employees that unwed pregnancy constituted grounds for dismissal.[133] The federal district court reasoned that, without an explicit school board policy, the plaintiff had no means of knowing that pregnancy out of wedlock would result in termination. The New Mexico Supreme Court held that a school board's decision to dismiss an unwed, pregnant teacher was arbitrary and unreasonable based on the evidence presented.[134] Facts considered by the court were that (1) at the time of dismissal five other unwed mothers were teaching in the school system, and (2) the teacher had been rated above average in performance, recommended for reemployment by the principal, and supported by the community for continued employment. The court, however, did not address whether unwed pregnancy constituted justifiable grounds for dismissal as "immoral conduct." As discussed in chapter 8, in two cases the Fifth Circuit Court of Appeals found that dismissals of unwed, pregnant teachers impaired the equal protection clause of the fourteenth amendment.[135]

With increased attention being focused on individual rights, the issue of teacher homosexuality has been the focal point in a number of controversial dismissal cases. While these cases often have raised constitutional issues related to freedom of expression and privacy, courts also have confronted the question of whether homosexuality *per se* is evidence of unfitness to teach or whether it must be shown that teaching effectiveness has been impaired. Teachers can be dismissed for criminal convictions for violating antisodomy laws;[136] diverse opinions, however, have been rendered by courts regarding the status of homosexual teachers when criminal charges are not involved. According to the Supreme Court of California, immoral or unprofessional conduct or moral turpitude must be related to unfitness to teach.[137] Consequently, the school board does not possess the right to dismiss an employee simply because it does not approve of a particular private lifestyle.[138] In a case where a male teacher was involved in a limited one-week relationship with another male, the California court enumerated criteria for evaluating the fitness of a teacher.

> The board may consider such matters as the likelihood that the conduct may have adversely affected students or fellow teachers, the degree of such adversity anticipated, the proximity or remoteness in time of the conduct, the type of teaching certificate held by the party involved, the extenuating or

> aggravating circumstances, if any, surrounding the conduct, . . . the likelihood of the recurrence of the questioned conduct, and the extent to which disciplinary action may inflict an adverse impact or chilling effect upon the constitutional rights of the teacher involved or other teachers.[139]

The particular circumstances of a case are important in determining whether a teacher can be dismissed for homosexual conduct. Two California decisions are illustrative. In the first case, a teacher's professional certificate was revoked for immoral conduct after he made sexual advances to a plainclothes policeman on a public beach.[140] Upholding the revocation, an appellate court noted that the teacher had a history of homosexual behavior which justified barring him from contact with students. In contrast, the state supreme court overturned the dismissal of a teacher who was charged with immoral conduct for sexual advances to a police officer in a public restroom.[141] Evidence indicated that this was an isolated incident, posed no threat to students, and did not attract public attention.

Although the California decisions suggest that evidence of impaired teaching effectiveness must accompany a teacher's dismissal for homosexuality, not all courts have agreed. In 1977 the Washington Supreme Court upheld a teacher's dismissal for immorality after he admitted to a school administrator that he was a homosexual.[142] The board's dismissal action was based entirely on the fact that the teacher was a homosexual; immoral conduct was not alleged. The Washington high court concluded that mere knowledge of the teacher's homosexuality was sufficient to establish an impairment of teaching effectiveness, and the United States Supreme Court declined to review the case.[143]

Some terminations have been based on evidence of inappropriate sexual conduct and *not* on the homosexual nature of the conduct. For example, an Oregon appeals court upheld the dismissal of a teacher for "immorality" (defined as "reprehensible sexual conduct") after the teacher was observed engaging in homosexual activity in an adult bookstore booth during an undercover investigation.[144] The court noted that, although much of the community concern expressed over the teacher's action related to the homosexual nature of the behavior, the crucial point for the court was that the teacher did in fact act improperly by engaging in public sexual intercourse.

While a large number of the cases involving the discharge of teachers for immorality involve sexual conduct, immorality is broader in meaning and scope. As one court noted, it involves "conduct which is hostile to the welfare of the school community."[145] Such hostile conduct has included, among other things, dishonest acts, criminal conduct, and drug-related conduct. Several recent cases illustrate the range of misconduct resulting in charges of immorality.

Disparaging comments to students may constitute immorality. The

Supreme Court of Nebraska found a teacher's statements in a classroom that subjected black students to humiliation and public ridicule to be immoral.[146] In the court's opinion, it was immoral for the teacher to teach white students by example that it is proper to engage in such conduct. The court considered the conduct to be as immoral as teaching students how to cheat on examinations. A Pennsylvania court found a teacher's reference to a student as a "slut" and "prostitute" in the presence of other students also to be immoral.[147] The court noted that "such statements are crude and ill-advised when used by a teacher in a public school environment."[148]

While criminal conduct does not always justify dismissal for immorality, state law may establish a nexus. For example, Alaska statutes define immorality as "an act which, under the laws of the state, constitutes a crime involving moral turpitude."[149] A conviction for unlawfully diverting electricity was held by the state high court to be such a crime. Under Georgia law, conviction for submitting false tax documents was sufficient to substantiate dismissal of a principal for moral turpitude.[150] Other dishonest conduct that has been found to substantiate charges of immorality include misrepresenting absences from school as illness when in fact the teacher attended a conference unrelated to work,[151] taking school property without permission (return of the property did not mitigate the charge),[152] and instructing a student wrestler to lie and cheat during a wrestling tournament.[153] In the absence of a statutory specification, however, the West Virginia Supreme Court held that a school board could not conclude that a conviction for a misdemeanor was *per se* immoral conduct.[154] The Washington high court also held that a conviction for grand larceny, standing alone, was generally not sufficient cause for dismissal; evidence that a teacher pled *nolo contendere* to a charge of shoplifting did not establish that the teacher was unfit to teach.[155]

INSUBORDINATION

Insubordination, another frequently cited cause for dismissal, is generally defined as the willful disregard for or refusal to obey school regulations and official orders.[156] Teachers can be dismissed for violation of administrative regulations and policies and even though classroom performance is satisfactory; school officials are not required to establish a relationship between the conduct and fitness to teach.[157] Kentucky law illustrates a typical definition of insubordination as:

> . . . including but not limited to (1) violation of lawful rules and regulations established by the local board of education for the operation of schools, and (2) refusal to recognize or obey the authority of the superintendent, principal or any other supervisory personnel of the board in the performance of their duties.[158]

Many state laws and court decisions require that insubordinate acts be "willful and persistent." In general, a single incident, unless severe or substantial, is inadequate for dismissal action.[159] In a Minnesota case, a teacher's continuous refusal to complete program evaluation forms resulted in insubordination charges.[160] The Minnesota Supreme Court, upholding the dismissal, defined insubordination as "constant or continuing intentional refusal to obey a direct or implied order, reasonable in nature, and given by and with proper authority."[161] The Wyoming Supreme Court presented an opposing view on whether repeated refusals to obey orders were necessary to justify dismissal.[162] The court concluded that the dismissal of a teacher who refused a split assignment between two schools was proper. In the court's opinion, repeated refusals were unnecessary if other elements of insubordination were present, such as reasonableness of the order and direct refusal to obey. Similarly, a Kansas teacher's dismissal was sustained for a one-time refusal to obey the superintendent's direct order to supervise recess,[163] and a Missouri teacher's termination was upheld when she refused to teach an assigned course.[164]

With the plethora of regulations enacted by school districts, wide diversity is found in types of behavior adjudicated as insubordination. Dismissals based on insubordination have been upheld in cases involving refusal to abide by specific school directives, unwillingness to cooperate with superiors, unauthorized absences, and numerous other actions. Since conduct is measured against the existence of a rule or policy, insubordination is more readily documented by a school board, and thus may be more supportable than most other legal causes.

Numerous dismissal cases involving insubordination have resulted from the inappropriate use of corporal punishment. Corporal punishment is not limited to actions involving "paddlings" but is defined broadly to include use of physical contact, such as slapping, pinching, and kicking.[165] If the school board has adopted policies prohibiting corporal punishment or prescribing procedures for its administration, teachers must strictly adhere to board requirements. Dismissal of an Illinois teacher was upheld because he failed to follow prescribed procedures which specified that a teacher must explain the reasons for the punishment to the child and must have another adult present while administering corporal punishment.[166] Shaking students and shoving them into chairs and the wall, along with general physical attacks on students, exceeded an Oregon board policy which limited physical discipline to the use of a paddle.[167] Administering physical punishment on five occasions over a two-year period in opposition to an established policy was held to constitute "willful and persistent violation" of regulations in a Missouri school district.[168] A Washington teacher's discharge was upheld because he continued to use corporal punishment after repeated warnings to cease.[169] In a similar case, a Philadelphia teacher who administered corporal punishment on several different occasions was warned that continued use could result in dismissal.[170] Challenging the board policy, the teacher contended that corporal punishment was legally permissible under state law. The court affirmed the board's prerogative to determine whether corporal punishment would be allowed, and concluded from the evidence that the teacher's action showed intentional disregard for school regulations.[171] In contrast to the preceding cases, the Colorado Supreme Court invalidated a teacher's dismissal for insubordination in connection with excessive use of corporal punishment because the school board had not adopted regulations pertaining to this disciplinary technique.[172] A Pennsylvania court found a single infraction of a policy prohibiting corporal punishment was neither severe nor willful and persistent.[173]

Insubordination charges often have resulted from conflicts arising from the administrator/teacher relationship. For example, a teacher cannot refuse to meet with a principal to discuss classroom matters. A Florida teacher's discharge was upheld for refusal to meet with her principal to discuss leaving her class unattended.[174] An Arizona teacher's continuing refusal to meet with his principal for the purpose of improving teaching skills supported dismissal.[175] In another Arizona case, termination was supported by a teacher's refusal to respond to a principal's request for information about a discipline incident.[176]

Teachers cannot ignore reasonable directives and policies of administrators or school boards. The Fifth Circuit Appellate Court found that insubordination was established because a teacher allowed boycotting students to attend classes in violation of a school policy and refused to attend two football games, as all male teachers were required to do.[177] Where a teacher's remarks to an unauthorized assembly of students encouraged disobedience of the principal's orders, the Sixth Circuit Court of Appeals upheld the teacher's dismissal based on insubordination.[178] The dismissal of an Iowa teacher was supported by a preponderance of evidence that he "persistently violated, ignored and demonstrated a nonsupportive attitude toward administrative policies, procedures, rules and directives . . ."[179] Violations included numerous incidents (misuse of copying machine, failure to notify administrators that he would be absent, creation of schedule conflicts) that showed a persistent pattern of insubordination. Other instances of insubordination justifying dismissal have included violating a school directive to retain final examination papers,[180] taking personal leave without permission,[181] abusing sick leave,[182] refusing to sign an attachment to a contract,[183] failing to abide by residency requirements,[184] failing to acquire board approval of supplementary materials used in classroom,[185] violating reasonable grooming regulations,[186] and refusing to cease religious exercises in the classroom.[187] The key determination is whether the teacher has persisted in disobeying a *reasonable* school policy or directive.

Neglect of Duty

Neglect of duty arises when a teacher fails to carry out assigned duties. This may involve an intentional omission or may result from ineffectual performance. In a Colorado case, neglect of duty was found when a teacher was absent from class for observance of certain holy days after having been denied permission for leave.[188] The discharge of a Louisiana teacher for locking three preschool handicapped children in a room while she attended to chores unrelated to her classroom was upheld based on willful neglect of duty.[189] The Supreme Court of North Carolina found that habitual use of alcohol during the school day supported dismissal.[190] Neglect of duty also was found when a teacher persistently refused to inform the superintendent if he would be returning from a leave of absence.[191]

The United States Supreme Court upheld the dismissal of an Oklahoma teacher for "willful neglect of duty" in failing to comply with the school board's continuing education requirement.[192] For a period of time, lack of compliance was dealt with through denial of salary increases. Upon enactment of a state law requiring salary increases for all teachers, the board notified teachers that noncompliance with the requirement would result in termination. Affirming the board's action, the Supreme Court found the sanction of dismissal to be "rationally related" to the board's objective of improving its teaching force through continuing education requirements.

The Supreme Court of Nebraska addressed what constitutes "just cause" in a dismissal for neglect of duty where a teacher had failed on several occasions to perform certain duties and at other times had not performed duties competently.[193] Evidence revealed that the teacher had not violated any administrative orders or school laws, had received good evaluations (only three of twenty categories had been noted as needing improvement), and had been recommended for retention by the administrators. In the opinion of the court, the facts did not support just cause for dismissal. The court cautioned that in evaluating a teacher's performance "incompetency or neglect of duty [is] not measured in a vacuum nor against a standard of perfection, but, instead, must be measured against the standard required of others performing the same or similar duties."[194] It was not demonstrated that the teacher's performance was below that expected of other teachers in similar positions.

The West Virginia Supreme Court held that missing one parent-teacher conference was not sufficient to justify dismissal based on neglect of duty.[195] In a later case, the same court also held that a teacher's unintentional distribution of pornographic cartoons to eighth-grade students was insufficient to establish neglect of duty.[196] Having failed to review the materials, the teacher was unaware of their objectionable content. A Louisiana appellate court also concluded that a teacher's removal of a gun from his car when physically attacked by a student did not warrant dismissal for neglect of duty.[197]

Unprofessional Conduct

Approximately fourteen states identify either unprofessional conduct or conduct unbecoming a teacher as a cause for dismissal.[198] A teacher's activities both inside and outside of school can be used to establish grounds for discharge. Dismissals for unprofessional conduct, neglect of duty, and unfitness to teach often are based on quite similar facts. For instance, a New York teacher was dismissed for unprofessional conduct for being absent after having been denied permission for a leave, whereas a Colorado teacher in a similar situation was charged with neglect of duty.[199] A Maine school board classified a teacher's unauthorized absences as unfitness to teach.[200] It must be remembered that causes for dismissal are usually identified in state statutes, but are defined through case law and various administrative rulings in individual states. Consequently, there are wide variances in the meaning of the same legal cause.

Courts have upheld dismissal for unprofessional conduct based on a number of grounds, such as arrest for alleged shoplifting,[201] serving liquor to two female students,[202] use of abusive language to other school personnel,[203] indictment for possession of cocaine with intent to distribute,[204] failure of a teacher's children to attend school in violation of the compulsory attendance law,[205] refusal to attend faculty in-service meetings and to supervise children during recess,[206] engaging in sexually suggestive behavior with a mannequin on front lawn of home,[207] and indictment on welfare fraud charges.[208] As with incompetency cases, courts often require prior warning that the behavior may result in dismissal.[209]

Unfitness to Teach

Unfitness to teach covers a wide array of teacher behavior.[210] An Illinois appellate court defined unfitness as "conduct detrimental to the operation of the school."[211] Under this definition, the court held that improper sexual conduct toward students constituted unfitness. The question of incapacity as unfitness was addressed by a New Jersey court.[212] In this case, a male teacher who underwent a sex change operation was dismissed on the ground that retention would result in psychological harm to students. The court concluded that the teacher's presence could potentially result in emotional harm to students, and, therefore, dismissal was appropriate. The judiciary has recognized that a determination of fitness or capacity may extend beyond actual classroom performance.

Two decisions from the Supreme Court of Maine dealt with dismissals for one-time incidents that allegedly affected fitness to teach. In the first case, a teacher who was a licensed gunsmith inadvertently brought a gun and ammunition to school in his jacket.[213] The gun was stolen from his room but later returned. The school board initiated dismissal proceedings for "grave lack of judgment." Overturning the board action, the court held that one isolated incident does not represent such "moral impropriety, professional incompetence, or unsuitability" as to warrant unfitness to teach.[214] The second case involved a teacher striking a student across the face with his hand during a voluntary basketball game.[215] The blow was severe, causing the loss of one tooth, damage to another, and extensive bruises. In this case, as opposed to the first, the court concluded that the single incident was sufficient to justify dismissal because of its direct impact on the teacher's effectiveness as a coach. Dismissals for one-time incidents, regardless of the grounds, are always scrutinized closely by courts.

Mental, emotional, or physical disorders can constitute unfitness to teach or incapacity.[216] To establish incapacity, health conditions must be severe and interfere with a teacher's ability to perform in the classroom.[217] It should be noted, however, that dismissals based on physical disabilities can under certain circumstances impair federally protected rights of handicapped employees. As discussed in chapter 9, the Eleventh Circuit Court of Appeals concluded that a teacher with tuberculosis was handicapped under Section 504 of the Rehabilitation Act of 1973 (which bars discrimination against otherwise qualified handicapped individuals in federally assisted programs), and thus could not be summarily dismissed because of the disease.[218]

Rather than discharging a teacher for unfitness, state law may permit a school board to place a teacher on an involuntary leave of absence when found to be medically unfit to teach. New York law provides that the superintendent of schools, upon recommendation of a building principal, may require a tenured teacher to submit to a medical examination to determine mental fitness to teach. According to the New York courts, this law also empowers a school board to place a teacher on involuntary leave of absence without a hearing. The Second Circuit Court of Appeals, however, has recognized that such action by the school board must be followed by a fair postsuspension hearing, as suspended teachers do not relinquish their procedural due process rights.[219]

Other Good and Just Cause

Not unexpectedly, "other good and just cause" as a ground for dismissal often has been challenged as vague and overbroad. Courts have been faced with the task of determining whether the phrase's meaning is limited to the specific grounds enumerated in the statute or whether it is a separate, expanded cause. An Indiana appellate court interpreted it as permitting termination for reasons other than those specified in the tenure law, if evidence indicated that the board's decision was based on "good cause."[220] As such, dismissal of a teacher convicted of a misdemeanor was upheld even though the teacher had no prior indication that such conduct was sufficient cause. Similarly, an Ohio appellate court concluded that "other good and just cause" was separate and distinct from other causes listed in the statute identifying reasons for terminating tenured teachers' contracts; a teacher's refusal to report to work during a labor dispute was found to establish "other good and just cause" justifying discharge.[221]

The Second Circuit Court of Appeals found "other due and sufficient cause" to be:

> . . . appropriate in an area such as discipline of teachers, where a myriad of uncontemplated situations may arise and it is not reasonable to require a legislature to elucidate in advance every act that requires sanction. Some general "catch-all" phrase may be incorporated to ensure that the legislature's inability to detail all matters meant to be proscribed does not permit clearly improper conduct to go uncorrected.[222]

The appellate court declined to rule on the vagueness of "other due and sufficient cause," but rather noted that courts generally assess the teacher's conduct in relation to the statutory grounds for dismissal. That is, if the specific behavior is sufficiently related to the causes specified in state law, it is assumed that the teacher should have reasonably known that the conduct was improper. In this case, where a teacher repeatedly humiliated and harassed students (and school administrators had discussed the problem with him), the court concluded that the teacher was aware of the impropriety of his conduct.

Reduction in Force

In addition to dismissal for causes related to teacher performance and fitness, legislation generally permits the release of teachers for reasons related to declining enrollment, financial exigency, and school district consolidation. While most state statutes provide for such terminations, a number of states also have adopted legislation that specifies the basis for selection of teachers, procedures to be followed, and oftentimes provisions for reinstatement. These terminations, characterized as "reductions in force" (RIF), also may be governed by board policies and negotiated bargaining agreements.

Unlike other termination cases, the burden of proof is shouldered by the employee challenging a RIF decision. There is a presumption that the board has acted in good faith with permissible motives. Legal controversies in this area usually involve questions related to the necessity for the reductions, board compliance with mandated procedures, and possible subterfuge for impermissible termination (such as denial of constitutional rights, subversion of tenure rights, discrimination).[223]

If statutory or contractual restrictions exist for teacher layoffs, there must be substantial compliance with the provisions.[224] One of the provisions most frequently included is a method for selecting teachers for release. In general, reductions are based on seniority, and a tenured teacher must be retained rather than a nontenured teacher if both are qualified to fill the same position.[225] Oregon statutes require that both legal qualifications and seniority be considered; a teacher lacking legal qualifications would not be permitted to teach while a permanent, legally qualified teacher with more seniority was dismissed.[226] Along with seniority, merit rating systems often are included in the determination of reductions. School districts in Pennsylvania use a combination of ratings and seniority; ratings are the primary determinant unless no substantial difference exists in ratings, and then seniority becomes the basis for layoff.[227] The Nebraska Supreme Court concluded that a school board could include noneducational factors such as contribution to the school activity program in selecting teachers for release.[228] Guidelines or criteria established by state or local education agencies must be applied in a uniform and nondiscriminatory manner.[229]

While the fourteenth amendment requires minimal procedural protections in dismissals for cause, courts have not clearly defined the due process requirements for RIF. Thus, procedural rights of employees vary according to interpretations of state law, bargaining agreements, and board policy. A Michigan court found no need for a hearing over staff reductions, because there were no charges to refute.[230] The court emphasized that the law protected the released teacher, who, subject to qualifications, was entitled to be hired for the next vacancy. Alternatively, a Pennsylvania commonwealth court held that a hearing must be provided to assure the teacher (1) that termination is for reasons specified by law, and (2) that the board followed the correct statutory procedures in selecting the teacher for discharge.[231]

Preference in reemployment often is given to the teacher who is released because of unavoidable staff reductions.[232] A teacher, however, must be certified for the available position. A French teacher whose tenure was in the secondary academic area was found to be unqualified to teach English or science because of lack of certification in those subjects.[233] Although statutes often require that a teacher be appointed to the first vacancy for which certified and qualified, courts have held that reappointment is still at the board's discretion. The terms certified and qualified are not synonymous. A Michigan appeals court recognized that a teacher could be certified in an area but, in the opinion of the board,[234] not necessarily qualified. Additionally, a board is generally not obligated to realign or rearrange teaching assignments to create a position for a released teacher.[235]

REMEDIES FOR WRONGFUL TERMINATIONS

An important element of due process is the right to appeal an adverse employment decision of a school board to a higher authority, such as a court of law. The legal cases cited in this chapter illustrate the variety of issues appealed to courts. Several points are important to note regarding judicial review. First, courts generally will not interject themselves into school board review proceedings until all aspects of the administrative appeal process have been exhausted. A teacher alleging denial of due process must first use established administrative procedures prior to resorting to judicial review. Second, in reviewing teacher termination actions, the judiciary does not substitute its judgment for that of the school board. Rather, courts examine cases to determine if the school board failed to accord the teacher procedural protections, impaired substantive constitutional rights, or was arbitrary and capricious in its decision. If upon review it is found that protected rights have been violated, courts attempt to redress the wrong by framing an appropriate remedy.

Depending on employment status, judicial remedies for the violation of employment rights may include reinstatement with back pay, compensatory and punitive damages, and attorneys' fees. The specific nature of the award depends on individual state statutory provisions and the discretion of courts. State laws often identify damages that may be recovered or place limitations on types of awards. Unless state provisions restrict specific remedies, courts have broad discretionary power to formulate equitable settlements.

Reinstatement

Whether or not reinstatement is ordered by a court as a remedy for school board action will depend on the protected interests involved and the discretion of the court, unless specific provisions are included in state law. If a tenured teacher is unjustly dismissed, the property interest gives rise to an expectation of reemployment. Reinstatement in such instances is usually the appropriate remedy. A nontenured teacher, wrongfully dismissed during the contract period, is normally entitled only to damages, not reinstatement.

While reinstatement is generally ordered when property rights are at stake, it is not appropriate for the impairment of liberty interests related to reputation, since no right to continued employment existed. Ordinarily, a successful liberty claim would require only an opportunity to clear one's name. The Tenth Circuit Court of Appeals, however, noted that reinstatement is not absolutely foreclosed if a teacher can prove that he or she would have been retained had full procedural due process been provided.[236] Although substantiation of such a claim is difficult, if proven that the actual reason for the nonrenewal of a teacher's contract is retaliation for the exercise of protected constitutional rights (e.g., protected speech), reinstatement would be warranted.[237]

The failure to comply with procedural requirements in nonrenewals and dismissals may result in reinstatement. When statutory dates are specified for notice of nonrenewal, failure to strictly comply with the deadline provides grounds for reinstatement of the teacher. Courts may interpret this as continued employment for an additional year[238] or reinstatement with tenure if nonrenewal occurs at the end of the probationary period.[239] In contrast to the remedy for lack of proper notice, the remedy for failure to provide a required or appropriate hearing is generally a remand for a hearing, not reinstatement.[240]

Damages

As discussed in chapter 8, judicial decisions in recent years have increased the potential for teachers to recover monetary damages when their constitutional rights, such as freedom of speech, are violated. Under Section 1983 of the Civil Rights Act of 1871, both school officials and school boards are liable for payment of damages to teachers for violations of federally protected rights. Individual school officials may claim qualified immunity for actions taken in "good faith;" however, disregard of constitutionally protected rights or impermissible motivation may demonstrate a lack of good faith. While *individuals* possess a certain degree of immunity, *school boards* are not protected against liability for the impairment of federal rights, even if their members or employees have acted in good faith. The Supreme Court's interpretations of Section 1983 have significantly expanded the likelihood of teachers recovering damages from school systems, and, therefore, more and more teachers are turning to federal courts for restitution.[241]

Monetary damages may be significant for wrongful terminations if a teacher is able to demonstrate substantial losses. A Delaware federal district court decision cited earlier illustrates the factors considered by courts in ordering relief.[242] The court found that a principal who had been assured of contract renewal if his performance was satisfactory was entitled to due process before termination of employment. The failure of the school board to provide procedural protection resulted in a judgment against the board and its members. The court held that the injured individual should be compensated for lost salary, out-of-pocket expenses, physical and mental stress, and injury to reputation in the amount of $51,000. In addition to the compensatory damages to repay the principal for harm inflicted by the board, the court found that punitive damages were appropriate. The sole purpose of punitive awards is to deter school officials and others from committing similar offenses in the future.[243] In this case, a jury award of $77,500 in punitive damages was found to be excessive and was reduced to $7,750. The First Circuit Court of Appeals did not find awards of $39,000 against a superintendent and $26,000 against a principal excessive in a wrongful termination when evidence showed that the school officials repeatedly retaliated against a teacher for exercising her protected speech rights.[244]

The following cases are illustrative of the diverse circumstances that have resulted in awards of damages. Back pay for five years and all other emoluments and fringe benefits were awarded in the wrongful dismissal of a Louisiana teacher for displaying a gun to defend himself when physically attacked by a student.[245] Wrongful dismissal of a teacher for admission of homosexuality resulted in payment of the balance due under a contract and an additional one-half year's salary.[246] Denial of a continuing contract to a Florida teacher for her relationship with a member of the opposite sex entitled the teacher to reimbursement for "any economic loss sustained," including legal expenses.[247] The termination of a tenured New York teacher without due process merited consideration of back pay and other employment benefits but not damages for emotional distress and mental anguish because only subjective evidence of such injury was presented.[248]

Given the success teachers have had in securing damages to compensate for injuries associated with wrongful terminations, school officials should ensure that dismissals or other disciplinary actions are based on legitimate reasons and accompanied by appropriate procedural safeguards. However, as the above cases indicate, courts have not awarded damages unless the evidence shows that a teacher has suffered actual injury. In 1986 the Supreme Court reiterated that compensatory damages are intended to provide full compensation for the loss suffered but are not to be based on a jury's perception of the value of the constitutional rights impaired.[249]

Attorneys' Fees

Attorneys' fees are not automatically granted to the teacher who prevails in a lawsuit, unless authorized by state or federal law. Although some state courts may exercise discretion in awarding attorneys' fees, fees are generally dependent on statutory authorization. At the federal level, however, Congress's enactment of the Civil Rights Attorneys' Fees Award Act gives federal courts discretion to award fees in civil rights suits.[250] Congress viewed the earlier disallowance of attorneys' fees as a significant bar to individuals who might seek judicial relief.[251] In congressional debate concerning attorneys' fees, it was stated that "private citizens must be given not only the right to go to court, but also the legal resources. If the citizen does not have the resources his day in court is denied him."[252]

Receipt of fees at either the state or federal level requires the teacher to be the prevailing party; that is, damages or some form of equitable relief must be granted to the teacher. Without an award of damages, the teacher is not considered the prevailing party, and attorneys' fees are denied.[253] Courts base the amount of fees to be awarded on time involved, current hourly rates, skill required, uniqueness of the issue, statutory provisions, and other appropriate considerations.

Because Section 1983 does not require exhaustion of state administrative proceedings before initiating litigation, the Supreme Court has denied the award of attorneys' fees for school board administrative proceedings conducted prior to filing a federal suit. Unlike Title VII's explicit requirement that individuals must pursue administrative remedies, plaintiffs can bring a Section 1983 claim directly to a federal court. In a wrongful termination case, a Tennessee teacher was awarded attorneys' fees as a prevailing litigant for the time spent on the judicial proceedings but was unsuccessful in persuading the Supreme Court that the local administrative proceedings were part of the preparation for court action.[254]

Although it has been established that the plaintiff who prevails in a civil rights suit may, at the court's discretion, be entitled to attorneys' fees, the same standard is not applied to defendants. When a plaintiff teacher is awarded attorneys' fees, the assessment is against a party who has violated a federal law. Different criteria must be applied when a prevailing defendant seeks attorneys' fees. The Supreme Court has held that such fees cannot be imposed on a plaintiff unless the claim was "frivolous, unreasonable, or groundless."[255] While awards of damages to prevailing defendants have not been common, in some situations, such awards have been made to deter groundless lawsuits.[256]

CONCLUSION

An area of general concern among teachers is employment security. Through state laws and the Federal Constitution, extensive safeguards exist to prevent arbitrary or capricious actions of school officials. Most states have adopted teacher tenure laws that precisely delineate teachers' employment rights in termination proceedings. Additionally, in the absence of specific state guarantees, the fourteenth amendment ensures that a teacher will be afforded procedural due process when a property or liberty interest exists in employment. Legal decisions, interpreting both state and federal rights in dismissal actions, have established broad guidelines as to when due process is required, the types of procedures that must be provided, and the legitimate causes required to substantiate dismissal action. Generalizations applicable to teacher employment termination are enumerated below.

1. A teacher is entitled to procedural due process if dismissal action impairs a property or liberty interest.
2. Tenure status, defined by state law, confers upon teachers a

property interest in continued employment; tenured teachers can be dismissed only for cause.

3. Courts have generally held that probationary employment does not involve a property interest, except within the contract period.
4. A probationary teacher may establish a liberty interest, and thus entitlement to a hearing, if nonrenewal imposes a stigma or forecloses opportunities for future employment.
5. When a liberty or property interest is implicated, procedural due process requires, at a minimum, that a teacher be notified of charges and provided with an opportunity for a hearing.
6. Full procedural rights in a dismissal hearing include representation by counsel, examination and cross-examination of witnesses, and a record of the proceedings; however, formal trial procedures are not required.
7. An adequate notice of dismissal must adhere to statutory deadlines, follow designated form, allow the teacher time to prepare for a hearing, and specify charges.
8. The school board is considered an impartial hearing tribunal unless bias of its members can be clearly established.
9. The burden of proof is placed on the school board to introduce sufficient evidence to support a teacher's dismissal.
10. Causes for dismissal vary extensively among the states, but usually include such grounds as incompetency, neglect of duty, immorality, insubordination, unprofessional conduct, and other good and just cause.
11. Incompetency is generally defined in relation to classroom performance—classroom management, teaching methods, grading, pupil/teacher relationships, and general attitude.
12. Immoral conduct, as the basis for dismissal, includes dishonest acts, improper sexual conduct, criminal acts, drug-related conduct, and other improprieties that have a negative impact on the teacher's effectiveness in the school system.
13. Dismissal for insubordination is based on a teacher's refusal to follow school regulations and policies.
14. Declining enrollment and financial exigencies constitute adequate cause for dismissal of tenured teachers.
15. An improper dismissal can result in an award of damages, reinstatement, and/or attorneys' fees.

NOTES

1. Adler v. Board of Educ., 342 U.S. 485, 493 (1952).
2. An earlier version of the procedural due process section appeared in Nelda

H. Cambron-McCabe, "Procedural Due Process," *Legal Issues in Public Employment*, Joseph Beckham and Perry Zirkel, eds. (Bloomington, IN: Phi Delta Kappa, 1983). As noted in chapter 1, the fourteenth amendment restricts state, in contrast to private, action. For employees in a private school to assert a constitutional right to due process in connection with termination proceedings, they must establish that the private school is sufficiently involved in state activity to trigger the limitations imposed by the fourteenth amendment. The Supreme Court has recognized that mere regulation by the state may be insufficient to evoke constitutional protections in private school personnel matters. The Court rejected a suit for damages against a private school for allegedly unconstitutional dismissals, reasoning that there was no "symbiotic relationship" between the private school and the state. Rendell-Baker v. Kohn, 457 U.S. 830 (1982). Although the private school received some public funds and had to comply with a variety of governmental regulations, the Court reasoned that the school was not fundamentally different from other private contractors performing services for the state. It is not impossible, however, to establish that a private school is sufficiently entwined with the state to constitute "state action," and such determinations must be made on a case-by-case basis.

3. *See* Board of Regents v. Roth, 408 U.S. 564, 577 (1972).
4. *Id.* at 573.
5. *See* Goodrich v. Newport News School Bd., 743 F.2d 225 (4th Cir. 1984); Atencio v. Board of Educ. of Penasco Independent School Dist., 658 F.2d 774 (10th Cir. 1981).
6. See chapter 8 for a discussion of teachers' constitutional rights.
7. This general rule of actual receipt of notice would not apply, of course, if a statutory provision indicated other means of satisfying the deadline, such as requiring the notice to be postmarked by the United States mail by a certain date. *See* Andrews v. Howard, 291 S.E.2d 541 (Ga. 1982). *See also* Martinez v. Anchorage School Dist., 699 P.2d 330 (Alas. 1985) (a notice picked up by the teacher after the statutory deadline but on the day a registered letter probably would have arrived met the statutory intent).
8. State *ex rel.* Peake v. Board of Educ. of South Point Local School Dist., 339 N.E.2d 249 (Ohio 1975). *See also* School Dist. RE–IIJ, Alamosa County v. Norwood, 644 P.2d 13 (Colo. 1982).
9. Stollenwerck v. Talladega County Bd. of Educ., 420 So. 2d 21 (Ala. 1982); Ledbetter v. School Dist. No. 8, 428 P.2d 912 (Colo. 1967).
10. Lipka v. Brown City Community Schools, 271 N.W.2d 771 (Mich. 1978); Board of Trustees of Nogales Elementary School Dist. v. Cartier, 559 P.2d 216 (Ariz. App. 1977).
11. *See* Perkins v. Board of Directors of School Dist. 13, 686 F.2d 49 (1st Cir. 1982).
12. The Supreme Court of Montana found that a school board's proffered reason that it "could find a better teacher" was inadequate to meet the statutory requirement that teachers be given reasons for nonrenewal. Bridger Educ. Ass'n v. Board of Trustees, 678 P.2d 659 (Mont. 1984).
13. Wren v. McDowell County Bd. of Educ., 327 S.E.2d 464 (W. Va. 1985); Wilt v. Flanigan, 294 S.E.2d 189 (W. Va. 1982).
14. *See* Struthers City Schools Bd. of Educ. v. Struthers Educ. Ass'n, 453

N.E.2d 613 (Ohio 1983); Maxwell v. Southside School Dist., 618 S.W.2d 148 (Ark. 1981).

15. 408 U.S. 564 (1972).
16. 408 U.S. 593 (1972).
17. Roth, 408 U.S. at 575.
18. *Id.* at 577.
19. 408 U.S. 593 (1972).
20. *Id.* at 600.
21. Mt. Healthy City School Dist. Bd. of Educ. v. Doyle, 429 U.S. 274 (1977). *See* text with note 3, chapter 8 for a discussion of the first amendment issue in this case.
22. *See* Board of Regents v. Roth, 408 U.S. 564, 572 (1972).
23. *See, e.g.*, Longarzo v. Anker, 578 F.2d 469 (2d Cir. 1978); Buhr v. Buffalo Public School Dist. No. 38, 509 F.2d 1196 (8th Cir. 1974).
24. Schreffler v. Board of Educ. of Delmar School Dist., 506 F. Supp. 1300 (D. Del. 1981).
25. Vail v. Board of Educ. of Paris Union School Dist., 706 F.2d 1435 (7th Cir. 1983), *aff'd by an equally divided Court*, 466 U.S. 377 (1984).
26. Martin v. Unified School Dist. No. 434, Osage County, Kansas, 728 F.2d 453 (10th Cir. 1984); Robertson v. Rogers, 679 F.2d 1090 (4th Cir. 1982).
27. *See* Perkins v. Board of Directors, 686 F.2d 49 (1st Cir. 1982); New Castle-Gunning Bedford Educ. Ass'n v. Board of Educ. of New Castle-Gunning Bedford, 421 F. Supp. 960 (D. Del. 1976); Schaub v. Chamberlain Bd. of Educ., 339 N.W.2d 307 (S.D. 1983). *See also* Wells v. Hico Independent School Dist., 736 F.2d 243 (5th Cir. 1984), *cert. dismissed*, 106 S. Ct. 11 (1985) (grievance policy and procedures did not create a property interest).
28. *See* Schaub v. Chamberlain Bd. of Educ., 339 N.W.2d 307 (S.D. 1983) (a hearing may be available to a nontenured teacher, but the board is not required to speak, produce evidence, or even answer questions at the hearing).
29. *See* Ryan v. Aurora County Bd. of Educ., 540 F.2d 222 (6th Cir. 1976), *cert. denied*, 429 U.S. 1041 (1976).
30. *See* Haimowitz v. University of Nevada, 579 F.2d 526, 528 (9th Cir. 1978).
31. Harris v. Arizona Bd. of Regents, 528 F. Supp. 987 (D. Ariz. 1981).
32. *Id.* at 996.
33. Bishop v. Wood, 426 U.S. 341, 345 (1976).
34. *See* Codd v. Velger, 429 U.S. 624 (1977); Bishop v. Wood, 426 U.S. 341 (1976); Paul v. Davis, 424 U.S. 693 (1976).
35. *See* Moore v. Otero, 557 F.2d 435, 437 (5th Cir. 1977); Sullivan v. Brown, 544 F.2d 279, 283 (6th Cir. 1976); Danno v. Peterson, 421 F. Supp. 950, 954 (N.D. Ill. 1976).
36. Moore, *id.* at 438.
37. Hardiman v. Jefferson County Bd. of Educ., 709 F.2d 635 (11th Cir. 1983).
38. *See* Colaizzi v. Walker, 542 F.2d 969 (7th Cir. 1976), *cert. denied*, 430 U.S. 960 (1976).
39. Robertson v. Rogers, 679 F.2d 1090 (4th Cir. 1982); Longarzo v. Anker, 578 F.2d 469 (2d Cir. 1978); Buhr v. Buffalo Public School Dist. No. 38, 509 F.2d 1196 (8th Cir. 1974).
40. Cato v. Collins, 539 F.2d 656 (8th Cir. 1976).
41. Beitzell v. Jeffrey, 643 F.2d 870, 879 (1st Cir. 1981).

42. Codd v. Velger, 429 U.S. 624 (1977).
43. Gray v. Union County Intermediate Educ. Dist., 520 F.2d 803, 806 (9th Cir. 1975).
44. Ball v. Board of Trustees of Kerrville Independent School Dist., 584 F.2d 684, 685 (5th Cir. 1978), *cert. denied*, 440 U.S. 972 (1979).
45. Stachura v. Truszkowski, 763 F.2d 211 (6th Cir. 1985), *rev'd on issue of damages*, 106 S. Ct. 2537 (1986).
46. Vanelli v. Reynolds School Dist. No. 7, 667 F.2d 773 (9th Cir. 1982); Dennis v. S & S Consol. Rural High School Dist., 577 F.2d 338 (5th Cir. 1978); Lombard v. Board of Educ. of City of New York, 502 F.2d 631 (2d Cir. 1974), *cert. denied*, 420 U.S. 976 (1975); Bomhoff v. White, 526 F. Supp. 488 (D. Ariz. 1981).
47. Robertson v. Rogers, 679 F.2d 1090 (4th Cir. 1982); Gray v. Union County Intermediate Educ. Dist., 520 F.2d 803 (9th Cir. 1975); Bomhoff v. White, 526 F. Supp. 488 (D. Ariz. 1981); Harris v. Arizona Bd. of Regents, 528 F. Supp. 987 (D. Ariz. 1981).
48. Mathews v. Eldridge, 424 U.S. 319, 335 (1976).
49. This chapter focuses on procedural protections required in the termination of teacher employment. It should be noted, however, that other school board decisions such as transfers, demotions, or mandatory leaves, may impose similar constraints on decision making. For example, an Ohio court found that the transfer of a tenured teacher from a regular classroom position to a position as a permanent itinerant substitute violated the teacher's due process rights. Mroczek v. Board of Educ. of Beachwood City School Dist., 400 N.E.2d 1362 (Ohio C.P. 1979). *See also* Dunsanek v. Hannon, 677 F.2d 538 (7th Cir. 1982), *cert. denied*, 459 U.S. 1017 (1982); Stewart v. Pearce, 484 F.2d 1031 (9th Cir. 1973).
50. *See* Levitt v. University of Texas at El Paso, 759 F.2d 1224 (5th Cir. 1985), *cert. denied*, 106 S. Ct. 599 (1985) (under certain circumstances, a constitutional deprivation might occur when an omission of state or local procedures results in a denial of the minimal constitutional procedures); Goodrich v. Newport News School Bd., 743 F.2d 225 (4th Cir. 1984).
51. *See* Hoover v. Wagner Community School Dist., 342 N.W.2d 226 (S.D. 1984); Lee v. Big Flat Public Schools, 658 S.W.2d 389 (Ark. 1983); Andrews v. Howard, 291 S.E.2d 541 (Ga. 1982). *But see* Hoyme v. Board of Educ. ABC School Dist., 165 Cal. Rptr. 737 (Cal. App. 1980).
52. McDonald v. East Jasper County Dist., 351 So. 2d 531 (Miss. 1977).
53. Griffin v. Galena City School Dist., 640 P.2d 829 (Alas. 1982).
54. Benton v. Board of Educ., 361 N.W.2d 515 (Neb. 1985).
55. Board of Trustees, Laramie County School Dist. No. 1 v. Spiegel, 549 P.2d 1161 (Wyo. 1976). *See also* Lee v. Board of Educ. of City of Bristol, 434 A.2d 333 (Conn. 1980).
56. Wagner v. Little Rock School Dist., 373 F. Supp. 876 (E.D. Ark. 1973).
57. *See* Shipley v. Salem School Dist., 669 P.2d 1172 (Ore. App. 1983), *review denied*, 675 P.2d 492 (Ore. 1984).
58. *See, e.g.*, Haddock v. Board of Educ., 661 P.2d 368 (Kan. 1983); Turk v. Franklin Special School Dist., 640 S.W.2d 218 (Tenn. 1982).
59. 105 S. Ct. 1487 (1985). *See* Leslie Gerstman, "Minimal Procedural Safeguards for Dismissal of Tenured Public Employees," *Education Law Reporter*, vol. 24 (1985), pp. 695–710.

60. *See* Brouillette v. Board of Directors of Merged Area IX, 519 F.2d 126, 128 (8th Cir. 1975).
61. Valter v. Orchard Farm School Dist., 541 S.W.2d 550 (Mo. 1976).
62. Ahern v. Board of Educ. of School Dist. of Grand Island, 456 F.2d 399 (8th Cir. 1972).
63. Birdwell v. Hazelwood School Dist., 491 F.2d 490 (8th Cir. 1974). *See also* Crane v. Mitchell County Unified School Dist. No. 273, 652 P.2d 205 (Kan. 1982).
64. Birdwell, *id.*; Crane, *id.*; Ferguson v. Board of Trustees of Bonner County Unified School Dist. No. 82, 564 P.2d 971 (Idaho 1977), *cert. denied*, 434 U.S. 939 (1977). *But see* Wertz v. Southern Cloud Unified School Dist., 542 P.2d 339 (Kan. 1975) (refusal of a teacher to participate in a posttermination or "after the fact" hearing did not constitute a waiver of due process rights).
65. Pederson v. South Williamsport Area School Dist., 677 F.2d 312 (3d Cir. 1982), *cert. denied*, 459 U.S. 972 (1982).
66. Jones v. Morris, 541 F. Supp. 11 (S.D. Ohio 1981), *aff'd*, 455 U.S. 1009 (1982). *See also* Bates v. Sponberg, 547 F.2d 325 (6th Cir. 1976) (hearing not required in presence of authority with ultimate responsibility for discharge decision); Pagano v. Board of Educ., 492 A.2d 197 (Conn. App. 1985), *review denied*, 499 A.2d 60 (Conn. 1985) (due process fulfilled by full, trial-type evidentiary hearing held before impartial hearing panel).
67. *See* Withrow v. Larkin, 421 U.S. 35 (1975).
68. Weissman v. Board of Educ. of Jefferson County., 547 P.2d 1267 (Colo. 1976). *See also* Ferguson v. Board of Trustees, 564 P.2d 971 (Idaho 1977), *cert. denied*, 434 U.S. 939 (1977).
69. 426 U.S. 482 (1975).
70. *Id.* at 496–497.
71. *Ex parte* Greenberg v. Alabama State Tenure Comm'n, 395 So. 2d 1000 (Ala. 1981). *But see* Danroth v. Mandaree Public School Dist. No. 36, 320 N.W. 2d 780 (N.D. 1982) (a board member's wife, being a principal objector to the teacher, did not deny the teacher a fair and proper hearing).
72. Staton v. Mayes, 552 F.2d 908 (10th Cir. 1977), *cert. denied*, 434 U.S. 907 (1977). *But see* Welch v. Barham, 635 F.2d 1322 (8th Cir. 1980), *cert. denied*, 451 U.S. 971 (1980) (statements by two board members at trial that they could not think of any evidence that would have changed their minds about terminating the individual did not show the degree of bias necessary to disqualify a decision maker).
73. Keith v. Community School Dist. of Wilton, 262 N.W.2d 249, 260 (Iowa 1978).
74. *See generally* Withrow v. Larkin, 421 U.S. 35 (1975); Dale v. Board of Educ., 316 N.W.2d 108 (S.D. 1982).
75. deKoevend v. Board of Educ., 688 P.2d 219, 228 (Colo. 1984).
76. *See* McIntyre v. Tucker, 490 So. 2d 1012 (Fla. App. 1986); Board of Educ. v. Lockhart, 687 P.2d 1306 (Colo. 1984); Schmidt v. Independent School Dist., 349 N.W.2d 563 (Minn. App. 1984). *But see* Holley v. Seminole County School Dist., 755 F.2d 1492 (11th Cir. 1985) (board's attorney permitted to sit as hearing examiner); Breitling v. Solenberger, 585 F. Supp. 289 (W.D. Va. 1984), *aff'd*, 749 F.2d 30 (4th Cir. 1984) (no due process violation even though attorney who represented superintendent's case for dismissal also served as an advisor to the school board).

77. *See* Martin v. Ambach, 502 N.Y.S.2d 991 (N.Y. 1986); Munger v. Jesup Community School Dist., 325 N.W.2d 377 (Iowa 1982).
78. *See* Robert E. Phay, *Legal Issues in Public School Administrative Hearings* (Topeka, KS: National Organization on Legal Problems of Education, 1982).
79. Altsheler v. Board of Educ., 476 N.Y.S.2d 281, 281–282 (N.Y. 1984). *See also* Whaley v. Anoka-Hennepin Independent School Dist., 325 N.W.2d 128, 130 (Minn. 1982).
80. Schulz v. Board of Educ. of the School Dist. of Freemont, 315 N.W.2d 633 (Neb. 1982).
81. *See* Alabama State Tenure Comm'n v. Tuscaloosa County Bd. of Educ., 401 So. 2d 84 (Ala. App. 1981), *review denied*, 401 So. 2d 87 (Ala. 1981); Doran v. Board of Educ. of Western Boone County Community Schools, 285 N.E.2d 825 (Ind. App. 1972).
82. *See* Libe v. Board of Educ., 350 N.W.2d 748 (Iowa App. 1984) (board could consider polygraph results); Mondragon v. Poudre School Dist., 696 P.2d 831 (Colo. App. 1984) (student previously hypnotized during a criminal investigation could testify at dismissal hearing and results of teacher's polygraph test taken by police were admissible).
83. *See* Sutherby v. Gobles Bd. of Educ., 348 N.W.2d 277 (Mich. App. 1984) (relevant evidence from prior years can be introduced).
84. Goldberg v. Kelly, 397 U.S. 254, 271 (1970).
85. *See* Benke v. Neenan, 658 P.2d 860 (Colo. 1983); Vorm v. David Douglas School Dist. No. 40, 608 P.2d 193 (Ore. App. 1980); Baxter v. Poe, 257 S.E.2d 71 (N.C. App. 1979), *review denied*, 259 S.E.2d 298 (N.C. 1979).
86. Hollingsworth v. Board of Educ., 303 N.W.2d 506 (Neb. 1981).
87. Morey v. School Bd. of Independent School Dist. No. 492, 128 N.W.2d 302, 307 (Minn. 1964).
88. Jackson v. Independent School Dist. No. 16, 648 P.2d 26 (Okla. 1982).
89. *Id.* at 31.
90. 78 CJS § 202.
91. *See* Floyd G. Delon, *Legal Controls on Teacher Conduct: Teacher Discipline* (Topeka, KS: National Organization on Legal Problems of Education, 1977), p. 12.
92. Henry Black, *Black's Law Dictionary*, 4th ed. (St. Paul, MN: West Publishing Co., 1968), p. 906.
93. *See* Benke v. Neenan, 658 P.2d 860 (Colo. 1983).
94. Horosko v. School Dist. of Mt. Pleasant, 6 A.2d 866 (Pa. 1939).
95. Beilan v. Board of Public Educ. of Philadelphia, 357 U.S. 399 (1958).
96. *See* text with notes 174–176, *infra*.
97. Beilan, 357 U.S. at 408.
98. Mims v. West Baton Rouge Parish School Bd., 315 So. 2d 349 (La. App. 1975).
99. Whaley v. Anoka-Hennepin Independent School Dist., 325 N.W.2d 128 (Minn. 1982). *See also* Wickersham v. New Mexico State Bd. of Educ., 464 P.2d 918 (N.M. App. 1970).
100. Hamburg v. North Penn School Dist., 484 A.2d 867 (Pa. Commw. 1984).
101. Aulwurm v. Board of Educ. of Murphysboro Community Unit School Dist. No. 186, 367 N.E.2d 1337 (Ill. 1977). *See also* Board of Directors of Sioux City Community School Dist. v. Mroz, 295 N.W.2d 447 (Iowa 1980).

102. Conder v. Board of Directors of Windsor School, 567 S.W.2d 377 (Mo. App. 1978).
103. Mott v. Endicott School Dist., No. 308, 713 P.2d 98, 101 (Wash. 1986).
104. Celestine v. Lafayette Parish School Bd., 284 So. 2d 650 (La. App. 1973).
105. Myres v. Orleans Parish School Bd., 423 So. 2d 1303 (La. App. 1983), *review denied*, 430 So. 2d 657 (La. 1983).
106. Phillips v. Plaquemines Parish School Bd., 465 So. 2d 53 (La. App. 1985), *review denied*, 467 So. 2d 540 (La. 1985).
107. Jergeson v. Board of Trustees of School Dist. No. 7, 476 P.2d 481 (Wyo. 1970).
108. Lamar School Dist. v. Kinder, 642 S.W.2d 885 (Ark. 1982).
109. *See* Hatta v. Board of Educ., Union Endicott Cent. School Dist., Broome County, 394 N.Y.S.2d 301 (App. Div. 1977).
110. *See* Kinsella v. Board of Educ. of Cent. School Dist. No. 7, 407 N.Y.S.2d 78 (App. Div. 1978).
111. *See* Jones v. Jefferson Parish School Bd., 533 F. Supp. 816 (E.D. La. 1982), *aff'd*, 688 F.2d 837 (5th Cir. 1982), *cert. denied*, 460 U.S. 1064 (1983); Rainwater v. Board of Educ., 645 S.W.2d 172 (Mo. App. 1982); Childers v. Independent School Dist., 645 P.2d 992 (Okia. 1981).
112. Scheelhaase v. Woodbury Cent. Community School Dist., 488 F.2d 237 (8th Cir. 1973), *cert. denied*, 417 U.S. 969 (1974).
113. *See* Delon, *Legal Controls on Teacher Conduct*; John McCormick, " 'Immorality' as a Basis for Dismissing a Teacher," *School Law Bulletin*, vol. 16 (1985), pp. 9–13.
114. Horosko v. School Dist. of Mt. Pleasant, 6 A.2d 866, 868 (Pa. 1939).
115. *See generally* Floyd Delon, "A Teacher's Sexual Involvement with Pupils: 'Reasonable Cause' for Dismissal," *Education Law Reporter*, vol. 22 (1985), pp. 1085–1093; Annot.: Dismissal of Teachers—Sexual Conduct, 78 A.L.R.3d 19 (1977). *See also* Fisher v. Independent School Dist., 357 N.W.2d 152 (Minn. App. 1984) (dismissal upheld for sexual abuse of an elementary student that occurred twelve years earlier); Katz v. Ambach, 472 N.Y.S.2d 492 (App. Div. 1984) (touching and kissing of sixth-grade female students supported dismissal).
116. Weissman v. Board of Educ. of Jefferson County School Dist., 547 P.2d 1267, 1273 (Colo. 1976).
117. Denton v. South Kitsap School Dist. No. 402, 516 P.2d 1080 (Wash. App. 1973).
118. Clark v. Ann Arbor School Dist., 344 N.W.2d 48 (Mich. App. 1983). *See also* Coupeville School Dist. v. Vivian, 677 P.2d 192 (Wash. App. 1984) (dismissal supported by one-time incident of male teacher permitting two female students to drink in his home); Shipley v. Salem School Dist., 669 P.2d 1172 (Ore. App. 1983) (negative impact of sexual contact with student on teaching effectiveness was obvious); Potter v. Kalama Public School Dist., 644 P.2d 1229 (Wash. App. 1982) (inappropriate physical contact with female students adequate basis for dismissal).
119. Kilpatrick v. Wright, 437 F. Supp. 397 (M.D. Ala. 1977).
120. *Id.* at 399.
121. Thompson v. Southwest School Dist., 483 F. Supp. 1170, 1181 (W.D. Mo. 1980).

122. Ross v. Robb, 662 S.W.2d 257 (Mo. 1984).
123. *See* Golden v. Board of Educ., 285 S.E.2d 665 (W. Va. 1982).
124. Sullivan v. Meade Independent School Dist. No. 101, 530 F.2d 799 (8th Cir. 1976).
125. *See also* Yanzick v. School Dist. No. 23, Lake County Montana, 641 P.2d 431 (Mont. 1982) (cohabitation was known throughout the small community and had become a matter of class discussion).
126. Sherburne v. School Bd. of Suwannee County, 455 So. 2d 1057 (Fla. App. 1984).
127. Ross v. Springfield, 691 P.2d 509, 513 (Ore. App. 1984), *rev'd*, 716 P.2d 724 (Ore. 1986). *See* note 144, *infra*.
128. Fisher v. Snyder, 476 F.2d 375 (8th Cir. 1973).
129. *Id.* at 377.
130. *See* Reinhardt v. Board of Educ. of Alton Community Unit School Dist. No. 11, 311 N.E.2d 710 (Ill. App. 1974).
131. Brown v. Bathke, 416 F. Supp. 1194, 1198 (D. Neb. 1976). Upon appeal to the Eighth Circuit Court of Appeals, damages were awarded in this case because of the lack of a pretermination hearing, 566 F.2d 588 (8th Cir. 1977).
132. Drake v. Covington County Bd. of Educ., 371 F. Supp. 974 (M.D. Ala. 1974).
133. Cochran v. Chidester School Dist. of Ouachita County, Arkansas, 456 F. Supp. 390 (W.D. Ark. 1978).
134. New Mexico State Bd. of Educ. v. Stoudt, 571 P.2d 1186 (N.M. 1977).
135. Avery v. Homewood City Bd. of Educ., 674 F.2d 337 (5th Cir. 1982), *cert. denied*, 461 U.S. 943 (1983); Andrews v. Drew Mun. Separate School Dist., 507 F.2d 611 (5th Cir. 1975). *See* the discussion of constitutional privacy rights associated with lifestyle choices in chapter 8.
136. *See* Bowers v. Hardwick, 106 S. Ct. 2841 (1986).
137. Morrison v. State Bd. of Educ., 461 P.2d 375 (Cal. 1969).
138. *Id.* at 382.
139. *Id.* at 386. It should be noted that this case dealt with the revocation of a male teacher's certificate because of homosexual conduct. Although it was not a dismissal case, the criteria listed have been relied on in dismissals for immorality.
140. Sarac v. State Bd. of Educ. 57 Cal. Rptr. 69 (Cal. App. 1967).
141. Board of Educ. of Long Beach v. Jack M., 566 P.2d 602 (Cal. 1977).
142. Gaylord v. Tacoma School Dist. No. 10, 559 P.2d 1340 (Wash. 1977), *cert. denied*, 434 U.S. 879 (1977).
143. In 1985 the Supreme Court declined to review Rowland v. Mad River Local School Dist., 730 F.2d 444 (6th Cir. 1984), *cert. denied*, 105 S. Ct. 1373 (1985), in which the Sixth Circuit Court of Appeals upheld the nonrenewal of a guidance counselor who was terminated for revealing her homosexual preference. *See* text with note 26, chapter 8, for a discussion of the constitutional issues involved in this case.
144. Ross v. Springfield School Dist., 691 P.2d 509 (Ore. App. 1984), *rev'd*, 716 P.2d 724 (Ore. 1986) (high court remanded for the Fair Dismissal Appeals Board to articulate criteria for assessing immorality). *See also* Naragon v. Wharton, 572 F. Supp. 1117 (M.D. La. 1983), *aff'd*, 737 F.2d 1403 (5th Cir.

1984), in which the appellate court upheld the reassignment of a university graduate assistant from a teaching to a research assistantship based on her homosexual relationship with a student who was not in any of her classes. The court reasoned that the university's action was warranted because of the graduate assistant's impropriety in developing a "deep, personal romantic relationship" with a student which the university considered to be unprofessional and detrimental to the institution's best interests.

145. Jarvella v. Willoughby-Eastlake City School Dist., 233 N.E.2d 143, 145 (Ohio 1967).
146. Clarke v. Board of Educ., 338 N.W.2d 272 (Neb. 1983).
147. Bovino v. Board of School Directors, 377 A.2d 1284 (Pa. Commw. 1977).
148. *Id.* at 1288.
149. *See* Kenai Peninsula Borough Bd. of Educ. v. Brown, 691 P.2d 1034, 1036 (Alas. 1984).
150. Logan v. Warren County Bd. of Educ., 549 F. Supp. 145 (S.D. Ga. 1982).
151. Bethel Park School Dist. v. Krall, 445 A.2d 1377 (Pa. Commw. 1982), *cert. denied*, 464 U.S. 851 (1984).
152. Kimble v. Worth County R.-III Bd. of Educ., 669 S.W.2d 949 (Mo. App. 1984), *cert. denied*, 105 S. Ct. 331 (1984).
153. Florian v. Highland Local Bd. of Educ., 493 N.E.2d 249 (Ohio App. 1983).
154. Golden v. Board of Educ., 285 S.E.2d 665 (W.Va. 1982).
155. Hoagland v. Mount Vernon School Dist, 623 P.2d 1156 (Wash. 1981).
156. *See* Sims v. Board of Trustees, 414 So. 2d 431 (Miss. 1982); Annot., 78 A.L.R.3d 83 (1977).
157. *See* Sutherby v. Gobles Bd. of Educ., 348 N.W.2d 277 (Mich. App. 1984).
158. Ky. Rev. Stat. § 161.790.
159. *See* Belasco v. Board of Public Educ., 486 A.2d 538 (Pa. Commw. 1985), *aff'd*, 510 A.2d 337 (Pa. 1986).
160. Ray v. Minneapolis Bd. of Educ., Special School Dist. No. 1, 202 N.W.2d 375 (Minn. 1972).
161. *Id.* at 378.
162. Board of Trustees of School Dist. No. 4 v. Colwell, 611 P.2d 427 (Wyo. 1980).
163. Warner v. U.S.D. #468, 604 P.2d 295 (Kan. App. 1979).
164. McLaughlin v. Board of Educ., 659 S.W.2d 249 (Mo. App. 1983).
165. *See* Simmons v. Vancouver School Dist., 704 P.2d 648 (Wash. App. 1985).
166. Welch v. Board of Educ. of Bement Community Unit School Dist. No. 5, 358 N.E.2d 1364 (Ill. App. 1977).
167. Barnes v. Fair Dismissal Appeals Bd., 548 P.2d 988 (Ore. App. 1976).
168. Board of Educ., Mt. Vernon Schools v. Shank, 542 S.W.2d 779 (Mo. 1976).
169. Simmons v. Vancouver School Dist., 704 P.2d 648 (Wash. App. 1985).
170. Harris v. Commonwealth of Pennsylvania, 372 A.2d 953 (Pa. Commw. 1977).
171. *Id.* at 957. *See also* Lithun v. Grand Forks Public School Dist., 307 N.W.2d 545 (N.D. 1981) (teacher claimed that policy placing restrictions on use of corporal punishment was not publicized; however, since teacher had been specifically warned, continued violation of policy supported dismissal).
172. Nordstrom v. Hansford, 435 P.2d 397 (Colo. 1967).

173. Belasco v. Board of Public Educ., 486 A.2d 538 (Pa. Commw. 1985), *aff'd*, 510 A.2d 337 (Pa. 1986).
174. Seitz v. Duval County School Bd., 346 So. 2d 644 (Fla. App. 1977), *review denied*, 354 So. 2d 985 (Fla. 1978).
175. Siglin v. Kayenta Unified School Dist., 655 P.2d 353 (Ariz. App. 1982).
176. Fulton v. Dysart Unified School Dist., 651 P.2d 369 (Ariz. App. 1982).
177. Blair v. Robstown Independent School Dist., 556 F.2d 1331 (5th Cir. 1977).
178. Whitsel v. Southeast Local School Dist., 484 F.2d 1222 (6th Cir. 1973).
179. Johnson v. Board of Educ., 353 N.W.2d 883, 884 (Iowa App. 1984).
180. Moffitt v. Batesville School Dist., 643 S.W.2d 557 (Ark. 1982).
181. Board of Trustees of the Hattiesburg Mun. Separate School Dist. v. Gates, 461 So. 2d 730 (Miss. 1984).
182. Ward v. Board of Educ. of the School Dist. of Philadelphia, 496 A.2d 1352 (Pa. Commw. 1985).
183. Sims v. Board of Trustees, Holly Springs Mun. Separate School Dist., 414 So. 2d 431 (Miss. 1982).
184. Wardwell v. Board of Educ. of the City School Dist. of the City of Cincinnati, 529 F.2d 625 (6th Cir. 1976). *See* chapter 7 for discussion of residency requirements.
185. Fisher v. Fairbanks North Star Borough School, 704 P.2d 213 (Alas. 1985).
186. Morrison v. Hamilton County Bd. of Educ., 494 S.W.2d 770 (Tenn. 1973), *cert. denied*, 414 U.S. 1044 (1973); Lucia v. Duggan, 303 F. Supp. 112 (D. Mass. 1969).
187. Fink v. Board of Educ., 442 A.2d 837 (Pa. Commw. 1982), *appeal dismissed*, 460 U.S. 1048 (1982).
188. School Dist. No. 11, Joint Counties of Archuleta and La Plata v. Umberfield, 512 P.2d 1166 (Colo. App. 1973). *See* text with note 176, chapter 9 for further discussion of absences for religious reasons.
189. Cunningham v. Franklin Parish School Bd., 457 So. 2d 184 (La. App. 1984), *review denied*, 461 So. 2d 319 (La. 1984).
190. Faulkner v. New Bern-Craven County Bd. of Educ., 316 S.E.2d 281 (N.C. 1984).
191. Keene v. Creswell School Dist., 643 P.2d 407 (Ore. App. 1982).
192. Harrah Independent School Dist. v. Martin, 440 U.S. 194 (1979).
193. Sanders v. Board of Educ. of the South Sioux City Community School Dist. No. 11, 263 N.W.2d 461 (Neb. 1978). *See also* Eshom v. Board of Educ. of School Dist. No. 54, 364 N.W.2d 7 (Neb. 1985) (incompetency was supported by detailed evaluations comparing terminated teacher with other teachers).
194. *Id.* at 465.
195. Fox v. Board of Educ. of Doddridge County, 236 S.E.2d 243 (W.Va. 1977).
196. DeVito v. Board of Educ., 317 S.E.2d 159 (W.Va. 1984). *See* Shurgin v. Ambach, 451 N.Y.S.2d 722 (N.Y. 1982) (knowingly exhibiting a pornographic film to students established adequate cause for the dismissal of a New York teacher).
197. Landry v. Ascension Parish School Bd., 415 So. 2d 473 (La. App. 1982), *review denied*, 420 So. 2d 448 (La. 1982).
198. *See* Delon, *Legal Controls on Teacher Conduct*, p. 12.
199. Pell v. Board of Educ. of Union Free School Dist. No. 1, 313 N.E.2d 321

(N.Y. 1974); School Dist. No. 11, Joint Counties of Archuleta and La Plata v. Umberfield, 512 P.2d 1166 (Colo. App. 1973).
200. Fernald v. City of Ellsworth Superintending School Comm., 342 A.2d 704 (Me. 1975).
201. Caravello v. Board of Educ., Norwich City School Dist., 369 N.Y.S.2d 829 (App. Div. 1975).
202. Coupeville v. Vivian, 677 P.2d 192 (Wash. App. 1984).
203. Kurlander v. School Comm. of Williamstown, 451 N.E.2d 138 (Mass. App. 1983).
204. Dupree v. School Comm. of Boston, 446 N.E.2d 1099 (Mass. App. 1983).
205. Meinhold v. Clark County School Dist. Bd. of School Trustees, 506 P.2d 420 (Nev. 1973), *cert. denied*, 414 U.S. 943 (1973).
206. DiCaprio v. Redmond, 350 N.E.2d 119 (Ill. App. 1976).
207. Wishart v. McDonald, 500 F.2d 1110 (1st Cir. 1974).
208. Perryman v. School Comm. of Boston, 458 N.E.2d 748 (Mass. App. 1983).
209. *See* Board of Trustees of the Clark County School Dist. v. Rathbun, 556 P.2d 548 (Nev. 1976).
210. *See* William D. Valente, *Education Law: Public and Private*, vol. 1 (St. Paul, MN: West Publishing Co., 1985), pp. 437–439.
211. Lombardo v. Board of Educ. of School Dist. No. 27, 241 N.E.2d 495, 498 (Ill. App. 1968).
212. In re Grossman, 316 A.2d 39 (N.J. App. 1974).
213. Wright v. Superintending Comm., City of Portland, 331 A.2d 640 (Me. 1975).
214. *Id.* at 647.
215. McLaughlin v. Machias School Comm., 385 A.2d 53 (Me. 1978).
216. *See* Dusanek v. Hannon, 677 F.2d 538 (7th Cir. 1982), *cert. denied*, 459 U.S. 1017 (1982); Fitzpatrick v. Board of Educ. of the Mamaroneck Union Free School Dist., 465 N.Y.S.2d 240 (N.Y. App. 1983) (serious personality disorder established incapacity to teach).
217. Smith v. Board of Educ., 293 N.W.2d 221 (Iowa 1980) (temporary mental illness inadequate). *But see* Clarke v. Shoreline School Dist. No. 412, 720 P.2d 793 (Wash. 1986) (dismissal of visually handicapped and hearing impaired teacher upheld because he could not perform essential functions of teaching position).
218. Arline v. School Bd. of Nassau County, 772 F.2d 759 (11th Cir. 1985), *cert. granted*, 106 S. Ct. 1633 (1986). *See* text with note 173, chapter 9 for a discussion of this case.
219. Newman v. Board of Educ. of the City School Dist. of New York, 594 F.2d 299 (2d Cir. 1979).
220. Gary Teachers Union, Local No. 4, AFT v. School City of Gary, 332 N.E.2d 256, 263 (Ind. App. 1975).
221. Wheeler v. Mariemont City School Dist., 467 N.E.2d 552 (Ohio App. 1983).
222. diLeo v. Greenfield, 541 F.2d 949, 954 (2d Cir. 1976).
223. *See generally* Joseph C. Beckham, "Reduction in Force," *Educators and the Law*, S. Thomas, N. Cambron-McCabe, and M. McCarthy, eds. (Elmont, NY: Institute for School Law and Finance, 1983), pp. 81–95; Robert Phay, *Reduction in Force: Legal Issues and Recommended Policy* (Topeka, KS: National Organization on Legal Problems of Education, 1980).
224. *See, e.g.*, Sutera v. Sully Buttes Bd. of Educ., 351 N.W.2d 457 (S.D. 1984)

(school board's procedures for staff reductions have the force and effect of law and must be followed); Gassman v. Governing Bd. of Rincon Valley Union School Dist. of Sonoma County, 554 P.2d 321 (Cal. 1976).

225. *See* Birk v. Board of Educ. of Flora Community Unit School Dist. No. 35, 472 N.E.2d 407 (Ill. 1984) (school system must consider seniority in reducing counselors' contracts from ten months to nine months when based on declining enrollments).
226. Cooper v. Fair Dismissal Appeals Bd., 570 P.2d 1005 (Ore. App. 1977).
227. Pa. Stat. Ann. 24 § 11–1124.
228. Dykeman v. Board of Educ., 316 N.W.2d 69 (Neb. 1982).
229. *See* Green Forest Public Schools v. Herrington, 696 S.W.2d 714 (Ark. 1985).
230. Steeby v. School Dist. of the City of Highland Park, 224 N.W.2d 97 (Mich. App. 1974). *See also* Dorian v. Euclid Bd. of Educ., 404 N.E.2d 155 (Ohio 1980); Milne v. School Comm. of Manchester, 410 N.E.2d 1216 (Mass. 1980).
231. Fatscher v. Board of School Directors Springfield School Dist., 367 A.2d 1130 (Pa. Commw. 1977).
232. Bilek v. Board of Educ. of Berkeley School Dist., 377 N.E.2d 1259 (Ill. App. 1978).
233. Chauvel v. Nyquist, 371 N.E.2d 473 (N.Y. 1977).
234. Chester v. Harper Woods School Dist., 273 N.W.2d 916 (Mich. App. 1978). *See also* Dinan v. Board of Educ., 426 N.Y.S.2d 86 (App. Div. 1980).
235. *See* Zurlo v. Ambach, 442 N.Y.S.2d 486 (N.Y. 1981); Von Krog v. Board of Educ., 298 N.W.2d 339 (Iowa App. 1980). *But see* Beeman v. Board of Educ., Oyster Bay-East Norwich Public Schools, 494 N.Y.S.2d 27 (App. Div. 1985). *See also* Pennell v. Board of Educ. of Equality Community Unit School Dist. No. 4, 484 N.E.2d 445 (Ill. App. 1985) (while rescheduling of positions may not be required, bad-faith realignment of positions to avoid existence of a position for a tenured teacher is prohibited).
236. McGhee v. Draper, 639 F.2d 639 (10th Cir. 1981).
237. *See, e.g.*, Sterzing v. Fort Bend Independent School Dist., 496 F.2d 92 (5th Cir. 1974).
238. *See* State v. Grant Valley Local Schools Bd. of Educ., 375 N.E.2d 48 (Ohio 1978); Board of Trustees of Nogales Elementary School Dist. v. Cartier, 559 P.2d 216 (Ariz. App. 1977); Jackson v. Board of Educ. of Oktibbeha County, 349 So. 2d 550 (Miss. 1977); Neal v. Board of Educ., School Dist. No. 189, 371 N.E.2d 869 (Ill. App. 1977); Boyce v. Alexis I. duPont School Dist., 341 F. Supp. 678 (D. Del. 1972).
239. *See* Weckerly v. Mona Shores Bd. of Educ., 202 N.W.2d 777 (Mich. 1972).
240. *See* deKoevend v. Board of Educ., 688 P.2d 219 (Colo. 1984); DiCello v. Board of Directors of Riverside School Dist., 380 A.2d 944 (Pa. Commw. 1977).
241. *See* Maine v. Thiboutot, 448 U.S. 1 (1980); Owen v. City of Independence, 445 U.S. 622 (1980); Monell v. Department of Social Services of the City of New York, 436 U.S. 658 (1978).
242. Schreffler v. Board of Educ. of Delmar School Dist., 506 F. Supp. 1300 (D. Del. 1981).
243. The Supreme Court held, in City of Newport v. Fact Concerts, 453 U.S. 247

(1981), that punitive awards cannot be assessed against governmental bodies such as school boards.

244. Fishman v. Clancy, 763 F.2d 485 (1st Cir. 1985).
245. Landry v. Ascension Parish School Bd., 415 So. 2d 473 (La. App. 1982), *review denied*, 420 So. 2d 448 (La. 1982).
246. Burton v. Cascade School Dist. Union High School No. 5, 512 F.2d 850 (9th Cir. 1975).
247. Sherburne v. School Bd. of Suwanee County, 455 So. 2d 1057, 1062 (Fla. App. 1984).
248. Cohen v. Board of Educ., Smithtown Cent. School Dist., 728 F.2d 160 (2d Cir. 1984). *But see* Alaniz v. San Isidro Independent School Dist., 589 F. Supp. 17 (S.D. Tex. 1983), *aff'd*, 742 F.2d 207 (5th Cir. 1984) (jury award of $50,000 as compensation for mental anguish and emotional distress was upheld because evidence substantiated injury).
249. Memphis Community School Dist. v. Stachuras, 106 S. Ct. 2537 (1986). *See* text with note 77, chapter 8.
250. 42 U.S.C. § 1988.
251. Alyeska Pipeline Service Co. v. Wilderness Society, 421 U.S. 240, 247 (1975).
252. 122 Cong. Rec. § 17051 (Sept. 29, 1976).
253. *See* Harrington v. Vandalia-Butler Bd. of Educ., 585 F.2d 192 (6th Cir. 1978), *cert. denied*, 441 U.S. 932 (1979).
254. Webb v. Board of Educ. of Dyer County, Tennessee, 105 S. Ct. 1923 (1985). *See* North Carolina Dep't of Transp. v. Crest Street Community, 107 S. Ct. 336 (1986) (attorneys' fees could not be recovered in administrative proceedings independent of enforcement of Title VI of the Civil Rights Act of 1964).
255. Christiansburg Garment Co. v. Equal Employment Opportunity Comm'n, 434 U.S. 412, 422 (1978).
256. *See, e.g.*, Hershinow v. Bonamarte, 772 F.2d 394 (7th Cir. 1985).

11

Collective Bargaining

Employment of teachers has been dramatically affected by the advent of collective bargaining in the public sector. Traditionally, boards of education had unilateral control over the management and operation of public schools. As employees of the school board, teachers were only minimally involved in the decision-making process. To achieve a balance of power and a voice in school affairs, teachers turned to collective group action during the 1960s and acquired significant labor rights.

Diversity in labor laws and bargaining practices among the states makes it difficult to generalize about collective bargaining and teachers' labor rights. In the absence of a federal law covering public school employees,[1] state labor laws, state employment relations board rulings, and court decisions must be consulted to determine specific rights. Over thirty states have enacted bargaining laws, varying widely in coverage from very comprehensive laws controlling most aspects of negotiations to laws granting the minimal right to bargain. Still other states, in the absence of legislation, rely on judicial rulings to define the basic rights of public employees in the labor relations arena. This chapter presents an overview of the legal structure in which bargaining occurs and public school teachers' employment rights under state labor laws.[2]

EMPLOYEES' BARGAINING RIGHTS IN THE PRIVATE AND PUBLIC SECTORS

Although there are basic differences in employment between the public and private sectors, collective bargaining legislation in the private sector has been significant in shaping statutory and judicial regulation of public negotiations. Similarities between the two sectors can be noted in a number of areas, such as unfair labor practices, union representation, and impasse procedures. Because of the influence of private sector legislation on the public sector, a brief overview of major legislative acts is warranted.

Prior to the 1930s, private labor relations were dominated by the judiciary, which strongly favored management. The extensive use of judicial injunctions against strikes and boycotts effectively countered employee efforts to obtain recognition for purposes of bargaining.[3] Consequently, courts reinforced the powers of management and substantially curtailed the development and influence of unions. To bolster the position of the worker, Congress enacted the Norris-LaGuardia Act in 1932. The purpose of this federal law was to circumscribe the role of courts in labor disputes by preventing the use of the injunction, except where union activities were unlawful or jeopardized public safety and health. In essence, the legislation did not confer any new rights on employees or unions but simply restricted judicial authority that had impeded the development of unions.

Following the Norris-LaGuardia Act, Congress in 1935 passed the National Labor Relations Act (NLRA), commonly known as the Wagner Act.[4] While this act created substantial rights for the private employee, one of the most important outcomes was that it granted legitimacy to the collective bargaining process. In addition to defining employees' rights to organize and collectively bargain, the act established a mechanism to safeguard these rights—the National Labor Relations Board (NLRB). The NLRB was created specifically to monitor claims of unfair labor practices such as interference with employees' rights to organize, discrimination against employees in hiring or discharge because of union membership, and failure to bargain in good faith.

The NLRA was amended in 1947 by the Labor Management Relations Act (known as the Taft-Hartley Act). While the Wagner Act regulated the activities of employers, the Taft-Hartley Act was an attempt to balance the scales in collective bargaining by regulating abusive union practices, such as interfering with employees' organizational rights and refusing to bargain in good faith. Since 1947 other amendments to the Taft-Hartley Act have further limited union abuses. Federal legislation has restricted interference from both the employer and the union, thereby ensuring the individual employee greater freedom of choice in collective bargaining.

Although the National Labor Relations Act specifically exempted governmental employees, a number of state public employee laws have been modeled after the NLRA, and judicial decisions interpreting the private sector law have been used to define certain provisions in public laws. The recognition of the sovereign power of public employers, however, is clearly present in public labor laws. For example, many public laws require employers to bargain over "wages, hours, and other terms and conditions of employment" as in the NLRA, but this requirement is then restricted by "management rights" clauses limiting the scope of bargaining.

There are several basic differences in bargaining between the public and private sectors. First, the removal of decision-making authority from public officials through bargaining has been viewed as an infringement on the sovereign power of government, which has resulted in the enactment of public labor laws strongly favoring public employers. Public employees' rights have been further weakened by prohibitions on work stoppages. Whereas employees' ability to strike is considered *essential* to the effective operation of collective decision making in the private sector, this view has been rejected in the public sector because of the nature and structure of governmental services.[5]

Bargaining rights developed slowly for public employees who historically had been deprived of the right to organize and collectively bargain. President Kennedy's Executive Order 10988 in 1962, which gave federal employees "the right, freely and without fear of penalty or reprisal, to form, join, and assist any employee organization . . . ,"[6] was a significant milestone for all public employees. The granting of organizational rights to federal employees provided the impetus for similar gains at the state and local levels.

Until the late 1960s, however, the constitutional right of public employees to join a union had not been fully established. A large number of public employees actively participated in collective bargaining, but statutes and regulations existed in some states prohibiting union membership. These restrictions against union membership were challenged as impairing association freedoms protected by the first amendment. Although not addressing union membership, the Supreme Court held in 1967 that public employment could not be conditioned on the relinquishment of free association rights.[7] In a later decision, the Seventh Circuit Court of Appeals clearly announced that "an individual's right to form and join a union is protected by the first amendment."[8] Other courts followed this precedent by invalidating state statutory provisions that blocked union membership.[9]

Recent decisions have reinforced teachers' constitutional rights to participate fully in union activities. School officials have been prohibited from imposing sanctions or denying benefits to discourage protected association rights. For example, the Sixth Circuit Court of Appeals overturned a school board's dismissal of a teacher because of union activities.[10] An Illinois federal district court held that a school board infringed on teachers' rights by abolishing a differentiated staffing system and appointing only nonunion members to certain positions after a union was reestablished in the district.[11] Similarly, the Massachusetts federal district court found that retaliation against a teacher, through suspension and other hostile action, for using the negotiated grievance procedure was constitutionally prohibited.[12]

While the United States Constitution has been interpreted as protecting public employees' rights to organize, the right to form and join a union does not ensure the right to bargain collectively with a public employer. Individual state statutes and constitutions govern such bargaining rights. Whether identified as professional negotiations, collective negotiations, or collective bargaining, the bargaining process entails bilateral decision making in which the teachers' representative and the school board attempt to reach mutual agreement on subjects that relate to or affect the teachers' employment. This process is governed in the majority of the states by legislation granting specific bargaining rights to teachers and their professional associations. Courts, viewing collective bargaining as within the ambit of legislative authority, have restricted their role primarily to interpreting statutory and constitutional provisions. The judiciary has been reluctant to interfere with the legislature's authority to define the collective bargaining relationship between public employer and employees unless protected rights have been compromised.

Because of the variations in labor laws, as well as the absence of such laws in some states, substantial differences exist in bargaining rights and practices. A few states, such as New York, have a detailed, comprehensive collective bargaining statute that delineates specific bargaining rights. In contrast, negotiated contracts between teachers' organizations and school boards are strictly prohibited in Virginia and North Carolina. Under North Carolina law, all contracts entered into by public employers and employee associations are invalid.[13] Similarly, in 1977 the Virginia Supreme Court declared that a negotiated contract between a teachers' organization and the school board was null and void in the absence of enabling legislation.[14] The board maintained that its power to enter into contracts allowed it also to bargain collectively with employee organizations. The court, however, concluded that such implied power was contrary to legislative intent.

In contrast to Virginia and North Carolina, other states have permitted negotiated agreements in the absence of enabling legislation. The Kentucky Supreme Court has ruled that a public employer *may* recognize an employee organization for the purpose of collective bargaining, even though state law is silent regarding public employee bargaining rights.[15] The decision does not impose a duty on local school boards to bargain but merely allows a board the discretion to negotiate. This ruling is consistent with a number of other decisions permitting negotiated contracts in the absence of legislation. The power and authority of the board to enter into contracts for the operation and maintenance of the school system have been construed to include the ability to enter into negotiated agreements with employee organizations.

Unless bargaining is mandated by statute, courts have not compelled school boards to negotiate. Whether or not to negotiate is thus at the school board's discretion. Once a school board extends recognition to a bargaining agent and commences bargaining, however, the board's actions in the negotiation process are governed by established judicial principles. While the employer maintains certain prerogatives, such as recognition of the bargaining unit and determination of bargainable items, specific judicially recognized rights also are conferred on the employee organization. For example, there is a legal duty for the board to bargain in good faith. Furthermore, if negotiations reach an impasse, the board may not unilaterally terminate the bargaining process. Also, after signing a contract, the board is bound by the provisions and cannot abrogate the agreement on the basis that no duty to bargain existed. Hence, the school board is subject to a number of legal constraints once it enters into the negotiation process.

The diversity across states in protected bargaining rights for public employees has led many individuals and groups to advocate a federal bargaining law for all state and local employees. Supporting such a proposal are a number of national organizations, including the National Education Association, the American Federation of Teachers, and the American Federation of State, County, and Municipal Employees. In the mid-seventies a federal law appeared imminent, but was abandoned by Congress with the Supreme Court's decision in *National League of Cities v. Usery*.[16] This decision involved a challenge to the 1974 congressional amendments to the Fair Labor Standards Act (FLSA) that extended the federal minimum wage and maximum hour provisions to employees of state and local governments. The Court concluded that the amendments unconstitutionally interfered with the states' rights to structure the public employer-employee relationship.

The Supreme Court, however, overturned *Usery* in 1985, concluding in *Garcia v. San Antonio Metropolitan Transit Authority* that state and municipal governments must comply with the minimum wage and overtime requirements in the FLSA.[17] As a result of this decision, uniform collective bargaining legislation may again be considered by Congress. For the immediate future, bargaining rights seem destined to be controlled by individual state legislation or, in the absence of legislation, by court rulings.

STATUTORY BARGAINING RIGHTS OF TEACHERS

The majority of the states have enacted statutes governing teachers' bargaining rights, and school boards must negotiate with teachers in accordance with the statutorily prescribed process. Generally, public employee bargaining laws address employer and employee rights, bargaining units, scope of bargaining, impasse resolution, grievance procedures, unfair labor practices, and penalties for prohibited practices. Many states have established labor relations boards to monitor bargaining under the statute. Although the specific functions of these boards vary widely, their general purpose is to resolve questions arising from the implementation of state law. Functions assigned to such boards include determination of membership in bargaining units, resolution of union recognition claims, investigation of unfair labor practices, and interpretation of the general intent of statutory bargaining clauses. Decisions of labor boards are an important source of labor law since many of the issues addressed by boards are never appealed to courts.

Most state laws define the broad criteria for determining appropriate groupings of employees for bargaining purposes. Among the factors considered in assessing appropriateness of bargaining units are the similarity in skills, wages, hours, and other working conditions of the employees; the effect of overfragmentation; the efficiency of operations of the employer; and the administrative structure of the employer. Of these factors, similarity in skills and working conditions has been the most significant requirement. Disputes over appropriateness of bargaining units are usually resolved by state labor boards.[18]

State laws generally provide that the school board will negotiate with an exclusive representative selected by the teachers. Procedures are specified for certification of the bargaining representative, election of the representative by employees, and recognition by the employer. Once an exclusive representative is recognized by the state labor board, an employer must bargain with that representative. In addition to certification, state laws also address cause and process for decertification of the exclusive representative.

Like the NLRA, state statutes require bargaining "in good faith." A number of states have followed the federal law in stipulating that this "does not compel either party to agree to a proposal or to require the making of a concession."[19] Since good faith bargaining has been open to a range of interpretations, judicial decisions in the public sector have relied extensively on private sector rulings that have clarified the phrase. Good faith bargaining has been interpreted as requiring parties to meet at reasonable times and attempt to reach mutual agreement without compulsion on either side to agree. Failure of the board or teachers' organization to bargain in good faith can result in the imposition of penalties.

Statutes impose certain restrictions or obligations on the school board and the employee organization. Violation of the law by either party can result in an unfair labor practice claim. Allegations of unfair labor practices are brought before the state public employee relations board for a hearing and judgment. Specific unfair labor practices, often modeled after those in the NLRA, are included in state statutes. The most common proscribed labor practice identified in both public and private employment is that an employer or union will not interfere with, restrain, or coerce public employees in the exercise of their rights under the labor law. Among other prohibited employer practices are interference with the operation of the union, discrimination against employees because of union membership, refusal to bargain collectively with the exclusive representative, and failure to bargain in good faith. Unions are prevented from causing an employer to discriminate against employees on the basis of union membership, refusing to bargain or failing to bargain in good faith, failing to represent all employees in the bargaining unit, and engaging in unlawful activities such as strikes or boycotts identified in the bargaining law.

SCOPE OF NEGOTIATIONS

Should the teachers' organization have input into class size? Who will determine the length of the school day? How will extra duty assignments be determined? Will reductions in force, necessitated by declining enrollment, be based on seniority or merit? These questions and others are raised in connection with determining the scope of negotiations. "Scope" refers to the range of issues or subjects that are negotiable, and determining scope is one of the most difficult tasks in public sector bargaining. Public employers argue that issues must be narrowly defined to protect the government's policy-making role, while the employee unions counter that bargaining subjects must be broadly defined for negotiations to be meaningful.[20]

Restrictions on scope of bargaining vary considerably among the states. Consequently, to determine negotiable items in a particular state, the state's collective bargaining law, other statutory laws, and litigation interpreting these laws must be examined. The specification of negotiable items in labor laws may include broad guidelines or detailed enumerations. Many of the states have modeled their bargaining statutes after the NLRA, which stipulates that representatives of the employer and employees must meet and confer "with respect to wages, hours, and other terms and conditions of employment."[21] Pennsylvania[22] and Hawaii[23] have adopted identical language, while Florida[24] specifies only "terms and conditions of employment." A few states have elected to deal directly with the issue of scope by identifying each item that must be negotiated; Tennessee lists ten items, while Nevada lists approximately twenty.[25] In general, if specific statutory rights have been granted to teachers, they cannot be preempted by negotiation.[26] For example, the state tenure law may require extensive procedural protections for the termination of a teacher's employment that cannot be altered through a collective bargaining contract.

All proposed subjects for negotiation can be classified as either mandatory, permissive, or prohibited. Mandatory items must be negotiated. Failure of the school board to meet and confer on such items is evidence of lack of good faith bargaining. Permissive items can be negotiated if both parties agree; however, there is no legal duty to consider the items. Furthermore, in most states permissive items cannot be pursued to the point of negotiation impasse, and an employer can make unilateral changes with respect to these items if a negotiated agreement is not reached. Prohibited items are beyond the power of the board to negotiate; an illegal delegation of power results if the board agrees to negotiate these items. Since most statutory scope provisions are general in nature, courts often have been called upon to differentiate between negotiable and nonnegotiable items. The following sections highlight issues related to governmental policy and specific bargaining topics.

Governmental Policy

Defining managerial rights is one of the key elements in establishing limitations on negotiable subjects at the bargaining table. State laws specify that public employers cannot be required to negotiate governmental policy matters, and courts have held that it is impermissible for a school board to bargain away certain rights and responsibilities in the public policy area. Established boundaries distinguishing such policy issues from other items that can be negotiated vary widely among the states.

Educational policy matters are generally defined through provisions in collective bargaining statutes, such as "management rights" and "scope of bargaining" clauses. Policy issues are totally excluded as negotiable items in a few states; however, most states stipulate only that employers will not be required to bargain such policy rights. The excerpt below from the Pennsylvania Public Employees Act illustrates a typical provision.

> Public employers *shall not be required* to bargain over matters of inherent managerial policy, which shall not be limited to such areas of discretion or policy as the functions and programs of the public employer, standards of services, its overall budget, utilization of technology, the organizational structure and selection and direction of personnel.[27] (emphasis added)

To interpret policy rights in a particular state, judicial rulings should be examined.

The phrase "conditions of employment," as it is used in public employee bargaining laws, can include far-reaching policy matters since most decisions made by a school board either directly or indirectly affect the teacher at the classroom level. The Supreme Court of New Jersey narrowly interpreted the phrase to mean wages, benefits, and work schedules, thereby removing governmental policy items such as teacher transfers, course offerings, and evaluations.[28] A number of courts, however, have construed conditions of employment in broader terms. The South Dakota Supreme Court held that subjects that *materially* affect teachers' employment are negotiable.[29] Similarly, the Nevada Supreme Court ruled that items *significantly* related to wages, hours, and working conditions are negotiable.[30] The Pennsylvania Supreme Court concluded that an issue's *impact* on conditions of employment must be weighed in determining whether it should be considered outside the educational policy area.[31]

While courts are in agreement that school boards cannot be *required* to negotiate inherent managerial rights pertaining to policy matters, these rights are viewed as *permissive* subjects of bargaining in some states. That is, the board may agree to negotiate a particular "right" in the absence of statutory or judicial prohibitions.[32] If the board does negotiate the policy item, it is bound by the agreement in the same manner as if the issue were a mandatory item.[33]

Selected Bargaining Subjects

Beyond wages, hours, and fringe benefits, there is a lack of agreement among states as to what is negotiable. Similar enabling legislation has been interpreted quite differently among states, as illustrated by the subjects discussed below.

Class Size. Class size has been one of the most controversial policy subjects, and one that courts and state legislatures have been reluctant to designate as negotiable. It is not specifically identified as a mandatory bargaining item in any state law. By statute in Indiana, however, class size must be discussed with the exclusive representative, but there is no requirement to reach a negotiated agreement.[34] The Nevada Supreme Court interpreted the state collective bargaining statute as including class size among mandatory subjects by implication.[35] In response to this decision, the legislature revised the state law to exclude class size from a detailed list of bargainable items.[36] A number of other courts have found class size to be a permissive subject of bargaining.[37] Although the Wisconsin Supreme Court found class size to be such a *permissive* subject, the court held that negotiations on the impact of class size on teachers' conditions of employment would be *mandatory*.[38] Similarly, a Florida appellate court concluded that class size and staffing levels were not mandatorily bargainable but noted that the impact or effect of the implementation of these decisions would be mandatorily bargainable.[39] In Alaska, the state high court has declared class size a nonnegotiable item because of its effect on educational policy.[40]

School Calendar. Determination of the school calendar generally has been held to be a managerial prerogative.[41] The Maine high court's finding that the school calendar is a nonnegotiable managerial decision represents this position. The court stated: "[T]he commencement and termination of the school year and the scheduling and length of intermediate vacations during the school year, at least insofar as students and teachers are congruently involved, must be held matters of 'educational policies' bearing too substantially upon too many and important non-teacher interests to be settled by collective bargaining or binding arbitration."[42] An Indiana appellate court agreed, noting that the impact of the school calendar on students and other public interests outweighed teachers' interests.[43] In a later case, another Indiana appellate court concurred that mandatory bargaining of the school calendar is not required, but under state law it is a "working condition" that must be discussed.[44] An Oregon appellate court concluded that the calendar is a policy matter but found that a union's proposal relating to vacations and to definitions of the work year for salary determinations related primarily to working conditions and therefore must be negotiated.[45] In contrast to the prevailing view, the Wisconsin Supreme Court upheld a ruling of the Wisconsin Employment Relations Commission declaring the school calendar mandatorily bargainable. The court reasoned that the school board is "required to meet, confer and bargain as to any calendaring proposal that is *primarily* related to 'wages, hours, and conditions of employment' " and, thus, interpreted calendar issues as more closely related to terms of employment than to policy matters.[46]

Teacher Evaluation. Significant gains have been made by employee unions in securing the right to negotiate various aspects of teacher performance evaluations. Most states have not specified evaluation as a mandatory bargaining item,[47] but a number of courts have found it to be significantly related to conditions of employment, thereby requiring or permitting negotiations. While courts have been receptive to union proposals to negotiate the technical and procedural elements of evaluation, they have been reluctant to mandate the negotiation of evaluation criteria. The Supreme Court of New Jersey, concluding that criteria for evaluation cannot be negotiated, recognized that "[w]hile the policy established for evaluating tenured teachers intimately and directly affects the work and welfare of those public employees, it also involves the exercise of inherent management prerogatives."[48] The court, however, did uphold negotiation of procedural aspects beyond those required of the school board in the state board of education regulations. Similarly, the Supreme Court of Oregon held that proposals related to procedural fairness were subject to mandatory bargaining but, in contrast to the New Jersey court, concluded that, although the mechanics and use of evaluations were related primarily to educational policy, they were subject to permissive bargaining.[49] The Wisconsin high court concluded that "who will evaluate" was nonnegotiable, but held that the procedures to be used must be negotiated.[50]

While the Supreme Court of Nevada held that teacher evaluation is a permissive item,[51] it has been declared nonnegotiable by the Alaska high court.[52]

Reduction in Force. With declining student enrollments and financial exigency faced by many school districts, staff reductions in force (RIF) have become a threat to tenured as well as nontenured teachers. The threat has resulted in employee unions demanding input into decisions to reduce staff, criteria for reductions, and procedures for selecting teachers for release. Generally, courts have held that the decision to reduce staff and the criteria used to make that decision are educational policy matters and thus not negotiable.[53] The *impact* of reductions on employee rights, however, may necessitate negotiation of RIF procedures. The Supreme Court of Kansas held that the decision to reduce teaching positions was a nonnegotiable managerial decision, but concluded that the mechanics of staff reductions, such as how staff would be selected and procedures for recall, were mandatorily negotiable.[54] The Supreme Court of Wisconsin developed a balancing test for weighing employees' interests in wages, hours, and conditions of employment against the employer's right to make managerial policy decisions. If an item is "primarily related" to wages, hours, and conditions of employment, the item is a mandatory subject of bargaining; if not, there is no duty to bargain. Accordingly, the court found that notice and timing of layoffs were primarily related to employees' interest and had "a direct impact on the wages and job security," thus requiring bargaining.[55] The Supreme Court of New Jersey also found that procedural fairness concerning timely notice of release of teachers was negotiable; such a requirement did not pose a "significant interference with the exercise of governmental prerogative."[56] Similarly, the Massachusetts high court held that timing of layoffs and the number and identity of the employees were negotiable subjects.[57] The Supreme Court of Iowa also found the procedures for selecting teachers for layoff to be a proper subject for bargaining.[58]

Procedures negotiated by the employer and the teachers' union for reduction, however, must not violate the constitutional rights of any employees. The United States Supreme Court recently overturned a collective bargaining agreement that was designed to protect members of certain minority groups from layoffs.[59] The agreement ensured that the percentage of minority teachers would not fall below the percentage employed before any reduction in force. In the absence of evidence that there had been prior employment discrimination, the Court held that the plan violated the equal protection rights of nonminority teachers.

Nonrenewal and Tenure. Decisions to retain a teacher or grant tenure clearly are managerial rights and not mandatorily bargainable.[60] If a school board negotiates procedural aspects of these decisions, however, the provisions generally are binding. For example, collective bargaining agreements may entitle nontenured teachers to procedural protections that would not ordinarily be required under state laws or the fourteenth amendment.[61] The Supreme Court of New Hampshire held that state law did not prevent a school board from agreeing to provide probationary teachers with a statement of reasons for nonrenewal; the board still retained its managerial prerogative not to renew the teacher's contract.[62] Similarly, the Supreme Court of Ohio found that an agreement requiring written notification of the reasons for nonrenewal did not restrict the board's right "to nonrenew for any reason it deems necessary."[63]

Failure of school boards to follow negotiated procedures has resulted in arbitrators ordering reinstatement of discharged teachers. Permissibility of such awards, however, depends on how a school board's authority is interpreted under state law. The Supreme Court of Alaska rejected an arbitrator's reinstatement of a teacher, reasoning that school boards "possess the exclusive power, not subject to *any* appeal, to decide whether to 'nonrenew' a provisional employee."[64] The court noted that a range of other remedies was available for the board's violation of the negotiated nonretention procedures. In contrast, the high courts of Montana and Ohio concluded that reinstatement of teachers by an arbitrator did not usurp school board authority but simply provided appropriate relief for the board's failure to abide by negotiated procedures.[65]

UNION SECURITY PROVISIONS

To ensure their strength and viability, unions attempt to obtain various security provisions in the collective bargaining contract. The nature and extent of these provisions will depend on state laws and constitutional limitations. In this section, provisions related to union revenue and exclusive privileges are addressed.

Dues and Service Fees

Unions seek to require employees either to join or financially support the recognized bargaining agent. It is argued that such provisions are necessary to eliminate "free riders," since a union must represent all individuals in the bargaining unit. There are several forms of union security provisions. The *closed shop*, requiring an employer to hire only union members, does not exist in the public sector and is unlawful in the private sector under the NLRA and the Taft-Hartley amendments. The *union shop* agreement requires an employee to join the union within a designated period of time after employment to retain a position. While this agreement is prevalent in the private sector, it is not authorized by most public sector laws and is limited or proscribed in a number of states under "right-to-work" laws. The *agency shop* and *fair share* agreements are the security provisions most frequently found in the public sector.[66] An agency shop agreement requires an employee to pay union dues but does not mandate membership. A variant of agency shop is the fair share arrangement whereby the nonmember simply pays a service fee to cover the cost of bargaining activities. Approximately seventeen states have legislation permitting the negotiation of such fees.[67] Two states most recently enacting collective bargaining laws, Illinois and Ohio, have included agency shop as a negotiable subject.

The constitutionality of mandatory payment of agency fees by public employees was upheld by the United States Supreme Court in 1977 in a Michigan case, *Abood v. Detroit Board of Education*.[68] The Court rejected the nonunion members' first amendment speech and association claims, noting the importance of ensuring labor peace and eliminating "free riders." The Court, however, concluded that under the protection of the first amendment an employee could not be compelled "to contribute to the support of an ideological cause he may oppose as a condition of holding a job as a public school teacher."[69] Accordingly, the fee for a nonmember teacher who objects to forced contribution to political activities of the union must reflect only costs of bargaining and administration of the contract.[70]

While the Supreme Court's decision permitted the collection of an agency fee, it did not resolve a number of significant issues, such as: (1) What expenditures can be legitimately claimed by unions as related to collective bargaining activities? (2) What procedures are adequate or necessary to protect the interests of individuals challenging the union's apportionment of costs? (3) Can employees be discharged as a means to enforce an agency shop agreement?

Under the *Abood* ruling, the burden is placed on the nonunion employee to object to the union's use of the agency fee, and the union then must establish the proportionate share related to employee representation. The Supreme Court noted that there would be "difficult problems in drawing lines between collective-bargaining activities, for which contributions may be compelled, and ideological activities unrelated to collective bargaining, for which such compulsion is prohibited."[71] In subsequent cases, the Supreme Court and lower courts have attempted to define this dividing line as well as the procedural protections necessary to respond to nonmembers' objections.

In *Ellis v. Brotherhood of Railway, Airline, and Steamship Clerks*, a private sector case, the Supreme Court advanced a standard for determining which union expenditures can be assessed against objecting employees:

> [T]he test must be whether the challenged expenditures are necessarily or reasonably incurred for the purpose of performing the duties of an exclusive

> representative of the employees in dealing with the employer on labor-management issues. Under this standard, objecting employees may be compelled to pay their fair share of not only the direct costs of negotiating and administering a collective-bargaining contract and of settling grievances and disputes, but also the expenses of activities or undertakings normally or reasonably employed to implement or effectuate the duties of the union as exclusive representative of the employees in the bargaining unit.[72]

In applying this test, the Court upheld the assessment of costs related to union conventions, social activities, and publications, but disallowed expenditures related to organizing activities and litigation unrelated to negotiations, contract administration, and fair representation.

Although the above test was not established in the public sector, it has been applied in a number of cases involving public employees. Both the Third Circuit and Ninth Circuit Appellate Courts upheld the use of representation fees for lobbying activities under this test. The Third Circuit Court of Appeals reasoned that collective bargaining is "a process whereby unions must advance the collective interests of their members in a number of arenas."[73] Since many of the terms and conditions of public employment are established by state legislation rather than direct negotiations, a union would be severely handicapped in representing employees if unable to lobby. The court, however, distinguished representative lobbying activities from impermissible lobbying to advance a political or ideological position of the union. The Ninth Circuit Appellate Court also held that the significant effect of state laws on public employment "requires that public employee representatives be given broad authority to protect their members' interests before the legislature."[74] Similarly, the Supreme Court of New Jersey found that the expenditure of fair representative fees for lobbying was valid.[75] A California appellate court upheld use of fees for lobbying and electioneering, state and national affiliation, and publications.[76]

The constitutionality of union procedures adopted to respond to nonmembers who object to the agency fee has generated considerable debate. Generally, after a nonmember raises an objection, unions have provided a rebate of the portion of the fee unrelated to bargaining activities. However, in the 1984 *Ellis* decision, the Supreme Court found a *pure rebate* procedure inadequate. Characterizing this approach as an "involuntary loan," the Court stated:

> By exacting and using full dues, then refunding months later the portion that it was not allowed to exact in the first place, the union effectively charges the employees for activities that are outside the scope of the statutory authorization.[77]

Because other alternatives such as advance reduction of dues and escrow accounts exist, the Court found even temporary use of dissenters' funds impermissible. In the wake of *Ellis*, several lower courts have upheld procedures that provide advance reduction and/or placement of funds in interest-bearing escrow accounts.[78]

In 1986 further guidance was provided by the Supreme Court in determining the adequacy of union procedural safeguards to protect nonmember employees' constitutional rights in the apportionment and assessment of representation fees. According to the Court in *Chicago Teachers' Union, Local No. 1 v. Hudson,* constitutional requirements for the collection of an agency fee include "an adequate explanation of the basis for the fee, a reasonably prompt opportunity to challenge the amount of the fee before an impartial decisionmaker, and an escrow for the amounts reasonably in dispute while such challenges are pending."[79] While the contested Chicago union's plan included an advance reduction of dues, it was found to be flawed because nonmembers were required to file an objection in order to receive any information about the calculation of the proportionate share, and were not provided sufficient information to judge the appropriateness of the fee. The Court held that adequate disclosure required more than identification of expenditures that did not benefit objecting employees; reasons had to be provided for assessment of the fair share. In addition, the Chicago procedures did not ensure dissenting employees a prompt decision by an impartial decision maker. The Court went further than the *Ellis* prohibition on a pure rebate procedure and held that, even if an advance reduction is made, any additional amounts in dispute must be placed in escrow. This was found to be necessary to minimize the risk that any funds of an objector would be used for impermissible ideological activities.[80]

The Supreme Court's rejection of federal constitutional claims to agency shop provisions in the public sector does not mean that such measures will be permitted under state law. The Maine high court held that forced payment of dues was "tantamount to coercion toward membership."[81] The Maine statute ensures employees the right to join a union *voluntarily*. This was interpreted by the court as including the right to *refrain* from joining. Similarly, a Florida appeals court rejected a fair share checkoff requirement, finding that such an agency shop provision violated the state constitution.[82]

While representation fees do not violate the Federal Constitution and have been upheld in most states, legal controversy surrounds enforcement of the provisions.[83] Often collective bargaining agreements require employers to discharge teachers who refuse to pay the fee. In Pennsylvania, an appellate court overturned the dismissal of two teachers, stating that refusal to pay dues did not constitute "persistent and willful violation of the school laws" to justify dismissal.[84] An Indiana appellate court concluded that school districts cannot bargain away their responsibility to discharge teachers.[85] Several courts have attempted to reconcile labor laws that authorize the negotiation of fair share fees as a condition of employment with tenure laws that permit dismissal only for specified causes. The Supreme Court of Michigan has ruled that the state labor law prevails when it conflicts with another statute.[86] Accordingly, a tenured teacher who fails to pay the agency service fee can be discharged without resort to procedural requirements of the teacher tenure act. Similarly, the California Public Employment Relations Board has held that state law authorizing a service fee permits termination of a teacher's employment.[87] The California Attorney General, however, has stated that in such a dismissal procedural requirements of the teacher dismissal statute must be followed.[88]

Unions also have pursued enforcement of agency fee agreements in civil actions against nonmember teachers. The California Supreme Court held that a statutory provision permitting payment of a service fee *as a condition of employment* did not prescribe termination of employment as the exclusive remedy for noncompliance; the union and employer were free to negotiate other alternatives such as civil actions.[89] Ohio and Michigan courts have upheld the use of similar civil actions by unions to collect service fees from individual employees.[90] In the Michigan case, the collective bargaining agreement noted civil suits as the sole means of enforcement.

Exclusive Privileges

The designated employee bargaining representative gains security through negotiating exclusive rights or privileges such as dues checkoff, the use of the school mails, and access to school facilities. While exclusive arrangements strengthen the majority union and may make it difficult for minority unions to survive, they are often supported by courts as a means of promoting labor peace and ensuring efficient operation of the school system.

The exclusive privilege most often found in collective bargaining contracts is dues checkoff. Over half of the states with public employee bargaining laws specify dues checkoff as a mandatory subject for bargaining.[91] Unless prohibited by state law, most courts have upheld negotiated agreements between the designated bargaining representative and the employer denying rival unions checkoff rights.

In 1983, the Supreme Court clarified one of the most controversial security rights—exclusive access to school mail facilities.[92] The case focused on an agreement between the exclusive bargaining representative and an Indiana school board denying access to the interschool mail system and teacher mailboxes to all rival unions. One of the unions challenged the agreement as a violation of first and fourteenth amendment rights. The Supreme Court upheld the arrangement, reasoning that the first amendment does not require "equivalent access to all parts of a school building in which some form of communicative activity occurs."[93] The Court concluded that the school mail facility was not a public forum for open communication and thereby its use could be restricted to official school business. The fact that several community groups (e.g., scouts, civic organizations) used the school mail system did not create a public forum. The Court noted that, even if such access by community groups created a limited public forum, access would be extended only to similar groups—not to labor organizations. The Court's emphasis on the availability of alternative channels of communication (e.g., bulletin boards and meeting facilities), however, indicates that total exclusion of rival unions would not be permitted.

The Fifth Circuit Court of Appeals subsequently ruled, and the Supreme Court affirmed, that denial of access to the school mail to all teacher organizations did not violate the first amendment when other channels of communication were available.[94] However, the Court found unconstitutional a policy prohibiting individual teachers from discussing employee organizations during nonclass time or using the internal mail system or bulletin boards to mention employee organizations. Such limitations on an individual employee's expression would be permissible only if a threat of material and substantial disruption were shown.

It appears that exclusive use of communication facilities can be constitutionally granted to the bargaining representative or that use of facilities can be denied to all employee organizations. If rival unions are excluded from specific communication channels, other avenues must be available to avoid infringement of first amendment rights. Under state laws, however, exclusive access to use of mail and school facilities may be an unfair labor practice. For example, the Florida Public Employee Relations Commission adopted a policy that access rules discriminating against rival unions are invalid.[95]

In most states, school boards negotiate only with the designated bargaining representative. Under this exclusive recognition, other unions and teacher groups can be denied the right to engage in official exchanges with an employer. Recently, the Supreme Court held that nonmembers of a bargaining unit or members who disagree with the views of the representative do not have a constitutional right "to force the government to listen to their views."[96] The Court concluded that a Minnesota statute requiring employers to "meet and confer" only with the designated bargaining representative did not violate other employees' speech or associational rights as public employees or as citizens since these sessions were not a public forum. According to the Court, "[t]he Constitution does not grant to members of the public generally a right to be heard by public bodies making decisions of policy."[97]

However, if a public forum, such as a school board meeting, is involved, a nonunion teacher has a constitutional right to address the public employer, even on a subject of negotiation. The Supreme Court concluded in a Wisconsin case that a nonunion teacher possessed the right to express concerns to the school board.[98] In this case, negotiation between the board and union had reached a deadlock on the issue of an agency shop provision. A nonunion teacher, representing a minority group of teachers, addressed the board at a regular public meeting and requested postponement of a decision until further study could be made. The Court reasoned that the teacher was not attempting to negotiate, but merely to speak on an important issue before the board—a right any citizen possesses. The Court further noted that teachers have never been "compelled to relinquish their first amendment rights they would otherwise enjoy as citizens to comment on matters of public interest in connection with the operation of the public school in which they work."[99]

While union security provisions such as agency shop fees and exclusive use of specific school facilities can be negotiated, nonunion teachers' constitutional rights cannot be infringed. Safeguards must be provided to ensure that teachers have an effective mechanism for challenging financial contributions that might be used to support ideological causes or political activities to which they may object. If specific communication channels for nonmembers are restricted through the negotiation process, alternative options must remain open.

NEGOTIATION IMPASSE

Most comprehensive bargaining statutes address impasse resolution. An impasse occurs in bargaining when an agreement cannot be reached and neither party will compromise. When negotiations reach such an impasse, several options are available for resolution—mediation, fact finding, and arbitration. As discussed in the final section of this chapter, the most effective means for resolving negotiation impasse—the strike—is not legally available to the majority of public employees. Most state statutes address impasse procedures, with provisions ranging from allowing impasse procedures to be negotiated to mandating detailed steps that must be followed. Alternatives that are most frequently employed to resolve impasse are identified below.

Mediation is often the first step to reopening negotiations. A neutral third party assists both sides in finding a basis for agreement. The mediator serves as a facilitator rather than a decision maker, thus enabling the board and teachers' association jointly to reach an agreement. Mediation may be optional or required by law; the mediator is selected by the negotiation teams or, upon request, appointed by a public employee relations board.

Failure to reach agreement through mediation frequently results in fact finding (often called advisory arbitration). The process may be mandated by law or may be entered into by mutual agreement of both parties. Fact finding involves the efforts of a third party to investigate the causes for the dispute, collect facts and testimony to clarify the dispute, and formulate a judgment accordingly. Because of the advisory nature of the process, proposed solutions are not binding on either party. However, since fact-finding reports are made available to the public, they provide an impetus to settle a contract that is not present in mediation.

In a number of states, the final step in impasse procedures is fact finding, which may leave both parties without a satisfactory solution. A few states permit a third alternative—binding interest arbitration.[100] This process is similar to fact finding except that the decision of the arbitrator, related to the terms of the negotiated agreement, is binding on both parties. States that permit binding arbitration often place restrictions on its use.[101] For example, Ohio and Maine permit binding arbitration on matters of mutual consent,[102] Rhode Island allows binding arbitration only on nonmonetary items,[103] and Oregon merely provides that impasse procedures with final and binding arbitration may be negotiated.[104]

It is generally agreed that mediation and fact finding, because of their advisory nature, do not provide the most effective means for resolving negotiation disputes. Since the strike is prohibited among public employees in most states, conditional binding arbitration has been considered a viable alternative in resolving deadlocks. Although a greater balance of power is achieved between the school board and the teachers' association with binding arbitration, it has not been met with enthusiasm by public sector employers, who often view it as an illegal delegation of power. As a result, interest arbitration generally has occurred in the educational setting only on a voluntary or conditional basis.

If a collective bargaining agreement expires during the negotiation of a new contract, most courts have held that the school board is obligated to maintain the status quo regarding wages, hours, and conditions of employment until a new agreement is reached or until the required statutory impasse steps have been exhausted. The Supreme Court of Indiana emphasized that the maintenance of the status quo "serves to continue the balance in the bargaining power of the parties as well as provide the flexibility necessary to reach agreement. . . ."[105] Accordingly, the court found that a school board's denial of salary increments for experience and education violated the status quo. Some courts, however, have interpreted status quo to mean *no change* in the employer-employee relationship from the point of contract expiration and have found that built-in wage increments alter the status quo.[106] Other actions that have been found to violate the status quo are changes in insurance carriers, termination of professional dues deductions from teachers' salaries, changes in work rules, and termination of insurance coverage.[107]

GRIEVANCES

Disputes concerning employee rights under the terms of a collective bargaining agreement are resolved through the negotiated grievance mechanism. Grievance procedures generally provide for a neutral third party, an arbitrator, to conduct a hearing and render a decision. Depending on state law and the negotiated contract, the decision may be advisory or binding. Public employers, adhering to the doctrine of the sovereign power of government, have been reluctant to agree to procedures that might result in a loss of public authority. Allowing grievance procedures to include final decision making by a third party significantly lessens a school board's power, effectively equating the positions of the teachers' organization and the school board. Nevertheless, as bargaining has expanded, legislative bodies have favored binding arbitration as a means of settling labor disputes. Over twenty states have enacted laws permitting school boards to negotiate grievance procedures with binding arbitration, and several states require binding arbitration as the final step in the grievance procedure.[108] With the widespread acceptance of grievance arbitration, it has become one of the most contested areas in collective bargaining. These legal suits have challenged the arbitrator's authority to render decisions in specific disputes as well as the authority to provide certain remedies.

One of the primary issues in establishing a grievance procedure is the definition of a grievance, that is, what can be grieved. In the private sector, a grievance is usually defined as any dispute between the employer and the employee. Teachers' grievances, on the other hand, are generally limited to controversies arising from the interpretation or application of the negotiated contract. Arbitrability of a dispute then depends on whether the school board and union agreed to settle the issue by arbitration or whether the agreement evidences an intent to subject an issue to arbitration.[109] Decisions as to arbitrability are made by arbitrators, and such decisions are generally presumed to be valid when derived from the construction of the negotiated agreement. The Supreme Court of Iowa noted:

> Because arbitration is favored as a means of settling civil disputes without the expense and delay of litigation, arbitrability will be recognized "unless it may be said with positive assurance that the arbitration clause is not susceptible of an interpretation that covers the asserted dispute. Doubts should be resolved in favor of coverage."[110]

Recent disputes held to be arbitrable based on negotiated contracts include unsatisfactory teacher performance, suspensions resulting from declining enrollment, failure of a school board to schedule 180 days of instruction following a work stoppage, merit and equity pay raises, classroom observations, and assignment of out-of-class activities.[111] While a range of questions have been found to be arbitrable, courts, however, have ruled that issues related to nondelegable policy matters under state law are outside the scope of arbitration. For example, impermissible issues have involved tenure decisions, dismissal of employees, reappointment of nontenured teachers, and claims of employment discrimination.[112] Also, issues that are specifically excluded in the contract cannot be submitted to arbitration.

Arbitration awards or remedies also have been challenged. Again, as with arbitrability, courts have adopted a narrow scope of review, with many courts presuming the validity of awards. The deference afforded an arbitrator's award is evident from a recent Supreme Court decision. The Court stated that "[u]nless the arbitral decision does not 'draw its essence from the collective bargaining agreement,' a court is bound to enforce the award and is not entitled to review the merits of the contract dispute."[113] As long as an arbitrator's award can be interpreted as rationally derived from the language and context of the agreement, courts have found that it "draws its essence" from the agreement.[114] Courts do not interfere with arbitration awards simply because they would have provided a different remedy.

STRIKES

The majority of teachers are prohibited from striking by either state statute or common law. It is argued that there can be no true collective bargaining without the right to withhold services, which characterizes the bargaining process in the private sector. Except in a few limited cases, legislation and judicial rulings have consistently prohibited strikes by teachers. In those states that have legislation granting public employees a limited right to strike, certain conditions, specified in statute, must be met prior to the initiation of a work stoppage.[115] Designated conditions vary, but usually include: (1) the exhaustion of statutory mediation and fact-finding steps, (2) elapse of a certain time period prior to commencing the strike, (3) written notice of the union's intent to strike, and (4) evidence that the strike will not constitute a danger to public health or safety. In contrast to the few states permitting strikes, most states with statutes pertaining to collective bargaining for public employees have specific "no strike" provisions.

Courts have consistently upheld "no strike" laws and denied the right to strike unless it has been affirmatively granted by the state. Several early cases are still representative of the judiciary's posture on public teachers' strikes. In a Connecticut case, the state high court stated that permitting teachers to strike could be equated with asserting that "they can deny the authority of government."[116] The court in this case denied teachers the right to strike, emphasizing that a teacher is an agent of the government, possessing a portion of the sovereignty of the state. In a later case, the Supreme Court of Indiana issued a restraining order against striking teachers, affirming the same public welfare issue.[117] Addressing the legality of strikes, a Michigan appeals court declared that public employees have neither a common law nor a constitutional right to strike.[118]

A strike is more than simply a work stoppage; states define the term broadly to include a range of concerted activities such as work slowdowns, massive absences for "sick" days, "work-by-the-rule," and refusal to perform certain duties. For example, the Massachusetts high court found that refusal to perform customary activities, such as grading papers and preparing lesson plans after the end of the school day, constituted a strike.[119]

State laws, in addition to prohibiting work stoppages, usually identify penalties for involvement in strikes. Such penalties can include withholding compensation for strike days, prohibiting salary increases for designated periods of time (e.g., one year), and dismissal. Under New York law, teachers are assessed two days' pay for each strike day.[120] Massachusetts law does not allow for compensation of strike days, even if teachers are required to work additional days to complete the required school term.[121] Several states disallow any salary increases for striking teachers. For example, Florida law prohibits any increase in compensation for a period of one year after a strike.[122] Minnesota has a similar antistrike statute that prevents a salary increase for one year and imposes a loss of pay for strike days.[123] Until the Pennsylvania strike statute was amended, salary increases were prevented for a three-year period following a strike. Penalties for illegal strikes are also imposed on unions. Sanctions may include fines, decertification of the union, and loss of certain privileges such as dues checkoff.[124]

Despite the statutory prohibitions against strikes, an increasing number of teachers, as well as other public employees, participate in work stoppages each year. Public employers can request a court injunction against teachers who threaten to strike or initiate a strike. Most courts have granted injunctions, concluding as did the Supreme Court of Alaska that the "illegality of the strike is a sufficient harm to justify injunctive relief." [125] Failure of teachers to comply with such a restraining order can result in charges of contempt of court, with resulting fines and/or imprisonment. For example, teachers in a Maryland school district who refused to obey an injunction were found guilty of criminal contempt.[126] In Newark, New Jersey, refusal to comply with an injunction resulted in a contempt-of-court charge, with fines and imprisonment for teachers and an additional fine for the union.[127] An order imposing a fine of ten dollars per day on striking teachers was upheld by the Wisconsin Supreme Court.[128]

Even though the injunction has been the most effective response to strikes, a few courts have been reluctant to impose this sanction automatically. Other factors have been considered, such as whether the board bargained in "good faith," whether the strike constituted a clear and present danger to public safety, and whether irreparable harm would result from the strike.[129] Thus, evidence required by school boards to demonstrate sufficient cause for an injunction has varied according to the legal jurisdiction and the interpretation of applicable state statutes.

The procedures required for dismissal of striking teachers have received judicial attention. Courts have held that due process procedures must be provided, but questions arise as to the nature and type of hearing that must be afforded. The leading case on this issue involved Hortonville, Wisconsin, teachers who entered the school year without a negotiated contract and continued to work until the next spring, when they went on strike. After issuing two notices for the teachers to return to work, the board conducted a hearing and terminated the striking teachers. The Wisconsin Supreme Court ruled that striking teachers must be provided with an impartial and fair hearing, and that the board of education was not sufficiently impartial to serve as the hearing panel. On appeal, the United States Supreme Court reversed the decision.[130] The Supreme Court maintained that the involvement on the part of the board did not overcome "the presumption of honesty and integrity in policy makers with decision making power." [131] The Court further held that "[p]ermitting the Board to make the decision at issue here preserves its control over school district affairs, leaves the balance of power in labor relations where the state legislature struck it, and assures that the decision whether to dismiss the teachers will be made by the body responsible for that decision under state law." [132] While noting that the fourteenth amendment guarantees each teacher procedural due process, the Supreme Court concluded that a hearing before the school board satisfies this requirement.

State legislatures and courts consistently have refused to grant public school teachers the right to strike. Even in the few states where a limited right to strike has been gained, extensive restrictions have been placed on its use. Teachers participating in an illegal strike are subject to court-imposed penalties and, in most states, to statutory penalties. Refusal of teachers to return to the classroom can result in dismissal.

CONCLUSION

Because of the diversity in collective bargaining laws among states, legal principles with universal application are necessarily broad. Generalizations concerning collective bargaining rights that are applicable to most teachers are set forth below.

1. Teachers have a constitutionally protected right to form and join a union.
2. Specific bargaining rights are conferred through state statutes or judicial interpretations of state constitutions, thus creating wide divergence in bargaining rights among teachers.

3. School boards are not required to bargain with employee organizations unless mandated to do so by state law.
4. Collective bargaining must be conducted "in good faith," which means that the school board and teachers' organization attempt to reach agreement without compulsion on either side to agree.
5. Scope of negotiations is generally defined to include wages, hours, and other terms and conditions of employment, such as teaching load, planning time, and lunch periods.
6. Subjects related to managerial policy making, such as class size, evaluations, and school calendar, are not mandatorily bargainable but may be permissive subjects unless prohibited by law.
7. State legislation permitting the negotiation of an agency shop provision is constitutional; however, if a public employee objects to supporting specific ideological or political causes, the agency fee must reflect only costs of bargaining and contract administration.
8. To collect an agency shop fee, the union must provide adequate information regarding the basis of the fee, procedural safeguards to ensure a prompt response to employees who may object, and an escrow account for challenged amounts.
9. Unions may constitutionally negotiate exclusive privileges such as the use of school mail and dues checkoff; other communication options, however, must be available to rival unions.
10. Nonunion teachers have the right to express a viewpoint before the school board on an issue under negotiation between the board and union.
11. Impasse procedures for public sector bargaining are generally limited to mediation and fact finding, with the public employer retaining final decision-making authority.
12. Teacher strikes, except in limited situations in a few states, are illegal and punishable by dismissal, fines, and/or imprisonment.

NOTES

1. *See* text with note 16, *infra*.
2. The application of private sector labor laws to private schools, most of which are church related, has been controversial. Only private schools with a gross annual revenue of $1 million or more come under the jurisdiction of the National Labor Relations Board; however, the majority of private schools do not reach this income level. Furthermore, the United States Supreme Court has held that the National Labor Relations Board does not have jurisdiction over lay faculty in parochial schools in the absence of a clear expression of congressional intent to cover teachers in church-related

schools under the NLRA. National Labor Relations Board v. Catholic Bishop of Chicago, 440 U.S. 490 (1979). Recently, however, the Second Circuit Court of Appeals concluded that Catholic schools in New York come under the jurisdiction of the state labor relations board. Since the ruling involved bargaining activities of lay teachers regarding only secular employment practices, no infringement of the establishment clause or free exercise clause of the first amendment was found. Catholic High School Ass'n v. Culvert, 753 F.2d 1161 (2d Cir. 1985).

3. *See* Benjamin Taylor and Fred Witney, *Labor Relations Law* (Englewood Cliffs, NJ: Prentice-Hall, Inc., 1975), pp. 69–99, for a discussion of the use and control of labor injunctions.
4. The Wagner Act states that "employees shall have the right to self-organization, to form, join or assist labor organizations, to bargain collectively through representatives of their own choosing, and to engage in concerted activities, for the purpose of collective bargaining or other mutual aid or protection." 29 U.S.C. § 157 (1976).
5. *See* text with note 27, *infra,* for discussion of governmental policy issues.
6. 3 C.F.R. § 521.
7. Keyishian v. Board of Regents, 385 U.S. 589 (1967).
8. McLaughlin v. Tilendis, 398 F.2d 287 (7th Cir. 1968).
9. Atkins v. City of Charlotte, 296 F. Supp. 1068 (W.D.N.C. 1969); Dade County Classroom Teachers' Ass'n v. Ryan, 225 So. 2d 903 (Fla. 1969). *See also* American Fed'n of State, County, and Mun. Employees v. Woodward, 406 F.2d 137 (8th Cir. 1969).
10. Hickman v. Valley Local School Dist. Bd. of Educ., 619 F.2d 606 (6th Cir. 1980).
11. Lake Park Educ. Ass'n v. Board of Educ. of Lake Park High School Dist., 526 F. Supp. 710 (N.D. Ill. 1981). *See also* Jackson v. Hazlehurst Mun. Separate School Dist., 427 So. 2d 134 (Miss. 1983).
12. Gavrilles v. O'Connor, 611 F. Supp. 210 (D. Mass. 1985).
13. Winston-Salem/Forsyth County Unit of the North Carolina Ass'n of Educators v. Phillips, 381 F. Supp. 644 (M.D.N.C. 1974).
14. Commonwealth of Virginia v. County Bd. of Arlington County, 232 S.E.2d 30 (Va. 1977). *See* Littleton Educ. Ass'n v. Arapahoe County School Dist. 6, 553 P.2d 793 (Colo. 1976).
15. Board of Trustees of Univ. of Kentucky v. Public Employees Council No. 51, American Fed'n of State, County, and Mun. Employees, 571 S.W.2d 616 (Ky. 1978).
16. 426 U.S. 833 (1976).
17. 105 S. Ct. 1005 (1985). *See* Floyd G. Delon and Mark A. Van Zandt, "The Pendulum Continues to Swing: Garcia v. San Antonio Metropolitan Transit Authority," *Education Law Reporter,* vol. 26 (1985), pp. 1–11.
18. *See* Ohio Revised Code 4117.06. State law not only provides that the Ohio State Employment Relations Board determines the appropriateness of a bargaining unit but also stipulates that the Board's decision is "final and conclusive and not appealable to the court." A similar restriction in the Indiana labor law resulted in the entire statute being declared void because the provision was nonseverable from the remainder of the statute. Indiana Educ. Employment Relations Bd. v. Benton Community School Corp., 365 N.E.2d 752 (Ind. 1977).

19. 29 U.S.C. § 158(d).
20. *See* "Developments in the Law, Public Employment," *Harvard Law Review,* vol. 97 (1984), pp. 1611–1738.
21. 29 U.S.C. § 158(d).
22. Pa. Stat. Ann. 43 § 1101.701.
23. Haw. Rev. Stat. 89 § 9(a). The statute goes beyond the NLRA provision and in § 9(d) specifies those items which cannot be negotiated, i.e., retirement benefits, public employees' health fund, classification and reclassification, etc.
24. Fla. Stat. 447 § 301(2).
25. Tenn. Code Ann. 49 § 11; Nev. Rev. Stat. 228 § 150.
26. *See* San Mateo City School Dist. v. Public Employment Relations Bd., 663 P.2d 523 (Cal. 1983); Ottawa Educ. Ass'n v. Unified School Dist. No. 290, 666 P.2d 680 (Kan. 1983); Spiewak v. Board of Educ. of Rutherford, 447 A.2d 140 (N.J. 1982); School Dist. of the City of Erie v. Erie Educ. Ass'n, 447 A.2d 686 (Pa. Commw. 1982).
27. Pa. Stat. Ann 43 § 1702.
28. Ridgefield Park Educ. Ass'n v. Ridgefield Park Bd. of Educ., 393 A.2d 278 (N.J. 1978).
29. Aberdeen Educ. Ass'n v. Aberdeen Bd. of Educ., 215 N.W.2d 837 (S.D. 1974).
30. Clark County School Dist. v. Local Gov't Employee Management Relations Bd., 530 P.2d 114 (Nev. 1974).
31. Pennsylvania Labor Relations Bd. v. State College Area School Dist., 337 A.2d 262 (Pa. 1975).
32. *See* Colonial School Bd. v. Colonial Affiliate, 449 A.2d 243 (Del. 1982) (interpreted labor law as containing no provision for permissive subjects of collective bargaining).
33. *See* Scranton School Bd. v. Scranton Fed'n of Teachers, 365 A.2d 1339 (Pa. Commw. 1976).
34. Ind. Code § 20–7.5–1–4.
35. Clark County School Dist. v. Local Gov't Employee Management Relations Bd., 530 P.2d 114 (Nev. 1974).
36. Nev. Rev. Stat. 288 § 150.
37. *See* Fargo Educ. Ass'n v. Fargo Public School Dist., 291 N.W.2d 267 (N.D. 1980); National Education Ass'n-Kansas City v. Unified School Dist., Wyandotte County, 608 P.2d 415 (Kan. 1980); City of Beloit v. Wisconsin Employment Relations Comm'n, 242 N.W.2d 231 (Wis. 1976); West Irondequoit Teachers Ass'n v. Helsby, 315 N.E.2d 775 (N.Y. 1974).
38. City of Beloit, *id.*
39. Hillsborough Classroom Teachers Ass'n v. School Bd. of Hillsborough County, 423 So. 2d 969 (Fla. App. 1982).
40. Kenai Peninsula Borough School Dist. v. Kenai Peninsula Educ. Ass'n, 572 P.2d 416 (Alas. 1977).
41. *See* University Educ. Ass'n v. Regents of the Univ. of Minnesota, 353 N.W.2d 534 (Minn. 1984); Board of Educ. of the Woodstown-Pilesgrove Regional School Dist. v. Woodstown-Pilesgrove Regional Educ. Ass'n, 410 A.2d 1131 (N.J. 1980); Kenai Peninsula Borough School Dist. v. Kenai Peninsula Educ. Ass'n, 572 P.2d 416 (Alas. 1977); Board of Educ. of Mont-

gomery County v. Montgomery County Educ. Ass'n, 505 A.2d 905 (Md. App. 1986).

42. City of Biddeford v. Biddeford Teachers Ass'n, 304 A.2d 387, 421 (Me. 1973).
43. Eastbrook Community Schools Corp. v. Indiana Educ. Employment Relations Bd., 446 N.E.2d 1007 (Ind. App. 1983).
44. Union County School Corp. v. Indiana Educ. Employment Relations Bd., 471 N.E.2d 1191 (Ind. App. 1984).
45. East County Bargaining Council v. Centennial School Dist., 685 P.2d 452 (Ore. App. 1984).
46. City of Beloit v. Wisconsin Employment Relations Comm'n, 242 N.W.2d 231, 240 (Wis. 1976).
47. For an example of a mandatory provision, *see* Iowa Code § 20.1, *et seq.*
48. Bethlehem Township Bd. of Educ. v. Bethlehem Township Educ. Ass'n, 449 A.2d 1254, 1259 (N.J. 1982). *See also* University Educ. Ass'n v. Regents of the Univ. of Minnesota, 353 N.W.2d 534 (Minn. 1984) (evaluation criteria represent inherent managerial policy and therefore are not negotiable).
49. Springfield Educ. Ass'n v. Springfield School Dist. No. 19, 621 P.2d 547 (Ore. 1980). *See also* East County Bargaining Council v. Centennial School Dist., 685 P.2d 452 (Ore. App. 1984).
50. City of Beloit v. Wisconsin Employment Relations Comm'n, 242 N.W.2d 231 (Wis. 1976).
51. Clark County School Dist. v. Local Gov't Employee Management Relations, 530 P.2d 114 (Nev. 1974).
52. Kenai Peninsula Borough School Dist. v. Kenai Peninsula Educ. Ass'n, 572 P.2d 416 (Alas. 1977).
53. Township of Old Bridge Bd. of Educ. v. Old Bridge Educ. Ass'n, 489 A.2d 159 (N.J. 1985); Board of Educ. of Bremen Community High School Dist. No. 228 v. Bremen Dist. No. 228 Joint Faculty Ass'n, 461 N.E.2d 406 (Ill. 1984); Unified School Dist. No. 501 v. Secretary of Kansas Dep't of Human Resources, 685 P.2d 874 (Kan. 1984); Bethlehem Township Bd. of Educ. v. Bethlehem Township Educ. Ass'n, 449 A.2d 1254 (N.J. 1982).
54. Unified School Dist. No. 501, *id.*
55. West Bend Educ. Ass'n v. Wisconsin Employment Relations Comm'n, 357 N.W.2d 534, 543 (Wis. 1984).
56. Township of Old Bridge Bd. of Educ. v. Old Bridge Educ. Ass'n, 489 A.2d 159, 164 (N.J. 1985).
57. Boston Teachers Union v. School Comm. of Boston, 434 N.E.2d 1258 (Mass. 1982).
58. Shenandoah Educ. Ass'n v. Shenandoah Community School Dist., 337 N.W.2d 477 (Iowa 1983).
59. Wygant v. Jackson Bd. of Educ., 106 S. Ct. 1842 (1986). *See* text with note 74, chapter 9.
60. Under most state laws, tenure decisions have been found to be a prohibited subject. *See, e.g.,* Honeoye Falls-Lima Cent. School Dist. v. Honeoye Falls-Lima Educ. Ass'n, 402 N.E.2d 1165 (N.Y. 1980).
61. *See* text with note 6, chapter 10.
62. Appeal of Watson, 448 A.2d 417 (N.H. 1982).
63. Tracy v. Otsego Bd. of Educ., 453 N.E.2d 610, 612 (Ohio 1983).

64. Jones v. Wrangell School Dist., 696 P.2d 677, 680 (Alas. 1985).
65. Savage Educ. Ass'n v. Trustees of Richland County Elementary Dist., 692 P.2d 1237 (Mont. 1984); Struthers City Schools Bd. of Educ. v. Struthers Educ. Ass'n, 453 N.E.2d 613 (Ohio 1983).
66. *See generally* Perry A. Zirkel and Ellis H. Katz, "The Law on Agency Shop for School Districts," *Education Law Reporter,* vol. 26 (1985), pp. 567–577.
67. *See Education Week,* December 11, 1985, p. 1.
68. 431 U.S. 209 (1977). *See* Mary Aslanian-Bedikian, "*Abood* and Its Progeny: Conflicting Perspectives on Safeguarding Union Security Agreements and Individual Rights in the Public Sector," *Detroit College of Law Review,* vol. 1 (1984), pp. 23–46.
69. Abood, *id.* at 235.
70. Under Title VII of the Civil Rights Act of 1964, an employee who objects to payment of a service fee because of religious beliefs must be accommodated by being allowed to substitute a contribution to a charitable organization. *See* McDaniel v. Essex International, Inc. 696 F.2d 34 (6th Cir. 1982); Tooley v. Martin-Marietta Corp., 648 F.2d 1239 (9th Cir. 1981), *cert. denied,* 454 U.S. 1098 (1981).
71. Abood, 431 U.S. at 236.
72. 466 U.S. 435, 448 (1984).
73. Robinson v. State of New Jersey, 741 F.2d 598, 607 (3d Cir. 1984), *cert. denied,* 105 S. Ct. 1228 (1985).
74. Champion v. State of California, 738 F.2d 1082, 1086 (9th Cir. 1984), *cert. denied,* 105 S. Ct. 1230 (1985).
75. Matter of Bd. of Educ. of Town of Boonton, 494 A.2d 279 (N.J. 1985).
76. Cumero v. Public Employment Relations Bd., 213 Cal. Rptr. 326 (Cal. App. 1985) (rebate must be provided for the portion of the publication devoted to political issues). *See also* Abels v. Monroe County Educ. Ass'n, 489 N.E.2d 533 (Ind. App. 1986) (payment to state and national affiliates upheld as well as expenditures for social programs, professional development workshops, lobbying activities, and state and national conventions); Hazleton Area Educ. Ass'n v. Commonwealth of Pennsylvania, 503 A.2d 71 (Pa. Commw. 1985) (assessment against nonmembers of litigation costs related to arbitration violated their rights to refrain from assisting employee organization); Aio v. Hamada, 664 P.2d 727 (Hawaii 1983) (lobbying and publication costs were permissible charges).
77. Ellis, 466 U.S. at 444.
78. *See* Robinson v. State of New Jersey, 741 F.2d 598 (3d Cir. 1984), *cert. denied,* 105 S. Ct. 1228 (1985); Matter of Bd. of Educ. of the Town of Boonton, 494 A.2d 279 (N.J. 1985); San Jose Teachers Ass'n v. Superior Court, 700 P.2d 1252 (Cal. 1985), *vacated and remanded sub nom.,* Abernathy v. San Jose Teachers Ass'n, 106 S. Ct. 1372 (1986). Several states by statute have specified that reductions must be provided. For example, in New Jersey and Minnesota assessed fees cannot exceed 85 percent of the regular membership dues. N.J.S.A. 34: 13A–5.5(b); Minn. Stat. Ann. § 179.65 (2).
79. 106 S. Ct. 1066, 1078 (1986).
80. Several state courts had earlier held under *Ellis* that the entire agency fee could be collected if the union established an advance reduction amount. *See, e.g.,* San Jose Teachers Ass'n v. Superior Court, 700 P.2d 1252 (Cal.

1985), *vacated and remanded sub nom.*, Abernathy v. San Jose Teachers Ass'n, 106 S. Ct. 1372 (1986). *But see* School Comm. of Greenfield v. Greenfield Educ. Ass'n, 431 N.E.2d 180 (Mass. 1980) (employee who objects to fee cannot be required to pay until appropriate amount is determined).

81. Churchill v. School Adm'r Dist. No. 49 Teachers Ass'n, 380 A.2d 186 (Me. 1977).
82. Florida Educ. Ass'n/United v. Public Employee Relations Comm'n, 346 So. 2d 551 (Fla. App. 1977).
83. *See* William Kay, Karen Reinhold, and Kathy Andreola, "Legal Problems in Administering Agency Shop Agreements—A Management Perspective," *Journal of Law and Education,* vol. 13 (1984), pp. 61–76.
84. Langley v. Uniontown Area School Dist., 367 A.2d 736 (Pa. Commw. 1977).
85. Anderson Fed'n of Teachers, Local 519 v. Alexander, 416 N.E.2d 1327 (Ind. App. 1981). *See* Fort Wayne Educ. Ass'n v. Goetz, 443 N.E.2d 364 (Ind. App. 1982) (upheld agency shop agreement that did not condition employment on payment of fees).
86. Board of Educ. of School Dist. for City of Detroit v. Parks, 335 N.W.2d 641 (Mich. 1983).
87. King City Joint Union High School Dist., California Public Employee Relations Bd., Order No. 197 (March 1982).
88. 60 Op. Att'y Gen. 370 (1977).
89. San Lorenzo Educ. Ass'n v. Wilson, 654 P.2d 202 (Cal. 1982).
90. Jefferson Area Teachers Ass'n v. Lockwood, 433 N.E.2d 604 (Ohio 1982); Eastern Michigan Univ. v. Morgan, 298 N.W.2d 886 (Mich. App. 1980).
91. *See* John F. Lewis and Steven Spirn, *Ohio Collective Bargaining Law* (Cleveland, OH: Banks-Baldwin Law Publishing Co., 1983).
92. Perry Educ. Ass'n v. Perry Local Educators' Ass'n, 460 U.S. 37 (1983). *See* text with note 52, chapter 8.
93. *Id.* at 44.
94. Texas State Teachers Ass'n v. Garland Independent School Dist., 777 F.2d 1046 (5th Cir. 1985), *aff'd,* 107 S. Ct. 41 (1986). *See* Ysleta Fed'n of Teachers v. Ysleta Independent School Dist., 720 F.2d 1429 (5th Cir. 1983) (a policy granting access to the school mails to all employee organizations established a limited public forum and precluded school officials from imposing prior clearance of all materials to determine if they were in accordance with school policy).
95. School Bd. of Dade County v. Dade Teachers Ass'n, 421 So. 2d 645 (Fla. App. 1982).
96. Minnesota State Bd. for Community Colleges v. Knight, 104 S. Ct. 1058, 1065 (1984).
97. *Id.*
98. City of Madison, Joint School Dist. No. 8 v. Wisconsin Employment Relations Comm'n, 429 U.S. 167 (1976).
99. *Id.* at 175, quoting Pickering v. Board of Educ., 391 U.S. 563, 568 (1968).
100. Interest arbitration refers to reaching a contract agreement as distinguished from grievance arbitration which addresses enforcement of rights under the contract.
101. To avoid strikes among certain groups of public employees, interest arbitration may be mandatory. *See, e.g.,* Ohio Rev. Code § 4117.14 (D)(1).
102. Ohio Rev. Code § 4117 (D)(2); Me. Rev. Stat. 26 § 979.D(4).

103. R.I. Gen. Laws 28 § 9.3–9.
104. Ore. Rev. Stat. 243 § 706.
105. Indiana Educ. Employment Relations Bd. v. Mill Creek Classroom Teachers Ass'n, 456 N.E.2d 709, 712 (Ind. 1983).
106. *See* Fairview School Dist. v. Commonwealth of Pennsylvania, 454 A.2d 517 (Pa. 1982); M.S.A.D. No. 43 Teachers' Ass'n v. M.S.A.D. No. 43 Bd. of Directors, 432 A.2d 395 (Me. 1981).
107. *See* Smith County Educ. Ass'n v. Anderson, 676 S.W.2d 328 (Tenn. 1984); Alaska Community Colleges' Fed'n of Teachers v. University of Alaska, 669 P.2d 1299 (Alas. 1983); Grandinetti v. Commonwealth of Pennsylvania, 486 A.2d 1040 (Pa. Commw. 1985).
108. *See* William D. Valente, *Education Law: Public and Private,* vol. 2 (St. Paul, MN: West Publishing Co., 1985), p. 543, table 25. States requiring binding arbitration are Alaska, Florida, Illinois, Minnesota, and Pennsylvania.
109. *See* Cloquet Educ. Ass'n v. Independent School Dist. No. 94, 344 N.W.2d 416 (Minn. 1984); East Pennsboro Area School Dist. v. Pennsylvania Labor Relations Bd., 467 A.2d 1356 (Pa. Commw. 1983).
110. Iowa City Community School Dist. v. Iowa City Educ. Ass'n, 343 N.W.2d 139, 141 (Iowa 1983), quoting Sergeant Bluff-Luton Educ. Ass'n v. Sergeant Bluff-Luton Community School Dist., 282 N.W.2d 144, 147–148 (Iowa 1979). *See also* Fortney v. School Dist. of West Salem, 321 N.W.2d 225 (Wis. 1982); Scranton Fed'n of Teachers v. Scranton School Dist., 444 A.2d 1144 (Pa. 1982); Howard County Bd. of Educ. v. Howard County Educ. Ass'n, 487 A.2d 1220 (Md. App. 1985). *But see* Acting Superintendent of Schools v. United Liverpool Faculty Ass'n, 369 N.E.2d 746 (N.Y. 1977) (declined to adopt the presumption of arbitrability).
111. Trustees of Boston Univ. v. Boston Univ. Chapter, American Ass'n of Univ. Professors, 746 F.2d 924 (1st Cir. 1984); Cloquet Educ. Ass'n v. Independent School Dist. No. 94, 344 N.W.2d 416 (Minn. 1984); Iowa City Community School Dist. v. Iowa City Educ. Ass'n, 343 N.W.2d 139 (Iowa 1983); Howard County Bd. of Educ. v. Howard County Educ. Ass'n, 487 A.2d 1220 (Md. App. 1985); Ridley School Dist. v. Ridley Educ. Ass'n, 479 A.2d 641 (Pa. Commw. 1984); East Pennsboro Area School Dist. v. Pennsylvania Labor Relations Bd., 467 A.2d 1356 (Pa. Commw. 1983).
112. Neshaminy Fed'n of Teachers v. Neshaminy School Dist., 462 A.2d 629 (Pa. 1983); Teaneck Bd. of Educ. v. Teaneck Teachers Ass'n, 462 A.2d 137 (N.J. 1983); Board of Educ. of Carroll County v. Carroll County Educ. Ass'n, 452 A.2d 1316 (Md. App. 1982).
113. W. R. Grace and Co. v. Local 759, United Rubber Workers of America, 461 U.S. 757, 764 (1983).
114. *See* Iowa City Community School Dist. v. Iowa City Educ. Ass'n, 343 N.W.2d 139 (Iowa 1983); Howard County Bd. of Educ. v. Howard County Educ. Ass'n, 487 A.2d 1220 (Md. App. 1985).
115. A statutory limited right to strike exists in Alaska, Hawaii, Minnesota, Montana, Ohio, Oregon, Pennsylvania, Vermont, and Wisconsin. Although the Alaska public employee bargaining law permits most public employees to strike, the state high court has held that, since the law does not expressly grant teachers this right, they are prohibited from striking. Anchorage Educ. Ass'n v. Anchorage School Dist., 648 P.2d 993 (Alas. 1982).

116. Norwalk Teachers Ass'n v. Board of Educ. of City of Norwalk, 83 A.2d 482, 485 (Conn. 1951).
117. Anderson Fed'n of Teachers v. School City of Anderson, 251 N.E.2d 15 (Ind. 1969).
118. Rockwell v. Board of Educ. of Crestwood, 226 N.W.2d 596 (Mich. App. 1975).
119. Lenox Educ. Ass'n v. Labor Relations Comm'n, 471 N.E.2d 81 (Mass. 1984).
120. Lawson v. Board of Educ. of Vestal Cent. School Dist. No. 1, 315 N.Y.S.2d 877 (App. Div. 1970).
121. Mass. Gen. Laws 150E § 15.
122. Fla. Stat. 447 § 507. (5)(6).
123. Head v. Special School Dist. No. 1, 182 N.W.2d 887 (Minn. 1970).
124. *See* Buffalo Teachers Fed'n, Inc. v. Helsby, 676 F.2d 28 (2d Cir. 1982).
125. Anchorage Educ. Ass'n v. Anchorage School Dist., 648 P.2d 993, 998 (Alas. 1982).
126. Harford County Educ. Ass'n v. Board of Educ. of Harford County, 380 A.2d 1041 (Md. 1977).
127. Board of Educ. of Newark v. Newark Teachers Union, 276 A.2d 175 (N.J. Super. 1971).
128. Joint School Dist. No. 1, City of Wisconsin Rapids v. Wisconsin Rapids Educ. Ass'n, 234 N.W.2d 289 (Wis. 1975).
129. *See* Joint School Dist. No. 1, City of Wisconsin Rapids v. Wisconsin Rapids Educ. Ass'n, 234 N.W.2d 289 (Wis. 1975); Bristol Township Educ. Ass'n v. School Dist. of Bristol Township, 322 A.2d 767 (Pa. Commw. 1974); Timberlane Regional School Dist. v. Timberlane Regional Educ. Ass'n, 317 A.2d 555 (N.H. 1974); School Dist. for City of Holland v. Holland Educ. Ass'n, 157 N.W.2d 206 (Mich. 1968). *See also* Jersey Shore Educ. Ass'n v. Jersey Shore Area School Dist., 512 A.2d 805 (Pa. Commw. 1986) (strike resulting in a loss of state funds for failure to comply with state required minimum instructional days constituted clear and present danger).
130. Hortonville Educ. Ass'n v. Hortonville Joint School Dist., 225 N.W.2d 658 (Wis. 1975), *rev'd,* 426 U.S. 482 (1976).
131. *Id.,* 426 U.S. at 497.
132. *Id.* at 496.

12

Tort Liability

Other chapters in this book focus primarily on the legal resolution of conflicts between government interests in maintaining public schools and individual interests in exercising constitutional and statutory rights. In contrast, this chapter examines principles of tort law which offer remedies to individuals for harm caused by the unreasonable conduct of others. This branch of law involves civil suits, pertaining to the private rights of citizens, as opposed to criminal suits, initiated by the state to redress public offenses. Generally, a tort is defined as a civil wrong, independent of breach of contract, for which a court will provide relief in the form of damages. Tort cases primarily involve state law[1] and are grounded in the fundamental premise that all individuals are liable for the consequences of conduct that results in injury to others.

Tort actions can be grouped into three major categories: negligence, intentional torts, and strict liability. Negligence involves conduct that falls below an acceptable standard of care and results in injury.[2] Intentional torts are committed with the desire to inflict harm, and include actions such as assault, battery, false imprisonment, and trespass. Strict liability occurs when an injury results from the creation of an unusual hazard (e.g., the storage of explosives), and the injured party need not establish that the injury was knowingly or negligently caused. Seldom have allegations of strict liability appeared in education cases. Some school-related injuries have generated intentional tort actions, but the vast majority of tort cases involving school districts and educational employees have entailed allegations of negligence. Accordingly, this chapter primarily addresses the conditions necessary to establish negligence and the legal defenses employed by school personnel to rebut negligence charges. Brief discussions of assault and battery and defamation also are included.

ELEMENTS OF NEGLIGENCE

Negligence is a breach of one's legal duty to protect others from unreasonable risks of harm. A charge of negligence can result when the failure to act or an improper act causes injury to another person.[3] To constitute negligence, an injury must be avoidable by the exercise of reasonable care. The ability to foresee harm is an important factor in determining whether or not an individual's conduct is negligent; accidents do not constitute negligence.

Negligence cases include questions of law, which are determined by judges, and questions of fact, which are decided by juries. In some instances, a judge may conclude that there are no material factual issues to submit to a jury and thus return a directed verdict. Where a trial does take place, a judge can reverse the jury's decision if it is clearly considered erroneous. Judges, however, will not exercise this authority unless supported by overwhelming evidence.

Several conditions must exist to establish an individual's negligence.

1. There must be a *duty* on the part of the individual to protect another from unreasonable risks.
2. The duty must be breached by the *failure to exercise an appropriate standard of care*.
3. There must be a causal connection between the negligent conduct and the resulting injury (referred to as *proximate or legal cause*).
4. There must be physical or mental *injury* resulting in an actual loss.[4]

These conditions necessary to establish negligence are discussed in the following sections.

DUTY

Under common law, school officials have a duty to anticipate foreseeable dangers and to take necessary precautions to protect students entrusted in their care from such dangers. This duty may be reduced in some states by statutes providing qualified immunity for employees or denoting liability only for injuries resulting from willful or wanton misconduct.[5] The specific duties that school personnel owe students are to provide adequate supervision and instruction, to maintain equipment and facilities in good repair, and to warn of known dangers.

While educators have a duty to protect students under their supervision from foreseeable harm, school personnel do not have a duty to protect students under all circumstances. For example, if students arrive at school before the designated arrival time, school authorities do not have a duty to provide supervision. Educators, however, can *assume* a duty to care for students if they routinely arrive early and provide supervision. Under such an assumed duty to protect others from harm, courts will impose liability if a reasonable standard of care is not maintained.[6]

School officials' duty of care to students clearly encompasses activities on the school grounds during school hours, but a duty also may be owed after regular hours and away from the campus. Circumstances and the nature of the activity will determine whether a duty exists. For example, a Louisiana appellate court found that a school board was negligent in the injury of a kindergarten student for its failure to provide supervision of a track practice sponsored by a nonschool organization. Liability in this instance was created primarily by the school's distribution of a flyer assuring the parents that there would be "tight supervision."[7] The Supreme Court of Minnesota held that school officials' duty to supervise the activities of cheerleaders continued through the summer months because the cheerleading squad was approved and controlled by the school. In the absence of supervision by school personnel, a student injured in an automobile accident while bannering the homes of football players prior to the beginning of the school year was awarded damages.[8] A Washington appellate court, however, ruled that school officials did not have a duty of care to students participating in a party on senior "release day."[9] School personnel were not involved in planning the party, nor did they attend; knowledge of the party on the part of the faculty adviser and principal did not create a duty to supervise the event.

When a student is injured in the school setting, a teacher has a duty to provide reasonable assistance commensurate with his or her training and experience.[10] Provision of emergency first aid treatment to pupils has been upheld if the treatment has been reasonable. Courts, however, have recognized that students should not be moved or treated unless such emergency aid is absolutely necessary prior to the arrival of appropriate medical personnel. Liability has been assessed in instances where injured students have been negligently moved from playing fields during athletic events.[11] Improperly administered first aid also has resulted in liability. In 1979 an Illinois appeals court recognized that public policy considerations dictate an obligation to ensure that medical treatment undertaken by a school or its agent is competently rendered.[12] In a Pennsylvania case, two teachers were held personally liable for administering medical treatment to a student by holding his infected finger under boiling water.[13] The superior court held that the action was not reasonable and noted that the situation did not necessitate emergency first aid.

Increasing attention has been directed toward the school's duty to ensure the safety of pupils and employees against injuries inflicted by third parties. The school district's duty to ensure safety has been cited in several recent cases involving criminal assault. For example, an Oregon appeals court concluded that a school district had the duty to warn students of a reasonably foreseeable assault that occurred on school premises.[14] Where assaults have been unforeseeable, however, liability has not been assessed against the school district or school personnel.[15]

Given the substantial concern for individual safety at school, in 1982 California voters amended the state constitution to include the "right to safe schools." The provision stipulates in part: "All students and staff of public primary, elementary, junior high and senior high schools have the inalienable right to attend campuses which are safe, secure and peaceful." [16] In a recent decision, a California superior court ruled that students and teachers could recover damages from school districts if officials have not used "reasonable diligence" to provide a safe school environment.[17] The ruling requires school officials to act affirmatively prior to injury of students or teachers. In the case before the court, a student had been harassed by another student on numerous occasions, and while the mother complained to school officials, no action was taken to separate the students. The California constitutional amendment is unique, but with widespread concern about school safety, it might serve as a model for similar legal protection in other states.[18]

Standard of Care

The standard of care required in various school settings is governed by the reasonableness theory. In assessing the reasonableness of an individual's actions, courts determine whether a reasonable and prudent person would have acted in the same manner under similar circumstances. The reasonable person has been described as one who has "(1) the physical attributes of the defendant himself, (2) normal intelligence, (3) normal perception and memory with a minimum level of information and experience common to the community, and (4) such superior skill and knowledge as the actor has or holds himself out to the public as having." [19] Under this standard, a teacher's conduct is gauged by how a reasonable teacher, who has had special training to assume that role, would have acted in a similar situation.

The degree of care owed is determined by factors such as the age of the students, the environment, and the type of instructional activity. For example, young primary grade students require closer supervision and more detailed instructions than high school students. A higher level of care is required in laboratory classes, gymnasiums, and other environments where risk of harm is great. Variability in the level of care deemed reasonable is illustrated in a Louisiana case. This case involved the fatal injury of a mentally retarded student who darted into a busy thoroughfare while being escorted with nine other retarded students to a park three blocks from the school campus. An appellate court noted that the general level of care required for all students "becomes more onerous when the student body is composed of mentally retarded youngsters." [20] Furthermore, the court noted that this higher level of care becomes even greater when such a group of children is taken away from the school campus. Accordingly, the court found negligence in that one teacher was inadequate to supervise the group and the safest walking route was not selected.

Proximate Cause

For liability to be assessed, negligent conduct of school personnel must be the proximate or legal cause of a student's injury. Even in situations in which a recognized duty is breached by the failure to exercise a proper standard of care, liability will not be assessed if there is not a causal connection between the actions of school personnel and the injury sustained by a student. An intervening act, such as the negligence of a third party, may relieve school personnel of liability.

As in assessing whether the appropriate standard of care has been breached, foreseeability is essential in establishing proximate cause of an injury. A Maryland appeals court concluded that a teacher had no reason to predict an intervening event that caused injury to a fourth-grade pupil who was engaged in a program of calisthenics while the teacher was absent briefly from the room.[21] The injury occurred when another child moved from his position, contrary to instructions, and struck the plaintiff with his feet while performing the exercises. The court reasoned that the incident could have occurred with the teacher in the classroom; therefore, her absence was not the proximate cause of the injury sustained. Similarly, a Pennsylvania court held that a teacher who was monitoring the hallway as students returned from recess was not liable for damages when a student entering the classroom was struck in the eye by a pencil that had been thrown by a classmate. The court concluded that teachers are not "required to anticipate the myriad of unexpected acts which occur daily in classrooms."[22]

The existence of intervening events, however, does not necessarily establish that school employees' negligent conduct was not the proximate cause of an injury. A Tennessee appellate court held that a student's misuse of a drill press resulting in a serious head injury to a classmate did not relieve the teacher of liability when he had failed to provide adequate instruction and supervision.[23] The teacher had not instructed the students in the use of the specific drill bit, had not warned of the dangers associated with its improper use, and was absent from the shop during the use of the drill. In a California case involving a student who was killed while engaging in an unsupervised "slap boxing" match on school grounds, the state supreme court held that the negligent supervision provided by school personnel was the proximate cause of the student's fatal injury.[24] While noting that another student's misconduct was the precipitating cause of the injury, the court concluded that, with proper supervision, the dangerous "slap boxing" activity would have been curtailed.

The New York high court similarly concluded that a school district was liable for injuries to an eight-year-old student caused by improperly secured dangerous chemicals.[25] Although two fifteen-year-old student employees had taken the chemicals from an unlocked laboratory and left them on the school grounds where the young child later discovered them, this intervening act was not considered sufficient to relieve the school district of liability. According to the court, the unauthorized removal of the chemicals by a third party was foreseeable as a consequence of the school district's negligence. Even when an intervening event actually causes a given injury, if school personnel place students in a dangerous situation, or if they reasonably should anticipate special risks of harm, they will not be relieved of liability for their negligent conduct.

Injury

To receive an award of damages, a plaintiff must have suffered an actual injury from the negligent conduct of the defendant. Even if conduct is considered negligent, legal action cannot be sustained unless the conduct actually results in physical or mental injury. If an injury is caused by the negligent action of more than one individual, damages will be apportioned accordingly.[26] Compensation may include any direct financial loss (i.e., medical expenses or loss of income) as well as remuneration for pain and suffering. In the drill press injury previously noted, the injured student was awarded a total of $25,000 in damages; approximately $4,000 for medical expenses and the remainder for pain and disability caused by a permanent weakening of the skull.[27]

EDUCATORS' LIABILITY

Courts have recognized that school personnel must provide adequate supervision and instruction and must maintain school facilities and equipment in good repair. In legal suits alleging negligent conduct, plaintiffs assert that one or more of these duties have been violated. Unlike claims for damages for the impairment of federal rights under 42 U.S.C., Section 1983 where the theory of *respondeat superior* (master is responsible for the acts of the servant) does not apply, employees' negligent performance of their duties may result in school district as well as individual liability for damages. For such liability to be imposed on a school district, however, negligent conduct must arise within the scope of an employee's employment or authority. A school board is not liable for purely private acts.

A number of states have enacted legislation requiring school districts to indemnify or "save harmless" teachers for monetary losses for tortious actions that may occur during the performance of their assigned duties. A recent Ohio law requires such indemnification of teachers except for "willful and wanton" acts.[28] Generally, these laws also require school districts to assume the cost of legal representation if tort claims are filed against a teacher. In states with such laws, school employees can still be found negligent, but they are relieved of responsibility for any damages assessed by courts. Some states also have enacted statutes that provide partial immunity for the negligent acts of teachers. Illinois law, for example, confers *in loco parentis* (in place of parent) status on educational employees and stipulates that willful and wanton misconduct must be established in order for liability to be assessed in connection with strictly educational activities.

An overview of the general nature of school employees' duties is presented in this section. Caution should be exercised in generalizing from specific cases because slight variations in the factual circumstances can alter the final determination of negligence and liability.

Supervision

One of the primary responsibilities of teachers is to provide adequate supervision of students under their care. Depending on the activity, this may entail general or specific supervision. Students completing a routine written assignment at their desks would require only general supervision, whereas students attempting a new move in gymnastics would warrant specific supervision. As noted previously, teachers have a duty to safeguard students from reasonably foreseeable dangers. Proper supervision thus requires teachers to be aware of students' activities and the conditions surrounding those activities and to warn of potential dangers. Failure to provide such supervision can constitute negligent conduct.

A teacher, however, does not have a duty to keep each student under constant surveillance or to anticipate every possible accident that might occur; as noted, teachers cannot be held liable for unforeseeable injuries. Even if supervision is inadequate, a teacher will not be held negligent if it is established that the injury could have occurred as easily in the presence of proper supervision.[29] A Missouri appeals court concluded that a kindergarten teacher did not breach her duty of supervision simply because she was attending to other students when a child fell during recess while attempting to swing down from a jungle gym.[30] The court concluded that the teacher was not required to have each pupil in sight at all times. Similarly, a Louisiana appeals court held that a teacher was not negligent with respect to an injury sustained by a child who fell on a tree stump at recess.[31] The court reasoned that the stump was not so hazardous as to place a special duty on the teacher to anticipate harm.

Courts have not assessed damages against school personnel unless an injury might have been prevented by the exercise of proper supervision typically required by the circumstances. Two student injury cases involving rock-throwing incidents illustrate the importance of foreseeability of harm in determining the appropriateness of supervision. In one instance, where student rock-throwing had continued for almost ten minutes before the injury occurred, the court found the supervising teacher liable for negligence.[32] In contrast, in a situation where a teacher aide had walked past a group of students moments before one child threw a rock that was deflected and hit another pupil, no liability was assessed against the aide.[33] The court concluded that the teacher aide had provided adequate supervision and had no reason to anticipate the event that caused the injury.

A teacher's mere absence from the classroom is not sufficient to establish negligence. Whether a teacher exercised reasonable care in temporarily leaving a class unattended is assessed in relation to the reason for the absence, length of the absence, age and maturity of the students, classroom activity in progress, and history and make-up of the class. Recognizing that teachers do not have to be present at all times in a classroom, a North Carolina appellate court concluded that a teacher could not be held liable for a student injury that occurred in her classroom while she remained in the cafeteria to finish lunch.[34] Under the school's policy, students daily returned to the classroom in groups of six and were instructed to remain in their seats and complete class assignments noted on the chalkboard. The Supreme Court of Wisconsin, however, held that there were legitimate issues of negligence in a situation where a teacher left fifty adolescent males unsupervised in a gymnasium for twenty-five minutes. During this absence, a fourteen-year-old pupil was injured in a rowdy game.[35]

Proper supervision is essential in settings that pose significant risks to students, such as vocational shops, gymnasiums, science laboratories, and school grounds where known dangers exist. In a Louisiana case, negligent supervision was found when a teacher left his welding class unsupervised and a student suffered a severe injury to his hand while using a power saw.[36] A state appellate court concluded that when inherently dangerous equipment is used in a class, a teacher must provide supervision at all times. The District of Columbia school system was found to be negligent in the injury of a six-year-old because of its failure to supervise a construction site as children departed from school.[37] School officials warned children daily about the dangerous site but did not provide actual supervision.

Supervision of students to and from school has generated litigation. In an Indiana case, a school district was found negligent in failing to provide adequate supervision of students during the boarding of school buses. A student suffered serious injuries when struck by a school bus while he waited outside the school building. Finding that lack of supervision was the proximate cause of the injury, an appellate court upheld a substantial damages award.[38] Actual supervision of student passengers on school buses may be necessitated if there is reason to expect misconduct that might result in injury to students.[39]

The school's duty to protect truant students from injury was addressed by the California Supreme Court in 1978. The case involved a student who left school without permission and was struck by a motorcycle several blocks from school.[40] The trial court concluded that the duty of school personnel to protect the student from harm terminated when he became truant. The California Supreme Court, however, reversed the trial court's decision, reasoning that proper supervision might have prevented the student's truancy and subsequent injury.

Pupil injuries during field trips often have evoked tort actions challenging the adequacy of supervision. While greater care is required during field trips to unfamiliar places, school personnel are not held liable for every injury that occurs. For example, no liability was assessed in connection with the death of a student on a band trip who drowned when he dove into the deep end of the swimming pool at a hotel.[41] The state appeals court reasoned that appropriate supervision was provided by school personnel, who had not been informed that the student could not swim. In fact, the child's parents had given permission for him to use the pool. The court concluded that he voluntarily dove into the deep end, and thus drowned through no fault of the supervisors. The Supreme Court of Oregon, however, assessed damages against a teacher for an injury sustained by a student at a beach during a school outing.[42] The court concluded that the unusual wave action on the Oregon coast was a known hazard and that the teacher failed to take reasonable safety precautions.

Teachers and administrators, because of their special training to assume such roles, are expected to make sound judgments as to the appropriate supervision required in any given school situation. The adequacy of care is measured against the risks of harm involved. Reasonable actions in one instance may be considered unreasonable under other conditions. Courts assess the facts of each case in light of the attendant circumstances in determining whether supervision is proper.

Instruction

Teachers have a duty to provide students with adequate and appropriate instruction prior to commencing an activity that may pose a risk of harm. An Indiana appellate court concluded that a jury could infer that inappropriate instruction exposed students in a physical education class to an unreasonable risk.[43] A sixth-grade student injured her mouth when she collided with a wall while performing a vertical jump. Evidence indicated that the teacher did not demonstrate the exercise and, according to expert testimony, provided improper directions for performing the jump. In another physical education case, a teacher was found negligent for permitting two male students to engage in boxing without proper training.[44] One of the students was fatally injured, and the teacher was held liable for failure to provide adequate instruction in the basic principles of defense. Similarly, negligent instruction was found in a New York case when a teacher failed to follow the state guidelines for conducting a physical fitness speed test and did not instruct students to take necessary precautions.[45] Failure to provide adequate instruction also resulted in negligence being assessed against a Tennessee shop teacher.[46] The teacher had permitted a student to use a drill bit without any prior instruction, and another student who was assisting in the operation of the machinery was severely injured.

In some situations, teachers have successfully rebutted charges of negligence by establishing that proper instructions were given to the students but were disregarded. In a case involving a shop class injury resulting from a nail thrown by a student, the South Carolina Supreme Court concluded that the teacher was not negligent, since he had forbidden students to throw objects.[47] The court emphasized that the teacher could not be held responsible for an injury caused by a student who disobeyed orders. A North Carolina shop teacher's detailed instructions in the use of power saws absolved him of any liability when a student lost several fingers in an accident.[48] Prior to students using the saw, the teacher had spent twenty minutes reviewing the safe use of the equipment and another twenty minutes demonstrating the proper procedures.

While school personnel have a duty to provide appropriate instruction to protect students from unreasonable hazards, students must also act in a reasonable manner. Liability will not be imposed against school personnel if students completely disregard the instructions and warnings of teachers.

Maintenance of Facilities and Equipment

Some states by law protect frequenters of public buildings from danger to life, health, safety, or welfare. These "safe place" statutes have been used successfully by individuals to obtain damages from school districts for injuries resulting from defective conditions of school buildings and grounds.[49] However, such "safe place" statutes do not cover the use of facilities or the equipment contained in the buildings.

In addition to "safe place" statutes that make liability explicit for certain types of injuries, school officials have a common law duty to maintain buildings, grounds, and equipment in reasonably safe condition. Courts have awarded damages in suits involving student injuries if school employees were aware of, or should have been aware of, hazardous conditions and did not take the necessary steps to repair or correct the conditions. The Supreme Court of Louisiana held that a school board was negligent in permitting a plate glass panel to remain in the foyer of a gymnasium. Prior to the injury of the plaintiff student in this case, the board had sufficient warning that the glass was dangerous, as an identical panel in the foyer had been broken several years earlier and replaced with safety glass.[50]

The duty to provide reasonable maintenance of facilities, however, does not place an obligation on school personnel to anticipate every possible danger or to be aware of and correct every minor defect as soon as the condition occurs. For example, a student was unsuccessful in establishing a breach of duty in connection with an injury sustained on a defective door latch.[51] The state appeals court concluded that there was no evidence that any school employee had knowledge of, or should have had knowledge of, the broken latch. Therefore, a duty to protect the student from the resulting injury could not be imposed. In another case, an appellate court rejected a claim that, because a student's thumb was injured when a heavy metal door slammed on it, the door posed such a danger that a door stop and a closure were required.[52]

Allegations that school personnel have breached their duty to maintain equipment in proper condition often have arisen in connection with student injuries sustained during athletic events. In 1978 an Illinois appeals court concluded that football coaches had a duty to inspect equipment provided to team members and were liable for student injuries resulting from the failure to conduct such inspections.[53] In the same year, the Illinois Supreme Court held that a school district breached its duty to protect athletes from harm by providing an ill-fitting and inadequate football helmet to a student.[54] The Massachusetts high court also concluded that a school district was liable for supplying a defective helmet to a student hockey player. The court noted that the student had every reason to expect to be supplied with proper equipment.[55]

Damages have been awarded to students where injuries after school hours have resulted from unsafe playground conditions.[56] A student in Michigan was successful in obtaining damages for the loss of sight in his right eye.[57] He sustained this injury while playing among piles of dirt and sand on the playground after school. The area was not fenced, and prior to the incident parents had complained to the school district concerning the dirt piles and "dirt fights" among children playing there. The Michigan appeals court concluded that the school district breached its duty to maintain the school grounds in a safe condition.

However, the fact that a playground injury occurs after school hours does not always mean that liability will be assessed against the school district. If the conduct of the injured party, rather than the unsafe condition of the grounds, is the primary cause of the injury, the school district may not be held liable for negligence. To illustrate, a California appeals court concluded that a school district was not liable for the death of a student on school grounds after school.[58] Although the playground was accessible to the public, unsupervised, and in disrepair, the court concluded that the student's death resulted from his own conduct in performing a hazardous skateboard activity, not from the defective condition of the playground.

A controversial issue in the 1980s has been the public school's duty to remove asbestos materials from school buildings. During the mid-twentieth century, asbestos products were commonly used in schools and colleges, and recent medical research has linked the inhalation of airborn asbestos fibers to lung and stomach cancer and other lung diseases. Responding to the serious health threat, in 1980 Congress enacted a law requiring local education agencies to inspect buildings and take remedial action to assure the safety of students and school employees.[59] Several tort actions also have been initiated against school districts to recover damages for asbestos-related injuries.[60] In addition, numerous school districts are involved in individual or class-action suits against asbestos manufacturers to recover costs for asbestos removal from those who supplied the hazardous materials without testing the products or warning consumers of the potential dangers.[61] Suits for damages where asbestos materials in public schools have caused personal injuries seem likely to increase in volume and complexity. In 1986 the Third Circuit Court of Appeals noted that more than 30,000 suits have been filed against manufacturers and that an additional 180,000 claims will probably be filed by 2010.[62]

DEFENSES AGAINST NEGLIGENCE

Several defenses are available to school officials to rebut charges of negligence. Traditionally, the most effective defense for school districts has been governmental immunity, which is based on the common-law notion that governmental agencies cannot be held liable for tortious actions. While this defense has been employed frequently by school districts, it is not available to school employees. The defense of contributory negligence, which bars recovery by an injured party based on evidence that his or her action was a substantial factor in causing the injury, also has appeared in educational litigation. In some jurisdictions, comparative negligence has been used to award damages in relation to the fault of each party involved. Procedural defects in suits, such as failure to adhere to statutory requirements regarding notice of claim, also have been used to relieve defendants of liability for damages. Other defenses in educational negligence cases have included assertions that the injured party assumed the risk of a known danger or that the injury was caused by uncontrollable events of nature. Because they have appeared so frequently in school litigation, several of these defenses are discussed in this section.

GOVERNMENTAL IMMUNITY

The doctrine of governmental or sovereign immunity originated in the Middle Ages from the notion that "the king can do no wrong." Subsequently, this idea was translated into the common-law principle that government agencies cannot be held liable for the negligent acts of their officers, agents, or employees. Various reasons have been offered for applying sovereign immunity to school districts, such as the involuntary status of government agencies and their legal inability to pay tort claims, since public funds are to be used only for statutorily prescribed purposes.

While governmental immunity for torts still exists under common law, legislative and judicial actions have partially eroded the vitality of this doctrine in approximately half of the states.[63] In many states, immunity has been abrogated by legislation, and in others, the use of immunity has been curtailed by judicial decree. Ohio, one of the most recent states judicially to abolish governmental immunity typifies the general legal stance in this area.[64] The state high court rejected the claim that school districts and other governmental agencies were unable to pay damages based on the lack of public funds from which such judgments could be paid, as the legislature had conferred authority to purchase liability insurance. Further, the court found archaic the notion that an injured individual should be inconvenienced rather than the government. In summary, the court noted that "[p]ersonal injuries from the negligence of those into whose care they are entrusted is not a risk that school children should, as a matter of public policy, be required to bear in return for the benefit of public education."[65]

While many states still enjoy governmental immunity or aspects of immunity, statutory provisions may permit recovery for specific functions or activities of school districts. As noted previously, most states have enacted "safe place" statutes that waive immunity for injuries resulting from defective school buildings and grounds.[66] Workers' compensation statutes also can waive the immunity of school districts for employee injuries. Under such statutes, negligence on the part of the employer need not be established; employees can recover damages for accidental injuries as long as they are work-related. The mere fact that an injury occurs at school does not entitle an employee to benefits, however, unless it is established that the injury is job related. For example, a teacher's widow was unsuccessful in securing benefits after her husband was murdered at school.[67] The deceased was murdered by another teacher's jealous husband, and the court ruled that the action, taken for personal reasons, was not a risk associated with employment.

In addition to being restricted by specific state laws from using sovereign immunity as a defense, government agencies also cannot plead immunity if they maintain a public nuisance that results in harm to an individual.[68] A nuisance is defined as an annoyance that interferes with common public rights.[69] Swimming pools or ponds on school property are classified as attractive nuisances; therefore, school districts generally are not shielded by immunity if proper precautions are not taken to prevent public access to such areas.

In some jurisdictions, a distinction has been made between governmental functions and proprietary functions in limiting the immunity of school districts. Governmental functions, which are performed in discharging the agency's official duties, have been considered immune from liability. On the other hand, proprietary functions, which could be provided as easily by a private corporation, have been legitimate targets for tort actions. Courts have not agreed, however, as to which school functions should be considered proprietary in nature. Some courts have held that profit-making extracurricular activities are proprietary functions, while other courts have ruled that all extracurricular activities are part of the educational mission of the school district and thus protected by immunity.[70]

Several courts have rejected the governmental/proprietary distinction and have instead distinguished between ministerial (administrative) and discretionary (policy-making) functions in determining a school district's potential liability. For example, in 1977 the Massachusetts Supreme Judicial Court concluded that school districts were liable for negligence involving ministerial duties in the administration of policies, but were immune from liability for negligence associated with discretionary, policy-making activities.[71]

Despite judicial and legislative action limiting governmental immunity, this defense continues to be used in many jurisdictions to protect school districts against liability for negligence. In 1984 a Michigan school district successfully relied on governmental immunity to bar recovery for a student's injury resulting from a horse bite that occurred on a field trip to a farm.[72] The Supreme Court of Alabama invoked governmental immunity to preclude damages for pupil injuries alleged to have resulted from unsafe high-school gymnasium facilities.[73] Similarly, governmental immunity prevented a Texas student from recovering for burns received at a homecoming bonfire.[74]

In a few states in which the application of sovereign immunity has not been limited, courts have ruled that the purchase of liability insurance to indemnify school districts is unnecessary because it protects a government agency against a threat that cannot exist. Under such circumstances, courts have concluded that the use of public funds to purchase liability insurance is illegal.[75] In states authorizing the purchase of liability insurance to protect government agencies, conflicting rulings have been rendered as to whether the acquisition of such insurance waives the sovereign immunity of the school district. The Supreme Court of Missouri has held that the purchase of liability insurance does not prevent a school board from asserting the defense of governmental immunity,[76] while courts in Georgia and North Carolina have concluded that the purchase of insurance constitutes a waiver of immunity.[77]

With frequent legislative and judicial actions related to liability, the extent that governmental immunity applies in the various states continues to be modified. To fully understand school district or individual liability, educators should consult state laws and judicial rulings.

Contributory Negligence

School personnel, in defending against negligence charges, often claim that an injured student's own acts contributed to the injury. If contributory negligence is found, a student is precluded from recovering any damages. In assessing whether contributory negligence exists, students are not held to the same standard of care as an adult; rather their actions must be reasonable for a child of similar age, maturity, intelligence, and experience. Some courts have further classified minors according to a presumption of capability for negligence: (1) children under the age of seven are considered incapable of negligence; (2) children over the age of fourteen are presumed capable of negligence; and (3) children between seven and fourteen years of age are considered incapable of negligence, but the presumption can be rebutted.[78] Clearly, age is a factor in determining reasonableness of a student's conduct, with contributory negligence being difficult to substantiate on the part of very young children.

School personnel have been successful in claiming contributory negligence if they have been able to prove that a student was aware of, or should have been aware of, the consequences of specific actions and nonetheless engaged in dangerous conduct.[79] A North Carolina appellate court concluded that a fourteen-year-old student was contributorily negligent in an injury he incurred through the misuse of a power saw.[80] Immediately prior to the injury, the teacher had provided comprehensive instructions and warnings regarding the use of the equipment. Similarly, the Supreme Court of Tennessee barred damages in the fatal injury of a twelve-year-old student who was struck by a guy wire supporting a utility pole when he leaned out the window of a school bus. Considering that the student was "a bright, alert and intelligent young man" who had heard school monitors almost daily warn students not to have their hands or any parts of their bodies outside the bus windows, the court found that the student's action was the proximate cause of the injury and constituted contributory negligence.[81]

School personnel have been unsuccessful in using contributory negligence as a defense if a student was not aware of the hazardous nature of an activity.[82] For example, a student who was waiting for a teacher outside an area marked "danger" in an industrial arts class was injured when a cylinder exploded.[83] A state appeals court rejected the claim of contributory negligence, concluding that the student was acting appropriately in waiting outside the danger area and had no reason to expect the injury to occur. Another court, in remanding a student injury case for a jury trial, noted from the evidence that an eleven-year-old plaintiff did not necessarily realize the dangers involved in an unfamiliar and improperly taught jump in physical education. Thus, the record did not support the teacher's claim of contributory negligence.[84] Also, teachers who have provided inadequate supervision or instruction cannot assert that students are contributorily negligent.[85]

Assumption of Risk

Similar to contributory negligence, assumption of risk may be used as a defense to prevent recovery for an injury if a student is found to have assumed a risk of harm. Teachers, however, may encounter difficulties in using this defense because of the age and maturity level of students. The defense is based on the premise that the injured plaintiff understood that a specific situation was dangerous and could result in possible injury, and still voluntarily consented to participate. By assuming the risk, the plaintiff thereby relieved the defendant of any responsibility or duty to exercise care for the plaintiff's protection.

Assumption of risk has been used particularly for sports injuries in educational settings. While inherent risks are associated with athletics, courts are not generally inclined to hold that students understand the risks. As a Pennsylvania court noted in a case involving an eleven-year-old student injured in a hockey game, "[i]f by reason of his tender age and lack of intelligence, experience and information, [he] did not appreciate the dangers of floor hockey, assumption of risk is not a viable defense."[86] In an earlier Pennsylvania case, the state high court remanded a student injury case for jury determination, questioning a student's understanding of the risks involved in preseason football conditioning and the voluntariness of his participation.[87] The student suffered permanent blindness in one eye from an injury incurred in playing "jungle football," an exercise conducted without protective equipment and involving rough body blocks and tackling. Evidence indicated that the student did not understand the risks and, furthermore, felt that selection for the team was contingent on his participation. A Louisiana appellate court, however, concluded that a high school athlete who challenged a coach to a wrestling match did assume the risk of injury.[88] The student, who was one of the strongest athletes in the school, the starting guard on the basketball team, and the starting halfback on the football team, was found to know and appreciate the risk of injury in wrestling.

Some educators are under the mistaken impression that parents can waive their children's right to sue for negligence by signing forms granting permission for the children to participate in particular activities. While such permission slips indicate that the students assume *normal* risks associated with the activity, parents cannot waive their children's entitlement to appropriate supervision and instruction. For example, while a child may assume some risk of potential injury by engaging in a dangerous sport such as football or by participating in a field trip (e.g., swimming or roller-skating), school personnel remain responsible for providing supervision and instruction to safeguard the child from foreseeable harm. Even though a permission slip might stipulate that the school is relieved of all liability for injuries associated with a given activity or outing, such documentation would not preclude liability if the child were subjected to unreasonable risks of harm.

Comparative Negligence

Contributory negligence and assumption of risk have been used less frequently in recent tort suits since many states have modified or replaced these defenses with comparative negligence standards. Depending on the level of fault, liability is apportioned among negligent parties, which may include the plaintiff, defendant, and other intervening actors. State laws vary as to restrictions placed on recovery.[89] For example, in some states damages are assessed in direct proportion to the various actors' relative negligence, whereas in other states damages are awarded to a negligent plaintiff only if the defendant's negligence is judged to be greater than that of the plaintiff.

Notice of Claim

Procedural defects in the process of filing a tort action can preclude recovery by the injured party. Most states specify the form to be used when initiating a suit and the time period within which a claim must be filed. Such requirements are designed to afford defendants an opportunity to investigate the claim while the facts surrounding it are still relatively recent.

While most courts have upheld notice statutes when minors have been involved, a few courts have allowed late petitions to be filed as long as they have been filed within a reasonable period of time, such as one year, from the date of the injury.[90] For example, the Supreme Court of Utah held that a minor's period of disability resulting from a shop class injury should not be considered part of the elapsed time for purposes of limiting the filing of a suit for damages.[91] In ruling that special consideration should be given to minors, the court noted that children are incapable of bringing suit and are left unprotected unless parents file the claim. A California appeals court also concluded that a minor should not be penalized because his parents neglected to initiate a timely action.[92]

ASSAULT AND BATTERY

Although negligence cases have dominated educational tort litigation, a few intentional tort actions have been initiated. An intentional tort need not be maliciously planned, but may be committed if a person intentionally proceeds to act in a manner that impairs the rights of others. Intentional tort actions in school settings mainly have involved charges of assault and battery.

Assault consists of an overt attempt to place another in fear of bodily harm; no actual physical contact need take place. When an assault is consummated and physical injury occurs, battery is committed. A person wielding a knife and threatening harm is guilty of assault; the actual stabbing constitutes battery.

Assault and battery cases in the school context generally have focused on the administration of corporal punishment by school personnel. Courts have been reluctant to interfere with a teacher's authority to discipline students and have sanctioned the use of reasonable force to control pupil behavior. For example, an Oregon appeals court ruled that a teacher was not guilty of assault and battery for using force to remove a student from the classroom.[93] After the pupil defiantly refused to leave the room, the teacher held his arms and led him toward the door. The student extricated himself, swung at the teacher, and broke a window, thereby cutting his arm. Concluding that the teacher used reasonable force with the student, the court dismissed the assault and battery charges.

A Louisiana appeals court also dismissed battery charges against a teacher who gently kicked a student.[94] Testimony revealed that the student had repeatedly disobeyed the teacher and had turned around in his chair to talk to classmates when the incident occurred. The teacher, who was holding chalk and an eraser in his hands, pushed the student with his foot in the right buttock to gain the pupil's attention. The court rejected the battery charge, reasoning that the blow was of little force and resulted in embarrassment more than pain. The court considered this situation to be one of the few circumstances in which a kick would meet the test of reasonableness.

In another Louisiana case, however, a student was successful in obtaining damages for assault and battery.[95] The pupil sustained a broken arm when a teacher shook him against bleachers in the gymnasium and then let him fall to the floor. The court assessed damages against the teacher, reasoning that the teacher's action was unnecessary to discipline the student or to protect himself. Similarly, the Supreme Court of Connecticut awarded damages to a twelve-year-old student because a teacher used excessive force in disciplining him.[96] The student suffered a fractured clavicle when the teacher threw him into a movable chalkboard in the classroom and then pushed him into a wall in the hallway.

School personnel also may initiate assault and battery suits against students. For example, a Wisconsin appellate court awarded a teacher both compensatory and punitive damages in a suit for battery. The teacher was physically attacked by a student outside the school building while attempting to escort the student to the school office for violating a smoking rule.[97] Concluding that the student acted with malicious intent, the court did not find a punitive damage award of $23,000 excessive. Similarly, an Oregon appellate court assessed damages against a student when he struck a teacher who was attempting to stop him from leaving the classroom.[98] Because Oregon law stipulates that parents are financially responsible for damages caused by the intentional torts of their children, damages also were entered against the father.

DEFAMATION

While most tort actions have involved claims for damages that were due to physical injuries, some plaintiffs have sought recovery for injuries to their reputations. Generally, *defamation* is defined as a false or misleading communication that places another person in a position of disgrace, ridicule, or contempt;[99] the statements may be made intentionally or negligently. *Slander* is spoken defamation, and *libel* is written defamation.

Under certain circumstances, communication is considered privileged and cannot be the grounds for a defamation suit. Statements made by justices and state officials in carrying out governmental services are usually considered absolutely privileged. Qualified privilege is often applied to statements made by educational personnel, and such communication is immune from liability as long as it is made in good faith "upon a proper occasion, from a proper motive, in a proper manner, and based upon reasonable or probable cause."[100] Qualified privilege will not shield educators if statements are made with malicious intent. The mere transmittal of erroneous information, however, does not constitute evidence of malice, as long as the communication is believed to be accurate and is conveyed in good faith. Truth can be used as a defamation defense, but usually, even if the communication is true, educators must have made the statements with good intentions in order to thwart defamation charges.

Despite the recent interest in the privacy rights of students, there have been few defamation cases involving students. Most defamation cases pertaining to schools have been initiated by teachers challenging evaluations placed in their personnel files or statements made by parents to school officials. In one such case, an Arizona appeals court held that parents were not liable for defamation of character simply because they submitted to the school board a list of grievances against a teacher.[101] Similarly, in a California case, a vice-principal was unsuccessful in a defamation suit against a group of parents who had made several allegations about him to the school board.[102] The court concluded that communication between citizens and public officials who are charged with investigating activities of employees is privileged. In another California case, an appeals court rejected charges of libel against parents for writing a letter to a school principal in which they made derogatory statements about a teacher. The court stated:

> One of the crosses a public school teacher must bear is intemperate complaint addressed to school administrators by overly-solicitous parents concerned about the teacher's conduct in the classroom. Since the law compels parents to send their children to school, appropriate channels for the airing of supposed grievances against the operation of the school sytem must remain open.[103]

Similarly, the New York high court held that parents had a qualified privilege to present a complaint against a teacher to the school board. Under state law, such concerns must be expressed in writing. The court, in emphasizing the need to maintain open communication between parents and school officials, noted that "[t]o tell lay persons that the governing body which has ultimate responsibility for the well being of their children will not even hear their claim unless they publish a statement containing their complaint, and then subject these parents to liability for making the statement is counter productive." [104]

Public educators also have initiated defamation suits against the news media. The degree of success a teacher or administrator has in bringing a defamation suit may depend upon whether the person is viewed as a private individual or as a public figure or official.[105] The United States Supreme Court has recognized the importance of preserving citizens' rights to criticize the government and public officials.[106] Accordingly, the Court has held that a public official can recover damages for defamation only if there is proof of actual malice; that is, a statement was made "with knowledge that it was false or with reckless disregard of whether it was false or not . . ." [107] To be considered a public official an individual must have "substantial responsibilities for or control over the conduct of governmental affairs." [108] The Florida and Maine high courts have held that teachers are not public officials since their authority is generally limited to school children.[109] An Oklahoma appellate court, however, found that a teacher who was a well-known civil rights worker, radio show hostess, and author was a public figure.[110] The Ohio Supreme Court has held that a public school superintendent is a public official for purposes of defamation laws.[111] The court based its decision on the fact that a superintendent has substantial responsibilities for the operation of the school system and that the public is concerned with the performance of the individual. Even if school personnel are deemed to be public officials or figures, a recent Supreme Court decision indicated that public officials would not have to show actual malice to recover damages in a defamation suit if the defamatory statements did not pertain to issues of public concern.[112]

CONCLUSION

While all individuals, including school personnel, have a responsibility to act reasonably and to respect the rights of others, some negligent conduct is likely to occur and to generate claims for damages. Consequently, educators should be knowledgeable about their potential liability under applicable state laws and should ensure that they have adequate insurance protection to cover any awards that might be assessed against them. To guard against liability, teachers and administrators should be cognizant of the following basic principles of tort law.

1. All individuals are responsible for any harmful consequences of their conduct.
2. The propriety of a teacher's conduct in a given situation is gauged by whether a reasonably prudent teacher (with the special skills and training associated with that role) would have acted in a similar fashion under like conditions.
3. Teachers owe students a duty to provide proper instruction and adequate supervision, to maintain equipment in proper repair, and to provide warnings regarding any known hazards.
4. Teachers are expected to exercise a standard of care commensurate with the duty owed; with more dangerous activities, a greater care is required.
5. Foreseeability of harm is a crucial element in determining whether a teacher's actions are negligent in a given situation.
6. An intervening act can relieve a teacher of liability for negligence if the intervening event caused the injury and the teacher had no reason to anticipate that the event would occur.
7. The common-law doctrine that government agencies cannot be held liable in tort actions (sovereign immunity) has been abrogated by legislative or judicial action in many states; in states still adhering to this doctrine, certain restrictions have been placed on its use to defend school districts against negligence claims (e.g., "safe place" statutes, exceptions to immunity for proprietary functions or ministerial duties).
8. While sovereign immunity does not protect school employees from liability in tort actions, some states by law require evidence of willful or wanton misconduct in order for school personnel to be liable for negligent acts in connection with educational activities.
9. Contributory negligence can be used to relieve school personnel of liability if it is established that the injured party's own actions were a significant factor in producing the injury.
10. If an individual knowingly and voluntarily assumes a risk of harm, recovery for an injury is barred.
11. Under comparative negligence statutes, damages may be apportioned among negligent defendants, plaintiffs, and intervening actors.
12. Procedural defects in filing a claim can preclude recovery on the part of the injured party.
13. School personnel can be held liable for assault and battery if they use excessive or brutal force with students.
14. Educators are protected from defamation charges by "qualified privilege," whereby written or spoken communication cannot be the subject of tort actions as long as statements are made to appropriate persons and with proper intentions.

15. Public officials can recover defamation damages from the news media for statements pertaining to public issues only if actual malice is proven.

NOTES

1. The only exceptions involve cases brought in the District of Columbia and actions initiated under 42 U.S.C. § 1983, which entitles individuals to sue other persons for damages in connection with the impairment of federally protected rights. For a discussion of liability under Section 1983, *see* text with note 168, chapter 8.
2. *See generally,* William Prosser, *Law of Torts,* 4th ed. (St. Paul, MN: West Publishing Co., 1971).
3. *See* text with note 120, chapter 3, for a discussion of educational negligence/malpractice litigation in which plaintiffs have alleged that school districts breached their duty to assure student literacy upon high school graduation.
4. Prosser, *Law of Torts,* p. 143.
5. *See, e.g.,* Ohio Rev. Code, § 2744.07.
6. Titus v. Lindberg, 228 A.2d 65 (N.J. 1967).
7. Augustus v. Joseph A. Craig Elementary School, 459 So. 2d 665 (La. App. 1984).
8. Verhel v. Independent School Dist. No. 709, 359 N.W.2d 579 (Minn. 1984). *See* Rupp v. Bryant, 417 So. 2d 658 (Fla. 1982) (school was responsible for supervising club activities off campus).
9. Rhea v. Grandview School Dist., 694 P.2d 666 (Wash. App. 1985).
10. In some states, "good Samaritan" laws shield individuals providing treatment in emergency situations from liability. Because of the special duty of care surrounding the student-teacher relationship, such laws would not relieve a teacher of liability for unreasonable actions.
11. *See* Welch v. Dunsmuir Joint Union High School Dist., 326 P.2d 633 (Cal. App. 1958).
12. O'Brien v. Township High School Dist., 392 N.E.2d 615 (Ill. App. 1979).
13. Guerrieri v. Tyson, 24 A.2d 468 (Pa. Super. 1942).
14. Fazzolari by Fazzolari v. Portland School Dist. No. 1J, 717 P.2d 1210 (Ore. App. 1986)
15. *Seė* Pesek v. Discepolo, 475 N.E.2d 3 (Ill. App. 1985) (rape victim failed to state a cause of action against school district for inadequate supervision of a truant student when school district could not foresee that the student would commit violent acts); Vann v. Board of Educ. of School Dist. of Philadelphia, 464 A.2d 684 (Pa. Commw. 1983) (attack on school property after school hours not foreseeable). *See also* Kavanaugh v. Orleans Parish School Bd., 487 So. 2d 533 (La. App. 1986) (armed robbery of teacher in classroom was not foreseeable).
16. Cal. Const. art. I, § 28(C).
17. Hosemann v. Oakland Unified School Dist., No. 583092–9 (Cal. Super. 1986).

18. *See* George Nicholson, James A. Rapp, and Frank Carrington, "Safe Schools: Ancient Doctrine Rediscovered," *Education Law Reporter,* vol. 32, no. 3 (1986), pp. 871–881.
19. Kern Alexander and David Alexander, *American Public School Law* (St. Paul, MN: West Publishing Company, 1985), p. 457.
20. Foster v. Houston General Insurance Co., 407 So. 2d 759, 763 (La. App. 1981).
21. Segerman v. Jones, 259 A.2d 794 (Md. App. 1969).
22. Simonetti v. School Dist. of Philadelphia, 454 A.2d 1038, 1041 (Pa. Super. 1982), *dismissed,* 473 A.2d 1015 (Pa. 1984).
23. Roberts v. Robertson County Bd. of Educ., 692 S.W.2d 863 (Tenn. App. 1985).
24. Dailey v. Los Angeles Unified School Dist., 470 P.2d 360 (Cal. 1970). *See* Rupp v. Bryant, 417 So. 2d 658 (Fla. 1982) (failure of school personnel to supervise activities of a club was proximate cause of student's injury).
25. Kush by Marszalek v. City of Buffalo, 462 N.Y.S.2d 831 (N.Y. 1983).
26. *See* text with note 89, *infra,* for discussion of comparative negligence damage awards.
27. Roberts v. Robertson County Bd. of Educ., 692 S.W.2d 863 (Tenn. App. 1985).
28. Ohio Rev. Code, § 2744.07.
29. *See* Segerman v. Jones, 259 A.2d 794 (Md. App. 1969); text with note 21, *supra. See also* Patterson v. Orleans Parish School Bd., 461 So. 2d 386 (La. App. 1984) (no liability for injury resulting from child catching his hand in door when general, orderly procedures were employed for escorting students to restroom).
30. Clark v. Furch, 567 S.W.2d 457 (Mo. App. 1978).
31. Partin v. Vernon Parish School Bd., 343 So. 2d 417 (La. App. 1977).
32. Sheehan v. Saint Peter's Catholic School, 188 N.W.2d 868 (Minn. 1971).
33. Fagan v. Summers, 498 P.2d 1227 (Wyo. 1972).
34. James v. Charlotte-Mecklenburg Bd. of Educ., 300 S.E.2d 21 (N.C. App. 1983). *See* Simonetti v. School Dist. of Philadelphia, 454 A.2d 1038 (Pa. Super. 1982), *dismissed,* 473 A.2d 1015 (Pa. 1984) (absence from classroom to monitor hallway did not constitute negligence).
35. Cirillo v. City of Milwaukee, 150 N.W.2d 460 (Wis. 1967). *See* Alferoff v. Casagrade, 504 N.Y.S.2d 719 (App. Div. 1986) (foreseeable that the disruptive behavior that regularly occurred in teacher's absence could result in injury).
36. Lawrence v. Grant Parish School Bd., 409 So. 2d 1316 (La. App. 1982).
37. District of Columbia v. Royal, 465 A.2d 367 (D.C. App. 1983).
38. School City of Gary v. Claudio, 413 N.E.2d 628 (Ind. App. 1980).
39. *See, e.g.,* Blair v. Board of Educ., 448 N.Y.S.2d 566 (App. Div. 1982).
40. Hoyem v. Manhatten Beach School Dist., 585 P.2d 851 (Cal. 1978).
41. Powell v. Orleans Parish School Bd., 354 So. 2d 229 (La. App. 1978).
42. Morris v. Douglas County School Dist. No. 9, 403 P.2d 775 (Ore. 1965).
43. Dibortolo v. Metropolitan School Dist. of Washington Township, 440 N.E.2d 506 (Ind. App. 1982).
44. LaValley v. Stanford, 70 N.Y.S.2d 460 (App. Div. 1947). *See also* Brahatcek v. Millard School Dist. No. 17, 273 N.W.2d 680 (Neb. 1979).

45. Ehlinger v. Board of Educ. of New Hartford Cent. School Dist., 465 N.Y.S.2d 378 (App. Div. 1983).
46. Roberts v. Robertson County Bd. of Educ., 692 S.W.2d 863 (Tenn. App. 1985).
47. Hammond v. Scott, 232 S.E.2d 336 (S.C. 1977).
48. Izard by Izard v. Hickory City Schools Bd. of Educ., 315 S.E.2d 756 (N.C. App. 1984).
49. *See* Monfils v. City of Sterling Heights, 269 N.W.2d 588 (Mich. App. 1978); Hudson v. Union Free School Dist. No. 2, 391 N.Y.S.2d 487 (App. Div. 1977).
50. Wilkinson v. Hartford Accident and Indemnity Co., 411 So. 2d 22 (La. 1982).
51. Lewis v. Saint Bernard Parish School Bd., 350 So. 2d 1256 (La. App. 1977).
52. Narcisse v. Continental Insurance Co., 419 So. 2d 13 (La. App. 1982).
53. Thomas v. Chicago Bd. of Educ., 377 N.E.2d 55 (Ill. App. 1978).
54. Gerrity v. Beatty, 373 N.E.2d 1323 (Ill. 1978).
55. Everett v. Bucky Warren, Inc., 380 N.E.2d 653 (Mass. 1978). *See* Tiemann v. Independent School Dist. No. 740, 331 N.W.2d 250 (Minn. 1983) (use of vaulting horses with exposed holes where pommels had been removed posed question of negligence).
56. *See* Pichette v. Manistique Public Schools, 269 N.W.2d 143 (Mich. 1978); Zaepfel v. City of Yonkers, 392 N.Y.S.2d 336 (App. Div. 1977).
57. Monfils v. City of Sterling Heights, 269 N.W.2d 588 (Mich. App. 1978).
58. Bartell v. Palos Verdes Peninsula School Dist., 147 Cal. Rptr. 898 (Cal. App. 1978).
59. Asbestos School Hazard Detection and Control Act, 20 U.S.C. 3601, *et seq.*
60. The New Jersey Education Association has filed suit against asbestos manufacturers and 157 New Jersey school districts, seeking the establishment of a fund to cover the cost of annual physical examinations for school employees. *See School Finance News,* October 18, 1984, p. 5.
61. *See* In re Asbestos Litigation, 789 F.2d 996 (3d Cir. 1986), *cert. denied,* 107 S. Ct. 182 (1986); Johns-Manville Corp., 53 Bankruptcy Rptr. 346 (S.D.N.Y. 1985).
62. In re Asbestos Litigation, *id.* at 1000.
63. *See* William D. Valente, *Education Law: Public and Private,* vol. 2 (St. Paul, MN: West Publishing Co., 1985), p. 224. For a discussion of the abrogation of school district immunity in connection with abridgments of federal rights under Section 1983 of the Civil Rights Act of 1871 (42 U.S.C. § 1983), *see* text with note 179, chapter 8.
64. Carbone v. Overfield, 451 N.E.2d 1229 (Ohio 1983). In 1985, the Ohio legislature enacted a statute granting modified immunity to school districts, Ohio Rev. Code § 2744.
65. *Id.* at 1230.
66. *See* text with note 49, *supra.*
67. Gutierrez v. Artesia Public Schools, 583 P.2d 476 (N.M. App. 1978).
68. *See* Wilson v. United States, 425 F. Supp. 143 (E.D. Va. 1977).
69. Prosser, *Law of Torts,* p. 583.
70. *See* Richards v. School Dist. of City of Birmingham, 83 N.W.2d 643 (Mich. 1957); Sawaya v. Tucson High School Dist., 281 P.2d 105 (Ariz. 1955).

71. Whitney v. City of Worcester, 366 N.E.2d 1210 (Mass. 1977).
72. Davis v. Homestead Farms, Inc., 359 N.W.2d 1 (Mich. App. 1984).
73. Hutt v. Etowah County Bd. of Educ., 454 So. 2d 973 (Ala. 1984).
74. McManus v. Anahuac Independent School Dist., 667 S.W.2d 275 (Tex. App. 1984).
75. *See* Board of Educ. of County of Raleigh v. Commercial Casualty Insurance Co., 182 S.E. 87 (W.Va. 1935).
76. Lehmen v. Wansing, 624 S.W.2d 1 (Mo. 1981).
77. Thigpen v. McDuffie County Bd. of Educ., 335 S.E.2d 112 (Ga. 1985); James by James v. Charlotte-Mecklenburg Bd. of Educ., 300 S.E.2d 21 (N.C. App. 1983).
78. *See* Berman by Berman v. Philadelphia Bd. of Educ., 456 A.2d 545 (Pa. Super. 1983).
79. *See* Branch v. Stehr, 461 N.Y.S.2d 346 (App. Div. 1983); District of Columbia v. Royal, 465 A.2d 367 (D.C. App. 1983); Bartell v. Palos Verdes Peninsula School Dist., 147 Cal. Rptr. 898 (Cal. App. 1978); Powell v. Orleans Parish School Bd., 354 So. 2d 229 (La. App. 1978).
80. Izard by Izard v. Hickory City Schools Bd. of Educ., 315 S.E.2d 756 (N.C. App. 1984).
81. Arnold v. Hayslett, 655 S.W.2d 941, 946 (Tenn. 1983).
82. *See* Potter v. North Carolina School of the Arts, 245 S.E.2d 188 (N.C. App. 1978); Sansonni v. Jefferson Parish School Bd., 344 So. 2d 42 (La. App. 1977).
83. Danos v. Foret, 354 So. 2d 667 (La. App. 1977). *See also* Lawrence v. Grant Parish School Bd., 409 So. 2d 1316 (La. App. 1982) (simply warning fourteen-year-old student not to use power saw without explaining dangers did not render student contributorily negligent when he was later injured).
84. Dibortolo v. Metropolitan School Dist. of Washington Township, 440 N.E.2d 506 (Ind. App. 1982).
85. *See* Foster v. Houston General Insurance Co., 407 So. 2d 759 (La. App. 1981).
86. Berman by Berman v. Philadelphia Bd. of Educ., 456 A.2d 545, 550 (Pa. Super. 1983).
87. Rutter v. Northeastern Beaver County School Dist., 437 A.2d 1198 (Pa. 1981).
88. Kluka v. Livingston Parish School Bd., 433 So. 2d 302 (La. App. 1983).
89. Valente, *Education Law: Public and Private,* pp. 215–218.
90. *See* Rocha v. Lodi Unified School Dist., 152 Cal. Rptr. 307 (Cal. App. 1979).
91. Scott v. School Bd. of Granite School Dist., 568 P.2d 746 (Utah 1977).
92. Williams v. Mariposa County Unified School Dist., 147 Cal. Rptr. 452 (Cal. App. 1978).
93. Simms v. School Dist. No. 1, 508 P.2d 236 (Ore. App. 1973). *See* chapter 6 for a more detailed discussion of the legal issues involved in the administration of corporal punishment.
94. Thompson v. Iberville Parish School Bd., 372 So. 2d 642 (La. App. 1979).
95. Frank v. Orleans Parish School Bd., 195 So. 2d 451 (La. App. 1967).
96. Sansone v. Bechtel, 429 A.2d 820 (Conn. 1980).
97. Anello v. Savignac, 342 N.W.2d 440 (Wis. App. 1983).
98. Garrett v. Olsen, 691 P.2d 123 (Ore. App. 1984).

99. *See* Alexander and Alexander, *American Public School Law,* pp. 499–501.
100. Baskett v. Crossfield, 228 S.W. 673, 675 (Ky. 1921).
101. Sewell v. Brookbank, 581 P.2d 267 (Ariz. App. 1978).
102. Brody v. Montalbano, 151 Cal. Rptr. 206 (Cal. App. 1978).
103. Martin v. Kearney, 124 Cal. Rptr. 281, 283 (Cal. App. 1975). *See also* Nodar v. Galbreath, 462 So. 2d 803 (Fla. 1984) (parent's statement before school board concerning teacher's performance was conditionally privileged).
104. Weissman v. Mogol, 462 N.Y.S.2d 383, 386 (N.Y. 1983). *See also* Stachura v. Truszkowski, 763 F.2d 211 (6th Cir. 1985) (parent has first amendment right to petition government for redress of grievances); State v. Reyes, 700 P.2d 1155 (Wash. 1985) (statute prohibiting individuals from insulting or abusing a teacher on school grounds found to be unconstitutional); Commonwealth v. Ashcraft, 691 S.W.2d 229 (Ky. App. 1985) (statute providing that "no person shall upbraid, insult or abuse any teacher of the public schools in the presence of the school or in the presence of a pupil of the school" held to violate a parent's constitutional right to free speech).
105. For a discussion of the distinctions between private figures and public officials, *see* Gertz v. Robert Welch, Inc., 418 U.S. 323 (1974); Rosenblatt v. Baer, 383 U.S. 75 (1966); New York Times Co. v. Sullivan, 376 U.S. 254 (1964).
106. New York Times Co. v. Sullivan, 376 U.S. 254 (1964).
107. *Id.* at 279–280.
108. Rosenblatt v. Baer, 383 U.S. 75, 85 (1966).
109. True v. Ladner, 513 A.2d 257 (Me. 1986); Nodar v. Galbreath, 462 So. 2d 803 (Fla. 1984). *But see* Milkovich v. News Herald, 473 N.E.2d 1191 (Ohio 1984), *cert. denied,* 106 S. Ct. 322 (1986). Justice Brennan, dissenting in the Supreme Court's denial of *certiorari,* noted that public school teachers, as role models, exert significant influence in communities.
110. Luper v. Black Dispatch Publishing Company, 675 P.2d 1028 (Okla. App. 1983).
111. Scott v. News-Herald, 496 N.E.2d 699 (Ohio 1986). *See* Garcia v. Board of Educ. of Socorro Consol. School Dist., 777 F.2d 1403 (10th Cir. 1985), *cert. denied,* 107 S. Ct. 66 (1986) (school board members are public officials).
112. Dun and Bradstreet, Inc. v. Greenmoss Building, Inc., 105 S. Ct. 2939 (1985).

13

School Desegregation

Since 1954 school desegregation has generated a steady stream of litigation. Indeed, no other topic has had such a dramatic impact on the direction of education law; federal courts have assumed a more assertive posture in reviewing public school policies and practices as a result of desegregation litigation. Claims of discrimination based on sex, handicaps, age, and other traits often rely on precedents established in cases involving racial minority students. This chapter provides an overview of legal developments pertaining to school desegregation, with particular emphasis on activity in the 1980s.

FROM *PLESSY* TO *BROWN*

In 1896 the United States Supreme Court interpreted the fourteenth amendment's guarantee of equal protection of the laws as permitting state-imposed racial segregation. In this case, *Plessy v. Ferguson,* the Court reasoned that as long as blacks and whites were treated equally, racial integration was not constitutionally required.[1] Although *Plessy* involved segregated railway accommodations rather than schools, the Court cited an earlier Massachusetts case in which the state high court endorsed school segregation.[2] Subsequently, the Supreme Court explicitly ruled that the "separate but equal" doctrine applied in the public school context.[3]

By 1950, however, serious questions had been raised regarding the "separate but equal" precedent. In several higher-education cases, the Supreme Court concluded that separate educational programs offered for black and white students were in fact not equivalent and thus violated the equal protection clause.[4] Perhaps realizing that the federal courts might be placed in the uncomfortable position of evaluating whether segregated public schools throughout the nation were indeed equal, the Supreme Court finally agreed to reassess its interpretation of the equal protection clause as applied to public school segregation.

In its landmark 1954 decision, *Brown v. Board of Education of Topeka,* the Court repudiated the "separate but equal" doctrine, declaring that racially segregated public schools are "inherently unequal."[5] Because of the significant impact of this decision, the Supreme Court delayed an implementation decree for one year, soliciting friend-of-the-court briefs regarding strategies to convert segregated, dual school districts into integrated, unitary districts. The Court's 1955 implementation decree, *Brown II,* contained the often-quoted phrase that dual school systems must be converted to unitary school systems "with all deliberate speed." The Court stated that in designing and effecting desegregation remedies, the federal judiciary should be guided by equitable principles that grant courts "practical flexibility" in adjusting and reconciling public and private needs.[6]

In the numerous desegregation cases following *Brown I* and *Brown II,* federal courts have been faced with a two-pronged task. Initially, they must determine if the equal protection clause has been violated by official action or inaction that has maintained or perpetuated unlawful school segregation. Once such a violation is established, then courts must approve a remedy that is appropriate in nature and scope. Both of these tasks have been troublesome for the federal judiciary. The Supreme Court has recognized that there is no universal solution to the complex problems of desegregation and that the interests of state and local authorities in managing their own affairs must be considered in fashioning remedies.[7]

PHASE I: SOUTHERN DESEGREGATION

The *Brown I* decision established that the state may not deliberately isolate students because of race; legally sanctioned dual school systems, where attendance is conditioned on a student's race, violate the fourteenth amendment. During the next decade, the Supreme Court reacted to blatant attempts to thwart the *Brown* mandate, such as state officials' efforts to block desegregation in Little Rock, Arkansas,[8] and an attempt to close public schools in one Virginia county while maintaining public schools in other counties in the state.[9] However, the Court offered little guidance as to the specific conditions that offended the Federal Constitution. Some lower courts reasoned that as long as barriers to integration were removed (e.g., state laws and school board policies requiring segregation), the constitutional obligation was satisfied.[10]

Finally, in a trilogy of cases in 1968, the Supreme Court announced that school officials in systems that were segregated by law in 1954 were charged with an *affirmative duty* to take whatever steps were necessary to convert to unitary school systems and eradicate the effects of past discriminatory acts.[11] Thus, the notion of "state neutrality" was transformed into a requirement of affirmative state action to desegregate schools. The mere removal of barriers to school integration was not sufficient; the Supreme Court declared that desegregation remedies would be evaluated in terms of their *effectiveness* in converting from dual to unitary school systems. In 1969 the Court recognized that its "all deliberate speed" mandate had been ineffective and ordered the operation of dual school systems to be terminated "at once."[12] Fifteen years after the *Brown* ruling, however, the extent of this duty remained far from clear.

A 1971 decision, *Swann v. Charlotte-Mecklenburg Board of Education,* often is cited as the Supreme Court's first direct attempt to identify the characteristics of an unconstitutional dual school system and the steps required to attain a unitary, nonracial system.[13] Recognizing that the continued presence of a small number of predominantly one-race schools in a district did not necessarily mean that the district was still practicing state-imposed segregation, the Court placed the burden of proof on school authorities to establish that such schools were not the result of present or past discriminatory action. The Court also held that factors such as the quality of school buildings and equipment, the racial composition of teachers and staff, the operation of extracurricular activities, and the construction and abandonment of school buildings should be considered in determining the existence of state-imposed segregation. Although the Court cautioned in *Swann* that mathematical racial ratios were a desirable norm rather than a fixed requirement, the decision introduced into desegregation litigation the definition of a unitary school system as one with a sufficient degree of racial balance in a sufficient number of schools.

Regarding acceptable remedial action, the Court in *Swann* suggested pairing schools, consolidating schools, altering attendance zones, reassigning teachers, and using racial quotas as components of plans to attain unitary school districts. The Court also held that the practice of assigning students to the schools nearest their homes was not a valid basis for operating a school district if it failed to eliminate school segregation. Accordingly, the Court endorsed the use of reasonable student transportation as a permissible means to attain integrated schools, noting that the "soundness of any transportation plan" must be evaluated based on the time involved, distance of travel, and age of the students.[14]

Applying the criteria established in *Swann,* substantial desegregation was attained in southern school districts during the 1970s. Where unconstitutional segregation was found, federal courts exercised broad power in ordering remedies affecting student and staff assignments, curriculum, school construction, personnel practices, and budgetary allocations. Judicial activity was augmented by threats from the Department of Health,

Education and Welfare to terminate federal funds for school districts not in compliance with Title VI of the Civil Rights Act of 1964.[15] Whereas only about 1 percent of minority students in eleven southern states attended school with white children a decade after the *Brown* decision, by 1972 over half of the black students in the South attended schools with less than 50 percent minority enrollments.[16]

PHASE II: BEYOND SOUTHERN DESEGREGATION

Since the Court in *Swann* carefully limited its decision to states with a long history of school segregation by *official policy,* questions remained regarding what type of evidence—other than explicit legislation requiring school segregation in 1954—was necessary to establish that segregated schools violated the fourteenth amendment.[17] In essence, what distinguished unconstitutional de jure segregation (i.e., segregation created by state action) from permissible de facto segregation (i.e., segregation that occurs naturally through no fault of state officials)?

In 1973 the Supreme Court delivered its first decision involving a school district outside the South. In *Keyes v. School District No. 1,* the Court held that in "a school system like Denver's, where no statutory dual system has ever existed, plaintiffs must prove not only that segregated schooling exists but also that it was brought about or maintained by intentional state action."[18] The Court indicated that unconstitutional de jure segregation could be found in school districts other than those that maintained segregation by law in 1954 with proof that *discriminatory motive* accompanied segregated conditions. Thus, an assessment of "intent" became the key in distinguishing de jure from de facto segregation. Furthermore, the Court in *Keyes* concluded that a finding of segregative intent in a meaningful part of the school system created a presumption of de jure segregation in other parts of the system.[19] Unless the presumption was successfully rebutted, a districtwide remedy would be warranted. The *Keyes* decision essentially provided for a shifting of the burden of proof; once plaintiffs established purposeful segregation in enough schools, the defendants had to substantiate that other segregated schools within the system were not the result of intentional discrimination.

In 1974 the Supreme Court again addressed the legality of nonsouthern school segregation, striking down an interdistrict desegregation plan in *Milliken v. Bradley*.[20] The Sixth Circuit Court of Appeals had ordered a metropolitan desegregation remedy for Detroit and fifty-three suburban school districts, reasoning that intentional school segregation implicated the metropolitan area. The Supreme Court, however, disagreed and held that the plaintiffs did not carry their burden of proof in substantiating purposeful discrimination on the part of the suburban districts. The Court emphasized that a remedy must not be broader in scope than warranted by the constitutional violations uncovered. Since intentional school segregation was substantiated in the Detroit School District, the case was remanded for the formulation of a desegregation remedy for the Detroit system only.

Two years later, the Supreme Court explicitly rejected any inference drawn from its prior decisions that an equal protection violation could be established by showing that official actions had a segregatory effect, regardless of their intent.[21] The Court declared that "disproportionate impact is not irrelevant, but is not the sole touchstone of an invidious racial discrimination forbidden by the Constitution."[22] The Supreme Court also recognized that school districts do not have an affirmative duty to revise remedial efforts annually once a unitary school district has been achieved to the Court's satisfaction and resegregation results from demographic changes rather than intentional discriminatory acts of school officials.[23]

By 1977 most lower courts had abandoned the notion that the mere existence of segregatory conditions implied a constitutional violation. Courts, however, were struggling to identify the requisites of unlawful intent that would trigger a duty to eliminate school segregation. Some federal courts assumed that a presumption of unlawful purpose could be established if the natural, probable, and foreseeable result of public officials' acts perpetuated segregatory conditions.[24] Yet, courts were not in agreement regarding whether intent should be determined by this objective "foreseeable consequences" test or by a subjective standard, requiring evidence that official decision makers actually harbored a desire to segregate.[25]

In 1977 the Supreme Court rendered *Dayton Board of Education v. Brinkman* (*Dayton I*), reversing the appellate court's endorsement of a massive busing plan to reduce the racial identification of Dayton schools.[26] Remanding the case, the Supreme Court instructed the federal district court first to determine whether official actions were intentionally discriminatory, and if so, to determine how much "incremental segregatory effect" such violations had on the racial composition of Dayton schools compared to what the composition would have been in the absence of such violations. The remedy could address only the difference ascertained, and a systemwide remedy could not be imposed unless there was evidence of a systemwide impact of segregatory practices. The Supreme Court rejected the appellate court's findings of "cumulative violations" as ambiguous and insufficient to support a massive systemwide remedy.

After the Sixth Circuit Court of Appeals reinstated the original systemwide desegregation remedy, the Supreme Court was called on to review the case for a second time in *Dayton II*. By a one-vote margin, the Court affirmed the appellate court's decision in 1979.[27] This time, in contrast to *Dayton I,* the Supreme Court majority was satisfied that substantial evidence of the systemwide effect of segregatory practices had been presented, warranting the comprehensive remedy ordered by the appellate court. The majority concluded that the appeals court properly ruled that evidence of intentional segregation in the Dayton schools at the time of the *Brown* ruling triggered a continuing affirmative duty to eradicate the effects of the dual school system. The Court declared that a school board's conduct under an *unsatisfied duty* to eliminate school segregation must be assessed by the "effectiveness, not the purpose, of the actions in decreasing or increasing the segregation caused by the dual system."[28] The school board had an obligation to do more than abandon its previous segregatory practices; it had an affirmative responsibility to ensure that its subsequent actions did not perpetuate or reestablish the dual system. Finding numerous post-*Brown* actions that had the effect of increasing school segregation, the majority concluded that the scope of the constitutional violations justified the systemwide desegregation order.[29]

In a companion case in 1979, the Supreme Court ruled that the Columbus, Ohio, school board had not fulfilled its affirmative duty to dismantle the dual school system and had instead "intentionally aggravated, rather than alleviated" racial separation in the schools.[30] The Court concluded that the findings of purposeful segregatory practices with systemwide impact warranted the systemwide remedy imposed by the courts below.

These two decisions are particularly significant in that they appeared to belie the widely held perception at the time that the Supreme Court was retreating in the desegregation arena. Although the Court reiterated that evidence of intentional discriminatory acts is necessary to establish a constitutional violation and that the scope of the remedy must fit the scope of the violation, the Court allowed the consequences of actions to be considered in establishing discriminatory intent. More significantly, the Court reasoned that if school officials are unable to refute that intentional school segregation existed in 1954, their post-1954 acts must be assessed in light of their *continuing affirmative duty* to eliminate the effects of such segregation. Racially neutral actions cannot satisfy this duty; school officials must take affirmative steps to eradicate school segregation until unitary status is attained.

RECENT DEVELOPMENTS

Numerous school districts throughout the United States remain embroiled in desegregation controversies, with many having been in litigation for well over a decade and some for nearly three decades. Over 200 school districts with more than five million students are under court-ordered desegregation mandates; many other districts have voluntary plans in operation. Without question, voluntary or mandatory desegregation activities have had a significant impact on the operation of American public schools. While the Supreme Court's desegregation rulings reflected unanimous opinions from 1954 until 1971, decisions rendered since 1972 have been characterized by a divided vote. Some of these decisions have appeared inconsistent, and they have not provided clear guidance to lower federal courts charged with monitoring the implementation of desegregation decrees.

Although the Supreme Court has declined to review most appeals in desegregation cases during the 1980s, lower courts have been active in addressing challenges to desegregation plans involving numerous cities in all regions of the nation. Recent litigation has focused primarily on what constitutes acceptable desegregation plans, and the judicial scoreboard is mixed. While the federal judiciary has exhibited a greater commitment to protecting minority interests than have the other two branches of government, which have been more sensitive to political pressures, recently the judiciary has not been as aggressive in requiring massive student reassignment plans to integrate schools as was true a decade ago. It was assumed in the early 1970s that racially balanced schools would ensure equal educational opportunities, but other approaches to attain this goal have received increasing judicial attention.[31] This section contains a review of recent developments pertaining to interdistrict remedies, fiscal responsibilities, busing limitation measures, and alternatives to student busing.

Interdistrict Remedies

A controversial issue has involved the scope of judicial authority to order interdistrict remedies. With many cities facing an increasing minority population, it has been argued that meaningful school desegregation cannot be accomplished without pupil transfers between city and suburban districts. As noted previously, in 1974 the Supreme Court declared that cross-district remedies could be ordered only with evidence of a constitutional violation in one district that produces a significant segregative effect in another school district.[32] Applying this principle in a subsequent case, the Fifth Circuit Court of Appeals concluded that "there must be clear proof of cause and effect and a careful delineation of the extent of the effect" for school district lines to be disturbed in a desegregation decree.[33] More recently, the Fourth Circuit Court of Appeals also recognized that if a school district has not *caused* school segregation in a neighboring district, it has no constitutional obligation to remedy such racial imbalance in the other district.[34] While suits requesting metropolitan remedies in Detroit, Houston, Kansas City, and Cincinnati have been rejected, court-ordered interdistrict plans have led to school district mergers in some metropolitan areas, such as Wilmington and Louisville.[35]

In other situations, such as Indianapolis and St. Louis, interdistrict pupil transfers are being implemented in the absence of school district mergers. The Seventh Circuit Court of Appeals ordered a one-way busing plan for the Indianapolis metropolitan area; this plan required the busing of over 5,000 minority students from the Indianapolis schools to six suburban school districts.[36] The appeals court concluded that the state was responsible for the segregated conditions in the Indianapolis schools because of legislation that merged municipal governments but not school districts in Marion County, Indiana.

The St. Louis desegregation case is somewhat unique in that the St. Louis City School Board and twenty-three surrounding suburban districts agreed in 1983 to implement a desegregation plan that required each suburban district to accept inner-city minority transfers up to 15 percent of its total enrollment. Upon reaching this goal, the suburban districts no longer will be subject to judicial supervision. However, if the districts fail to meet the enrollment goal in five years, the city school district and black plaintiffs have the option of renewing court action. The federal district court recognized its authority to order the city board of education to increase the tax rate if necessary to support the desegregation settlement. Subsequently, the Eighth Circuit Court of Appeals held that the state could be required to pay for half of the costs of certain programs to improve the quality of education in nonintegrated schools, total capital and operating costs of magnet schools established under the settlement agreement, and half of the desegregation transportation costs.[37]

Although numerous interdistrict student transfers are being implemented and several states provide financial incentives for such efforts, courts in general remain reluctant to order desegregation remedies that include school district mergers. To illustrate, in 1985 the Eighth Circuit Court of Appeals reversed a lower court's order requiring school district consolidation among the Little Rock School District and two other school districts in Pulaski County, Arkansas, to achieve county-wide desegregation.[38] While finding interdistrict intentional segregation that justified interdistrict relief, the appeals court concluded that the lower court's remedial order was broader in scope than warranted by the constitutional violation and did not adequately consider alternative remedies or the importance of local school district autonomy in managing its own affairs. The appeals court suggested that the interdistrict violations could be remedied by making minor boundary adjustments between two of the districts, correcting segregative practices within each of the districts, improving the quality of nonintegrated schools, requiring the state to provide partial funding for compensatory and remedial programs for minority students, establishing a limited number of county-wide magnet schools, and maintaining judicial oversight to ensure implementation of such plans.

Fiscal Responsibilities

Without question, substantial costs have been incurred in desegregation litigation and in implementation of remedial plans.[39] Courts, however, have shown little sympathy when the lack of sufficient funds has been proffered as a defense for maintaining dual school systems. In some situations, such as Cleveland and Boston, federal courts have overseen the management of the school district's financial resources to ensure that desegregation activities are implemented.[40] In other situations, such as Buffalo and St. Louis, the judiciary has asserted its authority to order tax increases or additional municipal appropriations to implement desegregation decrees.[41]

In several cases school districts have argued that the state has been responsible for creating school segregation and thus should share in the costs of implementing remedial plans. In 1977 the Supreme Court ruled that the state of Michigan was required to underwrite half of the costs of remedial programs, inservice training, guidance and counseling services, and community relations programs in the Detroit School District's desegregation plan because the state played a role in creating the dual school system.[42]

More recently, other courts have required states to share desegregation expenses based on evidence that state action has perpetuated the segregated conditions. For example, Missouri was ordered to assume partial costs of preparing and implementing a plan to dismantle vestiges of the dual school system in Kansas City since the state had the authority to remedy the segregated conditions and did not take affirmative steps to do so.[43] As noted previously, the Seventh Circuit Court of Appeals assessed the cost of the one-way busing plan in Indianapolis against the state, reasoning that the state was responsible for creating the school segregation.[44] Also, Ohio was ordered to share the costs of implementing Dayton's desegregation plan because state officials had knowledge of segregatory practices in the school district and failed to take remedial action.[45] Similarly, Tennessee was ordered to incur 60 percent of the costs of the desegregation plan in the Nashville metropolitan area.[46]

Because school desegregation has national importance, the federal government has provided some financial assistance to further desegregation activities in local school districts. During the 1970s, numerous school districts received federal desegregation aid under the Emergency School Aid Act (ESAA).[47] After ESAA was folded into the block grant to state and local education agencies under Chapter 2 of the Education Consolidation and Improvement Act in 1981, large urban school districts reported a substantial reduction in federal aid devoted to desegregation activities.[48]

In some situations the federal government has promised aid as part of desegregation consent decrees in which federal, state, and local officials have agreed to cooperate in remedial efforts. The federal government's role in some of these decrees has been controversial. In a widely publicized case, the Chicago school board sued the federal government for allegedly defaulting on a promise to provide $103.8 million in desegregation aid to the school district. Pending the outcome of the case, the Education Department was barred from releasing grant funds under several programs of national significance. After an earlier order was vacated by the Seventh Circuit Court of Appeals, in 1985 the federal district court reiterated that the United States had willfully violated the 1980 consent decree and held that the Chicago school district was entitled to $17 million immediately and as much as $100 million in federal funds over a five-year period.[49] However, the Seventh Circuit Court of Appeals again vacated the lower court's order, reasoning that the federal government could satisfy its fiscal obligation by giving priority to Chicago in allocating funds and searching for funding sources outside of desegregation programs.[50]

Busing Limitation Measures

While compensatory instructional programs and magnet schools increasingly are appearing in remedial schemes, the reassignment of students among paired and clustered schools remains an important component of most desegregation decrees. Several courts have recognized that instructional remedies may be necessary, but are not sufficient in and of themselves to desegregate a school system.[51] Because pupil reassignment—inevitably involving busing—is often a feature of acceptable desegregation plans, this remedial tool has been the focus of substantial public attention and political controversy. In 1983 a federal judge observed: "Busing (the buzzword for mandatory student assignment requiring transportation) is a concept loaded with emotional content on both sides of the issue."[52]

Busing limitation bills that would eliminate the authority of federal courts to order busing of students beyond the school nearest their homes have regularly been introduced in Congress. Among provisions of the 1974 Equal Educational Opportunities Act (EEOA) was a restriction on busing (to situations involving segregative intent) and a stipulation that the assignment of students to neighborhood schools was not a constitutional violation.[53] Although the EEOA did not place a limitation on judicial authority to order pupil reassignment where constitutional violations were found, there have been several unsuccessful attempts to secure federal legislation that would restrict the role of the Justice Department in desegregation cases and curb federal judicial authority in imposing student transportation plans as part of remedial decrees.

Busing limitation measures also have generated state activity. The Supreme Court in 1971 struck down a North Carolina law forbidding the busing of students to create racially balanced schools, concluding that the provision unconstitutionally restricted local school authorities' broad discretion to formulate plans to eliminate dual school systems.[54] Nonetheless, other states have continued to consider busing limitation measures. In both Washington and California, provisions restricting the use of pupil transportation to attain integrated schools were passed by the voters in the late 1970s. Challenges to these measures resulted in Supreme Court decisions in 1982.

In *Washington v. Seattle School District No. 1,* the Supreme Court affirmed an appellate court ruling, striking down a statewide voter initiative, Proposition 350, which prohibited mandatory pupil assignment outside neighborhood schools for the purpose of improving racial balance.[55] Only three school districts with integration programs—Seattle, Pasco, and Tacoma—were affected by the initiative, and they joined numerous community organizations in challenging the provisions under the equal protection clause. The Supreme Court agreed with the Ninth Circuit Court of Appeals's conclusion that the initiative created an impermissible racial classification by treating pupil assignments for racial balance differently than assignments for other purposes. The appellate court also reasoned that the initiative was prompted by discriminatory motive and that it reallocated political power by "allowing a state-wide majority to usurp traditional local authority over local school board educational policies," which specifically burdened minority interests.[56]

In contrast, the Supreme Court upheld an amendment to the California Constitution, Proposition I, prohibiting mandatory busing except to remedy violations of the fourteenth amendment.[57] Prior to adopting Proposition I, the California Constitution prohibited de facto as well as de jure segregation, thus requiring remedial plans in school districts where violations of the Federal Constitution had *not* been established.[58] The Supreme Court concluded that California was not legally obligated to maintain more stringent standards than required by the fourteenth amendment, which only prohibits de jure segregation. In short, California's commitment to remedy de facto segregation by ensuring racially balanced schools could be altered by the voters in the state. Since Proposition I did not interfere with the authority of federal courts to order mandatory busing to remedy violations of the equal protection clause, the mere repeal of the additional state requirement was not considered sufficient to establish a federal constitutional violation without evidence of discriminatory motive. The majority rejected the assertion that Proposition I reallocated the decision-making process for minorities as was true with Proposition 350 in Washington.

The Court's approval of California's busing restriction indicates that once a state elects to go beyond fourteenth amendment requirements, it can subsequently repeal such action. The Supreme Court majority noted that Proposition I would nurture the neighborhood school concept, but emphasized that school districts could still undertake voluntary pupil reassignment programs and that mandatory busing could be ordered with evidence of a fourteenth amendment violation. Thus, busing limitation measures that would impede enforcement of the fourteenth amendment seem unlikely to withstand judicial scrutiny.

Alternatives to Busing

Because of the substantial opposition to busing and interdistrict pupil transfers for desegregation purposes, there is some sentiment that desegregation efforts should focus on improving the *quality* of educational programs rather than on pupil reassignment. Remedial programs, counseling and career guidance, and bilingual/bicultural education have been included in desegregation plans to overcome the effects of prior racial isolation.[59] Also, magnet schools, offering theme-oriented instructional programs, have been used in an effort to attract nonminority students to integrated schools by the lure of exciting curriculum alternatives. Federal funds have been made available to assist school districts in establishing such magnet school programs.[60] While instructional remedies traditionally were considered supplements to student reassignment plans, magnet schools and other efforts to improve the quality of instruction have become important components of desegregation plans currently being implemented in cities such as Baton Rouge, Chicago, Cincinnati, Detroit, and Nashville.[61]

Magnet schools have been established as an alternative to interdistrict busing in the Houston Independent School District (HISD). In 1980 the Justice Department had asked for the merger of the HISD with twenty-two surrounding suburban districts, but in 1983 the Fifth Circuit Court of Appeals ruled that the city school district had eliminated vestiges of segregation in its schools.[62] Rejecting the interdistrict remedy, the appeals court reasoned that the single-race schools remaining were the result of uncontrollable population shifts in the city characterized by an increasing minority and Hispanic population. In 1984 the Mexican-American Legal Defense and Educational Fund and the HISD signed a settlement designed to end twenty-eight years of desegregation litigation.[63] The settlement requires affirmative action to recruit blacks and Hispanics in administrative and teaching positions and establishes a goal of 40 percent white students at the twenty-five magnet schools designed to attract nonminorities back into the HISD, which currently has a white student population of only 19 percent. An unusual aspect of the plan requires the HISD to take affirmative steps toward the goal of having students score at or above national norms on several standardized tests and establishes a seven-member panel to monitor student achievement in the school district.[64] The agreement allows challengers to seek court-ordered enforcement of its terms for the five years that it will remain in effect.

In complicated litigation involving the Dallas School District, an alternative to massive pupil reassignment was approved by the Fifth Circuit Court of Appeals in 1985.[65] Previously, the federal district court had rejected a plan to give minority students the option of remaining in their neighborhood schools, thereby waiving their constitutional right to be transported to desegregated schools.[66] Subsequently, the school board proposed a plan to return 2,300 minority students in intermediate elementary grades to neighborhood schools that would be remedial in nature. The district court approved the plan, and the appellate court held that the district court acted within its authority in approving the remedial program calling for partial suspension of the previous pupil reassignment plan. Even though the modification established one-race remedial centers, the appeals court found it to be an appropriate remedy to attain the goal of closing achievement gaps in reading.

Two federal appeals courts have reached opposite conclusions regarding school boards' obligations to continue student reassignment plans once unitary status has been attained, and the Supreme Court declined to review both rulings. The Norfolk, Virginia School Board sought to end court-ordered, crosstown busing and to return to neighborhood-based schools and voluntary means to achieve desegregation. The federal district court approved the neighborhood school plan, and in 1986 the Fourth Circuit Court of Appeals affirmed this decision.[67] Since the school district had been declared unitary in 1975, the appeals court reasoned that school officials had satisfied their affirmative duty to dismantle the dual school system and had no continuing obligation to bus students, even though ten of the district's thirty-six elementary schools would become more than 90 percent minority. The appellate court noted that once a school district has been found to be unitary, challengers have the burden of proving the existence of discriminatory intent. This burden was not met by those contesting the school board's plan to eliminate busing for desegregation purposes. The court further recognized that the school board could legitimately consider the impact of "white flight" in designing a plan to stabilize school integration. The Justice Department supported the school district, arguing that the district had eliminated de jure segregation and should be free to implement any student assignment plan as long as purposeful discrimination is not involved. The Department claimed that it is time for Norfolk and many other school systems that have exhibited good faith compliance with court-ordered desegregation plans to "regain responsibility for running their public schools."[68]

However, the Tenth Circuit Court of Appeals rejected this reasoning and reversed the trial court's endorsement of the Oklahoma City School Board's plan to curtail crosstown busing.[69] Noting that the school district had achieved unitary status in 1977, the trial court found no evidence that school officials had subsequently engaged in purposeful discrimination. Thus, the trial court concluded that the school district's affirmative duty to desegregate its schools had been satisfied and continuing judicial intervention was unnecessary. Reversing, the appeals court concluded that the trial court erred in not reopening the case to allow plaintiffs to present evidence that the neighborhood school plan with racially identifiable schools was unconstitutional. Rejecting the contention that once a finding of unitariness has been entered, all judicial oversight to enforce the original decree is terminated, the appeals court reasoned that the Justice Department's position "ignores the fact that the purpose of court-ordered school integration is not only to achieve, but also to *maintain,* a unitary school system."[70] The court noted that the plaintiffs were not asserting that the school board should be legally responsible for demographic changes within the school system, but that the board intentionally abandoned a plan designed to achieve desegregated schools and substituted a plan with an apparant segregative effect.

Since the Supreme Court declined to review these conflicting appellate decisions, the applicable legal principles have not yet been clarified. Until they are, other school districts that have attained unitary status are likely to consider modifications in their desegregation plans, with greater reliance on voluntary means to achieve integrated schools.

An End in Sight?

The end of judicial monitoring appears to be in sight for some school districts that have been involved in lengthy desegregation litigation. For example, in 1985 a federal judge released the Columbus, Ohio, School District from court control over its desegregation plan, finding that the school board and administrators had acted in good faith in abiding with the court's orders.[71] Plaintiffs had argued that the school district should not be released from court jurisdiction because of alleged racial bias in student disciplinary practices. Specifically, a higher percentage of black students were expelled and subjected to other disciplinary measures in Columbus public schools. Finding no direct evidence that the discipline disparity resulted from racial bias, the judge awarded the school district unitary status.

Boston's desegregation litigation also appears to be drawing to a close after over 400 court orders spanning twelve years. Judge Garrity made national headlines in the mid-1970s when he ordered his own experts to create and monitor a desegregation plan after the Boston School Committee failed to develop an acceptable proposal. In 1982 the judge relinquished jurisdiction over two of the twelve areas he had monitored since 1972—special education and local business/school partnerships. In 1985 Judge Garrity announced that the court would retain "standby jurisdiction" to ensure that the school district complies with existing orders pertaining to student assignments, faculty desegregation, vocational education, facilities, and parent councils. The court relinquished oversight in connection with transportation, discipline, safety and security, special education, bilingual education, and pairings of academic and business institutions. Although the judiciary has not completely withdrawn from the case, Judge Garrity has indicated that Boston has demonstrated general compliance with the court orders and should be given the responsibility to monitor most of its own desegregation activities.[72]

Also in 1984, the Cincinnati Public Schools, the National Association for the Advancement of Colored People (NAACP), and the state of Ohio reached a settlement intended to end ten years of desegregation litigation.[73] The settlement gives school officials flexibility in using various voluntary means such as magnet schools, remedial instruction, and community education programs to achieve desegregated schools, and the state has agreed to provide $35 million for these programs. However, if the school district fails to meet numerical goals of reducing racial isolation in the schools within seven years, the NAACP retains the right to seek judicial enforcement of the settlement.

While the climate seems more conducive to negotiated settlements than was true a decade ago, the end of judicial monitoring of desegregation efforts is in sight for a relatively small number of school districts. Until unitary status is achieved, school districts operate under an affirmative duty to eliminate the effects of past purposeful discrimination. In most situations where unconstitutional school segregation has been found, the school districts remain embroiled in lawsuits and judicial oversight of their desegregation plans.

For example, the Denver school district is still involved in litigation. In 1985 a federal judge rejected the school board's request to declare the school district "unitary," and thus school officials developed a new proposal focusing on staff and instructional remedies and maintaining substantial student reassignment.[74] The same year, the Sixth Circuit Court of Appeals instructed the lower court to retain jurisdiction over desegregation activities in the Detroit school system. The appeals court overturned the federal district court's order disbanding the court-created monitoring commission and terminating jurisdiction over certain components of the desegregation plan (the code of student conduct and community relations program).[75]

Similarly, the Fourth Circuit Court of Appeals recently ruled that the federal district court had continuing jurisdiction in Prince George's County, Virginia, because unitary status had not yet been achieved to the court's satisfaction. An unusual aspect of this case was the appeals court's conclusion that the burden was on school officials to refute the presumption of discrimination established by the disproportionate number of minority students placed in special education classes. Similarly, since unitary status had not been attained, the burden was placed on the school district to disprove the inference of discrimination in the underrepresentation of minority students in the district's program for gifted students.[76]

In a somewhat unique desegregation case, a federal district court held that education and housing officials were jointly liable for school segregation in Yonkers, New York. Although the impact of housing patterns on school segregation has been noted in several cases, in this decision the court found municipal housing authorities legally responsible for the fact that schools in a portion of the school district remained primarily minority. The court noted that for forty years housing officials had located all low-income housing in a predominantly nonwhite section of the city. Since the court found that actions of school authorities perpetuated the segregated conditions created by the housing policies, joint liability was assessed.[77]

Although some school districts appear to have turned the corner in satisfying the judiciary that they are making good-faith efforts to equalize educational opportunities, the end of judicial oversight is not on the horizon for numerous other school districts. Courts seem more receptive to strategies other than pupil reassignment to remedy constitutional violations, but they remain willing to intervene in the internal affairs of schools if necessary to protect minority pupils' rights.

STAFF DESEGREGATION REMEDIES

Remedial plans requiring the reassignment of personnel to integrate school facilities have been common in desegregation decrees.[78] Federal courts have emphasized that faculty integration is an essential component of effective desegregation remedies. In 1969 the Supreme Court endorsed a lower court's order requiring a southern school board to carry out its duty to attain a unitary school district by moving "toward a goal under which 'in each school the ratio of white to Negro faculty members is substantially the same as it is throughout the system.' "[79] In the subsequent *Swann* decree, the Court reiterated that the white/black representation among faculty members in each school should approximate the district ratio.[80] More recently, the Third Circuit Court of Appeals upheld a collective bargaining agreement imposing transfers to ensure racially balanced faculties in the Philadelphia School District.[81] The rationale for staff reassignments in desegregation decrees is *not* to remedy employment discrimination, but to vindicate the constitutional rights of minority students by assuring them the equal educational opportunities guaranteed by the fourteenth amendment.[82]

The conversion from dual to unitary school systems often has been accompanied by a reduction in personnel, and in 1969 the Fifth Circuit Court of Appeals established criteria to prevent black teachers from bearing a disproportionate burden in consolidation efforts. The criteria announced in *Singleton v. Jackson Municipal Separate School District* provided that: (1) race must not be a factor in hiring, assignment, promotion, demotion, salary, or dismissal; (2) a reduction in professional staff must be made on the basis of "objective and reasonable nondiscriminatory standards"; and (3) nonracial objective criteria must be developed by the school board prior to any reductions.[83] During the 1970s courts often were called on to apply the *Singleton* criteria in assessing the legality of staff reduction activity in school districts dismantling dual school systems. This litigation was concentrated in the fifth federal circuit, where the bulk of court-ordered desegregation activity was taking place. Federal district courts and the Fifth Circuit Court of Appeals overturned several dismissals of black teachers and administrators where school boards had not applied preestablished objective criteria in making the decisions.[84] However, the number of cases initiated under the *Singleton* criteria has declined in recent years because major consolidation efforts necessitated by desegregation have been accomplished. Since 1980, few plaintiffs have been successful in relying on *Singleton* to obtain relief for their dismissals.[85]

Recent controversies have not focused on consolidation activities, but rather on efforts to give preference to minorities to attain or maintain racially balanced staffs in school districts undergoing desegregation during a period of declining student enrollments. The use of racial considerations in hiring and assigning staff has been upheld in court-ordered as well as voluntary desegregation plans where race-conscious remedies have been necessary to eliminate the lingering effects of school segregation.[86] The legitimacy of such employment remedies has been buttressed by two recent Supreme Court decisions upholding temporary racial preferences in affirmative action plans that benefit some employees who have not suffered discrimination. As discussed in chapter 9, in one case the Court upheld the voluntary adoption of race-conscious promotion goals, even though they placed obligations on the employer that a court might not be authorized to impose.[87] In the companion case, the Court endorsed the judicial imposition of a racial membership goal where a labor union had been found guilty of egregious prior discrimination against minorities.[88]

More controversial than racial preferences in hiring, assignment, and promotion practices have been efforts to protect minority employees from layoffs because such plans abrogate the seniority rights of nonminorities. Racial quotas in reducing personnel have been defended as necessary to compensate for the disparate impact of seniority-based staff reductions on minority employees who are disproportionately represented among recent hires. Some courts have ordered school districts to impose racial quotas in laying off personnel where the districts have *not attained unitary status*. For example, in 1982 the First Circuit Court of Appeals affirmed a district court's order requiring the Boston School Committee to hire black and white teachers on a one-to-one basis until the percentage of black faculty reflected the black population of Boston (20 percent), to protect minority teachers from layoffs, and to give absolute recall preference to minority teachers until the goal was attained.[89] The court reasoned that minority students were the identified discrimination victims and that they have a constitutional right to attend schools with teaching staffs reflecting the racial composition of the community. The Second Circuit Court of Appeals also upheld the imposition of hiring and layoff quotas to protect "the existing ratio of minority to majority teachers" in the Buffalo School District.[90] But the appellate court did not require the school district's teaching force to reflect the proportion of minorities in Buffalo and departed from the First Circuit Court of Appeals in concluding that race should not be a factor in recalling teachers. The Supreme Court declined to hear appeals in both of these cases, thus leaving the appellate rulings intact.

However, in 1986 the Supreme Court delivered a significant decision, *Wygant v. Jackson Board of Education,* striking down a school district's negotiated agreement that protected minority teachers from layoffs to maintain the percentage of minority teachers employed prior to any reduction in force.[91] In this case, in contrast to the Boston and Buffalo situations, the school district was not operating under a court-ordered desegregation plan. The Supreme Court viewed *Wygant* as an employment discrimination case rather than a school desegregation case. As discussed in chapter 9, the plurality opinion in *Wygant* rejected the contention that the racial composition of faculty should reflect the racial composition of the student body to provide minority role models for students. The plurality reasoned that racial classifications in layoff policies must be justified by convincing evidence of prior discrimination, and means employed must be narrowly tailored to remedy such discrimination. Finding that the contested staff reduction policy did not satisfy either criteria, the plurality noted that school officials had other means, such as hiring goals, to increase faculty integration.

Whether the continuing impact of a dual school system would constitute the necessary compelling justification for layoff quotas was not clarified by the Supreme Court in the *Wygant* decision, and federal appellate courts have rendered conflicting opinions on this issue. The Sixth Circuit Court of Appeals struck down a lower court's order imposing a quota of 20 percent minority teachers in the Kalamazoo School District.[92] The order, protecting minorities from layoffs, was found to abrogate the seniority rights of nonminority teachers and to be unnecessary to protect the constitutional rights of students. The appeals court declared that students "do not have a constitutional right to attend a school with a teaching staff of any particular racial composition."[93]

However, the Supreme Court declined to review the Boston and Buffalo decisions in which federal appellate courts upheld the judicial imposition of layoff as well as hiring quotas to vindicate students' constitutional rights.[94] Thus, the legal status of preferential layoff policies in desegregation plans remains ambiguous. There is some sentiment that such racial preferences in staff reductions are permissible in school districts where unitary status has *not* been attained. However, the *Wygant* decision casts doubt on the legality of layoff quotas in the absence of clear and convincing evidence of prior discrimination and where other means are available to attain legitimate desegregation objectives.

CONCLUSION

From the recent and pending decisions, trends in desegregation litigation are difficult to identify. Some courts have endorsed alternative remedies to pupil reassignment and have seemed less concerned about the existence of single-race schools than was true in the 1970s. However, other courts have continued to favor busing plans to reduce racial isolation, and most courts have retained jurisdiction over desegregation cases with the option of subsequent judicial review to ensure the effectiveness of the remedial action.

Although it has been well over a quarter of a century since the landmark *Brown* decision was rendered, desegregation of American public schools has not been accomplished. Segregated housing has exacerbated the problems associated with attaining integrated public schools. There are no signs of a decrease in desegregation litigation, and keeping abreast of the complicated developments in a single case is extremely difficult as appeals and remands travel back and forth among the various federal court levels. Despite the complexity of desegregation litigation, several generalizations can be ascertained from decisions to date.

1. School segregation resulting from state laws or other intentional state action (e.g., gerrymandering attendance zones, selecting sites for new schools to maintain racial isolation, assigning staff to perpetuate the racial identification of schools, and implementing student transfer policies that allow students to avoid desegregation) violates the equal protection clause of the fourteenth amendment.
2. Segregatory effect alone does not establish unconstitutional intent; however, the consequences of official actions can be considered in substantiating discriminatory intent.
3. Where a school district has *not* achieved unitary status, school officials have an affirmative duty to eliminate the dual school system; under such a duty, official actions or nonaction are assessed in terms of their effect on reducing segregation, and the burden is placed on school officials to prove that predominantly one-race schools are not the product of past racial discrimination.
4. School districts do not have an obligation to alter attendance zones or implement other remedies (e.g., student reassignment from neighborhood schools) *after* unitary status is attained and resegregation occurs through no fault of school officials.
5. The scope of the desegregation remedy cannot be broader than the scope of the constitutional violation.
6. States are not obligated to go beyond the requirements of the

fourteenth amendment in addressing desegregation and can repeal state mandates imposing additional requirements.

7. Interdistrict desegregation remedies cannot be judicially imposed unless there is evidence of intentional discrimination with substantial effect across district lines.
8. School districts cannot plead "lack of funds" as a defense for failing to remedy unconstitutional school segregation; the state can be required to share the costs of remedial plans if the state has played a role in creating or maintaining the segregatory conditions.
9. Magnet schools and voluntary transfer policies can be central components of desegregation plans as long as such remedies are effective in desegregating schools.
10. Racial preferences can be judicially imposed or voluntarily adopted in hiring and assigning personnel to advance school desegregation efforts; racial quotas in reducing staff cannot be adopted or imposed without clear evidence of prior discrimination or where less intrusive means, such as hiring goals, are available to remedy past discriminatory practices.

NOTES

1. 163 U.S. 537 (1886).
2. Roberts v. City of Boston, 59 Mass. (5 Cush.) 198 (1849).
3. Gong Lum v. Rice, 275 U.S. 78, 86 (1927).
4. *See* Sweatt v. Painter, 339 U.S. 629 (1950); McLaurin v. Oklahoma State Regents for Higher Educ., 339 U.S. 637 (1950); Sipuel v. University of Oklahoma, 332 U.S. 631 (1948); Missouri *ex rel.* Gaines v. Canada, 305 U.S. 337 (1938).
5. Brown I, 347 U.S. 483, 495 (1954). For a discussion of litigation leading to the Supreme Court's decision, *see* Robert Kluger, *Simple Justice* (New York, NY: Knopf, 1975). Since the equal protection clause applies only to state and not federal action, the Supreme Court relied on the due process clause of the fifth amendment in striking down segregated public schools in Washington, D.C. The Court reasoned that protected "liberties" embrace freedom from racial discrimination imposed by the federal government. Bolling v. Sharpe, 347 U.S. 497 (1954).
6. Brown v. Board of Educ. of Topeka (Brown II), 349 U.S. 294, 300 (1955).
7. *See* Milliken v. Bradley, 433 U.S. 267 (1977). Racial classifications are considered "inherently suspect" and are presumed invalid unless justified by a compelling state interest. *See* Loving v. Virginia, 388 U.S. 1 (1967); text with note 2, chapter 9.
8. Cooper v. Aaron, 358 U.S. 1 (1958).
9. Griffin v. Prince Edward County School Bd., 377 U.S. 218 (1964).
10. In Briggs v. Elliott, 132 F. Supp. 776, 777 (E.D. S.C. 1955), the federal district

court declared that "[t]he Constitution . . . does not require integration . . . [but] merely forbids discrimination."

11. Green v. County School Bd. of New Kent County, 391 U.S. 430 (1968); Raney v. Board of Educ., 391 U.S. 443 (1968); Monroe v. Board of Comm'rs of the City of Jackson, Tennessee, 391 U.S. 450 (1968).
12. Alexander v. Holmes County Bd. of Educ., 396 U.S. 19, 20 (1969) (per curiam).
13. 402 U.S. 1 (1971).
14. *Id.* at 30–31.
15. 42 U.S.C. § 2000d (prohibits discrimination on the basis of race, color, or national origin in federally assisted programs or activities).
16. *Twenty Years After Brown: Equality of Educational Opportunity* (Washington, DC: U.S. Commission on Civil Rights, 1975), pp. 46–47.
17. In the 1960s, some courts reasoned that school segregation did not warrant remedial action in school districts where segregation was not imposed by law. *See* Deal v. Cincinnati Bd. of Educ., 369 F.2d 55 (6th Cir. 1966), *cert. denied,* 389 U.S. 847 (1967); Bell v. School Bd. of Gary, Indiana, 324 F.2d 209 (7th Cir. 1963), *cert. denied,* 377 U.S. 924 (1964). In the early 1970s, however, several courts concluded that remedial action was required in situations where state action had encouraged racial imbalance in public schools, even though dual school systems were not required by law in 1954. *See* Booker v. Special School Dist. No. 1, Minneapolis, Minn., 351 F. Supp. 799 (Minn. 1972); Johnson v. San Francisco Unified School Dist., 339 F. Supp. 1315 (N.D. Cal. 1971).
18. 413 U.S. 189, 198 (1973).
19. *Id.* at 208.
20. 418 U.S. 717 (1974).
21. Washington v. Davis, 426 U.S. 229, 240 (1976).
22. *Id.* at 242. *See also* Austin Independent School Dist. v. United States, 429 U.S. 990 (1976); Metropolitan School Dist. v. Buckley, 429 U.S. 1068 (1977); School Dist. of Omaha v. United States, 433 U.S. 667 (1977) (per curiam); Brennan v. Armstrong, 433 U.S. 672 (1977) (per curiam).
23. Pasadena City Bd. of Educ. v. Spangler, 427 U.S. 424 (1976).
24. *See* Arthur v. Nyquist, 573 F.2d 134, 140–143 (2d Cir. 1978); NAACP v. Lansing Bd. of Educ., 559 F.2d 1042, 1046–1048 (6th Cir. 1977), *cert. denied,* 434 U.S. 997 (1977); Hart v. Community School Bd. of Educ., 512 F.2d 37, 50 (2d Cir. 1975); Armstrong v. O'Connell, 451 F. Supp. 817, 822–827 (E.D. Wis. 1978).
25. In 1977 the Supreme Court upheld a zoning decision that tended to perpetuate racially segregated housing patterns, reasoning that plaintiffs failed to carry the burden of proving that race was a motivating factor in the zoning decision. Arlington Heights v. Metropolitan Housing Development Corp., 429 U.S. 252 (1977). Two years later in a case involving alleged sex discrimination under the equal protection clause, the Court recognized that intent requires more than recognition of consequences: "It implies that the decision maker . . . selected or reaffirmed a particular course of action at least in part 'because of,' not merely 'in spite of,' its adverse effects upon an identifiable group." Personnel Administrator of Massachusetts v. Feeney, 442 U.S. 256, 279 (1979).

26. Dayton Bd. of Educ. v. Brinkman (Dayton I), 433 U.S. 406 (1977).
27. Dayton Bd. of Educ. v. Brinkman (Dayton II), 443 U.S. 526 (1979).
28. *Id.* at 538.
29. *Id.*
30. Columbus Bd. of Educ. v. Penick, 443 U.S. 449, 461 (1979).
31. *See* Richard King, "Desegregation, Busing and the Merger of Local School Districts," *School Law Bulletin,* vol. 16, no. 3 (summer 1985), pp. 15–20.
32. Milliken v. Bradley, 418 U.S. 717, 745 (1974).
33. Lee v. Lee County Bd. of Educ., 639 F.2d 1243, 1256 (5th Cir. 1981).
34. Goldsboro City Bd. of Educ. v. Wayne County Bd. of Educ., 745 F.2d 324 (4th Cir. 1984).
35. *See* Evans v. Buchanan, 416 F. Supp. 328 (D. Del. 1976), *aff'd,* 555 F.2d 373 (3d Cir. 1977), *cert. denied,* 434 U.S. 880 (1977); Evans v. Buchanan, 447 F. Supp. 982 (D. Del. 1978), *aff'd,* 582 F.2d 750 (3d Cir. 1978); Newburg Area Council Inc. v. Board of Educ. of Jefferson County, Kentucky, 510 F.2d 1358 (6th Cir. 1974), *cert. denied,* 421 U.S. 931 (1975). *See also* Gordon Foster, "Trends in Interdistrict Remedies," *NOLPE School Law Reporter,* vol. 8 (1979), pp. 145–155.
36. United States v. Board of School Comm'rs, 637 F.2d 1101 (7th Cir. 1980), *cert. denied sub nom.* Metropolitan School Dist. v. Buckley, 449 U.S. 838 (1980); United States v. Board of School Comm'rs, 677 F.2d 1185 (7th Cir. 1982), *cert. denied sub nom.* Orr v. Board of School Comm'rs, 459 U.S. 1086 (1982).
37. Liddell v. Board of Educ. of St. Louis, 567 F. Supp. 1037 (E.D. Mo. 1983), *aff'd in part, rev'd in part,* 731 F.2d 1294 (8th Cir. 1984), *cert. denied,* 105 S. Ct. 82 (1984). *See also* Liddell v. Board of Educ. of St. Louis, 758 F.2d 290 (8th Cir. 1985). For a discussion of the St. Louis plan, *see* Daniel Monti, "*Brown's* Velvet Cushion: Metropolitan Desegregation and the Politics of Illusion," *Metropolitan Education,* vol. 1, no. 1 (1986), pp. 56–61.
38. Little Rock School Dist. v. Pulaski County Special School Dist. No. 1, 597 F. Supp. 1220 (E.D. Ark. 1984), *aff'd in part, rev'd in part,* 778 F.2d 404 (8th Cir. 1985), *cert. denied,* 106 S. Ct. 2926 (1986).
39. Court costs alone have been substantial in some cases. For example, the Cleveland school board spent over one million dollars on desegregation litigation from 1974 until 1978. *See* Nathaniel R. Jones, "The Desegregation of Urban Schools 30 Years After *Brown,*" *University of Colorado Law Review,* vol. 55 (1984), pp. 543–544.
40. *See* Reed v. Rhodes, 662 F.2d 1219 (6th Cir. 1981), *cert. denied sub nom.* Ohio State Bd. of Educ. v. Reed, 445 U.S. 1018 (1982); Morgan v. Kerrigan, 530 F.2d 401 (1st Cir. 1976). *See also* Lee v. Macon County Bd. of Educ., 616 F.2d 805, 811 (5th Cir. 1980), in which the appeals court declared that "cost alone cannot justify continued infractions of constitutional principles."
41. *See* Arthur v. Nyquist, 712 F.2d 809 (2d Cir. 1983) *cert. denied sub nom.* Griffin v. Board of Educ. of City of Buffalo, New York, 466 U.S. 936 (1984); Liddle v. Board of Educ. of St. Louis, 731 F.2d 1294 (8th Cir. 1984), *cert. denied,* 105 S. Ct. 82 (1984).
42. Milliken v. Bradley, 433 U.S. 267 (1977).
43. Jenkins v. State of Missouri, 593 F. Supp. 1485 (W.D. Mo. 1984) *aff'd as*

modified, No. 85–1765 (8th Cir. 1986). *See also* Liddle v. Board of Educ. of St. Louis, 758 F.2d 290 (8th Cir. 1985); text with note 37, *supra.*

44. United States v. Board of School Comm'rs, 677 F.2d 1185 (7th Cir. 1982).
45. Brinkman v. Gilligan, 610 F. Supp. 1288 (S.D. Ohio 1985).
46. Kelley v. Metropolitan County Bd. of Educ. of Nashville and Davidson County, 615 F. Supp. 1139 (M.D. Tenn. 1985).
47. The Emergency School Assistance Program, 20 U.S.C. § 4052, later became the Emergency School Aid Act, 20 U.S.C. § 3192. For a discussion of federal categorical aid programs, *see Harvard Educational Review,* vol. 52, no. 4 (1982) (entire issue).
48. In a study of twenty-eight of the nation's largest school districts, it was reported that in the 1983–84 school year the districts were spending only one-fourth of the amount on desegregation activities that they had received under ESAA two years earlier. Richard Jung and Robert Stonehill, "Big Districts and the Block Grant: A Cross-Time Assessment of the Fiscal Impacts," *Journal of Education Finance,* vol. 10 (1985), p. 322.
49. United States v. Board of Educ. of Chicago, 592 F. Supp. 967 (N.D. Ill. 1984), *vacated and remanded,* 744 F.2d 1300 (7th Cir. 1984), *cert. denied,* 105 S. Ct. 2358 (1985), *on remand,* 621 F. Supp. 1296 (N.D. Ill. 1985), *vacated and remanded,* 799 F.2d 281 (7th Cir. 1986).
50. *See Education Daily,* August 22, 1986, pp. 3–4.
51. *See* Vaughns v. Board of Educ. of Prince George's County, 758 F.2d 983 (4th Cir. 1985); Kelley Metropolitan County Bd. of Educ. of Nashville and Davidson County, Tennessee, 687 F.2d 814 (6th Cir. 1982), *cert. denied,* 459 U.S. 1183 (1983); United States v. South Bend Community School Corp., 511 F. Supp. 1352 (N.D. Ind. 1981), *aff'd,* 692 F.2d 623 (7th Cir. 1982).
52. United States v. Board of Educ. of Chicago, 554 F. Supp. 912, 924 (N.D. Ill. 1983).
53. 20 U.S.C. § 1701–1758. Title IV of the Civil Rights Act of 1964, 42 U.S.C. § 2000c–6, authorizes the Attorney General to seek redress on behalf of individuals denied equal protection of the laws, but it also stipulates that "nothing herein shall empower any official or court of the United States to issue any order seeking to achieve a racial balance in any school by requiring the transportation of pupils or students from one school to another or one school district to another in order to achieve such racial balance." Both Title IV and the EEOA have been interpreted as preserving the authority of federal courts to remedy constitutional violations; thus, they do not restrict the judiciary in ordering remedies for intentional school segregation. *See* Michael Combs, "The Supreme Court as a National Policy Maker: A Historical-Legal Analysis of School Segregation," *Southern University Law Review,* vol. 8 (1982), pp. 222–225.
54. North Carolina State Bd. of Educ. v. Swann, 402 U.S. 43 (1971).
55. Seattle School Dist. No. 1 v. Washington, 633 F.2d 1338 (9th Cir. 1980), *aff'd,* 458 U.S. 457 (1982).
56. *Id.,* 633 F.2d at 1344.
57. Crawford v. Board of Educ., 458 U.S. 527 (1982).
58. In 1976 the California Supreme Court interpreted the state constitution as

requiring school boards "to take reasonable steps to alleviate segregation in the public schools, whether the segregation be de facto or de jure in origin." Crawford v. Board of Educ., 551 P.2d 28, 34 (Cal. 1976).

59. *See* Milliken v. Bradley, 433 U.S. 267 (1977); Evans v. Buchanan, 447 F. Supp. 982 (D. Del. 1978).
60. Education for Economic Security Act, Title VII—Magnet School Assistance, 20 U.S.C. § 4052. *See also* 34 C.F.R. Part 280. This law has been controversial because an amendment prohibited the use of the federal funds for instruction in "secular humanism." Subsequently, this restriction on the use of funds was removed. *See* note 98, chapter 2.
61. *See* Jones, "Urban Desegregation"; Dennis Doyle and Marsha Levine, "Magnet Schools: Choice and Quality in Public Education," *Phi Delta Kappan,* vol. 65 (1984), pp. 265–269; *Education Week,* February 20, 1984, pp. 1, 15; *Education Week,* January 8, 1986, p. 8.
62. Ross v. Houston Independent School Dist., 699 F.2d 218 (5th Cir. 1983).
63. *See Education Daily,* September 6, 1984, p. 7.
64. *Education Week,* November 21, 1984, p. 3.
65. Tasby v. Black Coalition to Maximize Educ., 771 F.2d 849 (5th Cir. 1985). *See also* Tasby v. Wright, 630 F. Supp. 597 (N.D. Tex. 1986).
66. Tasby v. Wright, 520 F. Supp. 683 (N.D. Tex. 1981), *aff'd in part, rev'd in part,* 713 F.2d 90 (5th Cir. 1983).
67. Riddick v. School Bd. of City of Norfolk, 627 F. Supp. 814 (E.D. Va. 1985), *aff'd,* 784 F.2d 521 (4th Cir. 1986), *cert. denied,* 107 S. Ct. 420 (1986).
68. *See Education Week,* December 12, 1984, p. 18; *Education Daily,* December 7, 1984, p. 5.
69. Dowell v. Board of Educ. of Oklahoma City Public Schools, 606 F. Supp. 1548 (W.D. Okla. 1985), *rev'd,* 795 F.2d 1516 (10th Cir. 1986), *cert. denied,* 107 S. Ct. 420 (1986).
70. *Id.,* 795 F.2d at 1520.
71. *See Education Daily,* May 7, 1985, p. 6. For a discussion of litigation involving the Columbus schools, *see* Martha McCarthy, "Dayton and Columbus: A Tale of Two Cities," in *School Law in Contemporary Society,* M. McGhehey, ed. (Topeka, KS: National Organization on Legal Problems of Education, 1980), pp. 36–58.
72. *See* Morgan v. Nucci, 620 F. Supp. 214 (D. Mass. 1985); *Education Week,* September 11, 1985, p. 10. For a discussion of litigation involving Boston, *see* Jones, "The Desegregation of Urban Schools," pp. 537–541.
73. The consent decree was signed after the federal district court removed the suburban school districts from the suit. *See* Bronson v. Board of Educ. of Cincinnati, 578 F. Supp. 1091 (S.D. Ohio 1984).
74. Keyes v. School Dist. No. 1, 609 F. Supp. 1491 (D. Colo. 1985).
75. Bradley v. Milliken, 772 F. Supp. 266 (6th Cir. 1985).
76. Vaughns v. Board of Educ. of Prince George's County, 758 F.2d 983 (4th Cir. 1985).
77. Yonkers Branch, NAACP v. Yonkers Bd. of Educ., 611 F. Supp. 730 (S.D. N.Y. 1985).
78. While staff remedies have been secondary to student remedies in most desegregation plans, the Atlanta settlement was a notable exception. In the 1973 Atlanta compromise, the terms of the settlement led to little if any integration

of students in the school district which had a predominantly minority student enrollment. Central features of the settlement were that half of the administrative positions as well as the superintendent would be black. *See* Calhoun v. Cook, 487 F.2d 680 (5th Cir. 1973).

79. United States v. Montgomery Bd. of Educ., 395 U.S. 225, 232 (1969).
80. Swann v. Charlotte-Mecklenburg Bd. of Educ., 402 U.S. 1, 19 (1971).
81. Kromnick v. School Dist. of Philadelphia, 739 F.2d 894 (3d Cir. 1984), *cert. denied,* 105 S. Ct. 782 (1985).
82. Prior to 1986 several federal appellate courts adopted the "role model" theory, concluding that students have a constitutional right to be educated in school districts with integrated faculties. *See* cases in notes 89 and 90, *infra. But see* text with note 91, *infra.*
83. 419 F.2d 1211 (5th Cir. 1970).
84. *See* Ward v. Kelly, 515 F.2d 908 (5th Cir. 1975); United States v. Coffeeville Consol. School Dist., 513 F.2d 244 (5th Cir. 1975); Wright v. Houston Independent School Dist., 393 F. Supp. 1149 (S.D. Tex. 1975).
85. *See* Lujan v. Franklin County Bd. of Educ., 766 F.2d 917 (6th Cir. 1985); MacDonald v. Ferguson Reorganized School Dist., 530 F. Supp. 469 (E.D. Mo. 1981); *The Yearbook of School Law,* Philip Piele, ed. (Topeka, KS: National Organization on Legal Problems of Education, 1981), p. 31; *The Yearbook of School Law,* 1982, p. 37.
86. *See* Kromnick v. School Dist. of Philadelphia, 739 F.2d 894 (3d Cir. 1984), *cert. denied,* 105 S. Ct. 782 (1985); Zaslawsky v. Board of Educ. of Los Angeles, 610 F.2d 661 (9th Cir. 1979); text with notes 89 and 90, *infra.*
87. Local No. 93, International Ass'n of Firefighters, AFL-CIO v. City of Cleveland, 106 S. Ct. 3063 (1986). *See* text with note 65, chapter 9.
88. Local 28 of the Sheet Metal Workers' International Ass'n and Local 28 Joint Apprenticeship Comm. v. Equal Employment Opportunities Comm'n, 106 S. Ct. 3019 (1986).
89. Morgan v. O'Bryant, 671 F.2d 23 (1st Cir. 1982), *cert. denied sub nom.* Boston Ass'n of School Administrators and Supervisors v. Morgan, 459 U.S. 827 (1982); Boston Teachers Union v. Boston School Comm., 671 F.2d 23 (1st Cir. 1982), *cert. denied,* 459 U.S. 881 (1982). The Boston School Committee was temporarily relieved of its 25 percent minority recruitment goal until all laid-off tenured teachers were recalled.
90. Arthur v. Nyquist, 712 F.2d 816 (2d Cir. 1983), *cert. denied,* 104 S. Ct. 3555 (1984). Prior to 1986, several courts also had upheld the *voluntary* adoption of affirmative action plans with layoff quotas to further school desegregation. *See* Wygant v. Jackson Bd. of Educ., 746 F.2d 1152 (6th Cir. 1984), *rev'd,* 106 S. Ct. 1842 (1986); Britton v. South Bend Community School Corp., 775 F.2d 794 (7th Cir. 1985), *vacated,* 783 F.2d 105 (7th Cir. 1986); Marsh v. Board of Educ. of the City of Flint, 762 F.2d 1009 (6th Cir. 1985), *vacated,* 106 S. Ct. 2240 (1986).
91. 106 S. Ct. 1842 (1986). *See* text with note 74, chapter 9.
92. Oliver v. Kalamazoo Bd. of Educ., 706 F.2d 757 (6th Cir. 1983).
93. *Id.* at 763.
94. *See* text with notes 89, 90, *supra.*

14

Conclusion: Summary of Legal Generalizations

Since World War II, courts have increasingly influenced the operation of American schools by interpreting statutory and constitutional mandates as they apply to students and teachers. Similarly, legislative bodies at both state and national levels have become assertive in enacting laws to promote educational equity and excellence. Citizens are demanding greater accountability from public education agencies and are becoming more knowledgeable in using legal tools to challenge arbitrary school practices. No longer are school personnel shielded from the critical eyes of legislators or justices, and there are indications that legal directives pertaining to schools will continue to increase in volume and complexity.

In the preceding chapters, principles of law have been presented as they apply to specific aspects of teachers' and students' rights and responsibilities. Constitutional and statutory provisions, in conjunction with judicial decisions, have been analyzed in an effort to depict the current status of the law. Many diverse topics have been explored, some with clearly established legal precedents and others where the law is still evolving.

The most difficult situations confronting school personnel are those where specific legislative or judicial guidelines are lacking. In such circumstances, educators must make judgments based on their professional training and general knowledge of the law as it applies to education. The following broad generalizations, synthesized from the preceding chapters, are presented to assist educators in making such determinations in their daily school activities.

GENERALIZATIONS

The legal control of public education resides with the state as one of its sovereign powers. In attempting to comply with the law, school personnel must keep in mind the scope of the state's authority to regulate educational activities. Courts have consistently held that state legislatures possess plenary power in establishing and operating public schools; this power is restricted only by federal and state constitutions and civil rights laws. Of course, where the federal judiciary has interpreted the United States Constitution as prohibiting a given practice in public schools, such as racial discrimination, the state or its agents cannot enact laws or policies that conflict with the constitutional mandate unless justified by a compelling governmental interest. However, if the Federal Constitution and civil rights laws have been interpreted as *permitting* a certain activity, states retain wide discretion in either restricting or expanding the practice.

For example, while the Supreme Court has rejected the assertion that probationary teachers have an inherent federal right to due process in situations involving contract nonrenewals, state legislatures have the authority to create such a right under state law. Similarly, the Supreme Court has declared that the use of corporal punishment in public schools does not abridge the Federal Constitution. Nonetheless, individual state legislatures can prohibit corporal punishment in public schools or require that certain procedures accompany its use.

Unless inherent rights are at stake, courts defer to the will of legislative bodies in determining educational matters. State legislatures have the authority to create and redesign school districts, to collect and distribute educational funds, and to determine teacher qualifications and curricular offerings. With such pervasive control vested in the states, a thorough understanding of the operation of an educational system can be acquired only by examining the individual states' statutes, administrative regulations, and judicial decisions interpreting such provisions. The existence of fifty separate state systems of public schools has produced wide divergence in operational practices that affect teachers and students.

Conditions for the employment of teachers are delineated through either statutes or state board of education regulations. For example, all states require that a teacher possess a valid teaching certificate based on satisfaction of certain minimum qualifications. Additionally, tenure laws define the permanency of the employer/employee relationship. Furthermore, the dismissal process for all teachers, tenured and nontenured, is circumscribed by state law and enforced by the judiciary. The scope of teachers' rights to engage in collective bargaining also is defined by state statute.

Like conditions of teacher employment, conditions of school attendance for students are specified in state law. Every state has enacted a compulsory attendance statute to ensure an educated citizenry. These laws are applicable to all children, with only a few legally recognized exceptions. In addition to mandating school attendance, states also have the authority to dictate courses of study and selection of instructional materials. Courts will not invalidate such decisions unless constitutional rights are abridged. Comparable reasoning also is applied by courts in upholding the state's power to establish graduation requirements, including the use of minimum competency tests as a prerequisite to receipt of a diploma. Courts have recognized that the establishment of academic standards is within the ambit of the state's legal authority.

It is widely held that local school boards control public education in this nation; local boards hold only those discretionary powers conferred by state law. Depending on the state, a local board's discretionary authority may be quite broad or narrowly defined by statutory guidelines, or somewhere between these extremes. School board regulations enacted pursuant to statutory authority are legally binding on employees and students. Hence, it is imperative for educators to become familiar with their respective state education laws and local school board regulations enacted to implement the laws.

All school policies and practices that impinge upon protected personal freedoms must be substantiated as necessary to advance the educational mission of the school. While the state and its agents have broad authority to regulate public schools, policies that impair federal constitutional rights must be justified by an overriding public interest. Although both school attendance and public employment were traditionally considered privileges bestowed upon individuals at the will of the state, this view has changed during the past three decades. The Supreme Court has recognized that teachers and students do not shed their constitutional rights at the schoolhouse door. The state controls education, but this power must be exercised within the confines of the Federal Constitution.

Any interference with protected individual rights must be proven necessary—and not merely convenient—for the operation of the school. In balancing public and private interests, courts weigh the importance of the protected personal right against the governmental need to restrict its exercise. For example, courts have reasoned that there is no overriding public interest to justify compelling students to salute the American flag and pledge their allegiance if such observances conflict with religious or philosophical beliefs. In contrast, mandatory vaccination against communicable diseases has been upheld as a prerequisite to school attendance, even if opposition to immunization is based on religious grounds. Courts have reasoned that the overriding public interest in safeguarding the health of all students justifies such a requirement.

If there are reasonable means of attaining the school's purposes that are less restrictive of individual freedoms, courts will require such alternatives to be pursued. However, restrictions can be placed on teachers' and students' activities if necessary to advance legitimate school objectives. As an illustration, the judiciary has recognized that students' constitutional rights must be assessed in light of the special circumstances of the school. Vulgar student expression that might be considered protected by the first amendment for adults can be curtailed among public school students to further the school's legitimate interest in maintaining standards of decency. Even students' protected right to express political views can be restricted if the expression would lead to a disruption of the educational process. Similarly, school authorities, although considered state officials, can conduct warrantless searches of students based on reasonable suspicion that contraband posing a threat to the school environment is secreted.

Constraints also can be placed on teachers' activities if justified by valid school objectives. Prerequisites to employment such as examinations and residency requirements can be imposed, if necessary to advance legitimate governmental interests. Furthermore, restrictions on teachers' rights to govern their appearance and make lifestyle choices outside the classroom can be justified in some circumstances where such choices have impaired teaching effectiveness. Although teachers enjoy a first amendment right to express views on matters of public concern, expression pertaining to private employment grievances can be the basis for disciplinary action. Even protected expression can be curtailed among teachers if it impedes the management of the school, working relationships, or teaching effectiveness.

Every regulation that impairs individual rights, whether at the school district, school building, or classroom level, should be reviewed periodically to ensure that it is based on valid educational considerations and is essential to fulfilling the school's mission. Such regulations also should be clearly stated and well publicized so that all individuals understand the basis for the rules and the penalties for infractions.

School policies and practices must not disadvantage selected employees or students. The inherent personal right to remain free from governmental discrimination has been emphasized throughout this book. State action that creates a suspect classification, such as race, has been evaluated with strict judicial scrutiny. In school desegregation cases, courts have charged school officials with an affirmative duty to take whatever steps are necessary to overcome the lingering effects of past discrimination. Similarly, intentional racial discrimination associated with student grouping practices, testing methods, or suspension procedures, as well as with employee hiring or promotion practices, has been disallowed. However, neutral policies, uniformly applied, are not necessarily unconstitutional even though they have a disparate impact on minorities. For example, prerequisites to employment such as tests that disqualify a disproportionate number of minority applicants, have been upheld as long as their use is based on nondiscriminatory objectives and justified by a business necessity. Also, the assignment of a disproportionate number of minority students to certain instructional classes is permissible if such placements are based on legitimate educational criteria that are applied in the best interests of students.

In addition to racial classifications, other bases for distinguishing among employees and students have been invalidated if such classifications have disadvantaged individuals. Federal civil rights laws, in conjunction with state statutes, have reinforced constitutional protections afforded to various segments of society that have traditionally suffered discrimination. Indeed, the judiciary has recognized that legislative bodies are empowered to go beyond constitutional minimums in protecting citizens from discriminatory practices. Accordingly, laws have been enacted that place specific responsibilities on employers to ensure that employees are not disadvantaged on the basis of sex, age, religion, national origin, or handicaps. If substantiated that such distinctions are the grounds for withholding benefits from certain individuals, school officials can be held liable for damages.

Federal and state mandates also stipulate that students cannot be denied school attendance or otherwise disadvantaged based on characteristics such as sex, handicaps, national origin, marriage, or pregnancy. Eligibility for school activities, such as participation on interscholastic athletic teams, cannot be denied to a certain class of students. In addition, disciplinary procedures that disproportionately disadvantage identified groups of students are vulnerable to legal challenge. Educators should ensure that all school policies are applied in a nondiscriminatory manner.

Courts will scrutinize grouping practices to ensure that they do not impede students' rights to equal educational opportunities. Nondiscrimination, however, does not necessitate the identical treatment of all pupils. Students can be classified based on their unique needs, but any differential treatment must be justified in terms of more appropriately serving the pupils. For example, students with learning disabilities can be provided with special services designed to address their deficiencies. In fact, judicial rulings and federal and state laws have placed an *obligation* on school districts to provide appropriate services to meet the needs of handicapped and non-English-speaking students. Other children, such as the gifted, are beginning to assert a similar right to instructional accommodations for their unique needs.

Procedural due process is required before students or teachers may be deprived of protected liberty or property rights. Due process is a basic tenet of the United States system of justice—the foundation of fundamental fairness. The fourteenth amendment, which has been widely used in educational litigation, stipulates that state action cannot deprive a person of life, liberty, or property without due process of law. The notion of due process has been an underlying theme in the discussion of teachers' and students' rights throughout this book. The nature of due process required is contingent upon the interest at stake and the procedures outlined in applicable state laws. Many state legislatures have been quite specific about the procedures that must be followed before an individual's protected rights may be impaired.

In the absence of greater statutory specificity, courts have held that, under constitutional guarantees, teachers cannot be discharged or disciplined without procedural requisites if property or liberty rights are implicated. A property claim to due process can be established by tenure status or contractual agreement or by action of the employer that creates a valid expectation of reemployment. A liberty right to due process can be asserted if the employer's action impairs the teacher's status in the community or opportunity to obtain other employment. Once established that either a liberty or property interest is at stake, due process requires, at a minimum, notice of the charges and a hearing before an impartial decision maker. The provision of due process does not imply that a teacher will not be dismissed or that sanctions will not be imposed. It does mean, however, that the teacher must be given the opportunity to refute the charges and that the decision must be made fairly and supported by evidence.

Students, as well as teachers, have due process rights. Students have a state-created property right to attend school that cannot be denied without procedural requisites. If this right to attend school is withdrawn for disciplinary reasons, due process is required. The nature of the proceedings depends on the deprivation involved, with more serious impairments necessitating more formal proceedings. Handicapped children have a right to procedural protections in academic placement decisions as well as in disciplinary matters. Since school authorities will never be faulted for providing too much due process, they would be wise to ensure that at least minimum procedural safeguards accompany any nonroutine change in a student's status.

Inherent in the notion of due process is the assumption that all individuals have a right to a hearing if state action impinges on personal freedoms. Such a hearing need not be elaborate in every situation; an informal conversation can suffice under many circumstances. The crucial element is for all interested parties to have an opportunity to air their views and present evidence that might alter the decision. Often, an informal hearing can serve to clarify issues and facilitate a mutual agreement, thus eliminating the need for more formal proceedings.

Educators are expected to follow the law, to act reasonably, and to anticipate potentially adverse consequences of their actions. Public school personnel are expected to be knowledgeable of federal and state constitutional and statutory provisions as well as school board policies affecting their roles. The Supreme Court has announced that ignorance of the law is no defense for violating clearly established legal principles. For example, ignorance of the Supreme Court's interpretation of establishment clause restrictions would not shield educators from liability for conducting devotional activities in public schools.

Educators hold themselves out as having certain knowledge and skills by the nature of their special training and certification. Accordingly, they are expected to exercise sound professional judgment in their daily activities. Reasonable actions in one situation may be viewed as unreasonable under other conditions. For example, in administering pupil punishment, teachers are expected to consider the student's age, mental condition, and past behavior as well as the specific circumstances surrounding the rule infraction. The failure to exercise reasonable judgment can result in dismissal, or possibly financial liability for impairing students' rights.

Teachers also are expected to make reasonable decisions pertaining to the academic program. Materials and methodology should be appropriate for the age of the students and the educational objectives. If students are grouped for instructional purposes, teachers are expected to base such decisions on legitimate educational considerations and to anticipate negative consequences that the grouping practices might have on selected students.

In addition, teachers are held accountable for reasonable actions in supervising students, providing appropriate instructions, maintaining equipment in proper repair, and warning students of any known dangers. A teacher must exercise a standard of care commensurate with the duty to protect students from unreasonable risks of harm. Personal liability can be assessed for negligence if a teacher should have foreseen that an event could precipitate a pupil injury.

In addition, educators are expected to exercise sound judgment in personal activities that affect their professional roles. While teachers do not relinquish their privacy rights as a condition of public employment, private choices that impair teaching effectiveness or disrupt the school can be the basis for adverse personnel action. As role models for students, teachers and other school personnel are held to a higher level of discretion in their private lives than expected of the general public.

CONCLUSION

One objective of this book, as noted in the introduction, has been to alleviate fears of educators who feel that the scales of justice have been tipped against them. It is hoped that this objective has been achieved. Courts and legislatures have not imposed on school personnel any requirements that fair-minded educators would not impose on themselves.

Reasonable policies and practices based on legitimate educational objectives have been consistently sanctioned by the courts. If anything, legislative and judicial mandates have clarified and supported the *authority* as well as the *duty* of school personnel to make and enforce regulations that are necessary to operate schools and to maintain a proper educational environment. While the federal judiciary in the latter 1960s and early 1970s expanded constitutional protection of individual liberties against governmental interference, federal courts in the 1980s have tended to reinforce the authority of state and local education agencies to control activities in public schools and make decisions that are necessary to advance the school's educational mission, even if such decisions impinge upon protected personal freedoms.

Courts, however, continue to invalidate school practices and policies if they are arbitrary, unrelated to educational objectives, or, in violation of protected individual rights without an overriding justification. Since reform is usually easier to implement when designed from within than when externally imposed, educators should become more assertive in identifying and altering those practices that have the potential to generate legal intervention. Furthermore, school personnel should stay abreast of legal developments, since new laws are being enacted each year, and courts are continually reinterpreting constitutional and statutory provisions.

In addition to understanding basic legal rights and responsibilities, educators are expected to transmit this knowledge to students. Pupils also need to understand their constitutional and statutory rights, the balancing of interests that takes place in legislative and judicial forums, and the rationale for legal enactments, including school regulations. Only with increased awareness of fundamental legal principles can all individuals involved in the educational process develop a greater respect for the law and the responsibilities that accompany legal rights.

Glossary

Absolute privilege: protection from liability for communication made in the performance of public service or the administration of justice.

Appeal: a petition to a higher court to alter the decision of a lower court.

Appellate court: a tribunal having jurisdiction to review decisions on appeal from inferior courts.

Arbitration: a process whereby an impartial third party, chosen by both parties in a dispute, makes a final determination regarding a contested issue.

Assault: the placing of another in fear of bodily harm.

Battery: the unlawful touching of another with intent to harm.

Certiorari: a writ of review whereby an action is removed from an inferior court to an appellate court for additional proceedings.

Civil action: a judicial proceeding to redress an infringement of individual civil rights, in contrast to a criminal action brought by the state to redress public wrongs.

Civil right: a personal right that accompanies citizenship.

Class action suit: a judicial proceeding brought on behalf of a number of persons similarly situated.

Common law: a body of rules and principles derived from usage or from judicial decisions enforcing such usage.

Concurring opinion: a statement by a judge or judges, separate from the majority opinion, that endorses the result of the decision but expresses some disagreement with the reasoning of the majority.

Consent decree: an agreement, sanctioned by a court, that is binding on the consenting parties.

Consideration: something of value given or promised for the purpose of forming a contract.

Contract: an agreement between two or more competent parties that creates, alters, or dissolves a legal relationship.

Criminal action: a judicial proceeding brought by the state against a person charged with a public offense.

Damages: an award made to an individual because of a legal wrong.

Declaratory relief: a judicial declaration of the rights of the plaintiff without an assessment of damages against the defendant.

De facto segregation: separation of the races that exists but does not result from action of the state or its agents.

Defamation: false and intentional communication that injures a person's character or reputation.

Defendant: the party against whom a court action is brought.

De jure segregation: separation of the races by law or by action of the state or its agents.

De minimis: something that is insignificant, not worthy of judicial review.

Dictum: a statement made by a judge in delivering an opinion that does not relate directly to the issue being decided and does not embody the sentiment of the court.

Discretionary power: authority that involves the exercise of judgment.

Dissenting opinion: a statement by a judge or judges who disagree with the decision of the majority of the justices in a case.

Due process: the fundamental right to notice of charges and an opportunity to rebut the charges before a fair tribunal if life, liberty, or property rights are at stake.

Fact finding: a process whereby a third party investigates an impasse in the negotiation process to determine the facts, identify the issues, and make a recommendation for settlement.

Governmental function: an activity performed in discharging official duties of a state or municipal agency.

Governmental immunity: the common law doctrine that governmental agencies cannot be held liable for the negligent acts of their officers, agents, or employees.

Impasse: a deadlock in the negotiation process in which parties are unable to resolve an issue without assistance of a third party.

Injunction: a writ issued by a court prohibiting a defendant from acting in a prescribed manner.

In loco parentis: in place of parent; charged with rights and duties of a parent.

Liability: an obligation one is bound by law to discharge.

Mediation: the process by which a neutral third party serving as an intermediary attempts to persuade disagreeing parties to settle their dispute.

Ministerial duty: an act that does not involve discretion and must be carried out in a manner specified by legal authority.

Negligence: the failure to exercise the degree of care that a reasonably prudent person would exercise under similar conditions.

Plaintiff: the party initiating a judicial action.

Plenary power: full, complete, absolute power.

Precedent: a judicial decision serving as authority for subsequent cases involving similar questions of law.

Prima facie: a fact presumed to be true unless disproven by contrary evidence.

Probable cause: reasonable grounds, supported by sufficient evidence, to warrant a cautious person to believe that the individual is guilty of the offense charged.

Proprietary function: an activity (often for profit) performed by a state or municipal agency that could as easily be performed by a private corporation.

Qualified privilege: protection from liability for communication made in good faith, for proper reasons, and to appropriate parties.

Remand: to send a case back to the original court for additional proceedings.

Respondeat superior: a legal doctrine whereby the master is responsible for acts of the servant (a governmental unit is liable for acts of its employees).

Stare decisis: to abide by decided cases; to adhere to precedent.

Statute: an act by the legislative branch of government expressing its will and constituting the law of the state.

Tenure: a statutory right that confers permanent employment on teachers, protecting them from dismissal except for adequate cause.

Tort: a civil wrong, independent of contract, for which a remedy in damages is sought.

Ultra vires: beyond the scope of authority of the corporate body.

Vacate: to set aside; to render a judgment void.

Verdict: a decision of a jury on questions submitted for trial.

Selected Cases

Index